Many Peoples, Many Faiths

AN INTRODUCTION TO THE RELIGIOUS LIFE OF HUMANKIND

FOURTH EDITION

Robert S. Ellwood
University of Southern California

Prentice Hall, *Englewood Cliffs, New Jersey* 07632

Library of Congress Cataloging-in-Publication Data

Ellwood, Robert S.,
    Many peoples, many faiths : an introduction to the religious life
of humankind / Robert S. Ellwood. -- 4th ed.
        p.   cm.
    Includes bibliographical references and index.
    ISBN 0-13-544149-8
    1. Religions. 2. Religion.   I. Title.
    BL80.2.E45 1992
    291--dc20   91-18345
                                                                     CIP

Acquisitions editor: Ted Bolen
Development editor: Diane Schaible
Editorial/production supervision: Mary McKinley
Copy editor: Betsy Torjussen
Interior design: Lisa A. Domínguez
Cover design: Maureen Eide
Prepress buyer: Herb Klein
Manufacturing buyer: Patrice Fraccio

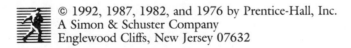 © 1992, 1987, 1982, and 1976 by Prentice-Hall, Inc.
A Simon & Schuster Company
Englewood Cliffs, New Jersey 07632

Printed in the United States of America

10 9 8 7 6 5 4 3

ISBN   0-13-544149-8

Prentice-Hall International (UK) Limited, *London*
Prentice-Hall of Australia Pty. Limited, *Sydney*
Prentice-Hall of Canada Inc., *Toronto*
Prentice-Hall Hispanoamericana, S.A., *Mexico*
Prentice-Hall of India Private Limited, *New Delhi*
Prentice-Hall of Japan, Inc., *Tokyo*
Simon & Schuster Asia Pte. Ltd., *Singapore*
Editora Prentice-Hall do Brasil, Ltda., *Rio de Janeiro*

For Richard Scott Lancelot Ellwood
May your faith be always adventurous

Contents

CHAPTER 3

LIFE AGAINST TIME:
The Spiritual Paths of India   55

CHAPTER 4

WISDOM EMBARKED FOR THE FARTHER SHORE:
The Journey of Buddhism   117

CHAPTER 5

DRAGON AND SUN:
Religions of East Asia 157

CHAPTER 6

ONE GOD, MANY WORDS AND WONDERS:
The Family of Three Great Monotheistic Religions 229

CHAPTER 7

KEEPING COVENANT WITH GOD IN HISTORY:
The Unique Perspective of Judaism 239

CHAPTER 8

SPREADING THE WORD OF GOD IN THE WORLD:
The Growth of Christianity   267

CHAPTER 9

SUBMITTING TO THE WILL OF GOD:
The Building of the House of Islam   337

C H A P T E R 10

LOOKING OVER THE SPIRITUAL HORIZON:
Religion Today and Tomorrow   381

Preface

For nearly two decades this introduction to the world's religions, *Many Peoples, Many Faiths,* has endeavored to combine factual information with empathetic writing that tries to convey something of the flavor of our planet's diverse religions and cultures. While striving for accuracy and depth, it is neither an encyclopedic compilation of data nor a survey of alternative philosophies. Instead it seeks to present something of the total human experience, made up as it is of an inseparable mingling of conceptual, worship, and social factors, of religious life past and present. The author hopes that his effort will implant in many readers a sense of the richness and facination of the areas of scholarship that lie behind the presentation of this experience, and will inspire at least some to explore them more deeply. The Fourth Edition of *Many Peoples, Many Faiths* was written to maintain the balanced and empathetic approach to the religions of the world toward which previous versions have striven. At the same time, it is recognized that in a world increasingly faced with very difficult challenges and with a growing awareness of current injustices, no human institution, religion included, can avoid challenge and criticism. New material has therefore been added to the introductory chapter on critical approaches to religion, and a new final chapter has been appended on religion in the context of present and future crises. Readers will be challenged to think about how religion has responded to present ecological and other travails, and what the possible future for religion may be.

Other changes and revisions have been made as well. I wish to thank James R. Lewis, of the Institute for the Study of American Religion, Santa Barbara, California, for helpful suggestions and corrections for the material on Sikhism. New material has been added on Confucianism in Japan; this perspective is important for understanding Japanese character and society, including the deep background of its present corporate culture and economic success. New material has also been added on Judaism, Roman Catholicism, and women in religion.

In this edition the Bibliography has been broken up into lists of Suggested Readings at the ends of chapters. New titles have been added, but it must be emphasized that these lists are by no means exhaustive; in many of the categories there are hundreds, even thousands, of valuable books. What I have tried to do is suggest a few books in each subject area, not so much for advanced research as for broader familiarization with the area. Most, therefore, are books written at a level accessible to beginning or middle level students. Many are textbooks with good further bibliographies. Books footnoted in the text but not cited in the reading lists are generally recommended too. In many cases, the books in the suggested reading lists have gone through a number of editions; the dates given may not represent the earliest or latest printing. Books marked with an asterisk are available in paperback. Again, these are only books representative of the wealth of material available in the study of the religious world; the inclusion or exclusion of a book should not be taken to reflect the author's own critical judgment in every case.

Questions for Review have been added to the end of each chapter to help students get involved in understanding and empathizing with different cultures and religions by taking an active role. The art and illustration program has also been greatly expanded in this edition, which will allow students more accessibility to foreign societies through visualization.

As always, true understanding of the many faiths of the many peoples of earth requires a mixture of knowledge and empathy. As you read this book keep the necessary facts in mind, but read it also with that human empathy which alone can furnish an understanding of what those facts mean to human beings for whom they are gateways to ultimate meaning.

I am indebted to many people who have helped to make this fourth edition possible. First, I would like to thank everyone at Prentice Hall who has worked on this book. Unfortunately, I cannot name them all here, but I would like to thank Ted Bolen, the Acquisitions Editor for Religion who has provided a wealth of guidance and has overseen this project; Diane Schaible, the Development Editor who has done much to improve the appearance of the fourth edition; and Mary McKinley and Rob DeGeorge, the Production Editors who tied it all together.

I also wish to acknowledge the readers who offered suggestions for improvement in this fourth edition. My thanks and appreciation to Roderick Hindery, California State University at Northridge; Daniel A. Brown, California State University at Fullerton; Jennifer Woods Parker, University of North Carolina at Charlotte; James Cook, Oakland Community College; James S. Dalton, Siena College; and Dale Bengtson, Southern Illinois University at Carbondale.

Many Peoples, Many Faiths

C H A P T E R 1

Understanding the World's Religious Heritage

CHAPTER OBJECTIVES

After studying this chapter, you should be able to

- Talk about what you mean by *religion*, and what a religion includes.

- Cite and interpret Joachim Wach's *Three Forms of Religious Expression*.

- Discuss the meaning of history and historical experience for religion.

- Explain the difference between an archaic religion and a founder-religion.

A NEW DAY OF RELIGIOUS ENCOUNTER

The religions of the world . . . the words themselves may evoke a cinerama of images, perhaps drawn from a host of movies and novels with east-of-Suez settings. Incense and temple gongs, yogis in strange contorted postures, ancient and enigmatic chants—all these and more sweep past our inner eyes and ears. For most often what fascinates us is that which is far away or long ago.

But the study of the religions of the world is no longer a matter of reading about exotic lands to which only the most intrepid travelers have voyaged. In today's pluralism and world community, almost any faith from anywhere is a presence and an option throughout the world. The temples of Hindu Americans and the mosques of Muslim Americans embellish larger American cities. American Zen centers, quiet with the great peace of the Buddha, teach Eastern meditation. Christianity and Judaism in all their manifold forms have long existed here side by side, just as they have been carried by American missionaries to the homelands of Hinduism and Buddhism.

All of this makes "now" an exciting time to study religion. We who come to the study of religion today bring with us expectations shaped by these times. The presence of many options, and ferment within most of them, are never just things outside a person.

All of this also indicates how complex religion is. It is now time to try to sort out this complexity by introducing some categories through which we can try to understand and "place" the different voices by which religion speaks. We shall present several sets of categories that classify, for the sake of trying to understand, the same religious phenomena in different ways. They may overlap and thereby seem inconsistent with each other; this is because none of them is "right" or "wrong," but all are simply different ways of looking at the same thing. The purpose is not to confuse or make the study of religion overly obscure, but merely to show that there are alternative ways of looking at it. Just as a plumber with a complete set of tools can do more than one equipped with only a hammer, so many angles of vision may make one better able to understand the broad scope of human religion than a single theory. We shall first suggest ways of looking at the religion of another culture, then describe three forms of religious expression, discuss descriptive and critical approaches, and finally outline the basic stages of religious history. In the process we shall, among other things, be working toward a definition of religion, but we may not reach that point even by the end of the book. For while most people have an idea of what they mean by the word *religion*—at least until they are asked—a comprehensive and satisfying definition has thus far eluded even the wisest; perhaps it is not possible.

DOORS AND WINDOWS
TO THE ULTIMATE

Suppose you were taking a trip to a country whose culture was completely foreign to you, and suppose that you wanted to find out the religion of that culture. Suppose, further, that because you cannot speak the language of the country well enough to ask anyone about it, you have to look for clues in what you see around you and what people do. What would you look for?

Most of what you see, of course, has an obvious explanation. Most things apparently meet understandable human needs for shelter, food, drink, security, and pleasure in this world. Most buildings up and down the streets are houses where people live, or shops where craftspeople work or merchants sell. Most of the people scurrying about are out on business or seeking recreation.

Once in a while, though, you may perceive something that offers no such "ordinary" interpretation. A structure may be neither home nor shop, yet obviously important, set apart, and perhaps elaborately ornamented. A human activity may be neither work nor play in the usual sense. It may not produce food nor exercise the body nor challenge one's skill in any common sense, yet clearly be of great importance and marked by a solemn or festive air. With both the building and the activity may be associated symbols and gestures that make no sense in terms of the usual affairs of this world yet are of deep significance to these people.

You suspect that these are places and practices connected to the religion of the land. You know that you could be wrong, of course; without considerable background information, certainty would be impossible. The special building might be a court instead of a temple; the activity a game or dance instead of a rite. Indeed, the rites of the state and of religion are often intermingled, and in many societies, games and dances have been done for reasons that combine their own intrinsic excitement with the sacred.

But you are aware of one thing: Traditional religion in innumerable different cultures affirms that human life has relationships and objectives beyond the ordinary, "this-worldly" plane—beyond ordinary labor and frolic. Structures, doings, and gestures that have no apparent meaning except in relation to invisible realities they express, or into which they "fit," may well be what is commonly called religion. They may vary from the rhetoric of preaching to the quiet of meditation, from the ornate garb and carefully stylized motions of ancient ritual to the gladsome tones of gospel music, but in any case they point to a belief that reality has more to it than the everyday, and that "otherness" impinges on human life and can be touched, channeled, and made manifest by special means.

Basic to religion is the assumption that we live in a "split-level" universe or, to use the expression of the historian of religion Mircea Eliade, that reality is "non-homogeneous." For the religious person, there is ordinary reality and "something else." Certain visible places, people, and events are more in touch with that "something else" than others. They are sacred places, persons, and rites.

Using relatively neutral terms derived from Buddhist thought, we may think of the two sides of this split-level universe—the ordinary and the Other—as conditioned and unconditioned reality, respectively. Let us start by talking about *conditioned reality*. To say something is *conditioned* simply means that it is limited or restricted. We are obviously conditioned in time and space. If we are living in the twentieth century, we are not also in the ninth with Charlemagne or in the twenty-fifth with Buck Rogers. If we live in Ohio or Oklahoma, we are not also in Hong Kong or on the planet Neptune. Further, we are conditioned by the limitations and habits of our minds. We can think about only one thing at a time, and we forget far more than we remember. Even the greatest genius can only know the tiniest fragment of what there is to know, or think more than the minutest fraction of what there is to think. Moreover, we continually build limits around ourselves when we, in effect, say such things as, "I'm a person who does this but not that," "I believe this but not that," or "I like this but not that."

Consider, however, what *unconditioned reality,* the opposite of all that, would be like. It would be equally present to all times and all places. Its knowledge, wisdom, and mental power would be unlimited and would embrace all that could possibly be known or thought. If it (or he or she) had preferences as to doing, believing, or liking, they would be based on omniscient wisdom, not the bundle of ill-informed fears and prejudices by which we too often act and react. Unconditioned reality would, in fact, be no different from the God or Ultimate Reality of religion and philosophy. It goes by different names and has varying degrees of personality, but in most religions, some unconditioned pole of reality stands over our very much conditioned everyday lives. Even the legions of secondary sacred entities that also inhabit the religious world—polytheistic gods, buddhas, bodhisattvas, angels, spirits—have their significance because they are in a special relationship to it and in some particular way refract chinks of light from unconditioned reality. We can illustrate conditioned and unconditioned reality and its names in various religions like this:

Unconditioned Reality

Brahman (philosophical Hinduism)
Nirvana (Buddhism)
Dao (Daoism)
Heaven (Confucianism)
God (Judaism, Christianity, Islam)

Conditioned Reality[1]

Maya (philosophical Hinduism)
Samsara (Buddhism)
Under Heaven (Daoism, Confucianism)
Choice of Death (Judaism)
The World (Christianity)
Realm of War (Islam)

One point remains to be added. For religion, the line between unconditioned and conditioned reality is not solid as it is above, as though the two realms were hermetically sealed off from each other. Instead, the main idea behind religion is that it is full of doors and windows, and much commerce plays between the two sides. Words and people pass through those invisible doors, and the world is full of places and occasions that are like windows to the other side. This porous borderline where the action is, is the realm of the religious.

Crossings are diverse. Revelations, angels, gods, and saviours are envoys from unconditioned to conditioned reality. All religions believe that certain teachings, practices (such as prayer or meditation, rites, and services), and modes of ethical behavior best express or fit in with the nature of ultimate reality and so are in themselves like the doors and windows. Certain persons or institutions also are held to be in especially close touch with unconditioned reality and so are like those portals. In a somewhat different sense, so are works of religious art, music, or literature. It is also possible for people themselves to move through the doors, so to speak, and enter the infinite kingdom of unconditioned reality: through prayer, mystical experience, or death.

Soon we shall collect the multiple doors and windows into three basic forms: the theoretical or teaching, the practical or worship, and the sociological or group life. Nearly all of the endless ways in which religion shows its awareness of unconditioned reality and of the possibility of tapping and revealing it in this world can be seen, for convenience, as connected to one of these three major forms of religious expression. We may, in fact, wish to think of religion as that in human life which expresses interaction with transcendent or unconditioned reality simultaneously through theoretical, practical, and sociological means.

Some will object that not all of what is ordinarily called religious, or which has to do with gods and the like, is really so much concerned with unconditioned reality. People go to church for family and social as well as for transcendent reasons. The prayers or chants that accompany the hunt or the planting of corn may be only tradition, or at best a particularized sort of magic without much ultimate reference. Yet I think that understanding religion should not always be limited by the conscious intention of the religionist (often hard to judge in any event) or by the explicit language of the example under study. Even if a person goes to church only to meet someone, or if a particular hunting chant only invokes a certain rather minor deity of the woods, something more is implied by the very existence of church and chant. In the church God will probably be spoken of and things done that make no sense if there is no God. As circumscribed as it may be, the hunting chant tells us there is more to the hunt than just human beings hunting. Both chant and church open up in back, so to speak, to a vision of an invisible world overlying the visible, in which beings all the way from Almighty God to woodland spirits interact with human life. For the thoughtful it probably begins with some notion of unconditioned reality, whose power all other saints and shrines engage in some particularized way. Even for those who just take it in its own terms, the invisible world tells us there is more than the ordinary. Religion can be conceived of as the doors and windows between unconditioned and conditioned reality; it can also be thought of as a laying out of maps of the invisible world.

MAPS OF THE INVISIBLE WORLD

All religions have attitudes in common that are unshared by nonreligious outlooks. They are all based on feelings, beliefs, and attitudes which imply that humans have needs other than the physical and live in an environment that includes more than physical reality. If people lived only to meet physical needs, an action such as "wasting" precious food to place it on the altar of gods, or "wasting" precious time on ceremonial acts, or "wasting" mental energy on anxiety about doing God's will would simply make no sense. Even if the purpose of the religious act was, say, just to ensure a good hunt, it is obviously achieving this end of meeting physical needs in a roundabout way that implies the existence of nonphysical reality.

Religion centers around those symbols, statements, and social forms that give visible expression to an invisible environment humans believe to be around them and an invisible true nature they sense to dwell within them. (We are speaking, of course, not of invisible forces like gravity, but of those that seem to have a living relation to our thoughts and feelings and social encounters.) We deal with this other reality by creating names and signs for it. In churches, temples, and shrines we make worlds in which the nonmaterial is as real and as visible as stars and cheese.

A particular kind of attitude also goes with this rapport with the nonphysical world. Humankind seems instinctively to feel nonphysical reality is more mysterious, more ultimate, and more powerful than the physical. It has to do with humanity's ultimate origins and most absolute relations. It has to do with that which cannot be surpassed—the point of origin beyond which one cannot go to a preceding stage, the relationship beyond which there is none more important, demanding, or final. This relationship is more than merely the last in a series; the very fact that it is ultimate and final puts it in a special category, different in size and kind from anything coming after. Oranges may come in all sizes, but none of them looks like the trees on which they grew, or the endless horizons of the old earth in which the tree is rooted, or the boundless space which is the mother of earth and sky. So the ultimate parent must always be endless, to fill up (as it were) the void that would otherwise lie behind it.

This kind of relationship has a different "feel" about it from that of other relationships. Indeed, even a relation with a particularized, finite deity who is only a fragment of the invisible world and not the endless parent, like a Shinto kami, has this "feel," insofar as one senses he is at least a token of the unbounded, coming from the same place, just as even a viceroy of a king has a certain majesty. The relation is one of solemn awe, or laughing festival with sport and song, or quiet contemplation alone. But whatever the mood, these moments will cloak themselves with finality; one will feel, if religion is alive, that "There is nothing more than this."

Yet religion is not just a subjective mood; it is also a spelling out in concrete expressions that bring to life in the visible, physical world the nonphysical realities that are subjectively felt. Religion is to the spiritual milieu what drawing and following maps is to the geographic environment. When people discover new environmental factors, they want to know how they are arrayed and where we stand in relation to them. The scriptures, temples, symbols, and holy places of religion are like the key or legend of a map. Just as a terrestrial map will have signs for roads, boundaries, swamps, and mountain ranges, so the former are "pointers" that religion has set up to indicate the topography of the spiritual world.

The history of religion is the history of these maps. Even as boundaries have shifted and cities have come and gone on the maps of the earth as empires have risen and fallen, so the religious map has changed over the centuries. But certain kinds of signs remain constant. These are the symbols put on the map by the basic forms of religious expression. For while the particulars of religion take almost countless variations, there are constants in the *kind* of expression that the religious consciousness takes.

THREE FORMS OF RELIGIOUS EXPRESSION

The sociologist of religion Joachim Wach (1898–1955) has provided one useful description of these constants. While the essence of religion may be beyond words, the religious experience, he tells us, *expresses* itself in three broad areas of human construction, which in turn engender other religious experience. These three forms of religious expression he called theoretical, practical, and sociological.[2] These categories will be referred to from time to time in this book in order to show the place and interrelationship of the various human religious activities of which we shall speak. It will be helpful now to get a preliminary idea of what is meant by each.

Theoretical Expression: What Is Said in Religion

The first level of religious expression, the *theoretical,* embraces essentially the verbal expression: what is said. Religions say things about certain basic, ultimate issues—how the spiritual universe is set up, what ultimate reality is, where the world came from and where it is going, and where humans came from and where we are going. Religions talk about how we know these things and how we are helped to get from here to the ultimate. They say these things in two fundamental ways: myth, or narrative story, and doctrine. In the history of religions, the term *myth* is used in a special way to denote stories that express in narrative form the central values of the society and the way it views what the world is and means. This is a usage different from the popular denotation of the word *myth*—a fable or a story that is not true. In the history of religions, no judgment is passed on the truth of a story by the use of this word, but only a statement of its function.

Practically all religions have stories that encapsulate the basic perception of the world and the human place in it in narrative form. The most important are often creation stories. They state an important view of the nature of the cosmos by, for example, telling of a God like that of the Judaeo-Christian tradition who created the universe from nothing and stands outside it; or who made the world by dividing up his own body in a primal sacrifice (as do some Hindu myths) and is thus himself the creation. These two examples imply very different relationships between God and the world.

Another important type of myth is the hero story, the story of the individual who is able to find the way back to the ideal state of the world at its beginning. He shows us the way from here to there and helps us along the way. He undertakes a mighty quest and experiences great anguish. But whether the model hero is a suffering saviour like Jesus Christ or a profound meditator like the Buddha says much about the central values of the community that cherishes the figures. Religions also have secondary model stories of miracles, saints, and conversions that express the map of the spiritual world and help to bring others inside it.

All developed religions have expression in doctrine as well. Doctrines are general, abstract statements that generalize from the narratives of creation, the hero's return, and the experiences of saints and believers. Doctrines are composed when people ask, "If this is what God did on this and that occasion, what can we say that is true of God all the time?" The answers are laid out in propositional form: God is loving, all-powerful, and so forth.

In the Judaeo-Christian tradition, for example, the narrative expression is found in the Biblical account of God's creation of the world; Moses' leading of the children of Israel out of Egypt; and the life, death, and resurrection of Jesus. Doctrinal expression comes in the creeds, catechisms, or general statements of church councils and theologians about the nature of God, the work of Christ, and the Holy Spirit, based on that narrative.

No problem dealt with by myth and doctrine alike is more important than that of the meaning of time. Although the subject is a partial digression, an understanding of two basic religious attitudes toward time will help to clarify a great deal that is raised in the following chapters. The difference lies in whether time is viewed as cyclical and endless or historical and linear.

In Hindu, Buddhist, and some Western philosophies, the universe is seen as everlasting, moving through great cycles of creation and destruction and creation again. There is no ultimately meaningful goal to time and history as a whole. The only real goal to human life is an experience of individual liberation from an existence that can result only in frustration or despair on the wheel of time. In this "cosmic" view of time, shared by some primitive religions and some very sophisticated philosophical systems, time essentially repeats itself, like the turning of the seasons or the rising and setting of the sun. And since time has no beginning or end, one cannot speak of "progress" or even "history" except in highly relative terms.

But Judaism, Christianity, and Islam, in their scriptural traditions, view time as a line, beginning with the creation of the world and ending with the final judgment. In this Western, "historical" view, all the way through time there flows a purpose of which human history is a part. The acts of God in history—the creation, the giving of the Law by Moses, and for the Christian the incarnation of God in Christ—are decisive events that definitively color one's spiritual life. Retrospectively, it makes a tremendous difference whether one lived before or after the Exodus or Christ—one's spiritual world would not have been at all the same had one lived in pre-Mosaic or pre-Christian times. In the cyclical tradition, on the other hand, at any time or place there are inward paths open to the center. Time is like the rim of a wheel, with spokes running in to the hub; Buddhism, for example, speaks of 84,000 paths to enlightenment.

The rapid pace of change has made linear time seem most real to many modern people (whether religious or not and whether Eastern or Western) and has shattered the world view of many traditions.

In the modern world, whether in the great religions or in a philosophy such as Hegelianism or Marxism or even in the secular notion of "progress," we think that whether one lived in the Stone Age, the Middle Ages, the twentieth century, or some future paradise makes a vital difference in almost everything subjective as well as outward about one's life and in one's relation to God or absolute truth, inasmuch as these have been revealed in very different degrees of fullness in different ages. Some ideas comparable to this have obtained in the East, often in the reverse form that says times are getting worse, and so new forms of spirituality—Tantrism, the Buddhism of faith in Amitabha—have become appropriate. Movements based on future hope, as in the coming paradise of Maitreya, the next Buddha, have also played a role in the East. But the fundamental idea of the major Eastern spiritual philosophies is that truth and reality are timeless and so stand in equal relation to all times and places, being always available to the person of will and wisdom.

In any case, religion views time as being, like the geography of temple and rite, a map of the invisible spiritual and nonphysical world; it is not ordinary chronology. Time for religion is more like memory in a human being. One does not remember with equal clarity all the millions of events that happened in one's life. A person remembers certain key landmark events that serve to define and symbolize who he or she is. It may be that some very important events in one's life are chosen to be forgotten, or allowed to emerge only in ill-understood dreams and fears. Other scenes from childhood always come forth with striking vividness when one tries to remember the past, even though they may seem trivial incidents. Similarly, religions tell accounts of their origins and pasts—accounts such as the traditional lives of Jesus or the Buddha—which like bright recollections illuminate how they now experience what they are and their mappings of the spiritual world. The theoretical form of religious expression, narrative and doctrinal, replays and interprets these moments and so unveils the religion's view of time as well.

Practical Expression: What Is Done in Religion

The religious perpetuation of the past is a function of myth and doctrine, but it is a particularly potent function of the second of Wach's three forms of religious expression, the *practical,* referring to practices, which covers the visible and performed side of faith: worship, rite, pilgrimage, forms of devotion or meditation, and other personal or group activities. To stand out as especially religious actions, things done have to have an appearance that makes their religious character evident, and this is likely to be the case only if they follow patterns recognizable in the culture as "religious," neither just meeting ordinary needs in an ordinary way nor merely idiosyncratic. In other words, it will have to be a gesture that is traditionally religious, and so something that comes out of the religious past. Even in political demonstrations clergy are likely to wear clerical collars to show the religious nature of their actions.

One always experiences a religion as something that has persisted through time to the present; part of the sense of expansiveness it gives is a sense of free access to the past. Even religion's visions of the future tend to be put in language that suggests a renewed past: the descent of the heavenly Jerusalem, the coming of a future Buddha. Religious rites carry over from the past vestments, language, and the like that are obsolete in the rest of the culture. Thereby, they give people a larger milieu and, indeed, a sense of unboundedness, by getting them outside the narrow confines of the present. At the same time this perpetuation of an idealized past serves to reinforce the values of the continuing culture it celebrates.

But it would be a mistake to conceptualize the second of the forms of expression only in terms of obvious traditional rites such as an Orthodox Jewish Passover or the Muslim pilgrimage to Mecca. These are religious groups with colorful and highly structured rituals. But there are many others that may claim to be "not ritualistic" and have little more than a sermon or address by a leader in ordinary dress, or even just free-form discussions. Are we to conclude then that these groups have little or nothing of the second form of religious expression?

The answer is no. If it is a religious group at all, the meeting is for some purpose connected with the experiencing and transmission of the religion and therefore is part of the religion's message. In some faiths (like the Quaker), simplicity is as traditional and as much a way of forging links with the past as ornate ceremony is in others. It is a question of what the message is.

Highly ceremonial religions say that one best transcends oneself to make contact with the divine by losing oneself in the drama and aesthetic stimulation of a mighty liturgy, or religious ceremony. Simple religions say that one best achieves the same end by the removal of all outward stimuli (except probably the spoken or sung word). Informal religions say that one attains still the same end, or something like it, where one has the greatest freedom to express himself or herself—by releasing one's inner self in prayer group or discussion or "speaking in tongues," one also draws near to God.

In any case, it is clear that something is *done,* there is *praxis,* and so there is a "practical" form of expression. Whether worship is largely verbal or nonverbal, structured or spontaneous, traditional or modern, centered on one leader or highly corporate tells important things about the group and its real view of the nature of God and humankind—things which sometimes are not made explicit in the formal doctrine but which may nonetheless be unspoken assumptions that underlie much of what is really going on in this religion.

Sociological Expression: Kinds of Groups Formed by Religion

The forms of organization undertaken by religion, and the way they relate to the broader social context, are also part of religion's map. Generally, religion's structures fall into two types. These may be called the church type and the withdrawal-group type. The church, in this sense, is the broadly based religion that represents the normative spiritual values of a society and in which most people are involved by virtue of their membership in the society—Hinduism in India or Catholicism in Spain. This is the faith a person in a society belongs to if he or she has not made a self-conscious, deliberate choice to be something else. The church type of structure is often a comprehensive system allowing for individual variations and in practice not making extremely rigorous demands on anyone. (An exception would be when the dominant religion has real political power and uses it to enforce its strictures or impel social change, as in Puritan New England or countries affected by Islamic "fundamentalism.") In America, we would have to think of the "church" role being played in effect by a number of major denominations, which tacitly but effectively support a general American religious consensus in the minds of the majority.

Over against this consensus are the withdrawal groups, which express the experiences of those for whom personal commitment and experience are more important than the family and community functions of religion. They meet the needs of those who feel the faith or unfaith of the majority is not for them and want to define themselves more sharply by making a separate choice. Those groups, such as the Amish or Jehovah's Witnesses in the Christian tradition, representing a more intense and unbending commitment than the average to the religion that is the general tradition, are often called *sects.* Groups that combine separation with syncretism, new ideas, and emphasis on mystical experience, are often called *cults,* although that word should be used with caution since it has acquired a negative connotation.

The relation of a religion to the broader society tells its own story about the meaning of humankind's relation to the spiritual world—whether it is a wisdom widely if diffusely known or an esoteric wisdom well known by only a few intensely dedicated people. Other aspects of the collective life also tell their stories. There is a message about both God and humanity in whether the group is open or authoritarian; whether the leadership is charismatic, acting out of the radiant power of the leader's own experience, or whether it works through traditional, constitutional, or "rational" channels.

The Interrelationship of the Forms of Expression

In any religion, the three forms of expression work together to form a unified experience. It is usually a mistake to think that one comes first and the others follow after. Children learn about their mother-faiths more or less through all forms of expression at once—they hear the stories, see the special atmosphere of church or temple when taken by parents, and pick up the tone of social life as they play with friends and relatives who share it. Even an adult convert will probably be drawn by all three forms and will participate in all three simultaneously. They unite to form a single, almost indefinable experience, which points to the ultimate nature of the holy and becomes a part of the inner life of each person touched by it.

Descriptive and Critical Approaches

But, you may ask, is it enough just to talk, in a neutral way, about the shape of a religion's doors and windows as they open toward unconditioned reality?

Admittedly, it is not the purpose of a study such as this to decide on the ultimate truth or falsity of any religion. We are simply trying to know and understand them better. Even so, does one look on everything in the religious world—from a human sacrifice to the healing work of a Mother Teresa—with exactly the same understanding gaze? Can we not at least consider the social and cultural roles of religions from a critical as well as an appreciative perspective?

Important questions are now being raised around the world about religion and the oppression of women, about its role in maintaining exploitative family and economic systems, and in impeding "rational" attacks on current problems such as overpopulation through allegedly outmoded beliefs. In each case, both sides—the tradition and its critics—have much to say. But too much empathy can certainly get in the way of even seeing where the problems are, and world religions scholars are coming to realize they need to be a part of this discussion.

The approach to world religions by "Western" scholars has gone through three stages in this respect. Many nineteenth-century books on Primal and Eastern religion, though pioneering, have been criticized for the high-handed, judgmental tone they brought to their subject, usually on the assumption that "the West" and its particular concepts of reason and ethics were the standard by which all else was to be appraised. The next period, in reaction against all that, popularized instead a **phenomenological approach.** Using it, one is asked to set aside all one's own beliefs and biases and just look at a religion, concentrating only on seeing what is there. One strives to empathize with what the faith means to the people who hold it and to perceive inner relationships in its practices and symbols.

This stage was a most valuable corrective. But now we are realizing that pure phenomenology is not enough; there are some things about a religion one will not understand unless one asks critical questions such as those asked, for example, by the feminist critique of religion. The role of women in most traditional religions has generally been obscured by outward male dominance of the religion. Men have written the scriptures and doctrines and have been the faith's priests and spokespersons in large part. Criticism of that reality has led us to inquire what role women do have in religion and how it has affected their lives. These questions have opened up perception of things we probably would not have seen before.[3]

Furthermore, beneficial change will not occur unless questions are asked and criticism made. But fair and effective change also requires accurate information and authentic insight. For this reason, there remains a vital place for the phenomenologist's clear and unvarnished presentation of things just as they are, and his or her empathetic insight into the meaning of practices in a cultural context that may be quite different from the one of the observer.

If an attack is made, for example, on a certain religion's endorsement of war, one needs to be sure that there is a right understanding of the attitude under question as it is understood by believers, and in the framework of the faith's total life and practice, without preconceptions. (It would also be helpful to analyze to what extent it differs from the practice of one's own and other religions.) Then, with good standing, a critical statement can be made—that is, a statement which expresses a responsible judgment—to challenge the religion to reassess its position. It would also need to be clear to what values one is appealing in making the judgment, and why those values should be considered superior to those of the religion itself.

Our task in this book will be mostly descriptive. It is a work on the level of getting information and empathetic insight. But critical judgments made honestly on the basis of reliable knowledge and insight are not only justified but ultimately necessary. Readers are challenged to reflect on what their critical judgments might be as they read.[4]

PERIODS IN RELIGIOUS HISTORY

Religion is never static. We now come to the final way of categorizing religious phenomena, according to the period in which they flourished or from which they derive.

This historical approach can easily be the most deceptive of all. It fits in with the linear time concept, which, as we have seen, is particularly Western or modern but is only one way of viewing time. It can easily be taken to imply a gratuitous concept of automatic progress in which "later is better"; but whether or not one accepts this as true depends on values independent of historical periodization itself.

Most important, the historical approach can impede religious understanding because it is a frame of reference very different from the way most religious people in the present, and virtually all in the past, have understood their religion. Most people participating in a Jewish or Christian service do not give much thought—even if they know—to which hymns and customs are ancient, which are medieval, and which are modern. Until recently, the majority of people, being illiterate, had not the slightest idea outside of mythic accounts about the origin and historical development of their religion. To them it came in the form it was practiced in their village as a single, seamless totality in the present. Whether a rite was old or new, Stone Age or sophisticated, made little conscious difference if its origin was outside living memory. Historical analysis must be handled with great care when it is used as a way of understanding this kind of religious life.

Nonetheless, we shall now present a set of periods in the history of religion. Moreover, most of the material in this book on various religions will be organized in basically historical form—giving the life of founders or the teaching of original scriptures first, then the development of doctrine and devotional patterns, and finally the modern situation of the faith. Timeline charts will be provided to give the basic historical development of great religious traditions. All in all, the historical approach seems to be the most useful for a number of reasons; better for all its dangers than any evident alternative.

First, history represents the way we in the modern West tend to think when we approach the academic study of something like religion. We want the historical questions answered early on. Until they are, we do not feel we have enough of a "grip" on the subject, a clear enough picture of it, to ask anything else. Whether this is ultimately good or not, it is the way we approach social phenomena. When we hear about Confucianism, we want to know about Confucius and his life, then about his influence, even though a traditional Chinese would have experienced his influence before knowing about the great sage's life. (In this book we shall often try to convey something of this realism by starting with cultural impressions, then going on to answer the historical questions they stimulate.)

Second, history provides a convenient way to deal one by one with the many components—the different scriptures, beliefs, rites, and so forth—of any developed religion. These components have usually come from different times. By taking them in this way, they provide an object lesson in how religions change and grow, a process we can see around us, too, when we learn what to look for.

Third, the historical approach offers a far greater expansion of awareness in the study of comparative religion than does a merely contemporary slice; one can imagine not only what is going on today, but also medieval pilgrims and Stone Age wizards. The fact that a modern religionist may not be consciously aware of the time period in which her usages developed does not mean history is wholly irrelevant to understanding her experience—perhaps nonetheless she changes time-gears in devotional moments, slipping back into a medieval or Stone Age world. Knowing something about these worlds helps us to understand her now and increases our ability to appreciate what she is doing. Another thing that must be remembered is that the history of religion is largely cumulative: When a new period—or even a new religion—comes, it does not so much replace what went before as it just adds another layer on top of it, while the former still continues to live, perhaps with a changed name and role. Today in the Christian world there persist, with various rationales, customs such as Christmas trees and Easter eggs, which stem from the pre-Christian world of archaic hunters and agriculturalists.

Knowing about all these things is fascinating and can lead to various sorts of useful understanding—if we always bear in mind that it is only one dimension of religious understanding and can be very misleading as a guide to comprehending how religious people actually understand themselves and their faith.

Following are periods in religious history worldwide, starting with the earliest society.

Hunting Religion

The earliest human society of which we can speak is that of hunters and gatherers. Typically, spiritual power is focused in the sky, the world of animals, and the ecstatic individual. Often a "high god" above made the world and sustains it. A very deep relation exists between humans and animals; beasts have spirit as do humans, and to take them requires that they be enchanted, propitiated, and respected. The human custodian of spiritual power may be the shaman, an individual who has gained mastery over spirits and who knows the paths of the dead by means of a great initiatory experience. Commonly, the initiation of all members of society is important too; life is seen as a series of stages through which one passes, gaining appropriate power at each. Birth and death are likewise stages in this endless cycle, and the land of the dead is thought of as similar to this, though the ghosts of ancestors are potent and feared.

Agricultural Religion

The development of agriculture was as great a landmark in religion as in economic history. The transfer of attention from the forest to the planted field meant that the earth, as mother of all, grew in significance as the high god faded. Moreover, the development of agriculture brought home anew the relation of death to life, in the seed that seems to be dead but is born anew. Animal and human sacrifice to the powers of fertility and initiatory mysteries reached a high point in archaic agricultural society. Initiation was practiced particularly among men, as though to counter the newfound feminine spiritual power of the earth mother. Spiritual life became more and more tied to the cycle of the seasons, marked by spring planting rites and the autumn harvest festival.

Ancient Empires

One result of agriculture was a great increase in the number of people that could be sustained by a given tract of land in fertile areas. Moreover, the population was sedentary, bound to the soil and the seasonal round. This in turn made possible and inevitable trade on a large scale, the growth of towns, and the unification of large areas into great political units, each of which could be controlled by a small but mobile elite based in a major urban center. These were the ancient agricultural empires, such as those of Egypt, Mesopotamia, India, or China. Their first religious results were the enhancement and sophistication of motifs of archaic agricultural religion. The sacred king, like the pharaoh of Egypt, acquired an immensely exalted spiritual position as one who is initiated through a mystery of death and rebirth parallel to that of the plant and who performed the rites of spring and harvest. Polytheism reached an apex, for it is really a result of the union of a number of tribes, each with its own patronal deity, into a single society, and also of heaven being made to imitate the increased compartmentalization of human labor in the city and the bureaucratization of earthly government.

Religion Responding to History

Other, more deeply creative forces were also at work. The growth of trade and new imperial social organization led to writing, chronicles, and intercultural contact. Out of all this arose glimmerings of historical awareness—the realization that time seems to move irreversibly in one direction, that things have changed and will not change back. This discovery of history is always a crucial challenge to religion. Because religion points toward self-transcendence, it must somehow show that historical change is not the last word—that even if the old timeless world of the hunter or the planter's seasonal round is passing, something stands above history. Responses to history follow four main strands listed below, sometimes separated and sometimes intertwined.

Epic.   One possible response is to accept history but to see in it the unfolding of a purpose implanted in it from the beginning—the triumph of a particular people or dynasty, the defeat of the powers of darkness by the true God. Much of the great narrative literature that grows out of the era of the discovery of history has this basic motif: the Old Testament, the Kojiki in Japan, the Aeneid. In these the historical experience of wars and conquests, empires and disasters are part of a narrative with a beginning and an ending.

Ritual.   Another response is to keep certain rites, especially those of a court, a city, or an official priesthood, unchanged as a sort of frozen perpetuation of the past before the discovery of history and a symbolic area of experience untouched by it. In ancient Rome, the institution of the Vestal Virgins and the sacrifices of the city's priesthood remained virtually unchanged through all the historical vicissitudes of the empire. In ancient Japan, an imperial princess was sent far away from the court, to the vicinity of the Grand Shrine of Ise, where she avoided all Buddhist practice and even words. She represented the court before the great ancestral deities at Ise, not as it was but as it would like to be seen by the Shinto gods, as she took her place in the classic, purely Shinto rites of the Grand Shrine.

The Religious Founders.   The most consequential event of this era, however, was the emergence in the ancient world of the great international and national religions built upon the work of individual founders. Only a half-dozen or so persons have filled this awesome vocation, which has made their names more powerful in history than those of countless kings. They are Moses, Zoroaster, the Buddha, Confucius, Lao-tzu, Jesus, and Muhammad. It is interesting that out of the hundreds of thousands of years humanity has lived on this earth, all the major religious founders have lived within a span of less than two millennia—between Moses in the thirteenth century B.C.E. and Muhammad in the seventh century C.E.[5] In each case their work, sometimes only after several centuries during which a transformation of values was quietly permeating an older society, resulted in a new state, empire, or cultural wave that marked the emergence into history of vast populations.

The founder-religions—Judaism, Zoroastrianism, the Chinese faiths, Buddhism, Christianity, and Islam—have in common that they see in the life and words of the founder the exemplification and perfect statement of the ideal human life, and also in some way see him as empowering his followers to live it. Buddhism, Christianity, and Islam, especially, see the founder's religion as being transnational and transcultural, and have demonstrated this by missionizing it across many boundaries and seas. The founder-religions, especially the missionary ones, are a particularly creative sort of response to the discovery-of-history experience. By making the life of a single individual the pivot of history, they acknowledge its irreversible movement and at the same time give it a sharply focused central axis. By emphasizing the drama of a single and unique life as the bearer of revelation, they show that now, in the more complex, diversified, and chancy life of a "modern" society, the creative individual and not just the immemorial custom of a tribe is what counts.

Yet at the same time, they are religions which emerged in a time when traditions were still strong. They provided foci around which all manner of things new and old were consolidated—they all have expression on many levels, from folkways to philosophy to eccentric individualism. They could only have come into being in their historical form after or along with the development of writing, large political systems, and international trade. These have been their bearers—all make much of scriptures and political implications. Yet the founder-religions have come to be greater than particular times and places.

Wisdom.   Another path to transcending the onslaughts of history is through absolutizing states of consciousness or angles of philosophical vision in which the timeless shows its incomparable superiority over time. In India, at approximately the same time as the emergence of the founders, the tradition that was to become Hinduism produced texts such as the **Upanishads** and **Bhagavad-Gita;** in them the central theme is the unity of the individual self, who seems to suffer the vicissitudes of time and space, with the absolute, who changes not. These books, representing the composite wisdom of many sages, derive from much the same era as do the founders in other traditions.

Even in the founder-religions, a reaction in favor of mysticism and wisdom tended to set in a few centuries after the founder's day, and the same was true where polytheistic worship persisted. In either case, the wise urged a perspective that saw unity beyond the many gods or the comings and goings of founder-teachers. In the West, Neoplatonic, Stoic, and Epicurean philosophy fulfilled this role. In Judaism, books such as Proverbs and the apocryphal Wisdom of Solomon personified wisdom as a maiden greatly to be desired and through whom God made the world; to know her is to know the inner mystery of the way things work. In the same manner, from around the first century C.E., Mahayana Buddhism personified wisdom, **Prajnaparamita,** or the "wisdom that has gone beyond," a sort of perfect intuitive insight, as a goddess to be worshipped and desired. Christianity, especially in the Greek theologians and mystics, and Islam also, went through a stage in which the deepest emphasis was on understanding with mystically illumined insight the eternal realities of God and his relation to humanity and the creation that underlay the particulars of the revelation through Jesus or Muhammad.

The wisdom movements all had in common a highly sophisticated restatement of motifs of the shamanism and initiatory rites of the earliest religion: belief that through proper psychological procedures one can obtain perception into the inner laws of the cosmos and thus power over them. For this reason, wisdom religion is also an ancestor of modern science.

Medieval Devotion

Wisdom mysticism, however profound, did not allow for a full expression of emotional feelings. The Middle Ages in both Asia and Europe brought to flower a piety in which feelings of rapturous love and identification with god or saviour were preeminent. We speak of the love of Christ and the Virgin Mary in the devotion of medieval Europe, of passionate Sufi mysticism in Islam, of Krishna and other Hindu gods in India, and of Kannon and Amida in East Asian Buddhism. These movements, in which romantic love and religion interfuse, bespeak a new individualism and sensitivity in their stress on the feelings of the devotee. They were generally accompanied by rich artistic expression in images and paintings of the beloved deity.

Modernity

The real roots of the modern situation in religion go back as far as the end of the Middle Ages and are typified by such developments as the emergence of Pure Land Buddhism in Japan and the Protestant Reformation in Christianity. In both cases, emphasis was put on salvation not by involved spiritual practices or feelings but by a simple act of faith, which could be made as effectively by the laity as by monk or priest. What this really implied was a new exaltation of the secular world and the individual in it. The gradual breakdown of peasant culture based on the agricultural round meant a loss of the spiritual unity of communities. Now religion was something an individual could do wherever he or she was—in the fields or the shop or the home.

Later reform movements in Islam and Hinduism went the same direction as those in Christianity and Buddhism in rejecting the wisdom and medieval devotional approaches in favor of the supposedly plain and nonpriestly original teachings of the faith. One reason for the early modern reaction in the direction of simplicity

▲ Religious Pluralism: Muslim mosque in Cedar Rapids, Iowa.

▶ Theoretical Expression of Religion: Jewish teenager reading the Torah.

▼ Practical Expression of Religion: Colorful Greek Orthodox procession.

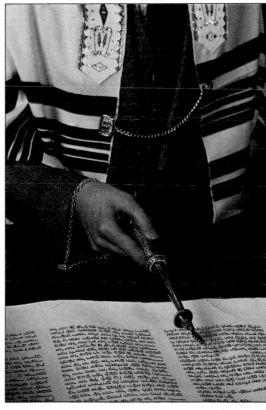

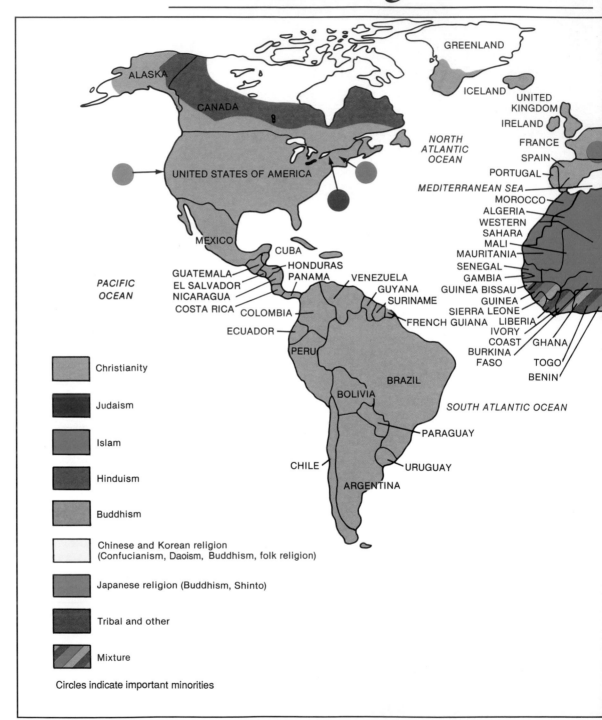

GREENLAND

ALASKA

CANADA

ICELAND

UNITED KINGDOM

IRELAND

NORTH ATLANTIC OCEAN

FRANCE

SPAIN

UNITED STATES OF AMERICA

PORTUGAL

MEDITERRANEAN SEA

MOROCCO

ALGERIA

WESTERN SAHARA

MALI

MAURITANIA

MEXICO

CUBA

HONDURAS

GUATEMALA

EL SALVADOR

NICARAGUA

COSTA RICA

PANAMA

VENEZUELA

GUYANA

SURINAME

SENEGAL

GAMBIA

GUINEA BISSAU

GUINEA

SIERRA LEONE

LIBERIA

PACIFIC OCEAN

COLOMBIA

FRENCH GUIANA

IVORY COAST

GHANA

ECUADOR

BURKINA FASO

TOGO

PERU

BENIN

BRAZIL

BOLIVIA

SOUTH ATLANTIC OCEAN

PARAGUAY

CHILE

URUGUAY

ARGENTINA

Christianity

Judaism

Islam

Hinduism

Buddhism

Chinese and Korean religion (Confucianism, Daoism, Buddhism, folk religion)

Japanese religion (Buddhism, Shinto)

Tribal and other

Mixture

Circles indicate important minorities

Religious Heritage

▶ Sociological Expression
of Religion: Jain Bahubalai
anointment.

▼ Religious Leadership:
Dalai Lama in Dharamsala,
India.

and faith certainly is the modern realization that we can do much to control and exploit the world through trade and technology, but to do so we must have a religion that can be practiced in the midst of worldly work and so can validate it. The modern faith cannot be too tied to a peasant outlook, or be too demanding of time or emotional energy, or too appreciative of mystical or emotional rather than rational and pragmatic states of mind.

However, this was not all that shaped the modern religious consciousness. This state of spiritual awareness is a collection of diverse and highly contradictory themes. The very trade and technological departures liberated by the religions of faith eventually began to undermine them, for they led to intercultural contact and scientific discoveries that made people wonder about the basis of faith. The new knowledge combined with the new secular freedom led to what is called "liberalism" in religion, essentially the statement of religious attitudes so as to fit with the normative social and scientific values of the cultural context.

Liberalism has, in turn, provoked its share of reactions, such as "integralist" Catholicism and fundamentalist Protestantism. In non-Western cultures the "crisis of modernity" has been exacerbated by the fact that it has meant coping not only with new social and scientific ideas and the changing conditions of life brought about by industrialization and urbanization, but also with an alien dominant culture—that of the West—often brought by colonial masters. There, traditional religions have responded, as in the West, in ways ranging from rigid rejection of the new to reformism based on traditional principles, like that of Gandhi, to undergirding militant nationalism, as in the Japan of the 1930s and 1940s, to lending support to radical revolution, as did some Buddhists in Communist China.[6]

It is clear, then, that religion is today in a state of flux and transition. But this has always been the case, although it has not always been quite so readily apparent. Yet each stage has always been melting into the next; there are always constant themes in religion, but their ways of expression shape themselves anew to some extent in each generation. The process is a complex interaction of tradition and new religious realizations, working through expression in word, act, and group formation, expressed through symbols or concepts that may be as old as cave art or discovered only yesterday.

FUNDAMENTAL FEATURES OF RELIGIONS

The fact that each of the world's religions has a history and encompasses each of the three forms of religious expression means that they all have common patterns. They usually ask and answer certain questions. All have a basic world view, ideas about God or ultimate reality, ideas about the origin and destiny of the world and of individual humans, a revelation or authority or mediation between the ultimate and humankind, standards about what is expected of humans—that is, patterns of worship, spiritual practices, and ethics or behavior—and an institutional or sociological expression.

In order to provide a convenient guide to these fundamental features, a chart has been prepared for each great religion. An introductory outline is presented below so that the reader can see what will be covered in each of the categories used.

It should be remembered that these charts can present only the dominant or traditional interpretation of the religion; variations often exist but cannot be taken into account here, although they may be in the text.

EVERY RELIGION A COLLECTION OF TENSIONS

It should never be forgotten that any actual religious tradition has within it something of all that has been presented. Buddhism, Christianity, Islam, and the rest have in them something of withdrawal from culture and something of affirmation of it; something of the Stone Age and something of modernity. Each may have special emphases, and each person within each may have his or her own emphases, but it needs to be grasped that all sides are there all the time. Categories such as those we have presented can help our understanding of religion, but they are not slots in which anything "out there," practiced by real living people, can be neatly dropped.

This should not surprise us if we recall that we as individuals are not just one thing all the time either. We may affirm parts of our culture and reject parts of it; we too may have something of the past and something of the present in us; all of us slowly change over the years. Every actual religion is not merely an abstraction but is rooted in the minds of thousands or millions of people and is fraught with such complexities; the religion may serve partly to simplify the complexities by setting up models and priorities, yet it cannot help but reflect them as well. Each religion turns out, in fact, to be not a simple solution to the basic tensions of life but a particular way of configuring them. It takes the chaotic complexities of human existence and causes patterns, or sets of polarities and priorities to emerge out of this morass, which help the individual to live in the midst of complexity.

In the same way, every religion throughout its history and in its full spectrum of expression will form more of a pattern, a configuration, than a straight line. Each religion has its own set of polarized attitudes toward acceptance or rejection of environing culture, toward the past and present, toward ordinary as over against ecstatic consciousness. It reflects, in other words, the great complexity and diversity of human experience even within one tradition. What distinguishes one religion from another is not only the unique founding and formal doctrine of each, but also the particular way each sets up its tensions and patterns—the particular points it lays out on its compass.

Certain areas of tension run through all religion. In virtually all we find individuals and movements representing polar positions on these axes: intellect versus feeling

Fundamental Features of Religions

Theoretical

Basic World View	How the universe is set up, especially in its spiritual aspect—the map of the invisible world.
God or Ultimate Reality	What the ultimate source and ground of all things is.
Origin of the World	Where it all came from.
Destiny of the World	Where it is going.
Origin of Humans	Where we came from.
Destiny of Humans	Where we are going.
Revelation or Mediation Between the Ultimate and the Human	How we know this and how we are helped to get from here to our ultimate destiny.

Practical

What Is Expected of Humans: Worship, Practices, Behavior	What we ourselves must do.

Sociological

Major Social Institutions	How the religion is set up to preserve and implement its teaching and practice; what kind of leadership it has; how it interacts with the larger society.

(trust in reason or in emotional experience as guide to truth), tradition versus innovation, affirmation versus rejection of culture, indigenous versus imported religion, finding the good in human society versus finding it in nature. But the symbols and personalities and concrete historical events that express these tensions in actual religion are manifoldly varied.

To illustrate each religious or cultural tradition as a collection of tensions, a series of thematic charts are included in this book. They should help the reader conceptualize the basic framework within which each tradition is working and how its leading figures and ideas relate to each other. There is nothing absolute, of course, about the reduction of each tradition to two pairs of opposites or in the particular terms that have—through a combination of arbitrariness and reflection—been selected to demarcate each chart. It is hoped, in fact, the reader will make his or her own refinements; like all schematizations, the charts are cruder than reality. But schematizations also supply signposts and symbolize that there are currents and prevailing tensions in reality that otherwise might be lost in its infinite multiplicity.

These charts, unlike the timeline charts, are nonhistorical; their thematic relationships and polarities exist within each major spiritual tradition across time as well as across denomination and sect lines. But it should be remembered that virtually nothing of significance that ever appears in the long history of a religion is ever really lost. Some whiff or savour will survive to keep it a putative part of every subsequent configuration of that tradition: Vedic rites can still be seen in India; even Protestant churches still sing medieval hymns.

It is time now to turn to the religions themselves.

SUMMARY

This chapter has tried to present some basic perspectives for understanding the religions of the world comparatively—that is, in terms of structures and patterns of thought, worship, and group life that might apply to more than one of them—and historically—that is, in terms of the ways human religion in general has developed over the centuries from the Stone Age to the present. We discussed religion as the "doors and windows" between conditioned and unconditioned reality and interpreted religion as a society's "map of the invisible world." We presented the three forms of religious expression: theoretical (narrative and doctrine), practical (styles of worship), and sociological (forms of group life). We reflected on ways in which both descriptive and critical approaches to religion are valid and important. We talked about the problems and possibilities inherent in discussing religion in terms of its history and summarized the major stages in the development of human religion. Finally, we indicated that each actual, living religion contains tensions and seemingly conflicting motifs which it tries to resolve into a pattern. (These will be presented in the case of each religion in the thematic charts.) This may make religion appear very complex and difficult; but if you will "look within" yourself, you will see that your own life is ordered in much the same way. By increasing your understanding of yourself as a human being, you will grow in your ability to understand the complexity of human religion.

QUESTIONS FOR REVIEW

1. Discuss whether or not you agree with the contention that today is a particularly exciting time to study world religions.
2. Explain the difference between conditioned and unconditioned reality, and religion's role regarding them.

3. Explain what is meant by calling a culture's religion its "map of the invisible world."

4. Name and explain Joachim Wach's three forms of religious expression.

5. Describe how religious doctrine develops from myths and narratives.

6. Compare "cosmic" and "historical" views of time.

7. Discuss what sort of messages might be transmitted nonverbally by the practical (style of worship) and sociological expressions of a religion.

8. Explain how the three forms of religious expression interact.

9. Present the values of both descriptive and critical approaches to the world religions. Give examples of both based on your own observation.

10. Discuss the advantages and possible pitfalls of a historical approach to understanding a religion.

11. Summarize the main periods in the history of human religion.

12. Indicate the main ways in which religion has responded to the experience of the "discovery of history."

13. Describe some common characteristics of founder-religions, especially Buddhism, Christianity, and Islam.

14. Explain some of the major characteristics of the modern experience and how religion has responded to them.

15. Discuss how religions both contain and try to resolve the tensions common to human existence.

16. Discuss whether or not you agree that the historical and comparative approach to studying world religions seems to make each offer partial truths relative to a particular culture, or do you think it is possible to find absolute meaning within any religion, and if so, of what kind.

SUGGESTED READINGS ON THE STUDY OF WORLD RELIGIONS

*BETTIS, JOSEPH DABNEY, ED., *Phenomenology of Religion*. New York: Harper & Row, 1969. A collection of basic papers by leading philosophers on "description of the essence of religion."

*DE VRIES, JAN, *The Study of Religion: A Historical Approach*. New York: Harcourt, 1967. A summary of the modern history of academic religious studies.

*ELIADE, MIRCEA, *Cosmos and History*. New York: Harper Torchbooks, 1959. A good basic approach to the history of religions; compares concepts of time in different types of religion.

*_____, *From Primitives to Zen*. New York: Harper & Row, 1967. A useful collection of texts and description arranged thematically.

*_____, *Patterns in Comparative Religion*. Cleveland: Meridian Books, 1963. A substantial cross-cultural treatment of basic religious symbols and themes, such as sun, moon, and agriculture.

*_____, *The Sacred and The Profane*. New York: Harper Torchbooks, 1961. An excellent basic introduction to the history of religions, elucidating such matters as the meaning of the temple, the festival, initiation, and myth.

FALK, NANCY A., and RITA M. GROSS, *Unspoken Worlds: Women's Religious Lives*. New York: Harper & Row, 1980. As the title suggests, a view into religious spheres too long lived in silence.

*HALL, T. W., ED., *Introduction to the Study of Religion*. New York: Harper and Row, 1978. Helpful presentations of basic perspectives.

KING, WINSTON, *Introduction to Religion: A Phenomenological Approach*. New York: Harper & Row, 1968. A good overview of different approaches and categories in the study of religion.

*LÉVI-STRAUSS, CLAUDE, *Structural Anthropology*. Garden City, New York: Doubleday, 1967. An important modern anthropologist's treatment of how myth, ritual, and shamanism create symbolic worlds.

*OTTO, RUDOLF, *The Idea of the Holy*. London & New York: Oxford University Press, 1958. A classic statement of the experience of the "numinous" from which religion begins.

SHARPE, ERIC J., *Comparative Religion: A History*. London, 1975; Peru, IL: Open Court, 1987. A useful story of the discipline.

*SMITH, HUSTON, *The Religions of Man*. New York: Harper & Row, 1958. A very readable and insightful survey.

SMITH, JONATHON Z., *Imagining Religion*. Chicago: University of Chicago Press, 1982. An engrossing critical look at several theories and issues in the history of religions.

*SMITH, W. C., *The Meaning and End of Religion*. New York: Harper & Row, 1962, 1978. A fresh approach to understanding religion as a phenomenon of human history.

*SPENCER, SIDNEY, *Mysticism in World Religion*. Baltimore: Penguin Books, 1963. The most authoritative survey of this area.

*STRENG, FREDERICK J., *Understanding Religious Life*. Belmont, CA: Wadsworth, 3rd ed, 1985. A good introduction to methodology in religious studies.

TURNER, VICTOR W., *The Ritual Process*. Chicago: Aldine, 1969. A highly stimulating set of essays on the meaning of rite and symbol.

*VAN DER LEEUW, GERARDUS, *Religion in Essence and Manifestation,* 2 vols. New York: Harper & Row, 1963. A classic thematic study containing a succinct statement of the phenomenological method.

*WACH, JOACHIM, *The Comparative Study of Religion*. New York: Columbia University Press, 1958. A brilliant treatment of the major concepts and problems in comparative religious studies from the author's point of view.

*_____, *Sociology of Religion*. Chicago: University of Chicago Press, 1944. A classic statement of the different kinds of religious groups, leaders, and forms of expression.

*WEBER, MAX, *The Sociology of Religion*. Boston: Beacon Press, 1963. A collection of basic writings by one of the seminal thinkers in this area.

The student is also referred to good encyclopedic treatments of particular topics, such as those in the *Encyclopedia Britannica* and Keith Crim, ed., *Abingdon Dictionary of Living Religions*. Nashville: Abingdon Press, 1981; and Mircea Eliade, ed., *The Encyclopedia of Religion*. New York: Macmillan, 1987.

CHAPTER 2

The Sacred in Sky and Soul:
PREHISTORIC AND TRIBAL RELIGIONS

CHAPTER OBJECTIVES

After studying this chapter, you should be able to

- Discuss common features of primal and tribal religions.

- Explain shamanism.

- Interpret the transition from hunting/gathering to agricultural religion.

- Discuss the importance of understanding early religion for human life today, including ways in which its themes can still be found.

THE FIRST HUMAN FAITHS

Behind the panorama of the great religions with their founders and scriptures—behind even the world of the ancient empires with their writing systems and sprawling political-economic entities out of which the former mostly emerged—hangs the backdrop of the religious world that went before. That was a religious world without written texts but rich in art, myth, and dance. It was the religious world of the ancestors of all living human beings for hundreds of thousands, perhaps millions, of years between the emergence of human culture as a distinct way of life on earth and the appearance of writing, large political units, and the rest of what makes up the form of human culture we call civilization. As such, it may be called *prehistoric* religion, for written history had to wait the invention of writing.

Away from the centers of civilization, forms of religious life continuous with the prehistoric have persisted—though in diminishing numbers—down to the present. We are speaking of societies characterized by two determinative features: They are nonliterate—that is, they do not have reading and writing—and they are organized in very small political units, such as tribes or clans. They may subsist by hunting and gathering only, or practice an archaic form of agriculture, or live as nomadic pastoralists. To further clarify the type of society of which we are speaking, let us note that it would not include nonliterate peasants in a large social unit; an empire or kingdom such as ancient Egypt or medieval England, in which a literate elite also existed; nor would it include tribal peoples, say Eskimos or Arab Bedouins, who have embraced a scriptural religion—Christianity or Islam—and are to that extent literate. As late as the nineteenth century, vast stretches of the earth, from Siberia to Africa, from Australia to the Americas, still supported such tribal societies, though under steadily increasing pressure. Their traditional forms of religion also flourished, though they were giving way to the efforts of missionaries even as the traditional ways of livelihood and social organization fell before the incursions of "civilized" traders, settlers, and colonial overlords. Today only remnants of tribal, nonliterate society and religion survive. But there is enough to provide a picture of what we think it was like.

To extrapolate from present-day tribal religion back to worldwide prehistoric religion is risky. Sometimes influences from the great religions have slipped in unostentatiously; sometimes the very fact that tribal religion was probably under seige by the time observers arrived has made a difference. Nonetheless, it seems safe to assume that at least the major themes of today's tribal religions are continuous with those of prehistoric religion, and in a single chapter we can do little more than examine major themes. So we will consider prehistoric and tribal religions together.

This type of religion has gone by many names among the literate. It has been called primitive, primal, basic, or archaic religion; it has been referred to as animism and shamanism. Problems exist with all these terms. Terms in the first set, of which *primitive* has been the most widely used, are acceptable insofar as they simply point to the fact that this is the style of religion that appeared first among humans. But the term *primitive* in particular has also acquired unjust and inaccurate connotations

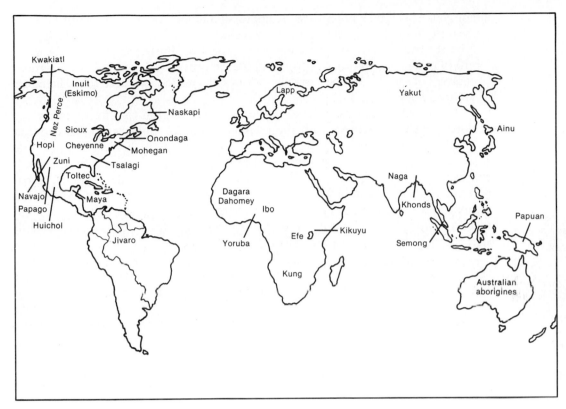

MAP 2–1.   Prehistoric and Tribal Religions

of crudity and barbarism, and "firstness" in any case is not the only characteristic of the religions in question. Having persisted down to the present, they have as long a sequence of development as any other faith; this development has just taken a different direction from that of religions employing writing and scripture and interacting with kingdoms and empires. **Animism,** or belief in souls or spirits, and shamanism, to be discussed later, allude to beliefs and practices widespread in prehistoric and tribal religions but of varying importance and also questionable as definers. Avoiding a single term for such an immense and diverse collection, we shall merely speak of prehistoric and tribal religions.

The substance of these religions is tremendously varied, for the roster of prehistoric and present-day tribes and nonliterate cultures, each with its own gods and rites, is almost endless; very many have undoubtedly been forgotten forever. Because of the immense variety, this chapter cannot hope to cover it in a systematic or culture-by-culture way. Our discussion is impressionistic and rather nonhistorical, although we shall take note of the religious significance of one important event in prehistoric "history"—the emergence of agriculture. Generally, however, our approach will be thematic, drawing from cross-cultural data to illustrate certain of the great motifs of nonliterate spirituality. Not all of these motifs are shared by all such cultures, of course. For specific data on particular cultures, the reader is referred to the literature of anthropology.

Mircea Eliade has used the expression **cosmic religion** to refer to a religious outlook largely coextensive with the religion of archaic hunters and farmers but with continuations down to the present.[1] Cosmic religion, he tells us, has little sense of history or of what was discussed in the last chapter as linear time. It finds and expresses sacred meaning in aspects of nature and human life—seasons, sacred rocks or trees, the social order, birth and death—without linking them to historical personalities or written documents as founder-religions do. Although the situation is full of ambiguities, reflecting on the cosmic religion experience is a good way to start meeting the prehistoric and tribal spiritual world.

Cosmic religion includes festivals of seedtime and harvest and the sacred trees and mountains around which the earth seems to pivot. It is the overlaying of our world by an "other world" of gods and goblins, of elves and spirits of the returning dead. It is the rites of hunting and archaic agriculture in a world where "everything is alive." It is the ecstasies of shamans who are believed to be able to control spirits and travel in trance to heaven or the underworld to recover strayed or stolen souls or to intercede with the gods.

The world of cosmic religion seems very remote to us at first glance. Yet many of its motifs, when communicated in fairy tales or African masks, come across as hauntingly beautiful or nightmarishly powerful. They hit one unexpectedly with all the impact of a half-remembered but very important scene from a dream or early childhood. Then again, countless survivals from the world of cosmic religion—from Christmas trees to the Muslim pilgrimage to Mecca—continue to flourish as much as ever with somewhat transmuted meanings. It could be argued that most popular religion, whether in Buddhist, Christian, or Muslim lands, is only a partially altered cosmic or primitive religion under another name.

Christmas, for example, is a festival of a religion deriving from the era of the discovery of history and commemorates a historical event, around which all history is believed to turn. But consider the Christmas symbolism—a celebration of light at the darkest time of the year, the inauguration of a new year, an ornamented tree representing a "cosmic tree" symbolizing the mystical center of the earth and a way of access to the divine world. This is not only pre-Christian in origin but expresses the cosmic religion kind of emphasis: the spiritual experience produced by the turn of the seasons, the sacred meaning of landmarks of nature like trees and mountains, the sheer immediate evocative power of symbols like light and glitter, the perennial importance to spiritual life of family and the sacred, set-apart time of festival.

Then there is our orange-and-black feast, with its atmosphere of jack o'lanterns and tales of witches amid frost and falling leaves. Perhaps the oldest holiday that is

A symbol of fertility, Venus of Willendorf c. 15,000–10,000 B.C.E.

a part of general American culture is Halloween. It is almost a pure survival of cosmic religion, and it incorporates no small number of its themes. On this night, children masked and costumed as ghosts, witches, and devils, or as pirates, cowboys, or monsters visit homes to receive candy with the threat of "tricks or treats."[2] Pranks ranging from soaping windows to putting a farmer's wagon on top of his barn are also sometimes part of Halloween. There are costume parties with spooky decorations and traditional games like bobbing for apples.

Perpetuated into Christian times as the eve of All Hallows or All Saints' Day, Halloween was originally the autumn festival of the ancient Britons and their Druid priests, called Samhain. It was the Celtic and Anglo-Saxon New Year. Like festivals of harvest and the new year everywhere, Samhain had motifs of settling accounts, kindling a new fire, the harvest moon, the celebration of first fruits, and the return of the dead to visit the living. It suggested a temporary return to the chaos before the world was created and thereby the release of the dark and uncanny denizens of chaos. Behind children's masks of monsters and witches, behind "tricks or treats" and bobbing for apples, lies the ancient cosmic religious orientation toward the turn of the seasons, rather than a historical event, as where reality is revealed. An important motif of cosmic religion is a feeling that the turn of the year is like a clock running down and coming virtually to a stop just before it is wound up again on New Year's Day. New Year's Day is like a recurrent Day of Creation to cosmic religion, and so the preceding eve is like replunging into that precreation flux when there were no controls. This is illustrated by the coming out of dark, grisly entities on Halloween, the ancient New Year's Eve, and our tradition of getting drunk on the modern New Year's Eve. In ancient Rome, the end-of-the-year festival was the Saturnalia, when masters and slaves exchanged roles in a gesture of turning upside down the ordinary structures of society.

May Day, another holiday celebrated mainly by children, continues the pre-Christian spring festival of ancient Britain, known as Beltane. As Halloween in the fall bore a mood of night, moon, the dead, and unwholesome visitants, so May Day is a celebration of day, sun, flowers, and all that is bright, warm, and fresh, although also supernatural. Dancing around the maypole was an ancient practice to encourage fertility; May baskets were gifts of the bounty of the enchanting White Lady who rode through the land awakening the miracle of spring. A center of this belief was the town of Banbury in central England; until modern times the visit of the White Lady was enacted on May Day in a pageant culminating at the ancient market cross in the town square. As the old rhyme has it:

> Ride a cock-horse to Banbury Cross,
> To see a fine lady upon a white horse,
> With rings on her fingers and bells on her toes,
> She shall have music wherever she goes.

Long after Christianity came, in fact, May Day celebrations were held in Banbury in which youths would gather boughs and make garlands, a maypole would be set up, and a girl would be chosen May Queen (formerly representing the goddess of fertility), who would ride to the festivities on a white horse.

It is interesting that the most colorful survivals of cosmic religion, May Day and Halloween, are kept mainly by children. Part of the world of nonliterate religion indeed seems childlike: wearing masks, keeping special days, believing in spirits, magic places, and gestures. Moreover, there is a sense in which the culture of children is always conservative. It retains lore in fairy tales, games, and holidays that have lost power in adult culture.

It would, however, be a grave mistake to think of such people as children. Adults among them are adult; their myths and symbols are full of evidence that people have passed through adolescence, experienced adult sexuality, married, and had children of their own. All these experiences are marked by rich ceremonies and

---

Fundamental Features of Prehistoric and Tribal Religions

Theoretical

Basic World View	The universe is a place animated by many spirits, some friendly and some not. Humans have a real place in the cosmos, which works by rules and cycles that can be known.
God or Ultimate Reality	Many gods and spirits; but perhaps a high god or unifying force over them.
Origin of the World	Either no point of origin, or created by the gods or a high god who may subsequently have withdrawn from activity.
Destiny of the World	Usually not clear.
Origin of Humans	Often children of gods or semidivine primal parents.
Destiny of Humans	Frequently to go after death to another world, not unlike this world, sometimes also to be reborn here in this world.
Revelation or Mediation Between the Ultimate and the Human	Myth, often told and enacted at festivals and by shamans; benign gods and ancestral spirits as helpers.

Practical

What Is Expected of Humans: Worship, Practice, Behavior	To undergo initiation; to honor and sacrifice to gods and ancestors; to observe tribal norms of behavior and taboos.

Sociological

Major Social Institutions	Tribe as a spiritual unit; shamanism.

permeate the rites of spring and harvest and the tales of the gods. Tribal people can think as rationally, and handle ideas as complex, as can any adults. Their symbol systems often convey as much complexity of information and insight as pages of writing or even mathematical equations.

Moreover, survivals such as Halloween and May Day contain only a few of the themes of early religion in its fullness. They suggest a typical (at least in temperate climates) seasonal emphasis, but the pantheon of gods and the full relation of the religion to society is less evident. Our holidays are, after all, only bits and pieces of forgotten faiths.

But we must now approach the world of prehistoric and tribal religion in its fullness. Although these religions do have rational world views expressed through rite and symbol and society, they do not have the formal written ideological statements that in other religions are all-too-tempting pegs for interpretation. We have to see what the unified experience and the particulars alike are themselves saying. Clifford Geertz has written that nonliterate religion

> . . . consists of a multitude of very concretely defined and only loosely ordered sacred entities, an untidy collection of fussy ritual acts and vivid animistic images which are able to involve themselves in an independent, segmental, and immediate manner with almost any sort of actual event.[3]

What we shall be examining, then, is images, and it is images—symbols, gestures, sacred art, and the mighty figures of myth—that stand out in the world of cosmic religion. It is from the accounts of heroes in story, from masks, from priests in the midst of a hunting rite, from carvings of ancestors, and paintings on rocks and caves that cosmic religion is learned. All of these go together to make up a cosmos in which spirit and matter are thoroughly interwoven, and everything is more than it seems as myth, rite, and art make the invisible visible. In this cosmos, human life is only complete in its total relationships—with family, tribe, ancestors, the Other World, and all spirits here and beyond.

GODS, SPIRITS, AND THE WORLD

Prehistoric and tribal religion has its demarcations between conditioned and unconditioned reality, its maps of the invisible world, and the colorful patterns they often are. Yet, as Geertz pointed out, they generally seem complex, only semiordered, and deeply intermingled with all of life. The images they imprint on the mind, however, borne by the powerful languages of myth and ritual, are unforgettable.

Most prominent of these images may be those of the time of human origins and the gods of that time, for there if anywhere is mastery of time and death. At the same time, humans are aware that the world is far from perfect and that if the creation was meant to be good, something must have gone wrong. Often an original or ultimate god will be portrayed as having made the world but now seems to have little concern for humankind except perhaps to enforce the moral law. A deity like this is spoken of as a **deus otiosus,** a "hidden god."

Sometimes a myth, comparable to the Garden of Eden narrative, accounts for the separation of humankind from primordial closeness to the creator. With the separation, death enters the world. The natives of Poso, Celebes Island, Indonesia, said that originally the sky where the creator dwelt was very near the earth, and he would lower gifts down on a rope to his children. Once he thus let down a stone, but the first men and women were indignant at such a useless gift and refused it. So the creator pulled it back up and lowered instead a banana. This they took. But the creator called to them, "Because you have chosen the banana, your life shall be like its life. Had you taken the stone, you would have been like it, changeless and immortal."[4]

Or, the creation itself may have been accomplished by lesser deities. Among the Semang, a simple hunting culture in Malaya, it is said the high god, Karei, lives in the sky and his wife, Manoid, in the earth. Their children are Ta Pedn, Begreg, Karpgen, and a daughter Takel; the thunder is Karei playing with his children. Karei's son, Ta Pedn, created everything; Karei himself made nothing. Karei merely enforces, as a firm and inexorable father-judge, the moral law. He requires that transgressors make a blood-expiation. It is said in fact among the Semang that Ta Pedn is good but Karei is evil.[5]

But though the creator high god (if there is one) may be far removed from ordinary human affairs, many much more involved spiritual entities range the intervening space. Lesser gods, perhaps offspring of the creator, like the children of Karei, may be closer presences in sacred mountains or the forests the hunter enters. Ancestral spirits are likely to be especially loved and feared, for they stay near their families to impart the strength that goes with the lineage, but they also punish individuals whose faults dishonor it.

Indeed, the concept of the soul as a separable, undying part of oneself is extremely widespread. But ideas as to what happens to it after death are mixed. In fact, a notion of several souls to accommodate the different prospects is common.

One idea is that the departed spirit remains close to hearth and home, becoming an ancestral soul that must be propitiated at a nearby grave or shrine. Sometimes these spirits are personified by dancers in ceremonies, often with masks. Another idea is that they go to a distant land of the dead, perhaps a known but remote island or mountain, perhaps a more mythical place like the Australian "Dreamtime" world. But usually this place is less a fanciful paradise than a mirror-image of this world, where life goes on much the same as here though perhaps more pleasantly, with days always mild and food always abundant. Finally, it is also sometimes thought that the dead reincarnate in the same tribe or family, perhaps after a stay in the alternative world. Sometimes one finds a concept of several souls evoked to deal with these varied destinies, one to become an ancestral spirit, and another to go to the other world.

But tribal religion is acted as much as it is thought. Among its best-known and most significant acts are initiations, scenarios that enact views concerning birth and death as stages through which the soul passes, and ancestors living and dead are seen as custodians of enabling power.

INITIATIONS

For most tribal cultures, life is a series of initiations, and it is through them that its most meaningful signs of status are bestowed, as well as the deepest mysteries of the ultimate meaning of human existence revealed. Birth and death are themselves initiatory experiences and so are a part of the series; the great ceremonial initiations enhance, ratify, recapitulate, and prepare one for what is imparted by these two deepest of all sacred mysteries.

Appropriately, initiation is a painful trial, like birth and death. Among the Papuans about Finsch Harbor in New Guinea, the initiation ceremony for all youths was held every ten to eighteen years, and the boys who underwent it ranged in age from four to twenty. The central feature, as in many such rites around the world, was circumcision or, more exactly, a ritual death and redemption of which circumcision is a lasting token.

At the appointed time, the young candidates are taken by the men of the tribe into the forest. The bull-roarers—flat elliptical pieces of wood, which when twirled make an unearthly roaring sound—are booming. Significantly, the word *balum* means both bull-roarer and ghost. The women of the tribe look on from a distance, anxious and weeping, for they have been told the boys are to be eaten by a balum or ghostly monster, who will release them only on condition of receiving a sufficient number of pigs. The women have therefore been fattening pigs since the ceremony was announced and hope they will be adequate to redeem their sons and lovers. There must be one pig for each initiate.

Deep in the forest, the boys are taken to a secret lodge designed to represent the belly of the monster. A pair of eyes are painted on the entrance, and roots and branches betoken the horror's hair and backbone. As they approach he "growls"—the voice of more hidden bull-roarers.

The pigs are sacrificed and eaten by the men and boys, for the monster demands only their "souls." The boys enter the lodge and undergo the circumcision operation. They remain in seclusion three or four months, living in that long hut inside the "monster." During this time they weave baskets and play two sacred flutes said to be male and female and to be married to each other. No women may see these flutes, which are employed only during such sacred seasons as this.

At the end of the seclusion period, the boys return to the village, but they return in a special manner that bespeaks festival and rebirth. They are first taken to bathe in the sea and then are elaborately decorated with paint and mud. As they go back to the village, they must keep their eyes tightly shut. An old man touches each on the forehead and chin with a bull-roarer. They are then told to open their eyes, and then they may feast and talk to the women.[6]

The 1990 accession rite of Japanese emperor Akihito. The Daijosai part of this ceremony is one of the oldest royal rituals to persist into the modern world.

Part of totem pole

In the New Hebrides island of Malekula, where a similar Melanesian culture prevails, the men spend their lives undergoing a series of higher and higher initiations, as they are able to obtain the requisite pigs (raised by the women) for sacrifice and feast. These achievements are memorialized in the imperishable tusks of the boars and by wooden markers like totem poles in the courtyard of the men's lodges; these become ancestral gods. By the spiritual power of the pigs, a man is enabled to pass the lair of Lehevhev, the terrible spider-woman who guards the road to the Other World. In the highest of these degree-rites, the initiates are garbed in masks and ghostly white webbing, as though they were already sacred ancestors with the dread power of one who has passed from death into unearthly life.

Besides these tribal rites, there are also special individual initiations. For some peoples, in fact, the initiation of all young men was more individualized than in New Guinea; the Pawnee young man was expected to remain alone in the bush until he personally received a dream or vision of his guardian spirit. There are also particular sacred individuals, especially kings and shamans, who are set apart by distinctive movements of the sacred.

SHAMANS

There are those who are singled out by the divine to receive special ecstatic powers for dealing with spiritual things. These are the men or women called shamans or, less precisely, medicine men or witch doctors. The **shaman** above all is one who, on subtle planes of perception or soul travel, moves freely between this world and the other. He knows the geography and dynamics of the invisible world. Thus, he can serve as guide of the souls of the dead and also as healer and intercessor.

The word *shaman* is Siberian, and it is in that land of endless birch and evergreen forests, broad rivers, wide skies, and dark subzero winters that its classic form is found, although shamanism, or closely related phenomena, appears in most parts of the earth. Indeed, it has been argued that shamanism is the prototype of much of the religious world.

Let us look at a few shamanistic performances and try to understand the common features of shamanism.

The Altaic shaman in Siberia wore brown leather and elaborate decorations of metal discs, bird feathers, and colored streamers. He entranced himself by beating a drum rhythmically for hours, sitting astride a horsehide-covered bench or a straw goose, and the beat of the drum was the pounding of the hooves or wings of these spirit-steeds as they bore him to the Other World. Finally, the shaman would dismount and, flushed with ecstasy, climb nine steps notched in a tree trunk. At each stage in the ascent he would relate the difficulties of his journey, address the gods of that level of the heavens, and report what they were telling him about coming events. Some of the episodes were comic, such as a burlesque hare hunt on the sixth level. The shaman's scenario is generally enacted with a rich dramatic sense for the right combination of spectacle, mystery, suspense, comic relief, and exalted sentiments. When the Altaic shaman had gone as high as his power permitted, he concluded with a reverent prayer of devotion to Bai Ulgan, the high god, and collapsed, exhausted.[7]

Peter Freuchen in his *Book of the Eskimos* describes a shaman's seance he attended.[8] He emphasizes that the shaman, named Sorqaq, prepared seriously for the exercise by fasting and meditation on the cliffs. Sorqaq was to contact a god who dwelt beneath the earth to find out why the tribe had been suffering a series of accidents. Nonetheless, he opened the session by telling those who attended that they were a bunch of fools for coming, that nothing he did would have any truth in it. The audience responded with cries of belief and encouragement. The shaman then sat naked upon a sealskin on a ledge in the igloo, and his assistant bound him tightly with sealskin thongs. His drum was placed beside him. The lights, except for one small flame, were put out.

Then Sorqaq began to sing, and his voice grew louder and louder. Soon it was accompanied by the beat of the drum and the rustle of the sealskin, which seemed to be flying about the room. The awful din rose to a crescendo, with everyone joining in the singing. Sorqaq's own voice then became fainter and seemed to be coming from farther and farther away.

The assistant suddenly put on the lights. Freuchen noticed that the audience was ecstatic—eyes gleaming, bodies twisting to the music of the shaman's song—like participants at a revival. Even more remarkable, the shaman himself was gone, his place on the ledge empty save for the drum and sealskin! Among the crowd the spiritual intensity grew, with people experiencing seizures and speaking in strange words, including a special seance language in which persons and objects are referred to by alternative terms.

Then the assistant announced that the shaman was returning. People went back to their seats and the lights were put out. The assistant told with what difficulty Sorqaq was swimming through the rocks beneath. His voice was heard growing in volume, once again the drum sounded louder and louder, and the sealskin crackled in the air. The room quieted after Sorqaq returned, and he was seen again seated on the ledge tightly bound in straps. He told what he had learned: "To avoid more tragedies, our women must refrain from eating of the female walrus until the winter darkness returns!" (Freuchen remarks that because they are considered basically unclean, it is almost always against the women that the taboos are directed.)

After the performance, Sorqaq said to Freuchen, "Just lies and tricks. The wisdom of our ancestors is not in me. Do not believe in any of it!"

These accounts should make evident that the shaman is distinguished from other types of religious specialists, such as the priest or the sorcerer, in part by the dramatic quality of his performance, with its semispontaneous appearance and the fact that the shaman seems to, and often does, undergo the psychic and physical changes attendant upon altered states of consciousness. Anthropological work has brought to light that taking hallucinogenic plants, such as the fly-agaric mushroom in central Asia and plants of the datura family in the Western Hemisphere, is a part of shamanism in many cultures.[9] The altered state of consciousness and the visions of the shaman, however valid spiritually in the context of the culture, are often facilitated by the well-known effects of these drugs.

That is not the case with all shamanism, however. Trance-induced altered states of consciousness in which radically nonordinary perception and audition are obtained are quite possible without the aid of drugs. Trances of this sort are often accompanied by violent trembling, swelling, discoloration, and berserk behavior, as well as divine utterance. Sometimes seemingly superhuman strength is attained; Tibetan shamans have been reliably reported to be able to twist strong steel swords into knots while in this state. But afterward the performer will be so exhausted as to sleep for days, and such shamans are said, in fact, to be generally short-lived.

The shaman is also distinguished by a related factor, the nature of his "call." Other religious functionaries may have entered into their role by heredity, choice, or apprenticeship. But in the case of the shaman, although these factors may play a part, the important point will generally be that he has passed through a powerful spiritual ordeal of selection, testing, and "remaking" by divine beings themselves.

Above all, he will probably receive an assisting spirit, who gives him supernormal powers and control over other spirits.

Here is a vivid account of the manner in which the Eskimo shaman received his power:

> The *angakok* consists of a mysterious light which the shaman suddenly feels in his body, inside his head, within the brain, an inexplicable searchlight, a luminous fire, which enables him to see in the dark, both literally and metaphorically speaking, for he can now, even with closed eyes, see through darkness and perceive things and coming events, which are hidden from others: thus they look into the future and into the secrets of others.
>
> The candidate obtains this mystical light after long hours of waiting, sitting on a bench in his hut and invoking the spirits. When he experiences it for the first time "it is as if the house in which he is suddenly rises; he sees far ahead of him, through mountains, exactly as if the earth were one great plain, and his eyes could reach to the end of the earth. Nothing is hidden from him any longer; not only can he see things far, far away, but he can also discover souls, stolen souls, which are either kept concealed in far, strange lands, or have been taken up or down to the Land of the Dead."[10]

One could move from this kind of experience to that of, say, the Buddha at the moment of his enlightenment, when it was not a question of an illuminating spirit entering him from outside. Rather, for the Buddha, all gods and spirits fell into secondary roles beside the pure, radiant, conceptless, horizonless, marvelous openness in which all thought of self vanishes. Reportedly, one who attains Buddha-consciousness, or Hindu liberation, is able to see all the intricacies of all lives past and present and to be in union with infinity.

The process of becoming a shaman is sufficiently violent to cause Mircea Eliade to speak of it as an "initiatory psychopathology." The future shaman's career begins typically with a "call" from a god or spirit, perhaps the primordial master shaman, in the form of "voices" or strange impulses or seizures. For a time, unable to escape from a supernatural world for which he is not prepared, he may be tormented by cruel spirits in his head and body. He may suffer extremes of anxiety and rapture, wander about the village in a dissociated manner, have fits, be unable to eat or drink, even become criminal. He is, in a word, what we in our culture would call insane.

In terms of his own culture, however, he is one marked by the gods as a possible candidate for a mighty vocation. However much he may want merely to be "normal," that can never be; the gods will not let their fingering-out of a person be scorned. He must either serve them or face the unspeakable terrors of their punishment in mind and body.

Even so, he will not necessarily succeed in becoming a shaman. There is a great test that lies ahead. He is already in the spiritual world. Now he must acquire power to master it. He has no choice; he must master it or it will destroy him. He can acquire this power only with the help of one who has it. He must find an initiator, either a great shaman in this world or a supernatural ally in the other, who will impart to him the techniques of control. In our terms, he must conquer his sickness and make it work for him. It must continue to produce knowledge-giving visions of the spiritual world, or the subjective world if one prefers, but only when he requests it to do so. His must become an insanity he can turn on and off at will, so as to learn the things only this state can teach, but he must not be enslaved by it.[11]

To arrive at this kind of control the novice must pass through a catharsis that is virtually a death and rebirth. Alone in the wilderness, in sickness, as aide to a senior shaman, he meets his crisis. Among the Eskimos, it is said that the future shaman must take out all his bones and count them; among the Australians that his soft viscera must be replaced by organs of quartz.

But however exclusive his call, shamanism is not lacking the social dimension of religion. The future shaman's spiritual attack, private as it is, is also a phenomenon

Navajo Indian shaman

expected in his society and has a conventional interpretation and resolution. Moreover, once the shaman has passed through his initiation, he has a role traditional in the society, which frequently has great prestige.

However genuine the call, the role—partly because of the conventional expectations—is not without an element of showmanship or even fraud, as the Eskimo shaman Sorqaq intimated. Perhaps his point of view was the same as that of Quesalid, a shaman of the Kwakiutl Indians of British Columbia, who told the anthropologist Franz Boas the story of his life. Quesalid said that he started out as a skeptic and associated with shamans to learn their tricks and expose them. Invited to join with them, he learned plenty: sacred songs, how to induce trances and fits, how to produce seemingly magical feats by sleight of hand, and much else. In the meantime, knowledge of his training spread, and he was invited by a family to heal a sickness.

Despite Quesalid's disbelief, he felt constrained to accept; the healing was a success. As more triumphs followed, word spread that he was a great shaman. Knowing such things as that the "sickness" he pretended to suck out of the ill person's body was actually made of down he had previously concealed in his mouth, Quesalid was at a loss how to interpret to himself what he was doing. Finally, he came to feel that the healings worked because the sick person "believed strongly in his dream about me," and he apparently felt that the deceptions were justifiable insofar as they helped people believe. Nonetheless, he proved the superiority of his method in competition with shaman colleagues and was contemptuous of most other shamans as charlatans, saying he had only known one he thought was a "real shaman," who employed no trickery he could detect and who would not accept pay.[12]

There are variations in shamanism. One major distinction is between the "traveling" shaman, such as the Altaic and Eskimo already presented, who goes to the distant heavens or underworld in his trance. The other is the "possession" shaman who, as it were, draws the gods to him rather than going to them, being possessed like a medium by gods and spirits in his performance and letting them speak through him.

A good example of the latter are the *miko,* or shamanesses, of Japan. Now disappearing, they played a substantial part in the popular religion of Japan in the past. They are found today mostly in the far northern part of the island of Honshu; every summer they gather there for a sort of convention on Mount Osore on the upper tip of that island. The Japanese shamans of this type are all female and, what is more, are all blind or nearly so. All were initiated into the vocation of shamanizing as young girls. While it precluded marriage (unlikely for a blind girl in any case in traditional society) it did provide a respected place in the village for girls who otherwise would have had slim prospects.

Blind girls became apprentices of older shamanesses at six or eight years of age. After a strict training involving fasts, cold-water ablutions, observing taboos, and learning shamaness songs and techniques of trance and divination, they were initiated.

For this rite, the novice wears a white robe called the death dress. She sits facing her mistress and other shamanesses; these elders sing and chant formulae

Main Themes of Prehistoric and Tribal Religions

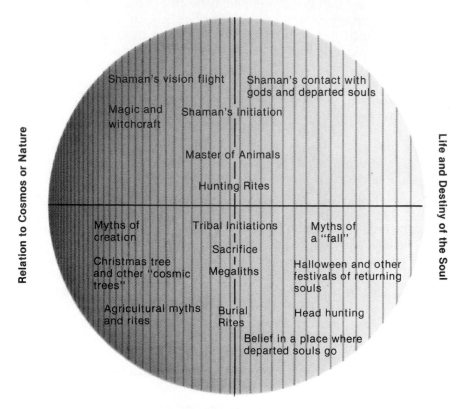

The Individual Religious Specialist

Relation to Cosmos or Nature

Life and Destiny of the Soul

Shaman's vision flight

Shaman's contact with gods and departed souls

Magic and witchcraft

Shaman's Initiation

Master of Animals

Hunting Rites

Myths of creation

Tribal Initiations

Myths of a "fall"

Sacrifice

Christmas tree and other "cosmic trees"

Megaliths

Halloween and other festivals of returning souls

Agricultural myths and rites

Burial Rites

Head hunting

Belief in a place where departed souls go

Religion as Tribal Cohesion

Thematic Chart 1. Here we see several of the aspects of primitive religion mentioned in the text set in a pattern that illustrates some possible ways of seeing their interrelationship. The chart shows that prehistoric peoples, like those in every age, saw themselves related to the cosmos or nature yet also as possessing something, symbolized in the concept of a soul, transcendent to nature and having a different destiny; and that religion served both to bind communities or tribes together and to provide scope for individuals like the shaman with a special calling in relation to the sacred.

and names of deities. Suddenly the mistress cries, "What deity possessed you?" When the candidate gives the name of a Shinto god or Buddha or bodhisattva (who will thereafter be her main supernatural patron), the mistress throws a rice cake at her, causing her to fall onto the floor in a faint. The elders then dash water onto her head as many as 3,333 times. Then they lie beside her and revive her with body heat. When she comes to, she is said to be reborn; she exchanges the death dress for wedding apparel, and a traditional Japanese wedding—with the traditional exchanges of cups of sake nine times—is performed. The new shamaness is the bride; her deity, the groom. Next a great feast of celebration follows, shared by relatives and friends of the new medium; she demonstrates her proficiency at communicating with spirits of the dead. For a week following, as a sort of divine honeymoon, she may live alone in a shrine of her deity.[13]

While doing field work in Japan in 1966, I visited a shamaness who consented to give me a "reading." One wall of the main room of her small house was taken up with altars—Shinto and Buddhist alike—reflecting the syncretistic nature of popular religion around the world. She sat on the floor facing the altars and sang in a sleepy, mystical tone as she swayed back and forth, going into a light trance. Then she called on the help of the sovereign gods, giving out a list of popular Shinto and Buddhist figures and calling on the patrons of the local mountains and districts. Next she received her modest payment, worked the 500-yen note in her hands slowly and placed it on an altar.

After this, she called down the guardian deity of my family, whom she said was Fudo, a bodhisattva prominent in popular Buddhism. He gave me such warnings as that I was in danger of having a cold in the next ten days, that my wife would become ill in the middle of the year, and a doctor from the south would help her to recover. This directional emphasis is doubtless due to the influence of Taoist geomancy, or the plotting of auspicious and unlucky directions, on folk belief in both China and Japan.

Next, the spirit of my grandmother was summoned. The miko had some diffidence about this request, since she had never before summoned a non-Japanese spirit. But she proceeded, and the shade of my American grandmother spoke in Japanese, and as though she were an oriental ancestral spirit.

She started by saying, "Except when it is difficult, offer me water. In this matter I am not happy. The good faith my grandson would show in offering me water as a parting gift would make me happy." She continued, however, to say that although a good doctor was not called when she died, she had had a long enough life and had no regrets; she was now happy in heaven but wanted to be remembered more by offerings of water, presumably at the small shrines of Buddhas and ancestral spirits found in a corner of a traditional Japanese home. She inquired about relatives, gave such advice as to watch out for pickpockets on vehicles, made a few minor prophecies, and promised to be with me.

The shamaness said nothing of much evidential value, but the session did provide a vivid insight into the shaman's role; to serve as a meeting ground between this world and the other, and as a reinforcer of popular spiritual lore. The altars and references to many faiths indicated that she was not tied to the systematic beliefs of any faith but was rather alive to the presence and powers of gods and spirits of any sort. She knew, so to speak, the secret shortcut paths to the Other World, and seemed to link them. One got a feeling that the real value of what she did was in the performance, with its atmosphere of mystery and belief in the survival of the deceased, rather than in the somewhat banal things the departed were made to say. In all this she was in the great tradition of shamanism.

ARCHAIC HUNTERS

Religion past and present concerns itself not only with crossing the bar to the Other World, but also with human needs here. Modern churches talk not only about salvation, but also offer prayers for harvest and good industrial relations. People have always viewed what is understood to be the source of their lives materially and subjectively to be at least a symbol, more likely the very presence, of the divine: the animal for hunters, the plant for agriculturalists, the king as giver of order for the ancient city and empire, the psychological sense of selfhood in the great ethical and salvation religions of individual decision and experience.

Thus, the relation of the archaic hunter to his game is far from mere exploitation. It is an important part of his religious life; going into the field, tracking, and killing the animal is, so to speak, an act of interplay with spiritual forces and in this respect is comparable to going to church or temple. Even though some tactics of the archaic hunter may seem cruel and ruthless, he sees his relation to the animal as that of one power or soul with another. To take the animal requires in some sense the consent of the animal or that of its divine masters, due propitiation for the wrong done to it, and proper magic to make anything happen at all.

It is necessary to prepare spiritually for a great hunt. Ceremonies set the hunters apart. Rites such as drawing a picture of the animal sought and charming it strive to attract the game, even as apologies to the animal may be offered. As the hunters leave for the field, a sacred silence may be observed; while out, they may observe taboos of diet, remain continent, and talk in a special vocabulary. They may stir up the animal's attention with a ritualized dance to draw it into an ambuscade or wait for it by a watering hole with a yogalike quietude. When it is taken and devoured, the remaining bones may be treated with respect, for the animal's soul may return to see how its remains were treated, or the bones may be mystically animated to make them magical instruments of great potency. Killing, in other words, entails all sorts of responsibilities. This is a different world of man-animal relations from that of the modern slaughterhouse or of many a modern sportsman with his high-powered rifle, telescopic sight, and desire for a "trophy."

Archaic hunters frequently believe in a divine "master of animals" who has control over the forest or a major species and is able to "open" or "close" the forest, making game available or impossible to find. Among the Naskapi Indians of Labrador, for example, the Caribou Man is said to live in a world of caribou hair as white as snow and deep as mountains. These mountains comprise the immense house of the Caribou Man, who is white but dresses in black. He is surrounded by thousands of caribou two or three times normal size, both live caribou and caribou ghosts. The animals pass in and out of his caribou paradise, along paths lined several feet deep with hair, and shed caribou horns, as the Caribou Man releases them into our ordinary world for the proper use of humankind.

No human is allowed within 150 miles of the Caribou Man's house. But yet it is said that a hunter who really comes to know the ways of the caribou, so that he can virtually think like one and share its life, and who observes all the proprieties in his hunting, not taking too much game and respectfully using every part of an animal he does kill—such a man becomes almost one with the Caribou Man and is always given what he needs.

When the Naskapi shamans address the animals, they say, "You and I wear the same covering and have the same mind and spiritual strength." This attitude governs their understanding of the animals that are so crucial to their survival in a harsh climate. Souls of animals circulate; the ghosts dwelling with the Caribou Man are waiting to be sent back into the world in fleshly bodies to be killed once again. It is therefore important that humanity live in reverent harmony with the biological and spiritual ecology of nature. Animals treated rightly will "play the game" and return to offer themselves as game to men again; those who are not will be enemies, now and hereafter.[14]

A comparable view of life is reflected in the bear sacrifice of the Ainu, a hunting people who live on Hokkaido, the northernmost island of Japan. They believe that an Other World reflects this one virtually as a mirror image; life circulates between there and here. When it is night here it is day there, and so forth. From time to time the Ainu took a small bear cub which they raised in their village and treated with great affection, like a spoiled child. When it had nearly reached adulthood, it was killed and sent back to the Other World in a long and elaborate rite, which was the greatest event in Ainu religious life. Before being sacrificed, the young bear was solemnly addressed. It was told that it had been sent into the world to be hunted and to remember how much care and love was showered upon it. They begged it not to be angry but to realize what an honor was being conferred upon it. They said that it was being sent back to its parents in the Other World, and they asked it to speak well of the Ainu before them. Finally, they begged the bear to come back into the world to be sacrificed again.[15,16]

ARCHAIC FARMERS

The beginning of agriculture, perhaps at several places, some 10,000 years ago and the subsequent spread of the practice of planting and harvesting produced probably the most far-reaching religious changes of any transition in the history of religion. In many ways we are still living in the age set in motion by the development of agriculture. The modern city is an extension of the village of the first sedentary planters. At least until the present century, the average person almost anywhere in the world was a peasant who lived close to the soil and seasons, and whose life and values were more like those of the archaic, Neolithic agriculturalists than those of contemporary technological society. It may be that today, as we finally move away from the world shaped culturally by the peasant farmer's way of life into a truly urban world of computers and space travel, religious changes as marked as those that separate the archaic farmer from the hunter will eventuate.

What was the development of agriculture, and why was it so important? First of all, it may seem strange that it should have taken us something like a million years to make such a seemingly simple and obvious observation as that seeds could be planted in the spring to produce plants in the fall where one wanted them, and that animals could be kept around the house. Second, it may seem just as strange that such a clearly mundane, economic matter should have such far-reaching religious significance as appears to be the case. In fact, these paradoxes are very instructive of the profound relation between religion—or, if one prefers, world view—and culture, and conversely of the deep impact such things as economic system and social organization have on religious forms. Each does much to determine what is, at least psychologically, available in the other sphere.

That it took people so long to discover such a simple thing as planting, despite the fact that we always needed food and that trees and herbs were setting examples by "planting" themselves all around every year, shows the interaction between what one expects to see because of one's concept of the way the world is and what one does, in fact, "see." For the hunter, with his magic and attention focused on the dramas of the animal, and the shaman, his faith centering around the master of animals who opens and closes the forest, plants and especially tiny seeds would be merely part of the background of life, scarcely noticed and never studied. The relation between seeds and new plants, even of those whose fruits he took or which his animals ate, would not have occurred to him. (Who knows how many more clues to unknown but equally important aspects of reality lie all about us every day but are not "seen"—and may not be for another million years—because our expectations about what there is to see closes our eyes even as we look directly at them!)

Every view of the world opens up some possibilities and makes inaccessible others which must wait for a different age. The world view of the hunter made possible a deep appreciation of the mysteries of animal life and our spiritual as well as material interaction with it. Yet, so much did the hunter see the human state as that of a being who wanders about the face of the earth under the sky, going whither the guardians of the forest directed and accepting what they chose to give, that it could not occur to him to "see" the possibilities of sedentary habitation on one small piece of land deliberately worked for all it could produce. The difference in attitude is well expressed in the words of a Native American who when urged by the United States government to take up farming on a reservation refused in these words:

> You ask me to plow the ground! Shall I take a knife and tear my mother's bosom? Then when I die she will not take me to her bosom to rest. You ask me to dig for stone! Shall I dig under her skin for her bones? Then when I die, I cannot enter her body to be born again. You ask me to cut grass and make hay and sell it, and be rich like white man! But how dare I cut off my mother's hair?[17]

These words were spoken in the last century, but they are an echo of the Paleolithic mind. For they come from the world which was before the discovery of agriculture—and they give us a hint of why for many peoples the introduction of agriculture seemed to be a kind of loss of innocence, or "fall," and its practice a way of life which, if more productive than hunting, was also somehow haunted by a sense of guilt that agricultural man felt but could never quite express save in myth and rite.

We do not know exactly how the discovery of planting took place. With its development the religious focus shifted to earth and tilled field for its metaphors. It shifted to the plant, which "dies" in the autumn to provide life for others, and then through the surviving seed comes back to life after a sort of burial in the spring.

But even though the introduction of agriculture resulted in considerable advancement in human living standards and culture, its discovery seems half-consciously often to have been regarded as an unlocking of forbidden knowledge, or to have involved a crime, a murder, which although it may have brought humankind wealth was spiritually a second "fall," putting humanity still farther away from the gods and primal innocence. (The second offense in the Bible after that of Eden was committed by Cain, tiller of the soil.) It will be said that the first plants were "stolen," or that the culture hero who introduced agriculture was a trickster or rebel against the primal gods, or that the first plants came from the body of a slain but innocent maiden.

Thus in the Kojiki, the ancient Japanese mythology, it is related that the moon god, Tsukiyomi, came down to earth and, going to the home of the food goddess, requested something to eat. She gave him a meal, but he considered it all repulsive food. In his anger he slew the food goddess and found in her body all sorts of food plants of a new sort—rice, beans, and so forth. These Tsukiyomi took back to heaven, and the High Goddess Amaterasu said they would be for planting in the broad and narrow fields of heaven and earth.

A myth from Ceram, in Indonesia, relates the same experience to the *dema*, divine creators and helpers who lived with man in mythical times. It tells us that a hunter long ago found a coconut on the tusk of a boar he slew. That night he was commanded in a dream to plant it. Immediately it grew into a great tree, and shortly after, a girl-child was born out of the tree after the hunter had spilled blood on it accidentally. He named her Hainuwele; in three days she was of marriageable age. Hainuwele then attended a great dance. For nine days she stood in the midst of the dancing area and passed out gifts to the dancers. Nonetheless, on the ninth day the dancers dug a grave, put Hainuwele in it, filled it in, and continued by dancing on it.

When Hainuwele did not come home the next morning, the hunter sensed that she had been murdered. He found the body, cut it into pieces, and buried the pieces in different places. The interred pieces gave birth to previously unknown food plants. The hunter carried Hainuwele's arms to a leading dema, Satane, who took them into the dancing ground, drew a nine-spiral figure with them on the ground and went to the middle of it. She said, "Since you have killed, I will no longer live here. I shall leave this very day. Now you will have to come to me through this door." Satane vanished through the mystic spiral into another mode of existence, and since then humans have been able to meet her only after death.

Farmers' Planting and Harvesting dance in Seoul, Korea.

After the agriculture-giving murder, the demas have no longer lived in companionship with humankind.[18]

Through stories such as this, a grim basic principle came to affect the agricultural world view even more than the hunter's: the principle of death for life. Agriculture seems to have brought out a new and darker sense of the interconnection of death and life. The interconnection was not unknown to the hunter; the Naskapi believed that by a reverent treatment of the bones of a slain beast, the soul of the animal could be influenced to return and offer itself again. The Ainu believed that by sacrificing the precious bear cub, they could persuade it and its relatives on the Other Side to return and replenish the supply of game.

But in agricultural society, all of this becomes more accentuated, often reaching a point that seems to us a grisly and perverse preoccupation with ritual death, whether animal or human. Religious headhunting, human sacrifice, and large-scale animal sacrifice are not genuinely primitive but are usually associated with agricultural societies and are a part of the mentality to which it gave rise. The meaning of sacrifice for early agricultural society can be ascertained by a few examples.

The Naga tribes of northeast India, archaic agriculturalists, were famous as headhunters. Heads from neighboring tribes were sought on several occasions—to grace the funeral of a chief, to settle blood feuds, and as an aspect of attaining manhood. A male could not marry until he had taken a head. Heads were presented at the harvest festival to placate the ancestral ghosts, and in some Naga tribes were placed on poles in the fields of growing crops, so that the life-power of the severed head would flow into the food plants. Headhunting was always undertaken with religious preparation; participants performed special rituals and remained apart from women both before and after a hunt.[19]

The relationship of headhunting to agriculture is even clearer in the case of the Jivaro of the upper Amazon. A Jivaro male who had taken and shrunk a head would perform a dance with it and two female relatives, usually his sister and his wife. He would hold the head in his outstretched hand, and they would hold on to him as they danced; this would empower these women to gain greater productivity from the crops and animals it was their province to tend. The dance seemed to make power flow from the head through the husband and then through his sister and his wife into the crops. After this rite, the head was no longer powerful and could be discarded like a squeezed lemon.[20]

The Khonds, a tribe in Bengal, offered a human victim to the earth goddess. The sacrificed person was supposed to be a volunteer but was often bought from his parents as a child. After he had been set apart for this grim vocation, he lived happily for years. Like the Ainu bear cub, he was well treated and looked upon as especially consecrated. Finally, at a great festival, also marked by an orgy to promote fertility (another important aspect of agricultural religion), the victim was decked with butter and flowers. The tribesmen danced around him, praying loudly for good crops and weather. After he was drugged with opium and killed, the priests cut his body carefully into pieces; these were buried with great ceremony in the fields to promote fertility.[21]

In many places, captives taken in battle were killed as sacrifices. Often among archaic peoples it was considered auspicious to place a human sacrifice under the foundations of a new building, or to kill a victim in connection with the launching of a new boat. In all of this, it is clear that human sacrifice meant a transfer of power from the victim to the sacrificer or his works, a concept prefigured in the murders that mark the beginning of agriculture in myth.

The sedentary character of agriculture in itself effected extensive changes in religion and culture. Because cultivation can sustain far more people than hunting and gathering on the same acreage, the advent of agriculture led to a marked increase in population in fertile regions. Inevitable results of this and related factors were the emergence of towns and cities, elaborate trade relationships, and an extensive division of labor. A flourishing agricultural economy could support not only the farmers, but also various traders, artisans, rulers, priests, and even a few scholars and philosophers. Finally, the susceptibility of the agricultural routine to commerce, taxation, and control, and its need in many lands for large-scale public works such as market roads and irrigation systems, led to writing and the ancient empires in which civilization as we know it emerged. The religious products of this new economy were far-reaching: elaborate polytheism mirrored in the heavens the new extensive division of labor and the coming together of many tribes; sacred scriptures were a first result of writing; even more far-reaching were the fruits of the leisure of priests, scholars, and philosophers.

But now we are getting away from prehistoric religion altogether. We must return to more immediate products of the discovery of the plant as miraculous life-giver. The sedentary farmer's closeness to the cycle of the plant made him extremely aware of the turning of seasons, especially planting and harvest. Out of this came such festivals as May Day and Halloween, associated with seedtime and harvest.

Sedentary agriculture also gave women a new importance. Perhaps it was women who first discovered planting; in any case, it is common in archaic farming societies for the men to continue going out on hunts (for game or heads) while the women maintain the tillages around home, which actually supply a large part of the food. (Indeed, in many societies, perhaps including modern Europe and America, the real economic base is domestic plants and animals, but the exploits of the hunt and war provide unique, though economically irrelevant, symbols of masculine status.)

Life in villages made the role of women as symbol of place, home, and social continuity important. More significant, the common association of earth and plant with mother and child made the spiritual power of the feminine increase with the growing importance of the soil and plant. Most of the great goddesses of antiquity—Isis, Demeter, Ishtar, Kali, Amaterasu—clearly stem from the powerful agricultural mother of archaic farming culture.

These developments did not fail to produce reactions on the part of the men. Some of the men's initiations that are kept most secret from the women and which most obviously imitate women's mysteries, such as those from New Guinea, emerge from archaic planting societies. Sometimes these movements take extreme shape in their reassertion of the remaining masculine virtues of group loyalty, strength, warlikeness, and spiritual skill, such as headhunting or the Leopard Society of West Africa. One men's society in Melaesian New Britain, the Dukduk, traveled from place to place with the function of enforcing the law in a rough-and-ready way wherever they landed.

An interesting penultimate reaction of masculine interests is megalithism, or the erection of giant stone monuments such as those at Stonehenge. A period of making bigger and bigger constructions of this type as temples, observatories, or tombs in many parts of the globe just before the breakthrough to ancient civilization occurs. They are found in England, Malta, China, and Japan, and they are succeeded by even greater edifices, such as the pyramids and ziggurats of Egypt, Mesopotamia, and Meso-America. It is as though the megalith were an extension of the custom in many men's lodges of erecting great totemlike figures as memorials of initiatory feasts and of ancestors.

The last overt reaction is what has been called the Patriarchal Revolution. At the onset of the ancient civilizations—whether in Egypt, Mesopotamia, India, or China—we see a vigorous assertion of masculine primacy in powerful sovereigns and a corresponding suppression of feminine religious figures, whether queens, goddesses, or shamanesses. In China and Japan, we read of early edicts forbidding or limiting the work of various sorts of priestesses; the sexless asceticism of early yogis

Stonehenge, built about 800–1400 B.C.E. from bluestones up to thirty feet high in two concentric circles with astronomical significance.

and Buddhist monks says the same thing, in different words, as the ascendancy of the pharaoh who made Isis, the great goddess, his throne, but who identified himself with the male Ra and Osiris. We may ask ourselves whether now, after several thousand years, the pendulum is swinging again toward feminine values in religion and culture.

SUMMARY

Prehistoric and tribal religion, the backdrop of all later religion, is a vast and complex phenomenon. But it possesses certain basic themes which, in modified forms, appear centrally in later religion as well. It is, first of all, cosmic religion—concerned to show the relation of humankind to nature and the cosmos, it celebrates the turn of the seasons and places of special sacred power. It has myths telling of the creation of the world by divine powers, but often also adds a mythic account of a "fall" that explains why humanity is no longer as close to the creative powers as at the time of creation.

Second, primitive religion is concerned with the soul. Endeavoring to explain the diverse feelings people have within them, it sometimes tells of two or more souls. Confronting the eternal human dread of death, it describes the destiny of the soul in the afterlife: sometimes different souls have different destinies, sometimes one at least goes to an alternative world, sometimes another aspect of the self remains around its familiar haunts as a ghost, sometimes one is reincarnated in this world. The spirits of ancestors or unappeased ghosts are usually feared and propitiated.

Initiations are very important for many primitive peoples. They serve the end of social cohesion by inducting adults into the tribe after proper training and a potent shared experience, and they often serve the end of individual fulfillment as well by giving status and perhaps secrets of value in the soul's journey after death. Initiations involve a process of separation, marginality when one is separated from the social structure but close to divine powers, and reincorporation of the individual into the social order.

The shaman is usually a person with a very special and personal, often lonely, initiation. He or she is believed to have powers of controlling spirits, healing, and confronting the gods, expressed through dramatic scenarios of trance and dance.

The religion of hunting peoples expresses the hunter's sense of dependence on the animal. He knows that the animal, and often a "master of animals" deity in charge of a species, must be kept in good spirit if game is to be taken. A hunt, then, is something for which one prepares spiritually, and after which one celebrates if it is successful.

Agriculture gave a tremendous impetus to human culture but seems often to have been perceived as a sort of fall from a purer state. The religion of agriculturalists tends to involve more blood and sacrifice, and more antagonism between the sexes, than that of hunters. Agriculture tore the earth deeply, but also allowed the rise of sedentary societies, great increases in population, and finally the ancient empires.

QUESTIONS FOR REVIEW

1. Explain the meaning of *cosmic religion*.
2. Interpret the thematic chart to show how some features of early religion are more related to individual needs and others to tribal needs; some more to humanity's relation to the cosmos or nature and others to the destiny of the individual soul. Notice that some features more than others combine an interest in two or more of these motifs, as indicated by their placement on the chart.
3. Discuss what human problems and experiences lie behind common myths of gods and spirits.
4. Talk about what early myths may be trying to say through their accounts of the soul, its often multiple character, and its destiny in the afterlife.
5. Explain the scenarios of initiation and their meaning in terms of the archaic interpretation of human life.
6. Understand shamanism and describe how a shaman characteristically acquires special powers and what he or she is believed able to do.
7. Present the main features of hunting religion and the world view that lies behind them.

8. Following the chart, explain some fundamental features of prehistoric and tribal religion.

SUGGESTED READINGS ON PREHISTORIC AND TRIBAL RELIGION

ALBRIGHT, W. F., *From The Stone Age to Christianity*. Baltimore: Johns Hopkins University Press, 1957. A standard survey from the point of view of Palestinian archaeology but casting much light on prehistoric religion in general.

CAILLOIS, R., *Man and the Sacred*. New York: The Free Press of Glencoe, 1960. A sparkling essay, including treatment of such topics as the sacred meaning of play and war in archaic societies.

DOUGLAS, MARY, *Purity and Danger*. Baltimore: Penguin Books, 1966. A classic study of pollution and taboo beliefs and practices.

*ELIADE, MIRCEA, *Shamanism: Archaic Techniques of Ecstasy*. New York: Pantheon Books, 1964. A masterful overview of the data and its meaning from the perspective of a historian of religions.

_____, *A History of Religious Ideas, vol. I: From the Stone Age to the Eleusinian Mysteries*. Chicago: University of Chicago Press, 1978. A highly literate outline of prehistoric and ancient religion as viewed by a distinguished historian of religion.

EVANS-PRITCHARD, EDWARD E., *Nuer Religion*. Oxford: Clarendon Press, 1956. A very influential study of the religion of one African people.

GILL, SAM D., *Beyond 'The Primitive': The Religions of Nonliterate Peoples*. Englewood Cliffs, NJ: Prentice Hall, 1982. A good introduction.

_____, *Native American Religions: An Introduction*. Belmont, CA: Wadsworth, 1982. An excellent beginning survey of the field.

*JAMES, E. O., *Prehistoric Religion*. London: Thames and Hudson, 1957. An orderly overview of the data.

*LESLIE, CHARLES, ED., *Anthropology of Folk Religion*. New York: Random House, 1960. A collection of fascinating essays on topics ranging from the Krishna cult in India to Haitian voodoo.

*LOWIE, ROBERT H., *Primitive Religion*. New York: Grossett & Dunlop, 1952. A classic text.

MARINGER, JOHANNES, *The Gods of Prehistoric Man*. New York: Knopf, 1960. Authoritative summary of what is known about the religion of Stone Age humanity.

*RADIN, PAUL, *Primitive Religion*. New York: Viking Press, 1937. A book providing an important perspective; it emphasizes the place of individual differences and doubt among primitive people.

RAY, BENJAMIN, *African Religions: Symbol, Ritual, and Community*. Englewood Cliffs, NJ: Prentice-Hall, Inc., 1976. A competent overview of traditional religion on the African continent.

*REDFIELD, ROBERT, *The Primitive World*. Ithaca: Cornell University Press, 1953. A basic book by a great anthropologist; gives much attention to religion.

CHAPTER 3

Life Against Time:
THE SPIRITUAL PATHS OF INDIA

CHAPTER OBJECTIVES

After studying this chapter, you should be able to

- Know the major features of Hinduism as a religion, including basic terms and common concepts.

- Present the central message of the Hindu classics, such as the Upanishads and the Bhagavad-Gita.

- Be able to recognize the chief Hindu gods and their myths.

- Discuss the importance of Hinduism and other religions of India in the contemporary world.

THE FACE OF INDIA

I first entered India by plane from Kabul. I left the windswept, mountain-guarded capital of Afghanistan with its icy rivers, mosques, and scarfed and turbaned tribesmen bearing ancient rifles. I followed, at jet speed, the track over the famous Khyber Pass of countless invaders and pilgrims from the hard but exhilarating highlands of central Asia. With them, I dipped down into the heat-thick air of the Ganges basin. Long before, at the dawn of history, Indo-European cattle herders had taken the same trail, and after them Alexander and his Greeks, then Huns, Turks, and the cavalry of the opulent Mughul emperors. Indeed, in Afghanistan I had seen one evening the gardens of Babur, founder of the Mughul Empire, cool and leafy in a dramatic mountain glade, almost a fragment of a Muslim heaven, and recalled how after conquest had taken him to sultry Delhi the homesick monarch had yearned for this spot.

Others had come over the passes for reasons other than physical spoils, for India has never failed to draw seekers of all sorts: Chinese monks seeking authentic scriptures of the Buddha, the Enlightened One, that son of India whose *dharma* had half-conquered the Middle Kingdom; and God-intoxicated mystics of Islam who were partly to conquer India in turn.

As I winged over Pakistan and toward the Indian heartland, the dry, bare, scowling humps of the Hindu Kush Mountains were suddenly no more. It seemed the earth itself had dropped away or been smoothed out like a sleeve by an iron. Flat fields of watery green, veined with placid rivers and ponds shimmering with heat, peeked through the lazy summer clouds. Here and there a straight narrow road or railway gave furtive hints of human planning and industry; more common were villages and towns sprawled out into amebalike shapes.

Like me, most international travelers today arrive in India by air, landing at one of the teeming, steamy cities in the Ganges basin or along the coast—Delhi, Bombay, or Calcutta. The air terminal will be located some miles out of the city, and the visitor will get his or her first impression of this fabled land riding in a bus or cab through a brief patch of countryside and then the messy environs of the metropolis.

At first, visitors may be quite disappointed if their expectations about India were shaped by that genre of literature and art in which it emerges closer to Oz than this earth. They will see a dull flat land of green fields and brown dust or mud, depending on the season. The landscape will be suffused, if it is clear, with glaring heat and light. Yet for all the brilliance, the scenery seems to give a drained, faded impression, as though too much sun had leached it of the brighter colors. The monotony of the softly verdant fields is broken only by clumps or rows of stolid trees, or slow muddy rivers, or the dull white of humped cattle, or tiny homes and shops all drab with dust, rust, and water stains.

As the visitor enters the city, another experience unfolds: He or she is lost amid labyrinthine crooked streets, open-air shops, houses of earth and corrugated

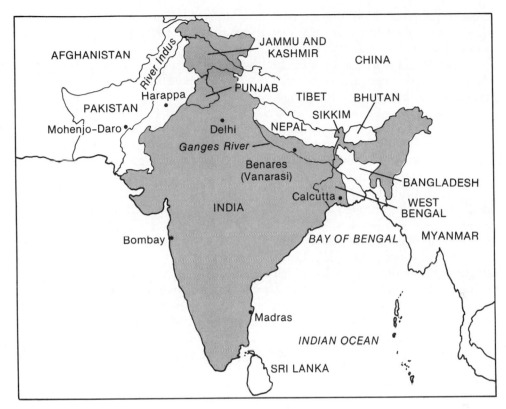

MAP 3–1. The Spiritual Paths of India

metal, and rain-browned official buildings. The narrow ways are thronged with oxcarts, horse-drawn wagons, countless bicycles, ancient buses and trucks, and once in a while a chauffered auto. On the most important streets as well as the byways, traffic may be backed up as a whitish inviolable cow ambles along or stands still, staring at the bustle of the human world with placid, indifferent eyes.

Above all there are people—women in many-hued saris, men in pants and pastel shirts, half-naked children. People are jammed into the streets like water being forced through a narrow funnel, jammed into buses and trains until they hang onto the railings and windows, crowding in and out of buildings, sometimes flaring up at each other, sometimes moving as though it were all a great dance.

On the surface, then, India may give an impression of drabness and grubbiness, not to mention the depressing signs of extreme poverty and hunger that are too often apparent. Families live and die in culverts or pallets on the streets; there are emaciated children and animals, thin adult faces deeply lined with toil and malnutrition, and hawkers and beggars in public places. India is indeed a harsh land, given to cruel extremes of flood and drought, heat and cold. The virile climate racks the tired, overworked soil year after year and wastes the far too many humans who swarm over it.

But for all that, one does not get the feeling of a sad, listless land or people. As soon as one's eyes and ears truly focus, vitality pops up everywhere like bright eyes from behind veils: craftsmen vigorously hammering metal, the glint of copper and brass in shops, lurid movie posters, the shining faces of children running and playing. Rather than listless, India is a country of strange and violent extremes. Everything—beauty and horror, life and death, rapture and anguish, love and callousness—seems to run to unbridled extremes; the beauty is more extravagant and the horror more terrible than in more temperate lands.

When I first left India after three weeks, I felt emotionally exhausted, as one does after passing through a major personal joy, crisis, or grief. India had been, in a real sense, all three. For life and beauty, I recalled warm eyes, flashing smiles, festivals full of colored streamers, bejeweled elephants and palanquins, and vigorous and sinuous dances. For grief, there was a madwoman lying ranting in the middle of the highway, ignored or left to her dream by the passersby; the ragged begging children; the indigents sleeping on streets by thousands night after night. India was not so much an interesting experience, in the casual sense, as an intense and unforgettable vision. As in a high dream, a door had opened a crack to let me glimpse something of an alternative world where the extreme potentials of human life in all directions—ecstasy, madness, depravity, extremes over which we in the West so often draw a veil—were starkly revealed.

Underlying these extremes and pervading them all is a great fact: the religion of India. For India has an intricate, invisible geography. It runs like girders beneath the dusty surface. Everywhere one sees the signposts of religion's map of this invisible world—bright temples of such unusual shapes as to seem almost botanical, little wayside shrines smeared with ochre and sprinkled with flower petals, sacred rivers lined with pilgrims and smoking funeral pyres, holy men covered with white ash and painted markings and matted hair, and cheap prints of startling divine beings with elephant heads or multiple arms. These religious outcroppings of the Other World are like jewels embedded in the ravaged face of India, like breakthroughs of a vein of emerald beneath a drab terrain.

UNDERSTANDING HINDUISM

The religion of the great majority of the people of India is Hinduism, and its guideposts of the invisible world have a distinctive flavor. The first real Hindu temple I visited was not in India but on the island of Fiji, where many people from India have settled. The air was humid and heavy; the place of worship was by the side of a road and was largely open-air. I first saw a large *lingam,* the half-phallic pillar which is the expression of Shiva. He is the absolute from which all cosmic energies, creative and destructive, derive; like sexuality, he is sheer life force, able to give the most stupendous joy and excruciating pain, to make and rip apart. In the presence of the lingam, I reflected that the Indian world view is deeply biological, tending always in the end to see the cosmos as a great living organism.

The lingam is not only sexual. Set as it is upon an oval base called the *yoni* (a name for the female organ), it could also be the flame in a lamp, or the axle of a wheel, or even the sun-packed heart of a spiral nebula—all symbols appropriate to God.

The Shiva lingam on Fiji was surrounded by open grillwork. Offering-pans of colored rice were put in front of the stone pillar, attracting squadrons of birds who flew through the grill to peck at it. Outside, facing the lingam, was an image of Nandi, the bull who is always Shiva's animal companion. Behind the bull was Ganesha, the elephant-headed son of Shiva, a great deity in his own right as remover of obstacles worldly or spiritual. The base of his statue was piled with rotting fruit, the remains of many offerings.

Ganesha

Another temple building stood a little way off. At first I did not go near it, for a priest, naked above the waist, was leading several sari-clad ladies in worship, and I hesitated to intrude. I later returned to gaze into the cavelike sanctuary. My look met the oval white spectral eyes of a black figure. A single oil lamp scarcely more than outlined the shape, but the eyes in that gloom were incredibly luminous; they have followed me since. This was Krishna, the marvelous child, divine lover, and hero. His languid poses, his impudent charm, his effortless omnipotence fascinate India because they are like the beguiling paradoxes of God. He is God himself, and when he came to earth long ago to counter the decline of righteousness, he brought with him the whole sensuous and rapturous ambience of his highest heaven— slow rivers, gemlike flowers cascading everywhere, the frolics of the *gopis,* or milkmaids, who eternally love him, all under a moon as big as one remembered from a childhood summer evening.

Legs flexed and eyes half-closed, Krishna would sound his flute deep in the woods, and the gopis, burning with intermingled human and divine love, would leave their legitimate husbands and dash into the forest of delights to revel with the young god. For the devotees of Krishna agreed with the troubadours of the Age of Chivalry in the West that extramarital love is a closer simile than the nuptial tie for the love of the worshipper for God, since the former is a passion freely given for the beloved's sake with no heed for the cost in shame and suffering, while the latter was (in old India and medieval Europe) probably a legal bond arranged in childhood by the families without regard for the individual's feelings. Deep in the forest, Krishna would dance with the milkmaids, miraculously multiplying himself so that each would think she alone was his partner. Or he would hide himself and make the gopis seek for him, sorrowing, that the celebration might be all the greater when he was found. Or he would steal the devotees' clothes while they were bathing in the river, to have them show their pure trust by emerging naked.

As an adorable but mischievous infant, too, Krishna was given to transcendent pranks. He once ate some dirt, and when his irritated mother opened his mouth to

HISTORY OF RELIGION IN INDIA

GENERAL HISTORICAL CONTEXT

End of Indus Valley
civilization

Consolidation of Indo-
European supremacy
in north

Kashi (Benares) prominent

Urban civilization
beginning in Ganges
basin

Invasion by Alexander 326

Mauryan Empire
321–185

Gupta Empire in N. 320–540;
classic Hindu period

PERSONALITIES AND MOVEMENTS

The Buddha 563–483

Mahavira c. 540–468

First Buddhist Council
c. 480

Buddhism prestigious

Ashoka r. 273–232

SACRED LITERATURE

Rig Veda

Brahmanans

Early Upanishads

Buddhist Tripitaka

Later Upanishads

Heart Sutra and other early
Mahayana writings

Yoga Sutras

| 1500 B.C.E. | 1000 B.C.E. | 500 B.C.E. | 1 B.C.E./C.E. |

Small states, largely
Hindu

Delhi sultanate (Muslim) 1211–1398

Small states, many Muslim ruled
Mughul Empire 1526–c. 1765

British rule
18th century–1947

Independent India,
Pakistan 1947–

Bangladesh 1971–

Nagarjuna c. 150

Kabir 1440–1518

Decline of Buddhism
in India

Nanak 1470–1540 fdr.
of Sikhs

Rise of Bhakti

Growth of Hindu Tantrism
Shankara c. 8th century
and Advaita Vedanta

Akbar r. 1556–1605

Ramakrishna 1836–86

Ramanuja d. 1137

Gandhi 1869–1948

Laws of Manu

Bhagavad-Gita

Lotus Sutra and other
later Mahayana sutras

Puranas

Tantras

Guru Granth Sahib

500 C.E.   1000 C.E.   1500 C.E.   2000 C.E.

check on it, she saw there the entire universe. He once stole some butter, but when his exasperated mother sought to tie him up in punishment, no matter how much rope she used it was never quite enough. In all this Krishna was as capricious and infatuating as God or a coy lover, for God also seems capable of playing cruel tricks on humans, yet we, like the gopis, continue to run after God, accept his changing moods, and feel something in us lifeless till we have once danced in abandon with him.

The crude paintings on the walls of the temple with the ghost-eyed Krishna told of these stories; there the milkmaids forever danced toward him in eager joy. Around the temple of this timeless passion ambled half-naked children, domestic animals, and countless birds.

In this temple and many others in India itself, I was struck by the continuity I felt between the temple and the riotous, rotting organic life around it. The Western church is usually dead but for cut flowers and tightly sealed against all nonhuman life. But through feast, sacrifice, or offering, the throbbing and dying life of the universe flows in and out of the Hindu temple like a vast tide of monkeys, cows, birds, flowers, and fruit. Indeed, the temples themselves, with their knobby unconventional shapes, seem almost more botanical than architectural. Like Hindu society itself, they grow out of the soil of India like prodigious plants, reaching away from nature yet still linked to its maternal arteries.

Betty Heimann has suggested that it is the *biological* flavor of Hinduism to which one must turn for understanding.[1] This is a deep insight, even if Hinduism presses biology much beyond where others might set humankind and nature, or mind and body, over against each other. But as in the lingam of Shiva, the biological and the divine are one unity. I have written elsewhere:

> Hindu society is not a contractual state, but a great organism. By means of the caste system, every individual finds his place through the biological process of birth and contributes to the whole like a cell of the body. . . . The fantastic numinous Hindu gods, dwelling in the dark cavelike interior of the temple (called the *garbha* or "womb"), are uncanny just because they are forms half-remembered, surfacings from the subtle deeps where mind grapples with such biological demi-gods as parents, sex, food, and shadowy recollections of the womb and the magically omnipotent infant. Yoga requires a skillful and persistent combined engineering of physiological and psychological forces. It says these two are ultimately one. It suggests the goal, *samadhi,* blissful unconditioned awareness, is the epitome or ultimate objective of the unceasing biological process. It is a total unveiling of that consciousness and perception which life seems to want, free of the limitations life ordinarily imposes. This attainment is, for Hinduism, the real transcendence. To Hinduism, the meaningful dualism is not of man and nature, or of mind and body, but of the infinite or unconditioned and the finite or conditioned. Mind, the unconscious, human society, and nature are all part of a biological continuum, all on one side of the dualism, because they are all alike conditioned; only the breakthrough which sees them all at once and so makes the many one moves to the other side. It is no blasphemy that birds and gods share the same offerings; it symbolizes they are alike in the circle of conception and consumption.[2]

Main Themes of Religion in India

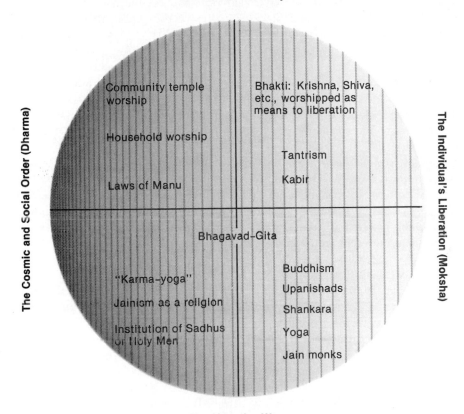

The Affirmative Way

Community temple worship

Household worship

Laws of Manu

Bhakti: Krishna, Shiva, etc., worshipped as means to liberation

Tantrism

Kabir

Bhagavad-Gita

"Karma-yoga"

Jainism as a religion

Institution of Sadhus or Holy Men

Buddhism

Upanishads

Shankara

Yoga

Jain monks

The Cosmic and Social Order (Dharma)

The Individual's Liberation (Moksha)

The Negative Way

Thematic Chart II.   The religious traditions of India, especially Hinduism, can be comprehended if it is seen that, like other religions, they strive to cover two often divergent objectives, sanctifying the social order and providing a path to inward liberation for individuals wholly absorbed in the spiritual quest. The means can be thought of as twofold also: These poles are also not unique to Indian experience, but perhaps each has never been expressed as extremely as there. The affirmative way means using things found in the realm of the many as means to the One; it is the employment of art, images, rites, temples, the social order, and so on to raise one's love to the infinite. The negative way is the ascetic way of denial; it finds the One by taking away all things that in their multiplicity and separateness are not the One.

This polarity is expressed in the basic polarity in Hindu thought and life—between *dharma* and *moksha*. Within the union that is life and the cosmos, these are the two lenses through which it ideally can be seen: as dharma, or the cosmic and social order; and from the perspective of moksha, or the state of liberation or unconditionedness.

The word *dharma,* related to our "form," is one of those terms so broad as to require more an intuition than a precise definition. It suggests the total order of the world as it is: the cosmic order, called *rita,* and flowing out of it the social order of human civilization, and finally the rites of the priests that sustain both. But dharma also implies righteousness in the sense that it means moral behavior that is in accord with the way things are. Humans and even the gods of nature can rebel against dharma, though they cannot escape the consequences that dharma imposes through *karma,* or personal retribution, just as one could attempt to defy nature by jumping off a cliff and trying to fly but would be met by the consequences. Finally, dharma includes ritual usages that uphold the great cosmic-social order by demarcating caste and sustaining the work of creation through "feeding" the divine forces that move it.

Actually, seeing the world as dharma means regarding life as ritual. It means that one suppresses one's individualistic predilections to harmonize with the swing of the total pattern, so that the world becomes like a great dance. There are rituals for rising, for brushing one's teeth, for bathing, for eating, for love, for study, for worship. One's personal dharma, *svadharma,* his or her particular steps in the great dance, are determined by individual birth and karma.

Karma, related to our word *car,* means basically action or activity, as in **Karma-yoga,** which we shall see means the way of union with God through right actions. But action always implies cause and effect, for nothing in this world acts or moves without an impelling cause. Therefore, Karma also refers to that chain of cause and effect set in motion by one's deeds in the world. Sooner or later, through inexorable laws of justice built into dharma, they rebound to affect one's own future. As one sows, so one reaps. Retribution or reward will include (but is not limited to) the state in which one is reborn—as a monarch or slave, a god or a dog.

This is the realm of endless and ultimately self-correcting change driven by striving and cause and effect in which we dwell. It is an interesting level, but in the end wearisome. However, it is not necessary to remain forever running with its tides and tossed hither and yon by the self-made waves of karma. There is always the possibility of leaping aboard a raft and skimming to a different level altogether, to a state as opposite to it as land to water. This is moksha, "leaping out," finding liberation. It is the final quest, after all other quests have run out.

According to the Laws of Manu (c. 100 C.E.), there are four basic goals that motivate people: pleasure (*kama*), gain (*artha*), righteousness (*dharma*), and liberation (*moksha*). Each has its own place and, indeed, its own "rituals," such as those for the first in the well-known *Kama-sutra.* But all except the last finally exhaust themselves in craving for something beyond that level.

We may imagine a young man starting out in life motivated mainly by pleasure—a playboy, a hedonist. But after a whirl at this he finds that pleasure alone, without direction or purpose beyond today, gives one a sense of disintegration. He feels that if he keeps up that way of life he will just keep wanting more and more to provide the same satisfaction, and that he will finally end up enslaved, more anxious to avoid losing pleasures and their symbols than enjoying them.

So next he decides to try instead for some real goals: getting ahead, making money, getting a big house and car (or, in ancient India, a chariot). This is the second stage, artha, and in time this goal is increasingly well met.

But still the man senses a certain inner disquiet. There is a quality of self-respect, or of desire for the respect of others, that he does not have. He wants not only to be successful, but also to be substantial, a solid, respectable citizen, a community leader. He wants to exemplify and uphold dharma in this world. So he becomes active in the PTA and Chamber of Commerce, and perhaps even gets into politics—highly motivated, of course. (Or, in ancient India, he is active in the *panchayat*, the local governing body of his caste, or is a faithful ritualist, or even a gracious and just king.)

Yet, when a busy day is done and he goes to bed, he may later wake in the middle of the night with an empty, despairing feeling, as though he were all straw and gnawing rats inside. What he is doing is good, yet somehow it means nothing, or rather it would mean nothing if it is all that people do, age after age, generation after generation, getting nowhere because it all has to be done time and time again, for all eternity. The big questions are now unavoidable: Why does nothing fully meet the unquenchable yearning in a person? What will become of me in the end? What is the real purpose of life and why is it so hard to discover? Who am I, anyway? He is now ready to tackle the last goal—moksha.

In India, these developments ideally would be in tandem with the four *ashramas*, or stages of life: student, householder, hermit, renunciant. But the first three goals—pleasure, gain, and dharma—would be dealt with in the householder stage, since the student was expected to practice continence and application, and was under obedience to his father and teacher. Then, after he had seen his first grandchild or his hair had begun to turn gray, he could retire to a hermitage to begin the quest for moksha and culminate it by becoming a *sannyasin*, or renunciant, a wandering monk free from all ties. His wife could accompany him if she desired. Of course, not more than a small percentage of the people of India, largely upper caste, have followed this regimen, and frequently the "retirement" of the last two stages is actually to a private room within the house. But the tradition is still alive and answers to something universal; one feels many westerners would be happier by accepting that in the last half of life pleasure and gain should be put aside in favor of another quest, which can be repressed but deep inside becomes more and more insistent.

There are many paths to moksha, bespoken by the many temples and teachers. There is the way of Krishna, through his garden of supernal love; the way of Shiva and the cosmic power of his lingam; and the ways of yogis outside of all such temples. In India, the quest would be undertaken under the guidance of a *guru*, a spiritual guide who would initiate the seeker into the path he was qualified to impart and direct him along. Later we will examine some of these paths.

Let us first look ahead to the goal. It may be given many labels—God-realization, identification with the absolute, supreme bliss, cosmic consciousness—but it is perhaps best spoken of by those more negative terms such as release, liberation, or freedom. For it is really beyond all concepts and labels. It is simply freedom. Not freedom

---

Fundamental Features of Hinduism

Theoretical

Basic World View	The universe is profoundly one. Even though it goes through surface changes and cycles, its ultimate nature as expression of the divine does not change.
God or Ultimate Reality	Brahman, the one Mind or Life, is the one reality. It expresses itself in all that is like a flame taking many shapes.
Origin of the World/Destiny of the World	The world goes through endless cycles of creation and destruction but has no real beginning or end.
Origin of Humans	Like the world, the individual has no known beginning. It goes through countless lifetimes, the nature of which is determined by karma.
Destiny of Humans	The series of lifetimes continues and may include episodes in heavens and hells. Finally, one transcends karma through God-realization.
Revelation or Mediation Between the Ultimate and the Human	The Vedic scriptures; the brahmin priesthood; the gods and God-realized Saints as expressions of the One; following one's *guru* as spiritual guide.

Practical

What Is Expected of Humans: Worship, Practices, Behavior	To follow *dharma* through rituals, behavior, and righteous deeds. If one seeks *moksha,* or liberation, one would practice yoga, meditation, or devotion under the guidance of a *guru.*

Sociological

Major Social Institutions	The caste system; temples as places of the worship of gods; holy men; the family; the brahmin priesthood.

---

in any political or individualistic sense but inner freedom from *everything* that circumscribes or conditions the sense of infinity one has within; that is, from all relation to the cause and effect of karma within or without. One is to rise above and master all this, to become as lithe and free as sunlight and clouds in the sky. Then one knows the answer to the secret of who one really is.

The prevailing Hindu answer is that, in the great quiet of meditation, in hearing the sonorous words of scripture, in the joy of devotion, the realization comes through that there *is* only One—**Brahman,** God—and that, as the Upanishads say, "Thou art that."

Phenomena and ideas such as these are some of the signposts on India's map of the invisible spiritual world, and they show ways in which the three forms of religious expression weave in and out of each other. We have seen hints of the two levels of theoretical or verbal expression: the myths of Krishna's delights, the symbolic potency of Shiva's lingam; and beyond them a flash of doctrinal putting-it-together in God as One and beyond time, and in the four stages of life, and the polarity of dharma and moksha that explains our fascination with these myths and symbols even in the midst of life. For the temples and images and myths are like reminders of moksha when we are not yet there. They are like colored glass between this world and the Other, letting us see the light from the moksha side.

In these same temples we see something of the practical or worship expression: altars yeasty with life, multiformed images, priests. We have also seen suggestions of the main streams of Hindu sociological expression: the caste system, which is the foundation of dharma in practice; the four stages of life, which define duties and possibilities within society; and the devotional movements, which have centered around the gods, such as Krishna, Shiva, and others. It now remains to examine Indian religion in more detail by putting it into historical perspective.

Brahma

THE RELIGION OF THE ANCIENT ARYANS

The Indus Valley, in what is now Pakistan, was the scene of a remarkable civilization around 2500 to 1500 B.C.E. Two cities some 400 miles apart, Harappa and Mohenjo-Daro, together with some smaller towns and villages, comprised it. Each city was laid out on a grid plan, and the houses, although often identical and severely functional, were technologically advanced; the plumbing has been equaled only by that of the Romans and the modern world. The writing of this culture has not been deciphered, and many mysteries about it remain, not least in its religion. The cities contain no obvious temples, though each does have a cloisterish complex, with a pool perhaps used for ritual bathing, on high ground above it which may have been the stronghold of a powerful priestly order. Enigmatic religious motifs appear on many of the seals and small art objects that have been found; these suggest a mother goddess, as one would expect in a highly sedentary agricultural society like this, phallic gods, sacred bulls, and in one case a deity in perhaps a yogic meditation posture. Some scholars have theorized that the sides of Hinduism that center around Shiva, bulls, the mother goddess, water ablutions, and yogic techniques come out of indigenous cultures related to that of the Indus Valley.[3]

But around 1500 B.C.E. a new people entered India. They conquered the cities of the Indus Valley. Being simple nomads, they did not replace them with a comparable material culture for many centuries, although spiritually they brought a different but equally impressive complex that was to provide the formal foundation of intellectual Hinduism. These were the Aryans, cattle herders who apparently came out of central Asia across the famous Khyber Pass into the hot plains. They were of Indo-

European stock, like most of the European peoples, and their Sanskrit language is related to Greek, Latin, Irish, German, and English. We have already seen cognates in our language to Sanskirt words such as dharma and karma.

The Aryans, very different from the Indus Valley folk, were an active, simple-living, and aggressive collection of tribes. The Vedas, the fundamental official scriptures of Hinduism, start out with the hymns and rituals of their priests. Their poetic style splendidly reflects freshness of vision, heroic virtues, and ritual precision.

Aryan society seems to have been composed of three classes: the brahmins or priests, the kshatriyas or warriors, and the common people. Each had its own pattern of life; of primary interest now are the brahmins. The group of words related to **brahmin** appear to come from a root meaning a magical force or spell.[4] From the earliest times, words of power that encapsulate the essence of a god or line of force in the cosmos, and so can be used to control it, have been employed by shamans and wizards. The brahmins used them in connection with their sacrificial rites. Just as through words of power and sacrifice the gods made the world, they said, so by words and sacrifice the gods could themselves be controlled. Thus, the sacrifices controlled the gods, and the brahmin priests controlled the sacrifice, becoming like higher gods themselves.

But this is getting ahead in the story. The oldest and most important of the Vedic scriptures is the Rig Veda, hymns to the gods sung while sacrifices were being presented; parallel to it are sets of songs and chants for auxiliary groups of priests and of charms called the Sama, Yajur, and Atharva Vedas, respectively. These Vedas in turn have sets of commentaries called the Brahmanas, Aranyakas ("Books of the Forest Schools"), and Upanishads. They offer ritual instructions but also, over the centuries, present more and more philosophical reflection on the meaning of the rites. The Vedas were transmitted orally and not actually committed to writing until recent centuries.

The original gods of the Aryans were vital, flashing, brilliant beings of sky and storm. They dwelt in the three levels of the known cosmos—sky, atmosphere, earth—and those of the middle atmospheric level act most vigorously.

The most popular deity was Indra, prototype of the Indo-European warrior and comparable to Thor in Germanic mythology. He wielded a thunderbolt and dwelt in the atmosphere where the action is. He was accompanied by the Maruts, a boisterous band of warrior-companions who rode chariots like the armies of ancient India. Every dawn was a victory for Indra. Abetted by the morning sacrifices of the priests, he and his Maruts would arise and defeat the demonic powers of darkness. Indra consumed countless cattle and, in preparation for heroic exploits, vast lakefuls of the sacred drink soma. Indeed, it was he who had originally found and taken soma from high in the mountains. Indra slew the monster Vritra in mythical times, but finally as his age gave place to another, was superseded by other gods closer to the heart of wisdom.

The Vedas present Dyaus—whose name is obviously cognate to the Latin Deus and Greek Zeus—as sky-father, but he is shadowy and remote, virtually a *deus otiosus*. Equally mysterious is the vague but profound-seeming figure of Aditi, light (or mind) beyond shadow or stain, and mother of the gods. Then there are two sky gods of somewhat more concrete personality, Varuna and Mitra, kingly figures whose main task is the upholding of rita, the cosmic laws. There are few female figures; such as there are, like Aditi and Ushas, the Dawn, seem passive and indistinctly conceived although the subject of lovely hymns. It is as though Aryans thought naturally in the ways of the masculine world—unlike the Indus Valley people and their fertility goddesses—and so the feminine appears as something rare.

In a sense, however, all the bright gods of the Vedas are elusive; all are described interchangeably as shining and benevolent, and each is addressed in turn as though he were the only deity, until finally we come to wonder if there is just one god who bears a series of names and parts. Yet there is a tremendous vitality and sense of personal forces at work in the Vedas. Nowhere is this paradox more apparent than in two further deities, Agni and Soma.

These are deities of the rituals. They are only barely personified but extremely important. Agni, whose name is cognate with the Latin *ignis* and our "ignite," is fire. Fire is the crucial mystery in the cycle of conception and consumption that keeps life in process; all its transitions, from sex through eating to death (in which we are eaten in turn, whether by microbe, worm, or tiger) are various gradations of oxidation, that is, of fire. This lively magician of life and death is Agni, and he is the central actor in the drama of the sacrifice, which miniaturizes the universe. On earth, it is said, he is fire; in the atmosphere, lightning; in the sky, the sun. Existing in principle in all strata, he is also the quick messenger of the gods; he bears prayer and sacrifice to them.

Soma is the drink of power and immortality which the gods consumed, especially Indra, and which was also manufactured, offered, and consumed in the sacrifices. It had an exhilarating, empowering effect: Indra fortified himself with Soma for the battle with Vritra; on another occasion he felt frenzied, exalted, as though he had passed beyond earth and sky, and asked himself rhetorically if he had been drinking Soma. The brahmins also sang:

> We have drunk the Soma, we are become Immortals,
> We have arrived at the Light, we have found the Gods,
> What now can hostility do to us, what the malice of mortals,
> O immortal Soma!

The question arises, What was Soma? The juice that is presently used in brahmin ceremonies under the same name does not produce any such effects. Many suggestions have been made. R. Gordon Wasson has argued that Soma was made from the fly-agaric mushroom, a hallucinogenic plant still employed by shamans in central Asia to induce altered states of consciousness. He points out that the cryptic Vedic allusions to the plant from which Soma is made do not speak of root or leaf, and in other respects seem compatible with the mushroom. Wasson also suggests intriguingly that the reason the secret of the original Soma was lost is that the fly-agaric only grows high above sea level; as the Aryans penetrated farther and farther into India, it was necessary to substitute for it.[5]

To understand Vedic thought, we must glance at what actually went on in the brahmin rites. It would be a great misconception to imagine a gorgeous ceremonial along the lines of a high mass or the processions and offerings of later devotional Hinduism. For while the brahmin rites required much preparation and many priests, outwardly they were quite plain. They were performed out of doors but often under a temporary shelter, in a quiet place with only the priests and the lay patron who was paying for them present. Three fire pits of different shapes—representing earth, atmosphere, and sky—and a grass-lined pit for preserving offerings and utensils were dug. Offerings of butter, vegetable, or flesh were placed into the fires; the plainest offering was just slowly pouring from two spoons the melted and strained butter (*ghee*) into the fire. While the offerings were being presented, other priests would chant the proper hymns; sometimes still another would just stand in the center, meditating on the whole procedure, unifying it in his thought.

Yet these relatively undramatic acts had to be done precisely right. The fuel and the fires were built with immense care as to detail; if a single syllable of the hymn was mispronounced or a single gesture wrong, the rite might be stopped and started all over again from the beginning. Much in contrast to the effusive and half-spontaneous dances and rapturous playlike swingings of flowers and food, lamps and water, of the later devotionalism, here all is crisp, sharp, and exact. It had the atmosphere of a modern laboratory experiment.

Indeed, the Vedic rites were a sort of science; while the premises may have been different from ours, the old brahmins saw themselves less as enthusiastic lovers of their gods than as technicians making precise adjustments in the cosmic order to correct an imbalance or produce some desired result. For the sacrifice was nothing less than "making the world" and calling into life the gods who rule over it; the purpose then was to meditate on what the cosmos is like and to make adjustments in it in such a way as to keep it on course or direct its power in desired directions: prosperity, the inauguration of a king's reign, a son, long life, immortality in heaven.

It was as though a reducing lens had been held up to the cosmos. The sacrificial spread was a miniaturization of the universe as a whole, made much smaller and its processes correspondingly speeded up. The fire was the destruction and transmutation of material—food—through heat that keeps the universe going. The words of the chants, the mantras, or "thought-forms," were sounds whose "vibrations" were in tune with the gods and the subtle currents of reality itself. On this "laboratory" world the priests performed their delicate technical operations; the rites to keep the universe on course and to help humans were like making tiny adjustments in a tremendously huge and intricate machine, perhaps only turning a single screw a quarter of a turn. But a trained technician, who knows exactly what he is doing, can by such minute modifications make the difference between whether the machine works as desired or not. Or so the brahmin priests understood their ritual activities.

But as time went on, as the brahmin sages pondered over and over the meaning of the rites, new questions arose. They thought of the web of vibrations, which the mantras and the miniaturization process seem to suggest, as orchestrating the universe. The whole was like a magic web that held the universe of humans, gods, and substance together, "the thread stretched out on which these creatures are strung together" (Atharva Veda 10:8:37), and within even this, "the thread of the thread," the fundamental unity, subtle beyond all sight yet inextricably there, beneath the world's romping multiplicity—Brahman, originally the power of the màntric charms that hold the world in course. Upon this secret the brahmin priest, who supervised and by his thought unified the sacrifice, was to meditate.

Other questions concerned Agni, the sacred fire. Fire is at the center of the world, and so of the sacrifices—but is it only the fire that burns visibly? What of the fire that burns within a person's own body—the fire of joy, of concentration, even of fever? Does this make the person also an altar, and a world?

In brahmin thinking, the sacrifice was "interiorized" to pave the way for philosophy and yoga.[6] *Tapas*—interior heat—was generated by the real sacrifice, which was within one. Through the asceticism of fasting and concentration, one built up tapas, and this power could be used by the adept to bless or curse or to gain cosmic vision. For the person *was* now the cosmos; one replaced with oneself the cosmic sacrifice; all without was also within, the greater in the smaller and the smaller in the greater. This is the secret of the Upanishads, the last and most philosophical commentary of the Vedas.

THE UPANISHADS

The texts called the Upanishads are presented as words about the inner or final meaning of things which would be imparted by a father or master to his most advanced pupils as the culminating stage of their learning; they are not for beginners, for until one has had enough experience of life, or has matured enough to ask the right questions, they would be only empty sounds. Far from preaching it to everyone, the wise jealously preserved Upanishadic wisdom for those ready for it. The ten to sixteen principal Upanishadic treatises, composed in the centuries after 500 B.C.E., were not published or taught widely but were passed on orally in secret at the right times.

Thus, the Chandogya Upanishad tells of a brahmin father who sent his son to study in a forest school. When the son returned, full of pride in his Vedic scholarship, the father deflated his son's ego and increased his wisdom by telling him of a further knowledge, "that knowledge by which we hear the unhearable, by which we perceive the unperceivable, by which we know the unknowable."

This arcane knowledge was that, as different things made of clay or gold go by different names, yet are still clay or gold, so all things are One Existence under many names. At the beginning this One Existence thought to himself, "Let me grow forth." "Thus out of himself he projected the universe; and having projected out of himself the universe, he entered into every being. All that is has its self in him alone. Of all things he is the subtle essence."

And the father adds the crucial words about the One to his son: That Art Thou.

Other analogies are used in this passage: one honey is made from nectar gathered by bees from many flowers; all rivers flow into one sea. The One Existent is the invisible essence of all things, like the "nothingness" at the heart of a seed of a giant tree. And after each example of the essence, the father repeats: That Art Thou.

This essence is Brahman. The great inner knowledge to which the wise ones of the Upanishads came is "Atman is Brahman." Atman is the innermost self, the "soul"; Brahman is the universal One Existent. "He is pure, he is the light of lights." All persons and all things are really Brahman, taking many shapes like fire taking the shape of every object it consumes, or air taking the shape of every vessel it enters.

As the Svetasvatara Upanishad puts it beautifully:

O Brahman Supreme!
Formless art thou, and yet
(Though the reason none knows)
Thou bringest forth many forms;
Thou bringest them forth, and then
Withdrawest them to thyself.
Fill us with thoughts of thee!

Thou art the fire,
Thou art the sun,
Thou art the air,
Thou art the moon,
Thou art the starry firmament,

Thou art Brahman Supreme:
Thou art the waters—thou,
The creator of all!

Thou art woman, thou art man,
Thou art the youth, thou art the maiden,
Thou art the old man tottering with his staff;
Thou facest everywhere.

Thou art the dark butterfly,
Thou art the green parrot with red eyes,
Thou art the thundercloud, the seasons, the seas.
Without beginning art thou,
Beyond time, beyond space.
Thou art he from whom sprang
The three worlds.[7]

The movement from Veda to Upanishad is well expressed in the Katha Upanishad. It begins with the account of a young man named Nachiketa. Nachiketa's crusty old brahmin father presented a sacrifice of the Vedic sort in which he was supposed to offer all his possessions but was careful to present only old and scroungy cattle. The boy, shocked by this, told his father he also was one of his possessions and asked him to whom he would give his son. The irritated parent responded that he would give him to Yama, the ancient King of the Dead.

Nachiketa, taking this very seriously, proceeded to the home of this king,

Death. Death was not at home, forcing Nachiketa to wait. When he returned, Death in compensation offered the sincere young brahmin three wishes, which he agreed to fulfill.

The first two wishes were clearly rooted in the traditional Vedic world. Nachiketa asked that his father's anger would be appeased; this wish concerned the finite social relations of patriarchal society. Second, he asked to know the fire sacrifice that led to heaven, for as we have seen, the power of the sacrifice extends from this world to the next. But this was only a finite matter, too, for life in the Vedic heavens extended only as long as the warping of cosmic energy by the rite lasted. Depending on one's skill and power, it might assure bliss for a very long time; but being just a matter of technical craft, it would ultimately wear down, for within the cosmos there is no such thing as perpetual motion or energy.

But the third question was a shift to another level of discourse. Nachiketa said, "When a man dies, there is this doubt: Some say, he is; others say, he is not. Taught by thee, I would know the truth. This is my third wish."

Understanding the thrust of the question, that Nachiketa is probing the fringes of an entire new spiritual world from that of the Vedic rites, and might well be ready to enter it, Death parried with him. He went through the time-honored conventions of the master seeming to frustrate and discourage the novice to test him. He informed Nachiketa that the gods themselves find the answer hard to understand and urged him to select some other favor. He urged him to select sons, cattle, elephants, gold, a mighty kingdom, or celestial maidens so beautiful as not to be meant for mortals.

But Nachiketa stood fast, pointing out that these things are only grasped for a fleeting day, then vanish like smoke . . . in the process, they wear away the senses. How can one desire them, he asked Death, who has once seen Death's face? There is a secret of imperishability and immortality that is beyond them, he insisted, and would not yield till Death had imparted it.

Inwardly well pleased, Death confirmed that there is another secret, one that cannot really be taught at all, but can be caught from a true teacher by the student who is truly prepared: that the Self within is the imperishable, changeless Brahman, the One beyond and in all these forms and changes. The mantra, or sound, that expresses Brahman himself, and whose recitation can give rise to his consciousness, is OM. The King of Death continues:

Om symbol

> The Self, whose symbol is OM, is the omniscient Lord. He is not born. He does not die. He is neither cause nor effect. This Ancient One is unborn, imperishable, eternal: though the body be destroyed, he is not killed.
>
> If the slayer think that he slays, if the slain think that he is slain, neither of them knows the truth. The Self slays not, nor is he slain.
>
> Smaller than the smallest, greater than the greatest, this Self forever dwells within the hearts of all. When a man is free from desire, his mind and senses purified, he beholds the glory of the Self and is without sorrow.
>
> Though seated, he travels far; though at rest, he moves all things. Who but the purest of the pure can realize this Effulgent Being, who is joy and who is beyond joy.

Formless is he, though inhabiting form. In the midst of the fleeting he abides forever. All-pervading and supreme is the Self. The wise man, knowing him in his true nature, transcends all grief.

The Self is not known through study of the scriptures, nor through subtlety of the intellect, nor through much learning; but by him who longs for him is he known. Verily unto him does the Self reveal his true being.

By learning, a man cannot know him, if he desist not from evil, if he control not his senses, if he quiet not his mind, and practice not meditation.[8]

Brahman and Atman
diagram

The Self—Atman who is really Brahman—is the only Being, the Sole Existent, the One Mind. He is everywhere yet indivisible. Brahman alone exists; all else floats insubstantial on the face of the shoreless ocean of his being, wisdom, and bliss, like reflections in an unstained mirror. Yet the ordinary consciousness grasps only the things and not Brahman, for the simple reason that Brahman *is* consciousness. In the same way, the eye cannot see itself or pliers grab itself. Brahman plays hide-and-seek with himself in the world, indwelling the myriad things while elusive to human thought and dream. Why? None of us groping about in the world of the many can fully know, just as those inside a house can only know incompletely the whole plan and shape of the structure. They would have to step through the door and look at it from outside as well.

The sages of India tell us there are doors which the wise and intrepid can find. As the end of the above passage tells us, it is through meditation, that is, quieting the senses and the mind, that the door to the infinite dimension can be unlatched. For it is the play of the senses and the mind that turn one away from one's true nature—Brahman—to the phantasmagoria of many things to which feeling and thought attach themselves like leeches.

It is as though a play had been going on for a very long time—not weeks and weeks but countless years. It has been going on for so long that the actors have forgotten they are merely playing parts and have come to identify themselves with the parts. They think that when one actor murders another, the victim is really dead, and the red gore on the floor is not ketchup but real blood. They think that when two members of the cast fall in love, or break up with tears and angry words, that these are absolute and final realities of life, not just events woven into the web of a greater drama with higher purposes beyond their ken. So the show becomes so mad, with the actors' involvement and anxiety rising out of control, that the prompter behind the stage must send out messengers to remind them that it is only a play . . . to remind them who they really are.

This is like the Upanishadic view of the world. The messengers are like the great sages who remind us of how things really are, the *rishis,* or seers, who composed the Vedas, the God-realized teachers who bring students into Brahman consciousness in all ages. But the difference is that in the Upanishadic vision there are not many actors but one actor—the One Mind—who is playing all the parts and is also the prompter. He who is playing the part of the one you love—and also the one you hate and the stranger to whom you are indifferent—is none other than the Self, of whom our outward-directed thoughts have been forgetful.

One other message from the Upanishads: The Mandukya Upanishad tells us that the Self, as consciousness, has three aspects—and beyond them, a fourth.

The first is the ordinary waking consciousness. It is you or I walking down the street, perceiving other objects and people as outside of oneself, and thinking of oneself as separate from them, while enjoying the pleasures of the senses.

The second aspect is the mental nature turned upon itself, enjoying a mental world created within the head. It is the dreaming state of consciousness and by extension of worlds of imagination, fantasy, and the deep archetypes of the unconscious. The images that dance behind the curtains of the mind in this state derive from things remembered by the senses and so come from outside, and except in advanced yogic states they are more or less out of control—we cannot usually tell ourselves what to dream. Yet although the second is not a divine state of consciousness but rather an inward turning of the first, it does have some similarity to Brahmanic consciousness; it is one mind growing a whole world of bright and transient forms, which do not exist elsewhere, out of itself.

The third aspect is the self in deep sleep without dreams. When all forms external and internal vanish into formlessness and mind and sense are still, like a windless lake in the midst of night, one enters the third state. Significantly, it is called the prajna state. *Prajna* means wisdom, not in the sense of factual knowledge about all sorts of things, which obviously would not apply, but that sharp, intuitive insight that simply *knows,* without the confusion of words or ideas from the world of the many. And what is known in this way, *all* that is known in this way, is Brahman.

In an important sense, then, the deep-sleep-without-dreams state is closest of these three to Brahman-consciousness. A fundamental principle of Hindu and Buddhist philosophy is that all outward, particularized perceptions and concepts, such as one has in the waking state, are really limitations. If you are thinking about one thing or a thousand, there are still millions of things you are not thinking about; and the very things you are thinking about cut you off from them, and so limit you. Only when this part of thought is quieted does the mind become like Brahman's— thinking of nothing in particular, and thus horizonless, infinite, in tune with the All. In deep sleep one is functioning just on the biological plane—and so becomes an integrated part of the dance of the atoms and galaxies, without being cut off by any individualizing thoughts from this infinite play of Brahman.

One could ask if all this means is that Brahmanic consciousness is like a return to the womb or even a wish for extinction. Certainly deep sleep is like a nightly return to the womb, or a miniature death, and it is well known that in every human being there is somewhere a deep undertow that desires the womb, or death. The unborn infant in the womb dwells in a world in which it is, to its knowledge, the only being, secure in warmth, darkness, moisture, delight. And is not this like the state of Brahman, Sole Existent, and so impervious and unthreatened, as well as and like the state of the mystic in Brahman-consciousness?

Of course, there is probably strength in periodic symbolic return to the womb, or to the other state in which no outward harm can come—death. Through the womb one can make contact with one's true parent, the universe; the womb was our link with the universe, for through it we tied in with the billions of years of life that made us and with the universal sources. Compared to these billions of years, one's brief conscious hour on the stage is of little magnitude. We may also return, we are told, more deliberately and purposefully in meditation. The gods themselves in India dwell in the womb of the temple and sit on lotus thrones, which are also womb symbols.

Yet the infant is born into this world. It leaves its world of total darkness for ours of half light and half darkness, of day and night, joy and sorrow. In the womb it is acquiring organs of whose use it has no glimmering: hands and feet, eyes and ears. It passes through a process that must seem to it like a death, but we on this side say, "Joy! A child is born into the world!"

In this world of half light and half darkness too, the wise say, we possess capacities of which we have little prescience: inexplicable drives to achieve and love even at risk to this flickering life, yearning for the infinite. These capacities are intended for use in another stage, which follows another birth that seems like a death in that it is an erasure of the manifold enchantments of the mind and senses. This is birth into the world of full light, the Brahman world.

That this end is really the fulfillment of the womb is the message of the fourth state. For the Mandukya Upanishad tells us that the true Self, OM or AUM, is the unification of all three other states. It is the state of a person who walks through the world bearing the gifts of all three. That person has the fearlessness and sense of oneness with the universe-home of the womb, or of one dead, or of Brahman. He has under control all the delights and occult powers of the inner dream world yet lives and works with acute capability in the outer world, for he knows things as they really are, down to their roots. In the vision of the Upanishads, such a person alone is a complete human being.

A TIME OF SPIRITUAL FERMENT

The spiritual movement of India around the fifth century B.C.E., which produced the "interiorization of sacrifice" of the Upanishads, produced other equally important results. Then as now, the culture of India was neither a monolithic unity nor divided into watertight compartments. Like America but more so, it was a mix of many colors; individual components can be distinguished, but at the same time the mixture as a whole was slowly stirring, blending, and receiving new inputs.

The Upanishadic vision is only one element in this mix. As the epitomizing expression of the classic lore of the most prestigious scholarly class, the brahmins, it enjoys a unique status and is accepted as authoritative, along with the rest of the Vedic literature, by all who consider themselves orthodox. But to think that it is *the* tool by which Hindu culture is to be interpreted, or that it plays a role in Hinduism exactly parallel to the Koran in Islam or the Bible in Christianity, would be to oversimplify.

Although reference to the Upanishads greatly illuminates the mentality that underlies India's gods, art, and institutions, one who tried to understand what was seen happening in an average Hindu village temple or pilgrimage center solely on its basis would be quickly at sea. It must be borne in mind that, through the centuries, the great majority of the people of India, illiterate and provincial, doubtless never heard much of the teaching of the Vedas directly. Indeed, as we have seen, these scriptures were considered unsuitable for any but advanced upper-caste students, and they were restricted until quite modern times. Chinks of their light might have reached the peasants through the lips of wandering holy men, or veiled in myth or song, but the people would know them as treatises no more than they knew the Sanskrit language to which the Vedas were traditionally confined, unwritten but passed privately by rote from brahmin teacher to disciple.

So it was that at the time the Upanishadic vision was crystallizing, much else was happening as well across the dusty face of India. Although its cities were shattered, much of the Indus Valley culture persisted, with its religious emphasis on fertility, the mother, purity, and (presumably) mystic states of consciousness attained by techniques of the yogic sort. Doubtless this heritage did much to influence the direction which the Upanishadic culmination of Vedism took. Not only did the Aryan thinkers in India move toward mystical monism rather than monotheism, as in Iran, but a doctrine as central to later Hinduism and Buddhism as reincarnation appears first in the Upanishads. In the earlier Vedas it is in very rudimentary form and can be supposed to be largely a contribution of the indigenous culture.

It was a time when the Aryan conquerors were pressing across northern India and had established control virtually to the Ganges Delta. No great unified empire had as yet arisen, although the sub-Himalayan plain was a patchwork of Aryan kingdoms large and small. Material civilization was still scanty, but spiritual and philosophical cultures were vigorous and moving ahead rapidly.

Spiritual teachers strolled from village to village in the company of bands of disciples, even as do **sadhus,** or "holy men," in India today. Typically, they would walk in the morning, arriving at their destination by noon, when they would beg food. In the afternoon they would rest and meditate; in the evening the townsfolk would gather around. The visitors—intriguing and the subject of much local talk because they came from "outside"—would pay for the hospitality they had been afforded with spiritual instruction, and doubtless also by telling news. The next day, unless a local magnate persuaded them to stay on as his guest, they would leave—possibly taking with them a local lad or two who had been impelled by a combined itch for adventure and hunger for higher things to leave home in the company of the peripatetic master.

Their teachings were wide-ranging and circumscribed by few dogmatic presuppositions, for these teachers were not brahmins defending the Vedic tradition, performing the sacrifices, and interpreting them now on Upanishadic lines. The brahmins were still mostly priests retained by courts or living in their own communities, hardly likely to go wandering among the common folk. But the new teachers, from other ranks of society, were looking for truth everywhere. One might be saying the world was created, another that it is eternal; one might be saying all is mind, another that there is nothing but matter.

One assumption that they shared in common, however, was that philosophical teaching was not to be merely abstract but was to aid in attaining a state of inner liberation. Each school should imply a spiritual path, and so could be tested empirically. Most, even many of the so-called materialists, advocated methods involving extremely rigorous self-denial and self-control.

One teacher, Vardhamana, called Mahavira ("Great Hero"), c. 540–468 B.C.E., was the founder of the Jain religion. We shall look at the Jain religion in more detail later.

Guatama Buddha, a contemporary of Mahavira, was among the many who roamed the eastern Ganges Valley with him. Many wanderers are now forgotten; but two, Mahavira and Siddhartha Gautama of the Sakya clan, called the Buddha, are not. Both founded faiths that have persisted through twenty-five centuries; both have symbolized for many the highest conceivable human state; both have structured the lives and blessed the deaths of innumerable spiritual children through the ages. Both moreover were of similar background; each was the son of a minor non-Aryan, indigenous ruler afforded more or less honorary warrior-caste (kshatriya) status; each was considered by his followers to be the last of a great chain of mighty teachers. Indeed, similar legends are told about the nativity and life of both, so much so that scholars once wrongly concluded they were the same person going by different names in two different religions.

Yet beyond this, their destinies differ, and far more so do the destinies of the two faiths. Jainism, profoundly Indian, has remained remarkably unchanged in teaching and practice through the ages, but at the price of remaining small and restricted to India. Buddhism has reached hundreds of times the numbers of Jainism, has spread over vast continental areas, has exfoliated into incredible diversities of sect and practice—and, again in contrast to Jainism, essentially died out in its homeland (although it has had something of a modern revival there) while spreading from Siberia to Ceylon, and from the Caspian Sea to Japan, not to mention its influence in the West.

While Mahavira taught a way of stern denial and control, the Buddha called his path the **"Middle Way,"** for it was a spiritual tack of dwelling in the calm spot of equilibrium between all polarities, such as asceticism and indulgence, love of life and desire for death, even being and nonbeing. The Buddha, we are told, had been brought up in luxury and had tried the extremes of fasting and asceticism, but he came to see both sides as forms of egotism. It should not be supposed, however, that Buddhism is any sort of easy-going, moderation-in-all-things philosophy. To hit the exact spot of equilibrium where one is in precise balance with the universe and so has all power is no easy act of spiritual archery. It involves neutralizing all the outward and subtle desires that keep us shooting impulsively this way and that, scarcely seeing the target, much less hitting the bull's-eye.

Although the Buddha and Buddhism are discussed in detail in the next chapter, it is important here to place the inception of Buddhism in its historical time and place, for despite the fact that Buddhism was to become the spiritual foundation of lands and ages remote from the India of the fifth century B.C.E., the Buddha was a son of India and of the special style of spiritual ferment of his day, as well as having much more to give. It can be observed too that Buddhism prospered in India, doubtless because of its close relation to the indigenous tradition and the moderation and attractiveness of its monks. They found favor in the homes of the mighty. In particular, they won the support of the Emperor Ashoka (r.c. 273–232 B.C.E.), one of the noblest rulers of all time.

Ashoka unified northern India and then, under Buddhist influence, ceased to make war, proclaimed tolerance for all beliefs, and promulgated noninjury to life. He reportedly sent the first Buddhist missionaries outside India, to Ceylon, Southeast Asia, and the West. While Ashoka was personally nonsectarian, supporting and approving worthy teachers of whatever persuasion, evidently the Buddhists were closest to his heart. His patronage gave Buddhism a prestige which, extended by various later kings, it was to enjoy in India for several centuries.

It is not clear to what extent India *was* Buddhist between around 300 B.C.E. and 400 C.E., but many of the greatest intellectual leaders and most prestigious educational institutions were Buddhist, and Buddhism set the tone and subject matter of the greatest of art and architecture in those days. Of course, the masses of people were in no sense exclusively Buddhist. At best they listened to Buddhist monks, offered flowers and fruit at Buddhist temples, and went on Buddhist pilgrimages, without neglecting the gods of tribe and caste or the ministrations of the brahmins either.

Indeed, to understand Buddhism it is helpful to realize that there is a sense in which one can say that Buddhism has seldom been *the* religion of a society, for it deals with personal liberation and not much with religion's role of legitimizing social institutions such as family and government. In "Buddhist" countries these are often taken care of by other traditions—Hindu, Confucian, Shinto. Nor is Buddhism intolerant of Hindu or other gods; it is glad to acknowledge them so long as they are seen as pupils of the Buddha, "teacher of gods and men." Rather, Buddhism is really the *samgha,* the order of Buddhist monks, dwelling *in* a society providing guidance for those ready for it, quietly available.

Yet there were ways in which Hinduism and Buddhism were consciously or unconsciously competitive. Even in the high tide of the Buddhist period, the Hindu tradition was providing responses and alternatives to the Buddha's way which would eventually supersede it in India itself, at the same time tremendously enriching and broadening the appeal of Hinduism in order to answer the questions raised by the Buddhist experience. But in so doing, Hinduism capitalized on the older religion's strong points as a total religious expression: Hindu concern was not only with liberation but also with the organization of society, the pluralism of spiritual paths and stages implicit in its polytheism. Let us now examine this new post-Buddhist Hinduism.[9]

THE NEW HINDUISM

The Laws of Manu

One Hindu response was the Laws of Manu (c. 100 C.E.) which as we know were a systematization of the Hindu view of society containing the teaching about the Four Ends of Man and the Four Stages of Life. The Laws also rationalize the caste system by speaking of the four great divisions of society, called *varnas* (literally "colors")—brahmins or priest-scholars, kshatriyas or rulers and warriors, vaishyas or merchants and craftsmen, and shudras or peasants. It is said that they come from different parts of the body of the primal man; brahmins from the head, kshatriyas from the arms, vaishyas from the thighs, and shudras (peasants) from the feet.

This pattern makes clear that the caste system, with all the evils it has brought, is a product of the Aryan invasion. The top three *varnas* are the original three Indo-European social groups, the shudras are descendents of indigenous peasant peoples conquered and subjugated by the Aryans, while the large population outside the four *varnas* altogether—now about 20 percent of the whole—popularly called "untouchables" and whose lives were routinely miserable, seem in large part descended from tribal groups brought into the Hindu system.

In all of this, the Laws of Manu are clearly trying to deal in a unified way with the two great but hard-to-reconcile poles of Hindu experience—dharma and moksha, or one's duty in society and liberation. So the two are seen as appropriate concerns for different stages of life, and through the caste system the social many is made manifestly compatible with oneness through the image of the great social organism, with each cell and organ playing its part, but some with much better roles than others.

The Yoga Sutras

What would one do during the course of seeking liberation? Can Hinduism compare with Buddhist meditation on this count? One important answer was given by the Yoga Sutras of Patanjali (c. 300 C.E.).[10] Buddhism had emphasized introspective meditation, with analysis of sensation and consciousness; the Yoga Sutras return to India's deeply biological, psychosomatic understanding of human nature as the background for liberation. Thus, hatha-yoga, the physical yoga of postures and breathing exercises, plays a major role in the spiritual quest; for rightly understood, breath and body are indispensable tools. Brought under control of spirit as precision instruments, they can facilitate states of consciousness that evoke the goals of spirit.

The goal of the yogi, the practitioner of yoga, is control of the modulations of the mind; in other words, *kaivalya,* "isolation," independence of the anxiety and limitations imposed by interaction with the changing world of sight and feeling and fantasy. This is done by getting the mind and body strictly under control by the exercises, and then using this control to withdraw attention from the outer world, so that the inner light shines unimpeded.

According to the Yoga Sutras, the process is comprised of eight steps, called limbs.

The first two are positive and negative moral rules aimed at a life of quietness, gentleness, and purity, for one's manner of life must be prepared and purified before yoga can hope to succeed. Releasing its potent spiritual forces into an unworthy vessel can, in fact, be most dangerous both to the individual and to society.

Then come the two steps of asana (posture) and pranayama (breath control) in which the psychosomatic powers are lined up to move in the one direction of liberation.

After the yogi gains control of his or her own bodily and emotional house in this way, the stage of the disengagement of the senses and attention from outer things becomes possible. This makes for acute inner, subtle ways of awareness. Just as a blind person develops especially sharp touch and hearing, so yoga tells us that when *all* the gross senses are withdrawn, other undreamed-of capabilities latent in the human being begin to stir, so that when they come to be mastered, the yogi has awareness of things near and far and the ability to use occult forces, beside which the ordinary senses and capacities are as an oxcart to a rocketship. The Yoga Sutras tell us how to read minds, walk on water, fly through the air, make oneself as tiny as an atom, be impervious to hunger and thirst, and so forth.

But these powers, doubtless tempting to many, are to be given up for an even greater goal—true liberation. This is the work of the last three steps, which are interior: concentration, meditation, and samadhi. Samadhi is the absolutely equalized consciousness of perfect freedom.

The Bhagavad-Gita

Both of these responses—the way of society and the way of the yogi—are brought together in the greatest Hindu statement of the period, the **Bhagavad-Gita.** Also composed somewhere around 100 c.e., it is really a section of the mighty epic called the *Mahabharata,* which has to do with a great war between cousins over the succession to the throne of an Aryan state. But the Bhagavad-Gita, or "Song of the Lord," can stand by itself once its setting is understood.

Prince Arjuna, whose charioteer is the heroic god Krishna in human form, is setting out to lead his army into bloody battle against the foe. Apalled at what he is about to do, Arjuna pauses in deep moral distress. The book is a series of answers that Krishna gives the prince in his irresolution. It discourses on why Arjuna can and must fight, but its implications go much further than this; the pacifist Gandhi greatly treasured this book, taking it as an allegory of the nonviolent struggle against injustice and for spiritual purity.

Krishna's first answer is along the lines of Upanishadic thought. He emphasizes that there is no reality behind talk of life and death, killing and being killed:

Some say this Atman   Unborn, undying,
Is slain, and others   Never ceasing,
Call It the slayer: Never beginning
They know nothing.   Deathless, birthless,
How can It slay   Unchanging forever.
Or who shall slay It?   How can It die
Know this Atman   The death of the body?[11]

But if it does not make any difference, the question could be asked, Why kill instead of not killing? This Krishna answers, in effect, "Because you are a kshatriya, a warrior, by birth and caste, and therefore fighting is your role in the drama of the universe; there is no honorable way you can shirk it, and right is on your side since the enemy has gone against dharma."

Further questions arise. Does this mean, then, that one born a warrior has no hope for salvation comparable to that of the brahmin whose hands are unstained with blood and who enacts the mystic sacrifices? Does it mean that he whose place in society makes it almost mandatory that he stay in the world cannot compete with one who is able to become an ascetic or a yogi?

No, replies Krishna. It is all a matter of how one lives in the world. The object is to become one with the Absolute, so that nothing in one's thoughts or deeds causes separation. But if Brahman is truly All, the world of the activist is just as much God as that of the recluse. Brahman is expressed through dharma as much as moksha if it is truly All—in the caste laws and all of life's stages together. One can realize God in acting as much as in meditation, if one's actions are as selfless as meditation and as passionless. Krishna teaches Arjuna the secret of karma-yoga, yoga in the midst of doing. The point is to be in the world impersonally, objectively, doing not out of personal desire for the fruits of one's actions but fearlessly and dispassionately, as it were by proxy for someone else, motivated solely by the duty and righteousness of the act. Then, with one's feelings not getting in the way, one's actions are a part of the great dance of the cosmos, of the life of the whole social and natural organism, and are as quiet and far-reaching as meditation.

You have the right to work, but for the work's sake only. You have no right to the fruits of work. Desire for the fruits of work must never be your motive in working. Never give way to laziness either.

Perform every action with your heart fixed on the Supreme Lord. Renounce attachment to the fruits. Be even tempered in success and failure; for it is this evenness of temper which is meant by yoga.

Work done with anxiety about results is far inferior to work done without such anxiety, in the calm of self-surrender. Seek refuge in the knowledge of Brahman. They who work selfishly for results are miserable.[12]

Traditionally, **karma-yoga** was interpreted in a highly conservative way to mean that one must accept the role given by caste. Some modern Hindus, however, see it instead as a view that liberates one for bold and selfless acts of service to humankind, however risky, unpopular, or likely to fail—if one is acting out of impersonal righteousness, rather than for the gratification of pocket or ego, which do not matter.

A philosophy like this does not satisfy all the spiritual needs of most people. However noble it may be, by itself it has a quality of dry resignation that does not answer one's thirst to *know* God. Yet something like karma-yoga can be an invaluable preparation for what seems to be its opposite, a religion of deeply felt awe and love in the presence of God. For only the person whose ego-self is unobtrusive can know God in any case.

This reflects the spiritual progression of the Bhagavad-Gita. After the Upanishadic and karma-yoga stages, the dialogue moves more and more into a sense of a mystical presence, nearer than hands and feet, which is with the one who had given up all selfhood to serve.

Now I shall tell you
That innermost secret:
Which is nearer than knowing,
Open vision
Direct and instant.
Understand this
And be free for ever
From birth and dying
With all their evil.[13]

Who burns with the bliss
And suffers the sorrow
Of every creature
Within his own heart,
Making his own
Each bliss and each sorrow:
Him I hold highest
Of all the yogis.[14]

Something else begins to arise in the tradition, a sense that the relationship of the individual and this presence can be one of love, and that love is greater than success or failure in keeping the formal obligations of law and rite.

Great is that yogi who seeks to be with Brahman,
Greater than those who mortify the body,
Greater than the learned,
Greater than the doers of good works:
Therefore, Arjuna, become a yogi.

He gives me all his heart,
He worships me in faith and love:
That yogi, above every other,
I call my very own.[15]

The greatest spiritual explosion, however, is yet to come. Nearness and love, in place of philosophy and duty, lead to a radically different relationship between humankind and God, and one far more analogous to the relationship of personalities than of persons to natural law. Moving into this spiritual sphere, Arjuna culminates the discourse by asking to see Krishna in his full splendor and glory. Krishna obliges:

Then . . . Sri Krishna, Master of all yogis, revealed to Arjuna his transcendent, divine form, speaking from innumerable mouths, seeing with a myriad eyes, of many marvelous aspects, adorned with countless divine ornaments, brandishing all kinds of heavenly weapons, wearing celestial garlands and the raiment of paradise, annointed with perfumes of heavenly fragrance, full of revelations, resplendent, boundless, of ubiquitous regard.

Suppose a thousand suns should rise together into the sky: such is the glory of the Shape of Infinite God.

Then the son of Pandu [Arjuna] beheld the entire universe, in all its multitudinous diversity, lodged as one being within the body of the God of gods.

Then was Arjuna, that lord of mighty riches, overcome with wonder. His hair stood erect. He bowed low before God in adoration, and clasped his hands, and spoke:

ARJUNA:

Ah, my God, I see all gods within your body;
Each in his degree, the multitude of creatures;
See Lord Brahma throned upon the lotus;
See all the sages, and the holy serpents.

Universal Form, I see you without limit,
Infinite of arms, eyes, mouths, and bellies—
See, and find no end, midst, or beginning.

Crowned with diadems, you wield the mace and discus,
Shining every way—the eyes shrink from your splendour
Brilliant like the sun; like fire, blazing, boundless.

You are all we know, supreme, beyond man's measure,
This world's sure-set plinth and refuge never shaken,
Guardian of eternal law, life's Soul undying,
Birthless, deathless; yours the strength titanic,
Million-armed, the sun and moon your eyeballs,
Fiery-faced, you blast the world to ashes.[16]

Here we see Krishna (as Vishnu), brighter than a thousand suns, express through endless multiplicity the same infinity which can also be expressed as the One, Brahman. God is here represented by the myriad things, and among them he is as an enthroned sovereign. But God as infinite series or infinite multiplicity also brings out the dark side of God: infinite series expressed through time as well as space; and in time all things perish, so God appears as destroyer—"By me these men are slain already," Krishna says a little later of Arjuna's foes. Hence, this vision too is a justification of Arjuna's fighting, and of much more as well.

Yet God as personal being, with whom one can have a relationship of knowledge and love, and who moreover comes among people as friend and brother like Krishna, engenders a new spiritual sensitivity too. It was a theme emerging in both East and West; at about the same time this narrative was composed, Paul was writing, "We have seen the glory of God in the face of Jesus Christ."

ADVAITA VEDANTA AND TANTRISM

Advaita Vedanta

The tradition of Hindu philosophy that has generally been most prestigious in India and is best known outside that country is Vedanta. The word literally means "the end [i.e., culmination] of the Vedas"; the school essentially centers itself on the teaching of the Upanishads, the last and most philosophic of the Vedas, concerning Brahman as one with Atman and as the Sole Existent. Other texts, such as the earlier Vedas and the Bhagavad-Gita, are interpreted in this light. As we shall see, theistic interpretations of Vedanta related to bhakti or Hindu devotionalism appeared, allowing some differentiation between God and the creation, and God and the human soul.

The most influential school of Vedanta among intellectuals, however, has been **Advaita Vedanta,** which may be rendered "Non-dualism in the Vedic tradition." Its leading exponent was Shankara (?700–732 C.E.), who argued forcefully and uncompromisingly for radical oneness in a universe of apparent manyness.

Commenting on the Upanishads, Shankara brought home in metaphysical language its intuition that there is only one reality, Brahman. Brahman only exists; all else—every idea, form, and experience—is "superimposed" on Brahman owing to our *avidya,* ignorance of the true nature of reality. What we see ordinarily is *maya,* often translated "illusion," but illusion has to be understood in the right sense, for maya is an appearance of Brahman and so is not unreal. The world is really there; it is not on a level with the pink elephants of the proverbial drunk. But it is not seen for what it is. Shankara liked to use the simile of a man who saw something lying on the ground and jumped, thinking it was a snake; he looked again and saw it was only a piece of rope. In the same way, we really see something when we see the world, but we misapprehend what it is we see; we think it is really many separate things, when actually it is "nondual"—it is but one "thing," Brahman.

Shankara's influence on the practical side of Hinduism was comparable to his philosophical influence. He reformed and promoted monasticism, establishing four great monastic centers of learning in the quarters of India. He tried to modify the harshness of caste distinction and encouraged devotion to the Hindu gods as aspects of the One. In all this, although he would not admit it was a goal, he was establishing Hindu parallels to the intellectual monasticism, subtle nondualist philosophy, and conditional devotion to Buddhas and bodhisattvas of Buddhism.[17]

Tantrism

Another movement starting in these centuries cut across both Hinduism and Buddhism and deeply affected the course of both. That is the complex and mysterious set of spiritual attitudes and practices called **Tantrism.** It is a road to enlightenment through powerful initiations, "shock therapy" techniques, the negation of conventional morals and manners, magical-seeming acts and chants, and the use of sexual imagery and ritual. Tantrism seeks through radical means to induce powerful consciousness-transforming experience, while preserving something of the technical aura of the old Vedic rites.

One reason why Tantrism's origins and teachings are so hard to trace is that it has often been the province of raffish and obscure segments of society who have expressed through it reaction against the current religious "establishment"—brahmins, princely rulers, Buddhist monks. It presented itself to left-out people as a secret, "underground" path far more potent than the official teaching, if one were bold enough to reject conventionality by accepting it. If the adept, it says, does not shrink back or go mad at its "steep path," in a single lifetime it can bring him or her to a state of realization and power that would take countless lives by ordinary means.

Roughly, the procedures of Tantra are this: The novice is initiated into the practice of a particular Tantric path by a guru; this impartation of power is said often to be physically felt and is extremely important. Being empowered, the aspirant then seeks identity with a deity like Shiva or Kali through magical evocations of the god's visible presence, visual fixation on diagrams (*mandala* and *yantra*) of his powers, and recitation of mantra that encapsulate his nature. By becoming one with the divinity, the aspirant hopes to share his or her cosmic realization and omnipotence.

In this process, the tantrist seeks to experience the god as the totality, the unity beyond all opposites—like male and female—indicated in the unity of god and consort-goddess.

To do this, one may liberate oneself from "partiality" by getting outside of structure—living independent of caste and morality. In some Tantric traditions, in specific rites, "forbidden" things—such as meat, alcohol, and sex—were partaken of, either symbolically or actually. Sexuality, in particular, is important to Tantrism, not only because of the "shock therapy" effect of sexual rites, but also because it is a tremendous evoker of energy, which the skilled practitioner can then sublimate to the spiritual quest, and because it is a symbol and sacrament of the Tantrist view of reality. In Hinduism, the male Tantrist identifies himself with a male deity like Shiva, the absolute, and his female partner with Shiva's consort, Shakti, who is the phenomenal universe; as the couple unites, they mystically unite the absolute and the universe in a flash of ecstasy.

But the rite cannot do this sacramentally, nor can moral reversal be spiritually efficacious, nor the sexual energies transmuted, until the novice is well advanced in a tantric sadhana, or path. Unless, for example, one has truly negated self and identified with the god, sex is merely lust and not participation in divine mysteries.

Tantrism had an influence far beyond the schools that taught it in its strictest form. All Hindu worship on a serious level is now likely to show some influence of Tantra, if only in the use of yantra and the repetition of the name and mantram of the deity over and over. It has also had a substantial impact on Indian art.

The important concepts of kundalini and the chakras come out of the Tantric tradition, although they are represented today in most yoga. They are an interiorization of the Shiva/Shakti dynamic. The kundalini, or "serpent power," is a feminine energy believed to dwell, coiled three and a half times, at the base of the spine. Through yogic techniques of posture, breathing, and concentration, the kundalini is awakened and aroused to be drawn up the spinal column. In the process it "opens" six chakras, "circles," or lotus-centers of dormant psychic energy located along the spinal column at the solar plexis, heart, neck, and so forth.

This, together with the withdrawal of senses from the outer world incumbent upon yogic practice, is said to produce remarkable states of awareness. The final objective, however, is only achieved when the kundalini reaches the inside of the skull where, with a psychic explosion, it awakens a 10,000-petal lotus that grants cosmic consciousness and God-realization. The awakening brings into the light an entire world within the head, replete with its own miniature mountain, lake, and sun and moon, and in its midst Shiva is enthroned.[18]

DEVOTIONAL HINDUISM

The early Middle Ages were times of realization of both the social and devotional promise of the Hindu reactions to Buddhism. In the process, Hinduism became a system integrating all the population of India into a loosely knit organism providing for a multitude of spiritual drives and social needs. New tribes and peoples throughout the land were brought into the system by being recognized as branches of major castes; thus thousands of subcastes, or *jati*, were created. The folk-gods of all these people were recognized as representations, or aspects, of one of the great gods of Hinduism—who by now owed as much or more to the indigenous traditions as to the Vedas. To these gods, devotion, the service of a loving heart, weighed more than legal righteousness or ritual.

Accounts of these gods, their myths and words and methods of worship, are presented in books called *Puranas,* deriving from the early Middle Ages. The devotional gods rejoice in colorful images and pictures, often being many-armed or animal-headed; they enjoy lavish temples and dramatic processions. It is this Hinduism that most moves the average Indian and is most conspicuous to the tourist.

As a spiritual path, devotionalism is *bhakti*—the way to liberation or moksha through losing one's egocentricity in love, love for the chosen god. Love is, for most people, the human drive in which one most readily forgets (if only now and then) self-centeredness. In these moments, one's feelings go outside of one's self to share in the subjective life of another human being through caring and empathy; it is a start, at least, in losing one's finite selfhood and expanding awareness toward the Infinite, and the best many of us do. Why not, then, bhaktists say, utilize this drive to propel the ultimate quest, for loss of self in the divine? Through the love of gods, whom one can visualize and adore, but who are themselves not separate from the absolute, one shares their nonseparateness, for one becomes what one loves.

The greatest theologian of bhakti was Ramanuja (born c. 1017). Although trained in Shankara's nondualist Vedanta, Ramanuja was of strong religious bent and a devotee of Vishnu. He criticized Shankara's system as both inconsistent and spiritually unsatisfying. If everything is Brahman, he argued, but this is not known because of avidya, ignorance, then this would mean that the ignorance lies in Brahman himself. Better to postulate a different model for the relation of universe and God than veiled identity—an organic model in which God is like the head and the cosmos the body, the two inseparable and interacting but having distinct modes of life. In this theistic system, God is personal and loving, and souls, in lifetime after lifetime, can respond to his love and grace, and by purifying themselves through bhaktic worship, draw near to him until they gain blissful eternity with him in a paradisal heaven. Through highly sophisticated philosophical argument, Ramanuja defended the religion of the love of a personal god, which was and is the faith of the great majority of his countrymen.

The devotional gods are best thought of as belonging to two families—the Vishnu family and the Shiva family. The difference can be thought of in this way: Vishnu and his religious system are somewhat like the Western concept of God, in that the masculine figures are heroic and dominant and the feminine figures rather demure; Vishnu as God represents not so much the cosmic totality as the forces on behalf of order or righteousness. He descends from highest heaven whenever righteousness declines in incarnate form, working to restore good in the world.

In the Shiva system, God is above all simply the absolute and so the union of all opposites—creation and destruction, male and female. Shiva and his consort goddess thus have equal prominence, and she is far from unassertive. But although they may appear in visions, they are not usually claimed to be born incarnate among humans.

Vishnu, it is said, slept over the cosmic ocean on a great serpent made up of the remains of the last universe before this one was formed; time is immense cycles of divine sleep and waking. When it came time for the cosmos to be made again, a lotus grew out of Vishnu's navel, and on the lotus appeared Brahma (not to be confused with Brahman), the creator god. He defeated the imps of chaos and fabricated the world. Then Vishnu uprose, seated himself in high heaven on a lotus throne with his consort goddesses Lakshmi (Fortune) and Bhu-Devi (the Earth). The serpent arched his hoods over the divine sovereign to make a canopy; the lesser gods attended him.

But as time progresses, the set moral order of the world (dharma) declines and the power of demons grows. To counteract the latter, Vishnu periodically enters the world in bodily form; these are called his *avataras,* or descents. The most popular list gives ten: as a fish, a tortoise, a boar, a man-lion, a dwarf, Parasurama (a brahmin hero), Rama, Krishna, Buddha, and Kalkin, the incarnation yet to come.

The most important are Rama and Krishna. Rama is the hero of the *Ramayana,* a great epic very popular among all classes in India and Southeast Asia. It relates that Rama was a prince of the ancient city of Ayodhya, but owing to intrigue was wrongly exiled from court. His brother and faithful wife, Sita, accompanied him as he went to live a simple life deep in the forest. But Sita was abducted by the demon Ravana and carried off to his palace in Lanka (Ceylon). Assisted by a monkey-army, especially the mighty monkey-hero Hanuman, Rama waged war against Ravana and prevailed. He received back his wife, was reconciled to his father, and finally presided over a long reign of peace and paradisal prosperity.

While Rama does not seem to have been considered divine at first, and his devotion did not become really popular until fairly recent times, he is now firmly established as an incarnation of Vishnu. He remains, however, essentially God as supreme human ideal: gentle, brave, devoted. Sita is the supreme model of the traditional Hindu wife, utterly pure and loyal. Hanuman's loyalty is also extolled; in north India his shrines are quite common, and in some cases he is shown with his breast torn open to reveal Rama and Sita reigning in his heart.

We have already spoken of devotion to Krishna. He appears in three basic modes: the marvelous infant, the divine lover, and the great hero of the *Bhagavad Gita*. His name means "The Dark One," and much of his worship, especially the agricultural and erotic elements, derives from the culture of the darker indigenous peoples. His commonest title is Govinda, popularly regarded as meaning "Cowherd" or "Cow-finder." Because of attempts of the king, Kansa, to kill him, he was brought up by a plain cowherd family. The homely tales of his youth are full of milk, butter, and the warm smells of cattle barns. In this simple and relatively innocent world, Krishna is delightfully naughty and much beloved.

Here it was that as a child Krishna ate the dirt and stole the butter. Here it was that he grew to manhood, and as a young man played his flute in the woods, enticing the milkmaids to share his divine delight. The *Srimad Bhagavatam*, the classic text of the life of Krishna which beautifully combines luminous simplicity with hints of the divine profundity beneath its surface, tells us:

> Sri Krishna is the embodiment of love. Love is divine, and is expressed in many forms. To Yasoda his foster-mother, the God of Love was her own baby Krishna; to the shepherd boys, Krishna was their beloved friend and playmate; and to the shepherd girls, Krishna was their beloved friend, lover, and companion.
>
> When Sri Krishna played on his flute, the shepherd girls forgot everything; unconscious even of their own bodies, they ran to him, drawn by his great love. Once Krishna, to test their devotion to him, said to them, "O ye pure ones, your duties must be first to your husbands and children. Go back to your homes and live in their service. You need not come to me. For if you only meditate on me, you will gain salvation." But the shepherd girls replied, "O thou cruel lover, we desire to serve only thee! Thou knowest the scriptural truths, and thou dost advise us to serve our husbands and children. So let it be; we shall abide by thy teaching. Since thou art in all, and art all, by serving thee we shall serve them also."
>
> Krishna, who gives delight to all and who is blissful in his own being, divided himself into as many Krishnas as there were shepherd girls, and danced and played with them. Each girl felt the divine presence and divine love of Sri Krishna.

Each felt herself the most blessed. Each one's love for Sri Krishna was so absorbing that she felt herself one with Krishna—nay, knew herself to be Krishna.

Truly has it been said that those who meditate on the divine love of Sri Krishna, and upon the sweet relationship between him and the shepherd girls, become free from lust and from sensuality.[19]

This is the very heart of Krishna bhakti devotion—this loss of self in the divine through the rapture of passionate love, until oneself, others, and the whole world become Krishna. His favorite among the milkmaids was the lovely Radha, whose image often stands beside his. However, he could not continue forever on earth—although he does in his heavenly world—in these pastimes of a divine youth. The time came for him to take up arms, slay the wicked king Kansa, take over his and later another kingdom, and work against the forces of evil. He slew demons all over India, took part (as we have seen) in the great battle of the Mahabharata, during which he delivered the Bhagavad-Gita. He was a worthy and magnificent ruler. Rukmini, a princess of Berar, became his chief queen among 16,000 wives, and he had 180,000 sons.

This happy estate, however, was not to last. In a scenario typical of European mythology but oddly unique in India, Krishna's chief men fell into a drunken brawl and soon had the whole capital city in a tumult. Krishna's brother, chief son, and best friends were all slain in the rioting. Unable to stop this disintegration into chaos, Krishna left to wander dejectedly alone in the woods. There a hunter accidentally killed him as he sat meditating. Like Achilles, his heel was his only vulnerable spot, and there an arrow struck. He then returned to his eternal spiritual world.

Krishna's story, then, begins with a divine infancy, flight, and murder of innocents, reminiscent of Christianity, and ends on a note more suggestive of Greek tragedy or some bleak Nordic myth than mystic India. But in between the aura of divine mystery about the pranks of infancy and the dalliance of love evokes the warm maternalism and poetic passions of India.

Devotion to Vishnu and Krishna takes equally expressive form. Vaisnavas, devotees of Vishnu or one of his forms, tend to be vegetarian, and flesh offerings are not used in the worship, only plant and dairy products. Some mark themselves with a V-shaped symbol on the forehead and perhaps upper arm.

Hinduism may take very austere forms in the case of renunciants who "interiorize" it all and worship without priest or temple. But it has never entertained much the Puritan idea that there is something virtuous about making ordinary worship drab. Rather, India (outside Buddhism) tends to feel that genuineness is found at extremes; whatever path a person takes, it should be taken all the way, with the abandon of the mystic or the lover. Ascetics may starve their eyes and ears as they starve their bellies, striving to find God in the all by negating him in any particular form.

The bhakta, the devotionalist, goes the other way and characteristically follows it without restraint; using the particular, the charming Krishna or the enigmatic Shiva, as stepping-stones to love of the All. This is the Hinduism of the temple, where nothing is spared of lights, music, flowers, jewels, pomp, incense, and offerings

Dancing Shiva or "Auspicious One" representing the Absolute Being.

to create an atmosphere of kingship, love, and heavenly delight, which takes the worshipper out of the ordinary and into the transforming circle of the sacred. Images of the god may be sheathed in gems worth a royal ransom; on festivals the bejeweled deities may be taken through the streets on festooned elephants or giant chariots.

Above all in the worship of Krishna, devotees lose themselves in graceful dance and chanting to exciting music. Women place images of the infant Krishna in tiny cribs and, calling themselves "mothers of the god," rock him back and forth as an expression of love. In devotional services, often images of Krishna and Radha are put together on the swing the bride and groom share in Hindu weddings, and are rocked back and forth. Always, the motive is put in terms of casting aside self-restraint and just asking, "What more can I do to show my love? What more can I do to please the beloved god, to make myself his indulgent mother, lover, or companion?"[20]

The Shiva family has a different feel about it. Instead of sunny Vishnu and playful Krishna, here is a fierce ascetic crowned with the mysterious moon, or a wild dancer whose hair is serpents, or one whose presence is simply the heavy stony pillar of the lingam. Rama was allied to an army of monkeys, but Shiva is companioned by a retinue of ghosts, and instead of the decorous Lakshmi or the charming Radha, his consort may be the grim Kali, of bulging eyes and tongue hanging out to lap the blood of her victims.

Yet Shiva and his family are also deities of immense power, mystic depth, and ultimate goodness. The difference is that while the Vishnu family, like the Western monotheistic God, represents in the divine all that is good, the Shiva family represents simply the all, the totality, the union that lies beyond all dualities of matter and spirit, creation and destruction—their "goodness" is in the wisdom that comes from initiation into this ultimate unity.[21]

Shiva is descended from the deity of the Vedas named Rudra. A cross-grained god who lived off to himself in the mountains, and who sang and danced in his solitude, Rudra could capriciously bestow healing herbs or send an epidemic. Worshippers called him Shiva ("Auspicious One") more in fearful hope than trusting love, for his lonely power was great. Shiva seems then to have assimilated much of the mystic and yogic divinity of non-Aryan religion. By the latest of the Upanishads he already is the All—and, indeed, to those who lack the eye of wisdom, the universe itself does seem to sing and dance like a mountain madman with more zest than moral precision.

Shiva, serpent-entwined, is a much more enigmatic figure than Vishnu; one is less sure how to read his subtle, ambivalent smile. His three most important representations are as the Lord of the Dance, the Master Yogi, and the Lingam. As Lord of the Dance, he dances with perfect equilibrium and pounds his drum down through all the changes of the world until the time comes for an age of the world to end; he then beats the drum louder and louder until its vibrations shatter the cosmos into its primal elements.

As the Master Yogi, he is seated high in the Himalayas, on skull-faced Mount Kailas, his body covered with the white ash that is a symbol of the ascetic's burning away of passion. He is seated on a tiger-skin pallet; his symbol, the trident staff, is in place beside him; the holy Ganges River leaps off the topknot of his long matted hair. He is sunk deep in meditation, and his concentrated thought is what sustains the world; if he were to cease his meditation for even a moment, the world would begin to vanish like a dream and "leave not a rack behind." The story is told, in fact, that once his consort came up behind him and playfully put her hands over her husband's eyes—but removed them in a hurry when she saw the mountains and forests fade and the sun and stars start to blink out.

Or as the cosmic Being, the sheer life-force and sole reality that underlies all that is, Shiva can be simplified and abstracted still further, to the still upright column of the lingam . . . the pivot on which the wheel of the universe turns, or the phallus of an unquenchable will to live.

As Shiva represents absolute Being, his consort-goddess, called his Shakti, or Power, is the whole of the phenomenal world, in all its bounty, danger, and change, forever wedded to the Absolute. She is thus a being of fierce splendor and power, and equal to Shiva just as in an even deeper sense the two are one. She is the fullness of the Eternal Feminine, the Great Mother and Mistress in all her moods, and she goes by countless names.

As Parvati, she is the world at rosy dawn, nature at its gentlest and loveliest. As Annapurna, she is the bountiful mother, the goddess of food and abundant harvest. But as Durga, the coloration shifts a bit; Durga is good, for she slew a mighty demon, but the Great Goddess in this form is more chancy-looking: she proudly rides a lion and wields a great sword.

Finally, in the form of Kali, she is also good and the object of the devotion of mild and wise saints. But she is good in a dark way that only the wise can understand, for on the face of it she is time and death. She bears a sword and carries the severed head of a victim said to be a demon, killed out of mercy lest his bad karma become too weighty. Her tongue hangs out, around her waist are the arms of other victims, and their severed heads are garlanded around her neck. She is dark, often standing or dancing on the prostrate white body of Shiva, the passive Absolute whose energy she draws upon. She is worshipped with offerings of male goats slain in her temples, and in the past has been presented human sacrifice.

All of this expresses that Kali is the phenomenal world of time, change, and multiplicity. In it, all that comes into being is sooner or later destroyed. So it is said that Kali will give birth to a child, fondle it at her breast, and then wring its neck.

The ways of Kali are not pleasant to contemplate, and one may wonder why such a goddess would be worshipped. Although the deities of other traditions, including the Western, also have their black sides, India is unrivaled in exuberance of expression of both the light and dark colors of the sacred.

But there are those who say that until Kali is fully understood and loved, one cannot truly find peace or know God, for peace and God are beyond the vicissitudes of creation and destruction, and one must confront them and pass through them first. They say Kali is standing there with her blood and her victims, and one cannot simply go around her; one day a person on the way to liberation must face her squarely, if not embrace her. Indeed, centering around Bengal there is a spiritual tradition called Shaktism, which focuses on the worship of the Great Mother; forgetting even Shiva, Shaktas hold that in Kali alone is the power of the universe and the wellspring of bliss.[22] Goddesses are also the main objects of worship in many villages.

Another style of devotionalism emerged at the very end of the Middle Ages on the spiritual frontier between Hinduism and Islam. The faith of Muhammad was then coming into India in force together with Muslim rulers. Eventually as many as a fifth of the people of India—the present populations of Pakistan and Bangladesh, plus a scattered minority in the Republic of India—became Muslim, drawn by Islam's practical advantages, the greater simplicity and human equality of this faith without image or caste and the attractiveness of many of its Sufi preachers and mystics.

However, the majority of Hindus, especially those of higher caste, remained Hindu and indeed became very conservative about it. The meeting of two cultures alien to each other, like Islam and Hinduism, produces two kinds of reaction. Some, generally the great majority, will respond with a conservative withdrawal into his or her own culture or faith. Especially if also politically subjugated, they will say, "They can take everything else from me; they will not take my faith," and cling to it all the more tenaciously and inflexibly. The ultratraditionalism for which Hindu society was famous until recently—rigid adherence to caste, rite, and the authority of past models—was not so much the heritage of the great creative periods of ancient India as it was a response, understandable in context, to the more recent centuries of Muslim and British rule, when it was the only possible vehicle for a Hindu sense of identity.

For others, the confrontation of faiths effects a different reaction. These are sensitive souls who say, "If one faith claims one truth and another a different truth, then is not everything we have taken for granted thrown into question? Perhaps reality is instead a truth beyond them both." There are some, from the great Mughul emperor Akbar (r. 1556–1605) to lowly weavers and washerwomen, who out of this situation were driven to adore a God beyond all particular places and rigidities of orthodoxy. The wandering ecstatic of a God in all persons and places, who is loved in a bhaktic way, became a new and attractive style of pilgrim. A good example is the poet Kabir (1440–1518). Alluding to the Kaaba in Mecca, the center of Muslim devotion, and Mount Kailas in Tibet, venerated as the abode of Shiva and a place of Hindu pilgrimage, he sings:

Kali standing on Shiva from whom she draws energy

> O servant, where dost thou seek Me?
> Lo! I am beside thee.
> I am neither in temple nor in mosque: I am neither in Kaaba nor in Kailash:
> Neither am I in rites and ceremonies, nor in Yoga and renunciation.
> If thou art a true seeker, thou shalt at once see Me; thou shalt meet Me in a moment
>   of time.
> Kabir says, "O Sadhu! God is the breath of all breath."
>
> It is needless to ask of a saint the caste to which he belongs;
> For the priest, the warrior, the tradesman, and all the thirty-six castes, alike are seeking
>   for God.
> It is but folly to ask what the caste of a saint may be;
> The barber has sought God, the washerwoman, and the carpenter . . .
> Hindus and Moslems alike have achieved that End, where remains no mark of distinction.
>
> If God be within the mosque, then to whom does this world belong?
> If Ram be within the image which you find upon your pilgrimage, then who is there
>   to know what happens without?
>
> Hari is in the East: Allah is in the West. Look within your heart, there you will find
>   both Karim and Ram;
> All the men and women of the world are His living forms.
> Kabir is the child of Allah and of Ram: He is my Guru, He is my Pir.[23]

A comparable mystic poet was Nanak, founder of the Sikh religion, which today numbers some 8 million. Nanak (1470–1540) had, like Kabir, strong ties to both the Muslim and Hindu traditions. He had an ordinary upbringing and marriage, but when he was about thirty he left his family to heed a call to the renunciant life. Then, when he was about fifty, a decisive special vision was granted him. God above and beyond human places and faiths came to him, Nanak said, and pledged him to worship and teach faith in his Divine Name.

The god of this revelation was neither the god exclusively of Islam or Hinduism but the one all-powerful, loving God who is above them both, who makes no unfavorable distinctions among mankind as to creed or caste but rather looks into the heart. He may be called by any name—Brahma, Rama, Hari, or Allah—so long as the worshipper recognizes that he is not limited to any of them. Sikhs love above all just to call the Lord Sat Nam, the True or Absolute Name. The repetition of his name is itself true devotion and equal to any pilgrimage to Mecca or Benares—in submission to it lies freedom. Here we see a fruitful combination of the fervent, loving devotion to one God of bhaktic Hinduism with the strong concept of submission to a personal and sovereign God, found in Islam.

Nanak spent a number of years, surrounded by disciples, as an itinerant poet and minstrel of this God. Here is one of his most expressive poems:

> Those who believe in power,
> Sing of His power;
> Others chant of His gifts
> As His messages and emblems;
> Some sing of His greatness,
> And His gracious acts;
> Some sing of His wisdom
> Hard to understand;
> Some sing of Him as the fashioner of the body,
> Destroying what He has fashioned;
> Others praise Him for taking away life
> And restoring it anew.
>
> Some proclaim His Existence
> To be far, desperately far, from us;
> Others sing of Him
> As here and there a Presence
> Meeting us face to face.
> To sing truly of the transcendent Lord
> Would exhaust all vocabularies, all human powers of expression,
> Myriads have sung of Him in innumerable strains
> His gifts to us flow in such plenitude
> That man wearies of receiving what God bestows;
> Age on unending age, man lives on His bounty;
> Carefree, O Nanak, the Glorious Lord smiles.[24]

Nanak believed he had been called to serve as the guru, or teacher, of this faith in the true God. After him, a succession of nine more gurus bore his authority. Following the tenth and last, the Holy Granth, the Sikh scripture comprised of poems of Nanak, Kabir, and others took the place of a living teacher. The story of how Sikhism became inevitably another religion, instead of a faith beyond all religion, is a colorful and fascinating one. It will be told later.

THE PRACTICE OF HINDUISM

The long past we have looked at is still present in India. Much has been poured into the melting pot of Indian culture over the centuries and millenia, but little (except Buddhism) has been lost. The earliest continues alongside the latest. As jet planes whine over modern Delhi or Bombay, brahmin priests still chant the Vedas and prepare the ancient fire rites. Hindu worship and social expression, while capable of change, move at a slower rate than intellectual or historical forces. Let us look at some of these phenomena.

In a devout Indian household, especially of the upper castes, the day begins early. It is understandable that dawn should seem the most apt time for worship in India. Not only is it natural that one should turn to God at the beginning of a day's activities, but the Indian dawn has a special quality. Except in winter, the day soon enough becomes wearisomely hot, muggy, or dusty. But for a short time, just before and during sunrise, it is as though an enchantment had fallen over the ancient land. The air is limpid, fresh, and inviting; dew gems the grass; all is as still and hopeful as the deep meditation of Shiva just before a new world streams forth from his thoughts. At this hour, the head of the household arises, splashes himself with water, and going out on his porch or rooftop says the Gayatri mantram, the morning hymn to the sun. He may place on his body sacred marks, indicating of what deity he is a devotee, who represents his "chosen ideal."

He then proceeds to the household shrine of the chosen deity. There he presents morning worship: he ritually chants praise and mantra of the deity, presents cups of water, washes the image, and offers food cooked by his wife. He may also study and meditate. If the household can afford it, the rites may be performed by a retained brahmin; otherwise, they must be done by the head of the household.

The household, in fact, is the real center of Hinduism, although of course its religious life is rarely seen by the foreign visitor, unlike that of the spectacular temples. But many devout Hindus never go to public temple. They express their faith through home customs and rites. To follow the home rites of one's caste and lineage is expected for social standing, at least in such matters as coming-of-age and marriage; worship at the temple is much more a matter of personal preference.

In the upper castes, there are samskaras, or sacraments, which mark the stages of life for boys, and would be marked by appropriate family ceremonies with a brahmin officiating: the child's birth, first eating of solid food, first haircut, and his attainment of manhood when he is invested with the sacred cord.

Weddings

No occasion is greater in Hindu family life than a wedding. For a woman, it is the decisive event in her life. She has no separate sacramental initiations; her marriage is the great initiation that sets up her spiritual framework. After marriage, it is with and through her husband that she formally worships the patron of the

Krishna or "Exalted One" who came to earth to counter the decline of righteousness.

Zoroastrian (Parsee) Haoma ritual.

The Golden Temple in Amritsar, India is considered the most sacred Sikh temple.

household—although women worship in the temples with other women. The wife does not present formal offerings at the household shrine, but prepares the offerings the husband presents, and in a deeper sense worships the god of whom her husband is family priest in *him,* since priest and god become identified.

A Hindu marriage is a long, exhausting ceremony lasting several days. There are offerings, formal meetings of the two families and of the bride and groom (who if they are of very traditional families would not have seen each other prior to the wedding day). There are vivid rites, such as the bride and groom sitting together on a swing and later binding their hands to each other, as the groom says, "I am heaven, thou art earth."

Funerals

Funerals, on the other hand, are not generally performed by brahmins, at least not by those of high status. Although a member of a class of funeral priests may officiate, the chief functionary at a funeral of a man is the deceased's eldest son, who lights his father's funeral pyre and when the skull becomes red-hot, cracks it with a stick. Bodies are brought from all over India to the banks of the Ganges, especially at Benares, to be burned; the ashes are thrown into the sacred river. Even if it is not possible to bring the body to Benares, the ashes may later be brought to that site.

All these rites suggest indirectly some of the great themes of Indian thought and point to both unities and tensions in Indian culture. The funeral fire reminds us of the Vedic sacrificial fire and tells us that death is but another stage in the cycle of conception and consumption through which the sacred fire dances. The sacramental structure of life and the role of the eldest son suggest the organic, biological view of life of which we have spoken.

Caste

Another usage that suggests the biological view of life is the caste system. Caste presents its own paradox: on the one hand, it suggests the organic unity of life; on the other, a desire for symbols of separateness—each group in its own place, not eating or mating with those outside a small unit. The basic dynamic in caste is the purity-impurity tension.

Although the ancient classification of society had only four great orders, the practical division of modern society is into thousands of *jati,* literally "births," with their own caste rules. They range from various types of brahmins through bankers, silversmiths, and farmers down to the "untouchables," to whose lot fell tasks such as sweeping, washing, and tanning hides.

The real principle of division is not occupation, as many think, but commensality—who can cook food for whom, who can eat with whom, and by extension, who can marry whom, or, for that matter, who can even come near whom without pollution. It is a question of relative purity and impurity. One is made impure by contact with a member of a lower caste—sharing water or food, being touched by the lower one's spittle. These contacts would require ritual purification. A basic principle is that products of the body pollute; thus barbers and washermen, handling hair and grime from human bodies, are low on the caste scale.

Caste has been legally abolished in modern India, though attitudes based on it remain in many places.

Water and Cows

So far we have dealt with aspects of the organic, dharma side of Hindu life—birth, marriage, death, caste. But even here, since caste itself is founded on a sense of the pure versus the impure, we get a glimmer of that basic thinking in terms of dualisms or polarities that carries up to the distinction of dharma and moksha. The moksha possibility is exemplified in other highly visible aspects of Hindu society: the holy man and the temple. But some things are simply pure and purifying in themselves; they stand as symbols of transition, on the borderline between the realm of dharma and that of moksha, and probably go back to days before the dichotomy of the two levels went beyond thinking of the impure and the pure. Two examples are water and the sacred cow.

There is a "tank" of fresh water near every temple not on a stream, river, or ocean, and the main places of pilgrimage, like Benares, are near rivers or the sea. The Ganges, flowing past Benares, is the most sacred water of all, streaming from the head of Shiva, and Hindus in the millions throng to it to bathe.

An unforgettable sight confronting every traveler to India is that of innumerable white humpbacked cows wandering freely about streets, marketplaces, and all but the busiest sections of cities. The gentle-eyed beasts, often no better fed than the masses of Indians but safe from slaughter, frustrate one as their slow ambling holds up traffic, but they are as much a part of India as the dust itself. The sensitive observer may see in their warm and much-beloved frames, which appear in the most unlikely places, a different concept of the relation of human and animal from the Western, one of living together rather than of superiority of human over beast. The cows all belong to someone, to whom they supply milk, and dung for fuel and plaster, but they seem also a public symbol, which indeed they are. They suggest the warm maternalism that India adores. Mohandas Gandhi, with his keen, non-Western perception, once remarked that the cow is really the most universal Hindu symbol, and cow protection its most expressive principle. Hindus, he said, may agree on nothing else, but they unite on the veneration and protection of the cow, a token of maternity, simplicity, nonmaterialism, and nonviolence. The products of the cow—its milk, urine, and dung—are purifying and used in purificatory rites.

Sadhus

Visible reminders of the moksha side of things are the numerous sadhus, the holy men of India. Virtually every Hindu village and homestead may from time to time have strange, yet familiar, visitors. They may be sons of the house or village, or from far away, but they will no longer be bound by family ties or have any claim other than charity upon the support of anyone.

The sadhu has in principle cut himself loose from society to be free for the greatest of quests. For what he represents—even if personally unworthy—he is welcomed and fed, his blessing sought and his curse feared. Sadhus have no centralized discipline like that of Western monastics, although most do acknowledge the absolute authority of their own guru, or in a few cases of an order. A sadhu may in turn establish his own "family," for disciples may join him and devout lay people may seek him out to become his spiritual pupils. To these the sadhu becomes formally a guru; he initiates them into his method, be it Vedantic, Tantric, devotional, or whatever. He takes on the burden of the disciples' karma and becomes their means of grace; followers worship the "lotus feet" of their guru. As the means to God for them, he becomes their personification and presence of God.

The way of life among sadhus varies greatly. Some wander as of old from village to village, teaching and begging. Some frequent temples and pilgrimage sites, where they seek alms and instruct in the appropriate devotions. Many are childlike, jovial spirits, going in merry bands from festival to festival. Others are unspeaking recluses deep in the woods, known only to a few who supply their meager needs. Some are charlatans, some are crazed, some are wise and learned, and some are true saints. Some were born to the holy life and have really followed no other. Some were prominent in business or civic affairs and only made the renunciation late. Some are devotees of Vishnu, wearing the V-shaped marks; others wear the three bars of Shiva and cover themselves with white ash. Traditionally, the ochre robe is the token of asceticism; some wear it, while others wear rags or nothing at all. Some shave their heads; others wear hair and beard as long and matted as old vines. But all are part of the pageant of Hinduism and are venerated by traditional Hindus. Insofar as they are God-realized, they *are* God, for they have become transparent to the God within, who is as much God as God anywhere. God is believed to be nowhere more present and visible than in his Great Souls: to venerate them is to venerate God. Their diversity, and the strangeness of some of them, only bespeaks the mystery and infinity of the Divine Sea, whose waves crest in its lovers.

Temples

The temple, through the medium of art and architecture rather than of a human life, also bespeaks the other side. Even as one approaches it, one senses the approach of another kind of realm. Here are lively people progressing upward in festive mood, and here are special shops selling flowers for offerings. The temple may be alive with monkeys and birds, with sacred cows grazing on the lawn, but it is also a throne room, and a brilliant image of the deity or a lingam stands toward the back. The arrangement and schedule of the temple are those of a king in his court. The deity is awakened in the early morning with conch trumpets, given his meals with regal ceremony, and presented entertainments of music and dance. There is even a siesta at midday when the curtains about his throne are closed. At regular

Meenakshi Temple in Madurai, Southern India—a temple city and important pilgrimage for Hindus.

hours he holds court; then his subjects come with their gifts, most commonly wreaths of flowers, which are handed to a priest, naked from the waist up, who takes them and tosses them over the image. He receives a token payment and often bestows on the worshipper a touch of color on the forehead as a blessing.

The interior of the temple is splendid and colorful, suggesting the heavenly delights of the pure realms of the gods, who in turn shatter like prisms the clear light of the Absolute into these gay colors. The gods too suggest that beyond mere purity is the playful delight of the divine, rolling out world after world. This warm and vivid atmosphere, of a piece with India's rain and sun, remains deeply impressed on a visitor long afterward.

Modern Hinduism

Hinduism has undergone slow changes in modern times, as it has all through its long history. Just as earlier problems were the meetings of Aryan and indigenous cultures, and of Hinduism and Islam, so the basic problem of thinking Hindus in the nineteenth and twentieth centuries has been the meeting of Hindu and Western values. How can the ancient faith respond to Western science, education, democracy, and the economic and social dislocations they bring? How does Hinduism fit in among the religions of the world? Dealing with questions like these while living in two worlds at once led Hindu intellectuals to produce a fascinating array of new philosophical and spiritual options, some of which have had considerable influence in the West.

One great influence was Ramakrishna (1836–86). Not an intellectual himself, this Bengali was in many ways a traditional Indian saint and mystic, deeply devoted to Kali the Great Mother, able to go into deep ecstatic trance, profoundly aware of God in all things. Yet he was also aware of modern religious pluralism, and after experiencing several religious traditions, including Islam and Christianity, from within to his own satisfaction, he taught that all religions are of the same essence and are paths to God-realization. Disciples of his, particularly Swami Vivekananda (1862–1902), brought his message to the West. In his writings and in the work of the Ramakrishna Order, he did much to make Vedantic Hinduism and the mysticism of Ramakrishna an intellectually vigorous and compassionate faith relevant to the modern world both in India and the West.

Undoubtedly the most significant of all modern Hindus was Mohandas K Gandhi (1869–1948), who led the movement for Indian independence through "truth force," the nonviolent resistance by noncooperation, demonstrations, and fasting, that Gandhi drew from the Jain's ahimsa and the Bhagavad-Gita's karma-yoga.

In the life of Gandhi, as in all else, we see the Indian religious tradition working once again to weave together in a new pattern the two realms where it has seen and known the one God—the social order and the infinite within the self.

JAINISM

We shall conclude this chapter with brief accounts of three of the smaller religions of India, Jainism, Sikhism, and the Zoroastrianism of the Parsees. Like the other religious minorities in the predominantly Hindu Republic of India—Islam, Buddhism, Judaism, and Christianity (to be considered in other contexts in this book)—they are not Hindu because they do not accept the authority of the Vedas or of the brahmin priesthood, even though they may accept some values associated with Hinduism.

As we have already noted, Jainism was established in its historic form by Vardhamana, called Mahavira, an approximate contemporary of the Buddha in the fifth century B.C.E. Mahavira is believed by his followers to have been the last in a series of Tirthankaras ("Crossing-Makers") who attained full liberation and taught the way to it. These men are honored as the greatest of *jinas* ("victors" or "conquerors"), from which the word Jain is derived. The ideal of conquering through great struggle is pervasive in Jain literature. But it is not a triumph over a human enemy that is lauded, for the foe is oneself and one's own material nature, which can be defeated by perseverance in asceticism or self-denial. This mood is often reflected in Jain art, which may portray the Tirthankaras as heroically rigid, immobile figures over which vines have extended their tendrils, in contrast to dancing or flute-playing Hindu deities.

Jainism teaches that sentient, feeling life dwells in all that exists—gods, humans, animals, plants, even stones, dust, and air. These *jivas,* souls or particles of life, are entrapped in the material shells of these substances as a result of karma. The Jain view of karma is somewhat different from the Hindu or Buddhist; for Jains it is more like a material coating that covers souls as a consequence of action based on desire and thereby condemns them to the suffering incumbent upon material existence.

One can look at it this way: Karma or action is inevitably directed toward some particular object and so "grows" the material form it needs to attain that object. If you want a piece of candy, you need an arm to reach out and grab it and a mouth with which to eat it. Karmic law says that in such matters you get what you want—but then you have to live with it. You now have a body so that you can enjoy candy, but you are also trapped inside that body, with all its limitations and capacity for pain—and you will have a very hard time getting out of it.

According to Jainism, since it was action that got us into the material predicament, it must be its opposite—quietness and abstention—that begins to reverse it, as well as suffering induced by asceticism that wears down the karmic shell until the soul can break free, floating up to the top of the universe to enjoy an eternity of bliss and omniscience.

Inflicting suffering on another soul, whether through cruelty or indifference or even apparent necessity, adds to one's burden of karma. For this reason, Jains go to great lengths to counter the callousness of the world toward life. Virtually all Jains are strict vegetarians and go so far as to put screens around lamps to keep insects from flying into them. Many Jain temples maintain homes for unwanted animals and hospitals for injured birds.

Practice differs, however, between laity and monks. The former essentially live so as to add no more to the burden of karma, in the hope of becoming a monk in some future life and ultimately attaining *kaivalya,* or liberation.

Monks, however, are determined to make real headway toward that goal in this lifetime. They not only practice the great Jain virtue of *ahimsa,* harmlessness, but undertake great asceticism—fasting, meditating in the hot sun, enduring discomfort—to wear down the karmic shell. Jain monks are divided into two orders: the Digambaras, who are naked, and the Svetambaras, who wear a thin white robe.

The high value placed on asceticism, however, has not inhibited a respect for learning and beauty among Jains. Monks go among Jain communities as teachers and preachers; a great number of the laity are well educated in the faith. Historically, Jain monks have played a very creative role in the letters and philosophy of India. Mohandas Gandhi, and through him such Americans as Martin Luther King, Jr., were deeply influenced by Jain teachings about harmlessness and nonviolence.

The Jains, typically merchants and bankers, are a prosperous and gifted class in India today, influential beyond what their numbers of only about 1.5 million would suggest. Their well-maintained temples are among the most exquisitely beautiful in India.[25]

Ahimsa

SIKHISM

The Sikh religion, as we have seen, arose early in the sixteenth century on the spiritual boundary between Hinduism and Islam. It answered to the needs of those who, perturbed by the coexistence of two mighty but conflicting faiths, sought a higher truth beyond them both. It taught the simple monotheistic worship of a God who can be called by many names so long as one does not limit him to any of them. Yet Sikhism, over time, became a movement with its own distinctive outlook and its own role in the complex and tumultuous history of India.

According to tradition, Guru Nanak, the first revealer of Sikhism, received his divine call at the age of thirty, when God came to him and charged him to teach humankind the worship of the true name of God through simple prayer, charity, cleanliness, and service. He was lost in the rapture of this experience for three days, and when he reappeared, he said to his companions, "There is no Hindu; there is no Muslim."

Nanak composed many psalmlike poems like the one quoted on page 95, which now comprise part of the Holy Granth, the Sikh scriptures. He inculcated in his growing band of followers an inclusive religion focused on the name of one universal, all-powerful and all-loving God, who makes no distinction among men and women on the basis of caste or creed but who looks into their hearts. The simple worship of God is sufficient; pilgrimage, ritual, or ascetic practices add nothing to it.

As the Sikh ("disciple") movement grew, the idea of the guru and of the Sikhs as a distinct community also became more and more important. Nanak was followed by a succession of nine gurus, each appointed by his predecessors, some of whom left distinctive stamps on the character of the faith. The Sikh fellowship, too, came to be clearly defined.

The fifth guru, Arjun (1563–1606), did much to make the religion institutional. He compiled the Sikh scriptures, the Granth, from the writings of Nanak, Kabir, and other poets and gurus. He enshrined it in the famous Golden Temple in Amritsar, which is Sikhism's most venerated site. A strong administrator, he organized local Sikh communities efficiently and pushed for a high measure of self-government for the movement as a whole. Arjun was martyred after he supported the wrong faction in struggles for power following the death of the great Mughul emperor Akbar. This event served virtually to absolutize the reforms of the great leader and to teach the Sikhs they would need to look out for themselves in an increasingly dangerous situation.

That lesson was not lost on Gobind Rai (1666–1708), descendant of Arjun and the tenth and last guru. The Mughul Empire in north India, with its many peoples and faiths, was deteriorating under the rule of the fanatically Muslim Aurangzib. Gobind advocated the right of the Sikhs to defend themselves and did much to enhance the military tradition for which Sikhism was to become noted.

In 1699 he inaugurated the Khalsa, the Sikh military fraternity. Standing before the great assembly of believers, Gobind asked if there were any here, now, today, willing to give their life for the faith. The crowd was astounded by this awesome request. But finally five brave men came forward. Gobind took each into his tent, a thud was heard, and when he came out his sword was dripping with blood. But finally he led the five out before the terrified assembly. They were unharmed, the blood had been that of a goat, but the men were now accounted heroes and the first members of the Khalsa. Though of different caste background, they drank *amrit,* sacred nectar, together and were to wear five tokens: uncut hair covered by a turban, a comb, a steel bracelet, a special pair of undershorts, and a *kirpan,* or two-edged dagger. They took the surname Singh, "lion." Others rushed to join the Khalsa, pledging never to turn their backs on an enemy. Gobind took to the field with some success but died of wounds inflicted in battle in 1708. Before he died, he is reported to have said that he would be the last guru in human form; after him the Granth itself would become the guru. In time, Sikh rulers governed states in the Punjab region until subjugated by the British in the Sikh wars of the nineteenth century.

The Sikhs have no formal priesthood. Their worship, reminiscent in some ways of Protestant Christianity, may be conducted by any qualified Sikh. It consists of hymns, prayer, scripture reading, sermon, and the sharing of food together, both in a sort of communion rite at the end of worship and in communal dinners afterwards. Private worship in the home morning and evening is also emphasized. In its mainstream form, it gives little place to asceticism or celibacy, though it teaches simplicity of life.

Sikhism, then, can be characterized as a monotheistic religion with a strong sense of community, a devotion to family life, a tradition of ethical and military virtues, and a belief that it worships a universal God beyond sectarian divisions.

ZOROASTRIANISM AND THE PARSEES

Another minority religion of India is that of the Parsees or Zoroastrians, heirs of a historically important creed, which was once a faith of a powerful neighboring country. Between Mesopotamia and India lies the vast expanse of the land called Persia or Iran. It is a land of paradoxes: nearly empty, yet the homeland of an ancient and immensely creative civilization; forbidding, with its endless deserts and stony mountain ranges, yet a country incomparably important as the transmitter of goods and ideas between East and West. From Alexander to Marco Polo, Persia was the portal of the East for intrepid Westerners; in China, foreigners of Persian or cognate race were the chief importers of ideas from the West. Perhaps astrology, of Babylonian origin, was introduced to Indians and Chinese by Persians. Even Buddhism came from India to China largely by way of central Asia, and its chief envoys to the Middle Kingdom included "blue eyes" like Kumarajiva.

Persia had, and Iran still has, a distinctive and splendid culture of its own. It has given its own gift of the magi to the religious world in Zoroastrianism, a faith now much diminished in numbers, but one which has had immense influence both East and West. Even after Persia formally submitted to the Muslim crescent, its ancient faith made rich contributions to the art, literature, and thought of Islam.

Wherever Persian spiritual influence has been felt, Zoroastrianism has given or reinforced three basic motifs: a battle between light and darkness as respectively good and evil; eschatology (or emphasis on an end to history), a divine judgment, and the making of a new purified earth; and the concept of paradise (a Persian word), an ideal heavenly realm with a divine court and abode of the blessed. In turn, these ideas have impelled religion in Persia and elsewhere toward monotheism, ethics, and a sense of the religious meaning of history. These Iranian contributions have done much to move Western religion away from mystical identification with the forces of nature or states of consciousness and toward "ethical monotheism."

Indeed, while the ancient Hebrews believed in one God who judged and punished those with whom he was angry in this life, it was not until after they had had some contact with Persia that such ideas as resurrection of the dead at the end of the world, a final judgment, the making of a new earth, and heaven and hell, became important in the Hebrew scriptures. These ideas, all part and parcel of Zoroastrianism, entered the Biblical tradition after the exile of the Judeans to Babylon, from which they were released by the great Persian king Cyrus; thereafter, contact between Jew and Zoroastrian was frequent. Today, ideas like final judgment and heaven and hell are important to traditional Judaism, Christianity, and Islam. (The exact nature and extent of Iranian influence on Judaeo-Christian eschatology is a matter of scholarly dispute, and other factors such as Greek and Egyptian influence and indigenous development play a part too. But nowhere in the ancient world, prior to late Judaism, Christianity, and Islam, is there an eschatological scenario with the grandeur of the Persian; one cannot doubt its vision would strongly stimulate those who came to know it.)

A visitor to modern Iran soon comes to grasp something of why this country was a homeland of eschatology. An immense, rugged, dry terrain not unlike the American southwest under infinite blue sky suggests the contingency of human life in a world alien to it, and the inescapable sovereignty of heaven. Here and there, like oases breaking the inhospitable contours of nature, the Persians have created islands of paradise in the midst of the desert: the Persian garden with its pool and ornamental trees, the cool mosque with its arabesques, even the Persian carpet and exquisite miniature painting or illuminated book. All suggest the theme of radical opposition between present environment and the visionary's hope.

The greatest son of Persia to perceive this vision, according to tradition, was the prophet Zoroaster (or Zarathustra; before 600 B.C.E.). The ancient Iranians were cousins to the Aryan peoples who invaded India. Prior to the time of Zoroaster their religion was similar to that of the Vedas. They worshipped gods such as Varuna and Mithra with sacrifice, chiefly of cattle, in the open air. They had a sacred drink, *haoma,* comparable to the Indic soma. The magi were a priestly class similar to the

Zoroaster

brahmins in Vedic India. Probably fire, *asha,* was of sacred importance in their rites in a way similar to the role of Agni in India. It is not clear to what extent eschatology, judgment, and paradise motifs were widespread before Zoroaster; no doubt they had some importance.

About Zoroaster too we have little reliable information, despite all the influence he had.[26] He came, according to tradition, from the East, was of prominent family, and probably was a priest. His wife was a daughter of a noble in the court of King Vishtaspa of Bactria or Balkh, a Persian area in what is now western Afghanistan.

Zoroaster had one of the most remarkably independent minds known to history, and he was less than satisfied with the customary rites. He was repelled by the sacrifice of cattle and the ecstatic intoxication of men who drank haoma. In his sight, the innocent, suffering eyes of cattle falling under the sacrificial knife represented the affronts the good always suffer from evil: They are like the cattle of God. The ritual, irresponsible bliss of haoma, too, had in this prophet's eyes little to do with the serious matters between God and man. But his criticisms made him unpopular and he was forced to flee.

Zoroaster wandered the mighty plains and towering mountains of his homeland striving to resolve his spiritual discomfit. Some say he spent ten years in this solitary quest. Finally, atop a great peak, he experienced a transcendent vision. He saw Ahura Mazda, as he named the high god, in all his splendor and glory above and beyond the old gods.

Zoroaster understood then that religion is not just religion but reflects an ongoing universal battle. Ahura Mazda and his forces of light are in combat against the legions of Ahriman or Angra Mainyu, the evil spirit also called the Lie, and the *daevas* who are in his following. Boldly, Zoroaster gave the dark army the name "daeva," meaning deva or god in the old polytheistic sense.

The great battle was a battle of Truth versus the Lie. Ahura Mazda was accompanied by six Amesha Spentas, Holy Immortals or Good Spirits, angels or perhaps aspects of God himself. Of the other gods, Varuna probably gave his name to Ahura Mazda; Mithra and a few others became aides in the courts of light. But the underlying monotheism of the vision of Zoroaster himself comes through strongly, together with a second-level dualism or belief in two polarized forces. Ahura is a god of goodness and morality, Ahriman is the Lie; humans must choose, out of free will, which side they are going to be on.

The battle of good and evil was the most satisfactory way Zoroaster could explain the ill he saw around him. Ahura Mazda, he believed, is only good; therefore he could create only good things and do only good deeds. Like all who wrestle with the problem of evil and find it very hard to explain its coexistence with an all-powerful good God, Zoroaster and his followers had difficulty explaining theologically the relation between Ahura Mazda and Ahriman—whether they are both eternal realities, meaning that Ahura's power is limited; or whether, as many thought, Ahriman is an offspring of Ahura who rebelled against him. But there is no question of the moral force of what Zoroaster was trying to say: that we are combatants in a war of ultimate significance and cosmic dimension, that no one can be just neutral in it, but that in every area of life, day by day, everyone must decide which lord he or she will side with, the Lord of Light or the Lord of the Lie.

Ahura Mazda, we are told, made this present world as a trap in order that his masterpiece, humankind, might ensnare the enemy. Humans are the bait—by drawing Ahriman, eager to tempt and win over humanity, into Ahura Mazda's world and by then freely choosing the good when tempted, humans weaken Ahriman's force and wear him down so that he can eventually be destroyed.[27]

Each person, then, is under judgment. Here the eschatology of Zoroastrianism comes in. While Zoroaster himself undoubtedly had strong eschatological ideas,

---

Fundamental Features of Zoroastrianism

Theoretical

Basic World View	The universe a battleground between good and evil.
God or Ultimate Reality	The good high God, Ahura Mazda, whose adversary is the evil force.
Origin of the World	Made by Ahura Mazda to entrap the evil force.
Destiny of the World	At the end of the age, to be remade as a new, pristine paradise.
Origin of Humans	Made by Ahura Mazda with free will to help trap and defeat the enemy.
Destiny of Humans	Judgment after death, sentence to paradise or hell; resurrection in the new world at the end of the age.
Revelation or Mediation Between the Ultimate and the Human	Revelation through the prophet Zoroaster; mediation by priests.

Practical

What Is Expected of Humans; Worship, Practices, Behavior	To choose the good, do right, keep pure; to maintain the faith by supporting its rites and institutions.

Sociological

Major Social Institutions	Temples, priesthood, a close-knit community; now mostly Parsees in India.

they have been preserved in a later form. That form centers on reward and punishment (although, in contrast to the Judaeo-Christian tradition, punishment in hell is not eternal), and on the making of a new world.

Zoroastrians said that on the fourth day after death, a deceased person had to cross the bridge called Chinvat, which connects humanity with the unseen world. The righteous will find it broad as a highway, and they will take it to enter the House of Song, where they will await the Last Day. Yet to the wicked, the bridge will seem narrow as a razor, and they will fall off it into hell.

But on the Last Day, Ahura Mazda will defeat evil. He will purify the entire world and reign over it. All persons will be raised in a general resurrection; the souls of the wicked, having been purified along with the earth, will be brought out of hell with their sentences terminated. All together will enter a new age in a new world free from all evil, ever young and rejoicing.

Just before the Last Day, it was said, Zoroaster would return in the form of a prophet conceived of a virgin by his own seed, stored in a mountain lake. A prophet would in fact appear in this way at 1000-year intervals during the 3000 years between Zoroaster and the renovation of the world.

Zoroaster was finally successful in converting the court of King Vishtaspa to his faith. The new religion was launched at about the same time as the great Persian Empire. Cyrus the Great (r. 559–30 B.C.E.), the first great Persian ruler, incorporated Mesopotamia into his realm, sent the Jewish captives home, allowing them to rebuild the temple in Jerusalem, and effectively unified Asia from India to the Mediterranean into an empire. It is not evident how much Cyrus himself was influenced by Zoroaster's teaching; the first Persian emperor is best known instead for his enlightened policy of tolerance and support of the faiths of all his diverse subjects. But Zoroastrian teaching spread rapidly; his successors, such as Darius and Xerxes, worshipped Ahura Mazda and claimed his protection.

The Zoroastrian priests, or *mobeds* (derived from magi), were great practitioners of magic as well as being profound philosophers. In the days of the Roman Empire (as the account of the visit of several of them to Bethlehem in the New Testament bears witness), they were a byword for astrologers and wizards. Zoroaster himself was accounted a great magician. However, many of those called magi around the ancient Mediterranean were probably only from Mesopotamia, where the occult arts flourished mightily. The Parthian Empire, Rome's great rival, ruled the Persian and Mesopotamian regions from 250 B.C.E. to 224 C.E.; it was a melting pot of polytheism, Zoroastrianism, Hellenism, Babylonian religion, and teachings from East and West, out of which mystical and esoteric movements bubbled continually. Among them were the influential Mithraism, worship of Mithra transformed into an initiatory mystery popular among Roman soldiers; and Manichaeism, an ascetic and syncretistic faith.

How widespread or exclusive a religion Zoroastrianism was in this period is disputed. Its heyday as an official, organized religion was the Sasanian Empire (224–651 C.E.). By this time Zoroastrianism had reincorporated haoma, sacrifices, and polytheistic elements—probably never lost in popular religion—and was fraught with priestly regulations concerning purifications, expulsions of demons, and the minute division of animals, insects, and so forth into the ranks of light and darkness. The Zend Avesta, the Zoroastrian scriptures, were compiled; although they contain the Gathas, hymns ascribed to Zoroaster himself,[28] there is much material of a later and more sacerdotal character.

After the fall of the Sasanian Empire, Persia was converted to Islam, and the minority of Persians who wished to remain faithful to the old religion were under pressure. Some—about 14,000—remain in Iran to this day. Others moved to the more tolerant atmosphere of India. Zoroastrians there, now called Parsees ("Persians") and living mostly around Bombay, number perhaps 150,000.

The Parsees in India have greatly prospered and are now one of the wealthiest classes in that nation. In large part this is due to their "work ethic," strong moral code, and philanthropy. They are well known for their fire temples and Towers of Silence.

Their Zoroastrianism is life-affirming. It says that the world, having been made good by Ahura Mazda, is to be accepted with thanks. One's basic duties are to confess the religion, take a mate and procreate offspring, and treat livestock justly; asceticism and world negation are not approved. The main places of worship are the clean, attractive fire temples, where a perpetual flame is kept burning as a symbol of the purity of God, being fed five times a day with prayers; here the scriptures are chanted and other rituals performed.[29]

The Towers of Silence are unique structures on which the bodies of Parsee dead are placed to be devoured by vultures. This custom reflects some basic Zoroastrian attitudes and some adjustments it has made.

Because the world is made by God and is good, and death is a pollution, a corpse cannot be consigned to any of the four elements—it can be neither exposed to the air, buried, given to the sea, nor cremated. The ingenious solution was to give the body to carnivorous birds. In Iran, bodies were apparently left for them on high mountains. In the flatlands of India, the Parsees instead built the remarkable Towers of Silence, over which vultures are always slowly wheeling; a corpse placed there will be completely stripped of flesh within an hour or two.

After death, the body is washed and clothed in white. It is shown to a so-called four-eyed dog (because he has two spots just above his eyes); this dog is believed able to detect whether life is extinct. After the body has been reverently taken to the Tower of Silence and left there, services are held to pray for the deceased as he crosses the Chinvat Bridge, and donations are made in his name to charity.

Purity is important to Parsees; elaborate rituals are prescribed for the expiation of pollution. Initiations of boys and girls into the faith of Zoroaster are occasions of colorful and joyful parties, processions, and rites. Even more elaborate is initiation into the hereditary office of *dastur,* or priest.

The faith of cosmic battle and renewal given us by Zoroaster, and once the religion of a powerful empire, has now declined in numbers. But no decrease can erase its immense influence on the history of religions, an influence that has touched the spiritual lives of countless millions past and present.

SUMMARY

India has been the cradle of several religions: Buddhism, Jainism, Sikhism. But the great majority of its people follow Hinduism, which can be taken to mean simply "the religion of India." As such, it embraces a vast diversity of gods, practices, and spiritual paths. It includes the worship of God through images and concepts and through taking them away. It strives to reconcile the following of dharma, the cosmic law and the way of righteousness in this world, and the quest for moksha, or liberation from all that is limiting to attainment of God-realization.

Hinduism has roots in the religion of both the indigenous agricultural peoples of India and of the ancient Aryan or Indo-European invaders. From the former, it probably received such features as fertility cults, mother goddesses, and yoga; from the latter it received the Vedas, its classic scriptures, and the rites of the brahmin priests. Beginning with brahmin sacrificial religion and its cosmic gods such as Indra and Varuna and Agni, the Vedas end with the "interiorization of sacrifice" in the Upanishads, with their message that Brahman, the universal Absolute, is one with Atman, the true self of each individual; Brahman, taking many shapes, is all that is, and only in knowing him is there joy.

During the period of the Upanishads (the last few centuries B.C.E. and the turn of the first millennium), other spiritual teachings were arising as well. The Buddha and Mahavira of the Jains taught inward paths to liberation not dependent on the Vedas. Patanjali and others taught the essence of yoga: self-control attained through virtuous life, postures, and ordered breathing, then withdrawal from the outer senses to reach mastery and freedom within. The Bhagavad-Gita, the great Hindu classic of this era, showed the direction religion was taking by beginning with teachings like those of the Upanishads and culminating in a great revelation of Vishnu that established the foundations of bhakti. In the process it also gave the karma-yoga teaching, which much later greatly influenced Gandhi, that one can know liberation through work in the world if that work is done selflessly. A little later, Advaita Vedanta, the philosophical teaching that speaks of the sole existence of Brahman, and Tantrism, the path to liberation through radical initiations and paradoxical practices, added their flavors to Hinduism. In the sixteenth century, the Sikh faith sought to worship the God above Hinduism and Islam.

The great majority of Hindus practice some form of bhakti, or devotion toward the gods. Bhakti believes that love for one's chosen deity is the easiest yet most supremely effective road to liberation. Hindu deities are numerous, but the major ones fall into two great families: the Vishnu family and the Shiva family. Vishnu represents the forces working for good in the cosmos; from time to time he comes to earth in the form of avatars, such as Rama and Krishna, to restore righteousness. Shiva, though also ultimately good, represents the life force and the totality; his consort or Shakti, the great goddess who goes by many names, such as Kali, Durga, and Parvati, is a powerful religious force in her own right.

Home and family are all-important centers of Hindu religious life. In a devout home, the head of the family offers daily devotions. In traditional India, one's caste was an important determinant of spiritual life; the power of caste is now weakening. Many Hindus worship in the colorful temples as well as at home, presenting garlands of flowers or other offerings to the divine images, perhaps with the help of a priest; temples are especially associated with pilgrimage and festival. Some Hindus, especially toward the end of life, become sadhus, renouncing the things of this world for the sake of the spiritual quest. They, like others serious about spirituality, may become disciples of a guru or spiritual teacher.

Modern Hinduism has made vigorous efforts to relate its ancient tradition to the modern world. Ramakrishna and his followers in the nineteenth century endeavored to show that the philosophical basis of the religion has universal value. In the twentieth century, Mohandas Gandhi drew from it to pioneer nonviolent methods of political and social change.

Jainism is an ancient Indian religion emphasizing life in everything and the liberation of the jiva or soul from bondage to karma or matter by self-denial.

Sikhism, emerging on the border of Hinduism and Islam, presented a simple monotheism taught by a lineage of true gurus.

Zoroastrianism is now diminished in numbers, but as the religion of ancient Persia, it was immensely influential. Deriving from the teachings of the prophet Zoroaster, it taught that the high god, Ahura Mazda, is engaged in cosmic battle against the forces of darkness. Humans are involved in the struggle and must choose which side to be on. Souls are judged and rewarded or punished after death; at the end, after Ahura Mazda wins, all will be resurrected and enjoy a new heaven and earth.

QUESTIONS FOR REVIEW

1. Turn back to the thematic chart for the chapter and explain how Hinduism has reconciled the "affirmative way" in religion—the way of moving toward unconditioned reality through devotion to divine images and ideas—and the "negative way"—the way to God by taking away all that is not God, all lesser images and ideas. See what persons, concepts, and practices are on each side and where they meet. Then from the same chart, explain how Hinduism reconciles the following of dharma, the divine order and the way of righteousness in the world, with the pursuit of moksha, liberation into divine infinity.

2. Interpret the view of human life indicated by Hinduism's four goals and four stages of life.

3. Present the main features of Vedic religion: its world view, its gods, the inner meaning of its sacrifices, how it set the stage for the development of later Hindu philosophy and religion.

4. Talk about the central message of the Upanishads.

5. Explain what is meant by Brahman.

6. Discuss the Buddha in the context of his times.

7. Understand the theory and practice of yoga.

8. Show how the thought of the Bhagavad-Gita moves from the insights of the Upanishads to those of bhakti, Hindu devotionalism.

9. Explain the philosophy of Advaita Vedanta.

10. Describe some features of the thought and practice of Tantrism as a path to liberation.

11. Describe the two main families of Hindu gods, as well as the mythology and worship of two or three deities in detail.

12. Explain how home and family are the main centers of Hindu worship for a large number of Hindus.

13. Interpret the fundamental meaning of the Hindu caste system.

14. Discuss the meaning and role of sadhus, or holy men.

15. Briefly describe typical worship in a Hindu temple.

16. Explain how Ramakrishna and Gandhi, each in his own way, related Hinduism to the modern world.

17. Talk about the insight of Hinduism that you found of most value for yourself.

18. Using the chart, summarize the fundamental features of Hinduism. How does it answer the great questions about God and the meaning of human life?

19. Give the fundamental features of Jainism.

20. Describe the Sikh religion.

21. Discuss basic themes of Zoroastrianism.

SUGGESTED READINGS ON THE RELIGIONS OF INDIA

General—Ancient

*BASHAM, A. L., *The Wonder That Was India*. New York: Grove Press, 1959. A masterly survey of classic Indian society with much attention to religion.

BROCKINGTON, J. L., *The Sacred Thread: Hinduism in its Continuity and Diversity*. Edinburgh: University of Edinburgh Press; and New York: Columbia University Press, 1981. A highly regarded introduction to Hinduism in all its periods and forms.

*COOMARASWAMY, ANANDA, *The Dance of Shiva*. Bombay: Asia Publishing House, 1948. A brilliant insight into the classic Indian mind through the gateway of art; invaluable for an understanding of the religion in depth.

DANIELOU, ALAIN, *Yoga: The Method of Reintegration*. New York: University Books, 1955. A concise and useful summary of the basic yoga texts.

*DEUTSCH, ELIOT, *Advaita Vedanta: A Philosophical Reconstruction*. Honolulu: East-West Center Press, 1969. A splendidly readable introduction to India's most prestigious philosophical tradition.

ECK, DIANA L., *Banaras: City of Light*. New York: A. Knopf, 1982. Brilliant insight into Hindu religion and culture through a study of its most holy city.

*ELIADE, MIRCEA, *Yoga: Immortality and Freedom*. New York: Pantheon Books, 1958. An invaluable overview of yogic concepts and literature.

*HOPKINS, THOMAS T., *The Hindu Religious Tradition*. Belmont, CA.: Wadsworth, 1971. A useful introductory text; particularly valuable for its treatment of Vedic ritual.

KINSLEY, DAVID R., *Hinduism: A Cultural Perspective*. Englewood Cliffs, NJ: Prentice Hall, 1982. A vividly-written introductory textbook.

*LANROY, RICHARD., *The Speaking Tree: A Study of Indian Culture and Society*. London and New York: Oxford University Press, 1971. A substantial, valuable interpretation, particularly for its psychological insights.

MORGAN, KENNETH W., ED., *Religion of the Hindus*. New York: Ronald Press, 1953. A collection of papers by Hindus written on a nonspecialist level; a good introduction to Hinduism.

O'FLAHERTY, WENDY P., ED., *Karma and Rebirth in Classical Indian Traditions*. Berkeley: University of California Press, 1980. Basic papers on a very important Hindu topic.

*___, *The Rig Veda: An Anthology*. Harmondsworth, England: Penguin Books, 1982. An accessible and well-introduced entry into the oldest religious literature of India.

*PRABHAVANANDA, SWAMI, AND CHRISTOPHER ISHERWOOD, *How to Know God: The Yoga Aphorisms of Patanjali*. New York: Mentor Books, 1969. An easy-to-read version of basic yoga text with commentary.

*___, *Shankara's Crest-Jewel of Discrimination*. New York: Mentor Books, 1970. The most accessible text of the nondualist tradition and a good introduction to the classic Indian metaphysical mind.

*___, *The Song of God: Bhagavad-Gita*. New York: Mentor Books. © 1951 Vedanta Society of Southern California. The most readable translation of this classic text, with an introduction by Aldous Huxley. Oriented toward an Advaita interpretation.

*PRABHAVANANDA, SWAMI, AND FREDERICK MANCHESTER, *The Upanishads: Breath of the Eternal*. New York: Mentor Books. © 1948, Vedanta Society of Southern California. A splendidly poetic and readable introductory translation of the most important of these basic texts. Oriented toward an Advaita interpretation.

*ZIMMER, HEINRICH, *Myths and Symbols in Indian Art and Civilization*. New York: Harper Torchbooks, 1962. A rich study; myth and symbol are as important as philosophy for understanding India.

*___, *Philosophies of India*. New York: Meridian Books, 1956. A brilliant and readable work by a scholar who understands the Indian tradition in a profound, if romantic, way.

Hindu Gods

BABB, LAWRENCE A. *The Divine Hierarchy: Popular Hinduism in Central India*. New York: Columbia University Press, 1975. A brilliant field study that provides insight into the workings of popular Hinduism everywhere.

CARMAN, JOHN B., *The Theology of Ramanvja*. New Haven: Yale University Press, 1974. Excellent insight into bhakti theological thought; aimed at interreligious understanding.

COOMARASWAMY, A., AND SISTER NIVEDITA, *Myths of the Hindus and Buddhists*. New York: Dover, 1972. An elementary retelling; well written and cumulatively gives a good insight into India.

DANIELOU, ALAIN, *Hindu Polytheism*. New York: Pantheon Books, 1964. A massive summary of data about the gods, mostly through selected translations of classic texts. Well illustrated.

HAWLEY, JOHN STRATTON, ED., *The Divine Consort*. Berkeley: University of California Press, 1982. Studies of the consort-goddesses of Hinduism.

*KINSLEY, DAVID R., *The Sword and the Flute*. Berkeley: University of California Press, 1975. An excellent study of Kali and Krishna.

_____, *Hindu Goddesses*. Berkeley: University of California Press, 1986. An intriguing account of the major Hindu goddesses and their place in the Indian pantheon.

O'FLAHERTY, WENDY P., *Asceticism and Eroticism in the Mythology of Siva*. London and New York: Oxford University Press, 1973. A landmark study of an important and complex deity, illuminating fundamental themes of Hindu mentality.

_____, *Hindu Myths: A Sourcebook*. Harmondsworth, England, and Baltimore, MD: Penguin Books, 1975. An authoritative introduction to Hindu mythology by a leading scholar in the field.

_____, *The Origins of Evil in Hindu Mythology*. Berkeley: University of California Press, 1980. A brilliant study that sheds much light on the whole of Hinduism.

*SINGER, MILTON, ED., *Krishna: Myths, Rites, and Attitudes*. Chicago: University of Chicago Press, 1968. A good, scholarly collection of papers on Krishna and his cultus.

Tantrism

*BHARATI, AGEHANANDA, *The Tantric Tradition*. Garden City, NY: Doubleday, 1970. A splendid, if sometimes technical, exposition of this often murky field.

*RAWSON, PHILIP S., *Tantra: The Indian Cult of Ecstasy*. London: Thames and Hudson, 1973. A lavishly illustrated popular treatment emphasizing the Hindu tradition.

Modern India

BRENT, PETER, *Godmen of India*. New York: Quadrangle Books, 1973. A fascinating picture of the role of "God-realized" holy men in India today.

ISHERWOOD, CHRISTOPHER, *Ramakrishna and His Disciples*. New York: Simon & Schuster, 1965. A very sympathetic picture of the influential saint of the last century, who through his followers continues to shape modern understandings of Hinduism.

IYER, RAGHAVAN, *The Moral and Political Thought of Mahatma Gandhi*. London: Oxford University Press, 1973. A masterful survey of the ideas of India's most influential man of the twentieth century.

The Jains

JAINI, P. S., *The Jaina Path of Purification*. Berkeley: University of California Press, 1979. A useful summary.

STEVENSON, MRS. SINCLAIR, *The Heart of Jainism*. London: Oxford University Press, 1915. Still the most readable overview, although dated; written from a Christian perspective.

The Sikhs

COLE, W. OWEN, AND PIARA SINGH SAMBHI, *The Sikhs: Their Religious Beliefs and Practices*. London and Boston: Routledge & Kegan Paul, 1978. An excellent introduction to the religion.

McLEOD, W. H., *Guru Nanak and the Sikh Religion*. Oxford: Oxford University Press, 1968. A valuable modern historical study of the faith's origins.

SINGH, TRILOCHAR, AND OTHERS., *Adi Granth: Selections from the Sacred Writings of the Sikhs*. London: George Allen & Unwin, 1960. A readable translation.

Zoroastrianism and the Parsees

BOYCE, MARY, *Zoroastrians: Their Religious Beliefs and Practices*. London and Boston: Routledge & Kegan Paul, 1979. Especially good on the medieval and modern thought and life of the religion.

*DUCHESNE-GUILLEMIN, J., *The Hymns of Zarathustra*. Boston: Beacon Press, 1963. Translation of the oldest parts of the Zend-Avesta.

*___, *Zoroastrianism: Symbols and Values*. New York: Harper Torchbooks, 1970. A short study by a prominent scholar.

*MASANI, RUSTOM, *Zoroastrianism: The Religion of the Good Life*. New York: Macmillan, 1968. An account by a modern Parsi Zoroastrian. Idealizing, but offers an unusual view of the religion from within. Easy to read.

MODI, J. J., *Religious Ceremonies and Customs of the Parsis*. London: Luzac, 1954. A useful reference.

*ZAEHNER, R. C., *The Teachings of the Magi*. New York: Macmillan, 1956. An excellent summary, based on a standard catechism of Zoroastrian doctrine.

CHAPTER 4

Wisdom Embarked for the Farther Shore:
THE JOURNEY OF BUDDHISM

CHAPTER OBJECTIVES

After studying this chapter, you should be able to

- Outline the traditional life and essential teaching of the Buddha.

- Discuss the major schools of Buddhism and how they spread to various parts of Asia.

- Present the importance of practice, especially meditation, in Buddhism.

- Talk about why Buddhism can be thought of as a particularly "psychological" religion.

A RELIGION
OF TRANSFORMATION
OF CONSCIOUSNESS

Buddhism is many things. On the flat Ganges plains east of Benares, it is an ancient enshrined tree, said to be a descendant of the very tree under which he who is called the Buddha, on the night of a full moon, ascended through the four stages of trance and attained full, perfect, and complete enlightenment. In Southeast Asia, it is steep-roofed temples, rich in gold and red, which house conventionalized images of the same Buddha, perhaps standing to teach, perhaps in the seated meditation posture of enlightenment, perhaps reclining as he makes his final entry into Nirvana. The images will probably be gilded, gleaming with transcendent golden light, and the figure's eyes will be half-closed and enigmatic. Around his head may be a many-pointed crown or a simple burst of flame. Outside the temple, saffron-robed monks of the Blessed One (as the Buddha is called) walk with begging bowls, seeking alms.

Lotus, a popular symbol of Buddhism and Hinduism

In the snowy Himalayas, Buddhism is a prayer wheel, a cylinder on an axle inscribed with a mantram such as "Hail the Jewel in the Lotus" and set up on a roadway or around a temple to be spun by passing pilgrims. In Japan, it is an old Zen monk making tea or contemplating the rocks in his monastery garden, as well as vigorous, dynamic young people organizing rallies that combine Buddhist chanting with marching bands and rock concerts.

What is it that ties this tradition together? Buddhism is not rooted in a single culture area, as is Hinduism, but is an international religion, a movement *introduced* in historical time into every society where it is now at home. It has deeply pervaded these cultures and deeply identified with them. But the perceptive observer never quite loses awareness that, on the one hand, this religion is not identical with all the spiritual life of the culture, and on the other hand, that it is a movement wider than the culture and has brought in gifts from outside.

All of this gives Buddhism a somewhat different atmosphere from the Hindu context out of which it emerged. Buddhism always combines something of the Indian spiritual tradition with very different cultures. Instead of the rich, heavy "biological" flavor of Hinduism, of which we have spoken in the preceding chapter, Buddhism has a more psychological thrust.

What is distinctive about Buddhist altars is that, instead of portraying the archetypal hero, mother, or cosmic pillar, as do Hindu altars, the image communicates a unified psychological state—profound meditation, warm compassion, or even unambiguous fury against illusion. Buddhist practices, too, are focused on strong and clear states of unified consciousness. Either they produce clear states or they draw power from beings who have achieved unfettered clarity.

Given this fundamental psychological thrust, let us briefly look at Buddhism in terms of the three forms of religious expression. We shall examine them in reverse order.

The basic sociological fact in Buddhism is the *samgha,* the order of monks. The monastic order is not a unified organization throughout the Buddhist world, and its structure and role vary. In modern Japan it is often no longer celibate. But almost always where there is Buddhism, there are men and women who have given up "natural" life and its goals to take formal vows that orient life in another direction, the realization of a different state of consciousness from the ordinary. Inseparably from this purpose, they are teachers and bearers of Buddhist tradition; and by their distinctive garb, monasteries and temples, and way of life, they make the Buddhist presence unavoidably visible in the midst of society.

Buddhist practice is, as has been indicated, immensely varied. But it centers around three foci: the imaged ideal of the Buddha, the transformation of consciousness, and the transformation of karma or practical destiny. The Buddha is revered and presented to the world as the fully realized being who teaches and epitomizes the true nature of all other beings. He attained realization through profound psychological self-analysis and self-control. Buddhist practice for transformation of consciousness works in the same way and so is most fully expressed in meditation, but it also includes chanting and ritual. Interaction with the Buddha, with his symbols, with the samgha, and following the ordinary moral teachings exposes even people not yet ready for full enlightenment to karma that shapes destiny for good; theirs may be equanimity here and a better rebirth later as a king or god.

Buddhist theoretical expression is concerned with the meaning of the Buddha, the transformation of consciousness, and the work of karma. Above all it is psychological in point of departure, for it is concerned with the analysis of human perception and experience. Buddhist thought is not a vague diffuse mysticism but a sharp precise intellectualism, which delights in hard logic and numerical lists of categories. It holds that ordinary life is unsatisfactory, for it is based on ignorance and desire, resulting in the inability to realize that there is no real "self." All entities within the universe, including human beings, are impermanent compounds that come together and come apart. The answer is a different kind of mind, a "wisdom mind," which finds the middle way between all attachments, uniting all opposites—being, like the Buddha, free of partiality toward any segment of the cosmos—and is therefore, in its unclouded clarity, open to all omniscience, all skill, and all compassion.

We shall now look at the life of the Buddha, to see how these themes are expressed in the traditional account of his quest and achievement.

THE LIFE OF THE BUDDHA

At the beginning of the tradition of which all these forms and much else are branches lies the life of one man, Siddhartha Gautama, of the Sakya clan, called the Buddha, dated by modern scholars approximately 563–483 B.C.E. The Buddha was born, according to tradition, at Lumbini, today about where the border of India and Nepal lies north of Benares. His father was ruler of a tiny state in the foothills of the Himalayas.

Large carved Buddha in Oya, Japan.

Tradition has it that a wise old brahmin came to the court and, observing certain remarkable signs on the infant's body, predicted the wonderful child would become either a world emperor or a Buddha, that is, an Enlightened One and World Saviour. The father, being more political than spiritual in orientation, preferred that his son follow the world emperor option. Realizing that if the gifted boy saw the suffering of the world he would be so moved by compassion that he would prefer to save humankind from pain than rule it from a throne, the king determined to shield him from any sight of ill. He built Siddhartha Gautama glorious pleasure palaces, equipped with everything from chariots to dancing girls to delight the heart of a young prince. All was surrounded by a high wall.

There, the future Buddha matured, married, and had a son. But even unbroken amusement palls eventually, and the prince persuaded his charioteer to take him down the road toward the nearby city. He took four trips in all and saw four thought-provoking sights: an aged man, a man suffering in agony from a hideous disease, a corpse, and finally an old wandering monk who appeared content.

Main Themes in Buddhism

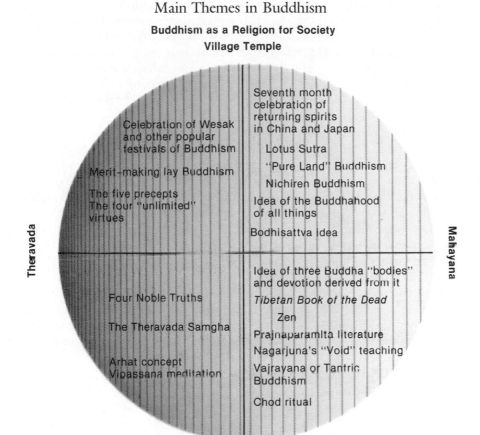

Buddhism as a Religion for Society
Village Temple

Celebration of Wesak and other popular festivals of Buddhism

Merit-making lay Buddhism

The five precepts
The four "unlimited" virtues

Seventh month celebration of returning spirits in China and Japan

Lotus Sutra

"Pure Land" Buddhism

Nichiren Buddhism

Idea of the Buddhahood of all things

Bodhisattva idea

Four Noble Truths

The Theravada Samgha

Arhat concept
Vipassana meditation

Idea of three Buddha "bodies" and devotion derived from it

Tibetan Book of the Dead

Zen

Prajnaparamita literature
Nagarjuna's "Void" teaching
Vajrayana or Tantric Buddhism

Chod ritual

Theravada

Mahayana

Buddhism as a Means of Liberation for Individuals

THEMATIC CHART III. Here we see that the fundamental tension in historical Buddhism is between the religion as a way for individuals, like the monk on the arhant or bodhisattva path, to seek absolute liberation from conditioned reality; and the fact that as the dominant religion of nations and cultures it has also had to serve ordinary men and women. Mahayana and Theravada Buddhism, however, have handled this tension in different ways. Nichiren Buddhism is discussed in the next chapter.

After this, Siddhartha saw even his dancing girls in a different light, and large disturbing issues clouded his mind.

What is the meaning of life, he asked himself, if its initial promise of joy ends long before its dreams can possibly all be fulfilled, in the old age in which one totters backward into infantilism again, or in sickness that can reduce a man or woman full of zest and hope to the state of a howling animal or finally to the apparently blank extinction of death? How can one be delivered from this ghastly witches' revel of birth, fancy, and pain?

Siddhartha did not know; but he knew that until these questions were answered, he could no longer live for anything else than finding their answers. The last sight, the itinerant monk with his staff and begging bowl, inspired him with the idea of a life wholly dedicated to finding the answers he sought. Not long after, in the middle of the night, the prince kissed his wife and son farewell without waking them and slipped off with his faithful charioteer to the banks of a river. There he exchanged his fine raiment for the coarse garb of a renunciant. He then proceeded alone on the great quest.

In his search he sampled the web of paths to realization that crisscrossed the spiritual map of India. He talked with brahmins. He worked with two teachers of trance meditation and went the route of extreme asceticism, getting down to one grain of rice a day and becoming so emaciated that his ribs and spinal column stood out as if he were a walking skeleton. But he found that neither philosophy nor fasting and self-control alone brought what he desired. He gave them up and went back to a moderate diet.

Then, late one afternoon, as he wandered not far from the banks of a river, he felt that the time had come. Purchasing a pallet of straw from a farmer, he seated himself on it under a huge fig tree. He placed his hand firmly to the ground and swore by the good earth itself that he would not stir from that spot until he attained complete and final enlightenment. All night he remained there, sunk in deeper and deeper meditation. Mara, an old god, buffeted him with furious storms and sweet temptations, but a wave of the Blessed One's hand was enough to dispel them. His consciousness refined itself by moving through four stages of trance, beginning with the calmness of the passions that concentration brings and ending with transcendence of all opposites. He also passed through several stages of awareness. First, he saw all of his previous existences. Then, he saw the previous lives, the interlocking deaths and rebirths, of all beings, and he grasped at the karmic forces at work; the universe became like a mirror to him. Finally, he saw with full understanding what principles underlay this web and how extrication from it is possible. He saw the mutual interdependence of all things and how egocentric ignorance leads sentient beings inevitably through desire to suffering, death, and unhappy rebirth. The Four Noble Truths (to be discussed later) appeared in his mind: All life is suffering; suffering is caused by desire; there can be an end to desire; the end is in the Eightfold Path.

Siddhartha Gautama was now a Buddha, an "Enlightened One," or "One who is awake." He is also called the Tathagata, an expression difficult to translate, meaning something like "He who has gone thus," in the sense of "He who passed beyond all bounds; one cannot say where he is but can only point in the direction he went"—referring to his overcoming of all conditioned reality in his enlightenment to become, one might say, "universalized." He was one with the universe itself and not any particular part of it in principle, even though, of course, he continued to have a physical body. (Another title commonly used in Asia is Sakyamuni, Shaka or Shakamuni in Japanese, meaning "Sage of the Sakya Clan.")

After remaining in meditation many days, he arose and went toward Benares.

On its outskirts, in Sarnath, the "Deer Park," he met five ascetics with whom he had been associated before, and who at first mocked him for giving up the austere life. He preached to them about the Middle Way and the Four Noble Truths. They were converted and became his first disciples.

As he wandered about teaching, other disciples came to join him, until there was a band of some sixty accompanying the Enlightened One. Upon entering the Buddha's order, each took the "Three Refuges" or "Three Jewels": I take refuge in the Buddha; I take refuge in the dharma; I take refuge in the samgha. The dharma here means the Buddha's teaching; the samgha is the order of monks. Thus, the Three Jewels affirm that the Buddha is the supreme embodiment of the potential of human life; his teaching tells how he can be emulated and what his wisdom is; the order is the custodian of the Buddha and dharma for future generations and the social context in which the potential can best be reached. We see here Buddhism taking the three forms of religious expression: There is an intellectual teaching; an emerging object of worship and a formal act of submission; and there is a sociological expression, the samgha, which today is probably the oldest continuing nonfamilial social institution in the world.

The life of monks was strictly governed by rules, of which the basic ten are prohibitions against (1) taking life, (2) taking what is not given, (3) sexual misconduct, (4) lying, (5) taking intoxicants, (6) eating after noon, (7) watching or participating in dancing, singing, and shows, (8) adorning oneself with garlands, perfumes, and ointments, (9) sleeping in a soft bed, and (10) receiving gold and silver. (These rules are still followed by Buddhist monks, although they are sometimes interpreted in an allegorical sense in northern traditions. Devout lay people often undertake the first five.)

The Buddha's ministry, which lasted forty-five years after his enlightenment, was generally successful. Of those to whom he preached, many were said to have become arhants—fully liberated beings who will suffer no more rebirths. Since being a Buddha is unique, the arhant state is the spiritual goal of the Buddha's disciples. When the band of disciples reached sixty, he sent them out as missionaries. Thousands came to the Buddha or his disciples seeking lay or monastic initiation, many from the highest ranks of society. Sometimes whole tribes or ascetic orders were converted at once. In time, an order of nuns was established. Valuable pieces of land were given to the order.

There was, of course, opposition. Certain brahmins murmured against the Buddha's doctrine. One disciple, Devadatta, egged on by a hostile king, became a "Judas" and tried to kill the Buddha, but his plots were foiled by the sage's perception. The Buddha's end finally came from eating tainted food; he died meditating in great peace surrounded by his disciples, passing again through the stages of trance, imparting final wisdom to the samgha, such as "Be ye lamps unto yourselves," "All compounds are transitory," and lastly, "Work out your own salvation with diligence." Breathing his last, he then transcended all particularized existence and joined Nirvanic consciousness.

This is the story traditionally told of the Buddha. Much of it is legendary, or a reading back of later Buddhist developments, but it is nonetheless important, for it presents the image of the Buddha that shaped the 2500 years of Buddhist history.[1]

BASIC BUDDHIST TEACHING

When the Buddha returned to preach to the five ascetics in the Deer Park after his enlightenment, he preached to them the Middle Way. When they first saw him and recognized him as one who had been with them but had left, they mocked him as a pleasure lover who had gone back to soft living. But when he opened his mouth to speak, they could not resist a wisdom which went beyond their mere pride in denying the flesh.

Of the Middle Way he said:

> Those foolish people who torment themselves, as well as those who have become attached to the domains of the senses, both these should be viewed as faulty in their method, because they are not on the way to deathlessness. These so-called austerities but confuse the mind which is overpowered by the body's exhaustion. In the resulting stupor one can no longer understand the ordinary things of life, how much less the way to the Truth which lies beyond the senses. The minds of those, on the other hand, who are attached to the worthless sense-objects, are overwhelmed by passion and darkening delusion. They lose even the ability to understand the doctrinal treatises, still less can they understand the method which by suppressing the passions leads to dispassion. So I have given up both these extremes, and have found another path, a middle way. It leads to the appeasing of all ill, and yet it is free from happiness and joy.[2]

The **Middle Way** becomes on its deepest levels an attitude that seeks to find the delicate, infinitely subtle point of absolute equilibrium between all extremes and polarities, from the obvious balancing off of asceticism and self-indulgence, to the recondite metaphysical reaches of eschewing attachment either to life or death, to desire for being or desire for nonbeing. Everything comes in pairs of opposites, the Buddha taught, in our world of partialities, multiplicity, and conditioned reality. The senses, the desires, the unexamined life get "hung up" on one side or the other in these pairs of opposites, thinking one side or the other is "better." The way of wisdom is to find a balance in the totality that includes them both—and so have the permanence and invincibility of the totality. The person of wisdom is stable like the sky, not like clouds now blown this way, now that, and finally dissipated.

The **Four Noble Truths** go deep into the psychological analysis behind the Middle Way idea, and the process to attain perfect equilibrium and totality. In his Deer Park sermon, the Buddha went on to say:

> What then is the Holy Truth of Ill [Suffering]? Birth is ill, decay is ill, sickness is ill, death is ill. To be conjoined with what one dislikes means suffering. To be disjoined from what one likes means suffering. Not to get what one wants,

also that means suffering. In short, all grasping at any of the five Skandhas involves suffering.

What then is the Holy Truth of the Origination of Ill? It is that craving which leads to rebirth, accompanied by delight and greed, seeking its delight now here, now there, i.e., craving for sensuous experience, craving to perpetuate oneself, craving for extinction.

What then is the Holy Truth of the Stopping of Ill? It is the complete stopping of that craving, the withdrawal from it, the renouncing of it, throwing it back, liberation from it, nonattachment to it.

What then is the Holy Truth of the steps which lead to the stopping of Ill? It is this holy eightfold Path, which consists of right views, right intentions, right speech, right conduct, right livelihood, right effort, right mindfulness, right concentration.[3]

These Truths can be summarized as consisting of two pairs. The first is

All life is suffering (or ill, or pain, or anxiety, or bitter frustration).
Suffering is caused by desire (or craving, or attachment).

This pair is the analysis of the ordinary human condition: a mad circle dance, fueled by ignorance, of suffering and desire chasing each other. The more we suffer, the more we want things to assuage or distract. The more we get, the more does anxiety that we shall lose them, and frustration at the transience of all things, build up further suffering. And so around and around.

Thus, the good news in the second pair:

There can be an end to desire.
The way out is the Eightfold Path.

Buddhism is sometimes thought of as a pessimistic religion, but that is so only in its assessment of the ordinary life governed by the suffering and desire of the first two Noble Truths. Buddhism is one of the most optimistic of religions in its vision of the ultimate potential of humankind once that syndrome is broken. For the third of the Noble Truths says suffering can be ended by the stopping of craving; at this point the vicious circle can be halted. One can throw sand in its gears and pull the plug on its turbulence.

Desire, then, is the vulnerable point at which the circle can be broken. It is vulnerable because there is something we *can* do about craving. Craving, or desire, the Buddha said, is like a fire, and any fire requires fuel. If fuel is taken away, the fire must die down. The fuel of the fire of desire is the many things to which the senses are attached. How does one pull back the senses from these attachments? By concentration or meditation, the last and culminating point of the **Eightfold Path,** which focuses one's awareness on something other than objects of desire and so lets the senses quiet down from burning for things they can never really have.

What is the goal of meditation? Ultimately, it is Nirvana, the state absolutely transcending all pairs of opposites, and so all conditioned reality, by the blowing out of all flames of attachment. In Nirvana, all conditioning, including the notion of being a separate individual self, is gone utterly beyond.

It must not be supposed that Nirvana is simply a state hardly distinguishable from annihilation. It is rather the opposite—universalization, the falling away of all barriers so that the mind becomes undifferentiated from horizonless infinity. The full, attractive, positive nature of Nirvana must be stressed. The word *Nirvana* is said to mean "extinguish" or "blow out," like blowing out a flame, yet it does not mean disappearance in a negative sense, but rather the blowing out of all the fires of desire which constrict us. It does not mean extinction of consciousness, but extinction of the desires that cage and enslave consciousness. Our present consciousnesses are usually bound up with relishing sensory input and the accompanying mind-fogging cravings and self-delusions. It is virtually impossible for us now to know what Nirvanic consciousness, genuinely free of all this, would be like. Nirvana is truly the opposite of life as we know it. But for all that, or rather because of that, in Buddhist literature it is portrayed as the Otherness that is utterly desirable, a sparkling and golden light, calm beyond all imagining.

Nor is the quest for Nirvana escapist. Far from being less alive, active, or useful, the person passed into it, if one can so speak—or brought near to it—is far more, infinitely more, of all of these, as well as blissful to an unlimited degree. But one simply cannot express in any words the meaning of these statements. All language comes out of making distinctions and so is bound up with the pairs of opposites that rack the conditioned world. Nirvana is beyond all opposites; it is what is left, so to speak, when the last of them are surpassed. Therefore, although we know from the unsatisfactory nature of life within attachments, contraries, and conditions that nirvanic transcendence would be supremely desirable and glorious, words cannot tell what it is, only what it is not, and those who have been there can only smile.

Nirvana is not merely an enhanced personal existence, as if it were just a heaven gained by good merit. As we have seen in both Hindu and Buddhist philosophies, personality or separate existence are finally viewed not (as we in the West tend to think) as vehicles for expanding awareness and joy but as limitations. However much one may learn, see, and experience, infinitely more is unlearned, unseen, and unexperienced. For the separate self is conditioned by being in some particular time and place, has a limited life span, and even the most brilliant human mind can comprehend only so much—a few grains of sand on the beach of the sea of the infinite universe.

In meditations leading to Nirvana, a different tack is taken—not the mind trying to comprehend through the senses and reason, but the awareness trying to break through their finitude. This can be done; sense and reason are a ring of fire whose fuel lines can be cut. Meditation does not destroy the mind but opens it up completely by breaking down the barriers, so that one simply is the nirvanic ocean and rides the tides of the infinite like a surfer riding the waves. Nothing cuts one off from infinity, so one sees, thinks, knows, does to an unlimited degree.

This is the state claimed for the Buddha after his enlightenment. He still walked the earth, but in a Middle Way manner, making no karmic waves, and at the same time his infinitely attuned mind was able to know all and see all. Although an ordinary-sized human being, so perfect was his equilibrium that he could, like the operator of a perfectly adjusted lever, work incalculable results. It is said that, deep in meditation late at night, his mind would move like a searchlight through the world, find people in spiritual need, and transport himself through his power over matter to that point, or even to several points simultaneously, to help.

When the Buddha died, or rather attained Nirvana absolutely, according to Buddhist belief an effect occurred that can only be called an implosion on the spiritual level. An implosion is the opposite of an explosion; it is what happens when a vacuum is suddenly created and all surrounding molecules of matter rush in to fill the void. The Buddha made no karma actively, as we do trying to grasp at things to fulfill desires. But his passing was like an implosion in the karmic field—suddenly there was nothing there—and a stream of karmic force (good karma) is still rushing in, striving to enter the gateless gate through which he had passed.

The best way to go in the direction he went, of course, is to meditate, emulating the means he used to get there. Next best, if one must act, is to act in ways that harmonize one with the onrushing waves of this stream flowing into the implosion void and let them bear one along. This is the meaning of being a Buddhist, accepting the Three Refuges. It is the meaning of the ordinary acts of kindness that follow the four "unlimited" virtues—unlimited friendliness, unlimited compassion, unlimited sympathetic joy, unlimited even-mindedness—and lead to rebirth in a very high heaven. It is the inner meaning of the merit-making acts of lay people toward the meditative monks, such as giving them food, clothing, and donations. It is the meaning of acts of pure devotion that win good merit, like having sutras read, gilding images of the Buddha, burning incense, and offering flowers at shrines.

NO SELF

One of the fundamental points of Buddhist psychology, and a key to understanding the whole system on a deep level, is *Anatman*—"no self." This Buddhist teaching can be compared to the Upanishadic doctrine that the Atman, the innermost self or soul, is really identical with Brahman. The Buddhist negative expression Anatman, or no self, is a difference of emphasis rather than a contradiction, for if the self is simply the one universal Brahman, it is also "no self" in any individualistic sense. But the difference points to the Buddhist tendency to psychological analysis rather than ontological statement.

Reflection on the idea of no self provides a line of insight into the meaning of the Four Noble Truths, the Middle Way, and the Buddhist experience. This is because the *fundamental* craving, or desire, that keeps us in the suffering-desire syndrome is the desire to be a separate individual self.

The first Noble Truth—that all life is suffering—tells us that there is something unsatisfactory, something anxious, frustrating, incomplete about all life as it is ordinar-

Chinese Bronze Buddha Amitabha, savior in Pure Land
Buddhism.

ily lived. (It does not mean that all life is excruciating pain or that there are no pleasant moments. The Buddha, who supposedly lived his first twenty-nine years in a round of extravagant pleasure, could hardly have said that. But what he does say is that there is something frustrating and unsatisfactory in life, and it can get worse and worse.)

The second Noble Truth tells us the reason for this sense of inadequacy in ordinary life is that we are always trying to cling to things—objects, persons, ideas, experiences—that are partial and not permanent, and so keep us in anxiety lest we lose them, as sooner or later we shall. Yet nonetheless we want to grasp.

The conclusion can only be that somewhere we have acquired a distorted idea about the whole nature and possibilities of human life—that we are basing life on a false premise. And just as when you try to do a complex mathematical problem with the wrong formula, sooner or later everything will begin to come out wrong, so it is with human life. According to Buddhism, the false premise that underlies all other delusion, suffering, and grasping is that one is a separate, independent, individual self—rather than a transitory compound of several elements completely interdependent with the whole universe.

Buddhism teaches that instead of being a "self," in the sense of a separate, enduring "soul" stuck in a body, we are all compounds made up of several different constituents. The five parts that make up a human being are called *skandhas;* the word *skandha* means "bundle" and reminds us that these constituents themselves are collocations of dharmas, the pointlike primary particles that flash out of the void. The human skandhas are form (the physical shape), the feelings, the perceptions (the "picture" the mind forms out of data transmitted by the sense organs), the inherent impulses (karmic dispositions), and the background consciousness. Note that both physical and psychological entities are brought together.

The problem is that when these five entities get together, they interact in such a way as to make the "person" think of herself as a separate individual self. Actually, although understandable, according to Buddhism this is a misreading of the data.

Consider what happens when you, as a collection of the five skandhas, walk down the street and meet another such collection. You interpret everything in terms of reinforcing the illusion that you are a "self," yet a moment's analysis would show how false this premise is.

As you walk, you could think, "I must be a separate individual self, for my physical body gives me the impression of being a detached unit, self-propelled and separate from other objects as I walk past them." (Not really true, for even the physical body is in continual and necessary interaction with the environment in the course of breathing and eating. It is only a certain perspective that makes me include the stomach when I say "myself," but not the field that grows the food it digests, or the sun that makes it grow.)

As you see the other person, you could say to yourself, "I must be a separate individual self or else why would I perceive that unit out there as other than myself?" (But it is not really "I" who sees the other; it is just a phenomenon of light waves hitting sensitive nerves. The skandha of the feeling senses then stimulates the skandha of perception to form a mental picture on the basis of this data.)

You may react emotionally to the person you see—with joy and desire if it is a person you love, with anger if it is someone you dislike. You may say, "I must be a separate individual self, for if I were not, who would be feeling these emotions of joy or anger?" (But these feelings are not a "self"—they are just something that comes and goes like billowing waves in response to data fed in by the senses, interpreted by the perception, and probably conditioned by the karma of patterns of behavior toward that person, or similar persons, carried over from the past along with much else.)

Finally, you may say, "I must be a separate individual self since I am aware of all this." (But the human capacity for self-consciousness is not itself a "self." It is just the skandha of consciousness that accompanies physical form, feeling, perceptions,

---

Fundamental Features of Buddhism

Theoretical

Basic World View	Reality is an indescribable unity. Humans find themselves in a realm of suffering governed by karma.
God or Ultimate Reality	Unconditioned reality beyond all opposites: Nirvana, the Void.
Origin of the World/Destiny of the World	While the cosmos may go through cycles, it has no known beginning or end.
Origin of Humans	An individual is a process of cause and effect rather than a self; to this there is no beginning.
Destiny of Humans	Unending lifetimes in this and other worlds, good or bad according to karma and merit. One then breaks through to attain the Nirvana state.
Revelation or Mediation Between the Ultimate and the Human	Through the Buddha, who attained full enlightenment, and the scriptures attributed to him.

Practical

What Is Expected of Humans: Worship, Practices, Behavior	To do good. Religious and moral works that gain good rebirth. To seek Nirvana by meditation or related practices.

Sociological

Major Social Institutions	Temples; the *samgha,* or order of monks.

and impulses—for it can neither generate nor erase the latter four, but it is just a mirror in which they reflect as they act and react.)

Through such analysis as this, Buddhism concluded that we are not separate individual selves, but collections of elements temporarily brought together and bound to break apart. A life that disregards this fact is basing itself on a false premise and can experience only the syndrome of anxiety and craving as it faces old age, sickness, and death.

Nonetheless, this collection perversely *wants* to be a separate individual self. From birth on, a human being asserts selfhood as the real reason for most of what he or she does. The newborn baby cries as if to say, "I must be a separate individual self or else who would be crying and who would be hungry?"

Through life, one wants to learn, to achieve, to be loved, to accumulate goods, to acquire fame, to become a saint, to win life in heaven—all for oneself, all as though to say, "I must be a separate individual self, for if I were not, who would be learned, famous, beloved, immortal?" Nevertheless, all these dreams bring their own syndromes of anxiety and craving, and the body and perhaps the mind fall apart before they more than begin to be fulfilled.

The Buddhist would put the question another way: *Who* is rich, famous, wise, holy, immortal? A name? A process? A set of memories? None of these is a *self*. Is there any *one* who can be abstracted from the round of rising and falling feelings and forms of a human life, who is independent of the continual flux of the universe? If there is no *one*, then we cannot properly think of the recipient of wealth, fame, wisdom, and so forth—but just that *there is* wealth, fame, and wisdom, or *there is* perception, anger, joy, but not as things to be grasped, or that anyone can grasp. For the Buddha's final words are reported to be, "All aggregates are transitory"— every compound, including the human, is unstable and will come apart.

The reason is **karma,** the force of universal action and reaction that keeps everything moving and changing. Your activities, mental images, and thoughts, even your desire to perpetuate yourself as a separate individual self set up "waves" in the cosmos around you as you try to gain this object or fulfill that dream. No energy is lost, and sooner or later the waves based on the false premise will come back to afflict and finally shatter the compound.

If there is no separate individual self, one might ask how Buddhism can talk as it does of reincarnation. What is there to reincarnate?

In one sense, of course, the answer is nothing. But karma also means that you get what you want; or rather, you continue to be what you think you are. Every cause, including the illusion of being a separate individual self, has an exactly corresponding effect. The illusion then becomes self-perpetuating, life after life.

It might be called a kinetic view of reincarnation. There is nothing solid taken out of one body and put in another, and a deceased person's skandhas are dispersed into the universe. But the karmic waves that one has generated continue to operate until the precise kind of energy they bear has been appropriately transferred, just as ripples may continue to spread on the face of a pond even after a dropped stone has hit the bottom. The karmic waves will move until they have put together another set of five skandhas having shape, circumstance, and dispositions that are what they are because of the karmic energies left by the previous person. In energy terms, then, if not actual substance, this person can be spoken of as the "reincarnation" of the other person.

THERAVADA BUDDHISM

The Buddhist world is now divided into two great traditions. Theravada ("Path of the Elders") Buddhism[4] is found in the nations of Sri Lanka (formerly Ceylon), Burma, Thailand, Cambodia, and Laos. Mahayana ("Great Vessel") Buddhism has spread throughout China, Korea, Japan, Tibet, Mongolia, Nepal, Bhutan, Vietnam, and corners of India and Soviet Asia.[5] Let us look first at **Theravada** Buddhism.

If you were to visit one of the Theravada countries, it would not be long before the practical and sociological expressions of Buddhism were evident to you, and through them you would perceive the wide and deep influence of Buddhism in these lands. You would be struck by the great number of temples dotting the

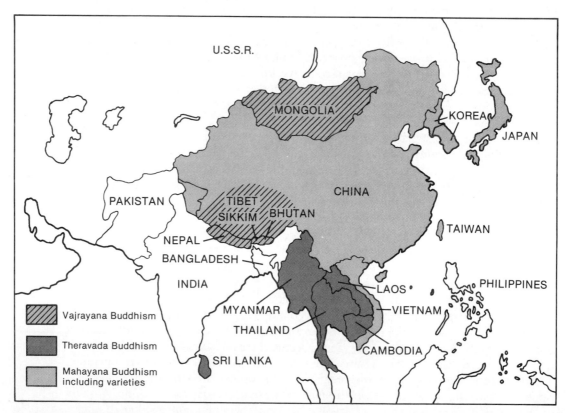

MAP 4–1.   The Journey of Buddhism

cities and lush tropical hills of the countryside. The temples are ornate and elaborate. Curved eaves mount up to pitched roofs. Soaring spires, in the case of large and lovely edifices such as the Shwe Dagon Temple in Rangoon, seem to catch the very soul of the East. Guarding the temple gates are fierce-looking mythological beings; these, like the sculpture and murals one may see of epic heroes, such as Rama and Hanuman, are gods borrowed from Hinduism. Shrines to indigenous spirits of nature and weather, *nats* in Burma and *phis* in Thailand, lurk in the temple shadows. Like the borrowed Hindu gods, they are pupils of the Buddha on another plane than the human.

Within the cool temple, however, it is the Buddha who is supreme; his image gleams richly amid lamps and delicate offerings of incense, flowers, fruit, and water. He may be seated, standing, or reclining; these three postures represent, respectively, the Buddha's enlightenment, teaching, and entry into Nirvana. Worshippers come and go doing worshipful acts of merit, which will benefit them in this and coming lives and prepare them for ultimate release into Nirvana.

On the streets walk monks in their saffron-yellow robes, their heads shaved and arms bare in the warm humid air. If it is early morning—Theravada monks do not eat after noon—each may be holding a begging bowl. At the door of a house he will stand silent, head lowered and hands upraised, accepting whatever the indulgent householder places in his dish.

Most of the monks are young, for in all the Theravada countries except Sri Lanka it is a custom (not always observed today) for every young man, from prince to peasant, to spend a year of his life as a monk. This experience serves to stabilize one's religious life and is an initiation into manhood. A youth would not marry until after he had served as a monk, and his closest lifelong friends are likely to be those with whom he shared this experience. But the great majority of men, of course, do not remain in the cloister. However, among the morning mendicants will be a few gentle old veterans of the monastic path, and they are afforded great respect.

If you followed one of the monks, you would return after him to a neighborhood temple with its attached monastery. Here the monks would gather after begging to consume the simple meals they had garnered. During the afternoon they will rest, study, and meditate.

The temple may be just a village or town *vihara*, rustic and no tourist attraction but a center of community life. Here, traditionally, children go to school, festivals public and private are celebrated, and the dead are remembered. For the plain people of the town, monks are counselors, healers, exorcists, and friends.[6]

Or the temple might be one of the popular places of pilgrimage, where the faithful hope to win merit by gilding the Buddha's image or burning incense before the Buddha's giant footprint—that significant and popular shrine which suggests that the Enlightened One was here, is no longer, but we can follow in the direction he went.

Or the monk you followed might be one of the many who throng the great national temples of the Theravada lands—the Temple of the Emerald Buddha in Bangkok, the Shwe Dagon Temple in Rangoon, the Temple of the Tooth in Kandy,

Theravada Buddhist monks in Thailand.

Sri Lanka. The skyward-curved towers of these splendid buildings, their pitched roofs and carved beams, their brilliant gold and color, their inner atmosphere of incense and contemplation, all murmur something of the sense of wonder and glory at the heart of Buddhism—and remind us it is far more than just a philosophy.

In theory, the main task of the monk in the monastery is meditation, for he is to emulate the Buddha himself, and it was through meditation that the Awakened One went thence. That the young novice is emulating the Buddha is shown by the procedure through which he enters the monastery, if only for a few months. He goes to the monastery dressed as a prince, accompanied by a friend who plays the role of the Buddha's charioteer. At the monastery, he will have his head shaved, don his coarse monkish robe, and, kneeling before the abbot, take refuge in the **Three Jewels.**

The monastic initiation of young men in some Theravada countries shows evidence of being a continuation of archaic pre-Buddhist initiations: the women weep as the boy departs; his teeth are scraped or blackened, suggestive of the ritual

Temple of 1,000 Buddhas.

knocking out of a tooth of older rites; he is often jostled and ridiculed as he tries to put on his unfamiliar robes.[7]

But the high point is movement in another direction. Upheld by the Three Jewels, the monk knows he is to emulate the silent image of the Buddha in the temple, with its serene and inward gaze. He is to explore and know through meditation the inward realm, and finally he is to break through it into the Unconditioned—Nirvana. He is to become an arhant, a perfected and enlightened one who has attained Nirvanic consciousness.

First, the monk must recognize that there are many worlds besides this one. Except for the animal world, the others are generally invisible, but they are accessible to inner organs of vision and are places of possible reincarnation. Like the shaman of old, the monk plunges into them through meditatively altered states of consciousness.

Hinduism and Buddhism speak of six *lokas,* possible "locales" or places where one can be reborn. These are, starting with the lowest:

The Hells
The Animal World

The Realm of Hungry Ghosts
The World of the Asuras or Ogres
The Human Realm
The Heavens of the Gods.[8]

The upper reaches of the heavens, although still part of conditioned reality and so not Nirvana, correspond to very rarefied states of consciousness. Attaining them is considered excellent spiritual exercise. Theravada Buddhism, then, has two basic kinds of meditation: samadhi meditation (which explores the *jhanas,* or higher states above matter and form) and vipassana meditation (which breaks through directly to Nirvana).

Samadhi meditation must begin with the practice of *sila,* ordinary morality and simplicity of life. It then moves to the technique of "one-pointed" meditation, focusing on one thing to concentrate the mind. There are forty traditional topics for this concentration, ranging from discs of various colors through Buddhist virtues to grisly objects such as the repulsiveness of digested food and gnawed corpses— these last considered salutary for those overattached to the lusts of the body. After learning to focus entirely on the object, one can then leave it behind to enter the calm of formless realms of thought.[9]

Nirvana itself requires a more direct thrust. The way is through **vipassana,** the meditation of insight. Instead of forty, it employs only three hard-hitting topics: the impermanence of all things, that all is "ill" or unsatisfactory in conditioned reality, and that one is not a real ego or self. Vipassana gets back to the fundamental Buddhist outlook of the Four Noble Truths and Anatman. The vipassana mediator analyzes himself until he realizes the truth of these three points. Then, as it were, in the gaps left by the breakdown of the ordinary ego-centered way of handling experience, flashes of nirvanic consciousness break through. The mediator is now "entering the stream." He continues in it until he is an arhant, one who has full continuous nirvanic realization and will not be reborn.[10]

Nirvana, the other shore, or the transformation of consciousness, is the goal of Buddhism. Yet it must not be forgotten that Nirvana, for most, is far away, and the life of the religion is something quite other than a direct quest for Nirvana or samadhi. Even among the monks, the great majority are perhaps more interested in passing exams, in community affairs, and in the daily monastic round than in assiduous meditation.

Theravada laity do not generally expect to make formal meditations in the manner of monks. Rather, for them the tableau of the Buddhist map of the invisible world—its temples, pilgrimage places, and cosmic lore—become ways they can align themselves with streams of good karmic force set in motion by the implosion of the Buddha's Great Departure. Buddhism, in other words, comes as a noble instrument for making merit, which will transform destiny to bring good things in this and future lives.

It must not be supposed, however, that the layperson's Buddhist orientation toward merit-making means a diminished Buddhist vision. It may well be richer than that of many monks. The splendors of the temples the layperson loves offer a glint of the Otherness of Nirvana itself, which illumines the mind on deep levels. The observant visitor often is made aware that popular attitudes toward time, human relations, and good or bad fortune in Theravada cultures reflect such basic teachings as no self, karma, and the Four Noble Truths. But the layperson relates to the Buddhist vision differently: through what he or she does rather than what is experienced in meditation.

The layperson tries to follow, as well as possible, the five precepts: not to take life, steal, engage in sexual misconduct, lie, or take intoxicants. He or she tries also to exemplify the four unlimited virtues: unlimited friendliness, compassion, sympathetic joy, and even-mindedness. Through the four unlimiteds, one can be reborn in a divine heaven.

Merit can also be made by donations of robes and food to the monks, building pagodas and making monastery improvements, undertaking pilgrimages, sponsoring a candidate entering a monastery or a formal scripture-reading, working for community good, or giving food to the poor and to animals. The relation of monk and layperson is mutually profitable in merit terms: The laity win merit by donations to the monks; the monks, by preaching and teaching to the laity and by giving them the opportunity to win merit through gifts. The relation of monks and laity exemplifies one of the deepest Buddhist doctrines, the interdependence of all things.

In Theravada countries, there are services in local temples four times a lunar month at the four main phases of the moon. The chief annual festival is Wesak in the spring, commemorating the Buddha's birth, enlightenment, and entry into Nirvana. In various places on this day, trees are watered, candles and incense wave in processions, and rockets blaze through the sky—in part, all aimed at producing the rain that will be so critical in the coming growing season.

A month later, the rainy period (May through July) begins in Southeast Asia. During this time, following the example of the Buddha himself, the monks remain in retreat in the monasteries. Many of the laity, in this Lentlike season, make a special effort to keep the precepts, or even enter the monastery temporarily themselves; for just the state of being a monk gives merit and benefit.

The monks and monastic life are like a reservoir of merit. The Buddha, the teaching, the order, and the laity are like concentric circles going around the absolute center, nirvanic consciousness. Every ring profits through interaction with its neighbors, especially the one next in.[11]

In the twentieth century, Theravada Buddhism has been caught up in the crises of nationalism, modernization, and ideological conflict that have tormented its corner of the world. In Sri Lanka and Myanmar, some monks played a vigorous role in the movement for independence from Great Britain; and postindependence leaders, especially U Nu in Myanmar, made much of Buddhism, in part as a symbol of the national non-Western culture. Other Buddhist monks have endeavored to reconcile Buddhism with modern science, democracy, or Marxism. In Thailand, the government has made the rural monasteries centers for official programs in health, agricultural improvement, and anticommunism. In Cambodia and Laos,

Buddhist life has been disrupted by war and the victory of Communist forces.[12]

Yet despite the incursion of modern problems, visitors to three of the five Theravada countries will still find cultures deeply shaped by centuries of Buddhism. The temples still gleam, and yellow-robed monks still walk the streets.

MAHAYANA BUDDHISM

The northern tier of Buddhist countries, including the great and distinctive Buddhist cultures of Tibet, China, and Japan, are in the **Mahayana** tradition. The style of being Buddhist and of exploring the meaning of the historical Buddha's experience is different from that of the Theravada Buddhism we have just discussed. It is a tradition almost as old as Theravada, although its mood and interests are not as conservative.

The first appearance of what was to become Mahayana was the school called the Mahasamghika ("Great Monastic Order"), which arose within the Buddhist order about a century after the Buddha's death. The points of difference with the Theravadins lay in the Mahasamghika's insistence that students and nonarhants be admitted to monastic meetings, that popular religious practices be reconciled with Buddhism, and that the Buddha was really a supramundane and perfect being who came into our midst as a teacher. These are theoretical points that led directly to Mahayana's universalism, accommodation, and transcendence, although it should be recognized that by the time it became the popular Buddhism of several countries Theravada had made its own adjustments in the same directions.

But through the early centuries of Buddhism, a consistently liberal and innovative party was pushing for more flexible forms of the tradition. By the first century C.E., they appeared as a distinctive tradition marked off by the fact that they accepted not only the *tripitaka,* the scriptures in the Pali language dealing with the Buddha's life and teaching and monastic rules accepted by the Theravadins, but also a growing body of Sanskrit scriptures called *sutras.* Acceptance of the body of sutra literature, rather than any particular doctrine, is the formal test of a Mahayanist.

Nonetheless, a broad consensus of attitude and doctrine runs through the Mahayana sutras, although they were written over several centuries and add up to a hundred times the bulk of the Christian Bible. (In theory, the sutras are put into the mouth of the historical Buddha and ascribed by commentators to various stages of his life; many are said to have been "hidden" for hundreds of years to await times when they would be most needed.)

These scriptures start from a universal rather than a historical perspective, holding that there is a universal true reality—the Void, Nirvana, Buddha-nature, dharmakaya—everywhere which is capable of being realized by anyone. Gautama Buddha realized it at the moment of his enlightenment, and so he manifests it and comes from it—but there are an infinite number of other Buddhas, too, and in a deeper sense everyone is actually an unrealized Buddha. Any means of attaining this realization is acceptable insofar as it works; the gradated practice of Theravada may be dispensed with, and techniques of devotion, chanting, even quasi magic, brought in from bhakti, Tantrism, and folk religion, can be employed.

In all of this the key figure is the **bodhisattva,** who becomes for Mahayana the ideal in place of the Theravadin arhant, and in many ways sums up the Mahayana vision. The bodhisattva is on the way to Buddhahood but holds back at its very threshold by compassion for the countless beings still in ignorance and suffering; he dwells both in Nirvana and the phenomenal world, having the power and reality of both; as a borderline figure, he also imparts grace and receives devotion.

All of Buddhism is built on the Buddha's experience of infinite consciousness at the moment of his enlightenment. Buddhism is all the various methods of apprehending that the way he saw the universe at that moment is the way it really is, and that all other ways are partial and thus erroneous. It is various ways too of interiorizing the same experience insofar as one can. In Theravada, this means "entering the stream" left by the historical Buddha.

In Mahayana, there is more emphasis that the world perceived by the Buddha at enlightenment is the true reality everywhere present at all times, and so it can be apprehended directly by a number of different means and through a number of mediators. The historical Buddha, although respected, is relatively deemphasized; in the final analysis, all reality is full of Buddhas and is one's teacher of Buddhahood, just as all reality is one's parents—everywhere one can see sages, gods, and Buddhas who are essentially aspects of one's enlightened mind, and the Buddha-nature is in every blade of grass and every grain of sand.

Visiting a Mahayana country, one is immediately struck by a difference in Buddhist tone from Theravada countries. There is still the great splendor and peace of the Buddhist temple. But now, instead of a single, solitary Buddha image on the altar, attended by mere gods and men, one will see radiant Buddha after Buddha, bodhisattva after bodhisattva, all transcendentally aware, but all in different moods and poses, from serene meditation to explosive wrath, and from deep withdrawal to many-armed compassionate activity.

This reflects that Mahayana is a "multimedia" way to Buddhahood. The "turning of the head" needful to see one's true Buddha-nature is not something that must be done only one way; since it relates to the ungraspable it cannot be put into a box. Thus, Mahayana has many methods, some very complex and some so simple as to seem insulting until one realizes that the simplicity is the point. Mahayana disdains none of the senses and no "level" of religion, from peasant folk faith to the most advanced metaphysical system.

Thus, Mahayana is Zen monks in Japan in long and immensely calm rows, "sitting quietly doing nothing." It is followers of Pure Land Buddhism chanting "Hail, Amitabha Buddha" and hoping to be brought into the "Pure Land" or Paradise of the Buddha of Infinite Light and Life from where attainment of Nirvana is sure— or perhaps just experiencing the "beingness" of doing the chant. It is Tibetan Tantric Buddhists blowing on trumpets of human thighbones and evoking through chanting and intense visualization the form of one's patronal spiritual ideal. Mahayana is finally the great peace of massive temples, the brazen images of supernal figures glowing dimly in incensed air.

Mount Hiei, the site of an ancient Buddhist monastery on the outskirts of Kyoto, in Japan, is a rich example of Mahayana. Here, amid stately moss-bearded old trees and fern-lined crystal streams, the visitor, almost as if in a Buddhist cafeteria, can wander from temple to temple. The Buddhas of each seem to personify states of consciousness as do Theravada images but suggest a greater variety of states of mind in relation to the world. Here may be a temple to Amida, the Pure Land Buddha who, in the far remote past, vowed that when he attained supreme enlightenment he would bring all who called upon his name into the western paradise over which he presided, from whence Nirvana is near at hand; this is a Buddhism of egolessness through dependence upon the help of another.

Down the road and past a stony cliff, there is a temple to Kannon, the bodhisattva commonly termed the Goddess of Mercy and often portrayed with many arms to symbolize her countless acts of mercy in answer to prayers in this world. The experience of receiving compassion from a great and enlightened being, even if for a seemingly trivial and worldly matter, can set one on the upward path by shaking out of oneself the conventional mindset; from a Buddha's perspective, nothing in the conditioned world is important and nothing is trivial, and no act of compassion is meaningless.

Another temple is dedicated to Dainichi, the Great Sun Buddha who personifies the absolute essence of the cosmos itself—Nirvana, reality insofar as it can be personified at all. In these and many other temples the multiplicity of ways to an experience beyond ways or words is expounded; the multiplicity helps defeat the tendency toward grasping by serving to baffle the human tendency to possessiveness over partialities.

This is not all. In Kyoto stands a temple with 3000 images of Kannon, all different. In the "esoteric" Buddhism of Tibet, Mongolia, and such sects as the Shingon in Japan, paintings (or even sculpture arrangements) called mandalas are popular. They arrange families of Buddhas and bodhisattvas in patterns that bring home both the diversity and unity of the psychocosmic forces they represent. As psychological analysis, they suggest the profound depth at which the human mind is continuous with mental and spiritual realities underlying the whole universe.

Also in Kyoto are famous Zen monasteries where proctors walk with a stick up and down in front of the silent, seated meditators, and incense burns before a tasteful image of the Buddha, most frequently Dainichi. Outside, there is an austere Zen garden, with its seemingly casual bits of rock and moss and raked sand—but as one looks at it, the mind may begin to whirl, and the rocks and moss become ships and islands on an endless sea, or nebulae and galaxies strewn through infinite space—anchorless reality spreading out of the horizonless mind of the Sun Buddha. And there may be a house for the tea ceremony, that typically Zen practice of doing something very ordinary, like serving tea, with a stylized but effortless grace that makes it expressive of the Buddha-nature of that moment.

The ultimate experience of Mahayana then is ineffable, and so can be "turned on" by many different means: meditation; the numinous wonder of a temple that causes one to forget oneself for a moment; the quasi-hypnotic rhythm of chanting; the magical concentration of evocation. The very fact that its view of nirvanic realization is so tremendous makes it accessible in seemingly easy and multitudinous ways— for it is already here; everyone is already a Buddha.

The **Lotus Sutra,** one of the most important of all Mahayana texts, tells us that a simple offering of flowers, or of a tiny clay pagoda, presented by a child to a Buddha, is of far more worth than all the proud efforts of an aspiring arhant. For any distance we can advance toward Buddhahood by our own self-centered efforts would be only as an inch to a thousand miles, but if one just forgets oneself in a childlike sense of wonder and giving, one is already there, for in that moment one's high walls of ego have vanished away. True, the temples and gilded images of Buddhist temples are meaningless from an ultimate point of view, but it is they that can bring us across, for they work with the natural effectiveness of bright baubles.

The Lotus Sutra also tells the parable of a father who, returning home to the house in which his children were waiting, was appalled to see it on fire and the children apparently unaware of the danger. Thinking quickly, he realized that if he shouted a warning, they might panic and be in a worse state. So instead, he cried out that he had new toy carts outside for them. Laughing and skipping eagerly, they ran from the house and were saved. Images, rites, devotion are like toys that draw us from the flames of desire and begin the process of self-transcendence.

The Buddha acts in a manner consistent with this view. The Lotus Sutra pictures him as like a rain cloud over all the earth which waters vegetation of all sizes and shapes equally. He is universal, ineffable reality who appears on different levels of reality in different forms, in countless worlds over and over again—as godlike heavenly Buddhas and bodhisattvas, and in the human worlds as teachers like Gautama. He is, in the climax of this astounding document, portrayed as descending in a tremendous, bejeweled temple to turn the wheel of his teaching in this universe.[13]

What is the inner story of how these kinds of Buddhist visions emerged? Something of the process can be seen in the Bamian caves in Afghanistan. In a deep green "Shangri-La" of a valley, there was for upward of a thousand years a great Buddhist monastery. This Buddhist center was apparently started during or shortly after the Kushan Empire had its brief period of glory in central Asia, stretching from the Persian frontiers to the Gobi Desert and covering much of northern India, under the great Emperor Kanishka (r. c. 78–103 c.e.). Kanishka was a vigorous (though tolerant) proponent of Mahayana, and his reign was at the time when the Great Vessel was clearly establishing its separate destiny and traits; he convened the Buddhist Council of Kashmir, which authorized commentaries of Mahayanist tendency. Although Bamian must have been of Mahayana bent from its beginning, one can feel that here and at monasteries like it, the Mahayana vision slowly took richer and richer form.

At Bamian, the deep walls of the canyon are honeycombed with the cavelike cells of the hundreds of monks who lived there in its heyday; the cliffs are dominated by two gigantic statues of the standing Buddha, the greatest 175 feet high, and several smaller images. What is left of the art on the walls of the caves, painted as aids to meditation, is of most interest, however. For over the course of centuries, from the first on, one can see shifts in perspective. The earliest work simply illustrates the Buddha himself; as time goes on there appear great wheels or circles of multifarious Buddhas, universes animated by Buddhas in all directions, of various colors and attributes. What the historic Buddha realized in the moment of his Enlightenment is seen more and more to be actually in everything, in every direction, in every aspect of human awareness, in their pristine form—and all of these are actually Buddhas, too, and can be portrayed as such. One can well imagine the profound meditations, the explorations of strange frontiers of consciousness and its symbols, which must have been undertaken in this majestic valley, and out of which the rings of cosmic Buddhas emerged.

THE VOID AND THE BODHISATTVA

The greatest philosophical force in the emergence of Mahayana was the teaching of Nagarjuna (c. 150–250 C.E.). His two basic principles are that **samsara** (the phenomenal world) and **Nirvana** are not different, and that the most adequate expression for this totality is "Void."[14]

That samsara is Nirvana and Nirvana is samsara means that one does not "go" anywhere to "enter" Nirvana. It is here and now; we are all in it all the time, and so we are all Buddhas. Experiencing getting up, walking down the street, or washing dishes as Nirvana rather than as samsara is simply a matter of how it is seen. The way to see it as Nirvana is with complete nonattachment and nonegotism, which means making nothing within the web of our experience more important or more prior than anything else. Neither self, nor any god, nor Buddha, nor the skandhas, nor any concept or idea or principle, are to be made into a basic upon which reality is constructed. None of these exist or persist of their own power. They are all "hollow"—impermanent, part of the flux of entities and ideas out of which the cosmos is constructed. All exist not of "own being" but in their interrelationships only.

The nirvanic vision, then, is to see all things, including (and this is perhaps the most difficult angle to get) oneself, the observer, equally and as an endless series of interdependencies and interrelationships. This universe neither starts nor stops anywhere. In it all things are continually rising and falling and moving in and out of each other, and nothing is stable except the totality itself, the "framework" in which this frameless and endless moving picture is situated.

Because the cosmos has no pivot or foundation or point of reference within itself (no starting or ending line), Nagarjuna believed the only adequate word for it is "Emptiness" or "Void." To say the cosmos is Void is not to say that nothing exists. The term "Void" is only a metaphor. But Emptiness or Void are the only appropriate words for Nagarjuna's cosmos, since any other word would imply some standard or "reality" to be grasped in order to understand it, and he taught that there is none. Void or Emptiness communicate the nongraspable quality of conditioned reality. Like the inside of a dewdrop or a soap bubble, Mahayana reality is, so to speak, done with mirrors—it is full of light and color, but everything is just a reflection of everything else, and there is nothing to seize. One who tries will be like a person who attempts to lasso a rainbow or bring home a sunset in a bucket.

The secret is the insight-wisdom called *prajna*. It is able to see things as they are without being attached at the same time to any structure of thought or theoretical concept. Theories try to make it possible to see things by interpreting them, but the use of such tools also twists them out of shape.

The importance of prajna came about in this manner: Mahayana began in part in discussion of the six *paramitas,* or areas in which one could attain Buddhist perfection: donation (giving of gifts), morality, patience, zeal, meditation, and prajna or wisdom.

The supreme *paramita* is **prajnaparamita,** the perfection of wisdom: It must be built on the foundation of perfection in the others. But it is prajna that gives the lightning flash of final insight uniting one firmly, invincibly through every corner of one's subjectivity with the marvelous Void itself, and so makes one as secure as it. This is prajnaparamita, the "wisdom which has gone beyond" or the "perfection of wisdom." The earliest distinctive Mahayana literature deals with it. Indeed, in devotional Mahayana, prajnaparamita (like wisdom in the Biblical Book of Proverbs) came to be personified as an initiating maiden greatly to be desired.[15]

The Bodhisattva

The great key figure in Mahayana thought is the **bodhisattva** ("enlightenment being"). Bodhisattvas, almost endless in name and number, dwell rank on rank in Mahayana heavens and flame out from countless Mahayana altars; there are also many of them, known and unknown, at work in this world. Virtually everything that is distinctive and of general interest in Mahayana is related to the bodhisattva and the bodhisattva's path; to understand this class of being, his meaning and methods, is to have the surest key to understanding Mahayana teaching, symbols, and practices.[16]

First, the bodhisattva epitomizes the ideal of samsara and Nirvana being not different, for he lives in both simultaneously. He is in the world but without attachments, and *therefore* he is able to see everything as it really is and to work with all power. He lives on the level of Void-consciousness.

Mahayana lore tells us that the bodhisattva is one who has taken a great vow to attain supreme and final enlightenment, however long it takes and at whatever cost, but at the same time to practice unlimited compassion toward all sentient beings, remaining active in this world without passing into absolute Buddhahood until all other beings are brought to enlightenment. Its fulfillment requires great sacrifice and suffering on his part. The Lotus Sutra portrays the bodhisattvas as superior to the Theravada arhants and "private Buddhas," who allegedly attain enlightenment for themselves only, falling short of the ideal of universal compassion.

In his work in the world for liberation of other beings, the bodhisattva is activated by two principles, skill-in-means and compassion. Both of these derive from his unconditioned awareness of the total interrelatedness of all things. Compassion is the ethical consequence of this knowledge; it is merely stating the fundamental Buddhist realization of "dependent coorigination" in ethical terms. If one truly realizes that everything in the cosmos is dependent on everything else, and nothing and no one can exist apart from the rest of it, the only logical consequence for behavior is love, which negates all egocentricity; for interdependency shows up the error of centering life around private goals. The bodhisattva—like the historical Buddha in a previous life—would think nothing of giving his physical body to feed starving tiger cubs, for he knows that body and time are all transitory and mean nothing, whereas compassion is affirming the basic truth of existence, and any holding back would be basing life on a false premise.

The bodhisattva's compassion is not merely a vague, diffuse force, well intentioned but capable of doing almost as much harm as good because of a lack of knowledge of all factors in a situation, as is the "compassion" of some. The bodhisattva's compassion is instead a sharp, precise instrument, for it is combined with the accurate insight that the bodhisattva's freedom from "thought-coverings" allows. This is what is conveyed in the attribute "skill-in-means." He is able to see all the karmic factors in a life situation and thus to know just what changes can be wrought to set a person's steps in the right direction.

Moreover, the same deep awareness, undistorted by any egocentricity, gives him a control of appearances in the world, which seems magical but is actually based on an unfathomably deeper awareness of subtle forces than the ordinary person has. He is able to take any apparition-body he wants, or rather that compassionate knowledge tells him would be most beneficial in a particular situation. Bodhisattvas have worked in the world, according to Mahayana scriptures and stories, as monks, abbots, orphans, beggars, prostitutes, rich men, and gods.

In his work in the world, the bodhisattva is able to make those small but precise adjustments in a situation that will achieve maximum effect. Even a bodhisattva or Buddha cannot change karma. No power whatsoever can do this. None can change the lot a person has earned by past deeds or convert the entire world, groaning as it is under the weight of eons of dark karma, at a single stroke. But the bodhisattva can work with subtlety and skill to bring one to make new resolutions through wise teaching, edifying experiences, and a whiff of the wonder of the other side.

Above all, the subtly skilled and compassionate bodhisattvas impart a sense of sublime serenity, save in some of the wrathful manifestations of the Vajrayana tradition. Whether the transcendentally tranquil princes of the Ajanta caves of India, crowned and holding flowers, or the many-armed and enigmatic-eyed Kannon of Japan, they impart a feeling of attainment so perfect as to be effortless and exude mercy like the perfume of a lotus. The concept of the bodhisattva, whose beauty has moved hundreds of millions, is the supreme achievement of Mahayana Buddhism. It superbly exemplifies the ultimate meaning of the Middle Way, and of dwelling at once in samsara and Nirvana.

MIND ONLY AND THE THUNDERBOLT VESSEL

Further developments in Mahayana thought and practice were in store. Some Mahayana thinkers, probably influenced in part by the developing nondualist Vedanta tradition in Hinduism, came to feel that merely to call the fabric of reality a void was inadequate. A new tradition, found in the Avatamsaka and Lankavatara Sutras and the thinkers Asanga and Vasubandhu (c. fourth century C.E.), said that what Nagarjuna had called Emptiness is more like mind, like pure consciousness in which particular forms or thoughts rise and fall. This position, called Yogacara or Vijnanavada and best labeled in English "Mind Only" or "Consciousness Only," was immensely influential.[17] Most important subsequent schools of Mahayana, including Zen and the Tibetan, are exponents of the Mind Only philosophy and are intellectually grounded on it as well as on Nagarjuna's Middle Way.

Buddhist Mind Only is comparable to idealistic philosophies of the West, such as that of George Berkeley. Mind Only holds that fundamentally only one clear mind or field of consciousness exists, the Buddha-nature or Nirvana. It is the basis of each person's own existence—we are therefore all Buddhas. But we do not realize this because we each "project" an apparent world of many different things, which we think we see outside of us but which actually is in our heads. It is really like an illusion made by the preconceptions and habitual but false modes of perception in which our individual karmas have bound us up and blinded us.

One can understand this by thinking of a movie projector. The screen is the one mind, the clear universal consciousness, without. The bulb in the projector is the one mind within, which is our own true nature. The reel of film is the "movie" put into the head by karmic forces reaching out of the past through preconception and habit to make us see and experience the kind of world they have made for us. We think we see forms—mountains and trees, cities and people, pleasure and suffering, joy and sadness—marching across the screen and invading our lives. But actually they are moving pictures cast by the reel running through our heads.

One might ask why, if each of us projects an individual "movie," we all seem to see the same world. Actually, this is not strictly the case; the world appears different to a child and to an adult, to people of different language and culture, and in subtle ways even to brothers and sisters. Yet admittedly there is general consensus on the "lay of the land." Mind Only philosophy says that this is because we carry over shared past impressions from collective as well as individual experience. This is called "store consciousness." Perhaps it would not be too much amiss to translate the concept by saying that the way we "see" the world is formed basically by human and community input, such as the common experiences of birth and having parents, language, education, and culture. What is added by individual karma is only like frosting—although it may be very important for individual destiny.

Mind Only, like most Eastern philosophies, is not just a theory. It is also a path to transformation of consciousness. It describes the projections and store consciousness as a prelude to teaching how to get beneath them and live without coverings on the unstained mirror of the one mind.

One method, developed by Zen, is simply through still meditation—"sitting quietly, doing nothing"—to settle down until one lives beneath the coverings and projections. (This will be discussed later.)

Another method is a kind of experiential shock therapy. One experiments with, as it were, taking out one reel and putting in another, until forced to recognize that one can in fact create any universe one wants; and so one knows that no reel is more "real" than any other, and only the one mind is "truly real."

This is the role of the psychic experiments and the visualizations of Buddhas and bodhisattvas, characteristic of the Tantric-influenced "esoteric" tradition in Mahayana. Through sacred and powerful words, gestures, and hard meditation, one creates before oneself alternative realities in which unlikely things are as real as rain. One may create a world in which one is a tree, or in which magic works, or where armies of gods battle in the sky, or—and this would be the goal—where Buddhas and bodhisattvas appear visibly on one's altar. Then one would "merge" with an evoked Buddha or bodhisattva and so share his bliss and enlightenment.

To do this, of course, one needed to have a good idea what the universe of innumerable Buddhas and bodhisattvas that Mahayana envisioned—in countless worlds, in aspects of one's mind, in great lineages—was like: what they looked like, how they were organized, how one went about contacting each one. Furthermore, in Mahayana each Buddha and bodhisattva may have his own heaven, a sort of aura around him from which entry into Nirvana through his aid is possible; these are different from the karmic heavens, also accepted by Mahayana, the highest of the six lokas. By devotion to a particular figure, one might enter his Buddha-heaven.[18]

One problem was that the Buddha-reality (reality as seen by the enlightened eye) was encountered in so many different "styles,"—in the Void, one mind, Nirvana; in the many transcendent Buddhas and bodhisattvas, which seemed more like gods in heaven than people of this earth; and finally in this world, where the historic Buddha and the bodhisattvas did their works of teaching and mercy. That problem led to yet another development in Mahayana, one that seems to have emerged in Mind Only circles. It is the *trikaya* concept, the idea of three "Buddha bodies," or more to the point, of three ways or levels in which the Buddha-essence is expressed.

The Three Forms of Buddhic Expression

First there is the dharmakaya, "truth body," what the universe ultimately is, the one mind through which the atoms and galaxies dance. It is the way the universe looks to a Buddha at the moment of his enlightenment and his entry into Nirvana, when all distinctions disappear and the universe and the Buddha's mind are absolutely one. This absolute nonduality is the Buddha-nature, the unstained mirror of the one mind, the Void, Nirvana.

The second form of expression is the samboghakaya, the "bliss body." It is the dharmakaya expressed in paradisal heavens ruled by radiant Buddhas and bodhisattvas, and it is represented in art and altar as golden Buddhas surrounded by gilded lotuses. But it must be remembered we are not talking about Buddhas or heavens literally "out there," but of the floating world of Buddhist reality, which is both (and neither) subjective and objective. In a profound sense, the samboghakaya is the absolute Buddha-nature insofar as it can be put into form—so it is now represented by the most luminous, "otherness" kinds of forms possible, those that come out of the realms of dream, vision, and artistic creativity.

The nirmanakaya, "marvelous transformation body," is the Buddha-nature expressed in this world of ordinary, "waking" reality. Because it is a world of seeing people and objects as separate, here the Buddha-nature comes to us as other persons—Gautama the Buddha and all the other Buddha-figures. This is only a development of the mighty concept of the Lotus Sutra that the Buddha-nature is really a universal reality without beginning or end, which comes into the world from time to time in apparent, apparition bodies.

It is evident that these three levels correspond closely to three states of consciousness in the Upanishads. **Dharmakaya** is the deep sleep without dreams, samboghakaya is the dream state, nirmanakaya is the waking consciousness—with Buddhist imagery applied to them.

The samboghakaya centers around figures called cosmic or meditation Buddhas, as presented in texts such as *The Tibetan Book of the Dead.* These are the images important in esoteric meditation. They are not Buddhas who were at one time historical human beings like Gautama, although sometimes legends about human lives in the remote past were given to them. Essentially, they are subjective-objective aspects of reality, which come into being in meditation and visualization as embodiments of aspects of the mind and the universe in their highest ratios. Each of the five in *The Tibetan Book of the Dead,* for example, corresponds among other things to one of the five skandhas, as though form, feeling, perception, karmic disposition, and consciousness are not merely inside human beings but reflect universal attributes or potentials that come into a lower level of manifestation in humans and a higher in this realm. Above all, they are forms that give shape to the wonder of the Buddha-nature; and by bringing them into being in meditation, one provides bridges toward it.

Vajrayana

The form of Mahayana that most developed these kinds of things is Vajrayana—the "Thunderbolt Vessel" or "Diamond Vessel." Today this is the Buddhism of Tibet, Nepal, Bhutan, and Mongolia, and it has much affected some schools in China and Japan. But like so much else, it originated in old India. It stems from a confluence of Mind Only Buddhism with the same forces that went into Hindu Tantrism, and it can be thought of as Buddhist Tantrism. In the end, Vajrayana produced colorful art, potent devotional techniques, and philosophy no less deep than that of any other Buddhism.

As we have seen, Tantrism had its roots in the adaptation of obscure indigenous rites by questing persons who hoped, in their secret conclaves, to attain greater power than the brahmin and Buddhist "establishments." These practices centered around magic spells, mighty initiations, and usages that sought to generate the power of a kind of shock therapy by deliberately defying ordinary caste, ritual, sexual, and dietary conventions.

Buddhist Tantrists took very seriously the dictum that samsara is Nirvana. To them this meant that nothing in the samsaric world is intrinsically evil and that everything can be used as a means to liberation. Above all, this is true of the passions, and the most potent among them is clearly the sexual. Rather than seeking to circumvent the passions, which only leaves them lurking behind in one's psyche as potential depth charges, one should wrestle with them, master them, and then deliberately arouse and direct their energy as dynamos of force for the breakthrough to the ultimate goal.

Needless to say, this is a dangerous tack, and the Tantric scriptures tell us that what the adept does would cost the ordinary bumbler eons in the hells. But Tantrists were nothing if not bold, and they prided themselves on their skill at dangerous occultism. Indeed, if samsara is Nirvana, it is necessary to bring all polarities together in the perfected human. The defiance of cultural prohibitions is a way of expressing this.

The dangers meant that secrecy was necessary, and much Tantric literature is veiled in a code called "twilight language." It meant also that only the qualified, or those supposed to be, were admitted, and that the student of these techniques had to work under the close supervision of a master, or guru. The one absolute in the Tantrist's world of inverted values was strict obedience to the master,[19] even if the master commanded, as some deliberately did, the most puzzling things—presumably to teach lessons about the emptiness of the universe.

By the early Middle Ages, Buddhist Tantra, like Vajrayana, had attained a literature and scholastic exponents. It became the prevailing form of Buddhism in some areas. Inevitably the rough edges were smoothed off; practices that violated conventional Buddhist morality were (since mind is all) translated into subjective meditations, restricted to marriage, or otherwise legitimatized, save in fringe groups. But it never quite lost its wildness either. Tantric adepts have always tended to be fierce, vivid, shamanlike characters, given to heroic spiritual strife deep in mountains or jungles, shunning the more staid academic and religious circles, and leaving behind beguiling tales of wizardry.

In Vajrayana thought, the dharmakaya is made equivalent to prajna (wisdom), and is regarded as feminine, the supreme mistress, the cosmic womb. The adept, from novice to Buddha, is masculine and personifies skill-in-means, seeking to penetrate and unite with prajna. Thus, in Tibetan art, the cosmic Buddhas and bodhisattvas are often shown locked in sexual embrace—as a "father-mother deity"—with their respective personifications of prajna: This represents the supreme enlightenment achievement. The great Vajrayana mantram of Avalokiteshvara, *Om Mani Padme Hum*—The Jewel in the Lotus—expresses all this, the union of Nirvana and samsara, of prajna and skill-in-means, and of the male and female principles. In the Vajrayana lands, it is chanted continually by priest and peasant alike, and is the message of a million prayer wheels and prayer flags.

A novice being brought into the Vajrayana path will be given by his or her guru a particular deity (a Buddha, bodhisattva, or female figure such as Tara representing an aspect of prajna) as patron, from out of the vast Vajrayana ranks that crowd the mandalas. He will then seek to evoke the patron's presence through concentrated means. He will study the deity's conventional picture, until it appears in his mind even when he is not looking at it. He will seek to unify himself to the deity's lines of spiritual force by repeating his mantra and making his mudra, or gesture, with his hands. Stemming from the Mind Only presuppositions, the practice strives to create for the adept a new universe revolving around his "god." Finally, it is hoped the deity will appear visibly on his altar to accept his client's worship. The student will then pull himself closer and closer to the deity until the ultimate goal is attained and he becomes one with his deity, shares his intimate embrace of prajna and his Buddha-enlightenment.

In the process, there is no lack of powers of sorcery the Tantrist can wield, generated as by-products of the mantras and supernormal friendship he possesses. But the true goal is enlightenment—realizing that all is mind, all gods, bodhisattvas, and Buddhas, and all souls and phenomena, arise out of mind and sink back into it. In this respect, far from being credulous, Vajrayana is psychologically both sophisticated and boldly experimental. It knows that the numerous celestial beings and forces it calls into service exist only in mind. They are projected out of it and then, once isolated and confronted, called back into it to reign over a liberated mind equal to their power. To learn this is to attain the true liberation.

Let us conclude this chapter on Buddhism with a description of one country with an unusual and fascinating Vajrayana Buddhist culture.

TIBET

Tibet, "Land of Snow" and "Roof of the World," has long had a very particular place in the imagination of the other peoples who dwell in lower, more prosaic places. For India, the realm behind the white ramparts of the highest mountains on earth, out of which the sacred Ganges flowed, was the abode of mystic Shiva and of mighty siddhas, wizard-adepts. For China, it was roughly Shangri-La, a paradise where the Queen-Mother of the West presided over a happy nation of Taoist immortals. For many in Europe and America, Tibet has been no less a land of magic and mystery, a cloudland of abominable snowmen and lost monasteries where occult lore is the specialty and weird psychic phenomena are everyday occurrences.

Although many stories about religious Tibet may be romanticized, there is no doubt that it would seem a very strange place to modern Occidentals. But it also is significant, for the real Tibet represents a unique and often profound interpretation of Buddhism and of the human experience.

In Tibet, as many as a quarter of the male population wore the reddish robes of monks, and the great thick-walled monasteries were centers of trade, finance, and government; there were even monk-soldiers who battled with each other. Other monks concerned themselves with complex meditations calling up the visible presence of strange, colorful deities of fierce or benign countenance, or perhaps with the casting of spells or the writing of histories.

The religion of the common people was equally colorful. Houses, as well as the squat, domed temples, were decked with bright prayer flags—pennants with brief mantras inscribed on them, flapping in the mountain wind. Prayer wheels—large drums around the outside of a temple, small ones held in the hand, each containing strips of paper inscribed with mantra—turned everywhere, sending out auspicious vibrations into the thin, crisp air. On holy days, particularly New Year's Day, brilliant dance pageants were enacted by the local priests and villagers wearing masks of grotesque demons and radiant heroes. Life in old Tibet was hard, and doubtless the ordinary people were, from our point of view, backward and exploited by their nobility and monk-rulers. But they were sturdy, immensely proud of their country and its religion, and according to travelers a cheerful folk.

The unique Tibetan spiritual culture was essentially a combination of indigenous shamanism with Tantric Vajrayana Buddhism imported from India, and allowed, by the unusual degree of isolation Tibet's geography afforded, to develop in its own way. From shamanism came the fierce desire of the man of power to undergo initiation, demonstrate his courage and vision, explore the infinite new worlds of the psychic plane, and manifest his accomplishments through preternatural talents. From Buddhism came a sophisticated philosophical framework by which to explain these things. One has acquired unlimited full power because one has become one with the universal, invincible void; one travels to strange realms because one is realizing that one creates all one sees out of the karma-twisted mills of one's own mind.

This combination, and something of the profound Tibetan point of view, is made evident in the well-known *Bardo Thodol,* or *The Tibetan Book of the Dead,* which is Tibet's most famous contribution to the world's religious thought.[20]

The Tibetan Book of the Dead is essentially an account of the experience of one deceased between death and, if that one is destined by karma to be born again, the next entry into a womb. In it all levels of the Mahayana Buddhist cosmos are touched. The deep Vajrayana teaching that we create our lives, and our own heavens and hells, out of mind is expressed.

The entity first starts with the "highest" level to encounter the "Clear Light of the Void," the **dharmakaya,** or absolute essence of the universe. It is of "terrifying brightness," and out of it comes a roaring louder than a thousand thunderclaps at once, the light and vibrancy of an entire cosmos. If the pilgrim recognizes this as one with his own true nature, however, he can merge with it and attain the ultimate

Tibetan monk painting a mandala which is used for meditation purposes.

liberation. Most, though, will be insufficiently prepared, shrink back, and lose the priceless moment of opportunity.

But there are other opportunities. The entity next faces, one at a time and then all together, a mandala of five great cosmic Buddhas in their "peaceful" aspects. They are like heavenly forms of the universal Reality. If the traveler through this, the Bardo realm, fails to recognize these as projections of her own mind and meditations, she will be frightened and pass quickly by; if she does so, she can simply reunite with it and be saved. The one who passes on will next encounter the same deities in their horrible, terrifying aspect, full of wrath, but with the same opportunity for recognition. If it is missed, the process of rebirth now takes hold firmly; the entity is propelled by winds of karma reaching hurricane force. He whips by flash visions of judgment and his future parents in copulation and finally swoons, forgetting all on a conscious level, to awaken in the womb of whatever animal or human is fated to give him the upcoming life. But even in these last stages the process can, with tremendous spiritual effort, be cut short and redirected. The most effective way is to meditate on the "father-mother" guru, the union of Buddha and Wisdom as male and female locked in erotic/ecstatic embrace, which is a popular subject of Tibetan sacred art. For the greatest power comes from the union of all opposites.

And, psychologically, the deepest polarity that needs to be rejoined is our partiality toward the male and the female.

This really expresses what Buddhism is about, for in the end all of its language, symbols, and practices are expressions of the union of opposites, the reconciliation of all polarities. From the Buddha's proclamation of a Middle Way, which finds infinite bliss in keeping a breathtakingly delicate balance between indulgence and asceticism, life and death, being and nonbeing, to the Tibetan vision of coupled father-mother gods in the Bardo sky, we have met with pointers to an experience of oneness, combined with awareness that it is one's self-made shell of ego encrustations that keeps one from it; out of this egg one has to break with a shout of awakening.

SUMMARY

Buddhism can be thought of as a religion with a psychological emphasis. It teaches the transformation of consciousness from attachment to ego, suffering, and objects of craving to the unattached bliss of Nirvana. Its fundamental teaching is that the Buddha, through his enlightenment, showed the way out of the wheel of rebirth or conditioned reality created by ignorance and attachment; its fundamental practice is meditation and comparable methods of transcending attachment; its fundamental sociological expression is the samgha, or order of monks in the succession of the Buddha's disciples.

The Buddha, among the first of the great religious founders, according to Buddhist tradition attained a state of perfect enlightenment after a spiritual quest. He then taught that liberation comes by following a Middle Way between all attachments; he taught the Four Noble Truths of suffering, attachment, and freedom from them in Nirvana through the Eightfold Path culminating in Right Meditation; he taught that the ego is the supreme delusive object of attachment, for we are really not egos but impermanent collections of parts.

Theravada Buddhism, the "Way of the Elders" predominant in the Buddhist parts of south and southeast Asia, adheres closely to these teachings. For monks, it emphasizes meditations leading to spiritual agility and nirvanic consciousness. For the laity, it emphasizes acts and attitudes that will lead to growth and good rebirths.

The Mahayana Buddhism of north and east Asia stresses the presence of "Buddha-nature," the essence of the universe as the Buddha saw it in his enlightenment, in all beings. Thus, the universe is spoken of as Void and as one with Nirvana, for there is nothing within it to be grasped. The Bodhisattva, an "enlightenment being" who realizes this and is at once in the world and Nirvana, is a key Mahayana figure. Because liberation is a matter of realizing one's own Buddha-nature, Mahayana teaches the accessibility of salvation to all and offers many diverse paths to the final goal. An important later Mahayana school is Mind Only, which holds that one creates reality out of one's mind. It led in turn to teaching about the three "bodies" or forms of expression of the Buddha-nature in the cosmos, in the heavens, and on earth, and to Vajrayana, the Tantric school of Buddhism, which presents rigorous initiation and training leading one to evoke or visualize helping Buddhas and bodhisatt-vas, among other techniques.

Vajrayana is the Buddhism of Tibet, a land which traditionally had a unique Buddhist culture. The Tibetan text best known in the West is the *Bardo Thodol,* or *The Tibetan Book of the Dead,* which describes after-death experiences and emphasizes that all one meets there is a manifestation of one's own nature.

QUESTIONS FOR REVIEW

1. Interpret Buddhism in terms of the three forms of religious expression.

2. Explain the thematic chart on Buddhism. Show through what forms a religion ultimately focused on individual liberation also functions as a religion for society. Point to the significant contrasts between Theravada and Mahayana Buddhism in both respects, as indicated by the chart.

3. Talk about the meaning of the Buddha's quest and enlightenment, as presented in traditional accounts of his life.

4. Explain basic Buddhist teaching: the Middle Way, the Four Noble Truths, no self, Nirvana.

5. Explain why meditation is so important in Buddhism.

6. Understand and be able to put into simple words the fundamental teachings of Nagarjuna that underlie Mahayana Buddhism: samsara is Nirvana, Void, or Emptiness, is the best metaphor for what we call reality.

7. Discuss the distinctive features of Mahayana: the Buddha-nature in all things, the bodhisattva concept, the "multimedia" approach to salvation, the sutras.

8. Mention some features of Mind Only (Yogacara or Vijnanavada) Buddhist philos-ophy and discuss its influence, especially its impact on spiritual practice as well as theory.

9. Explain the three "bodies" (trikaya) or forms or expression of the Buddha-nature as presented in developed Mahayana thought: the universal essence (dharmakaya), heavenly, and earthly (or transformative).

10. Discuss some features of Vajrayana, the Tantric Buddhism of Tibet, Mongolia, and elsewhere, especially its use of initiation and evocation, and its foundation in the Mind Only philosophy.

11. Discuss the scenario and deeper meaning of *The Tibetan Book of the Dead* (*Bardo Thodol*).

12. Using the chart, explain the fundamental features of Buddhism. How does it deal with the great questions of the nature of ultimate reality and the goal of human life?

13. Talk about the aspects of Buddhism that seem most meaningful to you.

SUGGESTED READINGS ON BUDDHISM

General

*BECHERT, HEINZ, AND RICHARD GOMBRICH, EDS., *The World of Buddhism: Buddhist Monks and Nuns in Society and Culture*. New York: Facts on File, 1984. A good survey for the general reader.

*BURTT, E. A., *The Teachings of the Compassionate Buddha*. New York: Mentor Books, 1955. A valuable set of excerpts from translated scriptures.

*CH'EN, KENNETH K. S., *Buddhism: The Light of Asia*. Woodbury, NY: Barron's Educational Series, 1968. A good introductory text, particularly for its country-by-country historical survey and its treatment of Buddhist cultural influence.

*CONZE, EDWARD, *Buddhism: Its Essence and Development*. New York: Harper Torchbooks, 1959. A masterful and vivid essay emphasizing Buddhist doctrine. Especially good on Mahayana.

*———, *Buddhist Meditation*. New York: Harper Torchbooks, 1969. A collection of texts on this topic; good editing.

*———, *Buddhist Scriptures*. Baltimore: Penguin Books, 1959. Another useful collection.

*———, *Buddhist Thought in India*. New York: Harper Torchbooks, 1962. A brilliant intellectual history, written with feeling, insight, and style.

*———, *Buddhist Wisdom Books,* London: George Allen & Unwin, 1958. Translations of two basic texts.

*COOMARASWAMY, ANANDA, *Buddha and the Gospel of Buddhism*. New York: Harper & Row, 1964. A sensitive essay from a Hindu point of view.

*DE BARY, WM. THEODORE, ED., *The Buddhist Tradition in India, China, and Japan*. New York: Modern Library, 1969. A useful collection of translated texts with good introductions.

GARD, RICHARD, *Buddhism*. New York: G. Braziller, 1961. A good introductory collection of translated texts and excerpts from studies.

LaFLEUR, WILLIAM, *Buddhism: A Cultural Perspective*. Englewood Cliffs, NJ: Prentice Hall, 1988. A good introductory textbook.

MORGAN, KENNETH, *The Path of the Buddha*. New York: Ronald Press, 1956. A series of interesting essays by modern Buddhists written for the general reader.

*ROBINSON, RICHARD H., AND WILLARD L. JOHNSON, *The Buddhist Religion*. Belmont, CA: Wadsworth, 1982. A vivid introductory textbook.

The Buddha

*PERCHERON, MAURICE, *The Marvelous Life of the Buddha*. New York: St. Martins Press, 1960. A popular account of the traditional story.

*RAHULA, WALPOLA, *What the Buddha Taught*. New York: Evergreen Press, 1962. A competent summary for the general reader by a modern Buddhist monk.

THOMAS, E. J., *The Life of the Buddha as Legend and History*. London: Routledge and Kegan Paul, 1924. A scholarly evaluation.

Buddhism in Southeast Asia

KING, WINSTON L., *A Thousand Lives Away*. Cambridge, Mass.: Harvard University Press, 1964. A fascinating description of Buddhism in modern Burma.

*LESTER, ROBERT C., *Theravada Buddhism in Southeast Asia*. Ann Arbor: University of Michigan Press, 1973. A clear, competent summary.

Tibetan Religion

*BERNBAUM, EDWIN, *The Way to Shambhala: A Search for the Mythical Kingdom Beyond the Himalayas*. Garden City, NY: Doubleday Anchor, 1980. An unusual book combining mountaineering and scholarship as it explores on several levels the meaning of the Tibetan traditions concerning a paradisal land called Shambhala.

*BLOFELD, JOHN, *The Way of Power*. London: George Allen & Unwin, 1970. A very clear statement. Sympathetic, emphasizes the Tibetan usage.

*DAVID-NEEL, ALEXANDRA, *Magic and Mystery in Tibet*. New York: University Books, 1965. A fascinating first-person account; not highly scholarly, but a stimulating introduction to old Tibet.

*EVANS-WENTZ, W. Y., *The Tibetan Book of the Dead*. New York and London: Oxford University Press, 1960. A translation of a famous and popular work, with introductions by Carl Jung, Lama Govinda, and others.

HOFFMANN, HELMUT, *The Religions of Tibet*. New York: Macmillan, 1961. A survey particularly useful on Bon.

SNELLGROVE, DAVID, *Buddhist Himalaya*. Oxford: Bruno Cassirer, 1957. A survey by a first-rate scholar; includes some travel narratives.

SNELLGROVE, DAVID, AND HUGH RICHARDSON, *A Cultural History of Tibet*. New York: Praeger, 1968. A standard resource.

TUCCI, GIUSEPPE, *The Religions of Tibet*. Berkeley: University of California Press, 1980. A standard work by a leading European scholar.

CHAPTER 5

Dragon and Sun:
RELIGIONS OF EAST ASIA

CHAPTER OBJECTIVES

After studying this chapter, you should be able to

- Cite the major religious traditions of China and Japan.

- Explain the different roles of Confucianism and Daoism in China.

- Interpret the relation of these spiritual traditions to East Asian societies today.

- Present the religious traditions of Korea and Vietnam.

THE EAST ASIAN SPIRITUAL WORLD

Some years ago, I encountered for the first time a non-Western religion in its homeland. That religion was Shinto and the country was Japan. I saw Japanese Buddhist temples on the same visit, of course, but it was Shinto shrines I saw first and which for some reason buried themselves most deeply in my memory.

I could not forget the *torii,* the gently curved archway that led into the precincts of a shrine, separating the noisy bustle of the street from the quiet shrine with its ancient architecture. The torii was like a mystic portal between one age and another, and even one dimension and another. In the midst of a modern industrial city, these plain but graceful halls of the *kami,* the Shinto gods, are set amidst sacred groves of gnarled old trees, and they communicate just a touch of the past, the natural, and the wondrous. In the countryside, where shrines grace mountaintops, clear rushing streams, or inlets of the sea, they lend an aura of the divine to vistas already beautiful.

I felt strangely stirred by these wooden shrines, simple and rustic in construction, with their pitched roofs and heavy doors. The porticos presented such understated but effective symbols of deity as zigzag strips of paper, immense rope lintels, and gleaming eyelike mirrors. I liked the way the shrines seemed never to clash with nature, but only to embellish it. If a divine kami-presence dwelt within the shrine, one felt, he (or she) was a deity who knew and respected the old trees in his parish down to their deepest roots and the insides of the ageless stones, as well as the grandmothers, young people, and babies who lived in the streets around his shrine-home. While musing on dreams of the mythic past, the kami watched with spirit-eyes the frenetic life of a modern nation.

Nor were these kami-presences forgotten. One feature of postwar Japan that has surprised many outside observers is that Shinto, shorn of state control and ultranationalistic overtones but retaining its shrines under local and democratic admin-istration, has not withered away but has prospered as a popular religion. To be sure, few of those frequenting the shrines would call themselves exclusively Shinto. Most are also Buddhist, at least nominally, or members of one of the "new religions" of Japan. Many would hardly think of themselves as religious at all. Yet they may pause for a moment as they pass a shrine.

At a shrine of any importance, the visitor will not wait long before seeing a Japanese individual or family pass through the torii, wash hands and mouth in a basin, approach the shrine, clap twice, bow, murmur a prayer, and leave a small offering in a grill.

If the observer is fortunate, she may have the opportunity to be at a shrine festival, or *matsuri.* Then she will notice a dramatic change in the atmosphere of the shrine. Instead of a quiet, shy deity in a leafy refuge, the kami now becomes a dynamic presence in the midst of the people, calling explosive festivity into being.

First, pure offerings of rice wine (*sake*), vegetables, and seafood are very slowly presented to the kami by white-robed priests, together with green boughs of the sacred *sakaki* tree brought forward by leading laypeople.

Then, suddenly and startlingly, this mood of classical dignity breaks. Sacred dance in vivid and fantastic costume is performed. A carnival may be held on the grounds of the shrine, with everything from cotton candy to *sumo* wrestling. The kami-presence is carried through the streets in a palanquin (*mikoshi*) by running, sweating young men, who shout "Washo! Washo!" as they zigzag down the ways and byways of the kami's parish.

Shinto has a highly distinctive personality of its own, yet it also illustrates several characteristics of the religion of East Asia in general. In Shinto shrines, and also in Chinese and Japanese Buddhist and other temples, one senses a close harmony of the human and natural orders. The gods and guides of humankind dwell in virtual symbiosis with woods, streams, and mountains, suggesting that in a larger sense society is a part of nature, and kami, immortals, Buddhas, and humans are all parts of a greater cosmic unity.

Very often, then, the divine is finite and tied to particular places. There may indeed be an indefinable universal divine principle that underlies all particular manifestations of the divine and is infinite. But the individual gods one can know are limited, although impressive, as if no more than glorified human beings. Indeed, in China for the last 2000 years, nearly all deities except Heaven and Earth themselves were conceived of as having once been humans who acceded to divine status by exemplary merit. Their ranks and titles were confirmed by the emperor as though they were simply another class among his subjects—and the emperor alone was permitted to worship Heaven and Earth directly. In Japan, although only occasionally entitling gods, the government assigned the status of the various shrines.

East Asian religion has tended to see a world in which gods and humans both have places and interact with each other more by agreement and respect than on the model of master and slave. To be sure, Chinese and Japanese worship is capable of mystery, awe, and wonder. Buddhism, particularly through the Mahayana philosophies and techniques described in the previous chapter, has made spiritual culture aware of mystical and metaphysical profundities oriented toward the infinite. Yet it all finally comes down to a human-centered view of mystery and metaphysics— the Chinese and Japanese are rarely forgetful that these things are important to humans insofar as they enrich human life and help validate its central institutions, the family and the state. Religious style is likely to be more restrained and pragmatic than the ecstatic abandon of the Hindu bhakta or the hard surety of the crusader. Religion is not that kind of commitment; rather, it is part of a ring of relativistic commitments whose real center is inflexible norms or propriety for human and divine relations: these are the true obligation. The value center, in other words, is propriety and one's means of integration into family and community.

The sociological expression is extremely important in understanding religion in East Asia. In particular, "natural" sociological units—family and community— for most East Asians *are* one's link with the infinite. It is through worship of one's particular ancestors that one expresses filial relation to the primordial infinite ancestors—Heaven and Earth. It is through one's particular kami or patronal deity that one integrates oneself into the hierarchy of the divine. It is through reverence to particular Buddhas and bodhisattvas that one acknowledges tacitly the unbounded wisdom a Buddha represents.

All these features come together when one thinks of East Asian faith as being centered in a "one world" concept. There is no god or heaven outside the world system of which we are a part here and now. Gods, heavens, hells, society, nature, family, and individual are all parts of a single unity of which humankind is (at least for humans) the pivot. This means the individual has to be a part of the whole; if there be only one unified system, it is absurd to try to opt out of it. On the other hand, it means that one is under no obligation to emphasize one part of the system more than another—heaven more than this world, a god more than family. All are parts of the same thing, so one's approach is according to one's circumstances or bent. Most would probably agree that a balanced outlook is wisest.

Some commentators have so stressed this supposedly "humanistic" and "this-worldly" East Asian attitude as to suggest that religion, life after death, heavens, and supernatural entities are unimportant to the Chinese and Japanese. At least in regard to traditional society, such an assessment is very wide of the mark. Whatever some rationalist philosophers may have held, popular culture was certainly not behind any other in energy and expense devoted to worship of gods, propitiation of spirits, and assurance of a good fate on the other side of death.

But it is fair to say that this concern, real as it was, is given a special quality by an overarching perception that the visible and invisible realms are parts of one unity, like the obverse and reverse sides of a coin, and that what is really important to humanity is the continuation and well-being of individual, family, and societal human life on both sides. Except for the most mystical of Daoists and Buddhists, this perpetuation of the good life for humans was the supreme good. The apparatus of religion was appreciated by the many who accepted it for the contributions it could make to the good life here and hereafter. It was a map of the invisible world that interlocked with this world.

The interaction of mystery and community was made very evident to the author in Hawaii, when visiting the annual festival of a large interrelated group that had immigrated in the nineteenth century from a single village in south China. The deity on the brightly-decked altar in the community hall was Kuan Di, a stern military god who is considered a strong protector against evil forces. He was a famous general back in the third century C.E., who was so exemplary in his heroism and righteousness that after his death an emperor declared him a god. He became well known and worshipped all over China.

As members of the community entered the hall, they lit sticks of incense and set them upright before the deity. Spread before Kuan Di were also food offerings, including a roast pig, paper boxes and houses, and firecrackers.

Then an old Daoist priest vested in a red-and-green robe put on a peculiar black cap. He stood before the altar, waved incense, and opened a worn liturgical book. Also on the altar were esoteric symbols of the Daoist craft: scissors, a measuring stick, and the character for Dao, the mystic universal unity.

The *jiao* or Daoist service offered by the priest had nothing directly to do with the community. It was essentially a priestly rite, although performed in the community's presence. Through chanting occult formulae, the officiant called up a series of high spirits—the spirits of the eighteen stars of the Big and Little Dipper, the Three Pure Ones—hierarchical rank upon rank, a celestial court like the old imperial bureaucracy. Each level contained fewer but more powerful entities than the one below it. Meditatively, then, the adept brought the cosmos into greater and greater unity until Yin and Yang, the two ultimate polarities into which all other multiplicity is resolved, alone remained. Then the priest merged them and stood before the ritually presented great Dao itself, the endless, incomprehensible stream down which all things visible and invisible flow. He did not become Dao, but he stood before it in awe.

In a real Daoist temple, such as one can still find on Taiwan, this *jiao* ritual might be performed in a great ceremony involving several priests and lasting for days at an important festival—and the ritual would be secret, the temple closed to all but the priests participating. In Hawaii, however, the members of the community were mostly seated in a big half-circle around priest and altar, many talking and laughing quietly—not out of disrespect, but just because priest, rite, spirits, community, Kuan Di, the Dao itself, are all part of one big family in which one feels at home. The incoming spirits *wanted* the community to be happy and prosperous, to enjoy the good things of life, good food and good companionship—they were in fact inducing the ripples of merriment and kindly gossip starting to roll around the room as waves in the tide of Dao.

Suddenly the tempo changed. The esoteric part of the mystery was over. The spirits were dispatched by burning the paper offerings outside in a big fire; the firecrackers were set off. The roast pig was quickly cut up and served. Everyone received a heaping plate of food and turned to enjoy a lavish banquet; a leading community official discreetly handed the priest of Dao the traditional bright red envelope containing payment for his services.

ANCIENT CHINA

To get a perspective on the specifics of East Asian religion, let us begin with China, and at the beginning. One of the most distinctive features of the Chinese mentality is its feeling that the Chinese people and the soil on which they live are inseparable and have been together as far back as tradition goes. In most other major societies, a tradition of having come from some other place and conquered the land in which the people now dwell is a feature of incalculable weight in the national image. Consider the significance of the Exodus and the taking of the Promised Land to the Israelites, the journey of Aeneas from Troy to Italy for the Roman mystique,

HISTORY OF RELIGION IN CHINA AND JAPAN

MAJOR ERAS–CHINA

Zhou (1123–221)

End of Shang

Qin (221–206)

Han (206 B.C.E.–220 C.E.)

PERSONALITIES AND EVENTS–CHINA

Court rituals

Laozi (?)

Confucius (551–479)

Zuangzi (c. 300)

Mencius (372–289)

Tung Zhungshu
(179–104) and Han Confucianism

MAJOR ERAS–JAPAN

Prehistoric

Protohistoric

PERSONALITIES AND EVENTS–JAPAN

Shamanism very
influential

Clan period

| 1500 B.C.E. | 1000 B.C.E. | 500 B.C.E. | 1 B.C.E./C.E. |

3 Kingdoms (220–265)

Jin (265–420)

Yuan (1280–1368)

Ming (1368–1644)

6 Dynasties (420–589)

Qing (1644–1911)

Sui (589–618)

Republic (1912–)

Tang (618–907)

People's Republic on
Mainland (1949–)

Song (960–1280)

Han synthesis

High point of
Buddhism

Ge Hong (283–343)

Zhu Xi (1130–1200)

Beginning of Chan and
Pure Land Buddhism

Neo-Confucianism
dominant

Huineng (638–713)

Wang Yangming
(1472–1529)

Taika (645–710)

Kamakura (1185–1333)

Muromachi (1333–1568)

Nara (710–784)

Momoyama (1568–1600)

Heian (794–1185)

Tokugawa (1600–1867)

Modern (1868–1945)

Postwar (1945)

Introduction of Buddhism
(early 6th century)

Honen (1133–1212)

Hakuin (1685–1768)

Zen dominant
Dogen (1200–53)
Eisai (1141–1215)

Confucianism dominant
culturally

Kojiki (712)

Kobo Daishi
(773–835)

Shinran (1173–1262)

Nationalism

Esoteric Buddhism

Nichiren (1222–82)

New Religions

500 C.E.   1000 C.E.   1500 C.E.   2000 C.E.

the importance of Indo-European invasions in both ancient India and Northern Europe, the myth of the conquest of Japan by the first emperor Jimmu for Japanese nationalism, or the immigration and pioneer motifs in America's national consciousness. In China, there is none of this. Instead, the Chinese have felt a quieter but even more secure assurance that they have always been in China, were created there, and belong there as surely as the rivers and mountains and rice fields.

A sense of place, of the cycles of nature, and of lineage were fundamental to the religious outlook of the earliest known Chinese, as they have been ever since. One of the oldest motifs of Chinese religion is the Earth-god. The cultural line that led to Chinese civilization began around 4000 B.C.E. in tiny villages in the Yellow River basin where millet, vegetables, and pigs were raised. The central sacred feature was often a stone or mound, like a concentration of the forces of the soil into a central focus; these mounds are the ancestors of the city-god temples of today, as well as the great Altar of Heaven in Beijng, built like an artificial mountain where the emperor offered worship at the winter solstice.[1] Worship was also offered very early to the spirits of rivers and of rain, the latter immemorially represented as the dragon, for the rivers and rain bless the fertile earth with moisture.

In burial and ancestrism, continuity of the three identity-giving factors of family, ancestors, and place was emphasized. Burial, the return of the tiller of the earth to its bosom, has always been very important in China. As the peasant works his fields, he may see on the side of an overlooking hill the site he has selected for his tomb. He knows that from there he will in spirit watch his progeny generation after generation work the same fields. At the tomb, at the family shrine with tablets bearing the names of ancestors, and in the home shrine, his descendants will remember him with offerings of food and drink, and with information concerning family events. This reverence may be tinged with awe and dread, for even the humblest family head grows mightily in power when he returns to union with the invincible earth itself, and he can reach out from the grave to bless those who keep bright the family honor or to afflict its enemies.

The concern with burial goes as far back as Chinese culture. Neolithic farmers buried children in urns under the house, and adults in reserved fields. In the first period of real civilization, the Shang, great pits were dug in the earth for the burial of a king. In what must have been a scene of incredible barbaric horror and splendor, the deceased monarch was interred brilliantly ornamented with jade, together with the richly caparisoned horses who had borne his hearse, hundreds of sacrificed human retainers and prisoners, and a fortune in precious objects.[2]

The Shang dynasty and its successor, the Zhou,[3] lasted from about 1750 to 221 B.C.E. The basic motifs of religion in these eras represent in developing form the fundamental ideas of Chinese religion and philosophy.

The thinkers of those days talked of a supreme ruler or moderator of the universe, Di or Tian, usually translated "Heaven," who gave rain, victory, fortune or misfortune, and regulated the moral order. All things ultimately derived from Tian, but it was more a personification of natural law than a real personality and was not directly worshipped; Heaven was like the high god of many archaic peoples.

Main Themes of Chinese Thought and Religion

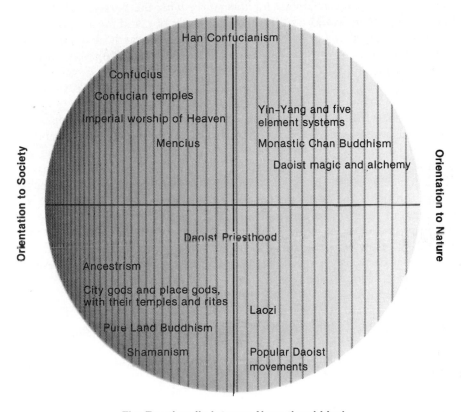

Ideal of the Rational, Controlled Life

Han Confucianism

Confucius

Confucian temples

Imperial worship of Heaven

Yin–Yang and five
element systems

Mencius

Monastic Chan Buddhism

Daoist magic and alchemy

Orientation to Society

Orientation to Nature

Daoist Priesthood

Ancestrism

City gods and place gods,
with their temples and rites

Laozi

Pure Land Buddhism

Shamanism

Popular Daoist
movements

The Emotionally Intense, Nonrational Ideal

THEMATIC CHART IV.   The Chinese tradition is marked by polarities between the Confucian ideal of a rational, virtuous life in a well-ordered society which expresses the Dao; and the Daoist ideal of a life close to the wildness of nature and giving full rein to feeling and fantasy.

Other gods, lesser but more accessible to worship, were those of sun, moon, stars, rivers, mountains, the four directions, and localities. These were given offerings, some seasonally, some morning and evening. Above all were the ancestral spirits, treated to meals and remembrance, and expected to intercede on behalf of the living with Tian.

The dead, in other words, were made a part of life. They could communicate with the living through the lips of shamanesses and oracles, and unpropitiated ghosts of the dead were much feared. There were also myths of culture heroes who combatted floods, built irrigation systems, and taught the people agriculture; if not directly worshipped, such figures as Yu and Hou Ji had marvelous births, precarious and miracle-fraught childhoods, and lives of self-sacrifice and superhuman works comparable to those of divine heroes and saviours elsewhere.

The Shang era is most famous for divination with the "oracle bones." The procedure was that kings would ask their ancestors questions, and the answers would be determined by cracks made in a tortoise shell when it was heated over a fire. Thousands of these bones, with the questions and sometimes the answers inscribed on them in an archaic form of writing, have been preserved.

Archaic Chinese religion is also noteworthy for the importance it gave to ceremonial. Highly stylized and exact rites were performed for each season, for gods and ancestors, and for the major occasions of life. These were done at court and apparently had their parallels among the common people as well. Court ceremonies were elaborate affairs; as we have seen, they sometimes involved grisly but solemn animal and human sacrifices.

Divination, the seasonal cycle, and ceremonialism all suggest one basic principle that has run through Chinese thought from the beginning—that the universe is a unity in which all things fit together. If humanity aligns itself with it, all will fit together for us as it does for nature. On this assumption, traditional Chinese lived with the turning of the seasons, and in their ceremonies strove to make life into an image of their harmony. Divination is based on the same world view, for it presumes that if the world is a unity, each fragment of it—like a tortoise shell—must contain clues to what is happening or will happen in other parts.

The unity in which all things fit together is called the Dao (Tao). The word is most often translated "way," and it originally meant a road but can also mean "speak." Among philosophers it came to mean the inexpressibly broad track down which all things roll; in philosophical writing, it has been translated by such terms as "way," "nature," "existence," and even "God."

CONFUCIANISM

Dao—how to know it, live it, and construct a society that exemplifies it—is the great theme of Chinese thought and the religious expressions closely related to it. Never was this more the case than in the last two centuries of the Zhou dynasty, 403–221 B.C.E. Called the "Warring States" period, this was an era when, because the emperor had been reduced to a powerless figurehead, rulers of feudal states battled unceasingly with each other. Although it was a time of cultural and material advance, people felt that all sense of restraint and morality had been lost. Even the rough warrior codes no longer held, and society was caught up in a madness of rapacity, intrigue, and violence punctuated by a depraved brutality in which prisoners were routinely killed by slow and horrible means. The peasants, exploited in the best of times, suffered most.

Yet this was a time of creativity for the human spirit. New concepts that could be the foundation of high civilization emerged, if only because thoughtful people were forced to ask themselves such questions as, "Where did we go wrong? How can we get society back on the right track and find the Dao? How can a sensitive individual find meaning in the midst of so much crassness?"

In asking how to get back on the track of Dao, the Chinese believed there were three realms where Dao could be experienced: nature, human society, and one's own inner being. The question was, How are these to be lined up, with what priorities, and with what techniques for ascertaining the "message" of the Dao?

The answers fall into two categories: Confucian and Daoist. (There were other schools that have not survived or did not develop significant religious expression.) The basic difference was that Confucianists thought the Dao, or Tian (the will of Heaven), as they often called it, was best found by humans within human tradition and society, and so was explored through human relationships and rituals and by the use of human reason. The Daoists thought that reason and society perverted the Dao; that it was best found alone in the rapture of merging with infinite nature and the mystical and marvelous.

The difference is comparable to that between rationalists and romantics in the West. Needless to say, Confucianism in China has been mainly associated with moralism and the ruling "establishment" elite together with their education system. Daoism, on the other hand, is linked with sensitivity of feelings, with artists and poets, and with all sorts of colorful, bizarre, "nonestablishment" things—from fairy tales to unusual sexual techniques, from exorcising devils to revolutionary secret societies and esoteric temple rites.

Confucius

But it is important to recall that relatively few Chinese would think of themselves as exclusively Confucian or Daoist or Buddhist. In the lives of most people, features from all sides would have a place. Confucian attitudes would undergird family and work ethics; Buddhism would help to answer questions about what happens after death; a dash of Daoist color would meet esthetic and spiritual needs in family and personal life. (It has been said that Chinese officials were Confucian at work and Daoist in retirement.)

The Confucian tradition is named after the philosopher Confucius (551–479 B.C.E.). We must distinguish Confucius the man of his time from the almost-deified, impossibly wise and remote figure of the Confucian educational tradition and state cult. But at the same time we must remember why this particular man was selected as the symbolic embodiment of that tradition.

First, we must take into account the winsome, wise, persuasive, and utterly sincere personality of Confucius himself. Born in the feudal state of Lu (modern Shantung) as the son of a minor official or military officer, Kong Fuzi—to give Master Kong his Chinese rather than Latinized name and title—received an education and sought employment by a prince. He was a member of a class called *ru*, who were specialists in the "six arts"—ceremonial, music, archery, charioteering, history, numbers—and so custodians of what passed in those days for a classical and cultivated tradition. But Confucius had great difficulty in finding a position, apparently because he was too outspoken about proper conduct on the part of rulers and seemed hopelessly to have "his head in the clouds." He had to settle for a role that to him seemed second best, but in the long run it proved far more epochal than that of government minister. He became a teacher. Among his students were young men who were successful in attaining practical influence and who over the years—and through subsequent generations of students over the centuries—reshaped the values and structures of Chinese statecraft, education, and social organization. It was they who understandably added honor upon honor to Confucius's memory until temples redolent of incense and sacrifice enshrined his name.

Confucius was not revered just for himself but because he was associated with the classical literature that was the real bedrock of the traditional culture. Five books, which existed in early form by the time of Confucius and which were the basic texts of the ru, are now often called the Confucian classics. These are the *Book of History,* the *Book of Poems,* the *Book of Change* (the famous *Yi Jing*), the historical *Spring and Autumn Annals,* and the *Book of Rites.* Tradition said, with greater or less exaggeration, that Confucius had written parts of them and edited them all; in any case, he was the symbol of their authority.

Four other books from shortly after the time of Confucius are also canonical and bear the putative seal of the master's authority: the *Analects* (containing the remembered words of Confucius himself), the *Great Learning,* the *Mean,* and the *Book of Mencius.*[4] (Mencius was the next best known philosopher in Confucian tradition.)

These books are important because they reflect basic Chinese values and ways of thinking. Their tradition went back before Confucius and continued after him. Confucius is not a peerless sage because he created this tradition; on the contrary, he is unequalled because the tradition "created" him and he reflected it faithfully.[5]

It was not unfair to Confucius to honor him as the embodiment of the tradition, for the burden of his teaching was above all to maintain this heritage and apply it fully and properly. He was a creative and deeply principled conservative. He believed that the way to get society on the right track again was to go back to the example of ancient sage-emperors. The basic structures of society, he felt, were adequate. The needful thing was to convince people they must act in accordance with the roles society has given them. The father must act like a father; the son, like a son; the ruler must be a real ruler like those of old, wise and benevolent; the ministers of state must be true civil servants, loyal and fearless and self-giving.

This change to becoming what one "is" (called "rectification of names") must first of all be within. One must be motivated by virtue, or *ren,* a typically vague but eloquent term suggestive of humanity, love, high principle, and living together in harmony. It is the way of the *jun-zi,* the superior man, who, as the Confucian ideal suggests, is a man at once a scholar, a selfless servant of society, and a gentleman steeped in courtesy and tradition; as an official and family head, he continually puts philosophy into practice.

Confucius conceded that this noble ideal is enforced by no outside sanctions except the opinion of good men, for it was based on no belief in divine rewards or punishment after death. Its sincere practice in this life might, as often as not, result in exile and hunger rather than honor from princes. Yet in the end it draws men by the sheer attractiveness of the good and by the fact that it embodies Dao, and so to follow ren is to align oneself with the way things are.

There follows a fundamental satisfaction from acting in accordance with the real nature of things that the virtueless devotee of passion and gain can never know, and that finally makes such a person's life hollow. For Confucianism has generally believed that the basic nature of humankind is good. It is only perverted by bad external example or bad social environment, and people will turn naturally to the good when good examples and social conditions are present. To make them present is the weighty responsibility of the ruler, advised by Confucian sages.

External influences, then, can aid in the inner development of ren. This leads to another very important Confucian term, *li*. It indicates rites, proper conduct, ceremonies, courtesy, doing things the right way. Despite a professed lack of concern about ghosts and gods, for Confucius the performance of rituals was extremely important.

It may seem to us excessive that a man at the height of his career, upon the death of his father would go into retirement for three years, wearing sackcloth, wailing through the day and night, eating only tasteless food. It might seem that the government of a nation ought to have better things to do than spend endless hours and money in the preparation and execution of seasonal ceremonies, one after the other.

But li needs to be understood as Confucius understood it, not as cold or mere "formalism" but as a supremely humanizing act. Animals act out of the lust or violent emotion of the moment, but humankind can rise above this in the societies it creates, and li exemplifies this potential. Li expresses a society that becomes a great dance and thus incarnates harmony. In ritual, everyone acts out proper relationships and has a structured place. Ritual generates order in place of chaos and nurtures "rectification of names." It can be hoped that if a person acts out, if only ritually, the proper conduct of his or her station in life often enough, in time he or she will interiorize the action, and the inner and outer will become one, the ritual father a true father, the ritual prince a true prince. Li, then, is meant to stimulate ren, even as melodious music induces calmness and heroic poetry valor.

It is within society that humanity comes to its best, for here the mutual stimuli of ren and li can be operative. Here is the key point of difference with the Daoists, who contended that society, or at least its regulations and rituals and mandatory relations, obscured the Dao. For Confucius, it was precisely in these social expressions that the Dao became visible and "spoke" to humankind. Society for Confucius was founded on five relationships: ruler and subject, father and son, husband and wife, elder and younger brother, friend and friend. In all of these, proper behavior, li, was required to give what is simply biological or spontaneous the structure that makes it into human society, calm and enduring for the benefit of all.

The cornerstone relation is the second—father and son. A son was expected to negate his own feelings and individuality in deference to the wishes and pleasure of his father in "filial piety."[6] It was in this relationship, which (at least according

---

Fundamental Features of Confucianism

Theoretical

Basic World View	The universe a unity under heaven, of which humans are an integral part. For humans, family and society are the most important links to the universe.
God or Ultimate Reality	"Heaven," regulating the world and moral order.
Origin of the World/Destiny of the World	Vague, but world originates from heaven and proceeds through interaction of Yin and Yang and the five "principles" or elements.
Origin of Humans	Vague; ultimately from heaven and earth.
Destiny of Humans	No stress on afterlife except in terms of ancestrism. Ideal is to live a good life in this world through family and society.
Revelation or Mediation Between the Ultimate and the Human	The teachings of Confucius and the classics; mediated by the educational system.

Practical

What Is Expected of Humans: Worship, Practices, Behavior	To observe official and ancestral rites; to honor parents and meet other ethical obligations. One works for a good society by exercising benevolence and practicing mutuality with others.

Sociological

Major Social Institutions	Great importance of family and of elite class; aligned to state under empire.

---

to Freudian psychoanalysis) is the most feeling-laden and difficult of all, that fundamental attitudes of ren and li and societal orientation were to be learned. It was as though to say, If love and virtue are to be learned truly, they must be learned at home and by making this hard but all-important relation the pivot. Father-son becomes the primal model of an interpersonal relationship, and in Confucianism it is in interpersonal relationships that man is humanized and Dao is manifested. If this relationship can be rectified, then all other relationships will also fall into place.

One might ask, Why is the relation between father and son, rather than that between mother and child, the key? Perhaps it can be looked at in this way: The mother-child relationship is essentially biological, fraught with deep feelings and instincts that humankind shares with most of the higher animals. The father-son relationship, on the other hand, is more *social* in nature. This is not to say, of course, that the father does not have a biological role and some instinctual equipment to go with it.

But in many archaic societies, the father's biological role does not in itself establish social responsibility for a child. Rather, the crucial factor is the father's taking responsibility for the child *in his social role* as head of the household. The role is defined by his picking up the child, giving him a name, and recognizing him as his ward and heir. In other words, the father-son relationship is the most basic relationship inextricably intertwined with the social as well as the biological components of human culture, such as language (giving a name), moral responsibility, family as a legal entity, and the combination of privilege and repression that makes learned behavior—all that flows into li and ren—possible.

It is therefore significant that in Confucianism, with its emphasis on human society as the key bearer of the Dao for human beings, the father-son relationship— the primal social, structured relationship—should be central; but that Laozi, whose Daoism emphasized the natural and biological and spontaneous as better than the social for manifesting Dao, should several times use the mother-child relationship as a metaphor for the relation of a person with Dao.

Needless to say, this perspective has meant that Confucianism, like many another traditional religion and social order, has presumed and established an essentially male-centered world view and society. Women, while given a place in the pattern of relationships, have found that place to be distinctly subordinate. They were to defer to the authority first of their fathers, then of their husbands, and finally of the sons whose birth and nurturance was their supreme function in life, since it was through sons that the family line would continue. Only male ancestors were venerated. (We have not hesitated to use the terms *man* and *mankind* in the discussion of Confucianism, for this usage certainly conforms to the Confucian outlook.)

Subsequent Confucian philosophers talked about human nature and how society can best be organized to manifest the Dao within it. Mencius (372–289 B.C.E.), for example, held that human nature is basically good and is only impeded by an evil social environment, while Xunzi (fl. 298–238 B.C.E.) said that man is basically evil in the sense of being self-centered and needs education and social control to become good.

We must give more attention, however, to the ways in which Confucianism clearly took the three forms of religious expression, presenting a unified structure of teaching, rites, and sociological forms. In a real sense, they have always appeared discretely in the true centers of Confucian values, that is, in the "natural" units of family and traditional community, since Confucius wanted to enhance and sanctify these units. He did not want to establish a center of sacred value elsewhere. It was the family and community that his teaching was about and for which his rituals were performed, and they made their own sacred community. The secular was the sacred.

But as Confucianism became a quasi-state religion in the Han dynasty (206 B.C.E.–220 C.E.) and after, it found it needed a quasi-theology, a quasi-divinity, and a quasi-priesthood with its own rites. Quasi-divinity it found in Confucius himself, and quasi-priesthood in the powerful class of Confucian scholars who staffed the bureaucracy of the empire. Confucius, as the peerless infallible sage, was seen as a sort of mystic king, with a true right to rule the inward kingdom of ideas and values upon which the outer realm, administered and educated by the mandarins, was based.

This kind of thinking, which may be called the Han synthesis because it generously incorporated Daoist and other traditional motifs into Confucianism, was the work of Dong Zhongshu (c. 179–104 B.C.E.) more than of any other individual. His thought is like that of cosmic religion in that it is interested in the total interrelationship of all things rather than free, personal ethical and political questioning.

Dong presented a doctrine of correspondences, in which humanity and nature are parts of an interwoven web. A portent in heaven may be related to a forthcoming event on earth, and the moral decisions of a ruler may affect the prevalence of rain in his nation's fields.

Unlike many moderns, traditional Chinese did not see people and nature as separate, going by different laws. Instead they assumed that humanity, human history, and government cooperate with nature and are controlled by the same laws. It is as though we were to say that perpetual motion is as impossible in the history of a nation as in mechanics if it is a true law. To further the comparison, it would be as though we then said that the nation must have a public ritual once a year to counteract its slowing down and to wind the energy up again.

For Dong, the key to the whole web of correspondences of which life is woven is the Yang-Yin concept. This theory had very early origins in occult speculation connected with astrology, alchemy, and *Yi Jing* divination, but it did not emerge fully into the mainstream of Chinese philosophy until the Han synthesis gave it place.

In this view, the Dao—that is, all the 10,000 things—is divisible into two great classifications: Yang things and forces, and Yin things and forces. Fundamentally, Yang is associated with the masculine and Yin with the feminine. But their respective meanings go much beyond gender. Yang is what is male, but also day, sky, spring, and all that is bright, clear, hard, assertive, growing, moving out. Its symbol is the dragon. Yin is female, and also night, earth, moisture, autumn and harvest, spirits of the dead, and all that is dark, underneath, recessive, pulling in, connected with the moon, mysterious. Its symbol is the tiger, which must be thought of as Blake's "Tyger, tyger burning bright/In the forests of the night"—emblematic of the arcane, inward, unfathomable, yet unescapable in human life.

It must be emphasized that Yang and Yin are by no means "good" or "bad." Neither is "better" than the other. They are both neutral, like gravitation. To keep going, the universe needs both and they need to interact in a balanced way. Too much of either brings disaster, just as rain and sun are both necessary in their places, but too much of either brings flood or drought.

Yang and Yin

The task of humanity is to keep these two eternal antagonists and partners, the dragon and the tiger, in proper balance, for our place is between them, and we are finally to interiorize them both. An elaborate art called *feng-shui* arose to determine, according to Yang-Yin "bearings," the most auspicious locations for houses and tombs and temples, between, say, a rock considered Yang and a tree determined as

Chinese New Year celebration.

Yin. (Much more was involved in the full system of feng-shui and of correspondences, too: the values of the five "elements" or modes of natural activity—fire, water, earth, metal, and wood—each of which corresponded with seasons, colors, tones, and so forth.) Finally, particularly in esoteric Daoism, one sought through alchemical potions and yogic practices to bring to equilibrium the two forces within oneself, and thus achieve immortality—for it is Yin-Yang imbalance that results in decay and death: one who has them in as perfect harmony as the great Dao itself will be as deathless as the great Dao. Confucianism has always emphasized finding a balance, and keeping away from too much or too little of anything.

The ritual year, both at the imperial palace and in the humblest village, strove to "work" Yang and Yin. The object was to support what the Dao, through the respective force, was doing at that time. The first half of the year, the time of growing and outgoing of nature as it awoke from the sleep of winter, was the time of the dynamic, rain-giving dragon. The Chinese New Year is marked by a parade through the streets of a gigantic, weaving dragon borne by many men. In midsummer, to consummate Yang, dragon boat or horse races are held, and then to inaugurate the Yin months of ingathering and the darkening of days, the lion or tiger dances are held. The traditional harvest festival when (as at Halloween) the dead return is full of Yin symbolism—it is at night, and cakes in the shape of the moon, decorated with moon castles where immortals live, are placed in the courtyards.

In the Han period, this sort of ideology also became political as a part of the new "synthesis" Confucianism. The emperor was Yang, the people Yin, and the ruler was to serve as activator of proper response by the ruled. Moreover, the sovereign was mediator between Heaven and Earth, the midpoint in a triad of Heaven, Earth, and human society. In his lawgiving he was representative of Heaven, the great origin, to the people; as chief priest in his worship he represented humankind before Heaven. In all this it was his responsibility to promote the proper working of Yang and Yin; if deterioration in nature or society became evident, it would be widely said that the sovereign had lost the Mandate of Heaven, that is, the right to rule as representative of Heaven.

This thinking fit the needs of the ru, or scholar class, who studied this kind of lore, enacted the rites, and made Confucius the symbol of learning and authority. His cultus grew apace. In 56 C.E., sacrifices to Confucius were ordered in all schools; by the end of the empire in 1912 he had (in 1908) been declared coequal with Heaven and Earth themselves, as though to say the best of human culture was no less a great thing than cosmic nature.

The importance of this scholar class in Chinese tradition can hardly be overemphasized. Three things set them apart: They were bearers of the ongoing tradition as dynasties rose and fell; they were unique as a class able to read and write well; in theory they were not a hereditary aristocracy, but an elite of brains who attained their positions in academic competition. As both teachers and administrators, they were indispensable to generations of rulers who found that sooner or later they had to conform to the values and usages of this class since they could not rule without its support.

The role of these Confucian scholars, called mandarins, meant that the real focus of power was not the sword but the pen, and that the vessel of cultural continuity in this society was a class of refined elites who scarcely hid their disdain of the rough soldier, but who made the written language and ability to wield it elegantly the supreme symbol of superiority over the toiling masses. This situation involved no small flourishing of class privilege, yet it also enabled a rudimentary democracy, for the means of entry into the privileged class was through education and the civil service examinations. In nearly all periods there were young men of humble background who managed to succeed in that grueling ordeal.

Dynasties periodically rose and fell, and with the transfer of the Mandate of Heaven a peasant or outlander might well come to the throne. There was no official nobility, and all families experienced years of bad fortune as well as good. The Middle Kingdom, then, did not know the domination of intermarrying noble lines like the Bourbons and Hapsburgs of Europe century after century; what lasted instead was the gray-gowned meritocracy of the learned.

Confucian followers burning incense at the tomb of deceased great scholars in Korea.

This class naturally developed its own internal traditions and "style." Its members grew fingernails inches long to prove that they did not do manual labor. Anything in writing, however trivial, was treated by them with respect and would be reverently burned rather than thrown out. They would typically be skeptical of beliefs concerning ghosts, spirits, gods, and an afterlife, but would treat such beliefs among the common people (or even the womenfolk in their own households) with a disdainful tolerance. It was better the masses believe in such things than that their discontent with their lot in this life get out of hand. In this spirit, the mandarin scholar appointed governor of a city would conduct the rites of the city-god, even to whipping the image of the deity when that divine protector failed to protect his people from misfortune. He would, however, know that beliefs like this were unworthy of a philosopher.

On a more serious level, the ru would manage the execution of the state ceremonies, culminating in the emperor's worship at the Altar of Heaven in the middle of the night at the winter solstice and the worship of Earth at the summer solstice. The drama of the midwinter worship of Heaven has been described by many observers prior to 1911. In icy darkness broken only by flaring torches, the sovereign and his ministers, clad in the heaviest furs, would arrange elaborate presentations of food, wine, and cloth on the huge tiered mountain of masonry in Peking called the Altar of Heaven, and the emperor would read an elegant prayer. In principle, only the emperor, as mediator, could worship Heaven and Earth, the greatest ultimates known; others had to be content with ancestral and divine intermediaries. For the

Confucianist, these rites were of grave importance as expressions of li; they were contributory to making society into a vast harmony or dance rather than a mere collection of thinking animals.

Another set of rituals were of special meaning to the Confucian elite. These were the major sacrifices to Confucius himself, held at the vernal and autumnal equinoxes, significantly midway between the two great rites of Heaven and Earth. These would be conducted at the temples of Confucius located in the more important cities. Although formerly they contained images of Confucius, since the Middle Ages they gave tribute to the superior worth of writing in the eyes of devotees of the philosopher by presenting only an upright tablet with the inscription "Confucius the Wise and Holy Sage," flanked by similar tablets to the master's disciples. At these rites, the local scholar-rulers would gather; kowtow (kneel deeply so that the forehead touched the floor) before the altar; present offerings of a whole slaughtered bull, pig, and sheep, together with wine and vegetables; offer a tribute; present music and dance supposed to be from the time of Confucius; and feast on offerings.

Understanding this ritual, as enacted by presumably skeptical scholars for one whom no one considered exactly a god, creates difficulty for the Westerner accustomed to quite different styles of thought. Clearly, it was an act of reverence and sacrifice that was less than divine worship, yet more than Western civil ceremonies. It was somewhere between what might be done at the Arlington National Cemetery on Memorial Day and a cathedral service, with the difference that animal victims were sacrificed in a way that Westerners consider barbaric—despite the slaughter of thousands daily with less ceremony in our stockyards.

Apart from their value simply as li, the Confucian rites can be thought of best in connection with the ancestral system. The Confucian scholars greatly valued their own family shrines and lineages; yet they were also, as a special called-out class, members of another "family," a spiritual clan of all their vocation. Of this literati family the supreme scholar Confucius was the ancestor.

A word should be said about the Neo-Confucian movement, which began in the eleventh and twelfth centuries during the Song dynasty and became the authoritative interpretation of the Confucian intellectual tradition. Partly in response to the issues raised by Daoist and particularly Buddhist thought, Neo-Confucian philosophers greatly enhanced their tradition's metaphysical foundation. It became a comprehensive world view concerned with the nature of mind and the ultimate origin of things, and with simple methods of meditation, as well as a social philosophy, although it never lost the ideal that the philosopher finds joy in the midst of family and social life, not in permanent withdrawal from them. Two leading Neo-Confucianists were Zhu Xi (or Chu Hsi, 1130–1200) and Wang Yangming (or Wang Shouren, 1472–1529). Zhu Xi taught that one great ultimate is manifested in the principles of the myriad separate things, as the light of the moon is broken onto many rivers and lakes. Through reflection on particulars, especially human morality, one can know the ultimate. The more idealistic Wang Yangming taught that the principles are actually within the mind itself, and so the supreme requisite is sincerity of mind. Through reflections such as these, the spiritual and intellectual side of Confucianism was given a transcendence that made the practice of Confucian rites and virtues a more deeply religious way, even a sort of mysticism in the midst of a life of service.

But the most important impact of Confucianism on China was in the area of moral and social values. Although ancestrism, the family system, and the ideal of selfless work for the common good have pre-Confucian roots, Confucianism gave these values ultimate prestige through the civilized centuries. It was of a piece with Confucianism that all important families had ancestral shrines in which the names of parents, grandparents, and great-grandparents were lined up on higher and higher shelves for each generation, and worship was offered them, as it was at the tombs and in the home. Inseparable from ancestrism was the Confucian-based family system in which loyalty and filial obedience were obligations that gave precedence to no others. Confucianism too underlay the Chinese "work ethic," the high regard for diligence and productivity for the honor and prosperity of one's family name. Without the mental image of the wise and sober sage from the state of Lu, and the words from his or his followers' pens, China would be very different from what we have known it to be for more than twenty centuries.

DAOISM

Confucianism, even in its most expansive forms, does not exhaust the spiritual heritage of China. Few people can be wholly devoted to sober virtues all the time, and the Chinese are no exceptions. There is another side that demands its due. This is the side of human personality that is attracted to what expresses the private fears, fancies, and aspirations of the individual. It is the side that feels for communion with nature, mystic rapture, imaginative works of art and letters, rebellion against social conformity, inward fear of evil, and love for gods. This side affirms the needs of *personal* life against the demands of structured society, and it affirms the place of the feeling, symbol-making, nonrational side against the cool, word-oriented rational side. In China, all this side has danced about under the broad umbrella of the Daoist tradition.

Perhaps we can understand the role of Daoism in China by thinking of the cultural situation in America in recent decades. First, there is the "establishment" and its values: the major institutions of business, government, education, and church, upholding the usual values in family life, behavior, and the legitimate organization of society. This side corresponds more or less to what Confucianism has undergirded in China.

Then there is what was called in the 1960s the "counterculture." It consists of people who have to varying degrees "dropped out" of the establishment. They were preoccupied with a gamut of things—living in the woods, writing poetry, painting, chanting, engaging in new styles of marital and sexual life, or trying to reach "altered states of consciousness" by meditation, yoga, and drugs. Some got involved in revolutionary movements. If there is a unifying idea, it is that one must above all be true to what one is in the depths of one's personal self—one must "get oneself together" and "do one's own thing."

In China, parallels to these counterculture features have appeared in connection with the Daoist tradition, most of them as major and recurring themes. As one would expect from this, Daoism has been many things to many different people and has taken an immense variety of forms over the centuries. It has included hermit poets, temples with lavishly robed priests burning clouds of incense before resplendent gods, and "underground" secret political societies. It has ranged from "nature mysticism" to occult quests for immortality to the rites of spiritualists who call up the dead.

Some commentators have talked about a "pure" philosophical Daoism and a "degenerate," "superstitious" religious Daoism. But, as usual, such presuppositions get in the way of real understanding. It is more instructive to comprehend how all of Daoism forms a unity of experience around a single pole, focusing on the feeling-oriented, nonrational side of life. Here it is simple to move rapidly from mysticism to occultism to revolution and back, and from "nature" to the most elaborate religious robes and rites, so long as they express something imaginative and personal.

Daoism in China is really a tapestry of countless strands of folk religion, ancient arcana going back to prehistoric shamanism and private vision. But its supposed founder is the sage Laozi (Lao-tzu). Appropriately for such a romantic tradition, he is more legend than fact, and his very name suggests anonymity, for Laozi just means "The Old Man." Stories say that the bearer of this epithet was an older contemporary of Confucius, and indeed that Confucius once met him, found him hard to confront, and said, "Of birds I know that they have wings to fly with, of fish that they have fins to swim with, of wild beasts that they have feet to run with. For feet there are traps, for fins nets, for wings arrows. But who knows how dragons surmount wind and cloud into heaven? This day I have seen Laozi and he is a dragon."

Laozi was, according to tradition, a "dropout." It is said he was an archive-keeper at the Zhou court and a popular fellow who kept a good table. But he became disgusted with the grasping and hypocrisy of the world, and at the age of eighty left his job, mounted a water buffalo, and wandered off to the west. At the western portals of the empire, the gatekeeper is reported to have detained him as his guest, refusing to let him pass until he had recorded his wisdom. So the Old Man wrote down the book called the *Dao de jing* (Tao te ching) and then departed in the direction of Tibet, becoming mysteriously lost to the world.

Other ways may be found to interpret the emergence of the Daoism of the *Dao de jing*. Some have pointed out that at the time of Confucius there were apparently a number of fairly well educated people around, more than there were government or literary jobs available; Confucius's own difficulty in finding a position may testify to this. Such persons, unable to work at the level of their abilities and too proud to return to the fields, formed a floating intellectual class for whose way of life early Daoism could provide at best an inspiration and at worst a rationalization.[7]

Others have noted that, on the other hand, the *Dao de jing* does contain a political philosophy aimed at rulers as well as reflections for the solitary individual;

太上老君

Laozi, the supposed founder of Daoism, riding an ox.

it must not have been intended only for people without place. Still others have seen in it the veiled but rather technical manual of a yogic school.[8] In sum, the origin of the *Dao de jing* is as mysterious as its meaning; each reader must get from it what he or she can.

Let us now look at the message of this book ascribed to Laozi, Daoism's traditional founder. It is a book about the Dao, that universal way or track down which all the 10,000 things roll and which is their substratum and the only lasting thing there is; the name *Dao de jing* means something like "The Book of the Dao and How to Apply Its Strength."

Although a book about the Dao, it begins with the curious affirmation that nothing can be said about its subject matter:

> Existence [the Dao] is beyond the power of words
> To define:
> Terms may be used
> But are none of them absolute.
> In the beginning of heaven and earth there were no words.
> Words came out of the womb of matter.[9]

There is no word, this means, that is an adequate symbol for the Dao. That is obvious when we consider that all human words come out of finite human experience; they do convey something of what really is, but only as human beings with their limited sensory equipment and limited field of experience have known it. When someone says to you the word *tree,* certain images pop into your mind. But these images derive only from your own limited experience with trees.

The image you have may be of a tree in your backyard as a child, or one that you saw in a picture book when you learned the word; you let this tree represent for you all the trees theoretically covered by the word. The word says little about all the trees you have not seen, or about how trees are experienced by other people or animals, much less about how a tree experiences itself! The word *tree* is really only a very pale thing, calling up a few tentative hints of what "treeness" means to a human being who is alien to a tree's life. It scarcely touches the vast untapped richness contained in the reality of trees "out there"—how they were in ages past before humankind arose, what they may be like on other planets, what they seem like to squirrels and birds who live in them, how they "feel" deep down in their own lives.

If this is true of something that is still only a part of creation, how much more must the limitations of language apply to the infinite whole. Add to the limitations of our experience the fact that language by definition cannot really apply a meaningful label to the whole since the purpose of words is to categorize the particular: We use them to distinguish one thing from another; to call something *rice* implies there are other things that are not rice from which it needs to be distinguished.

Even to use a word ostensibly for the whole, such as *Dao* or *existence,* does not avoid this limitation. All these words can do is point in a certain direction of comprehension, but they cannot make clear there is really nothing comparable to Dao or existence from which it could be distinguished.

Philosophical discussion like this may begin to open up the kind of realizations that seized the writer of the *Dao de jing.* But for him the book was no mere metaphysical nitpicking—nothing would have more won his contempt.

Rather, these reflections opened up a different, ecstatic mode of being in the world. Once you realize that the Dao which flows in and through everyone and everything cannot be labeled and put in a box, you can respond to it in a different way: with simple wonder, turning to it as an infant turns to its mother. The first chapter ends, "From wonder into wonder Existence [the Dao] opens." Elsewhere we read, "Can you, with the simple stature of a child, breathing nature, become, notwithstanding, a man? . . . Can you, mating with heaven, serve as the female part?" And again, the writer, seeing himself as a misfit in artificial society although marvelously near the Dao that others miss, says, "All these people are making their mark in the world, while I, pigheaded, awkward, different from the rest, am only a glorious infant still nursing at the breast." (We have already noted that, just as the father-son relationship was the cornerstone of Confucianism, so the *Dao de jing* makes becoming feminine, or becoming a child in a mother's arms, a basic image for the relationship of the individual with the great Dao.)

In the seemingly weak stance of the female or the child is tremendous strength—the strength of water that wears down the hardest rock, or wind and rain that can come and go as they wish. In yielding, bending with the wind like a supple tree and then springing back renewed, is a vital strength that will weave its way subtly through all the permutations of the Dao. But that which is stiff like a man standing on tiptoe will break and fall. We are told the best ruler is he who guides his people unobtrusively, so that they say, "We did this ourselves."

Making comparisons are inimical to this way of life, for they induce partial views and keep one from seeing life and the Dao whole:

> People through finding something beautiful
> Think something else unbeautiful.
> Through finding one man fit
> Judge another unfit . . .
> Take everything that happens as it comes,
> As something to animate, not to appropriate . . .
> If you never assume importance
> You never lose it.[10]

This outlook has political implications, and they are quite contrary to the elitism of "getting the best man for the job" of the Confucianists. There is also an attack on the philosophy of advertising: Nothing would be more contrary to Daoist political and economic ideas than our system of choosing leaders through elective competition and creating prosperity by encouraging consumption.

> It is better not to make merit a matter of reward
> Lest people conspire and contend,
> Not to pile up rich belongings
> Lest they rob,
> Not to excite by display
> Lest they covet.[11]

Elsewhere, we are told in the *Dao de jing* that the ideal community would be a village of simple, hardworking, prosperous farmers, so unsophisticated that they did not even use writing but kept records with knotted cords, and so content that even though they could hear the dogs barking and the cocks crowing in the next village, they never visited it.

Needless to say, this approach was quite at odds with the Confucianists' earnest talk of cultivating virtue and their moral norms such as filial obedience. Laozi instead refers back to a primordial paradise where people lived simply in harmony with the

Dao spontaneously. Only when deterioration sets in, he thought, did rules and norms appear, and they were both cause and effect of the deterioration.

> When people lost sight of the way to live
> Came codes of love and honesty.
> Learning came, charity came,
> Hypocrisy took charge;
> When differences weakened family ties
> Came benevolent fathers and dutiful sons;
> And when lands were disrupted and misgoverned
> Came ministers commended as loyal.[12]

In other words, what for the Confucianists was the very essence of true civilization, for the Daoists was the token of decay and hypocrisy. To them, true virtue, like that of nature or of a child with eyes full of wonder, could never be forced by bookish ethics. If we got rid of formalized learning and duty, Laozi said, people would be a hundredfold happier and would do naturally what they now resist just because they are told to do it.

Here we can see clearly the Daoist reaction against ordinary conventions of thought and behavior. It is but a step from this generalized sense of wonder and of the limitations of ordinary words and attitudes to affirmation of the most extraordinary seeming ideas: the possibility of deathlessness, the reality of fabulous secrets, powers, and worlds. In fact, even the *Dao de jing* appears to affirm that one who is in inseparable harmony with the Dao is as immortal as the Dao is, and that through the way of yielding one can find mysterious powers so great as to seem miraculous. But it remained to subsequent Daoist writers to make this potential of Laozi's vision more explicit. The first and greatest is Zhuangzi (Chuang-tzu died, c. 300 B.C.E.).[13]

Little is known of Zhuangzi apart from his book, but it is enough. Written in a vivid, fanciful, and humorous style, it immediately brings the reader into a world of expanding horizons. One is first told of strange marvels, as though from tales of Sinbad—of an immense fish thousands of miles long that changes into a bird just as large and flies to a celestial lake in the south. The writer then juxtaposes these examples of the fabulously large with mention of the tiny motes in the air that make the sky blue, and tells us that to a mustard seed a teacup is an ocean. As the reader's imagination is swung violently from the microscopically small to the immensely huge, from the fairy tale antipodes of the mind to the homey, he or she gets a sense of mental vertigo. One feels that one is spinning and things are coming unfastened.

That is just what Zhuangzi wants one to feel, for he wants to shake the reader loose from the ordinary way of seeing things. Zhuangzi wanted a person to be free—above all, free from oneself, one's own prejudices, partial views, categories, and from judging everything in terms of oneself. To this Daoist, man is *not* the measure of all things. The way the universe happens to appear to a biped six feet tall is no more the way it is than the way it appears to a fish, a mote, an eagle, or a star. Only the Dao itself is the measure.

In the same way, the ordinary rational waking consciousness is no more the measure of all things than the world of dreams and fancy and of the improbable. Zhuangzi tells us he once dreamed he was a butterfly, and when he awoke he did not know whether he was Zhuangzi who had dreamed he was a butterfly or a butterfly dreaming he was Zhuangzi. The dream world, in other words, is just as real as any other.

Unlike the sober Confucianist, Zhuangzi delights in the world of fantasy rocks and leviathans, wizards who can fly over the clouds, and islands of immortals. The world of the unconscious and the imagination, he is saying, is just as much a manifestation of the Dao as the rational—and may indeed better lead us to comprehending the Dao. At least it opens us to that sense of wonder and infinity beyond all limits which is necessary to comprehend the Dao—for the Dao is precisely the unbounded.

This was the direction in which Daoism went. A later Daoist thinker, Ge Hong (283–c. 343 C.E.), put it even more clearly, both in his life and in his writing. He lived during the three and a half centuries (221–589 C.E.) of division and political confusion that disturbed China between the fall of the Han dynasty and the relatively stable and unified Sui (589–618) and Tang (618–907) dynasties. Extensive but ephemeral conquests in the north by various nomadic peoples and Chinese cultural expansion in the south, combined with the inability of the nation to come together under a single leadership, shaped the uncertain social background of the periods between 221 and 589—a time which nonetheless was culturally quite creative. Buddhism spread extensively, Daoism revived, and brilliant new forms in art and literature emerged to express the visions of these new, and newly personal, spiritual visions.

Confucianism was still accepted as normative, but the collapse of the social order based on its Han synthesis version discredited it for many; in any case, a view of life oriented toward the communication of value through social usages and interpersonal obligations simply cannot "work" well in a time of social confusion. Many will be driven to look for more personal paths that promise inner meaning in spite of what is going on around one.

For some the answer was Buddhism, flowing into China from India via central Asia. For others—skeptical perhaps as the Chinese tend to be of imported gifts—it was some form of the Daoist heritage. They turned back to the books of Laozi and Zhuangzi, which by then already formed part of a counterculture constellation that included the heritage of various late Han "revivalistic" movements promising healing and magic on the popular level and a complex pattern of occult learning on the more sophisticated. Some of it, such as the Yin-Yang and "correspondences" thought, was also part of the Han synthesis. But the last was now more personalized; what had been a key to imperial rites was now the privilege of the informed individual striving to solve personal problems. (In the same way, in the West the astrology that was once the recourse of princes now "belongs" to everyone who reads a newspaper.)

To this effect it is interesting that Ge Hong's book, the *Baopuzi,* contains what are called Outer and Inner parts. The Outer presents conventional Confucian teaching; the Inner offers Daoist material centering on the achievement of personal

---

Fundamental Features of Daoism

Theoretical

Basic World View	The universe is one, yet always moving and changing.
God or Ultimate Reality	The Dao, the great Way down which the universe moves.
Origin of the World/Destiny of the World	It is an expression of the Dao without a known beginning or end.
Origin of Humans/Destiny of Humans	An expression of the Dao, to share in its never-ending evolution. One may become immortal by mastering the Dao and its power.
Revelation or Mediation Between the Ultimate and the Human	The teachings of Laozi and other sages. Benign immortals or gods can be honored and serve as helpers.

Practical

What Is Expected of Humans: Worship, Practices, Behavior	To live spontaneously and close to nature; in more formal systems, to meditate and perform rites that draw one close to gods and immortals.

Sociological

Major Social Institutions	Temples, monasteries, the Daoist priesthood.

---

immortality through alchemy and yogic techniques. It is as though to say that while Confucianism may still be adequate for social ideology, a new self-consciousness and sense of social failure has made Confucianism hollow without something for the individual as well.

This quest for personal immortality was a basic theme of the new Daoism, and with it came interest in the worlds of miracles and of immortal supernatural beings the quest implied and almost predicated. It had, as we have noted, philosophical roots in Laozi's implication that harmony with the Dao is immortality, and in Zhuangzi's, that truth is found in unfettered openness to all levels of consciousness and all possibilities, however fantastic.

The consequent distinction between Confucian and Daoist styles of thinking is very clear in a fictional debate that Ge Hong composed between a Confucianist and a Daoist on the possibility of immortality. The Confucianist argues that every living thing that anyone has ever heard of dies and that belief in immortality is therefore untenable nonsense. Baopuzi, the Daoist, responds that there are exceptions to every rule, and that just because things of which we know die, we cannot say that everything in this universe of which we really know so little *must* die. In effect, the Confucianist says, "You can't prove immortality," and the Daoist says, "You can't prove there isn't immortality." Perhaps little is proved in this particular argument except that, for Confucianists, the instinctive response to a query is the safe, rational, common-sense answer, and for Daoists, the romantic, speculative approach open to nonrational, "mind-blowing" possibilities. The cleavage is temperamental and comparable to the gulf between Enlightenment rationalism and the Romanticism that followed it in the West.

Other Daoists of the "interim" period followed lifestyles that seemed almost to repudiate the importance of personal immortality (as did earlier Zhuangzi), so much did they emphasize spontaneity. To them, living with the Dao meant a *feng liu* ("wind and stream") life, acting according to the movement of "what was happening" day by day. Many were artists and poets, or at least esthetes, and the unplanned life, which savored the beauty of each event and the richness of each impulse, well suited the temperament of their callings. Philosophical works that went with this Daoist stance, such as the *Guo Xiang's* Commentary on the *Zhuangzi* and the *Liezi,* made much of Dao as being *wu-wei,* nonbeing or not doing, in the rather technical sense that the Dao is not a "thing" or a "cause" and does not produce by plan or through work. Instead, all things just flow out of it freely or spontaneously in an endless stream of flux and change; the person who is attuned to Dao lives his life in this way.[14]

It was religious Daoism, however, with its popular gods and quest for immortality, that took lasting institutional form. Its roots are complex, reach far back into the murky past, and are far from adequately traced.[15] We have noted that magical techniques to attain deathlessness, and yogic practices to control breath and induce joy, may be reflected in the *Dao de jing* and are very ancient. We have also mentioned that in the Han period, popular religious movements emphasizing healing and revolution were attached to the *Dao de jing* tradition. For example, Zhang Ling in the second century C.E. started a revivalistic healing movement that established itself as a state within a state in mountainous areas. Zhang Ling said that Laozi had appeared to him from the realm of spirits and had given him a sword and other apparatus by which he was able to exercise control over the spiritual world. Zhang was called Heavenly Teacher, and his direct descendants (sometimes misleadingly called the "Daoist Popes") have continued the title to the present. They dwelt on a Dragon and Tiger Mountain in central China, exercised a tenuous spiritual authority over Daoist priests in the south, and sold mysterious charms that were distributed far and wide.

The popular Daoist religious system, which embraces the "Daoist Pope" and his charms and priests, presents a rich and colorful face. Perhaps no religion in the world has had a more vast pantheon of gods—many said to have been once human beings who became immortal and finally reached divine status. Some gods are ancient, although many were "appointed" to divinity by Tang and especially Ming (1368–1644) emperors.

This recalls the extensive interaction between Confucian and Daoist, as well as Buddhist, systems in China. Not only did the emperor, in designating approved worship, act out the role of mediator between heaven and earth assigned by Confucian thought, but the pantheon itself exemplified a heavenly reflection of the earthly bureaucracy manned by Confucian officials. Many of the deities, like Kuan Di, were originally earthly officials immortalized in the heavenly court.

Supreme deity in religious Daoism was the Jade Emperor, a personal high god for the masses ineligible to worship Heaven directly; he was enthroned in the Pole Star. Around him was his court: the Three Pure Ones—Laozi, the Yellow Emperor (mythical first sovereign of China), and Bangu (the primal man); the Eight Immortals, very popular in art and folk tales; and gods of literature, medicine, war, weather, and so forth. The gods and immortals lived in numerous heavenly grottos, in Islands of the Blessed to the east, and the Shangri-La of the Mother Goddess to the west, deep in the mountains.

The priests of this faith were a varied lot, affiliated with several different sectarian strands with differing specialties. Some were celibate and monastic; others, married. Some were contemplative, concerned above all else with perfecting in themselves the seeds of immortality. Some were custodians of lavish temples with huge and ornate images of the Jade Emperor and other worthies; to these temples believers would come to receive divination, have memorial services performed on behalf of their departed, and worship at important festivals, which were also occasions for carnival and feasting. Other Daoist clergy were mediums, male and female, who would deliver messages from the Other Side; some were sellers of charms, perhaps issued by the "Daoist Pope"; some were exorcists who performed dramatic rites of driving demons out of possessed persons and places.

Behind all of this lay the affirmation of immortality and of immortal entities; the panorama of religious Daoism made visible the invisible but deathless realm of gods and sages who had won the priceless secret. Those who would reveal the secret were not lacking, however. Religious Daoism pointed to three main highways to immortality: alchemy, yoga, and merit.

Alchemy referred to the preparation of elixirs supposed, in combination with spiritual preparation, to circumvent death through manipulation of Yin and Yang and the five elements. Most were based on cinnabar or mercury ore (HgS); some seven Chinese emperors are said to have died of mercury poisoning as a result of taking this medicine of immortality! Yet, as scholars such as C. G. Jung and Mircea Eliade have pointed out, both Chinese and Western alchemy contain important spiritual and protoscientific insights that cannot be neglected by the serious historian of ideas.[16]

Daoist yoga is equally complex. Its central motif, however, seems to have been the holding of the breath to circulate it throughout the body inwardly, awakening the gods of various physical centers, and finally to unite breath and semen to produce an immortal "spiritual embryo" who emerges as new life within the self. As it flourishes, the old mortal shell can fall away like the chrysalis of a butterfly. Diet and sometimes sexual practices of the Tantric sort were important supports of this process.

More available to the masses who were not adepts was the hope of attaining immortality by merit. The idea was approached with typical Chinese concreteness. Some popular temples even had a large abacus or calculating machine in full view

Daoist worshippers at the Matsu Yen Dao Temple in Anping, Taiwan.

to recall to the faithful the reckoning of good and bad deeds that will be required. Various texts cite the number and kinds of good deeds—building roads, acts of charity, compassion to living things—that would win immortality at diverse grades; even one demerit, however, would require the aspirant to start at the beginning of his labors again.

Daoism is usually presented as but one of the spiritual traditions of China, and not the most prestigious in the eyes of traditional scholars. But the attitudes of religious Daoism came closest to the spiritual world of the vast majority of ordinary people. Even Buddhism and Confucianism became "Daoicized" in cultus though not in doctrine and morals; whatever their origin, most plain people thought of the Buddhas, bodhisattvas, and even Confucius himself as immortalized humans now become spirits and able to send down blessings from above. Daoist and Buddhist priests served interchangeably in many localities, but their major functions such as funerals and exorcisms and village festivals were Daoist (that is to say, popular Chinese) in style. To be sure, popular Daoism borrowed much from Buddhism—the use of images, clerical organization, and the bureaucratic model of its pantheon from Confucianism—but those are historical matters, not all readily apparent to the person on the street.

Daoism, as the pervasive tone setter of the nonestablishment side of Chinese life, has contributed those undying elements of cheerful fancy, fairy tales, colorful festivals, bright pictures, and striking spiritual practices that are as much a part of Chinese life as Confucian common sense.

BUDDHISM IN CHINA

Buddhism first entered China in the Han period, spread widely during the three centuries of disruption that followed the fall of that dynasty, and reached its peak of maturity and creativity during the Tang era.[17] It was chiefly brought in the caravans of traders, not directly from India but from central Asia. As one would expect, the new faith first took root in the major cities and among the aristocrats. In the late Han and post-Han times, as we have seen, many of this class were searching among occult, mystical, and aesthetic possibilities for a richer inner life than could be offered by a decaying social order and its tired Confucian rationale. The wilder side of Daoism naturally appealed to some of them. But the profound mysteries of Buddhism, brought by exotic blue-eyed foreigners and bearing a whiff of the mystic perfume of India, as well as a more substantial philosophical and ethical base, was to many even more appealing. It speaks of both the power of Buddhism and the dissatisfaction of those times, that until the modern Western influence and subsequent Marxist triumph, no outside cultural force other than Buddhism has ever succeeded in making a major impact on China.

In the period when Buddhism was taking root in China, it was quite fashionable among the upper echelons of society. Aristocrats entertained visiting Buddhist priests, commissioned the translation of scriptures, and built temples in the mountains to which they would retire for genteel retreats. They also built hospitals and orphanages in the cities in accordance with the dictates of Buddhist compassion.

Buddhism opened up a new world of artistic possibilities with its demand for massive sculpture, mystic painting, and temple architecture. Buddhism also broadened ethical horizons more than many were prepared to accept, with its very new (and very controversial) notions of universal compassion, monasticism, and the relative independence of religion from the state cultus. These emphases, although suggested in Daoism, went strongly against the Confucian grain, with its feeling that the arts are more frivolous than civil service and that obligation to family and sovereign is primary. In particular, the ideal of the celibate Buddhist monk stood contrary to Confucianism, which put family life and the subordination of self to society at the center of value.

But Buddhism also made its adjustments to China. Indeed, for a long time the Indian religion was considered a variant of Daoism—an illusion promoted by some Daoists who even claimed that Laozi, after disappearing into the West, had gone to India and become the Buddha. In the translation of Buddhist texts from Sanskrit to Chinese, Daoist and Confucian terms were used, with inevitable shifts in connotation. Thus, dharma became Dao, arhant became immortal, and Buddhist morality was couched in the terms of submission and obedience hallowed by Confucian usage.[18]

Even the monastic system was modified in the direction of supporting rather than challenging the Chinese family unit. Young monks acquired a filial relation to their teachers, in imitation of obedience to father, and moreover were expected to assist dutifully their natural families by devoting much attention to prayer on behalf of relatives living and dead. Sometimes boys were dedicated to the monastery by their families for this reason, or in fulfillment of a vow made in prayer, because it was considered beneficial for a family to number a monk among its members.

Finally, monasteries were brought under the control of the throne, which licensed them and regulated the number of ordinations they could perform.

On the level of popular religion, Buddhism accommodated itself to China even more thoroughly. As already mentioned, popular Buddhas and bodhisattvas came to be regarded as blessing-giving deities little different from indigenous gods, except perhaps more broadly compassionate. The bodhisattva Avalokiteshvara became Guanyin (Kannon in Japanese), the so-called Goddess of Mercy who answered prayers for healing, women in childbirth, and wanderers. Maitreya, the Buddha of the future who would bring to pass a new paradisal era, was transformed from the lean, elegant, poised contemplative of Indian art to the immensely fat, laughing Miluo of China, who suggests a heartier, earthier vision of the joys of the new age. He has also been associated with revolutionary religio-political movements. In fact, even the Indian origin of Miluo, as of other Buddhist figures, came to be forgotten. Folklore identified him with a popular wandering wise-fool monk of the tenth century.

Probably the most important contribution of Buddhism to popular religion was in concepts of life after death. Previously, the Chinese had known belief in survival as ancestral spirits, as ghosts, or as Daoist immortals in blissful hermitages. To this Buddhism added the novel ideas of reincarnation and of elaborately gradated heavens and hells. Both these notions, however inconsistent with each other and with indigenous belief, were widely received, even by many who understood little else of Buddhism.

Reincarnation appears as a popular theme in literature. The hells were described in religious tracts, temple paintings, and sculpture displays (such as the well-known Tiger Balm Garden in Hong Kong) with a blood-splattered realism that even the dullest countryman could not ignore. The officials of hell, presided over by Yanluo (originally the Indic Yama, whom we previously encountered in the Katha Upanishad), were Confucian bureaucrats. As a reward for years of conscientious service, they were allowed to continue in the same line of work on the other side, where they saw to it that demons administered horrendous (but not eternal) punishments for infractions of both Confucian and Buddhist moralities.[19]

On the intellectual level, a number of different traditions of Buddhist thought and practice were introduced into China. Only the broad, tolerant, and variegated Mahayana had any success, however. But within it, the Void school, Yogacara or Mind Only, and esoteric Buddhism or Vajrayana all had early followings at various monastic centers. On Mount Tiantai, the syncretistic Tiantai school endeavored to reconcile all styles of Buddhist thought into a system that made the Lotus Sutra the summit of many planes of accommodation in the Buddha's teaching; Tiantai, and with it the Lotus Sutra, became immensely important in Japan.

When the dust settled, however, two strands of Buddhism emerged as the most important in China: Chan and Pure Land. The concept of clearly defined denominations, like those of Christianity or even of Japanese Buddhism, is alien to China except for minority sectarian movements. But it has ended up that most monasteries in China proper followed largely Chan teaching and practice, and Pure Land Buddhism was most popular among lay followers. Significantly, both (while having ultimate Indian roots) are highly Sinicized styles of Buddhism, owing much to different sorts of Daoist belief. Both are variants of a realization, emergent early in Chinese Buddhism's independent development, that true enlightenment is a sudden, spontaneous happening rather than a laborious process.

Chan, the tradition better known under its Japanese name of Zen, means the school of *dhyana*, Sanskrit for "meditation."[20] For it, enlightenment arises unexpectedly, often suddenly, in the course of "sitting quietly, doing nothing" in meditation, or perhaps in response to an unconventional teaching gesture by a master. Chan enlightenment is really like following the Daoist concept of Wu-wei, not-doing, and so letting events happen spontaneously. The assumption is that what is truly spontaneous is the Dao at work—or in this case, one's true Buddha-nature—while what is planned is of human egoistic contrivance, artificial and inauthentic.

Chan teaching and practice is a "therapeutic" means of bringing people to inward realization of the basic ideas of Mahayana, especially the Void teaching of Nagarjuna and the Mind Only insight of Yogacara. What is distinctive about Chan is the fierce and direct means used to shake aspirants into inward realization of basic Mahayana truth. That was the truth of nondualism—that getting entangled in making distinctions keeps us from realizing that we and all else are the indivisible Buddha-nature now and forever. Chan masters claimed that their tradition was one of getting at the truth by "direct pointing" and that it was transmitted "outside the scriptures," in that it did not depend on words and letters but on immediate experience passed from master to disciple.

The experience, tradition said, began long ago when the Buddha silently handed a flower to a disciple named Kashyapa and smiled. The disciple smiled back and *knew*—the flower and smile conveyed a universe of wisdom indefinable by any words or books.

After Kashyapa, the secret of the smile was passed down through a lineage of "patriarchs" in India, until the twenty-eighth, a sage from India called Bodhidharma, brought the tradition to China, where it became Chan, in 520 C.E. To exemplify it, Bodhidharma spent years meditating in front of a brick wall and did not hesitate to tell an emperor to his face that all the temples he had built, all the scriptures he had ordered copied, and all the monks and nuns he had supported, had won him no merit whatsoever.

In several ways this account is fictitious and misleading. The line of patriarchs in India is undoubtedly an invention, and Chan was well on the way to formation in China even before the time of Bodhidharma. The claim of Chan to be "outside the scriptures" requires qualification, for the Heart Sutra and others are chanted and expounded in its monasteries, and Chan is nothing more than a means toward realization of the central Mahayana concepts that these sutras proclaim. But Bodhidharma does dramatize that Chan is interested not in learning for its own sake but in hard, sharp, direct realization—and that colorful stories and exaggerated making-of-points are among its armory of techniques.

So it is that the idea of Emptiness or Void, and of the Buddha being found only in one's own consciousness (for all sentient beings are Buddhas and need only to be awakened to realize it) is shown in Chan disparagement of conventional Buddhist piety. In some places Buddha-images were chopped up periodically. In the earlier days of Chan, monks worked in the fields like peasants. A disciple once went up to his master, who was apparently weighing out a harvest of flax, and asked him, "What is the Buddha?" The master, continuing with his work, answered, "Three pounds of flax."

Another master had a habit of remaining silent and merely pointing up his thumb when asked a question like this. A disciple, seeing this and thinking cleverly to himself that there was some occult significance to this gesture, began to imitate his mentor by holding up his thumb in the same way. One day the master saw the boy do this and, quick as a flash, he whipped out a knife and cut the thumb off. When the disciple had recovered himself, he approached the master once more and brought himself to ask again the question, "What is the Buddha?" As though nothing had happened, the master held up his thumb. At that, the disciple attained enlightenment.

Perhaps this anecdote is related to the Chan saying, "When a finger is pointing at the moon, do not look at the finger." Scriptures, practices, and a good master may indeed point to the moon (a Buddhist symbol of Nirvana). But the idea is not to look at them but at where they are pointing. For the reality to which Chan points, like the Dao of the *Dao de jing,* is prior to words and cannot be reduced to them. A Chan master was once asked what the "First Principle" is. He replied, "If I told you, it would become the Second Principle!"

Once again, the truth prior to words, which Chan and Zen radiate, is that one *is* the Buddha and in Nirvana now, in the "unborn mind" before thought, and that this realization is attained not by effort but by "doing nothing" and seeing who one is when one is not oriented toward doing anything. That "empty-handed" truth is well presented in a story of Huineng (638–713), called the Sixth Patriarch of Chan in China, author of the Platform Scripture, and the man most responsible for the development of the Chan tradition.

Huineng came as a youth to the monastery of the Fifth Patriarch, Hongren. Only a poor obscure novice from the far south, then considered on the fringes of civilization, Huineng was set to such menial tasks as pounding rice.

One day the Fifth Patriarch called the monks together and announced that he would make the Sixth Patriarch whoever of them could write a poem evidencing deep understanding and true enlightenment.

One promising monk, Shenxiu (who became patriarch of the later extinct "Northern School" of Chan), wrote:

> Our body is the tree of Perfect Wisdom
> And our mind is a bright mirror.
> At all times diligently wipe them,
> So that they will be free from dust.

The Fifth Patriarch said that these lines showed understanding. But he perceived that this rather pedestrian and moralistic approach did not come near the great breakthrough possible in Chan.

The next night, an anonymous verse appeared on the bulletin board. It read:

> The tree of Perfect Wisdom is originally no tree.
> Nor has the bright mirror any frame.
> Buddha-nature is forever clear and pure.
> Where is there any dust?

Here was the insight Hongren had been looking for. True enlightenment cannot consist of obsessively trying to wipe away symbolic dust particles, but it is the marvelous freedom of realizing that one's mind, one's self, and the dust are all equally "empty" and so unbounded. The Fifth Patriarch grasped that Huineng had written this poem, secretly called him in from the rice-pounding room, and made him his successor as Sixth Patriarch.

How was the realization of one's true nature to be attained? By not striving to attain it. How does one reach a state of not-striving? Chan masters used several means. The most important is meditation: just sitting, doing nothing, striving for nothing, attaining nothing. However, Chan sitting does mean a definite posture and long hours. It produces a situation of nonstriving in which something can happen.

Many masters found that other techniques could hurry along the process of reaching nonstriving in their pupils. Some would fiercely scold, strike, and beat the disciples when they showed signs of trying too hard while missing the point, like the pupil who got his thumb sliced off. All this was intended as shock therapy to knock the novice out of the rut his thinking was in to a different perspective.

Many masters used the enigmatic Chan anecdotes, riddles, and sayings (known in the West by the Japanese names *mondo* and *koan*) such as, "What is the sound of one hand clapping?" or "Where was your face before you were born?" While these puzzles can be answered in terms of the Void and Mind Only philosophies, the real point is that such conundrums bring the ordinary, rational "monkey mind" to a stop. They stop its perpetual chatter by feeding it something it cannot handle in its usual way. Perhaps, Chan says, if the relentless mental process can be quashed for just a moment, the mind will have a chance to see what it is when it is not chattering and chewing.

But liberating what is genuinely free and spontaneous within is not easy. Unlike some shallow romantics, Chan does not confuse true spontaneity with mere self-indulgence. Liberation is not doing what you want to do, for the tradition is well aware that what the ordinary, unenlightened person thinks he or she wants to do is merely the operation of those attachment-rooted desires which, fulfilled or not, can only enslave one in the bitter syndrome of craving, anxiety, and despair. The life of a well-ordered Chan monastery was very much the reverse of a hedonistic life; through the deprivation techniques of celibacy, scanty food and sleep, hard work, long meditation in freezing halls, and on top of that sometimes physical and verbal abuse, it was hoped that the monk would find out who he is apart from the desire-wrought illusion of being a separate person.

When success comes, then the seeker is truly free—for he lives on the level of spontaneous enlightenment and Buddhahood everywhere, even in the most trivial aspects of life. One master, Huihai, when asked if he did anything special to live in the Dao, replied, "Yes; when hungry I eat, when tired, I sleep." When asked how this way differed from what ordinary people did, he replied in effect that ordinary people do not just eat when they eat, but they use eating as an occasion to let the desire-stimulated imagination run wild, thinking of what food one would like, or having conceits of how the food one is eating symbolizes one's prosperity, lifestyle, and the like; similarly, ordinary people do not just sleep when they sleep, but they lie on their beds awash with waves of restless worries, fancies, and lusts. The goal of Chan, however, is just to eat when you are hungry and sleep when you are tired—nothing more.

In the same vein, another master, Qingyuan, said that before he studied Chan for thirty years, he saw mountains as mountains and waters as waters. When he had made some progress, he no longer saw mountains as mountains and waters as waters. But when he got to the very heart of Chan, he again saw mountains as mountains and waters as waters.

The other important style of Chinese Buddhism, Pure Land, likewise evokes the freedom of nonstriving and nondependence on one's ego-self. A highly seminal early Chinese Buddhist philosopher, Daosheng (d. 434), spoke for both Chan and Pure Land when he argued that enlightenment has to be a sudden leap. Since it is a leap into the indivisible, he said, one can no more go through gradual stages of partial enlightenment than one can jump across a chasm in several steps.

But in Pure Land the structure is different; one has freedom from gradualism, striving, and self by dependence on the marvelous help of another, Amitabha Buddha, who can instantaneously and effortlessly give, out of his endless store of merit and grace, assurance to all who call upon his name that they will be reborn in his Pure Land where full enlightenment is easily available.

Amitabha, called Emiduo in Chinese and Amida in Japanese, is the Buddha in the West of the esoteric Mandala and *The Tibetan Book of the Dead,* and his Pure Land is also called the Western Paradise. It was said that countless ages ago he was an aspirant who, in setting foot on the path, vowed (the "Original Vow") that if he attained full and perfect enlightenment, out of compassion he would bring all who called upon his name into his Buddha-paradise (an enlightenment world that surrounds a Buddha like an aura, in which his devotees can dwell; not to be confused with the desire-heavens among the six lokas). Amitabha's paradise is described in marvelous terms. There are jeweled trees linked by gold threads, fields of lapis lazuli, and perfumed rivers that give off music.

While the scriptures that describe the Pure Land and Amitabha's Original Vow derive from India, it was only in China, Korea, and Japan that Pure Land became an important and distinct form of Buddhism. This was partly because, like Chan, it could easily be related to Daoist ideas—in this case, not only effortless and spontaneous release, but also popular belief in paradisal realms to the West where immortals dwelt amid fairy-tale loveliness.

In China and Japan, Amitabha became, for vast numbers of worshippers, virtually the only Buddha (assisted by Guanyin, who as mercy-working bodhisattva has generally been closely linked to Pure Land Buddhism). Amitabha came to be in effect the universal Buddha-nature; and placing trust in him, an act of release negating the individual ego in favor of harmonizing it with Nirvana or the universal. The Pure Land experience, then, ideally is not really different in character from the enlightenment experiences described in quite different words by other Buddhists.

These two doctrinal traditions, usually working closely together and not seen as inconsistent, formed the basis of Chinese Buddhism in recent centuries. The nation boasted scores of large monasteries. They followed a Chan regimen for the most part, modified by concessions to Pure Land, esoteric practices, and the economic necessity that Buddhist monks perform funeral and memorial rites; for many these rites were quite time-consuming, but they kept monks in touch with the lay public.

Monastic novices were ordained by a rite that included burning incense in several spots on the candidate's shaved head, a painful practice leaving scars intended to exemplify the bodhisattva vow to work and suffer at whatever cost for the salvation of all beings. The monasteries were headed by an elected abbot, and they were flourishing economic units busy with administering lands and dealing with pilgrims. The monks would often devote themselves to meditation and work on half-year shifts. Four monasteries on mountains in the four directions were especially important as pilgrimage centers. The roads to them would be lined with colorful shrines and hermitages; travel to these places for the sake of a vacation, enjoyment of natural beauty, and spiritual renewal all together was very popular. Many monks traveled frequently from one monastery to another in a manner akin to the wandering students of medieval Europe. Others might become hermits.

The majority of those who were students in a major monastery, however, would be receiving training like a seminarian and would sooner or later become priests in village temples. There the priest would live a fairly easy life, unless he were given to much study or spiritual practice, keeping his temple in order as a place for prayer and performing funerals, memorial rites, and other services as his parishioners required and could pay for them. Although the priest probably had Chan training, the temple would doubtless give principal encouragement to the Pure Land and Guanyin devotions as being more suitable for the laity. However, among more sophisticated urban lay Buddhists, especially of more recent times, many took one or another of the monastic vows, such as celibacy or vegetarianism, as a lay associate of a major temple and received advanced training in meditation or other practices from a distinguished master.

RELIGION IN TRADITIONAL CHINA

We began by observing that East Asian religion is generally religion of the particular place and social unit, deeply rooted in soil and family. We have, however, devoted much attention to exploring historical tracks made by the Confucian, Daoist, and Buddhist traditions; this has necessitated portraying them as three major traditions extending through time as though they were great independent causes. It is not possible to understand religious China fully without this historical and philosophical background. But in popular religion they unite to form a single spiritual world. It is now time to refocus on the particular to see how they are combined in practice.

Consider a single family in old China, the Changs. They live in a home in the countryside: the setting and ornamentation of the house itself reflects some ideas we have discussed, for when it was built its location was carefully determined so it would be at the meeting point of Yin and Yang forces in the environment and would be spiritually protected. Open places and straight lines dissipated the benevolent breath of nature and encouraged invisible evil forces; for this reason the house was situated between a sunken pond and a bamboo grove, and the road up to it was curved.

The Changs took very seriously the veneration of their ancestors. In three places they were memorialized: in the home at a small shrine to tablets bearing their names; in the chapel of the Chang clan or extended family where large tablets would be set up, rank on rank rising on higher and higher tiers the further back up the generations one went; and at the cemetery. A bit of water, incense, and food would be presented daily at the household shrine. Several times a year, the clan shrine and cemetery would be visited, cleaned, and given larger offerings and a report on family events. Ancestrism, combining very old spiritualist beliefs with Confucian filial piety toward departed parents and grandparents, was most important.

The biggest annual holiday was New Year's. At the end of the year, debts would be settled and the house cleaned. On New Year's Eve, the picture of the protective "kitchen-god," which had been hanging in the house all year, would have its mouth smeared with honey, to put it in a good mood, and would then be burned—for it was believed that this deity would then ascend to the court of the Jade Emperor to give his report on the merits and demerits of the family for the past year. On New Year's Day, itself, members of the Chang family would be gathered from far and wide, and extensive offerings of food and drink—plus a plate of soup set outside for lonely spirits without family to care for them—would be placed with bows and prayers before the family shrine, full of ancestors and protective gods. Then the family would join in a feast. Outside, they would hear firecrackers and doubtless see a Yang dragon parading down the road, animated by the feet of many men.

The Harvest Festival in the autumn would have a different, Yin sort of atmosphere, being oriented toward the moon, night, and returning spirits. Round cakes would be made, and tables set up in the courtyard of the house, both showing the fabulous palaces of the moon where Daoist immortals dwelt.

In the Chang household, sober Confucianism would have its due as well as Daoist fancy. The sons would bow to their father, and if educated, they would study first and foremost the Confucian classics. When the elder Chang died, the sons would mourn for him according to Confucian ritual—although somewhat modified and shortened—kneeling before the father's portrait or tablet, wearing a gown of rough sackcloth, and eating coarse and tasteless food.

For the funeral and subsequent memorial rites, Buddhist or Daoist priests would be called in. They would chant sutras or prayers, and burn elaborate paper houses and imitation money offerings to be used by the deceased on the Other Side. They would pray to the protecting city-god to serve as his advocate before the dread court of Yanluo. The family might discuss the possibilities before the deceased amid the many hells, heavens, and paths back to reincarnation in this world. They might well consult a medium, of Daoist ties, who would contact the departed spirit to find out what the disposition of his case had been, and how he fared, and what the living could do to help him. There were even shamanistic Daoist priests who cut themselves with knives in order to take on themselves the after-death suffering of their clients.

For answers to problems in this life, the Changs might consult a diviner who would use the ancient *Yi Jing*. He would throw coins or sticks to determine which of the sixty-four "hexagrams," or sets of six lines (some unbroken Yang lines; some broken Yin lines) unfolded the meaning of the situation in question. The text in the *Yi Jing* for that hexagram would suggest, in fairly cryptic language, whether favorable or unfavorable lines of force were in operation, whether it was a time for action or waiting, and the like. This book, now popular in the West, is perhaps the oldest extant Chinese book in its most ancient parts; it is one of the Confucian classics, yet it also expresses a Daoistic philosophy. In its own way it epitomizes a Chinese world view that underlies both traditions based on a profound sense of the continual, rhythmic interaction of visible and invisible forces within a unified world process to which humankind must gently and wisely accommodate itself.[21]

From time to time a representative of the Chang family would go to one of the temples in the locality. The temples could vary from tiny edifices with images the size of a doll, to huge structures with giant, superhuman gods of awesome countenance. Some would be Daoist, some Buddhist, some mixed. But it should be realized that they were homes of the gods, not generally places of congregational worship. When Mr. Chang or another of the family visited the temple, it was generally to ask a favor or pay respects, as one would to a powerful neighbor. Most frequently the visit would be to ask advice of the deity, done by throwing two woodblocks, drawing a printed oracle, or perhaps consulting a medium retained by the temple. Sometimes the family representative would make an offering of incense or paper temple money in thanksgiving for a favor, or in response to a vow. This worship would be done especially at earth-god shrines—humble but ubiquitous temples to deities of the soil older and closer to the people than any of the major faiths, in the spring for the crops, and in the fall in thanksgiving for the harvest. Food might be presented to the deity, but it would be brought back home for a feast.

At irregular intervals, depending on local custom, the temple would hold a great festival. Brilliant red candles would be burned around the divine image, priests would perform elaborate rituals such as a secret Daoist *jiao,* and villagers and visitors alike would throng the temple with offerings and divinations. The temple courtyard would be set up like a fair, with booths and amusements and colorful pageantry. There would be ranks of offerings, particularly pigs, presented by families and businesses. Here the Chang family might well be represented, and the family members (except women in a traditional middle and upper class family) would delightedly attend.

If Mr. Chang were of the mandarin class, he would also go to the nearest Confucian temple at the two equinoxes to join with his peers in the old dances and offerings presented to the Wise and Holy Sage by his latter-day disciples. He would probably also take part in the rites of the city-god, the protector of the town, honoring him with thanks and perhaps punishing him when misfortune struck, for his cultus was part of the official religion.

Then again, one day Mr. Chang or someone else in the family might become pious, or at least acquire a wanderlust, and go on a pilgrimage to some Buddhist or Daoist monastery on a cloud-wrapped mountaintop or an isolated island. There he would break his routine by living with the monks for a spell, sharing their meals and conversation, and renewing his spirit in a setting of exalted beauty.

The Chang family, then, would be touched by the attitudes and institutional life of all three of the great traditions, and by ancestrism and the earth-gods as well. This combined experience is nowhere better expressed than in the first part of the old Chinese fantasy novel *Monkey.*[22] In it, the Buddha and the Jade Emperor visit and consult with one another; dragon-kings, bodhisattvas, and sages with the secret of immortality move in and out of the narrative—yet the monkey-hero, like the sturdy peasant farmers of China, when needful employs both wiles and wonders to combat authority, even the hosts of heaven itself, to preserve the autonomy of himself and his household.

RELIGION IN THE PEOPLE'S REPUBLIC OF CHINA

Today this tradition is broken irrevocably. It still survives in Taiwan, Hong Kong, Singapore, and other Chinese outposts outside the People's Republic of China; but on the mainland, for that vast majority of Chinese who represent a quarter of the earth's population, the situation is very different. To understand how such an immense cultural and religious change could come about, it is necessary to know something of the history of China during the long, wrenching, and often dreadful hundred years from the middle of the nineteenth to the middle of the twentieth century. During this time, China underwent tremendous shock and change, not the least to its traditional ideological and religious systems.

The fundamental factor that made the shocks of this era even more climactic and catastrophic than those that accompanied earlier changes of dynasty was the incursion of the Western powers—demanding trade, missionary rights, and often inordinate influence on Chinese affairs. Trouble began in earnest with the Opium War of 1839–42, when Great Britain brought the Chinese imperial regime to its knees for the sake of preserving its trade in opium with China, which the government of the latter had properly tried to control. Britain won a large indemnity and forced the opening of five ports to British trade and residence; she also received Hong Kong. In the Second Opium War, 1856–60, Britain and France together obtained, after capturing Peking and burning the vast imperial summer palace, further port concessions, the right of foreign residence and travel in the Chinese interior, and full freedom for Christian missionary activity together with legalization by China of the profitable opium trade.

The impact of these humiliations, and of the countless subsequent little humiliations inflicted upon a proud people by the presence of privileged and often insensitive and exploitative foreigners, went far beyond the immediate terms of the treaties forced by these wars. The weakness of the Qing regime before the Westerners inevitably tended to discredit it, and in the eyes of many thoughtful persons the whole system upon which it was based, down to its ideological and religious roots, seemed anachronistic and discredited as well. A host of alternatives, ranging from reactionary to radical, arose to try to fill the void.

The most important in the nineteenth century, as well as the most interesting religiously, was the Tai Bing, "Great Peace," revolution, which controlled large portions of south China between 1850–1864. Its founder was Hong Xiuchuan. He was a visionary and failed civil service examinee who, having had contact with a Baptist missionary from America, believed that Jesus had appeared to him and pronounced him his "younger brother," with a commission to reform China on the pattern of the Kingdom of God. Hong and his followers advocated equal distribution of wealth, equality of the sexes, strict morality, and a disciplined society. Riding the crest of widespread discontent, the Tai Bing revolution was initially successful and established its capital in Nanjing. But eventually, weakened by internal dissension, it was suppressed by the imperial government with the help of Western officers. The episode was another blow to Qing power and prestige nevertheless, and the subsequent Nationalist and Communist movements alike were clearly partially inspired by the Tai Bing.

In 1912, after other traumatic vicissitudes, such as the Boxer Rebellion (with its roots in magical Daoism) of 1900, the lingering death of imperial China was finally consummated with the establishment of a republic. Inspired by Western democratic idealism, its history was, in reality, rocky and sometimes ignoble. The central government was rarely able to control either large-scale corruption or the power of avaricious local warlords, and just after it seemed in the late 1920s that it might be beginning to make headway against China's immense problems, the republic was dealt further staggering blows by Japanese military incursions and World War II.

During the period of the Republic, Confucianism declined in influence with the disestablishment of the state cultus, Buddhism experienced a modest revival, there was considerable Christian missionary activity—and the Communist Party of China, full of high dedication and radical solutions, flourished more and more.

Upon the triumph of Communism in 1949, numerous missionaries and Buddhist monks, together with the Daoist "pope," fled to Hong Kong and Taiwan. But the bulk of their followers remained behind to contend as best they could with the new regime. That government, the People's Republic of China, was not a state which professed any sympathy for religion.

In accordance with general Marxist theory, Chinese Communism saw religion as essentially the product of feudal conditions and bound to fade away as the circumstances of alienation and exploitation between classes disappeared. More specifically, religion was held to have two roots, the "social" and the "cognitive." The social root refers to the fact that exploiting classes have used religion to help secure their position by teaching the masses submission to their lot through the lips of gods, priests, and missionaries. The cognitive root of religion is its origin in the backward, prescientific understanding of nature in the countryside.[23] The Communist society, Chinese Marxism taught, would eliminate both these roots and so allow religion to fade away. But policy has veered sharply between letting social evolution take its natural course and trying to force its hand.

To comprehend Chinese Communist attitudes and policies toward religion fairly, we must consider the condition of Chinese religion in the previously discussed era of traumatic change that led up to 1949. It is quite a different picture from that of Western religion in the same century. The creative periods of Chinese religion were long since past, despite abortive attempts at Confucian and Buddhist philosophical revival. In the eyes of their many critics, the former was eclipsed by historical change, while Daoist and Buddhist priests were either anachronistic relics who catered to gross superstition for fees, or monastic mystics removed from the world and seemingly unconcerned with the awesome problems of changing China. The Catholic and Protestant missionaries who swarmed over China, while purveyors of more up-to-date medicine and education, were in the eyes of the Communists, despite individual exceptions, too closely aligned with the imperialistic powers and therefore only imperialists of another kind.

Communist reaction passed through several clearly defined stages. The first (1950–52) was a period of consolidation of the new regime. All foreign elements were forced out of China; this meant a mass exodus of missionaries together with many Christian Chinese clergy and believers. Religious bodies remaining on the mainland were pressured into forming themselves into "patriotic" organizations. In 1950, the Protestant National Christian Council adopted a Manifesto rejecting foreign missionary aid and supporting the new government's policies of independence and social transformation. A Patriotic Association of Chinese Catholics was gradually built up by a combination of indoctrination and persecution of recalcitrants to loosen the Chinese Catholic Church from its international connections. By 1958, Catholic dioceses were making their own bishops independent of the Vatican, and Catholicism in China was a schismatic and autonomous church. A Chinese Buddhist Association was formed to similar ends in 1953. It represented both Chinese Buddhism and the Chinese diplomatic line in international Buddhist gatherings, and at home assured that Buddhist monks and clergy engaged in appropriate self-criticism, shared in the manual and mental labor of constructing a new China, and that those allowed to remain as Buddhist spokesmen or temple incumbents maintained the right ideological stance. While Confucianism was only criticized and Daoism received little consideration, some Buddhist institutions were permitted to survive in the People's Republic, chiefly as showplaces to enhance the new China's image in the rest of the Buddhist world.

The period of 1952 to 1960 was a time of relative cooperation between the new society and the reorganized religious bodies. There was an increasing tendency to align religious thought with Marxism. This was particularly true among "patriotic" Buddhists, who did not hesitate to compare the Marxist utopia with Nirvana—since in both desire is eliminated—and the revolutionary struggle with the tortuous quest for enlightenment. But the 1950s were also a time when persecution of uncooperative religionists was harsh. Innumerable churches and temples—those not designated as showplaces—were confiscated for more productive use as schools or warehouses, and the great majority of monks were defrocked to join the workers in factory and field. In particular, the great Buddhist religious and cultural tradition of Tibet was brutally extirpated.

Nonetheless, in the early 1960s reports came of a resurgence of religion, particularly Buddhism. Accounts of foreign visitors interested in religion between 1960 and 1965 indicated that, at the least, religion of all sorts was ostensibly being practiced routinely and without hindrance; churches and temples, while far diminished in number from before the revolution, were in full swing. But it was the proverbial calm before the storm.

The Great Cultural Revolution of 1966 to 1969, with the young Red Guards in its vanguard, swept through China, leaving virtually no locale or institution untouched. Fired by a drive to suppress all that was old and a desire, perhaps contrived by the aging Mao Zedong himself, to renew revolutionary fervor at the expense of social stability, its cohorts disrupted education, harried enemies, defaced monuments of the past, and left nearly all religious places ransacked and closed. Such religious life as survived went deep underground.

Much was made in this period by outside observers of the religious character of "Maoism" itself. Certainly the phenomena suggested such an interpretation. Chinese

Communism had a "sacred history" repeated over and over in dramas and monuments. Its great programmatic rallies had a quality little short of sacred ritual. The famous "little red book" containing the sayings of Chairman Mao was read like scripture and, carried constantly about and eagerly held up by the faithful, doubled as a holy talisman. Above all, Mao himself was hymned and praised in language that made him hardly less than deity.

Yet if Maoism was a religion, it turned out to be one of the world's most ephemeral. After the Great Cultural Revolution had run its course by around 1970 and the need for a return to normality was apparent to almost everyone, fervent Maoism was definitely in recession and more traditional religion recovered its foothold. Following the death of Mao in 1976 and the subsequent purging of the "Gang of Four," who allegedly wanted a return to the policies of the Cultural Revolution, little more was heard of it.

The pragmatic leadership that subsequently governed China took a generally nonextremist stance toward religion, allowing a return to the conditions of the early 1960s. It sought above all the stability that is necessary for solid advances in education, technology, and the standard of living. Moreover, its desire to improve relations with the United States and other Western nations led it to avoid giving any impression of oppressing religions, especially Christianity. International, as well as internal, considerations have also led this regime to adopt a conciliatory attitude toward China's much larger Muslim population (about 5 percent, mostly minorities located in the far north and northwest). Pressure was considerably eased on Tibetan Buddhism.

Reports from China in the 1980s have indicated that certain religious institutions were flourishing, although discreetly controlled. Catholic churches, for example, were full but still had little relation with Rome. In assessing such reports, however, one must never forget that only a very small percentage of China's vast population is religiously active in any sense—far less than, for example, in the Soviet Union. The real religious significance of contemporary China lies in the fact that it, a quarter of the world's people, is beyond doubt the most thoroughly postreligious, secular society the world has yet seen. Its success in the years to come in meeting both the material and subjective needs of its citizens will provide data for very searching critiques of religion and secularism alike.[24]

In 1989, however, news from China was full of foreboding for the future of freedom—religious or other—in that ancient land. First, unrest in Tibet led to severe repression. Then, in May and June, vast peaceful "pro-democracy" demonstrations by students in Tiananmen Square, in the heart of Beijing, the capital, attracted worldwide attention and sympathy, only to be brutally suppressed with much loss of life by the army. The students were clearly in the venerable Confucian tradition of the scholar, without regard for personal risk, remonstrating the government on behalf of virtue. Significantly, they were also quoted as citing outside apostles of nonviolent activism, such as Thoreau, Gandhi, and King. The government, in turn, represented the classic Chinese tradition of authoritarian control at its harshest.

SHINTO IN JAPAN

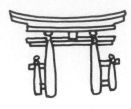

Torii

Let us now return to the Shinto shrine in the grove as we move from China to Japan. Comparably to the Chinese city-god and ancestral chapel, the shrine expresses Japanese religion's rootedness in place and family. But typically the Shinto shrine will have a light, lean construction, contrasting with the heavy and ornate quality of Chinese temples. Shinto shrines, and the Shinto religious complex, have distinctive attitudes and practices to go with the unique architecture. If we were to remain around a Shinto shrine and observe its activity, we would see things happen that would bring out four basic affirmations that are inherent in Shinto: affirmation of tradition, of life in this world, of purity, and of festival.

Virtually every Shinto shrine has its unique set of traditions: what festivals are celebrated, what rituals are performed. Some are ancient and some less so, but all strongly link the present with the past; they appear in the midst of modern Japan like time capsules from earlier centuries. The traditions of some shrines present brilliant spectacles drawing vast throngs of tourists; others are of only local interest. But in any case, the observer will note that while Shintoists may have little idea exactly why a rite is performed in a certain manner, or what it means theologically or philosophically, the action will be done in a precisely prescribed way.

The fire to cook the offerings may be started with a traditional fire drill, a ring of evergreen may be set up in the same way each year for people to walk through to remove pollution. What is really being affirmed is not so much the importance of this or that particular custom as the importance of having tradition itself, of living in the presence of visible carryovers from ages gone by, with all their color and evocative power. For millions of modern Japanese, living in a rapidly changing technological world, this role of embodying a traditional past they do not want entirely to lose is the most important function of Shinto, and one very precious to them.

The affirmation of tradition is clearly related to the motif of affirmation of life in this world. Shinto, the religion of clans and their communal spirit, of joyous festivals and bountiful harvests, affirms the good things of this world and the natural relationships. Its land of the dead is shadowy and its mystical and intellectual life relatively undeveloped. But in the exuberant festivals of harvest, or the stately splendor of ancient dance and ritual, Shinto comes into its own. Most Japanese tend to think of Shinto as religion concerned with the high and happy moments of this life, and Buddhism with somber and profound things, such as suffering and death. People are married and babies are blessed in Shinto shrines; funerals and memorial services are held in Buddhist temples.

This affirmation is related to another important Shinto motif: the distinction between purity and pollution. Shinto shrines, demarcated off by their torii, represent pure spaces in the midst of a polluted world. Upon entering the shrine precincts, one washes, and rituals begin with the symbolic sweeping away of impurity with a green branch. What is fresh, lively, and bright is pure; what is stagnant, decaying,

Main Themes of Japanese Religion

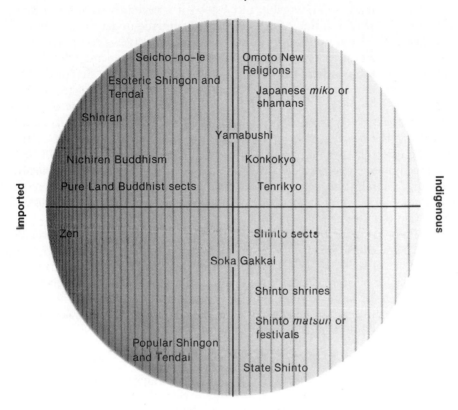

Individual Experience

Seicho-no-Ie

Esoteric Shingon and Tendai

Shinran

Nichiren Buddhism

Pure Land Buddhist sects

Zen

Omoto New Religions

Japanese *miko* or shamans

Yamabushi

Konkokyo

Tenrikyo

Shinto sects

Soka Gakkai

Shinto shrines

Shinto *matsuri* or festivals

Popular Shingon and Tendai

State Shinto

Imported

Indigenous

Community Religion

THEMATIC CHART V. Not only has Japanese religion and culture long been sharply aware of the distinction between traditions indigenous to Japan and those motifs imported from the Asian mainland or (more recently) the West, it has also long been riven by two modes of experiencing the gods, rites, and religious personalities of both: as sanctifiers of stable community life and as shamanistic conveyors of intensity and new revelation.

sick, or dying is impure. Blood, disease, and death are the most impure things. A dead body would not be brought into a shrine; on the rare occasion of a Shinto funeral, the rite is held at another place. Through its avoidance of impurity, Shinto affirms the persistence and superiority of life and joy.

The fourth motif is festival. As we have seen, the quiet, inactive shrine in its wood or beside its stream may have an air of still purity, but it is not until the kami is stirred to vigorous life by the drums of a matsuri, or Shinto festival, that the full color and dynamism of the divine side of reality is manifested. For one who has been at a matsuri, the sylvan quietude of the shrine on ordinary days, when only individual worshippers approach it to clap twice and pray, has a feel of expectant waiting about it. The still drum plainly visible on the open porch at the front of the shrine, and the dance pavillion, remind one of another mood.

To fully understand Shinto worship and festival, it is necessary to have a mental picture of the structure of a shrine. After the visitor has entered under the crossbeams of the torii and passed the purificatory font, he or she approaches the porch with its drum, *gohei,* or zigzag paper streamers, and other accouterments; this is the *haiden,* or hall of worship, where the laity pray and sacred dance is offered. Behind it, but visible from the front, is a second segment with a curious eight-legged table for offerings; this is the *heiden,* or hall of offerings. Behind the table, the observer will note a set of extremely steep steps leading up to a massive, richly ornamented door. It leads to the *honden,* an enclosed room much higher than the rest of the shrine and the symbolic dwelling place of the kami himself. In this room will be a heavily wrapped object called the *shintai,* "body" of the god—an old sword, mirror, inscription, or something else—which from ancient times has been the sacred presence of divinity in this shrine, in a manner somewhat analogous to the reserved sacrament in a Roman Catholic church.

Formal Shinto worship occurs at varying intervals, depending on the importance of the shrine. Some small shrines without a resident priest will enjoy offerings only two or three times a year; others will have services monthly, or every ten days, or daily in a few major shrines. Special rites commissioned on behalf of families and groups are common at larger shrines too. The spring and fall festivals will usually be the most important matsuri. However, many shrines also have very colorful and dramatic midsummer rites directed against evil influences. New Year's is a time of considerable shrine activity too, especially for private visits.

All full Shinto worship follows a basic structure. It can be remembered by a series of four words beginning with the letter *P:* purification, presentation, prayer, and participation.

First, a priest, dressed in white or perhaps lightly colored garments and a high black hat (derived from ancient court costumes) may, according to local usage, wave a branch or stick with paper or sprinkle salt or water over the heads of the people gathered in the courtyard as a rite of purification.

Then the priest will enter the shrine and present the offerings, very neatly arranged, before the kami-presence on the eight-legged table—or on very important occasions he will open the great doors and lay them on the floor of the honden. The presentation is accompanied by dramatically accelerating drumbeats and perhaps the eerie tones of reed flutes. The offerings, mostly fruit, vegetables, rice, seafood, salt, water, and rice wine, are borne up and arranged with reverent care.

Then, all in order on the altar, the priest reads a formal prayer, either silently or in a high chanting voice.

Next follows one of several possibilities, depending on the elaborateness of the occasion and the resources of the shrine. While the offerings are still on the altar, formal dance may be presented as part of the offering and as a representation of the divine presence to the worshippers. At the close of the service, individuals

Shinto priestess in Meiji Shrine, Tokyo.

may present as an offering a small branch, as though to show their participation, and as a kind of holy communion partake of a tiny bit of the wine and perhaps other offerings. (Prior to this, the offerings had been solemnly removed from the altar.)

Particularly at the main annual matsuri, vivid local activities affording everyone participation in the festival spirit occur. These will be as exuberant as the offering and prayer were solemn, suggesting a dramatic, divine change of pace as the kami-spirit animates his people. The kami may be borne through the streets in a palanquin by young men zigzagging and shouting. All over the shrine grounds, booths are set up as for a carnival, with cotton candy stalls and sumo wrestling exhibitions. As soon as the offerings are removed, it is understood that the solemn part is over, the booths are opened, and crowds throng onto the carnival grounds with laughter and squealing children.

In some great shrines, splendid parades, historical pageants, folk dances, medieval horse racing or archery performances, fireworks, indeed an almost endless variety of traditional activities, may be parts of the "participation" aspect of the matsuri. Some are rustic fairs little known outside the locality; some take months of professional preparation and draw spectators from around the world.

So far we have described only Shinto shrines and worship, saying nothing about the particular deities who are the recipients of this worship. This is not inappropriate, for to most Japanese the name and story of a particular kami means little; it is the shrine, worship, and festival itself that counts. A partial exception is the familiar

---

Fundamental Features of Shinto

Theoretical

Basic World View	Universe is pluralistic, having many gods. It is growing and changing. Nature, humanity, and the divine are not sharply separated.
God or Ultimate Reality	Many kami.
Origin of the World	Generated by the gods.
Destiny of the World	Unknown, but historical progress has meaning.
Origin of Humans	Descended from kami.
Destiny of Humans	Unclear; perhaps to become kami or merge with kami.
Revelation or Mediation Between the Ultimate and the Human	Myths; traditions, and festivals of shrines where one approaches the kami presence.

Practical

What Is Expected of Humans: Worship, Practices, Behavior	To remember and celebrate the gods, remain pure and sincere, enjoy life. Support the societies of which kami are patrons.

Sociological

Major Social Institutions	Shrines, with the *ujiko* community of each. Family, work, and regional ties with particular shrines important.

Inari shrines, distinguished by their red torii and stone foxes, to which people go to pray for prosperity. But Shintoists are far from having the kind of relation to their kami as Hindu bhaktas with Shiva or Krishna; Japanese religion, like the Japanese temperament, is much more reserved and formal.

Nonetheless, the kami do have names and myths. In many cases they are only local. But there is also a national myth in which some of the shrine kami appear, recorded in two of the oldest books in Japanese, the *Kojiki* (712 C.E.) and the *Nihonshoki* (720 C.E.), compiled by order of the imperial court to present its divine descent and commission.[25] Not all important shrine kami have major roles in this myth. But it is important for two reasons: It illustrates many of the basic Shinto motifs, and it explicates the relation between Shinto and sovereignty.

The *Kojiki* and *Nihonshoki,* although written early in the sixth century, often reflect the world of prehistoric religion. In those days, the Japanese were divided into *uji,* or clans. Each had a kami who was the spiritual guard and guide of his people. The clan chieftain was the priest who presented offerings and prayer to this deity, usually at an outdoor altar by a stream or on a hilltop, for this was even before the day of shrine buildings. It appears that a woman, probably wife or relative of the chief, served as official shamaness and would go into trance and deliver messages from the clan deity regarding matters of state.

One clan, ancestors of the present imperial family of Japan, seems to have long had an ill-defined paramountcy among the clans out of which the Japanese state emerged. The early emperors themselves had a consort or princess who served as oracle. Indeed, if reports of Chinese travelers and mythical histories are to be believed, on one or two occasions the shamaness herself ruled as a sort of sorceress-queen.

Although each clan had its own divine patron, people were aware that their own kami was but one, although the one they knew best, of a larger pantheon of gods. Early Shinto prayers speak of "the gods of heaven and the gods of earth." The religious world view centered on feeling that there were two classes of gods, of sky and soil, and that the world advances through dynamic interaction between the two. The fundamental pattern in Japanese myth is for male gods to descend from heaven, marry female kami of the earth, and produce children who, as sons of both earth and heaven, have great and versatile power; the greatest heroes and clan kami are of this type.

This pattern fit well the religious outlook of farmers after the introduction of rice agriculture between 300 B.C.E. and 300 C.E. It was believed that the heavenly kami descended on top of mountains in the spring, and villagers would ascend to greet them with festivity. They would be brought into the fields to mate with the female kami of the soil and rice, work to bring in the crop-child, and then be thanked and sent off at the harvest festival.

The national myth in the *Kojiki* and *Nihonshoki* tells us that in the beginning the High Kami in heaven sent the primal parents, the male Izanagi and the female Izanami, down from the High Plain of Heaven. They indulged in a virtual orgy of procreation, giving birth to islands and gods, until Izanami was burned to death upon the birth of the fire-god. Izanagi tried to bring his wife out of the underworld, but he was unable to do so because she had already eaten of its food. Izanagi then exchanged boasts with Izanami about the greater power of life than death. He bathed in the ocean to cleanse himself of the pollution of the underworld; from his washings were born several great gods, above all Amaterasu, the lovely goddess associated with the sun and ancestress of the imperial house. Here we see two Shinto themes: the affirmation of life and the importance of purification.

In heaven, Amaterasu once hid herself in a cave when her brother greatly offended her at the harvest festival; she was drawn out when a goddess did a ribald dance and another kami held up a mirror to the solar goddess's curious emerging face; this story suggests the Shinto affirmation of festivity and reminds us that ancient mirrors are often symbols of deity.

Later, Amaterasu gave the same mirror (now said by tradition to be enshrined as sacred object in the Grand Shrine of Ise) to her grandson, who was sent down from heaven to establish the line of sovereigns on earth. This brings us to another aspect of Shinto, its relationship to the Japanese state.

During the period of modern nationalism in Japan up to 1945, this mythical divine descent of the imperial house and the accompanying ancient belief that the emperor is himself in a mysterious sense a "manifest deity" was used (often in a rather cynical way) to focus extreme loyalty and to justify militaristic policy. The ancient role of the emperor, however, was one of sacred kingship in the priestly sense; in most periods of Japanese history, he has exercised very little real power. He has a special role toward the kami, however, which is well expressed in the Daijo-sai, the harvest festival as celebrated by the emperor after his accession.[26]

Before ending a discussion of Shinto, a word must be said about the Grand Shrine of Ise, a site that beautifully combines all the motifs of this religion. The Grand Shrine, located on the east coast south of Nagoya, is really two major shrines about five miles apart—one dedicated to Amaterasu and said to enshrine the mirror she gave to Prince Ninigi; the other dedicated to Toyouke, goddess of food. The shrines are set amid splendid old trees not far from clear streams in which pilgrims purify themselves. In the vicinity are a number of lesser shrines and places where the offerings of food and cloth are prepared by ancient means. As the shrine of the chief imperial ancestress, Ise has long had a special relation to the imperial household; emperors report important events to the goddess, and offerings from the imperial household are presented by envoys in ancient court dress on important festivals. In a very interesting rite of renewal, every twenty years the shrines are taken down after new shrines, exactly identical to the old, have been erected with many traditional ceremonies in lots adjacent to the old sites; at the Harvest Festival, the sacred objects are moved with impressive solemnity from the old to the new shrines.[27]

The word *Shinto* actually means "The Way of the Gods," and the *to,* "way," is the Chinese Dao. Shinto is a broad path offering a pattern of rites, attitudes, and subtle experiences that harmonize humankind with the many faces of its spiritual environment in the context of an ancient culture.

Shrine Shinto is just one part of a complex Japanese religious synthesis related to Shinto. From the beginning of historical times until the late nineteenth century, Shinto and Buddhism coexisted in a sort of symbiosis. Shinto and Buddhist places of worship would be put together, a pagoda in the courtyard of a shrine or a small shrine in the precincts of a temple. The kami was considered a protector, pupil, or form of manifestation of the Buddha; one school made it the other way around. In any case, Buddha and kami were a unified display of the sacred for the average worshipper, and not in competition. Only in 1868 did a new, modernizing government require the separation of Shinto and Buddhism, in its eagerness to make Shinto a vehicle for nationalistic expression. The present distinctiveness of Shinto and Buddhist places of worship dates from that time.

Confucianism and Daoism, early imported from China, have also been important factors in general Japanese spirituality. Both were influences shaping the earliest organization of Japanese society on the continental model. In the Heian period, formal education as well as the formal organization of the bureaucracy was Confucian in pattern. Daoist-related directional taboos and calendric gods appear in Heian literature; by early modern times these beliefs and much else of religious Daoism had worked their way down to affect Japanese folk religion. This effect can be seen in the account of the Japanese shamaness in Chapter 2.

Neo-Confucianism, introduced through Zen, was important in Japan particularly in the Tokugawa period (1600–1867), when it was virtually a state ideology, although it rarely took explicitly religious expression in Japan. Japanese Neo-Confucian thinkers greatly emphasized obligation and loyalty to one's feudal lord, as in *bushido*, or the samurai knightly code, to the emperor, as well as to parents; their importance in forming general Japanese values is great. In the modern nationalistic period, the Japanese Confucian concept of high loyalty to the sovereign combined well with the Shinto myths of imperial divine descent to give nationalism a moral and sacred aura.

These themes come together in Japanese ancestrism. Ancestral memorial tablets are most often on home Buddhist altars, just as funerals are usually conducted out of Buddhist temples. Yet ancestrism is related to Shinto since (although whether this was originally the case is debatable) the kami have come to be widely regarded as ancestors or relatives to the families of which they are patrons, on the model of Amaterasu and the imperial family itself. Confucian teachings of loyalty and filial piety gave great impetus to ancestrism in Japan as well.

Mention should also be made of Christianity in Japan. Catholicism was brought in by Francis Xavier and his Jesuit missionaries in 1549; the Jesuits were later supplemented by Franciscans. For several decades—times of immense social disorder in Japan—they were remarkably successful. But around the turn of the century, and especially after the accession of Tokugawa power in 1600, Christians suffered horrible persecution and finally seemed to be eliminated entirely. Yet when the first modern Catholic missionaries came to Japan in 1868, they were surprised to be met in some towns and villages by people called *kakure Kirishitan,* "hidden Christians," who had kept a garbled "underground" version of the earlier missionary faith alive for two and a half centuries. Protestant churches were established after 1868 as well.

BUDDHISM IN JAPAN

Nearly as common as Shinto shrines, and also of graceful wooden architecture but without the torii, are the Buddhist temples of Japan. However, the Buddhist edifices are likely to be larger than the shrines, with room for throngs of worshippers within. The temple will be dominated by imposing Buddhist images, some perhaps large and of a deeply glowing gold. These images personify a spiritual force that is not as old in Japan as the kami, who go back to misty prehistory, but is as old as history itself. For with the coming of Buddhism to Japan came writing, new models for art and governmental organization, many material boons of continental civilization, the keeping of records, and consciousness of history.

Buddhism arrived in Japan from Korea in the early sixth century. Early Japan long had closer ties with the Korean peninsula than with China proper, even to the extent of maintaining military and trading settlements there. In the sixth century, Buddhism had just come to Korea from Tang China, and in China itself it had only been a strong influence for some three centuries. It still was a young and dynamic enthusiasm in that part of the world, and the *Ninonshoki* says a Korean king, anxious to cement an alliance, sent the Japanese emperor a Buddhist image and scriptures.[28]

But we must remember that as new as Buddhism seemed then, that faith already had behind it nearly a thousand years of development. Mahayana, Tantrism, temple architecture, sutras, images, mandalas, schools such as Chan and Pure Land—all these had reached mature forms before Buddhism touched the shamanistic and nearly unlettered people of old Japan.

Buddhism came, therefore, as a powerfully more sophisticated culture, with splendors of art and subtleties of concept undreamed of before. It was far from well understood, but it was a force and a presence that could hardly be avoided. As they have done repeatedly since, the Japanese responded initially with debate between the desire to keep their culture intact and the desire to be open to everything foreign that seemed advanced and advantageous; then as later, they swung between extremes on each hand. But from then on, Buddhism was an increasingly deeply rooted part of Japanese culture.

The first great Buddhist era was the Nara period (710–84), named after the first permanent Japanese capital, established in that ancient and beautiful city in order to provide a court in the continental model. The government, immensely proud of its new Buddhist culture, lavishly endowed temples and monasteries. The lovely Nara park, with its shrine and pagoda and tame deer, is a momento of this era, as is the magnificent Great Buddha in the Todaiji temple. The latter is really the Sun Buddha, Vairocana, and indicates that from the beginning Japanese Buddhism was shaped by the more expansive and mystic forms of Mahayana. This temple belongs to the Kegon denomination, which emphasizes the presence of the Buddha-nature in all things—every blade of grass and every grain of sand. The giant Buddha Vairocana is really the Dharmakaya, and behind him is sculpted a great array of smaller Buddhas, to indicate that the Sun Buddha is reflected as in countless mirrors in the Buddhas of innumerable worlds.

The artistic and mystical splendors of Nara were not without price, however. The temples claimed great holdings of tax-free land and received valuable gifts from wealthy patrons. But the result was a larger gulf between the elite and the peasants, and a greater exploitation of the latter.

Nonetheless, the countryside also had some glimmer of the power of the new Buddhism. Although the official "six sects" of Nara Buddhism with their sophisticated glories belonged to the world of the aristocrats, the country people had their own version of the Buddha's path. It was a Buddhism in continuity with the old religion of shamans and Shinto mountain gods, a shamanistic Buddhism comparable to that of Tibet: rustic magicians, healers, and diviners under nominal Buddhist influence, called *ubasoku,* ranged the countryside.[29]

Passerby praying at Buddhist shrine in Tokyo.

Thereafter, down through the centuries, two kinds of Buddhism—the official-orthodox and the popular-shamanistic—have existed as poles in Japan. The shamanistic side has most recently emerged in some of the new religions of today. But there has also been continual movement toward rapprochement between the two poles. Even in the Nara period, the Emperor Shomu, when he wished to raise support for the building of the Great Buddha as a sort of national cathedral, was forced to call on the great popular ubasoku leader Gyogi (670–749) for assistance and make him chief Buddhist priest of the nation.

The Buddhist denominations that flourished in the next period, the Heian, advanced the reconciliation, for they combined power at the highest levels of society with ancient mountain and shamanistic themes. The capital was moved from Nara in 781 and established in the new city of Heian (modern Kyoto) ten years later. The basic reason for the move was the excessive political role of the priesthood in the former site, which culminated in an ambitious court chaplain's becoming romantically involved with an empress. Perhaps, lay authorities thought, if Nara teeming with monks is left behind, a new and better start can be made elsewhere.

But on Mount Hiei, the northeast guardian of the valley where the new capital was situated, there dwelt a hermit named Saicho, known posthumously as Dengyo Daishi (762–822). His enthusiasm was the Lotus Sutra as interpreted by the Tiantai school in China, which made it the final and culminating expression of the Buddha's teaching—a comprehensive umbrella under which all sorts of practices from Pure

Land to esotericism could be seen as ways to realize the eternal Buddhahood in all things, which makes all things absolutely real just as they are.

Saicho gathered about him a group of disciples. When the capital moved to Heian the emperor made it possible for him to go to China to study at the great Tiantai monastery. When he returned in 805, he established the monastery on Mount Hiei called the Enryaku-ji, the home monastery of the Tendai denomination in Japan. For many centuries Mount Hiei was the most significant of all religious centers in Japan, for its nearness to the capital made it politically important, and its influence on the future spiritual history of Japan is incomparable. The monks of Mount Hiei often swept down to demonstrate before the palace until their demands were met, and future independent Buddhist movements—Pure Land, Nichiren, and even Zen—had roots in the comprehensive Tendai system, and their leaders trained on Mount Hiei. On this spectacular mountaintop, with its magnificent old mossy trees, clear streams, and isolated temples scattered deep in the woods, meditations were made which shaped the future.

A contemporary of Saicho, Kukai, posthumously called Kobo Daishi (773–835), founder of the Shingon denomination, was an even more remarkable personality. Many legends testify to his brilliance and charismatic power. Stories suggest that he spent long years in mental and psychophysical training in the tradition of the shamanistic Buddhists. Above all, however, he was interested in synthesis, in attaining the most comprehensive truth. In 797 Saicho wrote a book trying to synthesize Daoism, Confucianism, and Buddhism.

His remarkable intellect attracted imperial attention, and Kukai like Saicho was sent to China, where he stayed from 804 to 806. His bent led him to the study of Tantric Buddhism. Above all he was attracted to the Great Sun Sutra (*Mahavairocana Sutra*), with its teaching of esoteric practices by which an adept could become one with the essence of the universe. When he returned to Japan, Kukai established a great monastery on Mount Koya, some sixty mountainous miles south of Kyoto and still a fabulous treasury of art, history, and spiritual practice.

Shingon considers the Great Sun Buddha, known as Dainichi in Japanese and Mahavairocana in Sanskrit, to be the central deity, who personifies the Dharmakaya, the cosmic unitary essence. Kobo Daishi taught that one can become a Buddha in this body, in this lifetime, through the esoteric "three secrets" he taught: mudras (hand gestures), dharani (mystic chants), and yoga (meditation, including evocations).

Shingon uses rich symbols, rituals, and art. They are sacred because they manifest the Buddha-nature latent in all things—to make an image of the Buddha out of a piece of wood brings out the Buddha-nature of the wood, and in the process is a kind of meditation for the artist. Above all, Shingon makes use of great mandalas, which manifest the hidden realities and lines of force in the universe.[30]

The next period, the Kamakura (1185–1333), was a different kind of age with different values. The Heian order broke down in the Middle Ages basically for economic reasons, in which the wealthy, nonproductive monasteries played their part. Military leaders of clans in outlying regions rose up, and one house, the Minamoto, became supreme. While preserving the imperial institution in Kyoto, the new overlords established the political capital far away in Kamakura, on modern Tokyo Bay, under a shogun, as the ruler was called, who administered the nation in the emperor's name.

If Heian was dominated by the elegant refined courtier and the esoteric monk, Kamakura was characterized by the simple, direct warrior. Moreover, times were troubled, and pessimism was in the air. People talked of the Buddhist idea of the *mappo,* the last age, when doctrine and morality would deteriorate so much that one could be saved only by faith, if at all. To meet the new age, three new forms of Buddhism arose in Japan—Pure Land, Nichiren, and Zen.

Each in its own way represented a popularization of Buddhism as a path to liberation for the masses. Each also represented a radical Buddhist simplification. Kamakura Buddhism was a soldier's reaction against the deep metaphysics and ostentatious rituals of Heian. The soldier, in a time of disorder and death, wanted assurance of salvation, but his straightforward nature was not attracted by monasticism or beautiful but impersonal rites or subtle philosophy. He insisted on some simple and sure key to salvation, as dependable on the battlefield as in the monastic temple.

Hence, synthesis and mystery gave way to simple faith, popular preachers, and practical techniques. An age can be understood as well or better through the questions it asks as through the answers it gives; while the Heian period (like medieval Europe) asked, "How can all knowledge and spiritual experience be brought into a great inclusive system?" Kamakura Japan (like Reformation Europe) was asking instead, "How can I know that I am saved?" It was eager to shuck the brain-splitting mysteries of the cosmic mandala and the three Buddha-bodies and the rest, for a sure answer to this desparate question that anyone could understand. Its new forms of Buddhism—Pure Land, Nichiren, and Zen—can be called products of the Kamakura Reformation.

Let us look first at Pure Land Buddhism in Kamakura Japan. It has taken the form of two great denominations: Jodo (Pure Land), founded by Honen (1133–1212), and Jodo Shinshu (True Pure Land), founded by his disciple Shinran (1173–1262).

Amidism, or Pure Land, and chanting *"Namu Amida Butsu"* ("Glory to Amida Buddha," the conventional expression of the faith which brings one to the western paradise) had been known in Japan prior to the Kamakura period, both as a part of the Tendai synthesis and as a growing folk religion movement. But it was Honen who was the real founder of denominational Amidism in Japan.[31] He studied at Hiei, became a priest, and retired to a hermitage to meditate. He said that he read all the Buddhist scriptures five times but was not satisfied with religion as he had learned it. It gave him no peace in those troubled times. Then he achieved enlightenment by reading a book on Amida's vow. Salvation in accordance with Amida's vow was the peace he was seeking, for it depended not on one's own strength but on the strength of another.

On the Pure Land path, only the recitation of the Nembutsu (the *"Namu*

Amida Butsu") with faith is necessary; the power of grace it releases is always and immediately available; even sinners are pardoned if they call on Amida in sincerity.

Honen lived a long and successful life. Despite some reverses and persecutions, he was able to lay a firm foundation for Amidism in Japan. But he was a mild and quiet man, however saintly. It took another to make of this new faith a dynamic movement. That was Shinran, one of the most colorful and important of all figures in Japanese religion.[32] Sometimes called the Martin Luther of Japan, Shinran taught an even more radical salvation by faith alone than Honen, and he implemented it thoroughly—demanding married clergy, the removal of all figures in temples except Amida, and a new "secular" Buddhist way of life, for if salvation is by Nembutsu faith and that alone, he argued, all the rest of the vast baggage of Buddhist rites and rules is unnecessary.

Shinran much appreciated what Honen meant by entitling one of his books *Senchaku Hongan Nembutsu-shu,* "Writings on Choosing the 'Original Vow' and the Nembutsu." *Senchaku,* "choosing," was for Shinran the clue to the unique appeal of Amidism. It does not mean merely "shopping around" for the best way to be saved, but it implies a willingness to take a risk in faith.

The Jodo Shinshu denomination he created became the largest in Japan and was particularly popular among peasants and Japan's growing class of merchants and craftsmen. It soon enough lost its radical tone to inculcate conventional morality and to become instead the faith of a stable middle class, family centered and given to impressive temples and rites. But its clergy were the first to be married (indeed, the clerical office was commonly hereditary), its altars bear images only of Amida and Shinran, and its rites center on chanting the Nembutsu.

The militant Kamakura spirit in religion is supremely manifested in Nichiren (1222–82).[33] The son of a poor fisherman, Nichiren as an intelligent and perceptive youth was haunted by two questions. He wondered why, in the struggle between the old Heian regime and the rebellious warlords, the imperial armies had been defeated despite the countless incantations offered on their behalf by the Tendai and Shingon clerics. And he asked, like so many in his day, how one could experience the certainty of salvation. Both of these are serious themes, which were to become pillars of the faith he finally offered the world: the religious interpretation of historical event, and the quest for absolute self-integration.

In 1242 Nichiren went to study at Mount Hiei, where he stayed until 1253. Under the influence of Tendai, he became convinced the answer to his problems lay in the Lotus Sutra. Not only in its teachings, although they are the supreme expression of Buddhist truth, but in the gesture of accepting the Lotus Sutra as the sole bearer of Buddhist faith and authority. In 1253 he began a prophetic mission, urging the whole nation to return to the Lotus Sutra.

The "practical" expression of Nichiren's Buddhism was said by him to center on three points: the chanting of the daimoku, the chant *"Nam Myoho Renge Kyo"* ("Glory to the Marvelous Teaching of the Lotus Sutra"—although Nichiren people give it a deeper meaning of referring to the unity of the absolute and the phenomenal world through sound); the *gohonzon,* a scroll originally made by Nichiren containing names of the main figures in the Lotus Sutra set up as an object of concentration while chanting; and the *kaidan,* the "ordination platform." The last derives from Nichiren's insistence that his movement should have the right to ordain its own priestly succession; it can be taken to typify the movement's tendency to be a dynamic, exclusive, closely knit group. Another characteristic is veneration of Nichiren himself, for the prophet identified himself with a suffering bodhisattva in the Lotus Sutra, and most of his followers today believe him to be the bodhisattva or Buddha for this age, superseding Gautama, and refer to no other authority than him and the Lotus Sutra.

From the beginning Nichiren Buddhism had a rigorist quality; his disciples did not shrink from using contentious and disruptive means to spread the faith. While for several centuries his faith then settled down to become a fairly ordinary denomination, Nichiren's thought was not without its effect on Japanese nationalism and modernization. Since World War II, a new Nichiren movement, the Soka Gakkai (actually a lay organization within Nichiren Shoshu, the largest of the Nichiren sects), founded by persons who suffered persecution from the wartime nationalist regime, has grown remarkably. Placing special emphasis on the power of chanting to achieve results in this life, after the this-worldly promises of Nichiren faith to augur a new age of human fulfillment, this tightly organized order has shown the force of Nichiren as a prophet for the modern world. Thanks largely to the work of Soka Gakkai ("Value-creation Society"), Nichiren faith has been a potent force in contemporary Japan.[34]

Since the basic principles of Zen have already been presented in connection with its sources in Chinese Chan, it will be sufficient here just to make a few comments on its Japanese development. Chan was transmitted to Japan by two men, Eisai (1141–1215) and Dogen (1200–53). Both were priests educated at Mount Hiei, and both like many others were looking for something more. Each went to China, and each came in contact with one of two major traditions of Chan. Eisai brought back the Linji school, which became Rinzai in Japan; Dogen returned with the Cao-dong, Soto in Japan.

Besides being a denomination that administers temples, Zen in Japan is a distinctive esthetic and cultural influence. Zen cultural expression—in poetry, painting, the tea ceremony, the garden—suggests the Zen experience of the absolute in the ordinary and the natural in that perfect simplicity which comes out of perfect control. For example, let us look at the Zen garden. A Zen monastery may possess a garden with raked gravel and moss and gnarled trees. The objects will not be spaced in the geometric patterns of a European formal garden, as at Versailles, but in a seemingly natural and irregular way that nonetheless enchants and satisfies. Like all the other Zen arts, it manifests the truly natural by pruning and control.

Early one mild spring morning, I sat overlooking the world-famous stone garden of the Ryoanji Zen temple in Kyoto. This garden is simply a large rectangle of raked white gravel in which are set five rough boulders, "islands" of rock, with

Rock garden in Japanese Zen monastery.

bits of moss around them. The big stones are in a seemingly random pattern, yet one cannot quite leave them alone. For long periods I gazed at them, torn between the intellect's insatiable desire to make everything into meaningful relationships and the inherent meaninglessness of this, which was yet a work of art. Over and over again, I felt that I had almost but not quite seen the meaning of the rocks' relationship, that I knew it but could not quite say it. Finally, like a koan, the rocks and their relationship brought me up against the futility of the pattern-making mind in dealing with certain ultimates. In gazing at the garden, I saw now random bits of moss and stone, now a cluster of galaxies in the trackless void of space.

CONFUCIANISM IN JAPAN

Confucianism is an "invisible" but profoundly pervasive spiritual presence in Japan. With one or two exceptions, it presents no eye-catching shrines like Shinto or splendid temples like Buddhism. Yet its influence on the structures and values of Japanese society can hardly be overestimated. However, diverse their metaphysical positions, the practical, this-worldly ethics of all accepted religions in Japan are essentially Confucian in character, stressing family, loyalty, harmony, and fulfilling obligations. More than anything else, Confucian values have made Japan the industrious, harmonious, hierarchical, sometimes repressive web of intricate loyalties and mutual obligations that it is. And more than anything else, these values lie behind Japan's burgeoning success as a world-class economic power. It is vital, therefore, to understand something about the Japanese adaptation of Confucianism, which in certain ways is different from what it meant in China.

Confucianism has been taught in Japan since the earliest arrival of continental influence. There was a Confucian university during the Heian period. Confucianism's Japanese heyday, however, was the Tokugawa era (1600–1867), when it flourished as the state ideology and also as the main inspiration of several popular or deviant philosophical movements.

Hayashi Razan (1583–1657), with his son and grandson, were custodians of the regime's official Confucianism, based on the Neo-Confucianism of Zhu Xi. Hayashi bitterly opposed Buddhism, regarding its "no self" doctrine as useless to the practical needs of society. He emphasized instead the Confucian ideal of a good society as the supreme good. To this he added Zhu Xi's basic concept of imitating the *li*, or principles of things—above all one's own *li*, or true inner nature. Hayashi said that one's *li* (*ri* in Japanese) is inherent yet must be cultivated. When this is well done by everyone, then society would create itself properly and harmoniously. A truly good society, then, would be one whose institutions allowed expression only to the true *li* of each person and class. The ideal social order could, then, as odd as that may seem to modern democratic eyes, be the highly regimented and hierarchical society to which the Tokugawa rulers aspired, not always successfully. As the cement of this structure, Japanese Confucianists emphasized *chu*, loyalty, as to one's feudal overlords and later to state and emperor, even more than *ko*, filial piety. All this suited well the needs of the Tokugawa shoguns, and it contributed substantially to the philosophy of *bushido*, the way of the warrior or *samurai*.

Very influential popular movements also inculcated broadly Neo-Confucian values. The Shingaku (heart-learning) of Ishida Baigan (1685–1756) embraced worship at both Shinto and Buddhist sites, but made central the cultivation of the heart's original purity, holding that human nature is one with the natural moral order. Shingaku taught respect for the social order and its laws, seeing in them human expression of that natural moral order—a characteristic Neo-Confucian perspective and one well calculated to produce a hard-working, law-abiding society.

Ninomiya Sontoku (1787–1856), the "peasant sage," was a vigorous advocate of rural welfare, who taught people of the impoverished Japanese countryside how to budget, plan, and cooperate. As a philosopher, his basic concept was *hotoku,* "returning virtue," a sense of obligation from out of the individual's dependence on nature and human society. Life, he said in good Confucian manner, is a process of cooperation, of returning good in gratitude for what is received.

Loyalty and obligation—the two values that have shaped Japanese social character more than any others—are deeply rooted in Confucianism. (Some say they go back even further than Confucianism, to the life of the archaic village and tribe, but certainly they have been articulated in historical times through Confucian language.) Loyalty in Japan goes beyond literal filial piety to apply to anyone who can be seen as in the *place* of a parent. Thus, feudal lords and many others have made extensive use of adoption to continue their line when suitable natural heirs were not forthcoming. Moreover, the concept has been extended to include loyalty of students to teachers, workers to their employer or corporation, even gangsters to their underworld bosses, and of subjects to state and sovereign. In Japan these obligations could, and often did, take precedence over family. That was because they were based on another key principle, the *on-giri* relationship, that of *on,* or benefaction, and *giri,* the resultant supreme obligation to repay by work and loyalty; this makes the benefactor a "parent substitute."

Although outer forms may continually change, these attitudes are virtually as alive today as ever. No understanding of contemporary Japanese politics or corporate life is possible without a grasp of how Confucian values make such institutions complex networks of loyalties and obligations, or of how the other Confucian-based ideals of harmony and cooperation make decision-making a sort of consensus-seeking process—one often quite mysterious to outsiders. For loyalty does not form an autocrat out of the recipient. Rather, the Japanese way tends to make superiors—including the emperor—figureheads and facilitators, and to exalt the collective responsibility and consensus decision-making of the whole family, group or "network" involved.

Japan, then, is a fundamentally Confucian society, and a very effective one that in many ways displays the tradition's potential for making human life work smoothly in the twenty-first century as well as in the days of the Ancient Sage. But it is Confucianism with a difference, without the mandarins or the rituals—save as the former are now captains of industry and the latter, the interpersonal courtesy for which Japan is famous.[35]

THE NEW JAPANESE RELIGIONS

One of the most fascinating of all contemporary religious phenomena is a set of groups called *shinko shukyo,* "newly arisen religions," in Japan. Although most of them have earlier roots, they grew and flourished tremendously in the postwar years of disillusionment with traditional life, including conventional Shinto and Buddhism. The "Golden Age" of these religions was the 1950s, when many were growing at fantastic rates and in some the original charismatic leader was still alive. But in the last quarter of the century they are still very much a part of the Japanese scene.

The new religions present a vividly diverse panorama of doctrines and practices. Tenrikyo ("Religion of Heavenly Wisdom") members perform sacred dances with gestures of sweeping movement to symbolize clearing away spiritual dust. Members of Perfect Liberty, believing that "Life is art" and that all aspects of life need to be integrated into a total work of art, emphasize sports and when possible have a golf course near their church. The Church of World Messianity offers *johrei,* in which the "Divine Light of God" is "channeled" through the cupped hand of one who administers it to a recipient.

Nonetheless, they have significant common characteristics as well. They are founded by strong shamanistic figures. In this they represent a very old Japanese pattern repeated in such men as Kobo Daishi, Shinran, and Nichiren, and more recently in figures such as Miki Nakayama (1798–1887), foundress of Tenrikyo, one of the oldest and most prototypical of the new religions.

Miki was of prosperous stock, but she and her husband became increasingly poor amid the economic decline and social trouble of Japan during the first half of the nineteenth century, before its remarkable modernization. Times of change and upheaval, of course, are generally productive of new religious movements. Then, when she was forty-one, in 1838, Miki's oldest son suffered a severe pain in the leg while working. An exorcist was called; he gave a series of treatments. In this ritual, it was customary for a female assistant, really a medium, to go into trance. She would then be possessed by a deity who would reveal the cause of the illness and to whom prayers would be addressed for healing. On one occasion the regular medium was unable to be present, and Miki took her place.

The deity who spoke through Miki's lips said that he was the True and Original God, and that he wished to use Miki's body as a shrine to save the world. From then on, she lived wholly as the vessel of this holy one, known to Tenrikyo as the Father-Mother God. Through her came the sacred scriptures of the religion, the lovely divine dances, and the site of its great temple, located where it is believed the creation of the world began and where divine dew will fall from heaven to mark the inception of the paradisal age. There is a shrine to Miki herself at this temple, as in all Tenrikyo churches.

Tenrikyo shows roots in old shamanistic motifs, but also emphasizes belief in one God. This belief contrasts with Shinto polytheism.

In all the new religions we see evidence of syncretism. Ideas from East and West are combined into new mixes; Jesus is quoted in their literature along with the Buddha. Seicho-no-Ie, for example, a group teaching that "All is perfect," draws both from the Western "New Thought" positive-thinking tradition, and from Mahayana belief in the universal unstained One Mind.

Modernity is particularly apparent in belief in a coming paradisal new age. Far removed from traditional pessimism, the new religions have an intense optimism about the human future. Soon, by divine action, this weary world will be transformed into a paradise. Humanity has a glorious future, not in some distant heaven, but here in this world, and all will partake in it through reincarnation. Indeed, the new age is foreshadowed in the life of the founder and the communal experience of the group.

Communal life is especially represented in the Sacred Center. Like Tenri City of Tenrikyo, Soka Gakkai's new glorious temple on the slopes of Mount Fuji, and the headquarters of Perfect Liberty with its super golf course near Osaka, the new religions tend to have gorgeous centers, often large communities, which are places of pilgrimage and show what the world will be like when the new age comes in.

The new religions have closely knit organizations. Everyone is taken seriously and given a part. This makes them appealing to the dislocated millions moved far from ancestral shrines to impersonal industrial cities by modernization.

The new religions emphasize that an individual makes his or her own world, health, and prosperity, through the attitude of his or her own mind. Like the "positive-thinking" philosophy in the West, and partly influenced by it, they tend to place full responsibility for one's condition in the individual—a ramification of the modern isolation of the individual, in contrast to archaic village or tribal society and religion. Part of this is expressed in their concern for healing, but it goes further than that.

It is not possible here to discuss individual new religions in detail. Some perspective may be provided, however, by noting that they fall into three main groups.[36]

First, there are the "old" new religions, which go back to the early nineteenth century, to the time of the breakdown of old social patterns before modernization. Two from this era are important today: Tenrikyo, already discussed, and Konkokyo. The founder of Konkokyo, Bunjiro Kawate, called Konko Daijin, also had a shamanistic vision in which a folk religion deity revealed himself to be actually a monotheistic high god. The major distinctive rite of this religion is a practice of personal spiritual guidance somewhat comparable to Roman Catholic confession.

Second, there are the Nichiren groups: Soka Gakkai, already discussed, affiliated with the Old Nichiren Shoshu denomination, and two new groups which also venerate the Lotus Sutra—Reiyukai and Rissho Kosei Kai.

Third, there are the Omoto groups. Omoto, meaning "great source," was the name of a group founded by a peasant woman, Nao Deguchi, and her son-in-law and adoptive son, Onisaburo Deguchi (1871–1948). The latter was a colorful spiritualist, mystic, organizer, and social commentator, with a remarkable genius for religious creativity. Omoto emphasizes the existence of a spiritual world (Onisaburo and Nao delivered much information about it in trance), the coming of a new age and a new messiah, healing, mental powers, the creation of paradise on earth, the religious importance of art. The three most important new religions in the Omoto tradition are World Messianity, Seicho-no-Ie, and Perfect Liberty.

The founders of the first two were at one time associates of Onisaburo Deguchi. The Church of World Messianity has emphasized the Omoto teaching about the coming of a new age marked by increase in the divine light (channeled through johrei) and has carried over modifications of certain Omoto techniques. Seicho-no-Ie has emphasized the mind-is-all philosophy and meditation techniques of Omoto, as well as borrowing from Buddhism and Western "New Thought." Perfect Liberty, while apparently not directly influenced by Omoto, shares its emphasis on art, wholeness, and personal spiritual guidance; this is the religion that makes much of sports and says "Life is art," but it also has a procedure for members to receive individual written answers to spiritual or personal problems, and a special prayer technique with symbolic gestures.

This is the story of Japanese religion: a long pilgrimage from ancient clan kami to modern philosophies of health and success, but preserving profoundly shamanistic and charismatic themes all the way through.

RELIGION IN KOREA

Korea has been called the "Bridge of Asia." This peninsula, reaching from the mainland toward Japan, has long been a melting pot of religious and cultural influences, and a pathway by which they have been transmitted to Japan. As we have seen, Buddhism first entered the latter from Korea. At the same time, with a population of some 60 million (now divided between the Republic of Korea in the South and Communist-ruled North Korea), Korea is an important cultural sphere in its own right.

Korean religion may be looked at in terms of five constituents: indigenous shamanistic faith, Buddhism, Confucianism, modern new religions, and Christianity. These are the main ingredients in the contemporary Korean religious melting pot, together with a dash of Daoism from China which is, among other things, represented in the Yang-Yin symbol found on the Republic of Korea's flag, but which is less of a definable stratum than the preceding five.

The ancient indigenous religion of Korea is comparable to early Shinto, to which it is probably related. It presents a myth of the origin of the Korean people in the union of a god descended from heaven who made a she-bear into a human and mated with her; their son, Tangun, was the founder of Korean society. He then worshipped the high god of heaven, Hananim. Shamanism was very important, persisting today in the role of *mudangs*, colorful shamanesses who may perform a rite called *kut* to drive away evil spirits and restore good fortune.

Buddhism came into Korea late in the fourth century C.E. and quickly took hold owing to patronage by rulers of several Korean kingdoms. Buddhist influence was all in the Mahayana tradition; monastic life has come to be predominantly Son (Zen), while lay Buddhism has focused on Pure Land faith and the worship of the bodhisattva Kwanseum (Avalokiteshvara; Chinese Guanyin, Japanese Kannon), the heavenly bestower of mercy. The great Buddhist temple and monastic centers of Korea tend to be in isolated places, quiet retreats often stocked with invaluable Buddhist libraries and works of art.

The golden age of Korean Buddhism was the early Middle Ages. The Yi dynasty (1392–1910) favored Confucianism and tended to restrict Buddhist activity. National temples performed Confucian rites, and Confucian (especially Neo-Confucian) values deeply affected Korean life. The patriarchal family, filial piety, and the honor of traditional learning among the elite were as absolute in old Korea as anywhere, and the impact of centuries steeped in Confucianism is far from gone today.

But in the nineteenth and twentieth centuries, the closed Confucian cultural world of the Korean "Hermit Kingdom" was harshly violated by Western and Japanese incursions, ranging from extensive Christian missionary activity to bitterly resented Japanese rule, to war and the shocks of modernization. These traumatic events have created an ardent sense of Korean cultural identity and messianism reflected in several new religious movements. Tonghak ("Eastern Learning") was founded in the 1860s and renamed Ch'ondogyo ("Way of Heavenly Teaching") in 1905; it inculcated the worship of the God of Heaven but combined features of shamanism, Buddhism, and Confucianism. It also advocated social change against the anachronistic, ultraconservative Yi dynasty, and it lay behind a great rebellion in 1894 which nearly toppled that regime and produced in turn the Sino-Japanese War of that year. Another group, which combines Christian, shamanistic, and messianic features, is that founded by the Rev. Sun Myung Moon, known in the West as the Unification Church.

Christianity, brought by Catholic and Protestant missionaries, has been more successful in Korea than in most other parts of East Asia except the Philippines, embracing nearly 20 percent of the population of South Korea in the 1980s.[37]

RELIGION IN VIETNAM

Situated on the southeast corner of the Asian mainland, Indochina is an area where Indian and Chinese cultural influences meet. Two of the Indochinese countries, Laos and Cambodia, are Theravada Buddhist and more oriented traditionally in the Indian cultural direction. The third and largest, Vietnam, has sometimes experienced Chinese rule and has been more dominated culturally and religiously by its great neighbor to the north. In the early centuries C.E., however, the southern tip of Vietnam, then the kingdom of Funan, was a center of Indianization.

But China ruled major parts of Vietnam, mostly in the north, for more than a thousand years, from 111 B.C.E. to 939 C.E. Despite ardent Vietnamese resistance to their rule, the Chinese succeeded in Sinicizing Vietnamese culture to no small extent. This is reflected in the dominance of Mahayana Buddhism, largely in the form of Thien (Chan or Zen) Buddhism, and in the traditional role of a Confucian mandarin elite imbued with the values of that tradition. However, these institutions have become thoroughly Vietnamized; in recent centuries, monk and mandarin alike have embodied Vietnam.

Like the other societies of Southeast Asia, Vietnam in the nineteenth and twentieth centuries suffered severe shocks that gave rise to new questions about the nature of its spiritual identity. The decades of French colonial rule, the missionary presence of Roman Catholicism, the demise of the traditional Confucian order in China itself, and some thirty-five years of war and confusion all left traumatic marks. Vietnamese felt caught between a Catholicism frequently benign but associated with alien rule, a moribund Buddhism, and a Confucianism linked to a social order clearly passing away. In this situation it is not surprising that, not only did Communism win support, but highly nationalistic "new religions" gained large followings. The two most important new movements, Hoa Hao and Cao Dai, both controlled whole provinces and fielded their own armies in the complicated struggles of Japanese, French, and various Vietnamese forces during the 1940s and 1950s. They continued as powerful factors in Vietnamese life until the unification of the country under the Communist Hanoi regime in 1975.

Hoa Hao was a Buddhist movement with Theravada leanings that sought to restore "pure" Buddhism. Cao Dai, on the other hand, was a highly syncretistic church based on spiritualistic communications, reminiscent of Daoist sectarianism. It embraced Confucian morality, such Buddhist doctrines as karma and reincarnation, and spiritist mediumship, while possessing an organizational structure under a pope clearly inspired by Roman Catholicism.

Since 1975, religious activity generally has been severely curtailed in Vietnam itself, but Buddhism, Catholicism, and Cao Dai continue to be practiced in Vietnamese refugee communities around the world.

SUMMARY

The religion of East Asia has emphasized the unity of the cosmos and the integration of the individual with nature as well as with family and society. Ancestrism has been an important way of meeting both ends. It has, however, also been a religious tradition deeply influenced by outstanding individual teachers and leaders.

Confucianism, deriving from the teaching of Confucius and other philosophers as well as from ancient Chinese attitudes, is perhaps the most pervasive spiritual force of all in East Asia. It has emphasized the importance of inward virtue and the obligations of the individual to family and society, and of rites and forms through which these are expressed. Daoism, with its stress on mystical unity with all of nature and with such "nonrational" aspects of human life as love of beauty, fantasy, and personal immortality, has provided compensation for the rational and ethical character of Confucianism. Both sought to align human life with the Dao, the universal Way, or with the will of Heaven; for Confucianism it was supremely found in a good society; for Daoists, in nature, beauty, fantasy, and mystical experience outside the corrupting influence of society.

Hardly less influential in East Asia has been Buddhism. In China, it was considerably affected by Daoism. Its main forms were Chan (Zen in Japan), emphasizing meditation and nature, and Pure Land, emphasizing rebirth in paradise through faith in Amitabha. In the popular religion of traditional China, Confucianism, Daoism, and Buddhism combined with ancestrism, seasonal festivals, and local deities to make up a colorful complex.

In the contemporary China of the People's Republic, this tradition has been largely broken. Religion, while still practiced, is circumscribed, and China is generally a secular society.

In Japan, Confucian values have been and still are important, but formal religion has been mainly a matter of the indigenous Shinto faith and Buddhism, imported at the dawn of Japanese history. Shinto is the worship of the kami or polytheistic gods of clans and places. The kami are housed in simple but lovely shrines and worshipped either privately or in community *matsuri* that stress tradition, purity, and the festive spirit.

Japanese Buddhism has centered more around major leaders and has changed character through the production of new denominations with major changes in historical eras. Its earlier forms, such as Kegon, Shingon, and Tendai, stressed comprehensiveness and often used esoteric forms. The new denominations of the Medieval Kamakura period—Pure Land, Nichiren, and Zen—moved in the direction of the simplification and popularization of Buddhist salvation.

In modern Japan, a number of New Religions have arisen in response to times of rapid change.

Two other important East Asian countries, Korea and Vietnam, also share a heritage of Confucianism and Buddhism in the Chinese Chan and Pure Land styles, and in the context of a modern experience devastated by upheaval and war, they have generated major new religious movements.

QUESTIONS FOR REVIEW

1. Discuss the main general features of East Asian religion: its stress on cosmic unity, its orientation toward family and society, and its practicality.
2. Interpret the meaning of the important theme of ancestrism.
3. Discuss the thematic chart for Chinese religion, showing how it brings out aspects of Chinese religion oriented toward society and those oriented toward nature, and how it sorts out those aspects that stress a rational approach to ultimate meaning and those that give vent to the nonrational side of human nature.
4. Talk about the meaning of Dao.
5. Present the main features of Confucianism. Be sure to distinguish the features of philosophical Confucianism and the religious aspects of Confucian worship, but also show how the two fit together in traditional China through the values and role of the mandarins.
6. In the same way, explain the main features of Daoism (Taoism), distinguishing between the outlook of the Daoist philosophers and religious Daoism, but also indicating how they are related.
7. Discuss the main forms and features of Chinese Buddhism, explaining how Buddhism was modified through interaction with Chinese culture.
8. State the major points of popular religion in traditional China, such as ancestrism, seasonal festivals, and relation to family and place.

9. Explain what the attitudes and policies toward religion of the People's Republic of China have been and what has happened to religion under its rule.

10. Explain the thematic chart on Japanese religion, showing the importance of tension between imported and indigenous features in the spiritual history of Japan and of its individual and community aspects.

11. Discuss the principal features of Shinto.

12. Discuss Buddhism in Japan, stressing the role of the great leaders who have shaped it and how its character has changed with changing historical periods.

13. Interpret the general characteristics of the "new religions" of Japan.

14. Using the charts, explain the fundamental features of Confucianism, Daoism, and Shinto. How do they answer the great questions about the nature of ultimate reality and the meaning of human life?

15. Describe the religious traditions of Korea.

16. Summarize the religious heritage of Vietnam.

SUGGESTED READINGS ON EAST ASIAN RELIGION

Chinese Religion

AHERN, EMILY M., *The Cult of the Dead in a Chinese Village*. Stanford: Stanford University Press, 1973. A good introduction based on field research of this very important facet of Chinese popular religion.

BAITY, PHILIP CHESLEY, *Religion in a Chinese Town*. Taipei: Orient Cultural Service, 1975. A valuable study based on field research in Taiwan.

BAUER, WOLFGANG, *China and the Search for Happiness*. New York: Seabury Press, 1976. A brilliant study of Chinese religion and popular culture, emphasizing the role of paradises and other symbols of ultimate happiness; valuable insights into religion.

*BLOFELD, JOHN, *I Ching*. New York: Dutton, 1968. The most readable translation of this classic.

BREDON, JULIET, AND IGOR MITROPHANOW, *The Moon Year*. Shanghai: Kelly & Walsh, 1927; reprinted New York: Paragon Press, 1966. A report of Chinese religious and traditional customs centering around the festival calendar.

EBERHARD, WOLFRAM, *Guilt and Sin in Traditional China*. Berkeley and Los Angeles: University of California Press, 1967. Analyzes popular morality books and fiction, together with popular concepts of heaven and hell; invaluable for understanding popular Chinese religious concepts.

*FUNG YU-LAN, *A Short History of Chinese Philosophy*. New York: Macmillan, 1960. A sound, well-written summary.

JOCHIM, CHRISTIAN, *Chinese Religion: A Cultural Perspective*. Englewood Cliffs, NJ: Prentice Hall, 1986. A fine introductory textbook.

JORDAN, DAVID K., *Gods, Ghosts, and Ancestors: The Folk Religion of a Taiwanese Village*. Berkeley and Los Angeles: University of California Press, 1972. An illuminating report of field research.

*Thompson, Laurence G., *Chinese Religion: An Introduction*. Belmont, CA: Wadsworth, 1969. An excellent beginner's book that integrates all levels and periods of Chinese religion into a unified picture.

*———, *The Chinese Way in Religion*. Encino, CA: Dickenson, 1973. A valuable collection of translated texts and studies, with good introductions.

Wolf, Arthur P., ed., *Religion and Ritual in Chinese Society*. Stanford, CA: Stanford University Press, 1974. A collection of anthropological studies on popular religion.

*Yang, C. K., *Religion in Chinese Society*. Berkeley and Los Angeles: University of California Press, 1961. Advanced but a landmark treatment of the sociology of religion in China.

Confucianism

*Bahm, Archie J., *The Heart of Confucius*. Harper & Row, 1971. Simple translations of two basic Confucian texts, *The Mean* and *Great Learning,* with an introduction that gives useful explanations for beginners of basic Chinese philosophical terms.

*Ch'u Chai, and Winberg Chai, *Confucianism*. Woodbury, NY: Barron's Educational Series, 1973. A useful introduction to Confucian philosophy from an intellectual history point of view.

*Creel, H. G., *Confucius and the Chinese Way*. New York: Harper Torchbooks, 1960. A standard book on the life, thought, and influence of Confucius.

*Fingerette, Herbert, *Confucius—The Secular as Sacred*. New York: Harper Torchbooks, 1972. A brief but stimulating interpretive essay.

Nivison, David S., and Arthur Wright, *Confucianism in Action*. Stanford: Stanford University Press, 1959. A classic account of how Confucianism worked as the ruling ideology of imperial China's officialdom and educational system.

*Ware, James R., *The Sayings of Confucius*. New York: Mentor Books, n.d. A readable translation of the Analects.

Daoism

*Blofeld, John, *The Secret and Sublime: Taoist Mysteries and Magic*. London: George Allen & Unwin, 1973. A personal, anecdotal narrative giving a lively picture of the Daoist world.

*Bynner, Witter, *The Way of Life According to Lao Tzu*. New York: Capricorn Books, 1962. A free but very readable translation of the *Tao Te Ching*.

Girardot, Norman J., *Myth and Meaning in Early Taoism*. Berkeley: University of California Press, 1983. An excellent scholarly study.

Goullart, Peter, *The Monastery of Jade Mountain*. London: John Murray, 1961. A vivid, atmospheric account of Daoist life in pre-Communist China.

Lagerwey, John, *Taoist Ritual in Chinese Society*. New York: Macmillan, 1987. Daoism as it functions in modern Chinese society.

*Merton, Thomas, *The Way of Chuang Tzu*. New York: New Directions, 1969. A sensitive mystical interpretation of a seminal Daoist thinker.

*Rawson, Philip, and Lazslo Legeza, *Tao: The Eastern Philosophy of Time and Change*. New York: Avon Books, 1973. A groundbreaking explication of Daoist philosophy and its expression in religion, art, and symbolism.

*Saso, Michael R., *Taoism and The Rite of Cosmic Renewal*. Pullman: Washington State University Press, 1972. A rare scholarly account of Daoist religious ritual, with much insight into religious Daoism.

————, *The Teachings of the Taoist Master Chuang*. New Haven: Yale University Press, 1977. Religious Daoism through the eyes of the modern practitioner.

*Welch, Holmes, *Taoism: The Parting of the Way*. Boston: Beacon Press, 1957. The best general introduction to all sides of Daoism.

Buddhism in China

*Blofeld, John, *The Wheel of Life*. Berkeley, CA: Shambala Press, 1972. An autobiographical book that offers, through the author's exploration of Buddhist China, rare insights into its manifold variety.

*Ch'en, Kenneth, *Buddhism in China: A Historical Survey*. Princeton: Princeton University Press, 1964. An authoritative introduction.

Welch, Holmes, *The Practice of Chinese Buddhism 1900–1950*. Cambridge, MA: Harvard University Press, 1967. An excellent account of Chinese Buddhism before the revolution; especially good on the actual life of monasteries and temples and on popular devotional practices.

————, *The Buddhist Revival in China*. Cambridge, MA: Harvard University Press, 1968. Buddhism in modern China prior to 1949.

————, *Buddhism Under Mao*. Cambridge, MA: Harvard University Press, 1972. A thorough study of Buddhism in Communist society.

*Wright, Arthur F., *Buddhism in Chinese History*. Stanford: Stanford University Press, 1959. A brief, vivid, and reliable treatment of the introduction and assimilation of Buddhism in China.

Religion in Japan

Blacker, Carmen, *The Catalpa Bow: A Study of Shamanistic Practices in Japan*. London: George Allen & Unwin, 1975. A carefully researched and beautifully written summary of Japanese shamanism.

*Earhart, H. Byron, *Japanese Religion: Unity and Diversity*, 3rd. ed. Belmont, CA: Wadsworth, 1982. A fine introductory text, historically oriented. Excellent bibliography.

*————, *Religion in the Japanese Experience: Sources and Interpretations*. Encino, CA: Dickenson, 1974. A useful collection of texts and examples of modern scholarship.

Ellwood, Robert S., and Richard Pilgrim, *Japanese Religion: A Cultural Perspective*. Englewood Cliffs, NJ: Prentice-Hall, Inc., 1985. A survey of Japanese religion and its interaction with culture.

*Hori, Ichiro, *Folk Religion in Japan*. Chicago: University of Chicago Press, 1968. A collection of readable essays by a prominent Japanese scholar.

Kitagawa, Joseph M., *Religion in Japanese History*. New York: Columbia University Press, 1966. An authoritative historical survey, emphasizing the modern period.

Smith, Robert J., *Ancestor Worship in Contemporary Japan*. Stanford, CA: Stanford University Press, 1974. The best study of this important aspect of Japanese religion.

Buddhism in Japan

*Bloom, Alfred, *Shinran's Gospel of Pure Grace*. Tucson: University of Arizona Press, 1965. A highly insightful interpretation of Pure Land Buddhism.

*Dumoulin, Heinrich, *A History of Zen Buddhism*. New York: Pantheon, 1963. A standard work, covering this tradition in both China and Japan.

Eliot, Sir Charles, *Japanese Buddhism*. London: Routledge and Kegan Paul, 1959. An older book but still useful as a reference, especially on the various denominations.

*Hoover, Thomas, *Zen Culture*. New York: Random House, 1977. An excellent overview of the interaction between Zen and Japanese culture.

*———, *The Zen Experience*. New York: New American Library, 1980. Zen through the perspective of its great masters, both Chinese and Japanese.

*Kapleau, Philip, *The Three Pillars of Zen*. Boston: Beacon Press, 1967. A fascinating introduction to Zen methods and thought. Contains accounts of modern Zen experience.

*Saunders, E. Dale, *Buddhism in Japan*. Philadelphia: University of Pennsylvania Press, 1964. A useful historical survey.

*Suzuki, D. T., *Zen Buddhism*. Garden City, NY: Doubleday, 1956. One of many books by this well-known writer who has successfully communicated much of the Zen spirit to the West.

Shinto

*Kageyama, Haruki, *The Arts of Shinto*. New York, Tokyo: John Weatherhill, 1973. A well-illustrated treatment that gives insights into some little-known sides of Shinto.

*Ono, Sokyo, *Shinto: The Kami Way*. Rutland, VT: Charles E. Tuttle, 1967. A basic introduction, representing the point of view of a leading modern Shinto scholar.

Ross, Floyd H., *Shinto: The Way of Japan*. Boston: Beacon Press, 1965. A readable introduction, in some places communicating a personal perspective.

New Religions of Japan

Hardacre, Helen, *Lay Buddhism in Contemporary Japan: Reiyūkai Kyōdan*. Princeton: Princeton University Press, 1984. A representative study of one Buddhist-based new religion, utilizing careful field research and good sociological insight.

*McFarland, H. Neill, *The Rush Hour of the Gods*. New York: Macmillan, 1967. A well-researched, sometimes critical overview of several of the groups.

Offner, Clark B., and Henry van Straelen, *Modern Japanese Religions*. Tokyo: Rupert Enderle, 1963. A carefully done study emphasizing healing in the New Religions.

*Thomsen, Harry, *The New Religions of Japan*. Tokyo and Rutland, VT: Charles E. Tuttle, 1963. A readable basic report on the major new religions.

CHAPTER 6

One God, Many Words and Wonders:
THE FAMILY OF THREE GREAT MONOTHEISTIC RELIGIONS

CHAPTER OBJECTIVES

After studying this chapter, you should be able to

- Understand the unique features of monotheistic religion, and their relation to the historical period in which monotheism as we know it emerged.

- Discuss the relation of the major Western monotheistic religions to each other.

THE NATURE
OF MONOTHEISTIC RELIGION

Monotheistic religions are those professing belief in one all-powerful and personal God, and in no other gods. The largest and most influential of these faiths today are Judaism, Christianity, and Islam, each of which will be discussed at length in the chapters that follow. Here we are concerned to show how these three are a family, for they all explicitly go back to one source, the experience of one God of the ancient Hebrews recorded in the Old Testament. The God of Judaism, Christianity, and Islam is the God of Abraham and Moses and the prophets; these fathers in faith are venerated by all three.

As we have seen, there are other monotheisms too: Zoroastrianism, Sikhism, and in a sense bhaktic Hinduism and Amidist Buddhism. Overtones of monotheism appear in the primal high god and in nondualist Hinduism and Buddhism. But for all that, these three monotheisms are a family—though Zoroastrianism may have had no small impact on their development—and they are uniquely bound together in origin and history. Even their quarrels—and never have other religious hatreds and persecutions matched those among and within these three—have the special bitterness of family fights, as an ancient kinship one does not want to honor makes rage all the worse.

Yet these three religions, for all their shared past and common beliefs, should not be thought of as in a separate category from all other faiths. To do so would be to overemphasize the first of the three forms of religious expression, the theoretical—that is, the myths, doctrines, and ideologies, which usually include what historical awareness there is among believers—and neglect the message of the other two: the practical or worship and cultus; and the sociological, or types of groups formed. For in the last two forms of expression we find divergences both among and within the three faiths every bit as great as between one of them and, say, what is found in Hinduism or Shinto.

Thus, the following discussion of the characteristics of the monotheistic traditions may appear full of qualifications, exceptions, and statements that this or that trait is shared by other traditions too. That is because religious life simply is that way. A distinctive belief, such as belief in one personal God, does not necessarily make the religion different in practice all the way through—and different people may experience the same religion in different ways. There is certainly a distinctively monotheistic style of relation to God, a relation of interpersonal awe, love, and obedience unshared by polytheism or mystical monism. But not everyone in a monotheistic tradition is really concerned with that sort of relationship to God, or feels one ought to be. For many the practice aspects of a monotheistic religion—worship, law, customs, society, mysticism—are what is important.

What is more, we find striking parallels in patterns of worship and styles of religious groups which seem to pay little heed to whether the faith is theoretically monotheistic or polytheistic. Religious activity throughout the world could be classified according to way of worship—that is, whether images are used or not, whether pilgrimages are important or not, and so forth. Or, it could be classified according to types of groups formed—whether monasticism is normative, whether there are "services" with a congregation—instead of in the usual way, according to formal beliefs. By these classifications, the lines would be quite different from what we are used to, and they would cut across some of what are termed "religions," to link parts of one with parts of another in a far different corner of the world. For most people, style of worship and group have a deep, half-conscious impact on attitudes which may well exceed that of formal belief.

Within the monotheistic family itself, the messages communicated by the practical and social forms, including art and architecture, could hardly be more contrasting. Compare the Muslim mosque in the Alhambra in Granada with a Spanish Roman Catholic church. The mosque is of clean lines, devoid of pictures or images, the worshippers who pray in it having been oriented only by a bare niche in the wall to the direction of Mecca. Yet far from giving an impression of mere barrenness, the cool, still arabesqued interior of the mosque is in an almost indescribable way symbolic of fullness and light. It turns thoughts to God, for all that is not God is expunged; nonrepresentational designs of arabesque fantasy line the walls and dome, raising the mind beyond image to dimensions of meditation where God is pure spirit.

The traditional Spanish Roman Catholic church also evokes feelings of wonder and awe, but in a very different way. Here one typically is confronted with richness and diversity of forms to rival a jewel box. The altar is a gleaming shape of gold and brocade, and behind it the reredos reaches to the ceiling, an ornate waterfall of gilt, lights, and statues of saints. Indeed, images are not exhausted at the altar but continue around the church, each in its own little chapel—of sorrowful and bleeding Christs; of the Blessed Virgin Mary, Queen of the Universe in imperial crown and robe; of St. James of Compostela on his horse, and so on. Apostles, monks, nuns, bishops, kings, each unique yet each part of a larger mosaic, suggest that in this church the power of the beam of monotheistic light is shown by the many different colors and forms into which it breaks as it interacts with the world. This faith appears close to polytheism, though it is not that. Yet neither is it the clear, austere monotheism of Islam, whose simplicity, oddly enough, is matched by the rustic grace of many shrines of that most polytheistic of religions, Shinto.

On the other hand, if one were to compare a Quaker meetinghouse or a New England village church with the mosque, one would feel, at least, in the same world. Orders of monks and nuns bring Roman Catholic and Eastern Orthodox Christianity closer to Buddhism, in this particular sociological respect, than to most of their Protestant, Jewish, and Muslim neighbors. Many different grids can be laid over the religious world to produce different configurations of similarity and difference.

Nonetheless, the three monotheistic faiths have common features, both historically and practically. All have their roots in what Karl Jaspers has called the "axial age." The impact of this period, covering centuries and capable of flexible definition,

HISTORY OF THE THREE MAIN WESTERN MONOTHEISTIC FAITHS

GENERAL INFLUENCES

Pyramid texts

Sumerian decline

Egypt and
Mesopotamia
dominant in Near
East

Trojan War

Zoroaster

Cyrus

Persian Empire

JUDAISM

Abraham

Moses

Exodus (c. 1290)

Judges

David (r.c. 1000–962)

Solomon (r. 961–922)

Early prophets:
Amos, Elijah

Exile (586)

Jeremiah, Isaiah

Return from captivity in
Babylon (538)

Most Wisdom literature

Apocalyptic literature

CHRISTIANITY

ISLAM

| 2000 B.C.E. | 1500 B.C.E. | 1000 B.C.E. | 500 B.C.E. |

Alexander

Hellenistic
Culture

Roman Empire

Byzantine Empire

Renaissance

European
preeminence

French & American
revolutions

Feudalism

Marxism

Maccabees (165)
John the Baptizer
Temple destroyed (70)
Talmud

Jewish dispersion
throughout Europe, Asia
& N. Africa

Maimonides (1135–1204)
Zohar (1275)
Kabbalah

Hasidism
Reform
Conservative
Holocaust
State of Israel
(1948)

Jesus (c. 30)
Gospels (60–100)
Paul (d. 62)   Constantine (r. 312–37)

Council of Nicaea (325)
Augustine (354–430)

Conversion of Europe

Rise of medieval papacy
Monasticism

Separation of
Eastern Orthodox
and R. Catholic
churches (1054)

Crusades
St. Francis (1181–1226)

Aquinas (1225–74)
Medieval
Catholicism
Medieval
"heretics"
Luther (1483–1546)
Calvin (1509–64)
English Ref. (1534)
Radical Reformers

John Wesley
(1703–91)
American
Christianity

Muhammad (570–632)
Muslim conquests
Rise of Sufism
Baghdad Caliphate
(750–1258)
Avicenna
(980–1037)

Al-Ghazali
(d. 1111)

Al-Arabi (d. 1290)

Islam spreads to India,
Malaysia, Indonesia
Rise of Ottoman
Empire

Sufi orders and devotion
prominent

Growth of Islam in
Africa

Nationalism

| 1 B.C.E./C.E. | 500 C.E. | 1000 C.E. | 1500 C.E. | 2000 C.E. |

"Sacrifice of Isaac" by Rembrandt illustrating God's covenant with Abraham.

yet in retrospect a distinctive historical "moment," is marked in certain fundamental ways. (It has been discussed in Chapter 1.) Human consciousness emerged from cosmic religion into a state in which it was apparent that things change and do not change back, that human history is a process in which the new and more complex is always unfolding. This increasing consciousness of history suggests a force, greater than seasonal natural forces, that governs this larger process. Awareness of history also makes possible monotheism's central pivot in history—the distinctive revelation, prophet, and scripture—which can give meaning to the new and more complicated historical world.

Each monotheistic religion, then, traces itself back to a historical founder, such as Moses, Jesus, Muhammad, or farther east, Zoroaster and Nanak. Monotheism is never a simple continuation of something growing out of a timeless past, even though it may embrace important elements of cosmic religion. The idea of a special revelation through a known historical figure, who at a known point in time gave an authoritative word from the one personal God, which the monotheistic faith proclaims, seems to be inseparable from monotheistic expression.

Thus, monotheism generally has strong roots in the teaching of great individuals. It tends to stress intense individual commitment and emphasis on verbal expression. This means that the written word, scripture, is of great importance in monotheistic religion. While other religions also have constantly studied and chanted scriptures, in the monotheistic religions scriptures (characteristically short and clear-cut compared to Vedas or Sutras) are especially decisive statements of law and belief as well as mystical hymns, monastic rules, and philosophy. They are to be universally proclaimed and are given through the founder, or at least are fruits of a process started by him, at the pivotal moment. These scriptures are written; significantly in the axial age writing also emerged.

In keeping with its linkage to the discovery of history, monotheism is inevitably tied to what we have spoken of as a linear concept of time. While the idea has played different roles in different times and places, Zoroastrianism and the three monotheisms now under discussion have taught that the world was created by God at the beginning of time and is moving toward a climax at an equally definite end: the coming of the Messiah, the final judgment, the making of a new heaven and earth. Monotheisms are, in other words, eschatological.

Finally, it can be noted that monotheisms arise or become socially important in periods of rapid cultural change; that is, in conjunction with the emergence of national cultures and political institutions—ancient Israel, the Arabs at the time of Muhammad, Christianity in the flux of the Roman world and subsequently providing a cultural focus for the dying Roman Empire and the new European nations. (Of course, other axial age religions, such as Buddhism and Confucianism, have done this too.) Monotheism, with its idea of a universal God who can legitimatize one sovereign and one law below, helps greatly in a transition from tribalism to nationhood.

But monotheism also, by its own intrinsic logic, is universalist, for if there is but one God with one message, it must be for all people everywhere. This is modified considerably in Judaism, with its idea of the "chosen people" with a special calling by the one God; but even so, the chosen people are to mediate a blessing to all the families of the earth. In Islam and Christianity, monotheism and belief in one revelation have at various times served as an ideological undergirding for the creation of empires uniting many cultures and people—even though as we have seen systematic polytheism can also serve this function. But an international, universal gospel serves especially well as a dynamic for the vigorous missionary expansion of culture. It is usually personal monotheism, then, or a psychologically similar form of Buddhism, such as those of Kamakura Japan, that strongly missionizes and spreads cross-culturally.

Monotheism is like a river running through religious history. The obscure springs where it arose are located very far back indeed, doubtless with the primordial high god of archaic hunters. The river flows through the fertile lowlands of the inevitable polytheism of archaic agricultural religion, with its emphasis on the marriage of heaven and earth to produce the divine harvest-child, and of the ancient empires uniting the local gods of many tribes and towns into an organized composite. Even then, however, monotheism glimmered faintly in the usual concept of a controlling universal principle, associated with an often vague but sovereign deity: Tian, Varuna, Amon, Zeus. In the ancient Judaism of Abraham, Moses, and the prophets, the river first emerges as a distinct current: It is then fed by tributaries such as Zoroastrianism and Greek philosophy, and at the same time it spreads out like a delta to form its three main branches. Sometimes these branches flow torrentially; more often they become slow, amiable, domesticated streams and millponds, which coexist comfortably with diverse landscapes of cosmic religion, folk religion, and local culture. But the river never quite stops moving toward a destination.

QUESTIONS FOR REVIEW

1. Discuss the nature of monotheism.
2. Explain why the present great monotheistic religions have their origin in the period of the "discovery of history."
3. Tell why those religions have given an important place to a single individual founder, to revelation in history, and to scripture.
4. Discuss the relationship of Judaism, Christianity, and Islam to one another.

SUGGESTED READINGS

Hebrew Scriptures/Old Testament

*ALBRIGHT, W. F., *From the Stone Age to Christianity*. Garden City, NY: Doubleday, 1957. A scholarly guide to Palestinian archaeology, emphasizing its relation to the Old Testament and its meaning for philosophy of history.

ANDERSON, B., *Understanding the Old Testament*. Englewood Cliffs, NJ: Prentice-Hall, Inc., rev. ed., 1986. A standard introductory textbook.

*BUBER, MARTIN, *The Prophetic Faith*. New York: Macmillan, 1949. A study by a famous Jewish theologian.

FLANDERS, HENRY JACKSON, ROBERT W. CRAPPS, AND DAVID A. SMITH, *People of the Covenant: An Introduction to the Old Testament*. 3rd ed., New York: Oxford University Press, 1988. A good standard introduction.

*GASTER, T. H., *Dead Sea Scriptures*. Garden City, NY: Doubleday, 1964. A semipopular overview of these important finds and their meaning.

HARRISON, ROLAND KENNETH, *Introduction to the Old Testament*. Grand Rapids: Eerdmans, 1969. A standard text written from an evangelical perspective.

HESCHEL, ABRAHAM, *The Prophets*. New York: Harper & Row, 1962, 1969. A brilliant introduction to the spirit of prophetic religion in ancient Israel by a very distinguished Jewish thinker.

*PRITCHARD, JAMES B., *The Ancient Near East in Pictures*. Princeton: Princeton University Press, 1954. A fascinating survey by a distinguished archaeologist.

TRIBLE, PHYLLIS, *Texts of Terror*. Philadelphia: Fortress, 1984. A powerful look at controversial Biblical passages from a religious feminist perspective.

CHAPTER 7

Keeping Covenant with God in History:
THE UNIQUE PERSPECTIVE OF JUDAISM

CHAPTER OBJECTIVES

After studying this chapter, you should be able to

- Present the ancient and modern history of Judaism.

- Discuss the uniqueness of the Jewish religion.

- Explain the importance of practices and observances in Judaism as a way of life.

JEWISH UNIQUENESS

Every religion is unique in its own way. But none perhaps is as distinctive or has as remarkable a history as that of the Jews. Judaism seems always to be the exception to every rule of history, just as Jewish thought or even the mere presence of the Jewish community has so often pointed up the limitations of whatever "universal" truth and practice someone else has tried to lay out. Toward the ancient empires and polytheisms, toward Eastern mysticism and Christian salvationism, toward modern nationalism, dictatorship, communism, mass culture, and disbelief, Judaism— or at least some Jews—have always said "Yes, but. . . ."

They have not opposed all of these things: Judaism, for example, has had mystical thinkers worthy of comparison with those of India, and also its share of skeptics, and it has been and is today expressed in nationhood. But it has always been wary of making an "ism" out of them and then saying that mysticism, or skepticism, or nationalism is the end of meaning and truth, that when you have that, "you've arrived." Jews have always had a tendency, fired by centuries of living as a minority "different" from the majority culture of whatever nation they happen to be inhabiting and honed by centuries of hard study of the bristly legal texts of their law, to say, "Yes, but perhaps there's another side—maybe there's more than just this one thing."

The questions have not always been put verbally. The mere presence of the Jewish community as an all-too-visible exception to a nation's spiritual and cultural homogeneity has stated them more eloquently than words. Needless to say, such questions, whether verbal or implicit, are not always welcome to those who prefer to leave the waters of mystical or cultural unity unruffled. Jewish "differentness" and the awkward queries it implies for others have given Jews much suffering. But they have persisted in making the question felt and have thereby also pressed human society not to settle for partial truths.

Jews have been exceptions from the beginning of the tradition among the Israelites of the Hebrew scriptures (which Christians call the Old Testament). They were developing toward the monotheism of a personal God while polytheism became richer and richer among their neighbors.

Why this reliance on one God, and finally the belief that he is the only God and sole king of the universe, developed uniquely among the Israelites is hard to say. It may have arisen in part out of the climatic situation of pastoral peoples wandering over the face of the hard desert. The fact that humans are like aliens in these lands, caring for flocks that would die were they not taken to pasture and well by shepherds, suggests that God in the infinite desert sky above is as "other" from earth as humans are from desert, yet he guides his people as a shepherd his flock. That the shepherd, like Abraham, sets up an altar and worships the same God in many different places, wherever his wanderings take him, implies that his God is universal, not tied to place or nature like an agricultural deity. (Yet, although the early monotheists were pastoralists, many pastoralists did not become monotheists.)

Main Themes of Judaism

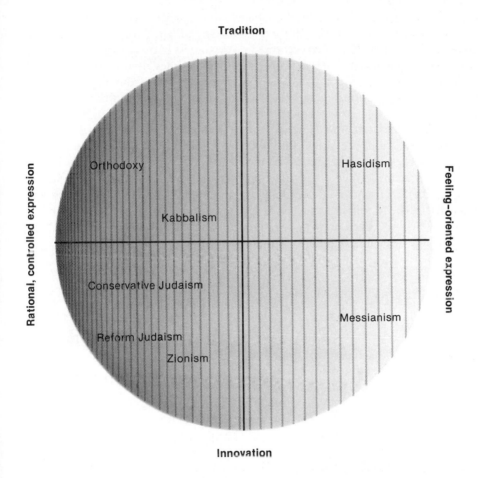

THEMATIC CHART VI. In Judaism, polarity between intellectual and emotional modes of religious expression has been particularly marked, modified by the fact that both have been used as conveyors of both traditionalist and innovative visions in Judaism, and by the fact that both came together in actual Jewish community and family life.

The traditional Jewish interpretation is simply that God, for reasons of his own, himself selected this people and made himself known to them. This did not mean that he meant to make their life smooth and easy; the call involved heavy responsibilities and frequent suffering. He established a covenant, or agreement, with them that they would worship him, follow his Law, and be faithful to him; on his part God would preserve them throughout history, even to a consummation at the end of history when the meaning of this relationship would be made known. A core, at least, of Jews have maintained this trust; no people so dispersed as they have been for 2000 years, so much a minority and so persecuted, has ever kept a faith intact for so long.

This faith has not been *centered* on belief in an afterlife, or an experience of salvation in personal or mystical terms, or a philosophy, or a technique of meditation, or even a set of doctrines. It has been centered on awareness of this unique relationship with God, but it has taken different forms at different times. It was first God who called Abraham from Mesopotamia, and the Israelite people from Egypt, as they viewed it. Then the relationship was one of God helping them win their wars and establish their nation. Next the relationship was expressed chiefly through following an elaborate law they believed God had given them to show their differentness, with unusual stipulations regarding food, work, worship, and much else. In modern times, still other views of the special relationship have been put forward. But in any case, what has made Jews stand apart has not been any special elaborate beliefs or exotic spiritual attainments but something harder to pin down—varying ways in which a sense of being different has been expressed, which in turn have helped to create the difference. Together with this sense is a belief, at least traditionally, that it is the one God who initiated and sustains it.

THE ANCIENT STORY OF JUDAISM

The ancient religion of Syria and Palestine, and no doubt of the earliest Hebrews, was related to that of the major Semitic civilization, the Mesopotamian. These peoples were all Semitic (except the Sumerians) and believed in common deities, like the Great Mother Ashtoreth (Ishtar) and the dying-rising vegetation god Tammuz or Baal. The account in the Book of Genesis tells us that Abraham, father of the Hebrews, came out of Ur in the Valley of the Two Rivers, affirming still more strongly the common cultural background. This is reinforced by many passages in the Hebrew scriptures, from the obvious parallels between the flood story featuring Noah in Genesis and that of Utnapishtim in Babylon (though the monotheism of the former and the polytheism of the latter afford quite a difference in tone), to the reference in Ezekiel to the practice in Israel of "wailing for Tammuz"—of which the prophet much disapproved. The difference was that the Hebrews were originally herdsmen Semites, like the Arab Bedouins of today, in contrast to the more numerous and prosperous sedentary agriculturalist Semites of Mesopotamia and the fertile regions of Syria and Palestine who worshipped fertility-giving lords of the land such as Baal.

However the Hebrews—wandering herdsmen originally on the fringes of the great Semitic civilizations—had their own God. They were familiar with the Baals and Ashtoreths and Marduks, for from time to time they must have come into the cities to trade and could not help but notice the massive temples, the powerful priests, the sacred prostitutes. But for themselves, at sacred stones and mountaintops deep in the desert they knew better than anyone else, they worshipped their own

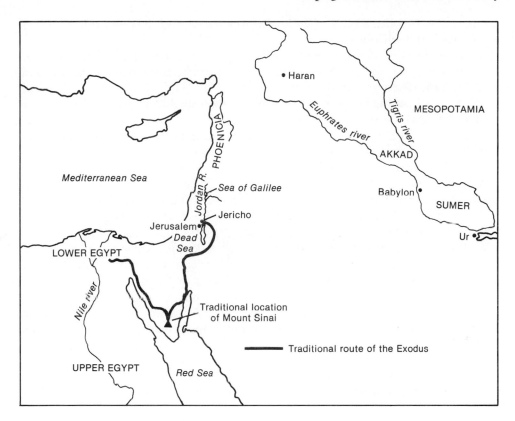

MAP 7–1.   The Unique Perspective of Judaism

God, Yahweh, who was not tied to one place but could be served wherever the tribe wandered.[1] Moreover, he was not pleased with the offerings from the cultivated field but preferred instead the odor of roasting flesh from the herds of his own poor but free people, as the story of Cain and Abel tells us (Gen. 4:3–5).

It was not until most of the Hebrews themselves became agriculturalists after settling in the land of Canaan (Palestine) that the issue of the Baals and Ashtoreths became acute. Should the tribes stay with a god of the desert after they had become people of the soil, or go to the Baals and their kin, whose province seemed to be the agricultural way of life? Many understandably took the latter option.

But there were always those, led by the prophets, who contended that the Hebrews should continue to worship Yahweh even in the new way of life. This was because Yahweh was particularly connected with basic rules of the nation, the Law of Moses, and with inspiration (originally more or less shamanistic in type) that seized the nonpriestly spiritual leaders called prophets. Because they harked back to the nomadic period with its simpler ways, the parties favoring continuing loyalty to Yahweh had a rigid, conservative appearance, and the other side doubtless a suggestion of judicious flexibility.

Ironically, the faith in Yahweh had far more future to it and apparently far more potential for adjusting to various cultural levels, from planting to modern industrial; the desert god of the Hebrews lives today, while the Semitic agricultural religion, which seemed the height of sophistication in 800 B.C.E., did not outlive the cultural level it served.

A statement like this is, of course, only one side of the situation. A deity can keep the same name and become different, or change names and remain the same. The "wailing for Husain," which is a part of Islam in some sections of Iraq, India, and even Trinidad today, seems in direct continuity with the ancient near eastern wailing for Tammuz. Although the name of Yahweh was kept among the agricultural Hebrews, his worship evolved to include farming feasts and offerings, and these in turn have been retained among Jews long after they became urban.

It is no mark against Yahweh if his worship undergoes development, regardless of what the case may be with other gods. For a fundamental feature of the Hebrew scriptures is what we have spoken of as a historical or linear concept of time, in which God himself imparts new revelations in history. A picture steadily emerges of the relation between God and the Children of Abraham as like a dialogue in which God's faithfulness is always constant; but as his people are more or less loyal to their pledge, the situation takes different forms: reward for obedience and punishment for disobedience. It is a history in which God is himself acting and revealing more of himself. The Books of Deuteronomy and Chronicles in particular interpret the history of Israel in these terms, as do the prophets regarding the events of their day. One can think of it as a graph, with the high peaks representing the moments when Israel was seen as close to God and the low points the periods of apostasy.

The story begins with a very high point, the creation of the world and the placing of Adam and Eve in the Garden of Eden. But suddenly the graph falls to near the bottom as the primal couple disobey God in the matter of eating the forbidden fruit and are expelled from the original paradise. From then on, the dealings of God with the people of Israel are really a part of his plan to bring humankind back to the original high level of relationship.

The story of Noah, the ark, and the flood tells us that the process began as God exercised judgment toward the fallen world, and also mercy as he saved one righteous family, and specimens of the animals, in the destruction of the wicked. But the plan did not really get underway until Abraham and his family were called to leave Ur of the Chaldees, in order to go to a new land which God promised to give Abraham, where he would make of him a mighty nation. This was not for Abraham's sake alone, but was part of a plan for the good of the whole earth, for God said "by you all the families of the earth will bless themselves" (Gen. 12:1–3). The ancient city of Ur has been excavated, and it has been verified that there were people called Hapiru (Hebrews) in Ur, a Sumerian capital, before roughly 2000 B.C.E., when it appears Abraham and his people left for the Promised Land by way of Haran, a city in northern Mesopotamia which was a center of the cult of Sin, the moon-god.

This Covenant of God with Abraham was ratified by Abraham's sacrificing to God, and it was confirmed by God's giving Abraham a son, Isaac, in his old age. The promise then passed to Isaac and to his son Jacob, also called Israel, the name by which the Hebrew people became known. Under Abraham, Isaac, and Jacob, the line on the graph clearly moved upward; for all their human failings, a new relationship was being established between God and humankind in the patriarchs. Indeed, the sharp difference between Hebrew religion and some others could scarcely be more evident than in the personalities of the father of faith, Abraham, and his son and grandson. They are not mystics or meditators, magicians, or philosophers, but shrewd, barely literate, sometimes coarse, obscure wanderers on the edge of civilization, who fought and made love and drove hard bargains and (at least in the case of the young Jacob) were not above trickery to get their ends. In the Bible, however, it is not the self-purification or spiritual achievements of a yogi or adept or Buddha that makes one available to God to advance his work. It is rather that the one God, with true omnipotence, is able to reach to the "bottom of the barrel" if he wishes and select whomever he wants, however unpromising.

Very hard times came in the latter days of Jacob, and he went down to Egypt (where Jacob's son Joseph had been taken earlier and risen to power) to try to buy food. But in time the Children of Israel ended up in bondage there, and this was a low point on the graph, for the God of the patriarchs and his worship may have been nearly forgotten.

After 400 years, we are told, this situation was reversed through the labors of Moses, the most outstanding figure in the Hebrew scriptures. Moses appears as a member of the oppressed Hebrew class in Egypt who nonetheless advanced high in the service of the pharaoh. But he killed an Egyptian he saw beating a Hebrew and was forced to flee to the deserts of Midian (now northwest Saudi Arabia), where he kept the flocks of distant kinsmen. There God spoke to him in a vision of a burning bush, and Moses returned to Egypt to lead the Hebrew people out of bondage. He succeeded, and the event was fraught with great drama. Moses and his brother Aaron pronounced ghastly plagues upon Egypt to force pharaoh's hand, culminating in the death of the firstborn, save those of the Hebrews, who marked their homes with sacrificial blood so that this final plague would pass over them. That night, too, they ate a hurried meal in preparation for the flight from Egypt; this is commemorated in the Passover.

The Exodus probably occurred about 1300 B.C.E., although some date it a couple of centuries or so earlier. The narratives of the parting of the Red Sea, so that the escaping slaves could thwart their last pursuers, and of the forty years of wandering in the desert, are well known. At Mount Sinai, in the midst of this trek, the final definition of the covenant, or agreement, between God and Israel was made. Amid the thunder and lightning of a great storm, Moses on the mountain received the Ten Commandments and the rest of the law recorded in the Torah, or the first five books of the Bible containing the "Law of Moses." At this point, the line on the graph moves sharply up.

Moses himself died before he could lead Israel into the Promised Land; this difficult and warlike task was undertaken by his successor, Joshua. Gradually, a nation was put together from an assortment of restless herding and raiding tribes, who were at best a rough democracy under emergent leaders called "judges." (It must be pointed out here that scholars believe the Book of Judges contains the oldest material in the Bible that can be accepted as history in the ordinary sense, some of it having been written virtually on the scene. The accounts of the patriarchs, Moses, and the Exodus are of inestimable importance for the Judaeo-Christian-Islamic religious outlook and certainly reflect real events, but they reach us in the form of tradition rather than of strictly historical documents.) As the Hebrews adapted to the agricultural way of life indigenous to Palestine, sedentary institutions like kingship came to seem more and more appealing. Finally, it is written that God consented to the anointing of the first king, Saul, though Yahweh expressed only reluctant approval through the prophet Samuel for this development, indicating the conservative nature of the Yahwist and prophetic faith.

Saul, however, proved unworthy of the kingship; he failed to liquidate completely the people and flocks of the Amalek folk, as Samuel said Israel was commanded to do by the Lord. David, who was designated by Yahweh to succeed Saul, began his reign c. 1000 B.C.E. He was succeeded by one of his sons, Solomon.

Under Solomon a great temple to Yahweh was built in which all the ritual prescriptions of the Law of Moses for temple worship could be carried out; from the time of Moses until then Yahweh had been worshipped in a movable shrine called the tabernacle. After Solomon, the kingdom divided into Israel in the north and Judah around Jerusalem, and the glory of the people began to decline.

During these times the line on the graph, as read by devout later historians, wavered up and down like a fever chart. In the time of Joshua and the judges, it was presumed that whenever Israel won, the Lord was pleased with them; when Israel lost, it was because there had been sin. But then came the early prophets, such as Samuel, Elijah, Elisha, and Nathan, and after them writing prophets—Amos, Isaiah, Jeremiah, and the rest—who argued this was not necessarily the case. The prophets were apparently originally members of a class of seers who entered into some sort of visionary, divinatory trance, not wholly unlike a shaman's, and there gave out the direct word of God for a situation. As in the case of Samuel reproving Saul even as the king stood victorious over the Amalekites, or Nathan reproving David at the height of his glory for having taken Bathsheba, another man's wife, the word of the Lord that came through these envoys could well indicate God was displeased even when his people seemed successful. It could still happen that they were forgetting the fullness of God's commandments. Even in prosperity, they might, as Amos said, be too much "at ease in Zion" and sell the needy for a pair of shoes.

The low point in this period came in 586 B.C.E., when the Babylonians took

Jerusalem, destroyed the temple, and carried off leading citizens to Babylon for a life of exile and servitude. Prophets like Jeremiah blamed this on the failings of the king and nation. When, some decades later (the year 538 B.C.E. is often given), Cyrus of Persia took Babylonia and allowed the exiles to return and the temple to be rebuilt (an event celebrated in Isaiah Chapters 40 to 66 and described in Nehemiah and Ezra), it seemed a marvel beyond hope or belief, a victory of God when all was darkest, and is so sung in Isaiah 58:8 and many passages of similar power:

> Then shall your light break forth like the dawn,
> and your healing shall spring up speedily;
> your righteousness shall go before you,
> and the glory of the Lord shall be your rear guard.

Or in a psalm like 126:

> When the Lord restored the fortunes of Zion,
> we were like those who dream.
> Then our mouth was filled with laughter,
> and our tongue with shouts of joy.

Yet for all that, the religious experience of Israel was not fully satisfied with the Return, for it was also a return, like all such, to the ambiguities of ordinary life in history. There were new problems and new challenges. These were faced by the new temple and, even more significantly, by a new affirmation of Judaism as a religion of the Torah, or Law of Moses, and by new developments in literature and belief. The last centered on a literature of wisdom and the growth of a belief in a Last Day and a Messiah. But first let us look at the story of those times.

FROM THE SECOND TEMPLE TO THE TALMUD

Some twenty years after the first Jews were permitted to return to Jerusalem by Cyrus the Great in about 538 B.C.E., the foundations of a smaller but nonetheless adequate second version of the temple were laid in the Holy City by Zerubbabel and Haggai. It was completed in 515. But the work of rebuilding Jewish society in the land of Israel—of which the reconstruction of the temple was an important aspect—is epitomized in two men who subsequently were leaders in the religious and political spheres respectively, Ezra and Nehemiah. Each has his book in the Bible. The promulgation of the **Torah,** or Law, by Ezra in 444 B.C.E. and the people's assent to it (Nehemiah Chapters 8–10) is of immense religious importance, for it vividly displays the changes that exile and distance from the site of the temple had wrought in Judaism.* Though the temple was rebuilt, the religion became more and more what it ultimately would become, a religion of the synagogue and the written word, rather than of temple and sacrifice.

Although details are unclear, tradition has it that the text of the Torah and, eventually, that of the entire Hebrew Bible was edited and finalized over these years by an assembly of learned scholars called the Great Synagogue, founded by Ezra. These developments must have been accelerated by exile, when Jews had to make do religiously without temple rites and were far from their homeland. Instead it was necessary to gather, to pray and to sing what they could recall or had written down, to hear the words of the wise and of the books proclaiming the Law and the words of men of God, to eat and drink and hold festival in accordance with the Law, and to remember. This is the essence of synagogue life to this day, as a people becomes a community to learn and to manifest its common life in things solemn and joyous. Though the temple was rebuilt, more and more Jewish communities near and far worshipped mainly in the synagogue style, and within a few centuries this form of worship prevailed.

Here is that history. After the Return, the land of Israel remained a province of the Persian Empire, locally ruled (no doubt as far as possible under the emerging Law) by the Chief Priests of the restored temple and lay leaders such as Nehemiah, a Jew who had risen high in the civil service and arranged to have himself appointed governor of Judea. In 331 B.C.E., Alexander the Great conquered the Persian Empire and, with it, the homeland of the Jews. Alexander's empire, after his early death, was divided among his leading generals: Egypt going to the house of Ptolemy and Syria to that of Seleucus. Palestine went at first to Egypt but was later transferred to the Seleucids. In 168 B.C.E., the Syrian ruler Antiochus IV, after seeking to impose Greek civilization, desecrated the temple and prohibited the practice of Judaism.

This led to a rebellion much celebrated in Jewish lore. The Maccabee brothers mounted a campaign to drive out the oppressor. Then, in 165, they relit the lamps of the holy temple, a joyous event commemorated in the festival of Hanuka. For

---

* Most scholars believe that the Law read by Ezra at this time was essentially what is known at the Priestly Code, the legal, ritual, and moral prescriptions contained in the Book of Leviticus and large parts of Exodus and Numbers, or a portion of that code. Much earlier, before the Exile, the righteous king Josiah (r. 640–609 B.C.E.) had promulgated a book of the Law, which was probably essentially the Biblical Deuteronomy. Certainly the Law has a long history, much of it now lost, prior to Ezra. But Ezra's recitation and the people's response is of immense importance, for it represents the triumph of the Torah—and so of the Torah's God—as the supreme, unquestioned authority in normative Jewish religion. Before, especially before the purgation of exile, we read much of the admixture of Yahwist religion with various forms of paganism and idolatry. On another level, the charisma of the prophets, profoundly inspiring and disturbing, had reached its height in figures such as Isaiah, Jeremiah, and Ezekiel before and during the exilic era. It had then shared pride of place with the emerging Torah tradition, but now quickly fades also, subordinated to a scriptural text that contained (though in legal rather than poetic form) the Yahwist and Mosaic values for which the prophets had stood and, in time, their own "books." (The poetic tradition was perpetuated in the "wisdom" books of the Bible, such as the Psalms, large parts of which are certainly post-exilic.) After Ezra, we hear nothing of idolatry within Judaism and very little of fresh prophecy. Judaism from this point on was basically the religion of the Torah and its elucidation, and Jewish identity intimately bound up with the life of the Torah.

over a century thereafter (167–63 B.C.E.), Judea existed as a tiny and precariously independent state, first under the Maccabees, then their descendants, kings of the Hasmonean house, who increasingly combined high priestly and royal functions in Jerusalem. Rome brought the Holy Land into its empire in 63, ruling sometimes directly, sometimes through client kings such as Herod the Great and his lineage.

During these difficult years, the Jewish religious tradition, based on the now-established Torah, was being consolidated by a succession of distinguished rabbis, men such as Hillel, Gamaliel, and those of the school known as the Pharisees. They composed commentaries and case-applications of the Law, in part validated by the contention of the Pharisees that there was an oral Law given to Moses as well as the written, the former living in Judaism's succession of teachers and giving guidance to their exposition of the latter. These labors were compiled in the Mishnah (c. 200 B.C.E. to 200 C.E.) and the Gemara (c. 200 to 500 C.E.); both together make up the great multivolumed text known as the Talmud.

Next to the scriptures, no book is of more importance to Judaism than the multivolumed Talmud. It is a vast and ever-fascinating collection of religion, folklore, ethics, and jurisprudence, and it is the text to which all learned Jews instinctively turn first for illumination of the tradition's thought on virtually any issue, though its role is understood differently by liberal and Orthodox authorities.[**]

The new age brought forth other responses too. Jewish tradition divides the Hebrew Scriptures into three parts: the Torah; the Prophets, which also includes historical books; and the Writings, containing other books of history, such as Ruth and Esther, and the "Wisdom" literature—Psalms, Proverbs, Job, Ecclesiastes, and the Song of Solomon. Although the Wisdom Books incorporate much pre-exilic material, they were compiled in their final scriptural form in the days of the Second Temple or even later. These works are often called Wisdom Books because they are primarily concerned with presenting timeless words of devotion, reflection, moral advice, and philosophy. They are remarkably diverse; to one whose view of the Bible is chiefly shaped by those parts concerned with God's Law, judgment on sin, or calls to faith, passages in the Wisdom Books may seem amazingly skeptical or speculative.

Messianic belief also has pre-exilic roots, but it flourished most in the atmosphere of extreme alternating hope and disillusionment, and of the precarious national exis-

---

[**] It is important to point out that Jewish Orthodoxy does not mean the kind of direct, unmediated adherence to the scriptural text characteristic of Christian Fundamentalism. Rather (as in the case of so-called Muslim "Fundamentalism," with its insistence on strict adherence to the Shariah, the Islamic law developed case by case over centuries by its recognized interpreters), Orthodoxy does *not* mean individual recourse to the original Biblical Law but acknowledgment both of its divine inspiration and its legitimate interpretation and application by a recognized succession of rabbis, down to the rabbinical courts operative in Orthodox Judaism today. The findings of this succession are recorded in the Talmud and the later "responsa" of eminent jurisprudents. Rabbinical decisions, like those of any court, are bound to honor and take into account precedent, though variations along accepted lines may be mooted. The "fundamentalism" of Orthodox Judaism, though, lies in the literalistic acceptance of Talmudic and subsequent rabbinical teaching, not *directly* in scriptural literalism. Though the Hebrew Torah is believed to be literally inspired by God, word by word and even letter by letter, its explication is beyond the power of the unaided individual human intellect and requires the authoritative guidance of the tradition.

tence that characterized Israel after the Return. Prophetic proclamation of God's judgment led to growing expectation of a final, culminating judgment of the entire world and the making of a new, purified heaven and earth. Related to this idea was the believing hope that, before that great event, a Messiah (the word means "Anointed One," for anointing with oil was the way of designating a king in ancient Israel), or sublime hero and king, would be sent by God; he would defeat Israel's enemies and rule in perfect justice and peace. Many expected even nature to be bountiful beyond imagining in the messianic age.

MEDIEVAL AND MODERN JUDAISM

Just as one sees changes in Judaism from the desert wanderers' religion of Abraham or Moses to the temple of Solomon, spiritual center of a kingdom and of a largely farming society, so has it continually adjusted to new situations through its long subsequent history. There was the destruction of the first temple and the Exile to Babylon; but the temple was rebuilt, as we have seen. It was destroyed again by the Romans in 70 C.E., and from then on Judaism made a transition to a way based on the home-centered ethical and ceremonial precepts of the law, without the temple with its bleating animals, its heavy smells of blood and incense, and its richly vested priests. The transition was not as difficult as might seem, for it had already been made in effect everywhere in the widely dispersed Jewish community except Jerusalem. Worship outside the city was held in synagogues, "gathering places," and consisted of prayer and study of the Scriptures, without sacrifice. Jewish scholars, especially in Babylon where a large community had remained even after the return from the Exile, prepared out of close argumentation the vast commentaries on the Law called the Talmud, which made it both precise and flexible enough to be applicable to the new times in which Jews were more likely to be an urban minority than rural farmers and herders. Pilgrimage to the temple had once been the main bond of worldwide Jewry; now cohesion lay in the "Fence of the Torah," following the Law as interpreted by the Talmud, which gave inwardly and in the eyes of others a separate identity in a world of change and confusion. There were other kinds of flexibility, too; Philo Alexandria (first century C.E.), for example, interpreted the scriptures allegorically in terms of Platonic philosophy.

The "Fence of the Torah" style of Judaism persisted through the Middle Ages and into modern times, as Jews dwindled to very small numbers in their homeland (first ruled by Christians and then by Muslims) but became important minorities in European and Near Eastern cities, and spread as far as India and China. When they did not suffer persecution, they generally flourished, and many Jews rose to prominence in Christian or Muslim societies. Their education and diligence, fruits of the careful study that the law required, were frequently superior to that of their neighbors.

► *Construction of the Temple of Jerusalem Under the Order of Solomon* by Fouquet.

▼ *Story of Moses* by Raphael showing Moses with the Ten Commandments or covenant between God and Israel.

▶ Yom Kippur or Day of
Atonement children's
service.

▼ Circumcision, a rite of
passage which takes place
eight days after birth.

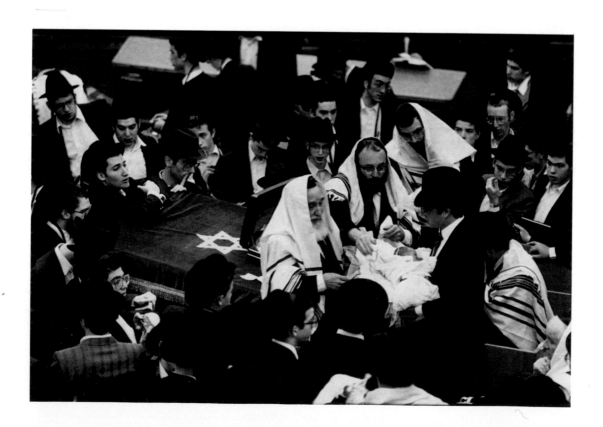

The Western or "Wailing" Wall of the Temple in Jerusalem
destroyed in 70 C.E.—a sacred site of pilgrimage.

Several new developments colored medieval Judaism. The form of Jewish mysticism called the **kabbala** had its supreme expression in the *Zohar*, or Book of Splendor, probably composed within a developing tradition by Moses de León in Spain about 1275.[2] Based on finding deeper, allegorical meanings in the words and letters of the Hebrew Torah which point to metaphysical realities, it held that God in himself is infinite and incomprehensible, but that his attributes provide windows of insight into God as he relates to humanity. As topics of meditation, certain basic attributes of God drawn from the Scriptures are arranged into a pattern of male-female polarities and on different levels in the hierarchy of spiritual things called the "kabbalistic tree." Meditation on their dynamic interaction provides a subtle and often profound spiritual path.

Kabbalism had many areas of influence, from magic to messianic movements. The most important was the more popular form of Jewish mysticism called Hasidism. This was a pietistic movement that started in Eastern Europe in the eighteenth century through the teaching of Ba'al Shem Tov (1700–60). Hasidism was a feeling-oriented reaction against rabbinic emphasis on learning and legalism, and against stifling social conditions; it taught Jews to follow the Law but to make it an expression of fervent love for God. (The colorful stories and doctrines with which its venerated *tzaddiqim* explained the meaning of love for God and the symbolism of ritual law were deeply dyed with kabbalistic lore. They emphasized pious love and the wisdom of the person of simple devotion.) Music, dancing, and even uncontrolled ecstatic behavior were frequently part of Hasidic worship. Small but vigorous groups of Hasidic background, such as the Lubovitcher movement, which has done much to encourage a return to Orthodox practice, are still active in Israel and America.[3]

Another strand of modern Judaism, the liberal and rationalistic, has roots both in certain ancient schools and in the thought of the medieval philosopher Moses Maimonides (1135–1204), whose commentaries on the Talmud and law codification made use of Greek philosophy and presented a smooth, logical face to the faith. It was not until the eighteenth-century Enlightenment, however, that this lineage exercised its full influence on Jewish life. Particularly in Germany, Jewish leaders and thinkers such as Moses Mendelssohn (1729–86) emphasized acculturation to non-Jewish European life and the critique and defense of Judaism through philosophy. In the end—although this was not Mendelssohn's intention—many Jews in Western Europe became more or less secularized, like countless Christians of the same period, more interested in the mainstream of European culture than the law and the synagogue.

Modern Jewish life is a conflux of several forces. It has been touched by traditional Orthodoxy, Hasidism, and Enlightenment secularization and liberalism. It is influenced also by the bitter effects of persecution in Russia in the late nineteenth and early twentieth centuries, and by a milder but ugly antisemitism widespread in Europe and America, restricting Jewish participation in many areas of life. Jewish immigration to America provided a reservoir of strength there; the American Jewish population is about 6 million.[4]

Most horrible of all Jewish experiences was the "Holocaust" under Nazism, in which some 6 million Jews perished before and during World War II, and traditional Jewish life in Europe was devastated. All Jewish life since then has been interwoven with sorrowful remembrance of this terrible event and with the attempt to cope with it. It has deeply affected Jewish-Christian dialogue. The determination that it not happen again has immensely strengthened support for an independent Jewish homeland.

Thus, a major force in modern Judaism is the movement known as Zionism, which led to the establishment of the state of Israel. Zionism, the effort of Jews to make a national homeland of their own, preferably in Palestine, began late in the nineteenth century as a response to the frustrations of confinement and prejudice in Europe. Palestine, though never without a Jewish community, had been mainly Muslim for a thousand years and was then part of the Turkish Empire, but European Jews began settling there in the 1890s, often forging out new lifestyles like that of the agricultural communes called *kibbutzim*. Against all probability, the global vicissitudes of the twentieth century led to the birth of the state of Israel in 1948. This was, of course, just after the Holocaust, and the population of the new nation was enriched by many survivors of that tragedy. They wanted to make it a place of refuge for Jews everywhere facing persecution. Israel includes Jews of all types, from the most secular to the extremely Orthodox and Hasidic; Israel is also a center of Jewish learning. Israel is important today as a cultural and religious focal point for world Jewry; it is important to many Jews also to be able to know there is one small place in the world that is free and definitely Jewish.

American Judaism is not homogeneous but is divided into three major traditions. **Orthodox** synagogues teach the full following of the Law, or Torah, and are quite traditional in Talmudic scholarship, theology, and forms of festival and worship. **Reform** Judaism, which calls its places of worship temples rather than synagogues, has roots in the German Enlightenment experience. It is liberal in attitude, oriented more to the prophets than the Law, and believes the essence of Judaism does not involve following the Law legalistically. Many Reform Jews follow it hardly at all save for major festivals, though they refer to its underlying principles in thinking about ethical and moral questions. Between the Reform and Orthodox camps is **Conservative** Judaism, which takes the Law seriously as a guide to life but believes that its provisions can and should be adjusted to suit the conditions of modern living.

JEWISH BELIEFS

Judaism is often presented as a religion in which the importance of formal, theological doctrine is minimized. In a real sense this is true. No dogma is as significant to most Jews as adherence to the Jewish community, a relationship many feel better expressed through practice—participation in the Sabbath worship, festivals, customs, and observances traditional to the community—and through a living sense of being part of the Jews' long history, than in creedal affirmations. Jewish theoretical and ideological expression, both on the part of theologians and of ordinary believers, has accordingly been remarkably free and varied. Practitioners of Judaism as a religion, or as a communal tradition, have ranged from literal believers in God as presented in the scriptures to agnostics and atheists.

Nonetheless, it is fair to say that over the centuries a broad theological consensus has survived among the majority of serious Jews. A conventional touchstone for its delineation has been thirteen principles of faith put down by the great medieval thinker Moses Maimonides:

1. God is Creator and Guide.
2. God is One in a unique way.
3. God does not have a physical form.
4. God is eternal.
5. God and God alone is to be worshipped.
6. God has revealed his will through the prophets.
7. Moses is the greatest of the prophets.
8. The Torah was revealed to Moses.
9. The Torah is eternal and unchanging.
10. God is all-knowing.
11. God gives rewards and punishments.
12. The Messiah will come.
13. The dead will be resurrected.

Whether interpreted strictly or liberally, these principles appear to have four main emphases. First, they affirm the existence of a God who is creator and sustainer of the world and who is absolutely one without a second. This expresses the uncompromising monotheism which is Judaism's central religious theme and most distinctive gift to humanity. Second, the principles affirm that this God is an active God, in some way continually involved in human history. He has revealed his will through prophets and scripture in the context of history and is preparing a messianic culmination of history. Third, they affirm the complete religious adequacy of Judaism; its greatest prophet, Moses; and its Torah. Fourth, they powerfully elucidate depth, meaning, and righteous judgment in individual human life, as they affirm that God knows each life thoroughly, bestowing rewards and punishments to each in a manner not fully specified. By speaking of personal resurrection Maimonides avows the eternal significance of each individual life.

Like all creeds, this statement cannot be wholly detached from its historical context; in this case, Judaism lived amidst Christianity and Islam. The opening stress on God's oneness, incorporeality, and eternity as metaphysical categories reflects the profound influence of Greek thought on the philosophical expression of all three faiths, and so establishes common ground. On the other hand, the principles indirectly distinguish Judaism from Christianity by making no allowance for the Trinity or the Incarnation of God in Christ, insofar as these tenets compromise God's oneness and bodilessness. They also clearly deny both Christian and Muslim assertions that Moses and the Torah were succeeded by greater prophets and more perfect scriptural revelations; and of course they disallow that the Messiah has already come. (Asked about the last point, most Jews will respond that while they much admire the Jew called Jesus as a heroic figure and great rabbi, he was not the kind of Messiah they expected and still anticipate, for after two thousand years the world is still painfully far from the reign of peace, justice, and abundance that prophecy declared the Messiah's age would bring.)

At the same time, some dimensions of Judaism are not mentioned in the principles. Most conspicuous is the concept of Jews as a "chosen people" having a special covenant relationship with God. As we have seen in connection with the traditional establishment of that covenant with Abraham, the momentous pact was not made with that patriarch alone but with all his descendants, and it was not for their sake alone but for the blessing of all the human race. For Jews this "specialness" has certainly brought as much or more suffering as blessing by any ordinary worldly measure, though its inner, spiritual worth is immeasurable in such terms. In any case, most Jews are well aware of their peculiar role as—to extreme extents—the blessers and sufferers of the world, and religious Jews give this experience special meaning as the product of their divine chosenness.

The problem of combining existence in historical time, so inseparably intertwined with chosenness, with Judaism's transcendent monotheism has been a crucial issue in modern Jewish thought. This has been all the more true since recent history has dealt Jews both opportunity and horror to unprecedented degrees: emancipation, the Enlightenment, moves into the mainstream of Western culture; immigration to the New World; pogroms and the unspeakable Nazi Holocaust; the rebirth of Israel as a state. In all this, the God of Israel has often been easily left behind, as though irrelevant to such new ways of life or such raw terror. Yet, some would say, never has the heart of Jewish faith been more needed. Here are three examples.

Franz Rosenzweig (1886–1929) insisted that divine revelation within historical time must be central to any religion which truly revolves around God and not merely on philosophical idealism or moral consciousness. This revelation is a relation between the eternal God and finite, time-bound individuals, a discourse between the divine subject as (to us) Thou and the dependent and autonomous I. This "I–Thou" relationship became the key concept of Rosenzweig's friend Martin Buber (1878–1965), who was also heavily influenced by Hasidism. Without diminishing the importance of the divine-human I–Thou, Buber made the I–thou concept a keystone of all authentic interpersonal relationships, in which the other is not simply an "it" to be used like an impersonal object, but a "thou," full of inwardness and subjectivity like that of the "I."

Abraham Joshua Heschel (1907–72), a Jewish thinker whose ideas often took mystical wing under kabbalistic and Hasidic inspiration, celebrated the holiness hidden in all things and the possibility of intense, passionate relationship between God and humans; Jewish practices sanctifying the whole of nature and life facilitate both realizations. Yet, as we shall see, Heschel also wrote of Judaism's particular emphasis on the manifestation of the sacred through time, whether in the stream of history or the annual round of festivals and holy days.

We must now turn to such sacred observances in Judaism. Before we leave the company of wise men, however, we might make one final observation: that both of the last two, Buber and Heschel, shared to the full the vicissitudes of modern

Jewry. Both were raised in the rich traditional, scholarly Jewish culture of Eastern Europe; both were compelled to leave the Europe of Hitler's Storm Troopers to end their days in two relatively safe havens for Jews—Buber in Israel and Heschel in the United States.

JEWISH LIFE

Let us examine some of the specifics of Jewish life. It should be remembered always that there are various degrees of observance and various attitudes toward the importance of, for example, the dietary laws and strictness of Sabbath-keeping. The differences are not only between the serious and the lax; Jews of equal inner commitment, insofar as this can be gauged, may place the emphasis on different strands of the tradition. (Differences of these kinds are, of course, found between the various traditions of all major religions.)

But throughout all of Jewish life a special chord reverberates. It is made up of a tradition of respect for education, awareness of history, and a sense of being an often-persecuted minority group, as well as the specific festivals, customs, and religious rites of Judaism. The close family and community life of Judaism reflects

The bride and groom under the chuppa or wedding canopy with their parents touching their heads in blessing at a Reform Jewish wedding.

this tone, through whichever of several possible styles of Jewish life it is expressed. There is always some sense of Jewish identity, too; it has often been commented that every Jew, however nonpracticing and secularized, knows that he or she is a Jew.

The sociological bedrock of Jewish life is the family. With only very few possible exceptions, such as the prophet Jeremiah and perhaps the Essene communities of Hellenistic times, religious celibacy has had no place in Judaism. One of the most consistent themes of all Jewish history, after the theme of being a special called-out

---

Fundamental Features of Judaism

Theoretical

Basic World View	Universe is made by God but is an arena of humans to live in and enjoy, exercising free will, in cooperation with God's guidance.
God or Ultimate Reality	In traditional Judaism, a sovereign, personal, all-good creator God.
Origin of the World	Created by God.
Destiny of the World	Will be led by God through historical vicissitudes, until finally a messianic age brings it to a paradisal state.
Origin of Humans	Created individually by God.
Destiny of Humans	Chiefly in this world; with divine help and human cooperation, the human condition can become better and better until a paradisal age is reached.
Revelation or Mediation between the Ultimate and the Human	The scriptures, especially the Torah, or Law, and its traditional interpretation in the Talmud.

Practical

What Is Expected of Humans: Worship, Practices, Behavior	To honor and serve God by following the Law of Moses in letter or spirit, to maintain the identity of the people, and to promote the ethical vision of the great prophets and humanitarians. Jewish customs are followed in the home as well as in the place of worship.

Sociological

Major Social Institutions	After the Jewish people as such, the basic unit is the congregation of Jews, forming a synagogue or temple. Jewish family life is also very important.

covenant people, is that of the holiness of marriage and the procreation of children: a fundamental religious duty for the wisest and holiest rabbi as well as for any other Jew. It is not a concession to the weakness of the flesh but a sacred as well as a joyful way of life and a part of the covenant:

> The whole world depends on the holiness of the union between man and woman, for the world was created for the sake of God's glory and the essential revelation of His glory comes through the increase of mankind. Man must therefore sanctify himself in order to bring to the world holy people through whom God's glory will be increased. . . .[5]

It is in the family, then, that religious observances begin. The Sabbath, festivals, and the dietary rules all involve, especially in Orthodox tradition, much more that is done at home than in the synagogue with the community as a whole—the Sabbath meal and prayers, holiday blessings and customs like Hanuka lights and the Passover meal in which the head of the family is the religious leader, the hours spent preparing food according to religious regulation. Beside this, the synagogue is not where religion "happens" so much as where one receives instruction and inspiration to make it happen in its true locus. But under the changed conditions of modern life the tendency, especially in the more liberal traditions, is to express Jewish identity more through synagogue, temple, or community participation and less through the complicated and time-consuming home actions in their traditional forms. Even so, it must be emphasized that the home can still be a place where Jewish identity in its moral and cultural meaning is learned and deeply felt.

The cornerstone of Jewish practice is the observance of the **Sabbath.** This period of twenty-four hours from sunset Friday to sunset Saturday commemorates the Lord's day of rest after the work of creation, and it is intended for the rest and refreshment of both body and soul. On it no work is done, and there is feast and celebration and nourishment for the body and mind and soul at the table and the synagogue. Far from being an onerous burden or a time of negative prohibition, the classical Jewish literature sees the Sabbath as a bountiful gift to God's people, as a lovely bride to be welcomed with eager love.[6]

Traditional Sabbath observance begins with concluding one's ordinary business, bathing, and putting on fresh garments reserved for that festive day on Friday afternoon. After sundown, the previously prepared Sabbath meal is eaten, with traditional Sabbath dishes and prayers and blessings over the food and the full cup of wine.

On the next day there is public worship in the morning and late afternoon. Synagogue or temple worship consists basically of reading from the Torah and the other Scriptures, prayers, and chants. But the atmosphere of the worship will vary considerably from one tradition to another. In Orthodox synagogues, men and women will be on separate sides; the liturgy will be in Hebrew; and the preservation of many ornate ritual customs, as well as in some cases a certain Hasidic exuberance expressed, perhaps, in swaying or dancing to the music, will suggest that this is the Judaism most in continuity with that of Old World Europe. In Reform temples, the service will be plain and dignified, with more emphasis on the sermon. Conservative synagogues will follow a middle course. However, Reform and Conservative worship, like that of some once-staid Christian churches, is today in a new way discovering the Jewish heritage of lively music, dance, and chant, especially in services for young people.

The most important object in any Jewish place of worship is the Torah, the scroll of the Law, in its large ornamented box, called the Ark, at the front of the hall. A lamp continually burns before it. Opening the door and curtains in front of the Torah, and finally removing it from the case for reverent reading, are major actions in the drama of the service.

FESTIVALS AND PRACTICES

Besides the regular Sabbath worship, the Jewish year is marked by several festivals. Although not really as important as the weekly celebration of the Sabbath—only the Sabbath is mentioned in the Ten Commandments—many Jews today observe something of the "High Holy Days" (Rosh Hashana and Yom Kippur) and the Passover if nothing else. The holidays can be divided into three groups. Because they follow the partially lunar Jewish calendar, the dates (like that of the Christian Easter) vary from year to year.

First are the **High Holy Days,** or "Days of Awe," which come in the autumn. Rosh Hashana, literally "Head of the Year," is kept as the anniversary of the creation and is the Jewish New Year's Day. Then, after a sacred season of ten days for repentance, comes Yom Kippur, the Day of Atonement. It is said to be the day when God reckons up the sins of every person for the previous year and, accordingly, sets their fate for the coming year. For some Jews this is only a metaphor, but it sets the tone of Yom Kippur, a day when each person in her heart assesses guilt and determines how to amend her life. The customs of the day create a backdrop for this inward strife and turning: fasting for twenty-four hours and a daylong synagogue service full of haunting, dirgelike music and corporate confession.

Three happier festivals are basically grounded in the agricultural society of ancient Israel and fit the seasonal cycle of all archaic agricultural religion yet also have meaning as commemorating the mighty acts of God on behalf of Israel recorded in the Bible; they orient the believer to God's work both in nature and in history. These are Passover in the spring, Shavuot in late spring or early summer, and Sukkot in autumn.

The Passover, or Pesah, recalls God's sparing, or "passing over," the firstborn of the Israelites and the hurried meal that the Israelites ate before leaving their enslavement in Egypt for the great events of the Exodus, the parting of the Red Sea, the receiving of the Law at Sinai, and the entry into the Promised Land. An impressive family rite, the Passover meal, or Seder, with its traditional foods (the paschal lamb, which is not actually eaten but is like a sacrifice, unleavened bread, roasted egg, vegetable, bitter herbs, wine, and so forth) and the question and answers between the youngest son and the father concerning the meaning of the symbols, is deeply loved in Jewish homes and is the Jewish holiday best known to Christians because of its association with the death of Jesus.

Shavuot, or Pentecost, seven weeks after Passover, was anciently a harvest festival for grain, and is also commemorated as the anniversary of the giving of the Law on Mount Sinai. Traditional Jews mark it by all-night study of the Torah, and it is a customary time for religious confirmation and graduation exercises.

Bright and colorful Sukkot is the autumn harvest festival for fruit and vegetables. When possible, "booths" are set up on lawns and in temples, gaily decorated with apples, pomegranates, gourds, corn, and the like. The booths are covered with straw, boughs, or palm fronds, but with spaces so one can see the stars. People eat, study, and sometimes sleep in them; like so much of Judaism, it is the sort of religious rite the children find exciting and unforgettable.

Finally, there are several minor holy days. Only two of the best known will be cited, Purim and Hanuka.

Purim, in February or March, commemorates the story recounted in the Book of Esther: how the Jews were saved from the wicked designs of Haman, chief minister of the Persian king, by Esther the queen and her cousin Mordecai. Like Mardi Gras, or carnival, in Latin countries, which comes at approximately the same time, Purim is the time when religion gives sanction to the role of comedy, buffoonery, and "letting go" in human life. Tradition says one may drink until one cannot tell the difference between "Blessed be Mordecai" and "Cursed be Haman." During the reading of the story in the synagogue, children gleefully make a tremendous racket with noisemakers whenever the name Haman is spoken. Strolling players and schoolchildren perform farces in which solemn rabbis and elders might be spoofed most of all.[7]

Hanuka comes at about the time of the Christian Christmas and has become popular in America partly as a result of this association. It commemorates the rededication of the temple in Jerusalem in 165 B.C.E., as we have seen. The event is too late even to have been included in the Jewish Bible, although the Books of Maccabees do appear in the Roman Catholic Bible and in the "Apocrypha" of some Protestant versions. The celebration is simple and is carried out in the home. An eight-branch Hanuka menorah, or candelabra, is lit, and a Hanuka song sung, over an eight-day period. On the first night cakes and gifts are presented to the children.

Jewish boys undergo certain rites of passage: circumcision, performed as a religious act, when eight days old; **Bar Mitzvah,** when the boy reads from the Hebrew Scriptures and begins the entry into manhood. In America, the Bar Mitzvah has often become the occasion of gala celebrations; in the Reform tradition, and to some extent in the Conservative tradition, a parallel festival for girls, the Bat Mitzvah, has been introduced. Reform Judaism also has a confirmation rite for young people of high school age, when commitment to the faith is expressed.

The Jewish dietary laws have had an immense role over the centuries in keeping the faith alive and its people together, for the rules of food preparation are so exacting they make it almost a practical necessity—if they are to be kept—for one to eat with, and therefore live in and marry within, his or her own community. Today, however, their observance varies; some follow them minutely, some give them only token honor such as refusal to eat pork, some feel they are entirely irrelevant to the modern world and observe them not at all.

No restrictions govern food from plants; the law deals only with killing and eating conscious life. The basic rules are that animals eaten must have a split hoof and chew the cud; this includes cattle and sheep but excludes a vast swarm: swine, reptiles, elephants, monkeys, horses, and all carnivorous beasts, among others. Of sea creatures, only those with fins and scales may be taken; of aerial creatures, birds of prey and insects are forbidden. Furthermore, meat must be slaughtered and prepared in special ways to be "kosher," or edible by those keeping the dietary rules. The rules also forbid the eating of meat and dairy products together, and expects that separate pots and plates will be used for each; the keeping of two sets of dishes (and a third for Passover) is a sure sign of a quite traditional Jewish home.

The tradition requires men to pray morning and evening and to give time to Torah study, although it never puts obligations on women that must be met at particular times except the purifications connected with the female cycle. Two styles of life in relation to God—the male dealing with word and schedule, the female with food preparation and home—are encompassed in Judaism.

In all these observances we see again that Judaism is not primarily oriented toward doctrine as its basis; one finds that ideas about God and such matters as the afterlife vary immensely, and that even many fairly orthodox observants profess to be skeptical or uninterested in them. Yet the Jewish faith continues to be intensely felt as a way of life here and now.

The reason may be that it is oriented toward time and history, rather than eternal ideas, as the source of human meaning and obligation. The Law is important because it comes out of past history and now controls present time, making time holy through demands on how it is spent and how biological events in time are sanctified. In turn, the Jewish hope of salvation is chiefly oriented toward future time. The tradition affirms that God will, in his time, send the Messiah, a hero heir to the greatest kings and prophets of old but greater than they, and in his day and through his work all evils on the earth will be rectified and an era of joy initiated. Some interpret this hope literally; others figuratively, in terms of a "Messianic Age."

Judaism is a religion whose centers of value are in time: tradition out of the past and hope for the future. We are beings in time and history, and we are to look to the tradition and our hopes, rather than to new revelation or mysticism alone to find what we need most to know and believe to live this human life as it is meant to be lived.

SUMMARY

The pioneers of the tradition of the great monothestic faiths were the ancient Israelites, the people of the Old Testament. Their self-understanding as a people with a covenant relation to God, who was leading them for his ultimate purposes through suffering and success in historical time, gave them a special attitude toward God and history and a scripture to interpret it. The scriptures contained the Torah, or Law of Moses— its first five books—giving the commandments God had given the people to set them apart and reveal the covenant relationship; histories, showing the course of the relation with God; prophetic books, giving the proclamations of divine spokesmen of what God says in particular situations; and wisdom books, with timeless poetry and philosophy from out of this historical experience.

The center of worship was the temple in Jerusalem. But around the beginning of the Christian era, because of the dispersal of the Jews and the destruction of the temple, worship and learning came to be centered around the synagogue, a gathering of the community for prayer and study. In the Middle Ages, Jews experienced widespread dispersion throughout Europe, where they were sometimes prosperous and sometimes persecuted. The mystical philosophy called kabbalism arose. Since the beginning of modern times in the seventeenth century, Judaism has seen the rise of the popular mysticism called Hasidism in Eastern Europe, trends toward rationalism and secularism in response to the Enlightenment, persecutions culminating in the Holocaust during World War II, further dispersal through immigration, and Zionism—the successful movement to create a Jewish state in the Holy Land.

Judaism has the highest regard for marriage and the family; ideally, Jewish religious life revolves around the home even more than the synagogue. Its chief expression is the Sabbath with its special observances. The High Holy Days and festivals are yearly landmarks of faith. Jewish distinctiveness and faith is also shown through the rites by which persons are brought into the adult community and among some by following dietary laws.

American Jews are divided among Orthodox, Conservative, and Reform schools of interpretation. All have in common a sense of a unique Jewish experience and mission in the world, and an emphasis on the sacred importance of time and history.

QUESTIONS FOR REVIEW

1. Talk about the thematic chart for Judaism, showing how this religion has produced both traditionalist and innovative expressions and has shown in various movements both feeling-oriented and rationalistic approaches.

2. Interpret the meaning to Judaism of the Jews as "chosen" or covenant people.

3. Discuss the Jewish scriptures (Old Testament) as a drama of the relation of God and humanity.

4. Summarize the history of Judaism from the second temple to the Middle Ages, and the emergence of the Talmud, the synagogue, and the rabbinical tradition.

5. Cite the main features of medieval Judaism, such as its dispersion and Kabbalistic thought.

6. Cite the main features of modern Jewish history: Hasidism, the Enlightenment and Jewish responses to it, immigration to the New World, persecution and the Holocaust, and Zionism.

7. Discuss basic Jewish beliefs and the perspectives of important modern Jewish thinkers.

8. Talk about the meaning and role in Judaism of the family, the Sabbath, the High Holy Days and festivals, and the dietary laws.

9. Discuss initiation into Judaism through circumcision and the Bar Mitzvah.

10. Interpret the meaning of Judaism as a religion oriented toward time.

SUGGESTED READINGS ON THE HEBREW BIBLE AND JUDAISM

Hebrew Scriptures/Old Testament

*ALBRIGHT, W. F., *From the Stone Age to Christianity*. Garden City, NY: Doubleday, 1957. A scholarly guide to Palestinian archaeology, emphasizing its relation to the Old Testament and its meaning for philosophy of history.

ANDERSON, B., *Understanding the Old Testament*. Englewood Cliffs, NJ: Prentice-Hall, Inc., rev. ed., 1986. A standard introductory textbook.

*BUBER, MARTIN, *The Prophetic Faith*. New York: Macmillan, 1949. A study by a famous Jewish theologian.

FLANDERS, HENRY JACKSON, ROBERT W. CRAPPS, AND DAVID A. SMITH, *People of the Covenant: An Introduction to the Old Testament*. 3rd ed., New York: Oxford University Press, 1988. A good standard introduction.

*GASTER, T. H., *Dead Sea Scriptures*. Garden City, NY: Doubleday, 1964. A semipopular overview of these important finds and their meaning.

HARRISON, ROLAND KENNETH, *Introduction to the Old Testament*. Grand Rapids: Eerdmans, 1969. A standard text written from an evangelical perspective.

HESCHEL, ABRAHAM, *The Prophets*. New York: Harper & Row, 1962, 1969. A brilliant introduction to the spirit of prophetic religion in ancient Israel by a very distinguished Jewish thinker.

*PRITCHARD, JAMES B., *The Ancient Near East in Pictures*. Princeton: Princeton University Press, 1954. A fascinating survey by a distinguished archaeologist.

TRIBLE, PHYLLIS, *Texts of Terror*. Philadelphia: Fortress, 1984. A powerful look at controversial Biblical passages from a religious feminist perspective.

Judaism

*BAMBERGER, BERNARD J., *The Story of Judaism*. New York: Schocken Books, 1970. A valuable introduction.

*BOROWITZ, EUGENE B., *Liberal Judaism*. New York: UAHC, 1984. An important statement of a non-Orthodox Jewish perspective.

*BULKA, REUVEN P., *Dimensions of Orthodox Judaism*. New York: KTAV, 1983. A survey of the Orthodox position and its varieties.

*FINKELSTEIN, LOUIS, ED., *The Jews: Their History, Culture, and Religion*. 2 vols., New York: Harper, 1949. A standard reference.

*FRIEDMAN, MAURICE, *Martin Buber's Life and Thought*. 3 vols., New York: Dutton, 1981–84. A comprehensive survey of Buber's contribution.

*GLATZER, NAHUM N., ED., *Franz Rosenzweig: His Life and Thought*. New York: Schocken, 1961. An introduction to this important thinker.

*HESCHEL, ABRAHAM, *Between God and Man: An Interpretation of Judaism*. New York: Free Press, 1965. The view of a very distinguished, moderately liberal modern Jewish thinker.

*KAUFMAN, WILLIAM E., *Contemporary Jewish Philosophies*. New York: Reconstructionist Press, 1976. An introductory survey of current Jewish theology.

*NEUSNER, JACOB, *The Life of Torah: Readings: The Jewish Religious Experience*. Encino CA: Dickenson, 1974. An anthology; emphasizes discussion of the Commandments.

*———, *The Way of Torah: An Introduction to Judaism*. 2nd. ed., Encino, CA: Dickenson, 1974. A good introduction; emphasizes Jewish history and way of life.

*ROSENTHAL, GILBERT S., *Contemporary Judaism: Patterns of Survival*. New York: Human Sciences, 1986. A valuable introduction to the history and ideology of the major Jewish traditions, Orthodox, Conservative, Reform, and Reconstruction.

*SELTZER, ROBERT M., *Jewish People, Jewish Thought*. New York: Macmillan, 1980. A sensitive interactive treatment of Jewish history and ideas.

*WAXMAN, MEYER, *Judaism: Religion and Ethics*. New York: Thomas Yoseloff, 1953. A clear survey of Jewish practice and moral attitudes today.

WOUK, HERMAN, *This Is My God*. Garden City, NY: Doubleday, 1959. A popular statement of the meaning of Orthodox Judaism by a well-known novelist.

Jewish Mysticism

*SCHOLEM, GERSHOM G., *Major trends in Jewish Mysticism*. New York: Schocken Books, 1961. Quite scholarly; the definitive work, especially on the kabbala.

*WEINER, HERBERT, *9 ½ Mystics: The Kabbala Today*. New York: Holt, Rinehart & Winston, 1969. A fascinating, easy-to-read account by a modern rabbi of visits to contemporary centers of Jewish mysticism; provides an incomparable insight into their spirit.

See also the *Encyclopedia Judaica,* 16 vols., Jerusalem, 1971.

CHAPTER 8

Spreading the Word of God in the World:
THE GROWTH OF CHRISTIANITY

CHAPTER OBJECTIVES

After studying this chapter, you should be able to

- Place the life and teaching of Jesus in historical context.

- Explain the historical development of the Christian religion.

- Summarize the teaching, practice, and institutional life of the major forms or denominations of Christianity.

- Discuss the position of Christianity in the world today.

THE SCOPE OF CHRISTIANITY

For the majority of Americans, Christianity is the most familiar form of religious expression. In fact, it probably shapes unconscious attitudes about what religion "ought" to be like.

In a sense this reaction is appropriate today, for in the twentieth century few countries have more influenced the world's religious history than the United States, except in a very different way the Marxist countries. Apart from countless indirect American influences on world culture and hence on religion, America has served in this century as chief bastion, financial resource, and exporter of its various forms of Christianity—from Roman Catholicism to Pentecostalism, the latter originating here in its present form in this century to become a Christian "third force" worldwide.

But Christianity is also an ancient faith with a long history, the greater part of it transpiring before America was settled by Europeans, and set in cultural environments immensely remote from ours. Most of the other major faiths, except Islam, are closer to 2500 than 2000 years old, the age of Christianity. But Christianity is scarcely behind any of them in the sense of antiquity breathed by its oldest shrines in the Old World. The comparatively new brick, glass, or wood churches that dot Christian America by the tens of thousands may give this religion an almost modern facade, but that is not the impression it gives in other places. In Europe the church buildings are often the oldest structures in an old city, giving a feel of the remote past.

The hymns and worship style *we* call the "old-time religion" largely date only from the nineteenth-century American frontier. Before that are eighteen other centuries of Christianity. Some of the forms it took in the past would seem almost as exotic as Tibet to us, and much of this history is relatively little understood or known by most American Christians.

In the waning days of the Roman Empire, Christians not only worshipped in underground burial tunnels called catacombs and met lions in the Colosseum, but wrote, argued, and took the faith to barbarian tribes who built churches on wagons to follow them on their wanderings. While western Europe was in the Dark Ages, worship in Constantinople—with its opulently robed priests, clouds of incense, and sonorous music—reached a splendor that visiting Russians reportedly said was closer to heaven than earth. In the tenth century, the Nestorian Church of the East, following the caravan routes, was planted from Mesopotamia to the imperial city of Tang China. A Christian church of Eastern Orthodox type has existed in South India since the fourth century at least. At the other end of the world, Irish monks let God guide their flimsy boats to remote islands and promontories, inhabited only by sea gulls, to build rough monasteries.

Then there are somewhat more familiar but no less colorful Christian images: medieval popes in monarchical splendor, crusaders, manuscript-copying monks, Canterbury pilgrims, Protestant reformers, visionaries of the Blessed Virgin Mary at Lourdes or Fatima, and missionaries on tropical islands. Christianity embraces worshippers at high masses and at silent Quaker meetings, people for whom the faith is a liberal charter and those for whom it demands the most rigorous conservatism on both social and theological issues.

JESUS

Like all major religions, Christianity has integrated into itself meanings and practices from many places where it has dwelt: The process begins with the Greek vocabulary of the New Testament itself. But there is only one focal point which brings together all this diversity: the last two or three years in the earthly life of Jesus of Nazareth, called the Messiah or Christ, in the first century C.E.

He appeared publicly in Roman-occupied Palestine around the year 30 C.E. Jesus was first visible as an associate of a man called John the Baptizer, an ascetic

Byzantine art: "Detail of St. John the Baptist."

who had lived in the desert and then had come into the Jordan Valley to preach fiery outdoor sermons calling on people to repent and change their ways, for God was about to judge the world and punish the wicked. Such apocalyptic expectation was rife at this time, all the more since the heavy hand of Roman tyranny seemed to block all nonsupernatural hope for the Jewish nation or for individuals, except those who curried favor with Rome.[1] The repentance John called for was marked by a ritual washing, or baptism, which he administered to his converts in the Jordan River.

Among those who received this baptism was a young man from Nazareth called Jesus (Joshua). Not much is definitely known about his background. The stories later told about his descent from David, miraculous conception, birth in Bethlehem, and childhood are hard to corroborate historically and are generally accepted or not on the basis of one's religious outlook; for Christians, they embody important religious truths about Jesus.

Shortly after Jesus' baptism by John, the latter was arrested and then executed. This arrest did not give Jesus the leadership of John's movement directly, but it did partly inspire him to gather disciples and start a ministry of his own, which was in some ways parallel to John's but came to develop distinctive characteristics.

Like John, Jesus began by proclaiming in his preaching that the **Kingdon of God** was at hand. The "Kingdom" meant the paradisal rule of God which would follow the apocalyptic distress and judgment. The Kingdom as a concept was intimately tied up with the work of the Messiah, who would inaugurate it.[2] Jesus also taught that people should repent of their former ways and live now as though in the Kingdom, in preparation for it. The principles for this way of life are assembled in the Sermon on the Mount in Chapters 5, 6, and 7 of Matthew's Gospel; the essence is to practice forbearing love and nonresistance of evil because God will shortly be dealing with it in judgment, and to be perfect even as the God who is to rule is perfect. By comparison, John's moral message was merely of repentance and following justice.

Unlike John, Jesus did not baptize, although his followers did. His work of healing was the major sign in his ministry of the power of the coming Kingdom, as baptism had been John's major sign. His miracles of healing the sick, the insane, the blind, and the paralyzed, and his other miracles such as feeding the 5000 with five loaves and two small fish, are presented as signs of the Kingdom's arrival. Healing was often understood as the exorcism of evil spirits from the disturbed. Jesus said, "If it is by the finger of God that I cast out demons, then the kingdom of God has come upon you" (Luke 11:20).

The nature miracles and healings bring to light another special feature of Jesus ministry, his aura of authority, and his mingling with both sexes and with all classes of society. Jesus taught everywhere, not only in synagogues but also by the lakeshore and in open fields. Instead of using close argument or extensive scriptural analysis, he used stories—parables—and simple but acute aphorisms to make his points; or, better, to catch up the hearer in the luminous web of his vision of the Kingdom's nearness—so near its power is already breaking through and is within reach of those who see its rising light.

Engraving of Jesus healing the sick by Gustave Dore.

Just as the Kingdom was for everyone, but in a special sense for the poor who had so little now, so did Jesus bring its message to everyone. He numbered among his associates fishermen, prostitutes, the revolutionary zealots, the despised tax collectors, and (though he also harshly upbraided them) members of the strict religious party, the Pharisees. He did not inculcate extreme asceticism, but rather was known as the teacher who came eating and drinking, and his illustrations show a sympathetic awareness of the ways and problems of ordinary life with its sorrows, joys, and innocent festivities.

After only a short year or two of this life, however, the young wandering preacher and charismatic wonder-worker of the Kingdom left Galilee, his homeland, and went down to Jerusalem shortly before the Passover. He clearly intended this journey, which God had laid upon him, to be a climactic appeal to Israel to accept the incoming Kingdom and reject perversions of religion. To this end he made certain dramatic gestures: He entered the pilgrim-thronged holy city in a sort of procession, and he caused a disturbance overturning the tables of the currency exchangers and the chairs of the sellers of birds and animals for sacrifice in the temple courtyard. He and his disciples then withdrew for a few days to live in suburban Bethany and to teach in the temple precincts.

But in the edgy political situation, these gestures combined with news of Jesus' popular appeal in Galilee understandably came to the concerned attention of Roman and Jewish authorities alike. They perceived revolutionary political overtones in the young prophet's activities and appeal. How far this perception was justified is much disputed by historians, but there is no doubt there were those among both supporters and opponents of Jesus who expected him to be at least the figurehead in an uprising against Rome, and perhaps against the collaborating Jewish elite as well.[3] This was an upshot neither the Romans nor the Jewish elite wished. Before the end of the week the decision had been taken and carried out to dispose of him.

Jesus was arrested with the help of a disgruntled radical among his disciples and hastily but decisively tried by the various authorities concerned, ultimately before the harsh Pontius Pilate, the Roman governor who throughout his tenure had shown no pity to protesters against Roman rule. (Indeed, Rome finally recalled him for excessive cruelty.) On Friday in Passover week Jesus was executed by being nailed to a structure made of two crossed beams set upright, the slow and agonizing death that Rome awarded to rebels. But the story did not end there.

THE EARLY
CHRISTIAN COMMUNITY

The drama of this tragic death of one so young, beloved, and appealing to many inevitably worked deeply into the minds of those who had been committed to his movement and caught up in his vision of the Kingdom. They tried to find ways to understand the man and the event in categories familiar to them. Some thought of the tradition of a coming Messiah, "Anointed One" or King (the title "Christ" is the literal Greek translation of "Messiah"), and wondered if, as some of Jesus' words and deeds suggested, he were this figure. In particular, they now conjoined the Messiah image with the poignant passages in Isaiah about the "suffering servant"— the hero who saves his people not by military victory but by undergoing excruciating pain, baring his back to the smiters, his cheek to those who plucked out the hairs.

Some thought of the words "Son of Man," which he had often used, words which his hearers would have recognized as referring to the mysterious judge who would descend on clouds at the Last Day in the current apocalyptic expectations; it was frequently ambiguous whether Jesus meant the title to refer to himself or another coming one, or if he meant both at the same time. Others, closer to the Greek religious tradition, thought of the titles "Lord" and "Son of God" used of Hellenistic kings and deities alike, or even of philosophical concepts like *Logos* ("Word" or "Principle") or *Sophia* ("Wisdom"), used to describe the creative power of God at work in the world, in connection with the enigmatic and unforgettable man from Nazareth. As to exactly how he thought of himself and his mission, in his own subjectivity, who can say? Almost all we know of him, including the words he is reported to have spoken, comes to us through the hands of those who saw him in light of categories such as the above. Beyond all the words, however, there is mystery—the mystery of one whose charm and sternness, magic and endurance of torture, empathy and remoteness, combined to make him both unknown and unforgettable. He had the combination of mystery and clarification of all great religious images and symbols.

Soon enough he was a supreme symbol of the ineffable mysteries of life, death, and God, all of which he somehow seemed to focus. His form and the instrument of his suffering were reproduced in gold and silver and gems around the world.

This kind of thinking took hold in the community of Jesus' disciples and followers. Historical Christianity has never been a purely individual religion. Even before the crucifixion, it was communal; the disciples, leaving job and family, formed a new social group around Jesus, and it was in the context of this group especially formed in expectation of the Kingdom that the teaching about the Kingdom and the wonders which foreshadowed it were imparted. The disciples were always at hand for Jesus' preaching and miracles, and it was they who were told the inner meaning of parables and signs. The disciples were a called-out group who knew the Kingdom of Heaven was at hand, and they lived for that reality.

On the Friday Jesus died on the cross, this community was dispirited and scattered; Peter went back to his fishing. But on the first day of the next week, word of a new event brought the community together again. It was reported by Mary Magdalene, a woman close to Jesus and the disciples, and then by Peter himself, that the tomb was empty and Jesus was walking in the garden where he had been interred. More such accounts were quickly bruited about: He had joined two disciples walking to Emmaus, and when they broke bread together he was known to them; the disciples were in a room with the doors shut, and he appeared in their midst; they were in a boat, and he appeared on the shore and cooked breakfast for them. He seemed the same and yet different in these postdeath appearances, as though partly in a different dimension. He ate. "Doubting Thomas" was able to touch his wounds to assure himself he was really the crucified one and not a ghost or imposter. Yet this Jesus was able to pass through shut doors and appeared or disappeared unexpectedly and by no pattern discernible to mortals. Finally, forty days after the first appearance in the garden, the resurrected Jesus appeared to them, we are told, in familiar Bethany. There, as they talked, he took them out to a nearby hill, blessed them, and was taken up into heaven.

By now, the nascent Christian community—the disciples, certain women such as Mary Magdalene and Mary the mother of Jesus, and peripheral followers—was vitalized and enthusiastic. The series of mysterious resurrection appearances, which came only to members of the community, greatly reinforced its thinking about who Jesus was along the lines of the categories mentioned above. The supreme event came when, during Pentecost, shortly after his ascension into heaven, those who were gathered in an upstairs room suddenly felt tremendously shaken by a spiritual force they were certain was the Holy Spirit of God mentioned in the Old Testament, and whose coming was remembered to have been promised by Jesus.

After receiving the Holy Spirit, the **apostles,** as the inner core of the group were now called, began preaching in the streets to the many peoples who crowded into the holy city. They preached basically that Jesus who had died was risen from the dead, that this event confirmed that he was and is both Lord and Messiah, and so all the scriptural prophecies about both the Jewish and universal roles of the Messiah and the Last Days were fulfilled or will be in him.

Many heard and believed. Most were Jews, but some of the earliest converts to the truth and significance of this new happening in Judaism were Greeks, probably of a class called proselytes, who, without undertaking the whole of the law, admired Judaism, worshipped its God, and accepted as much of its teaching and practice as possible. The incipient universalism of the Christian sect, with its proclamation of a new age when the reign of the Jewish God would be evident everywhere, and was now already present in Christ, eased the spiritual plight of such half-and-half people greatly—it was the breakthrough in Judaism for which many must have yearned.

PAUL

This role of Christianity in presenting Jesus as a manifestation of God who welcomed Jew and Greek alike was given preliminary definition by the council of the apostles described in Acts 15, where only a minimal adherence to the Jewish Law was required of non-Jews. But it was in the work of Paul, the most notable convert and missionary in the days of the early fellowship, that this universalism in Christ fully came through.[4]

Paul was originally called Saul. He was a strict follower of the Law and a persecutor of the new Christian sect. But while traveling from Jerusalem to Damascus in his anti-Christian efforts, at one place in the road he unexpectedly fell to the ground in a violent rapture; he experienced a vision of Jesus the Christ appearing to him and saying "Saul, Saul, why do you persecute me?"

Although he did not immediately begin his public missionary work, Paul was a great if controversial advocate of the new faith between about 45 and 62 C.E. His labors on its behalf took him through Asia Minor, Greece, and finally to Rome. More and more he saw himself as the apostle to the Gentiles (non-Jews), whose calling was to show that, in these days after Jesus, the Gentiles had been "grafted" into Israel as an alien branch onto an old tree, and so when they prayed in the name of Jesus, they had all the privileges and responsibilities of being God's people that had formerly been Israel's alone. But this did not mean, for Paul, that they had to follow the Law of Moses. They had only to believe the Gospel, or "Good News," about Jesus and have trust in him, and they would be brought into his oneness with God—not on their own merits, but as a free gift of God transmitted even as they were grafted into old Israel through Jesus Christ. His death on the cross, Paul said, broke the sway of sin and death in the world, and his rising again brought new life. By joining oneself to Christ by faith (not only belief, but a commitment of one's whole self) and the acceptance of baptism (the ritual immersion in water representing initiatory rebirth), one received new life in Christ, was no longer of this world which is passing away, but was entered into the everlasting reign of God.

CHRISTIANITY IN THE ROMAN WORLD

By now a number of interpretations of the Christian message and community had become articulated. Some still thought of Jesus primarily as the Jewish **Messiah** who would soon return to vindicate Israel. Some thought of Christianity as a continuation—one might say an "export version"—of Judaism, making its promises freely available to all apart from the social and dietary law. (One can compare the relation of Buddhism to Hinduism.) Others doubtless experienced Christianity as something closer to the well-known Greek mystery religions, the purveyor of a belief and an experience that would give a blissful state after death to one who received it; the death and resurrection of Christ provided for them the pattern of such a deliverance, which one needed only to appropriate for oneself. All of these, and other philosophical and religious themes as well, found their way into the letters of Paul to his churches and into an emerging Christian world view.

These ideas were stirring in groups that Paul and the other apostles established throughout the Roman world. They were usually fringe groups to the Jewish community, but they embraced many others as well—rich and poor, slave and free, but more of the dislocated than of the well established in the polyglot, spiritually mobile Mediterranean world. The destruction of the Temple by Romans in 70 C.E., mentioned in connection with Judaism, and the dispersion of Jerusalem Jews, had a profound effect on Christianity as well. By weakening severely the Jerusalem church with its links to Judaism, it allowed the more "radical," universalistic wing of Christianity represented by Paul to prevail, and the faith to become primarily a Gentile religion.

As the first century advanced, the life of the new Christian church naturally became more stabilized. One sign of this was the writing down and circulating of "standard" lives of Jesus. Four became accepted; there were others, more fanciful and tendentious, which were not. The first three of the Gospels, or lives of Jesus, are called the Synoptic Gospels; they obviously go together because long passages are virtually identical. The shortest, Mark, was evidently written first, probably between 65 and 70 C.E.; Matthew (c. 70–80) and Luke (c. 80) borrowed much from him and added much of their own. The fourth Gospel, John (its date is uncertain, but is probably late first century) is evidently written from a different point of view. Concerned to present Jesus as the light and life of the world, the eternal Logos or principle of God's activity revealed to the eye of faith, it contains much that is religiously beautiful and profound yet is perhaps less close to the historical facts about Jesus than the other three—though matters like this are the subject of continuing scholarly discussion beyond the scope of this book.[5]

Added to this growing corpus of Christian literature were the letters of Paul, written only 20 to 30 years after the crucifixion, much treasured in the churches he had founded; the Acts of the Apostles by Luke (probably written 85–90 C.E.); and other writings of varying caliber, some of which finally became part of the Christian Bible and some of which did not.

Another sign of stabilization was the emergence of normative Christian beliefs, rites, and church organization. This stage, sometimes called "early Catholicism" because it obviously represents the beginning of the course of Christian development that led to the structure of the medieval church, can be found as far back as the New Testament "Pastoral Epistles" (I and II Timothy, Titus) and the Epistles of Peter. There were formulas of belief slowly becoming standardized into creeds (for example, II Timothy 2:11–13); attacks on heretics (such as Titus 1:10–16); and a quieter, more sober and conventionally moralistic way of life. With the hope of many in the Christian community for an early appearance of the Lord in glory disappointed, the virtues of soundness and self-control were urged, being needed for a long-term sojourn as the children of light in the midst of a dark (but not yet passing away) world. The brilliant apocalyptic colors of the Gospels and the halcyon early days of Acts fade; concern turns to sorting out true from false doctrine and the proper qualifications and prerogatives of church officers and various classes of members, such as young men and widows.

Yet the church of those days had an appeal of its own. Each local church came to be headed by an *episcopos* ("overseer"—our "bishop" is derived from this Greek word), assisted by a council of *presbyteroi* ("elders"—"priests" or "presbyters" in English), and by *diakonoi* ("deacons" or "servers" whose special duty was caring for the needy). The churches apparently had many other categories of roles as well, from readers and healers to widows—each with special duties in worship and otherwise, and perhaps special places to stand during service. Everyone was to have a definite and important part. The church did extensive welfare work among its membership; like most such organizations in the Roman world, it was a mutual aid society as well as a religious fellowship.

The church met for worship early in the morning on Sunday (of course, just another ordinary workday then), the day commemorating the Resurrection, and perhaps on other days as well. To avoid legal problems, Christians often gathered quietly and, until late in the third century when churches began to be built, in private homes or catacombs. Worship combined scripture, prayer, and instruction with the Eucharist, the sacred communal meal representing the Last Supper which, as the Mass, Holy Communion, or Lord's Supper, remains the principal act of worship of Roman Catholic, Eastern Orthodox, and some Protestant churches.

The evidence suggests that a typical service in those days would have been as follows: At the back of the room, behind a table, sat the bishop, with his presbyters seated on either side. In front of the table would stand the deacons, probably two in number. The service would begin with readings from the scriptures of the Old Testament, with emphasis on the passages believed to prophesy the coming of Christ, and the Psalms, used as hymns of praise. Many people might take part in these readings. The bishop, and possibly others, would discourse on their meaning. Perhaps letters of the apostles and accounts from the life of Christ would be read too; gradually these came to be more and more a formal part of Christian worship, until they evolved into the normative collection known as the New Testament. The bishop would then pray at some length, and the Kiss of Peace would be exchanged. After this, everyone would bring up to the table a gift of bread or wine. The bishop, standing behind the table with the elders, would raise his eyes to heaven and offer thanks for this food. Then the people would come forward to receive a piece of bread from the bishop and a bit of wine offered in a chalice held by a deacon, believing this to be a sacred meal in which Jesus Christ is mystically known and his grace imparted.[6] Not to be confused with the communion was the *agape,* or love feast, held afterward as a social communal meal.

The other great service was baptism. This initiation into the Christian life was generally held on Easter Eve. Only those who had received baptism would take part in the communion just described; catechumens, or those receiving instruction, and also penitents going through a process of readmission after confessing a major sin, would remain at the service only through the first part. Instruction would be very long and thorough, lasting perhaps for two full years, and would be followed by careful intellectual and moral examination. Then during the week before Easter the candidates would be given a final exam by the bishop on Wednesday, would bathe on Thursday, fast on Friday, be blessed and exorcised by the bishop on Saturday, keep an all-night vigil, and finally, early on Easter morning, would be baptized in a font or by having water poured over them, and would immediately afterward receive **Holy Communion.**[7]

During this period, Christian intellectual life continued to increase the philosophical sophistication with which the faith was presented. Christian thinkers such as Clement of Rome, Clement of Alexandria, Origen, Justin Martyr, Irenaeus, Tertullian, and others moved the emphasis from showing the continuity of Christianity with Judaism to showing its compatibility with Greek and Roman philosophy, and its points of difference from it. This is natural, since the non-Jewish Greco-Roman world became increasingly the milieu of Christianity.

The tone of Christian thinkers ranged from the fiery Tertullian (c. 160–225), a former lawyer who thought that everything pagan was alien to Christianity and who deemed faith alone and a very strict moral life the only proper Christian way, to the mild Clement of Alexandria who, with his fellow Alexandrian Origen, emphasized that all truth leads to Christ who is the Word or creative principle known to philosophy. Some Christians went much further; the Gnostics combined Christianity with more esoteric and mythical elements of Greek and Asian thought. They were countered by the bishop of Lyons, Irenaeus, who emphasized the importance for Christians of following the traditions passed down from the apostles, particularly the truth of God's taking human flesh in Christ in order to undo the tangled knot of evil wrought in Adam, and thus to bring the creation back to himself by one who is flesh of our flesh. This was in conscious opposition to Gnostic ideas that, the flesh being evil or virtually worthless, the taking of flesh by God is only illusory or allegorical, and salvation means escape from the world through realization of one's true, divine nature.

During the same period, and largely in reaction to the same doctrinal disputes, the canon of authoritative New Testament scriptures was established. It was not finalized until a council of bishops at Carthage in 419. The final codification of scripture thus was fairly late and came after much of the development of Christian teaching, worship, and social organization. On the other hand, the selection was influenced by the fact that most of those books to be considered canonical were already accepted as authoritative; the last disputes were chiefly over the pastoral epistles, Jude, and the Book of Revelation, and whether the Epistle to the Hebrews was actually written by Paul. Many then as now were dubious about its Pauline authorship but accepted it anyway as part of the New Testament.[8]

Everyone has heard of the persecutions of Christians under the Roman Empire: of martyrs hung upside down on crosses, or burned at the stake, or thrown to the lions in the Colosseum. Indeed, there were ghastly persecutions, although they were sporadic and local until the third century. Often Christians in the empire lived undisturbed lives, and while they were not an officially recognized religion, the general policy was to tolerate all groups, however bizarre, that did not present a clear threat to the government. Tradition has it that the Emperor Nero (r. 54–68) instigated a persecution (in which the apostles Peter and Paul were killed) to deflect blame from himself for the disastrous fire at Rome; if so, it was limited to the capital.

In the third century, however, there were persecutions ordered for the entire empire under Decius (r. 249–51), Valerian (r. 253–60), and Diocletian (r. 284–305). By this time the numbers of Christians had grown quite visible, and troubles were increasing in the Roman state requiring both solidarity and scapegoats. In the face of external invasion and internal dissension, these emperors desperately wanted unity and did not yet realize that the empire and Christianity could converge and be mutually supportive, as they were to do within a century. Ironically, it was generally the most conscientious emperors who persecuted Christianity, for they took most seriously their responsibilities for unifying and strengthening the realm.

Usually the persecution was in the context of a drive for all subjects of the

Main Themes of Christianity after Constantine

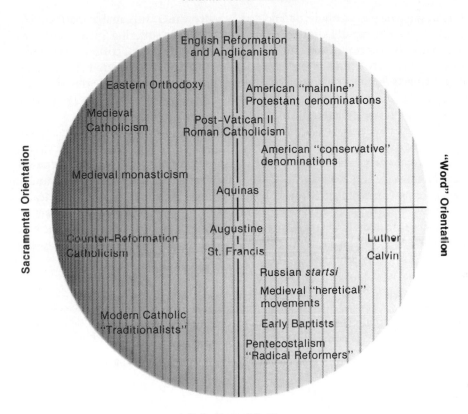

Affirmation of Culture

English Reformation
and Anglicanism

Eastern Orthodoxy

American "mainline"
Protestant denominations

Medieval
Catholicism

Post-Vatican II
Roman Catholicism

American "conservative"
denominations

Sacramental Orientation

Medieval monasticism

Aquinas

"Word" Orientation

Augustine

Counter-Reformation
Catholicism

St. Francis

Luther

Calvin

Russian *startsi*

Medieval "heretical"
movements

Modern Catholic
"Traditionalists"

Early Baptists

Pentecostalism
"Radical Reformers"

Rejection of Culture

THEMATIC CHART VII.   Throughout history, some Christians have emphasized the importance of the "Word"—preaching and studying the Bible—in Christian life; and others, the importance of Christianity's sacramental institutions—baptism, Holy Communion, priesthood, and so on—as mediums of the grace God gave to humankind in Jesus Christ. On both sides of this polarity have been those who have emphasized that Christians can and should accept, while sanctifying from within, the surrounding culture in which they find themselves; and others who have emphasized that Christians should see themselves as a "called out" people who have as little to do with it as they can. (On the chart, *culture* means the values, attitudes, and norms of the surrounding, contemporary society, not classical or "high" culture.)

empire to express loyalty to the sovereign, who was nominally regarded as divine. Few took this seriously, but it was expected that patriotism would be expressed by burning a bit of incense before a portrait or image of the emperor, an act regarded as offering divine honor. At the times of persecution, Christians might be summoned by the authorities and required to make this and comparable gestures or suffer imprisonment and possibly death. Christians, regarding the token gesture as idolatry, frequently refused it; this was taken as proof that they were subversive, and they suffered the consequences.

Greatest havoc was wrought by Diocletian, a dedicated and capable man striving desperately to save a rapidly disintegrating state but one suffering many problems and bad advice. By his time Christianity had numerous churches, costly possessions, and large numbers. He shrank at first from shedding blood, but ordered all Christian buildings, artifacts, and books destroyed, seeking thereby to weaken the obstreperous movement. That did not work, and before long his agents were working torture and death as well among the faithful.

It must be noted that among Christians a certain cult of martyrdom flourished. Those who died violently under the various persecutions were afforded heroic status, and the bones and graves of many became relics and shrines. Here began the veneration of saints. There were those who, if not explicitly seeking martyrdom, looked to the example of Jesus Christ and the earlier martyrs and were fully prepared for death. Thus Ignatius, bishop of Antioch, was taken to Rome in the days of Trajan (r. 98–117) where he met his death at the jaws of wild beasts in the ampitheater. Thinking no doubt of the Holy Communion, he wrote to the church at Rome while on his journey to death:

> I am God's wheat; I am ground by the teeth of the wild beasts that I may end as the pure bread of Christ. If anything, coax the beasts on to become my sepulchre and to leave nothing of my body undevoured so that, when I am dead, I may be no bother to anyone. I shall be really a disciple of Jesus Christ if and when the world can no longer see so much as my body. Make petition, then, to the Lord for me, so that by these means I may be made a sacrifice to God.

In this vein, he also said:

> The pangs of new birth are upon me. Forgive me, brethren, do nothing to prevent this new life.[9]

THE CHRISTIAN TRIUMPH

Not long in terms of world history was Christianity to dwell amidst the smell of beasts and blood, save in memory. In the early decades of the fourth century, Christianity emerged from its place as merely one of the competitors in the lavish spiritual marketplace to become first the dominant and then the sole official religion of the empire and, in time, of all Europe. This reversal happened with surprising speed. True, the church had done well during the long years of comparative peace since the end of the Decian persecution in 251. In some places, especially Asia Minor,

Christianity was the majority faith, and nearby Armenia had become the first officially Christian nation around 300. In many cities, including Nicomedia in Asia Minor (modern Turkey), to which Diocletian had moved his capital, there stood impressive churches, and members of the emperor's family as well as the lowly supported them until his persecution of the church.

Nonetheless, the reasons for the triumph of Christianity around 312 are not all immediately apparent. The faith of Christ had no greater prestige than the Neoplatonic mysticism favored by philosophers, or the Mithraism popular in the army, or the ancient polytheisms nostalgically upheld by patrician traditionalists. Indeed, it had been only a few years earlier (303) that, at the instigation of his son-in-law Galerius, the aging Diocletian imposed persecution.

But one of Diocletian's commanders, Constantine, who emerged in Western Europe after the former's abdication in 305 as an Augustus or "co-emperor," favored the Christian cause. Another co-emperor, the sadistic Maximin Daza, who continued persecution in the East, was deposed by a rival, Licinius. The latter met with Constantine in 313 to decree toleration, the so-called Edict of Milan. Thereafter, Constantine and Licinius ruled together.

Deep psychological currents favorable to Christianity apparently ran through the complex mind of Constantine. His mother, Helena, became a Christian, and at the famous battle of the Milvian Bridge, where he defeated a rival in 312, it is said he saw a cross in the sky and the letters IHS—the Greek beginning of the name Jesus, or the Latin initials for *In Hoc Signo,* "By this sign."[10]

After 323 Constantine was the sole emperor. He established his capital in Byzantium, later named Constantinople (modern Istanbul), and pursued policies favorable to Christianity, although he was not himself baptized until he was on his deathbed. In 325 he sponsored a council of bishops at Nicaea, which made most of what is now the Nicene Creed the standard of doctrine. But Christianity did not become the official religion, the only one whose open practice was possible, until the reign of Theodosius I (379–95).

While the great pagan temples were turned into churches or public buildings, and the centers of pagan learning dispersed, paganism lingered a long time in the countryside. In the course of becoming the dominant religion of society and subsuming all the roles and drives that had animated the former faiths—from folk religion to the mysteries to Neoplatonist philosophy—Christianity naturally underwent development. In church organization, the bishops remained in the cities where the faith had long held sway, becoming more and more the spiritual parallels of governors and magistrates. Successors of the *presbyteroi* of old, parish priests, ordinarily one to a church, strove to Christianize the archaic agricultural religion of the countryside. Festivals such as Christmas and Easter became colorful public holidays; pagan shrines and temples changed names. Moreover, the new faith spread rapidly among the restless Germanic tribes who were replacing Roman provinces with their rude kingdoms and dukedoms.

THE FOUNDATIONS
OF MEDIEVAL CHRISTIANITY

Let us look more explicitly at the changes Christianity underwent in terms of the forms of religious expression.

Theoretical expression became more and more solidified, particularly in regard to an understanding of the incarnation, or how God became human in Christ. This articulation took place by means of **General Councils,** meetings to which all bishops were invited. They sought to condemn heresy, or false teaching, and define correct, or orthodox, teaching. The councils had political overtones as well, for they were all held in the area of Byzantium, and the theological issues were often identified with parties or nationalities of political significance within the empire. In particular, issues were frequently polarized between Egypt and the northern part of the empire. The Bishop of Rome, being an outsider to Eastern squabbles, often could mediate these problems. This increased his authority and helped in the development of his office into the medieval and modern papacy.

There were four important General Councils. Nicaea in 325 affirmed, in the Nicene Creed, that Christ is of one substance or essence with God the Father; this definition opposed the Arians who held that Christ was only "like" God and a lower being sent as his envoy. Constantinople reaffirmed the Nicaean position in 381. Ephesus in 431 affirmed Christ was always God from his mother's womb (and so it called Mary his mother *Theotokos,* "God-bearer"), not a man who had been made Son of God. Chalcedon, in 451, affirmed that Christ is both True God and True Man, two natures conjoined in one person.

A similar matter that underwent theological refinement at about the same time, although never the subject of a General Council, was the doctrine of the Trinity. Christians had experienced God in three basic ways: as God the Heavenly Father, as the Son of God in Jesus Christ, and as the Holy Spirit who was promised by Christ and who filled the community in the upper room on Pentecost. Now it was written that these are three persons bound together in infinite love, who nonetheless are but one God.

In the West, Christians were less involved in the General Councils than in the East, but theological work continued there, too. The greatest Western figure was Augustine, a North African bishop who taught about the Trinity and about grace, God's free gift or help, among other topics. Concerning grace, Augustine emphasized that God takes the initiative in relations between himself and us. All begins with grace, for we cannot seek God or do things pleasing to him unless he first enables us, since we are naturally self-centered and do not truly seek God or do selfless acts on our own. In such terms as these Augustine explained "original sin" and "prevenient grace."

It is too easy, however, to stress the history of ideas in the church and forget that changes were going on in worship and social organization of just as immense consequence. As the church moved out of the spiritual underground of the great

Gothic Architecture: Reims Cathedral in France.

cities and into spacious buildings, typically modeled on the basilica or Roman court of law, or into the rural world of peasant and lord, the liturgy, or pattern of worship, also changed. It became expressive and ornate. The clergy wore symbolically colored garments and moved with slow ritual, accompanied by music and incense, to present and bless the bread and wine. In the West the language of the service was Latin; in the East, Greek. These tongues, especially Latin, quickly became "sacred" languages, like Sanskrit in India, as the vernacular changed and as numerous new peoples came into the orbit of the faith.

For the Christian population was rapidly growing and changing. During the fourth century virtually all the peoples of the old Roman Empire were at least superficially Christianized—even those of areas no longer Christian today, such as

North Africa, Egypt, Syria, Palestine, and Asia Minor. In the East, missionaries won converts in Ethiopia, Mesopotamia, Persia, and even India. In the West, as hosts of heathen invaders out for plunder and new land—Visigoths, Saxons, Vikings, Franks, and the like—swept across lands only barely brought under the cross in the waning days of the imperial order, the situation was often chaotic; this is the era known as the Dark Ages. By the year 1000, however, all but a few corners of Europe had been converted, and the rambunctious tribes had begun slow progress toward becoming nations. We cannot trace here the full course of this missionary effort, although its annals contain many fascinating and adventurous tales.

Let us look briefly at two examples, however: England and Ireland. Christianity came to Roman Britain in the third century. Apparently it was brought by unknown soldiers and merchants, although stories were told in the Middle Ages that Paul himself had visited Britain, or that Joseph of Arimathea (he who claimed the body of Jesus) had come there and planted the sacred tree known as the Glastonbury Thorn, a favorite place of pilgrimage. These legends are significant because they typify the believing world of medieval Christianity. The Celtic and Roman settler population had become widely Christian by the time Britain was cut off from Rome early in the fifth century.

Shortly afterward, massive invasions of Danes, Angles, and Saxons, still adherents of the old Germanic religion of Wotan and Thor, had pushed the Christianized Britons back to the far West, to what is now Wales and Cornwall and their vicinity. There they held out; the tales of King Arthur reflect in part the days of these belea- guered people, who still remembered something of Rome and Christ, as well as old Celtic religious motifs. But in 597 a missionary named Augustine (not the North African bishop) was sent out from Rome to Kent, the Saxon kingdom in the extreme southeast corner of England. Its king and people, through the agency of the king's Christian wife, were converted, and not long afterward all the Anglo-Saxon king- doms—Wessex, Sussex, Mercia, and the rest—had submitted to the faith of Christ.

Ireland's conversion was worked by the famous Patrick, who died in 461. The population was still tribal, and such organization as the church had followed tribal lines. It was full of zeal and its monks full of wanderlust. Missionaries from Ireland traveled to many parts of Europe. Ireland was Christian while England and much of the continent was not; in those confused times Ireland was a preeminent center of Christian learning and effort in the West.

The classical pattern of bishops, who governed the church in geographical areas called dioceses, and parish priests in each community was perpetuated wherever the church acquired a foothold. Moreover, the bishops of major cities became known as archbishops. The Council of Chalcedon made the bishops of five of the most important cities in the ancient empire—Constantinople, Antioch, Alexandria, and Jerusalem in the East, and Rome in the West—patriarchs, and the patriarch of Constan- tinople, the capital of the Byzantine Empire, was called ecumenical or universal patriarch; with this title, he is still the chief dignitary of the Eastern Orthodox Church, though only as "first among equals." On the other hand, the patriarch of Rome came to be called the pope. He had long been looked upon as the chief arbitrator of disputes and heir of the church which, having been associated with the apostles Peter and Paul themselves, had an apostolic tradition of unquestionable soundness. Indeed, it was said by many in the West especially that the pope, successor to Peter as bishop of Rome, was heir to those promises that Matthew's Gospel records Jesus as having given to Peter:

> You are Peter, and on this rock I will build my church, and the powers of death shall not prevail against it. I will give you the keys of the kingdom of heaven, and whatever you bind on earth shall be bound in heaven, and whatever you loose on earth shall be loosed in heaven. (Matt. 16:18–20)

Furthermore, in the confusion that attended the collapse of the empire, the popes, particularly strong popes such as Leo (r. 440–61) and Gregory (r. 590–604), emerged as dominant figures in both church and secular affairs, beacons of stability and hope in a dark and terrifying world. It is not surprising that by the Middle Ages, their sovereignty over the church in the West was firmly established.

One extremely important social development in Christianity was **monasticism.** In order to serve God better, and in search for security and purity in a corrupt and chaotic society, young men—and not long afterward, women—left society to remain unmarried and form communities focused on the worship of God. The monastic movement started in Egypt in the late third century when men such as Anthony and Pachomius went into the desert to pursue lives of prayer as hermits. Soon they were followed by disciples, and communities grew up. Before long the idea had spread throughout the Christian world. Benedict (c. 529) established the Benedictine monastic pattern, which became normative for the church in the West. Quickly monasteries became centers of both missionary work and the preservation of learning, and also orphanages, hospitals, and way stations.[11]

Parallel to monasticism was the general idea of celibacy for the clergy. There was a widespread feeling, based both on the examples of the apparently unmarried Jesus and Paul the apostle and on lingering aversion to the "passions" derived from Greek philosophy, that the celibate life was holier and closer to perfection than the married. The actual situation in the early church was mixed, however. In the East, the pattern that prevails in Orthodoxy to this day—that bishops should be celibate but the ordinary clergy may be married—was established at least by the time of the General Councils. In the West, partly in response to the social disruptions, regional churches and finally the papacy enjoined celibacy for all clergy, and this was observed (at least officially) everywhere in the West by the Middle Ages.

Patterns of popular Christian worship also evolved strikingly. One feature was devotion to the Blessed Virgin Mary, mother of Jesus Christ, and to other saints. It had roots in the early church's veneration of martyrs and in Christian belief that all who are in Christ, whether in this life or the next, are one family and so able to communicate with and help one another. Now this area of the faith grew and expanded: shrines and altars to saints and festivals for them appeared in both East and West; statues in the West and icons (sacred paintings) in the East, as well as saints' relics— bones, clothing—came to focus this devotion. The cultus, especially for the vast

---

Fundamental Features of Christianity

Theoretical

Basic World View	A world made by God, but fallen far from harmony with his will; Jesus Christ bridges the gap between God and humanity. In this situation faith and love are required.
God or Ultimate Reality	A sovereign, personal, all-good Creator God.
Origin of the World	Creation by God.
Destiny of the World	At the end of time, to be judged and then remade as a paradise of God.
Origin of Humans	Created individually by God.
Destiny of Humans	Judgment and resurrection on the last day; eternal life.
Revelation or Mediation between the Ultimate and the Human	Supreme self-manifestation by God in Jesus Christ the Mediator; revelation in Scripture and, especially in the Roman Catholic, Eastern Orthodox, and Anglican traditions. The tradition and authority of the Christian church.

Practical

What Is Expected of Humans: Worship, Practices, Behavior	To seek to know God, to worship him, to practice the ethics of love and service.

Sociological

Major Social Institutions	The Christian church, divided into many traditional denominations; also monastic orders, missionary works, numerous associations.

---

illiterate masses now Christianized, provided a deeply felt color and warmth. With it also came pilgrimages, journeys for the sake of devotion to Jerusalem and other holy places.

Christian life now had two basic emphases: the winning of eternal life in heaven and the avoiding of hell after death; and following Christian moral teachings while on earth. Although the Last Judgment, typically portrayed on the rear wall of medieval churches, was much regarded, like death it was chiefly seen as a narrow portal to heaven. Heaven was gained through the sacraments (baptism, Holy Communion, and the "last rites" especially) and by prayer, penitence for sins, and a moral life. Morality included doing those things that would make earthly society just and stable, a worthy prologue to heaven. Thus Christian moral teaching helped to make the medieval world, which idealized itself as an unchanging human estate lying between the time of Christ and the Last Judgment.

MEDIEVAL CHRISTENDOM

Let us look at the religious life of a medieval peasant, typical of the vast majority of people in Europe between 800 and 1500, and in many places until much later. His life would center around the village where his fellow peasants lived, the manor or castle of the lord, and the church. In some cases the lord would actually be a bishop or abbot; usually he would be a hereditary feudal lord who would spend much of his time leading his knights in combat with other lords and their knights, and who would probably name the priest of the church.

Most villagers would be illiterate or virtually so; the peasants and probably the lord and his household would consider reading beyond or beneath them; the priest might have a limited education in theology and would be able to recite the service in Latin. Education grew gradually more prevalent among both clergy and genteel laity as the Middle Ages wore on; but for the most part only bards, monks, lawyers, and Jews had anything that resembled real learning.

Their world was beyond the horizon of the peasant. As a serf, he was bound to the soil of the manor. He had never been more than a few miles from the village where he had been born and would live and die in sight of its church spire. The village was a shabby affair of mud, wattle, and thatch; above it loomed the imposing but grim castle or manor house of the lord. In theory, the serfs were obligated from birth to the service of the lord in the castle, although they had plots of their own as well as the lord's fields which they worked. The lord could employ them, tax them, and judge them at law as he saw fit. They could not marry without his consent, nor leave the estate. In practice, however, the relationship was complex and mitigated by custom, for the lord was also dependent on the serfs and lived close to them in an isolated community. Lord and peasant shared feasts in the great hall, and all but the greatest lords had to work alongside their peasants at harvest and were hungry with them during the cruel medieval winter if that year's harvest was poor.

The center of this community was the parish church. This stone building was an island of relative grace and color in a drab world. It would have vivid paintings and windows showing supernal things: a radiant saint, the wondrous Mother of God with her warm open arms and compassionate look, Christ judging high and low alike on the dreaded Last Day. At the front would be the richly decked altar, with its hangings, glowing cross, and flickering candles. A scent of incense might hang in the air. This place was of some manifestly different order from the cold, heavy castle with its endless fighting, or the drab village, with its often hungry and sick inhabitants. It was clearly the portal of another world of heavenly terror and joy, a magic lens that enabled a richer level of perception.

On Sunday morning bells from this church would ring out, and the lord and his family and knights would gather together with the peasants in the church for Mass, generally at nine o'clock. The priest in his vestments would stand before the altar and, with many bows and elaborate gestures, wavings of incense and strikings of bells, would celebrate the Mass. It was the same offering and blessing of bread which the early Christians had done in their catacombs and upper rooms, but the priest would be muttering now in an old and sacred tongue the words that made the wafers of bread and cup of wine the Body and Blood of Christ, for the saving of souls in his parish. He might also give a sermon. Priest and church were supported by glebe lands, fields of the manor set aside whose revenues went to this cause.

Besides Sundays, numerous festivals of saints broke the tedium and hard work of village life. Then would come special services, dancing, fairs, and traditional practices—some of them, like the Procession of the White Lady of Banbury (cited in Chapter 2), having clear pre-Christian background, but no less delightful to the peasants.[12]

There were other breaks in the rhythm too. Merchants and tradesmen were able to make pilgrimages to shrines where miracles were said to take place, like Chaucer's pilgrims to Canterbury. Some even went as far as Jerusalem. In other ways, too, the pattern of medieval life was often broken, for the Middle Ages were by no means the static "Age of Faith" sometimes imagined. Changes and dissidents were always present. The vicissitudes of war and weather—and often disease—swept continually through medieval town and countryside.

Rumors of the Crusades—that remarkable combination of bloodthirstiness and piety—must have reached almost everywhere. The Crusades expressed the very spirit of medievalism, but they helped to bring that age to an end by opening up contact with new ideas from the East and from the Greek culture better preserved there, as well as leading to deep-seated enmity between Christian Europe and Islam and between Eastern and Western Christianity.

In the year 1054, before the Crusades started (in 1095), came the formal rupture between the Eastern Orthodox and Western (Roman) Catholic churches. The official reason was the *filioque* question, whether the Holy Spirit proceeds from both God the Father and God the Son (as the Western version of the Nicene Creed stated), or from the Father alone (as the Eastern version had it), and a few other theological and ecclesiastical issues of similar quality. But the real issue was the growing authority of the papacy in the West (the word *filioque*, "and the Son," had been added to the Western Nicene Creed by authority of the pope, not of a General Council), and even more perhaps by wide cultural differences emerging between Western Europe and the Byzantine East. The split was effectively made irrevocable by the Crusades; the sack of Constantinople by soldiers of the cross in 1204 left a bitter legacy that made lasting reconciliation impossible.

The greatest Western religious thinker in the Middle Ages was Thomas Aquinas (c. 1225–74), the major figure of the style of philosophy known as scholasticism. Influenced by the Aristotelianism of the Muslim thinker of Cordova, Averroës, Thomas was concerned to distinguish between the realm of nature where reason holds sway and the realm of faith where revelation adds its gifts. The existence of God, shown by nature, is (he stated) knowable through reason alone. But the way to salvation can only be known by revealed Christian faith. The result of this philosophical and theological labor was a vast synthesis of Aristotelian science and philosophy, Christianity, and medieval experience, which summed up the vision of that age and has been the most important intellectual force in Roman Catholicism down to the present. In it, all beings under God—angels, humanity, matter, sound reason, and sure revelation—have their logical places and reasonable duties in reflecting God's glory, a vision expressed more poetically but no more powerfully in the *Divine Comedy* of Dante Alighieri.

The Middle Ages teemed with new religious movements centering in holy, charismatic personalities, increasingly so as time advanced. Most were reactions to the church in favor of "Gospel simplicity" and "inwardness." They favored asceticism, fervent religious feelings, and freedom of movement for religious persons in contrast to the comparative wealth, objective worship of shrine and sacrament, and rootedness in feudal village and agricultural patterns of the conventional church. The dissident movements were, significantly, strongest among the crafts and trades people of the burgeoning towns, although sometimes they swept through countryside districts on a wave of social protest. They were a combination of the age-old "holy man" ideal and the modern severing of religion from its rural roots; both motifs contrast with the medieval alliance of religious and feudal concepts, and of Christianity and agricultural religion.

Some of these movements, like that of Francis of Assisi and his friars, remained within the orbit of orthodoxy. Francis, the "Little Poor Man," lived and inspired many others to live a life of Christian perfection marked by poverty, universal love, and a new personal devotion to the human Christ in the manger and on the cross. His order of friars, or "brothers," wandering, begging, and relatively free from control by bishop or parish priest, transmitted this experience throughout Europe and soon enough to Latin America and the Orient.

Other such preachers, however, were considered heretical. Some, like the Albigensians or Cathari who were the object of brutal persecution in the thirteenth century, were, indeed, inspired by ancient Manichaeism as well as the new ideas of simplicity and inwardness; the Albigensians so honored spirit above flesh that they held self-starvation a noble thing. Others, like the Waldensians, Lollards, and Hussites, were more concerned to conform Christian life to the Bible according to their lights. The important thing to note is that these protests were challenges to the medieval order by a new, sometimes cantankerous but always deeply felt, individualism and rejection of the old corporate village faith of parish church and succession of festivals.[13]

THE REFORMATION AND LUTHER

The next development was the Reformation, which carried all these trends to their natural conclusion—a new style of Christianity. Perhaps the onset of change was abetted by the Black Death, or plague, which swept across Europe, wiping out something like a third of the population during 1348–50, disrupting traditional patterns of society, leaving many parishes without clergy, and on a deeper level going some ways to discredit the traditional faith and church. (People asked themselves,

"Why did good and bad alike succumb to the plague? Why did the prayers of the traditional church not protect us?")

At the same time, the prestige of the papacy as the unifying force in Europe and Christendom was greatly weakened by the abduction of the pope by agents of the French king in 1309 and the relocation of the papal residence in Avignon, under French domination, during 1309–77. Above all the papacy's image was tarnished by the resultant "great schism" of 1378–1417, when two "popes" reigned, one in Rome and one in Avignon, each claiming to be the true ruler of the church and each holding the allegiance of several nations.

Against this background, groups such as the English Lollards, followers of John Wycliffe, began around 1380 to demand such "reforms" as abolition of clerical celibacy, the use of images, prayers for the dead, pilgrimages, and elaborate vestments. They demanded that the clergy should chiefly preach and that the scriptures should be freely available to all in the vernacular language. In Bohemia and Moravia the Hussites, followers of John Hus (who died at the stake in 1415), made similar demands, particularly asking that the church manifest poverty and church lands be expropriated.

It was not until the sixteenth century, however, that new ideas came into their own at a time of the slow decline of feudalism, the rise to prominence of towns, and the corresponding shift of Christian emphasis (even in Catholic mysticism) from cosmic and sacramental religion to preoccupation with inner motivation and experience. It would be an oversimplification to say that these changes caused the Reformation. The modern mind was also shaped by Renaissance businessmen and intellectuals in Catholic Italy who shared many of the new attitudes yet did not become Protestant. But certainly social changes and the Reformation went together.

The Reformation was overtly focused on spiritual and theological issues, however. The man who by far most influenced its course, Martin Luther (1483–1546), was little concerned consciously with these matters of social history, for he was a scholarly friar of the Augustinian order since the age of 21, though his father—a strict, pious, enterprising civic leader engaged in the mining business in the small German town of Eisleben—was typical of the kind of man the Reformation would help to supersede knights, lords, and peasants. Nonetheless, it was Luther's deeply inward spiritual struggles that defined the issues, language, and direction of the Reformation.

In his monastery, Luther experienced grueling anxiety. His problem was that he felt himself a sinner, however blameless a life he lived as a monk. So long as he thought of it in terms of how much he had to do, what standards he had to meet, what religious acts he had to perform, and what devout feelings he had to feel, he could only live, it seemed, in a cruel uncertainty, which would virtually lead to madness if one were really serious about it—and Luther was nothing if not serious. He felt trapped; he was commanded to love God, but how could one love a God whose demands left one in such anguish? Could he ever know if he had done enough?

Then, in studying the Scriptures, Luther struggled with the lines "He who is righteous by faith shall live" (Habakkuk 2:4, Romans 1:17) until this saying provided a sunrise of new awareness that led to his doctrine of *sola fides,* "faith alone." He realized to the depths of his being that what set a person in right relationship with God was not the things he had been trying before, but simple faith—sincere belief, trust, and intention—and this as a matter of inner attitude was available to anyone at any time. In fact, it is not really a matter of what we do at all, for faith is first of all a gift—a grace (from *gratia,* meaning "free") from God—always free, always poured out in love, to which we only respond with sincerity of faith. When Luther realized this, all else appeared superfluous and likely to confuse. For this reason he insisted also on the principle of *sola scriptura,* the Bible alone as guide to Christian faith and practice, for he felt that salvation by grace through faith *was* the clear and central message of the Scripture, and that its obscuring had come about through overlays of human philosophy and ecclesiastical tradition.

Luther's new understanding of Christianity first brought him into conflict with its medieval version over the issue of indulgences. Indulgences were related to the doctrine of purgatory—a universally held medieval belief that there is an intermediate state between heaven and hell for those who die neither saints nor hopeless sinners; there souls suffer purging fires for a long or short time, until they have been cleansed of evil and justice is satisfied, and they can then await entry into the presence of God. Indulgences were certificates issued by the pope, under his power of binding and loosing, affirming that because the recipient had done an adequate number of acts of penitence and devotion, so many days—or possibly all—of his or her prospective suffering in purgatory had been remitted. This remittance was held to be made possible by the transfer to the penitent of something of the superabundance of merit attained by Christ and the saints; to this "treasury of merit" the pope held the spiritual key. Indulgences could even be obtained by one person on behalf of another, living or dead.

This profoundly medieval doctrine was not without its attractive side; it was a concrete way of stating the benefits accrued from such extra and innocent religious acts as pilgrimage, and it suggested, in the exchange of merit idea, that Christians deeply share in one another's lives and can bear one another's burdens. It was an implementation of the communion of saints. Indulgences are still made available in the Roman Catholic Church. But in Luther's day, indulgences were being widely distributed in Germany with little consideration but for the donation of money customarily given by the recipient; in effect, they were being used as a means of church fund-raising, and a special drive was on to raise funds for the building of St. Peter's Cathedral in Rome. Moreover, the theology behind indulgences went very much counter to Luther's new inner discovery of salvation by grace through faith only; the use they were being put to raised the hackles of nascent German nationalism, for many Germans felt they were being exploited for the sake of interests south of the Alps.

On October 31, 1517, Luther reportedly posted ninety-five theses, or points for debate, on the door of All Saints Church in Wittenberg, which served as the university's bulletin board. It was the eve of All Saints' Day, when many relics of the saints (a comparably questionable matter with Luther) would be exposed for veneration in that church. In the famous Ninety-five Theses Luther spoke against abuses of indulgences, relics, and the like, but the tone was not extreme, nor did he question papal authority or the doctrine of purgatory as such. He stressed the supreme value of inwardness and of sharing the sufferings of Christ more than prematurely trying to take advantage of heaven: a theology of the cross rather than a theology of glory.

This challenge started as a theological dispute but quickly escalated beyond what one would normally expect of such arguments among monks. Luther was engaged in a course that finally led to his rejection of papal authority as its logical outcome, and this in turn produced his excommunication by Rome in 1521. Public opinion in Germany tended to take Luther's side. Spurred on by his pamphlet "Address to the Christian Nobility of the German Nation," a sense of German national pride and identity, long smoldering under cultural and spiritual domination from southern Europe, was inflamed. When Luther was summoned before the Imperial Diet at Worms to defend himself, he may not actually have used the famous words, "Here I stand; God help me, I can do no other," but that was what he meant, and his defiance of resented authority deeply stirred many a German knight. But this did not please the young Holy Roman Emperor Charles V, who desired to continue the alliance between his throne and that of the pope.[14]

The test of inward faith, rather than rites, sacraments, or pious deeds, was congruous with a longstanding German mystical bent. The precise theological points at issue may have mattered less to the knights and people at large than to scholars, but the common folk grasped the implication that the new teachings meant all persons were fully equal before God. When Luther's German Bible and simplified services in the vernacular soon appeared, people well understood both the new orientation toward inward faith and the implicit Germanic self-affirmation.

Luther had hoped to see the church purified and Christians everywhere find new inner freedom and peace. It was a cause of grief and bitterness to him that one of the most conspicuous results of reform was conflict—theological, political, and military. In the following century conflict escalated into the devastating Thirty Years' War, finally settled at the Peace of Westphalia in 1648. Scandinavia, most of northern Germany, and small minorities elsewhere were thereafter Lutheran.

CALVIN

The most important reformer after Luther was John Calvin (1509–64). He was a Frenchman but is associated mainly with Geneva in Switzerland. As a young man he was a Renaissance humanist, but in 1533 he was converted to the Protestant movement that Luther had spearheaded. He immediately wrote his theological master-piece, *Institutes of the Christian Religion*. The brief first edition was published in 1536, but Calvin kept revising and expanding it until the definitive edition of 1559.

After 1541 Calvin lived in Geneva, which had recently thrown out its ruling bishop and become Protestant, and had invited him to take over leadership. Reluctantly (he much preferred a quiet scholarly life) he accepted. During his stay, Geneva became a kind of holy community of the Reformed faith, dominated by Calvin and other clergy, who enforced strict moral rectitude and correct belief in church and city government alike.

Calvin's theology is based on a strong contrast between the infinite greatness and power of God and the sinfulness of humanity. God's glory fills the universe; the division between the sacred and the secular is done away with, for all is sacred, and all that happens is due solely to his will, from life and death to the smallest seemingly accidental events here below. Nonetheless, humankind is in rebellion against God; God permits this in order that his mercy may be shown in the salvation of those whom he chooses, while divine justice is affirmed by the punishment of the rest. Those whom God chooses for eternal life do not have any merit of their own; they are recipients of his grace which, as Luther (following Augustine) had emphasized, must come before anything right that humans can do. The elect, those chosen through grace, will be marked by righteous life and a seemingly spontaneous and persevering predilection for true religion. Calvin's theology also emphasizes the mystical union of the Christian with Christ.

Calvin stressed, like Luther, the importance of the Bible alone as the normative guide for Christians. In church organization, he made greater changes than did Luther; doing away with bishops, he gave considerable place to local control and boards of elders, or presbyters. The sacraments of baptism and the Lord's Supper were greatly simplified in administration, and the preaching of the Word of God, the chief means by which people are called to faith and grace, was given new emphasis.

The theology and style of church life left by John Calvin has been much criticized; and indeed, when **Calvinism** appears without the panoramic world vision and inner piety of its best men and women, it can easily become harsh and rigid. But Calvinism's positive role in the making of the modern world must be appreciated. Calvinism contributed immensely to the development of democracy: indirectly through its new emphasis on the equality of all before God, for the elect might be found in any social station; and directly through the model of its presbyterian or congregational forms of church organization, which gave many sorts of people experience in decision-making responsibilities and did not fit as well with feudalism or absolute monarchy as did bishops. Calvinists insisted, as did other Protestants, that everyone should be able to read the Bible, and this gave much impetus to education. Finally, it can be noted that Calvinism appealed especially to the rising business class in western Europe. Its stress on the elect's sense of inner call, commitment, and righteousness in the midst of work in the world, rather than sacerdotalism or monasticism, and its stern ethics focusing on self-denial, hard work, and individual responsibility contributed to the psychology that made this class prosperous and, in fact, for several centuries second to none in worldwide influence. Sometimes prosperity was seen as in itself a sign of divine election and favor.

Today, churches known as Reformed, Presbyterian, or Congregational are from the Calvinist tradition, although Calvin's original message has been varyingly modified by them over the years. Calvinism became dominant in Holland, Scotland, and parts of Germany and Switzerland; the Puritan movement in England and America was Calvinist as well, and has had tremendous impact on life in those countries and their spheres of influence. Minority Protestant churches in France, Hungary, and some other parts of Europe are also Calvinist in background.

THE ENGLISH REFORMATION

In England the Reformation took yet another form. It is natural that this country of Wycliffe and the Lollards, and of emerging nationalism as well, should have harbored many people who responded enthusiastically to news of the events in Germany. Yet the English character has always exhibited a sense of pragmatism, moderation, and appreciation of tradition as well as a thirst for reform. All of this is evident in the English Reformation. Significantly, it did not receive its impetus from a wholly engaged reformer such as Luther or Calvin, but from a rather sordid political matter. The king, Henry VIII, had been an enthusiastic defender of the old faith against the reformers, but in the early 1530s desired to divorce his queen, Katharine of Aragon, since she had been unable to give him a living male heir. This step required a dispensation from the pope, which the latter, Clement VII, was unwilling to authorize. Therefore, Henry called upon Parliament to sever relations with Rome and make the king supreme head of the church in England; the resultant Act of Supremacy was passed in 1534. Henry was divorced and married again, not for the last time.

Although strained relations between Rome and England were no new thing, undoubtedly the continental reformation created an atmosphere conducive to taking this final step. But those who desired a more thoroughgoing reformation were initially disappointed. True, monasteries, convents, and pilgrimage shrines were dissolved promptly and their wealth divided among Henry's henchmen, but otherwise little changed; most of the same bishops remained in their sees, and the same celibate priests in their parishes, saying the same Latin mass. The king rigorously enforced Catholic doctrinal orthodoxy.

But after Henry VIII died in 1546, the dike could no longer hold. Calvinist influence now pouring in from Geneva overbalanced the conservative side. A new form of worship in the English language, the *Book of Common Prayer,* was produced in 1549; essentially, it perpetuated the basic structure of the old Latin forms but with substantial concessions to Protestantism on sensitive issues, such as its formal elimination of devotion to saints. It was over a century before the religious situation in England was fully stabilized, but the essential outline of its official form, the Church of England, was already apparent in the Prayer Book of 1549: continuity of church structure from the Middle Ages; English-language worship, which was Catholic in outline but designed to be nonoffensive to moderate Protestants; and a pragmatic mentality (which emerged more slowly), allowing for some divergence of theological opinion among individual clergy and members, especially between the Catholic and Protestant traditions which meet in the Church of England.

A minority in England maintained allegiance to the Church of Rome. Over the next two centuries, others separated themselves from Anglicanism (the Church of England) into more fully Protestant groups: Puritan (Calvinist), Baptist, Quaker, Methodist. We shall now examine the story of groups such as these.

RADICAL REFORM

Outside the great movements of Luther and Calvin, and that in England, and generally without the support of rulers, the Reformation stirred up the zeal of many who wanted many more far-reaching changes in the church, and often also in society. These movements typically stressed the need for personal conversion experiences, moral perfection, and a close following of the New Testament both in faith and social life. They varied from Anabaptists (indirectly the forebears of modern Baptists in England and America), who rejected the baptism of infants, insisting that Christians should have a personal conversion experience and be baptized only after it; and Mennonites, who were perfectionists, pacifists, and often communalists; to rationalistic Unitarians, such as Michael Servetus, who denied the doctrine of the Trinity and was burned at the stake in Calvin's Geneva.[15]

The non-Anglican Protestant groups of England have been particularly influential in world Christianity. That is because they have flourished wherever the far-flung British people have settled overseas—especially in a nation as large and powerful as the United States—and because they have generally been active in missionary work. Many of these Dissenters or Nonconformists, as they were called in England, emigrated overseas because of discrimination or persecution against them in the homeland.

British Nonconformity has its post-Reformation roots in the Puritan movement which began in the Church of England in the latter part of the sixteenth century. It was comprised of highly Protestant-oriented Anglicans who wished to "purify" the church of what they saw as persisting elements of Catholicism. Puritans wanted simple (though long) services emphasizing preaching, Biblical doctrine (with a Calvinist tone), moral earnestness, and an emphasis on the religious life and role of the laity. Some of them preferred the presbyterian or congregational forms of church government to the bishops of the established church.

By the 1580s, some Puritans realized that the Church of England was not going to change its basic character (which was based on the Catholic-Protestant compromise known as the "Elizabethan settlement") in the direction they wished. Some of them felt compelled by conscience to worship apart from it with like-minded believers as the "gathered church." They were called "Independents" or "Separatists." These persons were severely repressed; some emigrated, like the "Pilgrims" who established Plymouth Colony in 1620.

In the seventeenth century, the fortunes of Puritanism and dissent rose and fell dramatically, becoming entangled in fierce battles between king and parliament, old aristocracy and rising middle class, as England painfully wrenched itself into the modern world. In general, the Stuart kings of the century strongly supported episcopacy and the Church of England (when they were not Roman Catholic sympathizers), while Parliament and the rising middle class favored Puritanism. Religion was not the only issue, but it was an age when religious positions were taken very seriously and became flags of allegiance of classes and interests as well as passionately held convictions. These struggles climaxed with the Civil War between royal and parliamentary forces in the 1640s, the parliamentary Puritan victory and the beheading of King Charles I in 1649, and the subsequent rule of England by the faction controlled by Oliver Cromwell.

The 1650s, the decade of Cromwell's "Commonwealth," were rife with radical social as well as religious movements. The "Levellers" wanted to abolish all hierarchical distinctions in society. The "Diggers" were agrarian communalists who, though harassed by both the law and violent mobs, endeavored to cultivate common land they said should be made available to the poor. The "Ranters" showed the interaction of radical political and spiritual protest by bringing to such causes their rejection of all authority of scripture or creed, holding instead only to an inner experience of Christ that makes all equal and free. But hope that this radical decade signaled a new age in which the world would truly be "turned upside down" were dashed by the end of the Commonwealth in 1660. Most of these movements did not survive. One that did, and which has long preserved—though sometimes in rather fossilized form—the spirit of the age of Levellers, Diggers, and Ranters was the Religious Society of Friends, commonly called the Quakers. Founded in the 1650s by George Fox (1624–91) and others, the Quaker movement carried to one sort of logical conclusion the quest for earnestness, truly inward religion, and the equality of all believers. Quakers rejected all "outward" rites, such as baptism with water and ritualistic Holy Communion, wishing instead to be baptized and commune with God inwardly. They considered all persons to be equally ministers, and they were far ahead of their time in accepting the spiritual equality of men and women in the ministry. Quakers also refused on religious grounds such practices as oathtaking, removing one's hat before anyone but God, and participation in war. Their meetings for worship were conducted in silence unless anyone felt moved by the "Inner Light" to speak or pray.

In 1660, after Cromwell's death, the monarchy was restored, and Anglicanism was once again in the saddle. At first, despite the wishes of the new king, Charles II, for religious liberty, punishment was once again visited upon Dissenters. But gradually, as the bloody events since the Reformation made it clear that national uniformity in religion was a hopeless ideal, a trend toward accepting religious pluralism and liberty set in, culminating in the Toleration Act of 1689. It granted freedom of worship to all except Roman Catholics and Unitarians. Their emancipation was not to come until much later.

These dramatic events had momentous consequences for the emerging denominationalism of the English-speaking world, including America—then a thin ribbon of seaboard colonies on the east coast of the New World. On both sides of the Atlantic, Congregationalism became the successor of the independent Separatist congregations. English and American Baptists came from the same background; they were originally independent congregations who differed little from the others save in their rejection of infant baptism and their insistence that baptism can be given only to believers who have made a mature confession of faith. But as time went on, the general mood of Baptists shifted from Puritan Calvinism toward "Arminianism"—that is, emphasis on the individual's freedom to decide rather than on predestination. This is evident today in the tendency of Baptist preaching to stress the individual's responsibility to make a decision for faith in Christ.

The last great English dissenting movement was Methodism. It did not arise until the eighteenth century under the leadership of the Anglican clergyman John Wesley (1703–91). After a youthful conversion experience, Wesley became a powerful preacher who took all England as his parish, teaching the necessity of genuine conversion and the possibility of Christian perfection. This ministry, amid the social evils of the early Industrial Revolution (of which Wesley was well aware) in a time when the older churches were at a low ebb after the passions of the previous century, made a powerful impact. Societies and classes were formed in numerous communities to study and practice the Wesleyan approach. Although Wesley himself never intended that his movement should leave the Church of England, shortly after his death many of these groups, finding they could no longer keep their new wine in old bottles, became independent churches, both in England and in America. At least as many followers of Wesley remained within the Church of England to become the seedbed of a powerful Anglican evangelical movement.

THE CATHOLIC REFORMATION

During the period of the Protestant Reformation, far-reaching developments were also taking place in the papal church against which the Protestants had rebelled, the church known—in distinction from Protestantism—as Roman Catholic. These developments are sometimes known collectively as the Counter Reformation. But there was more to them than mere reaction to Protestant criticism, even though that formidable challenge certainly pressed Catholics to rethink and strengthen their tradition.

Some moves for Catholic reformation had been underway even before the Protestant reformers. The Fifth Lateran Council (1512–17), on the eve of their Reformation, accomplished little but kept the idea of internal reform alive. Church leaders such as Cardinal Ximenez de Cisneros (1436–1517) in Spain had worked diligently for the improvement of clerical education and standards. But after Luther and Calvin, such efforts cried out for considerably augmented energy and scope. The need was answered by widespread renewed emphasis on Catholic education and discipline, especially among priests, and above all by new religious orders such as the Capuchins (1528) and the Jesuits (1540), dedicated to missionary work abroad and to holding the line against Protestantism in Europe.

The new situation also called for even greater Catholic unity and clearer definitions of the Catholic position, especially in regard to issues raised by the Protestant reformers. In that task the Council of Trent (1545–63) is the centerpiece. At first attempting unsuccessfully to achieve reconciliation with the Protestants, the Council during a second phase beginning in 1551 sought above all to purify and then defend the traditional Catholicism of the Middle Ages and before. The result of the Council's decrees was a church clearly governed by the Pope and his "cabinet," or Curia; possessing a high degree of uniformity in doctrine and worship (centered in the Latin Mass); firmly maintaining such controverted teachings as Purgatory and the invocation of saints; sure of its own authority based on both scripture and tradition rightly interpreted by its *magisterium,* or teaching jurisdiction; determined to uphold high levels of training and commitment; prepared to win back what it could from the Protestants and to spread itself over the earth. This was essentially the style of Catholicism which was to prevail for four centuries, until the Second Vatican Council (1962–65) brought in equally significant redefinitions of Catholic life.

CHRISTIAN MYSTICISM AND DEVOTION

Before presenting the characteristics of the major branches of Christianity today, let us pause to look at the mystical and devotional side of the religion and its literary expression. Perhaps more than other religions, Christianity makes a clear-cut distinction between theological writing and mystical-devotional literature. Christian doctrine and thought have an objective and historical quality that makes it possible to understand them, at least superficially, without direct experience of the divine realities that lie behind them. Many would say that one can have saving faith without the sort of experience of God of which mystics and devotees speak. In this respect, Christianity shows its difference from a religion like Buddhism, in which the equivalent of salvation would have to be the ultimate transformation of consciousness represented by Nirvana. But mainstream Christian theology and preaching is generally more concerned with salvation than with mystical experiences to which not every Christian is called.

By mystical experience we mean experience interpreted as immediate contact with the divine, very frequently expressed in the language of unity: "I felt the oneness of all things," "I was united with God." Mystical writings describe this experience and how to attain it. Devotional writing presents prayers and meditations addressed to God or intended to lead one's mind toward union with him. Since the one who prays or meditates is still speaking *to* God or thinking *about* him, a certain distance, however filled with love and feeling, remains between that person and the divine. Devotion, then, falls short of the mystic's experience of sheer union; that is why the latter is sometimes said to be "beyond words," and mystics may shock the conventionally pious when they say that even prayer and meditation are practices to be surpassed.

Though not the same as the theological tradition, there is a Christian tradition of mystical and devotional writing worthy of comparison with that of any other faith and which cannot be neglected if one desires to comprehend the fullness of Christianity as a religion. Moreover, the Christian mystics, while they sometimes say startling and disturbing things, also say things (not infrequently at the same time) that go to the very heart of Christianity's esesntial meaning—or so many feel who have studied them long and deeply.

The Christian writer Charles Williams once described a long standing distinction between two kinds of mysticism and devotion: that of the "negation of images" and that of the "affirmation of images."[16] The term *image* is used in a broad sense to mean any kind of "picture in the mind" or conceptualization, as well as any kind of work of art that mediates between the self and God—whether, say, a painting of Christ or a specific belief about Christ or God. The way of the negation of images seeks oneness with God by taking everything from mind or eyes that is not infinite God himself—even the most holy pictures, concepts, or beliefs—holding that the truest ideas concerning God or the most sacred art are not the same as God and can easily become idols that stand in the way of real union with God. The way of the affirmation of images, while recognizing this danger, wishes nonetheless to climb by the ladder of images and ideas toward the God who lies behind them. As Williams pointed out, Christian mysticism and devotion have made generous use of both paths.

The first Christian mysticism after the New Testament veered in the direction of the negative way. Like the formal expression of doctrine in the same era—the period of the General Council—it was deeply indebted to Neoplatonic philosophy for its terminology and philosophical concepts. But instead of developing categories for laying out the Christian view of God, Christ, Holy Spirit, salvation, and so forth, mysticism was concerned to show how the soul inwardly rises to more perfect union with the One. Classical Christian mysticism was, therefore, less interested in borrowing Neoplatonic terms for theological purposes, than in mining the vein of Neoplatonism which instructs that in raising minds and hearts to the infinite we must pass beyond words and concepts.

The most influential Christian mystical writings of this sort are those of the writer who called himself Dionysius the Areopagite—the Greek philosopher of the Book of Acts who heard Paul on Mars Hill (Areopagos) in Athens. The union of Christianity and Greek thought symbolically suggested by this attribution is very apt, but the writings, which include *The Mystical Theology* and *The Divine Names,* are now believed to be by a Syrian monk of the sixth century.

"Dionysius" was a Neoplatonist and believed that God in his fullness and infinity is beyond human knowledge, and so is ultimately nameless and ineffable. Nothing we could say about him is adequate to the unbounded mystery of divine being. God is thus spoken of by Dionysius as a "darkness which is beyond light"— though the darkness is really due to an excess of light beyond what human faculties can handle, like the shadows that fall across the eyes when we try to look directly at the sun. The way to God, then, is through an "unknowing" by which human intellect and feelings, too frail for this sublimest task, are stilled in mystical contemplation. "We pray," Dionysius says, "that we may come unto this darkness which is beyond light, and through the loss of sight and knowledge may see and know that which is above vision and knowledge."

In the West, the great Saint Augustine, in his mystical writings, also expounded the Neoplatonist approach. He taught that the way of contemplation, by which one gazes inward, leads also to God, for the Light beyond all lights is also the light of the soul. In a famous passage of the *Confessions,* Augustine said, "Late have I loved Thee, O Thou Beauty of ancient days, yet ever new. . . . And, behold, Thou wert within, and I abroad." The same theme of the negative way is continued elsewhere, where he says, "He is best adored in silence, best known by nescience [unknowing], best described by negatives."

Augustine's immensely influential teaching on sin and grace has sometimes been considered inconsistent with his mystical Neoplatonism, yet it may reflect only another side of Christian experience ultimately convergent with mysticism. The basic teaching is that we are free to do whatever we want to do, but in our finitude and ignorance we turn from God to love the self and its gratifications, becoming more and more enmeshed in them. We can be extracted from this spiritual black hole only by help from outside, by God's grace which, working through other persons, scriptures, above all through Jesus Christ, presents the attractiveness of the good and God in a way persuasive enough to turn the will toward them—even as when a child is shown sweets, he will run toward them. But grace is not an external force in any simple sense; it is something that stirs deep within to make us dissatisfied with life as it is and sensitive to a new delight: "The good begins to be desired, when it begins to be sweet"; and "With a hidden goad Thou didst urge me, that I might be restless until such time as the sight of my mind might discern Thee for certain"; and "Thou has created us for Thyself, and our hearts are restless till they rest in Thee." Would it not be in stillness, and in the "unknowing" of the thousand things that make us restless, that these realizations arise?

The Neoplatonic tradition of Dionysius and Augustine had a renaissance in the late Middle Ages. We can mention here only three writers, the unknown author of the English classic *The Cloud of Unknowing,* the Flemish Jan van Ruysbroeck, and the German Meister Eckhart.

As the title suggests, the fourteenth-century *Cloud of Unknowing* tells us that the path to God is through the negative way, the way of unlearning or unknowing what we think we know about God. When knowledge falls away, all that is left is love, the best and only road to God. "Blind outreaching love to God Himself" is better than to "gaze on the angels and saints in heaven, and hear the happy music of the blessed." Jan van Ruysbroeck (1293–1381) says much the same thing: One must plunge into the Divine Dark which is Divine Light without map or support. One "must have lost himself in a Waylessness and in a Darkness," only inwardly cleaving to God with love and naught else.

Meister Eckhart (c. 1260–1328) presented the paradoxes and radical possibilities of Christian mysticism with unequaled force. He taught that the "God above God," the Divine Dark essence of God, is in "the core of the soul," but can be reached only as the mystic makes a final spiritual breakthrough by utter detachment. At this point he or she breaks beyond even God as God can be conceived, and lives in God by not knowing God in any conscious way. All that is experienced is the untrammeled joy and freedom of Being itself.

But during the same Middle Ages, something else was stirring as well. A Christian mysticism of the affirmation of images was coming to flower. It was not wholly a product of the Middle Ages, having roots in the piety of Paul and Augustine, but it found strong new voices in men such as Bernard of Clairvaux (1091–1153) and Francis of Assisi (1181–1226).

Bernard, famous as monastic reformer, ecclesiastical statesman, crusade preacher, and disputationist, was also a writer of great power and subtlety on the spiritual life. He reaffirmed tradition when he spoke of the highest stage of the spiritual progression as union with God in which the self is forgotten. But he was the father of modern Christian devotion by advocating loving and tender attention to the human life and form of Jesus and the Blessed Virgin Mary, as can be seen in the passionate language (in his celebrated series of sermons on the Song of Solomon), as well as the selflessness by which he expresses the love of the soul for the divine. The beginning of one of his image-laden hymns, "Jesus, the very thought of Thee, with sweetness fills the breast," is an example. Here mental images of Jesus and Mary, no doubt reinforced by picture and statue and sacred story, raise the soul toward love, not the negation of thought.

This trend was transformed into a movement by the well known and much-beloved Francis of Assisi. In his direct, exuberant way, Francis enacted what Bernard taught. He fervently promoted devotion to Jesus in the manger and on the cross, both affirmative pictures to which devotion could be affixed in mind and heart. Tradition credits the "little poor man" of Assisi with making the first Christmas crèche and with receiving the stigmata, or marks of the nails and crown of thorns and wounded side of Christ on the cross, in his own flesh. The Franciscan order, which burgeoned in the late Middle Ages, eagerly carried his style of devotionalism throughout Western Europe and later to the Spanish and Portuguese New World.

Protestant mysticism, like the Protestant movement generally, continued both negation and affirmation of images in its own way. The Lutheran and Calvinist discovery of a Christianity centered on inward faith and the inner workings of grace gave new life to the negative way. Although not the same as Augustinian or Dionysian mystical Neoplatonism, having no regard for its spiritual stages or unitive "states," Protestantism was partly influenced by the medieval version of that tradition. That relation was most explicit in those so-called "Protestant mystics," for whom the inward freedom of the Divine Abyss fulfilled the profoundest spiritual promise of the Reformation.

Protestant mysticism began in the age of Luther himself. Sebastian Franck (1499–1542) and his disciple Valentine Weigel (1533–88) were both Lutherans, the former a sometime preacher and the latter a pastor, and also both Dionysians. They wrote that God is beyond all notions, definitions, concepts, and thought, but is incarnate as the inner essence of humans. Weigel boldly affirmed that God knows himself through persons; it is in us that the Ultimate becomes person, consciousness, and will. Another German, Jacob Boehme (1575–1624), a shoemaker, is widely considered the greatest Protestant mystical thinker. Boehme spoke of the divine infinity beyond words and concepts as the Original Ground; its expression is through the interplay of opposites. All this is incarnate in humans. Boehme's thought, while often highly speculative, is psychologically and philosophically rich.

Dionysian mysticism found a congenial home in England as well, especially in the tumultuous seventeenth century. The group of thinkers called the Cambridge Platonists gave it an academic voice. They went contrary to the harsh spirit of the age by, from out of their mystical roots, stressing Christian wisdom and morality far above dogma, ritual, or form of church government. The most striking sociological expression of English Protestant mysticism was the Society of Friends (Quakers), already discussed. Quaker concepts, such as the Inner Light as the supreme religious authority, were only partially inspired, and then at second or third hand, by the Dionysian mystical tradition; but they did provide a new influx of the ancient mystical ideal of knowing and loving God better by moving beyond rigid ideas and doctrines *about* God.

But the mysticism of the affirmation of images found a Protestant mode of expression as well. Movements like seventeenth-century Pietism on the continent, and Wesleyan Methodism in eighteenth-century England, so stressed the importance of inwardly felt conversion in the believer that they easily led to positive devotional focus on the catalyst of the change, Jesus Christ. The result was a highly Christocentric Protestantism, still immensely powerful, which mentally pictures, prays to, and inwardly relates to Jesus himself. This Christian style is well expressed in such hymns as "O Sacred Head Now Wounded," or "He Walks with Me and He Talks with Me."

Roman Catholic mysticism during and after the Reformation era reflected comparable lines of development. The Roman church's greatest mystics and spiritual writers in this period tended also to be great founders or reformers of religious orders who labored on the spiritual, intellectual, and practical levels to enable their church to meet its new challenges. In particular this was true of the great sixteenth-century Spanish mystics: Ignatius of Loyola (1491–1556), founder of the Society of Jesus (Jesuits) and author of the celebrated *Spiritual Exercises;* John of the Cross (1542–91), monastic reformer and writer of the profound *Dark Night of the Soul,* which explores the stripping away of self and sense one must pass through to reach, through love alone, the unitive state; and Teresa of Avila (1515–82), also a reformer and spiritual writer of great perception on the stages of gain and loss leading to union, where even God is momentarily forgotten as he is gained. In these saints the spiritual path is definitely outlined on Dionysian principles, now as rigorously reinterpreted by the scholastic thought of Thomas Aquinas, but its austerity is sweetened more than a little by the use of sensual and romantic language in the tradition of Bernard.

In the next century, Roman Catholic leadership in exploring the spiritual life passed to France, where a group of devout and learned priests made the practice of meditation move further in the general direction of pietism through emphasis on picturing such subjects as the life of Christ in the mind and in filling oneself with affective feeling toward the saviour. One example is Jean-Jacques Olier (1608–57), founder of a famous seminary at the church of St. Sulpice in Paris.

The spirituality of the Eastern Orthodox Church has remained very conservative, long adhering in its essence to the Christian Neoplatonism of the early Christian centuries, yet also long remaining more deeply entwined with the lives of ordinary believers than has often been the case in the West. For this reason its major movements can appropriately be described in a general account of the Eastern Church. We shall now turn to a description of the three major branches of Christendom: Eastern Orthodoxy, Roman Catholicism, and Protestantism.

EASTERN ORTHODOXY

The branch of Christianity called **Orthodox** is the dominant religious tradition of Greece, the Balkans, and Russia; there is a scattering in other parts of the Near East, and of course it is found wherever immigrants from its homelands have come, including the United States. (A Russian Orthodox cathedral was established at Sitka, Alaska, as early as 1794). The Orthodox churches, about 160 million strong, are often called "Eastern" because their center of gravity is in Eastern Europe, although this faith is of worldwide importance. They are sometimes called Greek Orthodox, since the cultural and historical background is Greek; the tradition took its definitive form in the culturally Greek Byzantine Empire. But the majority of Orthodox are now Slavic rather than Greek. The Orthodox churches of various nationalities commonly go by national names, such as Russian Orthodox, Serbian Orthodox, Rumanian Orthodox.

Orthodoxy likes to speak of itself as the oldest Christian church, and indeed geography makes its churches continuous with those that Paul and other apostles founded or visited in places like Thessalonika, Corinth, and Cyprus. But the ritual and ethos of the present-day Orthodox churches is essentially the form in which it crystallized in the Byzantine period before the fall of Constantinople to the Turks in 1453. Since then, most Orthodox lands have spent long centuries under Muslim or Mongol rule, just as most of them have experienced Communist regimes that were cold toward church and religion. Both under the Byzantine Empire and sympathetic modern nation-states, and in a different way under the Ottoman Empire, the Orthodox Church has been very closely linked to the state and often controlled by it. This history, different from that of Christianity in the West, has inhibited outward development but has given Orthodoxy a deep relation to the national culture of several countries, and often a very rich inner spiritual life.

The word *orthodox* has varying uses and connotations in English. For the people of the Eastern churches it is an attractive and strong word, not primarily suggesting rigid and narrow attitudes. They believe, of course, that their churches alone preserve the correct, or orthodox, tradition of Christian teaching and life from earliest times. But they also like to point out that in Greek, *orthodox* can mean both "right teaching" *and* "right glory." The combination of these two gives insight into the world of Orthodox life.

A highly conservative mood informs the standard doctrinal teaching of the Orthodox churches. It is held that only a General Council can officially define doctrine, and only those seven councils held in Nicaea, Constantinople, Ephesus, and Chalcedon up to 787 are recognized. Moreover, Orthodox thought has been deeply influenced by Platonism with its assumption that what is most real and true is unchanging. Thus, central to Orthodoxy is the reality of the Trinity, God as three in one—an eternal mystery that undergirds the world. Next is the eternal reality of the incarnation of God in Christ, not only a historical episode but an eternal involvement of God in the material world, through struggle and suffering, making the children of earth divine, manifesting true glory.

On the one hand, this attitude has led to an exaltation of timeless contemplation, exemplified by devout Orthodox monks such as those living virtually out of history on Mount Athos in Greece, whom all serious Orthodox regard as ideals and as unseen givers of life to the church. The goal, Orthodox say, is to be deified in the sense of becoming "partakers of the divine nature," actual sharers in God's own life; contemplation raises us to this level.

Yet on the other hand, Orthodoxy greatly celebrates Christ's **Resurrection** and the anticipated Last Day when God will make the new heaven and earth and be all in all. These events represent the triumph of God's suffering work in the world as he makes it visibly what the contemplative knows inwardly it is: infused with divinity.

The worship side of Orthodoxy richly expresses these ideas. For one used to the plainness of much Western Christianity, a first visit to an Orthodox church can be an overwhelming experience. The service is long and may be in an unfamiliar tongue. But few will be untouched by the glowing color and the soaring, exotic music. The Divine Liturgy, as the main Sunday service is called, is also at heart the early church's offering and blessing of bread and wine. The ornate vestments shimmer richly, incense is swung into the music-laden air over and over, the book of the Gospel and the elements of bread and wine are brought out in procession.

Across a partition (the *iconostasis*) before the altar, and at the church entry and elsewhere, will be seen the icons—vividly colored stylized paintings of Christ and the saints. These, which the faithful reverently kiss and before which they burn candles, have a very special meaning in Orthodoxy. Made according to holy traditions, they are seen as radiating the divine glory of the subjects and so are like peepholes into eternity and the means of raising oneself to it. In fact, the whole Divine Liturgy is seen as an experience of moving up into another plane, or conversely a breakthrough of heaven to earth. The entire intricately wrought interior of the building may be backgrounded in gold, representing eternity.

The concept that the church makes available here on earth these experiences of the Other Side helps one understand the activity of people in Orthodox worship. People will often be coming and going throughout the long service, or getting up on their own to pray and light candles, perhaps with prostrations, at various icons. The sense of individual freedom suggests the church is more like a home than an institution. At the same time, Orthodoxy inculcates a deep sense of community within which this freedom is possible. A sense of simple belonging to the Orthodox community is an interior identity that goes beyond any particular forms of outward

Russian Orthodox ceremony.

expression. There is much that is important and traditional in matters of worship, fasting, and so forth, yet they hardly stifle the homey and spontaneous tone with legalism.

Something of the same feeling permeates other of the Orthodox forms of social expression; this was particularly the case in old Russia. No country except India has had as many wandering holy men as Russia before the Revolution; in some ways the Orthodox Christianity of "Holy Russia" was more Asian than Western in religious style. The *startsi,* holy monks or hermits, more often laymen than priests, familiar to readers of Dostoevsky, were venerated counselors and givers of blessing. Some remained in one place; some were perpetual pilgrims who wandered about the vast land—even as far as Jerusalem—with nothing but the clothes on their back and perhaps a sacred book or two, begging or remaining silent unless pressed to teach. There were also the "Holy Fools," perhaps idiots, madmen by conventional standards, or cripples, who would babble nonsense, meow like a cat in church, or castigate a czar for his sins, yet before whom even nobility might bow with humility, for they were seen as embodiments of the suffering Christ and of the irrational side of God here on earth.[17]

Thus, Eastern Orthodoxy has quite distinctive forms in the three areas of religious expression: theological emphasis on God in Trinity and incarnation as eternally unchanging yet present all through the world, even in the lowliest, and always breaking through in mystery and glory; a worship which expresses that glory; and social forms making room for tradition, homeliness, and spontaneity in individuals within a mystical community.

ROMAN CATHOLICISM

The Roman Catholic Church, the communion of Christians who recognize the supreme spiritual authority on earth of the bishop of Rome, the Pope, and who share much else as well, is the largest Christian body. Some 950 million people are within its spiritual, or at least cultural, orbit; it is the dominant religious tradition in most of Southern and Central Europe, Ireland, and Latin America, and is an important minority in English-speaking North America, Australia, and parts of Africa and Asia.

For many people both within and outside it, the Roman Catholic Church means an institution of monolithic uniformity and highly authoritarian direction. If this was ever true—and it never has been entirely—it is not today. Since the Second Vatican Council of 1962–65, this church has known considerable ferment and experimentation. Whatever it becomes, it can surely not return to what it was before, despite a trend back toward authoritarian uniformity under Pope John Paul II. In the late 1960s and early 1970s, I witnessed a very informal mass—with guitars, the congregation standing around the altar, and pentecostal "speaking in tongues"—in Los Angeles; a highly traditional Latin mass in Communist-ruled Budapest; and a dignified yet reformed mass in Japanese at Ise, not far from the great Shinto shrine, in which members of the congregation read various parts of the service. The Roman Catholic experience has never really been monolithic—even traditional pre-Vatican II worship did not have quite the same "feel" in Austria and Ireland or Brazil and Belgium—but now its variations are becoming more spontaneous and individual, less merely differences in national "style" and background folk culture.

But one thing outwardly links this realm together: acceptance of the **Pope** as symbol and guarantor of Christian unity. Even this sign has varied in appearance

Roman Catholic priest shaking hands with parishioners
during the sign of peace at Mass.

through the centures, with popes being weak and relatively little noted in some
centuries and in others, great potentates who played major roles in international
politics, lavishly patronized art, or exercised near-absolute control over the church.
Now understanding of the papal role, like much else, is changing. But its profoundest
meaning, as a token of the catholicity, or universality, of the church, is likely to
abide. With the papacy goes another characteristic that is also changing in nature,
yet is deeply ingrained in the Latin past and Catholic present—an acceptance that
some uniformity and centralized authority are good in the church, not only for
practical reasons, but also because of the opportunity they provide for love and
negation of egocentricity.

The papacy is far from being the only distinguishing mark of the Roman
Catholic Church, however, and many today would argue it is not one to be overempha-
sized, even though in some ways it symbolizes much that is distinctive about Roman
Catholic experience. Here are some other general characteristics.[18]

1. Affirmation of sacramentality and visible forms. This attitude, shared by Eastern Orthodoxy and many Anglicans and Lutherans, affirms the central importance of the sacraments, or acts by which divine grace is bestowed through material forms: water in baptism, bread and wine in Holy Communion. The seven **sacraments** recognized by the Roman Catholic Church are baptism, confirmation, penance (confession of sins and absolution or forgiveness mediated by a priest), Eucharist (the Mass or Holy Communion), marriage, ordination, unction (anointing of the sick and dying, part of the "last rites.") The same "sacramentality and visible forms" attitude also affirms the appropriateness of colorful ceremonies, vestments, and images. It affirms through them the presence of the numinous in the church and the necessity of the church appearing to the world as a visible, organized community. The fundamental assumption is that God's work is not wholly invisible and unpredictable, but that God does work through specific matter, people, and institutions; that the incarnation of God in Christ authenticates this experience and God's promises confirm it. For Roman Catholics, the affirmation of appearances and the sacramental principle are ways of emphasizing that the world was created to be good and that the church is a visible and specific work of God on earth by which he comes to the world through the things of the world.

2. The church as an instrument of mediation and communion between humans, including those departed—whether saints or sinners or mixed—and between humanity and God. This characteristic interprets the role given the invocation of the saints as heavenly helpers, prayers for the spiritual growth of those who have left this life, and the importance of the church as God's "extended family" to Catholics. The principle of mediation also interprets the importance of ordained priests, who have a definite role as teachers and as mediators of grace through the sacraments. The institution of the priesthood has an objective side. The Roman Catholic Church maintains a clear chain of doctrine, and priests and bishops are expected to uphold normative standards regarding devotional practices, celibacy of clergy, and moral issues such as abortion and birth control. The legal model is an inheritance of Roman law, to which is added the belief that Christ gave to his church a distinctive teaching authority.

3. The church is an organic and growing institution. Besides affirming the church's organization and authority, Catholics increasingly harbor another feeling about it too: awareness that the Christian fellowship, the church, is an organic, growing, and so changing institution. The papacy, general councils, and other organs of the church's teaching authority have power to direct this growth, yet it is believed to move under the guidance of the Holy Spirit, who is always helping Christians better understand the truth given them. Changes in rite and custom, like those undertaken on a large scale at the time of the Second Vatican Council (1962–65), and clearer definitions of what previously had been latent or unclear in doctrine (although doctrine itself does not change), accompany the church's pilgrimage down the ages. Papal infallibility, itself defined by the First Vatican Council in 1870, means that the Pope is preserved from error when he exercises this defining function in a formal way.

The Roman Catholic Church, then, is an institution highly visible, sacramental, legal, and yet changing. While it certainly claims continuity with the church of the early centuries and the Middle Ages, it is equally not the same in all respects now as then. Let us look at some specific characteristics of present-day Roman Catholicism.

First, some essential doctrines. God is said to be accessible to reason. Faith means intellectual assent. In other words, one can know by reason that there is a God apart from the Christian revelation, and faith is recognizing in the mind that this is so. This is all significant, for it indicates the partnership of religion and philosophy, and the belief, important to many Catholic attitudes, that there are basic truths upon which the Christian faith builds. The added revelation that comes through Christ is mediated through both scripture and tradition, the Bible and the church's lore interacting to cast light upon each other. Its basic points are the Trinity and the incarnation of God in Christ.

The Roman Catholic Church makes much of the Mother of Jesus, the Blessed Virgin Mary. This is fundamentally because her role guarantees the incarnation, but also because she is seen—in her acceptance of God's request that she bear his incarnating son—as a representative of the human race as it was before sin came. She is humanity responding perfectly to God's will and receiving the fullness of God's grace and reward. This is the meaning of the papally defined doctrines of the Immaculate Conception (1854), that Mary was herself conceived without original sin (the doctrine of the Immaculate Conception is not to be confused, as it often is, with the doctrine of the Virgin Birth of Christ); and of her bodily assumption into heaven, defined by the Pope in 1950, which makes her an exemplar of the Resurrection and heavenly reward of all the redeemed.

St. Alfonso Liguori (1696–1787) said, "What Jesus has by nature, Mary has by grace." The prerogatives of Mary, distinctively Christian even if corresponding to the paradigm of the pre-Christian Mediterranean goddesses like Isis and Cybele, and answering to the natural desire of many for feminine as well as masculine principles in religion, have made devotion to Mary notably popular; her power in heaven is held to be immensely great, and her benevolence virtually unconditional. Marian piety has reached a high pitch in the last hundred years or so with the two previously mentioned definitions. They were paralleled by the widespread belief in appearances of Mary to heal and prophesy at such places as Lourdes in France and Fatima in Portugal, now extremely popular pilgrimage centers, with their holy grottos or wells, their appealing statues of Mary appearing to artless peasant children, their dramatic torchlight processions, and their ongoing miracles. But post-Vatican II emphases somewhat reduced interest in this whole Marian complex.

Other significant doctrines include purgatory, already mentioned, and the canonization of saints, a process by which the pope (anciently, any bishop) declares that a given person of "heroic sanctity" is in heaven and so able to intercede on behalf of those who call upon him or her before the throne of God.

Worship is centered on the previously mentioned seven sacraments, although by no means is it limited to them. These include the initiatory rites of baptism and confirmation, and the Mass. This last, the ancient offering of bread and wine, was always said in Latin until Vatican II, except in certain churches using rites similar to those of the Eastern Orthodox. The priest stood at the altar in stately vestments, his back to the congregation, and at the supreme moments when the bread and wine became the Body and Blood of Christ, knelt and then elevated them, to the accompaniment of bells. At a "high mass" there would be a sermon, incense, and chanted music during the rite. Members of the congregation could follow the Latin service in a book with translations; even if they did not, the rich atmosphere, so expressive of numinous "otherness," and of the contrast between the sacred and the ordinary, was conducive to prayer and meditation. Now, the use of the ordinary language and a rather more informal mood, with the priest standing behind the altar facing the people as the host at a banquet, suggests something different: the church as a family of love, where the talents of all have a place.

Another sacrament is penance, the forgiveness of sins. Traditionally, one was expected periodically to make a private confession of his or her sins to a priest, generally in the small boxlike structure in churches called the confessional. The priest has authority to impose a penance—commonly a set of prayers to say—and to give absolution, or impartation of God's forgiveness for the confessed wrongs. Today, group confessional prayers recited in church are often used instead.

Marriage is another sacrament, for it is a gift of God and a means of grace. The Roman Catholic Church therefore has rules governing its members' marriages; since the marriage bond is sacramentally permanent, remarriage after divorce is a matter that requires legal procedures within the church, and there is disapproval of abortion and "nonnatural" means of birth control.

Roman Catholicism is abundant in spiritual life apart from the sacraments. Devotion to the Blessed Virgin may take the form of the rosary, with its repeated Hail Marys, or novenas, special sets of prayers on successive days, or pilgrimages to shrines. Today, creative diversity continues to emerge; the charismatic movement, for example, enriches Roman Catholicism with Pentecostal spontaneity and "speaking in tongues."

Roman Catholic social expression is complex and highly organized. At the head of the church is the Pope, whose seat is in Vatican City, a tiny independent state of which he is sovereign in the heart of Rome. He is elected by the College of Cardinals, an assembly of some seventy prominent archbishops, bishops, and a few others who have been named by a previous Pope to this dignity. The Pope is assisted by the Curia, a cabinet and bureaucracy whose department heads are generally cardinals. Beneath the papacy the church is divided into provinces, headed by archbishops, dioceses headed by bishops, and local parishes under their parish priests. Today bishops are generally appointed by the Pope, and parish priests by the bishop, although other arrangements (often with the state having a role) have obtained in the past and do today in some places.

Parallel to this hierarchy are the orders of monks and nuns—persons who have undertaken not only the celibate state but also vows of poverty and obedience. They usually live communally in monasteries and convents; devote much time to worship together and private meditation; and engage in educational, missionary, or charitable work—if they are not in an "enclosed" order whose task, instead, is a combination of labor, study, corporate prayer, and contemplation. The great orders, such as the active Franciscans, Dominicans, and Jesuits, and the more contemplative Benedictines and Cistercians (including Trappists), and their distinctive traditional garb, are well known. Today the "religious life," as this way is called, is also undergoing considerable modification, but it remains a bulwark of Roman Catholicism.

PROTESTANTISM

The term *Protestantism* is generally taken to include all non-Roman Catholic and non-Eastern Orthodox churches that directly or indirectly derive from the sixteenth-century Reformation in Northern and Western Europe. We have already looked at this event and some of its principles. For although the vast collection of Protestant denominations may suggest almost chaotic variety, they do have in common certain basic attitudes traceable to the Reformation. Even points upon which they differ tend to fall into certain predictable categories. Churches of the Reformation tradition vary from some Anglican and Lutheran churches that have worship and doctrinal emphases similar to those of the Roman church to silent Quaker meetings and Pentecostalist groups that stress spontaneous shouts and "tongues." But apart from a few exceptions, Protestant worship could not be mistaken for any other.

So far as theoretical expression is concerned, the central emphasis for most informed Protestants remains justification by God's grace through faith in Christ, and all that it implies. The important thing is that one's consciousness and feelings be centered on God, open to his will and grace. What is of value, then, is what evokes and expresses this centering. Thus, Protestantism in doctrine and story alike is inclined to apply the principle of parsimony. Cut away everything not essential to hearing and receiving the word of God in the scriptures; cut away all that might distract from one's personal relationship to God.

This simplification motif is clearly evident in worship. Protestant worship has generally become stylized. The typical service contains hymn, scripture, prayer, sermon, the offering, benediction, and a closing hymn. A simple service of Holy Communion is also offered, though not every Sunday in the majority of Protestant churches. The main participation of the congregation is in singing, although in some churches the people offer prayers as well. Otherwise the minister, as a trained religious specialist, is the principal communicator of the mainly verbal experience.

The power of words to communicate saving concepts, imagery, or emotions is central to Protestants; the scripture and sermon and hymns contain "the words of eternal life." Compared to the value placed on what is communicated through reading and hearing words and music, communication through other media is relatively distrusted by Protestants.

In social expression, the ideal is generally recovery of the New Testament church, since seldom (except in Anglicanism) is post-New Testament tradition given much authority. However, the New Testament scriptural paradigm means different things to different wings of Protestantism, and there is a considerable variety in modes of government. Some are ruled by bishops, some by boards of presbyters, some by the local congregation. In practice, the historical situation has also influenced structural form. After the Reformation, Protestantism had state church status in a number of countries; this meant that its organization had to fit in with the laws of the realm. On the other hand, groups such as the separatist Puritans in England who rebelled against that situation, being small and fairly powerless, had to focus on the local church as the important entity. In America after the Revolution, and particularly on the frontier, Protestantism was independent of the state and highly fluid. This led to a wealth of new forms of expression that usually were rooted in the authority of the local group or the charisma of the traveling evangelist.

The scope of Protestantism can be comprehended by stressing first its common themes and then by examining the poles existing in the expression of each.

In terms of theoretical expression, we have noted the centrality of salvation by God's grace through faith. But there are poles regarding the means of receiving grace and expressing faith: In the Lutheran and Reformed traditions, preaching and reading the scriptures are primarily the means; in Anglicanism, the sacraments may be equally important as objective means of grace; among Pentecostals and others at the opposite end of the spectrum, charismatic personalities, revivalists, and healers may in practice be primary means of grace. Similarly, the expression of grace ranges from an emphasis on the ethical life and good works (and here there is polarization between those who stress personal morality and those who stress Christian responsibility for society as a whole) to an emphasis on spiritual states and their expression through conversion, inward joy, and ecstatic phenomena like "tongues"—although of course the two sides are not necessarily incompatible.

The other major Protestant position, the sufficiency of Scripture alone, finds expression in diverse groups, ranging from those who stress that the Bible must judge church life to those, particularly some *Anglicans,* who—like Roman Catholics and Eastern Orthodox—would emphasize the importance of interpreting Scripture within the context of church tradition. (That is something everyone probably does to some extent, since it is inevitable that one will bring to one's understanding of those books written long ago and far away one's own experience in church life and language.)

There also is a difference between fundamentalist interpretations, which insist on a "literal" rendering of such points as the virgin birth and the miracles of Jesus, and "liberal" interpretations, which hold that Scripture must be interpreted in a way consistent with present-day historical and scientific knowledge. This distinction means in effect that fundamentalism often functions as a vehicle of resistance to modern culture, while liberalism tries to relate Christianity to the current scientific and scholarly world view. But on some issues the roles may be reversed.

A continuum is also seen in styles of worship: They range from the solemn and formal services of Anglicans, Lutherans, and Reformed to the folksy worship of many Methodists and Baptists and the often ecstatic meetings of Pentecostals. The most formal expression has generally been that of the "state church" Protestants of Europe and their American counterparts. But the recent growth of informal services and charismatic or Pentecostal phenomena all through Protestantism has changed this pattern.

Protestant social organization has in common the tacit or explicit assumption that the whole of the Christian church cannot be visible and entire in the world today; it is at best only the sum total of many Christian bodies, and its true membership cuts across all sorts of lines and is known only to God. Thus, all visible Protestant bodies are particularized, limited in their base to certain culture areas. They stress local or regional control, although this may mean anything from a state church to an independent congregation. Types of organization vary widely between churches that come out of the state church tradition, whether the Church of England or state Lutheran and Reformed churches in Germany, Scandinavia, Scotland or Holland, or their American branches, and those independent movements that sprang up as alternatives to them and usually had, at least originally, sectarian characteristics: charismatic leaders, local control, strict moral codes, and greater stress on subjective feelings.

The fluid Protestant style of Christianity is not restricted to Northern Europe and America but is as international today as any religious movement in the world. Its rapid geographical expansion began in the missionary enthusiasm of the nineteenth century, when the major Protestant nations were vigorous and expansive, and it has continued into the twentieth. Today, missionary-sending from Europe and America is less central to world Protestantism, although it is still important. But indigenous Protestant churches, some quite independent and some tied to older denominations, exist today nearly everywhere the missionaries went. Missionary educational work has been a very important factor in the emergence of new nations in many parts of the world. (Nineteenth- and twentieth-century Roman Catholic missionary work, of course, is of equal significance.) Today, in some parts of the Third World, especially Africa and Latin America, churches of broadly Protestant lineage founded by local prophets or Pentecostalists are the most active Christian force. They represent a quite different Christian style from that of staid "mainline" denominations, although one more similar to the radical reformers and the American frontier. Above all, they relate Christianity to local cultures in ways that European and American churches usually cannot.

AMERICAN DENOMINATIONALISM

We will now turn to American religion and its special style of spiritual life. The American Main Street, lined with big voluntarily supported Catholic, Protestant, and Jewish places of worship, really represents a map of the invisible world that is quite distinctive within both the Judaeo-Christian tradition and the religious world as a whole.

Because of the special nature of religious history in America, denominationalism is a key to understanding it. Even Judaism, Roman Catholicism, and Eastern Orthodoxy—all very important to American religious life—have had in practice to fall in with styles of social expression the American context creates.

The basic facts in American religious life are (1) immigration by peoples of numerous religious cultures and (2) the emergence of a new society with a need for cohesion and a sense of creating a new political and spiritual way of being in the world. These facts have created pluralism rather than a single official or heavily dominant religious institution, as obtains in most other societies. Yet they have also meant that most groups have found themselves affirming common American ethical and social ideals—democracy, patriotism, social concern—together with their distinctive doctrines and worship.

The general history of religion in America reflects these centrifugal and centripedal drives. In the colonial period, immigrants of diverse religious backgrounds settled in different areas, often in order to find a religious haven: Puritans in Massachusetts, Baptists in Rhode Island, Quakers in eastern Pennsylvania, Lutherans in western Pennsylvania, Roman Catholics in Maryland, and Anglicans in Virginia and the southern seaboard. During 1720–40 the movement for a deeper, more intellectually serious and also more feeling-oriented Christianity, called the Great Awakening, swept across parish, denominational, and colonial lines. The first vital expression of the American centripedal force, it paved the way for the Revolution in that it gave the populations of the thirteen colonies a new sense of being a distinctive American people with their own spiritual concerns, rather than just transplanted Europeans.

The Revolution, of course, brought the sense of national unity to a high pitch and culminated religiously in the First Amendment to the Constitution, which made the United States of America the first society in the history of the world to have not only religious toleration but genuine legal freedom and equality for all faiths and the absence at the national level of any official religious endorsement or support. In this situation, there were many who felt that, forced to stand on its own in a new society and shorn of feudal trappings, religion would wither away, or (as the concurrent Unitarian movement in New England suggested) become very "rational." But such was not to be.

Instead, during the period of westward expansion, nation building, and belief in a special American "Manifest Destiny" both geographical and spiritual, religion flourished in a cornucopia of forms. Evangelical revivals swept the frontier. They brought tremendous growth to the Methodist and Baptist churches, and they produced new denominations such as the Disciples of Christ. New movements, such as Spiritualism and the Latter-Day Saints, originated in upstate New York. There were utopian communes and numerous colleges planted in the name of religion. In an expansive era, the centrifugal and centripedal drives reinforced each other without great tension—and showed that far from weakening religion religious pluralism, with absence of state interference or support, can liberate it to flourish brilliantly.

But this primal "era of good feeling" was not to last. Just as Eden ended with the discovery of sin, so the optimism of the first decades after independence was darkened by the confrontation with the shadow side of American life—slavery. The middle decades of the nineteenth century were rent by controversy over slavery, and denominations were divided by it on North–South lines, so that we came to have northern and southern Baptists, Presbyterians, and Methodists (the Methodists were reunited in 1939, the Presbyterians in 1984). After the Civil War, most of the freed slaves entered exclusively black churches. For many decades, black churches were the only important institutions controlled by blacks, and their ministry was the only profession generally available to them. Out of the black churches came a distinctive style of religious life characterized by close community feeling, a free spiritual expression in which the important worldwide movement of Pentecostalism is rooted, and leaders in the civil rights movement such as Martin Luther King, Jr.

During the same years, and up until 1920, new immigration vastly increased American population with a mixed multitude. During the one decade of the 1840s, American Roman Catholicism grew by immigration from a small minority to the largest single church in the nation—a position it has held ever since. Jews, Eastern Orthodox, and German and Scandinavian Lutherans also immigrated in the millions during the latter half of the century. All this was in the context of great social change: the growth of cities, industry, widespread education, and life based on modern technology. The older Protestantism tended to react in two ways: a conservatism, which came to be known as fundamentalism and which sought to preserve the religious values of frontier revivalism and religious surety in a changing world; and the more liberal "social gospel" movement, which strove to correlate religion to new ideas in science and society, and to recover the old dream of making America into a new "people of God" through social reform.

The strands of this history are expressed in the panorama of American **denominations.** They are far from the whole story of American religion; the centrifugal "civil religion" drive toward a common American ethic and vision cuts across them, and important issues such as fundamentalism versus the "social gospel" have polarized denominations from within and have found expression in distinctive denominations. Indeed, "one issue" denominations without concomitant ethnic or sociological roots have not generally been very successful, and it seems that now the day of forming major new denominations is long since past—although the countervailing ecumenical drive toward unifying them has had only limited success.

But American denominational pluralism is an important phenomenon. Derived from the unique history of colonial settlement, the frontier flux, the slavery controversy, and immigration, it is as distinctive in its way as Tibetan Buddhism. No other society, except to some extent British Commonwealth nations such as Canada and Australia, which have had a superficially comparable religious history, approaches this particular form of sociological expression of religion.

The denomination in America is a voluntarily supported religious group for which its members feel responsible and which feels in practice responsible primarily for them, rather than, as a denomination, for the total spiritual life of the nation. (All this is quite different from most traditional religion and Old World Christianity.) The religious nation is seen as a composite of denominations, all legally and (in the minds of many) spiritually coequal. ("It doesn't matter what church you go to so long as you go.") They are sometimes competitive, sometimes cooperative; the complex webs they form are the outline of the map of the invisible world in America. Because this pattern is so different from that of Europe and is so rooted in the relatively brief American past, it largely accounts for the lack of a sense of the long ancient and medieval Christian history so characteristic of American churches.

Here is a glance at important Protestant denominations or traditions that express this map. Membership approximations are for 1991. For comparative purposes, it may be noted that the Roman Catholic Church has 55 million members in the United States; the Eastern Orthodox Churches, about 4 million. There are some 4 million Jews who are members of religious congregations, 4 million or more Muslims, and perhaps 500,000 Buddhists.

The Methodist family includes the United Methodist Church with some 9 million members; the Free Methodists, which is a conservative group split from it; and the predominantly black African Methodist Episcopal Church and African Methodist Episcopal Zion Church. As we have seen, Methodism stems from the eighteenth-century preaching of John Wesley and others in England. In America, Methodism greatly flourished on the frontier. But in the process of becoming a dominant faith, especially in the small towns of the South and Midwest, it inevitably became more moderate or liberal than in the heyday of frontier evangelism. In reaction to this, groups such as the Free Methodist Church and the Church of the Nazarene broke with Methodism around the turn of the twentieth century to keep intact the original Wesleyan conversion and holiness doctrines as they understood them.

The largest single block of American Protestants are the Baptists. The Southern Baptist Church has some 14.5 million members; it is virtually a way of life in parts of the South. The northern-based American Baptist Church has 1.5 million members. Two predominantly black National Baptist churches total some 9 million, and there are other smaller Baptist groups. Baptists in America derive from the seventeenth-century movements in England, inspired by "radical reformation" Anabaptists on the continent who stressed that baptism should not be given to infants but should be a sign following adult conversion. Baptists have always stood for religious freedom and have opposed state churches; they have tended to be conservative regarding scripture and personal morality.

The largest Lutheran church, the Evangelical Lutheran Church in America, with over 5 million members, was formed by a merger in 1987. The Lutheran Church—Missouri Synod (2.6 million), is a more conservative body. Although the Lutherans represent American expressions of state churches deriving from Luther's wing of the Reformation, unlike Methodists and Baptists who derive from European dissident movements, they were in practice heavily influenced by nineteenth-century pietistic movements, which explains differences between European Lutheranism and the sometimes more conservative American Lutheranism. Lutheran worship is generally stately and attractive, with majestic music and learned preaching; Lutheran people in America, largely of German and Scandinavian descent, are conspicuous in their loyalty to the church and its worship.

The Church of England, the state church that separated from Rome in the days of Henry VIII, is represented in America by the Episcopal Church, with some

2.5 million members. It was dominant in much of Colonial America, but great numbers of its nominal members were swept away by the frontier Methodist and Baptist movements after the American Revolution. Episcopalianism managed to recover strength and now represents a tradition similar to that of the colorful, rather ceremonial worship of the Church of England.

In 1984, the two major Presbyterian churches in America united to form the Presbyterian Church (U.S.A.) with 3 million members. American Presbyterianism represents the tradition of the state Church of Scotland and its affiliates in England and Ireland. Its theological heritage is Calvinist, its worship simpler and closer to the central Protestant structure than the Episcopalian. It has always emphasized a high level of education and preaching among the clergy.

Also in the Calvinist lineage are two groups representing wings of the Reformed Church in the Netherlands: the Reformed Church of America (340,000 members) and the Christian Reformed Church (220,000).

A Calvinist background is also found in the United Church of Christ, with some 1.7 million members. The UCC is a merger of the Congregational Church, whose heritage is the Puritan settlers from England in New England, and the German Evangelical and Reformed Church. By and large, Congregationalism and the UCC have moved away from the proverbial (though often misunderstood) narrowness of the Puritan to a liberal stance that permits no small diversity of expression. Its congregational organization allows each local church to elect its own minister and draw up its own statement of belief.

A numerically small but significant denomination of New England congregational background is the Unitarian-Universalist Church (179,000 members), a union of two very liberal bodies. It professes absolute freedom of belief; most of its members would reject such doctrines as the Trinity and the divinity of Christ, and many would reject belief in the traditional God in favor of religion centered on human needs and ends.

Another small but important tradition is that of the Religious Society of Friends, commonly called the Quakers. Starting from the ministry of George Fox in seventeenth-century England, Quakers rejected a paid ministry, sacraments (they do not baptize or partake of Holy Communion "outwardly"), and structured worship. A Quaker meeting consists of worshippers sitting in silence until someone feels moved by the Spirit to speak, which he or she may then do freely. Quakers first settled Pennsylvania; now the several Quaker denominations have about 120,000 members together. Some are still nonministerial and "unprogrammed"; these tend to be liberal socially and theologically. Others, usually more conservative in temperament, have ministers and organized worship services.

A number of denominations have originated in America. These are all further from European traditions, as one would expect, than the churches cited. There are the Churches of Christ, 1.6 million, the Christian Church (Disciples), 1 million, and the Christian Churches (1 million), which emerged out of the frontier "Restoration Movement" to recover the New Testament church, and are now moderate to fairly conservative evangelical churches. Pentecostalism, so dynamic worldwide that it has been called a Christian "third force," started in America and is represented by a variety of churches: several called Church of God, the Assemblies of God, the Pentecostal Holiness Church, and others. They emphasize the value of "speaking in tongues" as a sign of conversion and receiving of the Holy Spirit; worship life is spontaneous, immensely alive, and full of the expectation of miracles.

Other American movements include the Church of Jesus Christ of Latter-Day Saints (the Mormon church), with some 4 million members in America, based on the teachings of Joseph Smith, whom his followers believe found golden plates in upstate New York telling, among other things, that Jesus came to ancient America; the Church of Christ, Scientist, founded by Mary Baker Eddy, which emphasizes that God is all and therefore there is no disease save in distorted mind; and the Seventh-Day Adventist Church (687,000 members), which stresses that Christ will return again very soon, and also that Christians have an obligation to keep some of the Law of Moses, including worship on Saturday, the old Sabbath. There are churches in the New Thought tradition, such as the Unity churches and the Church of Religious Science, theologically liberal and stressing the power of mind to solve problems and bring joy. Spiritualist churches focus on communication by mediumship with the spirits of the departed to assure believers of immortality.

American Protestantism is indeed diverse. Not only do the denominations differ widely, but even within a single denomination one may find some members asserting that God is dead and that our concerns must be entirely secular, while others see visions and find God's hand at work among them in signs, miracles, and tongues. Yet the diversity is not infinite, and what holds it together is really more basic than its diversity: There is everywhere a fundamental belief in the importance of right inwardness, whether one means by that intellectual integrity, powerful conversion feelings, the Holy Spirit giving supernatural gifts, or positive thinking. There is a definite congregation and a weekly worship service (not the case in all religions), which usually focuses on singing, preaching, and prayer. A Unitarian and a Pentecostal church might seem quite different to an outsider, but the outsider would have no trouble in comprehending that they are related in a way neither is to a Zen monastery, Hindu temple, Muslim mosque, or even a Rumanian Orthodox or Italian Roman Catholic church. American Protestant churches represent numerous fine gradations of doctrine, worship, and sociological grounding, but all these are finally within only a certain portion of the much broader spectrum of human religion as a whole.

THE MODERN EXPANSION
OF CHRISTIANITY

Christianity calls forth more than the image of established cloisters and churches. It also evokes scenes from its geographical front lines: the Spanish friar building his sun-washed missions surrounded by native tribespeople of the Americas; the nineteenth-century Protestant missionary marching into the jungles of Darkest Africa or a "Cannibal Isle," Bible in hand.

These are pictures that call forth in us a profound diversity of responses; the missionary's front-line soldiering on behalf of the Cross has usually been controversial, both in the sending and the receiving countries. He or she has been admired for incredible heroism, and millions have been deeply grateful for the medical, educational, and spiritual benefits they have received. Yet the missionary's calling has also given rise to gnawing doubts about the right of one religion to impose itself upon people of another, about the relation of modern missions to Euro-American expansionism, and about the long-term impact of the missionary upon cultures around the world whose ancient ways have been challenged and sometimes shattered preemptorily.

The story of Christian missions since the days of Columbus is as complex as these responses imply. But one thing is certain: The Christian missionary endeavor together with European immigration in these five centuries has radically changed the religious map of the world. From being mostly the faith of a relatively small corner of the earth—Europe—Christianity has overwhelmed whole continents and islands across vast seas, and it is represented in nearly every nation of the earth; a quarter of the world's population is, at least nominally, under its spiritual sway.

At the time of Columbus's first voyage to the Americas in 1492, Christianity was gradually recovering from a low ebb. In the previous century the faith had been sorely weakened in numbers or morale by the Black Death, the Papal Schism, and Muslim advances in the East. The last culminated in the Turkish capture of Constantinople in 1453 and the final demise of Christendom's bulwark to the East, the Byzantine Empire.

But in the fifteenth century new life was stirring. Renaissance learning brought expansive new views of the world and the cosmos. As the Turks sealed off the old trade lines in the East, a growing economy in Western Europe sought new markets and new paths of trade. The two countries which were to play the leading role in the early stages of that quest, Spain and Portugal, completed their nation-building when Spain drove out the last of the Muslim rulers in the south of the Iberian peninsula in a long struggle ending in 1492. In those years Spain and Portugal stood proud, robust, full of enthusiastic Catholic faith, facing the broad Atlantic ready to conquer new worlds for king and Christ.

Portugal began first. Prince Henry the Navigator (1394–1460) and his successors sent intrepid explorers such as Vasco da Gama around the Cape of Good Hope and finally to India and beyond. Their followers raised the Portuguese flag at such exotic places as Goa and Malacca, laying the foundations of a far-flung empire. Commerce may have been its real dynamic, but kings and seafarers alike sincerely believed that they were acting at the will of God, and that the conversion of the infidel was the greatest objective of their brave voyages. King Manoel of Portugal (r. 1495–1521), called "The Fortunate," for under him some of his nation's supreme achievements were obtained, wrote to an Indian monarch that now it was the command of God that Portuguese go to India, and it would be "a wrong and injury to God to wish to resist His manifest and known will."

So also his people believed it would be wrong to deny the Christian faith to those in overseas places, though at first the Portuguese believed the Hindus, not

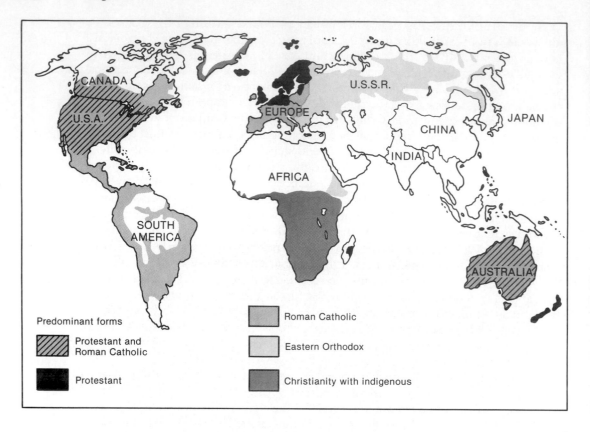

MAP 8–1. The Growth of Christianity

being Muslim, were Christian, their gods and goddesses renditions of Christ and his Mother. Priests accompanied the explorers and empire builders, both to minister to the spiritual needs of the Europeans and to baptize the heathen. Not a few of them were Franciscans, for members of that order had been adventurous missionaries since the time of Francis himself, who once went to the Holy Land to try to convert the Saracen.

   In the sixteenth century they were joined by Jesuits. The greatest of all missionaries of the Age of Exploration was the Jesuit Francis Xavier (1506–52) who, although Spanish-born, sailed from Lisbon and worked along the Portuguese lines of trade and conquest. He labored in the Portuguese Indian enclave of Goa with great success in 1542–45, then made converts on the Malay peninsula, and finally, as we have seen, was in Japan from 1549 to 1551. There it took him only two years to lay the foundation of Japan's remarkable first era of Christian penetration.

   The Portuguese career in India and the Far East was brilliant, but it flickered out in a century or so, save for such tiny colonial remnants as Goa and Macao, and only in such places did the Catholic faith brought by zealous missionaries put down deep roots. Of more lasting impact, from the religious point of view especially, was the work of Portugal and, above all, of its larger neighbor Spain in the New World. For it is well known that, while Portugal was navigating the stormy waters of the Cape to reach the fabled treasure of the East and to carry thence the treasure of the Gospel, Christopher Columbus had persuaded Ferdinand and Isabella of Spain to assist him in seeking a direct route west to that same treasure. He found not the East of the Portuguese rivals, but an entire new world to present to the Spanish monarchs.

Within a remarkable half-century of 1492, brutal but effective Spanish conquests had subdued the great centers of Native American civilization, Mexico and Peru, and had established colonial outposts from Argentina to the northern Caribbean. In the wake of the armies, missionaries baptized thousands daily, bringing the Indian masses nominally under the cross. Their work did not stop there. The Spanish priests built churches in imposing baroque style, often on the location of major pre-Christian temples. They devised ingenious ways to inculcate the rudiments of Christian faith in their illiterate charges; elaborate sacred dramas, simple hymns and chants, and colorful processions, as well as fiery preaching in both Spanish and native tongues, supplemented the mystery of the mass.

As the Spanish frontier advanced, its vanguard was typically the mission, such as the famous Spanish missions of California. Here, priests would pave the way for Spanish settlement, trade, and rule by domesticating the Indians into a mission-centered community, teaching them farming and simple industries while giving them paternalistic and today sometimes criticized, supervision. Most remarkable of all was the quasi independent mission-state that the Jesuits ruled in Paraguay between 1586 and 1756. Protecting the Indians of that inland nation from more warlike natives and European settlers, they established a peaceful society of beautiful communal farms and immense ranches, dotted with thirty-three garden cities. But in the end, the wealth of this earthly paradise attracted the greed of both Spain and Portugal, who drove the missionaries out and divided the land between themselves.

This was not the only case in which the missionaries were more on the side of the natives than of the colonizing powers. The priest Bartolomé de Las Casas (1474–1566) labored heroically for humane treatment of the Indians, preaching against abuses and traveling several times to Spain to obtain laws protecting the natives and at the same time mediating between the races in the New World whenever possible. To his later bitter regret, in his zeal to alleviate exploitation of the Indians, it was he who first suggested importing black slaves from Africa to work the plantations of the European settlers. But other dedicated priests, such as the celebrated Jesuit Pedro Claver (1581–1654), gave themselves to ministering to the miserable cargo of the slave ships upon their arrival in American ports. In the Portuguese colony of Brazil, the exploited found a friend in the Jesuit António Vieira (1608–97), whose long and varied career in Brazil, Portugal, and Rome included struggles for protection of Indians in the New World and toleration of Jews in Europe.

Despite such outstanding men as these, however, the quality of clergy in the

Santuario de Guadalupe, a Spanish Catholic mission in the American southwest.

Americas was not high, and the church suffered generally from passivity, a shortage of priests, especially American-born, and excessive government control. This dual heritage of a heroic few and general anemia is reflected in the strengths and weaknesses of Latin American Catholicism to this day.

Before leaving the Golden Age of Roman Catholic missions, a word must be said about the remarkable work of Matteo Ricci (1552–1610), an Italian Jesuit, and his companions in China. Coming to the East with the Portuguese, Ricci entered China through Macao in 1583 and finally reached Peking in 1601, where he remained the rest of his life.

Ricci and his Jesuits pioneered a new approach to missions. Before beginning work, they mastered the Chinese language and studied Chinese culture in depth.

Ricci became thoroughly Chinese in all nonessentials, wearing a mandarin robe and ingratiating himself with the intellectual class through his teaching of Western science and geography. While his number of converts was not large, he established the Christian church in China and won intellectual prestige for it through his own example. But his willingness to employ Chinese language and Confucian practices, such as ancestral rites, in Christian worship, created a longstanding controversy within the Catholic church. The "Rites Controversy," as it was called, was essentially over the significant issue of to what extent Christianity can adapt itself and its worship to the ways of the various lands to which it travels. The matter was decided against the Jesuits in the eighteenth century, but in 1939 the Vatican adopted a more liberal policy, and the Second Vatican Council expressed a considerable new openness toward local adaptations of Catholicism; in effect, vindicating Ricci's position. But also, as we shall see, Ricci's writings about China had a reverse impact on Europe as it groped toward the Enlightenment and modernity—an impact that casts light on another kind of influence the missionary movement has had.

The modern expansion of Christianity has come in great waves. The first, essentially Roman Catholic, followed the Spanish and Portuguese movement east and west. By the seventeenth century this wave had crested. In that century and the next, Christianity continued vigorous expansion, but far more through immigration than direct missionary activity. Christian Europeans, both Protestant and Catholic (especially from the British Isles, France, Holland, and Germany), settled in North America and South Africa, where their colonies formed the seeds of great nations of predominantly Christian faith.

The beginning of the nineteenth century saw the beginning of a new wave of European imperial and commercial as well as emigration expansion; this time— even as the old colonies of the New World won independence—centering on Asia, the South Pacific, Australia, and later Africa. Protestant nations such as Britain and the Netherlands and later Germany were most involved, as was also Catholic France. With this expansion came a new wave of missionary work in which those countries, as well as the United States, were most active.

With the loss of the American colonies, British interest turned substantially eastward to India, Australasia, and the archipelagos of the South Pacific, lately visited by Captain James Cook. This interest coincided with the late eighteenth-century rise of the evangelical movement, which fired missionary zeal. The stage was set for a new Golden Age of the missionary spread of Christianity, abetted by the expansion of Euro-American commerce, emigration, and colonial empires.

A good example is the voyage of *The Duff*. In 1796 a party sent by the newly formed London Missionary Society (interdenominational but predominantly Congregational and evangelical) sailed on a ship of that name to the South Seas to land missionaries on three island groups that Captain Cook had touched in his celebrated voyages only a few decades before. The majority went to Tahiti, and by 1815 most of the population was at least nominally Christian on that tropical paradise.

The story of missions in the South Pacific is a fascinating and provocative one, but the total number of people affected was small. We must now look at the impact of nineteenth-century missions in the great centers of non-Christian population.

Christianity in India has ancient roots; the Mar Thoma church there claims to have been founded by the apostle St. Thomas. The sixteenth-century Portuguese work also left a lasting heritage. But the British East India Company, which increasingly controlled the subcontinent in the eighteenth century, opposed missions on the grounds they might be disruptive. Nonetheless, in 1793 the first Protestant missionary to India, William Carey, arrived with a companion, John Thomas, a doctor. Carey combined preaching with a wide variety of activities that set the pattern of modern missionary work. He established medical and educational services, taught Bengali in college, translated the Bible, engaged in such scholarly work as translating the *Ramayana* into English, interceded with the government to effect reforms, and encouraged the training of native missionaries.

In Australia and New Zealand, missionaries combined ministry to settlers with efforts to convert and assist natives. Perhaps the story of New Zealand is of greatest interest. Anglican missionaries arrived on those islands in 1814, followed by Methodists in 1822; both were sent by the evangelical Church Missionary Society. That society tried to prevent the coming of white settlers to New Zealand, rightly believing their arrival would lead to bloodshed and exploitation of the Maori natives. Nonetheless, by the 1840s whites began to stream in; by this time virtually all the Maori had been converted at least superficially, but that did not prevent brutal conflict with their European coreligionists until they were "pacified." During this period the Maori were considerably reduced in number owing to disease, war, and the demoralizing disruption of traditional styles of life.

Christian progress in the midst of the great civilization of China has been understandably checkered. As in India, Christianity there had ancient roots, but the Nestorian church present in the Tang era completely vanished. The Catholic work founded by Ricci suffered increasing repression after his day, but it remained alive, often underground. Modern missionary work, both Catholic and Protestant, began after the Opium War treaties forced the admission of missionaries. Many turned to Christianity in the troubled China of the era between the Opium Wars and the Communist triumph; the old ways were widely discredited, and the educational and material offerings of the Western missionaries appealed to millions, as did their spiritual gifts. Yet missionaries were also resented and persecuted as hated foreigners, reminders of the humiliating treaties that had let them in, and scapegoats for China's distress. As we have seen, after the establishment of the People's Republic of China the Christian churches had to sever all foreign ties and sometimes suffered persecution.

In Japan, modern Christianity has never exceeded 1 percent of the population, yet it has had no small influence. When missionaries returned in the nineteenth century to the Island Empire, they found not only the "hidden Christian" remnants of the sixteenth-century Christian era, but also both xenophobic attitudes and a remarkable openness to anything Western—including Western religion. Among those most open were now younger samurai, members of the class leading Japan into modernization. Aided by exceptional educational and medical work, Christianity grew in the 1870s and 1880s but then slowed down as Japanese self-confidence and nationalism rose.

Sub-Saharan Africa has thus far been numerically the most successful of modern mission fields. This is despite the fact that black Africa has been the site of some of the worst evils of the white man's ways, from slaving to exploitative colonial empires. But Africans have been aware that missionaries have generally fought those evils and have brought many gifts. The best-known pioneer missionary was David Livingstone (1813–73), sent by the London Missionary Society, who combined the search for converts with important exploration. He was followed by others; conversion became virtually a mass movement helped by educational, agricultural, and medical work, and by the inevitable decline of traditional ways and beliefs as Africa became part of the modern world. Today, between 25 and 50 percent of the population is Christian in most of the sub-Saharan nations.

African Christianity has taken innumerable forms, however. Not only is virtually every denomination represented, but many new movements, often centering around local prophets and going further than would most missionaries to assimilate native attitudes and practices to Christianity, have sprung up on African soil. Missionary opposition to such traditionally accepted customs as polygamy has turned some to indigenous brands of Christianity as well as to Islam, which is also growing south of the Sahara. Africa today is a vital arena of religious life and change.

If the missionary movement has spawned numerous new forms of Christian life, it has also contributed immeasurably to Christian unity. From the beginning, Protestant missionary work has had an interdenominational aspect; as we have seen, groups such as the Church Missionary Society sent out workers of several churches. In the mission field, denominationalism often seemed less important than it had at home, and the visible unity of those working for the same great cause became more imperative. It is primarily out of the missionary endeavor that the modern ecumenical movement, dedicated to interchurch cooperation, understanding, and ultimately re-union, has arisen. In the nineteenth century various missionary conferences, regional or among allied denominations, were held; these culminated in the World Missionary Conference in Edinburgh, Scotland, in 1910, bringing together representatives of the missionary work of all major Protestant churches. It led directly to the World Council of Churches, the main ecumenical agency, which the Eastern Orthodox churches later joined. In more recent years Roman Catholics have also cooperated with the World Council as nonmember "observers" and have in other ways striven to promote ecumenical understanding.

The missionary enterprise has had a reverse impact on Europe and America, too, one doubtless unexpected at first. Just as missionaries shattered the isolation of countless tribes and nations around the globe, so have their reports shattered the complacency and spiritual isolation of the older Christian nations. They opened up a wide world which many perceived to be far more complex, spiritually as well as otherwise, than anticipated.

First, questions about the moral underpinnings of Christendom slowly began to arise in the minds of thoughtful Christians as a result of experiences such as that of the first Portuguese missionaries in Africa, who found that natives they had brought under the gospel of love quickly fell away when brutal slavers arrived flying the same flag as they.

Second, questions about the absolute superiority of Christianity could not help but be suggested by missionary reports of non-Christian cultures, which the unbiased mind could only see as equal or even in some ways superior to those in the West. In Asian countries such as India, China, and Japan, missionaries encountered civilizations and religions of great sophistication, and they found themselves regarded as barbarians. Missionary scholars were, in fact, among the first to translate and bring west the great spiritual classics of the East, many of which we have already studied, and which some in the West discovered to be as appealing as the Bible. The reports of Jesuits such as Ricci from Confucian China, with its respect for education, its civil service examination system, its apparently tolerant and primarily ethical religion, made that ancient empire seem something of a utopia to intellectuals in an early eighteenth-century Europe struggling toward democracy and just emerging from the bloody religious wars of the seventeenth century. The Chinese image had a significant impact on the emergence of the eighteenth-century Enlightenment ideals of reason, deistic religion, tolerance, civil service, and democracy—much more of an impact than Europe, despite those missionaries, had on China in the same century.

Nonetheless, on a worldwide scale Christian missions have been an overall success. For all those at home disturbed by questions, more were won to Christianity in Asia, Africa, and the Americas. Thanks to them and to European emigration, Christianity has become the most genuinely worldwide religion the planet has ever known. We must now examine its present status around the world.

CHRISTIANITY IN THE WORLD TODAY

As the tumultuous twentieth century draws to a close, Christianity remains numerically the strongest religion in the world. But it enjoys its preeminence in an anxious world full of strains, paradoxes, and ominous portents almost beyond imagining. In some places a new age of high technology, symbolized by space probes and sophisticated computers, is being ushered in. Yet a third of humankind goes to bed hungry every night, and the bodies and minds of children shrivel for lack of bread. Even as prospects of amazing progress in science, medicine, and all branches of learning gleam, not for centuries has the future been so feared. For beside that glittering computerized future (and what it might do to human values nobody knows) loom the grim shadows of the four horsemen of the Apocalypse: tyranny, war, economic disaster, and famine.

Just because of its phenomenal worldwide spread, Christianity finds itself today at all corners of the world's dilemmas. It is the church of wealthy consuming nations and the church of the starving, of countries old and new, of lands and classes with little in common and much reason to see themselves at cross-purposes.

In 1900 the most powerful countries were Christian, ruled by professedly Christian emperors, kings, and presidents. Moreover, it was widely boasted that Europe and America's Christianity had something to do with their manifest superiority over the rest of humanity. Not a few Christians prophesied that, since the day of the other religions and their outmoded cultures was clearly past, the whole planet might be converted within a generation.

By the last quarter of the century, the confidence of those expansive times was long gone. Wars and revolutions have brought atheistic regimes in the place of ancient Christian as well as Confucian thrones; movements of national independence have brought resurgent affirmations of Hinduism, Buddhism, and Islam; in Europe, America, and elsewhere immense social and intellectual changes have weakened the grip of the traditional religion, Christianity, on the minds of many.

Yet Christianity, chastened but quite alive, abides. In some places it is in recession, but in others it is growing. In some places it shows quite a different face from 1900; in others it seems to have changed little since 1900, nor indeed since 900. It retains its complex denominationalism, its amazing diversities of forms of worship and theological opinion, and its chronic inability to find a common voice with which to address a problem-ridden world. Yet it is still a presence to be reckoned with. We shall now review the status of Christianity in the late twentieth century.

In the region of its origin, the Middle East, Christianity still has a precarious foothold. The dominant religion in the heyday of the Byzantine Empire, it has long since been swamped by Islam. But though a small minority in most places, Christianity survives as remnants of ancient churches, Orthodox, Catholic, Monophysite, Nestorian, and more recently Protestant. Lebanon is half Christian (chiefly Eastern-rite Catholics, Orthodox, and Armenians) and half Muslim; the two communities have been engaged in bitter civil war. The Monophysite Coptic Church of Egypt, representing about 7 percent of the population, has lost political and social influence with the rise of a more militant Islam there as elsewhere, but it has undergone something of a spiritual revival. In Armenia and Ethiopia, on the northern and southern frontiers of the region, respectively, Monophysite churches are dominant as they have been for many centuries, but they face an uncertain future under Marxist governments and in the face of rapid change. All in all, Middle Eastern Christianity appears on the defensive, as it has been ever since the rise of Islam, but it shows no sign of losing the tenaciousness which has enabled it to survive for so long.

Christianity has been found in Europe since the days of the apostles, and on that continent more than anywhere else the great dramas of Christian history have been played. Here supremely was the land of 2000 years of active Christian history, with its kings, saints, theologians, and cathedral builders, and with its wars and persecutions.

In Western Europe in the late twentieth century one could easily get an impression that the weight of all this Christian past has finally produced a great weariness, that the religious drama has at last been almost played out. The splendid churches and cathedrals are still there, but attendance at them is low in most places, ranging from 10 or 15 percent of the population on an average Sunday in England and

France to 2 or 3 percent in Scandinavia; and the younger generation seems almost totally indifferent. Only in Ireland, with its running conflict between Catholic and Protestant factions, does religious passion seem high.

Yet, although interest in Christianity has dwindled in Western Europe as the century declines, it has not vanished. European Christian thinkers, if not now quite the equals of the greatest theologians of the past, continue to dominate the religion's intellectual life. There are signs of a growing dissatisfaction with sheer secularism, which might lead to a rediscovery of the Christian heritage, or to a turning elsewhere for solace.

In Communist-dominated Eastern Europe, the situation was strikingly different. Such countries as Orthodox Rumania and Catholic Poland claim a rate of church attendance of around 50 percent, the highest anywhere. During the Communist years, religion offered one of very few places in which people could espouse values other than those of the state, and the churches had an important role in the dramatic events of 1989 which toppled or much modified Communist regimes across Eastern Europe. Their place in the newly-emerging post-Communist societies remains to be seen.

Above all, Europe's greatest religious institution, the papacy, which shepherds Catholics both East and West, has found renewed vigor and meaning in the waning twentieth century. In a time dominated by mass media, electronic communication, and rapid jet-propelled transportation, there is a hunger for charismatic personalities. Far from appearing a mere medieval relic, the office of the pope when occupied by powerful and engaging personalities such as John XXIII or John Paul II has seemed well made to exploit those characteristics and focus the religious aspirations of such an age. Traveling the world in white robes, making pronouncements on numerous issues, all carefully recorded by press and television, the pope has been a constant and highly visible reminder of transcendent values. For Catholic and non-Catholic alike, despite problems on the part of some with aspects of papal theology and policy, the potential of such a position as a central Christian voice and a center of Christian unity seems to become more and more apparent; without doubt, the pope's is the single most important spiritual office in the world of the late twentieth century.

Christianity remains a small minority in most of South and East Asia, save for the Philippines. But in its interaction with the great non-Christian cultures of Asia, that faith has once again shown signs of creativity, perhaps heralding a future Christianity freer of Western civilization than today's. In India certain Roman Catholic monks have, as Christians, taken to living the life of sadhus, showing they are capable of the spirituality and self-denial so respected by India in its holy men. In Japan, dialogue between Christianity and Buddhism proceeds, and some Christians have found ways to incorporate Zen attitudes and meditation into their spiritual lives, even as Christian moral and social concerns have certainly influenced Buddhism.

China and Christianity each represent nearly 25 percent of the earth's population, yet there is less than 1 percent overlap in these populations. But that 1 percent is significant, especially that part of it in the People's Republic, for as we have seen it represents the persistence of Christianity in still another environment, long cut off from the rest of the Christian world.

We turn now to the Americas. In the United States, Christianity remains outwardly strong. In the early 1990s polls showed that weekly church attendance hovered as it had for two decades at about 40 percent of the population, well above most other traditional Christian countries. Diversity of religious choice, a generally positive public image of religion, and the lack of alienation from religion on the part of any important class or constituency seemed to have prevented here Europe's twentieth-century religious decline.

Yet despite widespread support and fervent religious activity on the part of some, especially evangelicals, some observers in the 1990s noted signs pointing toward possible future Christian decline in America as well. The church-attending population seemed to be getting older in many places, baptismal and church membership figures were stagnant or falling in large denominations, the "televangelist" scandals had hurt religion's image, and—on another level of concern—to more than one commentator it seemed that the intellectual quality of American Christianity was falling, and with it the capacity of religion to engage as it did in times past in serious interaction with the mainstream of American academic, cultural, economic, and social life. Whether these are passing or permanent problems is not yet clear.

Latin America is a region of religious as well as social and political turmoil. Once noted chiefly for the conservatism and passivity of its mostly Roman Catholic Christianity, it now finds itself swept by evangelical movements and by new attitudes on the part of Catholic leaders. In a region riven by great gulfs between privileged and nonprivileged, some priests and bishops have taken strong stands on behalf of the poor, speaking out and organizing such movements as parish cooperatives. Some have tried to mediate between warring factions in lands seething with unrest. The future of South and Central America is unclear, but certainly neither it nor its religion can again be what it once was.

In Africa, Christianity is lively, growing, and prone to divisions. While the majority of African Christians—as we have seen, 25 to 50 percent of the population of the sub-Saharan part of the continent—probably adheres to a mainstream denomination, it has been estimated that as many as 6000 new religious movements have arisen in Africa since 1880. Most present an African response of one sort or another to the presence of Christian missions. For example, in Zaire, The Church on Earth By the Prophet Simon Kimbangu, or Kimbanguist Church, was founded by Simon Kimbangu (1889–1951), who was converted in 1915 by Baptist missionaries and was at first a lay evangelist. But recalling a childhood vision of a man "neither black or white" appearing with a Bible, he became more and more an independent prophet, performing, it was widely rumored, many miraculous healings like Jesus himself. When he was imprisoned by the Belgian colonial authorities, the Christlike drama of his life, as it was seen by his growing number of native followers, was further advanced, and he was viewed as a living martyr and special prophet called to bring Christ to the Africans. His church is now a flourishing institution with widespread religious, educational, and social service works. While avoiding any direct political involvement, it played a part in the development of the modern African consciousness that led to independence and nationhood in the Congo and elsewhere.

Christianity in the world today, then, is widespread and diverse. Depending upon where and how one looks, it shows signs of both decline and vitality. But it remains a powerful spiritual influence.

SUMMARY

Throughout its 2000 years of history, Christianity has achieved a wide diversity of forms. But they all derive ultimately from the person, life, and teaching of Jesus. The teaching centers on the Kingdom of God, Jesus's proclamation of God's reign or rule, which is both present in the world and coming into it. Jesus was executed on a cross by the Roman authorities; reports spread among his followers that he had risen three days later from the dead. For the religious movement that formed around him, whose teachings were supremely articulated by the apostle Paul, Jesus was a divine saviour; through faith in him one could share his life eternally.

For the sometimes-persecuted early Christian church of the Roman Empire, Christian life was arduous. It centered around baptism, the major rite of entry into its fellowship, and the Holy Communion, the sacred meal which repeated Jesus's Last Supper before his crucifixion.

After the triumph of Christianity under the Emperor Constantine, Christianity faced new problems and opportunities. Doctrinal differences were resolved by General Councils, which emphasized that Jesus Christ is of one substance with God the Father, truly God and truly human. Christian worship became more elaborate; the church became the official religion of the empire, and over the next few centuries converted most of Europe. The medieval style of Christianity that followed seemed outwardly to express the stable social order and steady round of festivals and Sunday masses that were the medieval ideal; but beneath the surface were tensions that gave rise to radical movements and set the stage for future developments.

The sixteenth-century Reformation was sparked by the monk Martin Luther's conviction that salvation was not won by the amount of one's piety or good works but was freely given by God as grace and received by faith. In opposition to medieval church life, he proposed an alternative style centered on scripture, preaching, and the ideal of inward faith. The second great reformer, John Calvin, emphasized the sovereignty of God and his calling of people by grace to his service and salvation. The Reformation in England was more conservative than that on the continent, resulting in a church with both Catholic and Protestant features. On the other hand, England was a main center of Radical Reform—movements of more extreme Protestants who favored a simple church of believers, social change, and separation of church and state. From out of the radical wing of the Reformation came such denominations as those of the Congregationalists, Baptists, Quakers, and, later, Methodists.

Christian mysticism and devotion has run deep over the centuries, in two great though sometimes converging channels: the way of the negation of images, which seeks to know God by taking away all words and concepts less than God; and the way of the affirmation of images, using ideas and mental images to lift one to God.

Both have expression in each of the three main divisions of Christianity: Eastern Orthodoxy, Roman Catholicism, and Protestantism. But in these and other respects, the three show differences as well.

Highly traditional, the Orthodox church centered in Eastern Europe presents firm doctrine, ornate worship, and a deep affiliation with the cultures of the countries in which it is predominant. Its spiritual life combines freedom with a feeling for the meaning of corporate church life and the resurrection of Jesus.

The Roman Catholic Church is distinguished by the papacy, a sense for the importance of combining freedom with order, and an emphasis on the sacraments in Christian life. In it, traditionalism combines with a capacity for change.

Protestantism displays wide diversity but generally is characterized by relative simplicity of worship, emphasis on scripture and preaching, and often a desire for local and democratic control of church government.

During the last 500 years, Christianity has expanded to become the largest and the most worldwide of religions. Beginning with the work of Catholic missionaries in the wake of Vasco da Gama and Christopher Columbus, Christianity has expanded remarkably through a combination of missionary work and European emigration. The nineteenth century, when Protestant as well as Catholic missionaries were active, was particularly a period of growth.

In the late twentieth century, Christianity faces many problems and many prospects. It remains a worldwide faith, with much variation in its appearance from one part of the world to another.

QUESTIONS FOR REVIEW

1. Summarize the life and central teaching of Jesus.
2. Explain, on the basis of the Thematic Chart, how some Christian groups have accepted the surrounding culture, some have rejected it, and some have found a mediating position between these extremes. Relate these different attitudes to the role Christianity has played in various historical times and places, and the emergence of new Christian movements. Then, also on the basis of the Thematic Chart, discuss varying Christian positions toward emphasis on Word and emphasis on sacraments.
3. Summarize the basic teaching of Paul the apostle.
4. Give a description of life in the early church: its forms of worship, way of life, organization, and fundamental beliefs.
5. Explain the reasons for persecution of Christians under the Roman Empire and the Christian attitude toward martyrs.

6. Interpret what the triumph of Christianity under Constantine meant to the religion. What new problems appeared together with new opportunities? What new forms of Christian life arose?

7. Summarize the meaning and teaching of the first four General Councils.

8. Trace the development of medieval Christianity and outline its major features.

9. Interpret the nature of Martin Luther's basic religious experience and cite the main points of his teaching.

10. Explain some fundamental features of Calvinism.

11. Outline the course of the Reformation in England and tell how and why it was different from that on the continent of Europe.

12. Discuss the nature of Radical Reform, explaining who the Puritans were and the background of such denominations in the English-speaking world as Congregationalists, Baptists, Quakers, and Methodists.

13. Interpret the meaning of two kinds of mysticism and devotion—that of the negation of images and that of their affirmation—and trace the course of both within Christianity.

14. Summarize the main features of Christian teaching, practice, and church organization and life within Eastern Orthodoxy, Roman Catholicism, and Protestantism. Be sure to include variations within each of these major branches of Christianity.

15. Trace the history of the expansion of Christianity in the last 500 years, referring to the worldwide role given Christianity and the questions it has raised.

16. Describe the situation of Christianity today in various parts of the world.

SUGGESTED READINGS ON CHRISTIANITY

General

ELLWOOD, ROBERT S., AND JAMES B. WIGGINS, *Christianity: A Cultural Perspective*. Englewood Cliffs, NJ: Prentice Hall, 1988. An introductory textbook.

GERRISH, BRIAN A., *The Faith of Christendom: A Source Book of Creeds and Confessions*. New York: World, 1963. A helpful collection of primary materials on Christian belief.

LATOURETTE, KENNETH SCOTT, *A History of Christianity*. New York: Harper & Brothers, 1953. A massive, well-written history emphasizing the expansion of Christianity.

*NIEBUHR, H. RICHARD, *Christ and Culture*. New York Harper Torchbooks, 1956. A classic study of different ways Christianity has related to its cultural environments.

PELIKAN, JAROSLAV, *Jesus Through the Centuries*. New Haven: Yale University Press, 1985. A remarkably insightful and informative study of how Jesus has been perceived in art, devotion, and theology in the various periods of Christian history.

SMART, NINIAN, *The Phenomenon of Christianity*. London: Collins, 1979. A good phenomenological study of the varieties and commonalities of Christianity.

*TILLICH, PAUL, *A History of Christian Thought*. New York: Harper & Row, 1968. A leading Protestant theologian's view of the topic.

*UNDERHILL, EVELYN, *Mystics of the Church*. London: J. Clarke & Co., 1925. A semipopular account by a distinguished scholar: emphasizes Roman Catholic figures.

———, *Worship,* London: Nisbet & Co., Ltd., 1936. A view of Christian worship and its meaning which tries to be sympathetic to all traditions. Written before the modern liturgical movement, but a classic.

WALKER, WILLISTON, *A History of the Christian Church,* rev. ed. New York: Scribners, 1984.

The New Testament

BORNKAMM, GUNTHER, *Paul*. New York: Harper & Row, 1971. Widely regarded as the best study of the apostle's life and thought.

BROWN, RAYMOND E., *The Birth of the Messiah*. Garden City, NY: Doubleday, 1979. A major work on the birth and infancy stories of Jesus.

———, *The Community of the Beloved Disciple*. New York: Paulist Press, 1979. Study of the background of the Gospel of John by a distinguished scholar.

DELLING, GERHARD, *Worship in the New Testament*. Philadelphia: Westminster, 1962. A useful treatment of the field.

FIORENZA, ELIZABETH SCHUSSLER, *In Memory of Her: A Feminist Theological Reconstruction of Christian Origins*. New York: Crossroad, 1983. A seminal study of the New Testament church from the perspective of its meaning for women.

GRANT, ROBERT M., *A Historical Introduction to the New Testament*. New York: Harper & Row, 1963. A standard overview of the New Testament from the perspective of its setting in time and place.

KEE, H., *Understanding the New Testament*. Englewood Cliffs, NJ: Prentice-Hall, Inc., 4th ed., 1983. A standard textbook.

———, *Community of the New Age*. Philadelphia: Westminster Press, 1977. Studies in the Gospel of Mark.

LADD, GEORGE ELDON, *A Theology of the New Testament*. Grand Rapids: Eerdmans, 1974. An excellent presentation of the evangelical perspective; monumental scholarship.

MEEKS, WAYNE A., *The First Urban Christians: The Social World of the Apostle Paul*. New Haven, CT: Yale University Press, 1983. An important study providing fresh insights on the sort of people who became early Christians and the role of the Pauline church in their lives.

RICHARDSON, ALAN, *An Introduction to the Theology of the New Testament*. New York: Harper & Row, 1958. A standard, fairly conservative work by a distinguished scholar.

The Early Christian Church

GOUGH, MICHAEL, *Early Christians*. New York: Praeger, 1961. A valuable, well-illustrated survey oriented toward archaeology.

PAGELS, ELAINE, *The Gnostic Gospels*. New York: Random House, 1979. A new view of Gnosticism and the early church based on recently discovered Gnostic texts.

*ROBINSON, JAMES M., ED., *The Nag Hammadi Library in English*. San Francisco: Harper & Row, 1977, 1981. Translation of the important recently discovered Gnostic documents.

*WADDELL, HELEN, *The Desert Fathers*. Ann Arbor: University of Michigan Press, 1957. A good translation, with a beautifully written introduction. Gives a vivid picture of the earliest Christian monastics.

WAND, J.W.C., *A History of the Early Church*. London: Methuen, 1937. A well-written work; traditional point of view.

Eastern Orthodoxy

FEDOTOV, G. P., *A Treasury of Russian Spirituality*. London: Sheed & Ward, 1952. A fine anthology of the mysticism of Eastern Christianity.

LOSSKY, VLADIMIR, *The Mystical Theology of the Eastern Church*. London: James Clarke, 1957. Fairly scholarly, and a brilliant treatment of the topic.

*WARE, TIMOTHY, *The Orthodox Church*. Baltimore: Penguin Books, 1963. A good, solid introduction.

ZERNOV, N., *Eastern Christendom*. London: Weidenfeld & Nicolson, 1961. A sympathetic popular introduction.

Roman Catholicism

*ADAM, KARL, *The Spirit of Catholicism*. New York: Macmillan, 1929. A profound but fairly simple essay, written from a personal point of view.

BAUSCH, WILLIAM J., *Pilgrim Church: A Popular History of Catholic Christianity*. Notre Dame, IN: Fides, 1973. A modern treatment.

BRANTL, GEORGE, *Catholicism*. New York: Braziller, 1969. A useful anthology.

*McKENZIE, JOHN, *The Roman Catholic Church*. Garden City, NY: Doubleday, 1971. A standard resource.

RAHNER, KARL, *Teachings of the Catholic Church*. New York: Alba, 1967. A summary by a modern liberal Catholic theologian.

Protestantism

DILLENBERGER, JOHN, AND CALUDE WELCH, *Protestant Christianity*. New York: Scribners, 1954. A historical introduction.

*DUNSTAN, LESLIE, *Protestantism*. New York: Braziller, 1961. A useful anthology of historical material.

HAVERSTICK, JOHN, *The Progress of the Protestant*. New York: Holt, Rinehart & Winston, 1969. A lavishly illustrated popular history of Protestantism.

MacINTOSH, HUGH ROSS, *Types of Modern Theology: Schleiermacher to Barth*. New York: Scribner's, 1939. A fine introduction to the most talked about modern Protestant theologians.

*MARTY, MARTIN E., *Protestantism*. London: Weidenfeld & Nicholson, 1972. A survey of Protestant attitudes on a number of issues; good bibliography.

NICHOLS, JAMES HASTINGS, *Primer for Protestants*. New York: Association Press, 1951. A well-done basic introduction to traditional Protestant attitudes.

*NIEBUHR, H. R., *The Kingdom of God in America*. New York: Harper & Brothers, 1937. A seminal history of the interaction between Protestant attitudes and American history.

PAUCK, WILHELM, *The Heritage of the Reformation*. Glencoe, IL: Free Press, 1961. An authoritative historical statement.

*VON ROHR, JOHN ROBERT, *Profile of Protestantism*. Belmont, CA: Dickenson, 1969. A good basic textbook.

*TAWNEY, R. H., *Religion and the Rise of Capitalism*. London: John Murray, 1926. A statement of the often-discussed thesis that Protestant and capitalistic attitudes have reinforced each other.

WILLIAMS, GEORGE, *The Radical Reformation*. Philadelphia: Westminster, 1962. The standard book on this aspect of the Protestant Reformation.

American Religion

*AHLSTROM, SYDNEY E., *A Religious History of the American People*. New Haven and London, CT: Yale University Press, 1972. A substantial but readable story of American religion, emphasizing periods and broad themes. Reliable and highly recommended.

BEDNAROWSKI, MARY FARELL, *American Religion: A Cultural Perspective*. Englewood Cliffs, NJ: Prentice-Hall, Inc., 1984. A descriptive survey of American religion in its diversity and cultural impact.

BELLAH, ROBERT N., *The Broken Covenant*. New York: Seabury Press, 1975. A study of American "Civil Religion": use of Christian-derived myths, salvation themes, taboos, and the like in political and social life.

JAMES, JANET W., ED., *Women in American Religion*. Philadelphia: University of Pennsylvania Press, 1980. Articles on American religious women in all their diversity, from Colonial Quakers to contemporary Roman Catholic sisters.

MILLER, WILLIAM LEE, *The First Liberty: Religion and the American Republic*. New York: Knopf, 1986. Bound to become a classic study of the first amendment to the U.S. Constitution; on religious freedom and separation of church and state, and the story of its interpretation and application.

RABOTEAU, ALBERT, *Slave Religion*. New York: Oxford University Press, 1978. Important study of a significant, but in some circles little known, sector of American religious history.

*ROSTEN, LEO, ED., *Religions of America*. New York: Simon & Schuster, 1975. Questions and answers about the basic beliefs and practices and the major American religions and denominations; a good introduction. Valuable statistical information as well.

Eugene Gordon

CHAPTER 9

Submitting to the Will of God:
THE BUILDING OF THE HOUSE OF ISLAM

CHAPTER OBJECTIVES

After studying this chapter, you should be able to

- Discuss the basic teachings and practices of Islam.

- Explain the historical role of the Islamic faith.

- Summarize the major schools of Islam.

- Interpret the place of Islam in the world of today.

THE MEANING OF ISLAM

Over 900 million of the world's population adhere to the faith of Islam, the youngest of the world's great religions. Despite important variations within Islam, it is also the most homogeneous and self-consciously international community of the three giant cross-cultural faiths: Buddhism, Christianity, and Islam.

Islam is a community that does indeed cut across many cultures. Non-Muslims often envision Islam as the faith of romantic (and now tremendously oil-wealthy) Arab sheiks and caravaneers, but only a minority of Muslims are Arab, and only a

Thematic Chart VIII.   Like most spiritual traditions, Islam seeks both to create community and come to terms with the diversity of individuals. It also is polarized in practice between two models of the spiritual path, each of which has its own community-forming and individual-expression style; the way of the law-follower and the way of the saint.

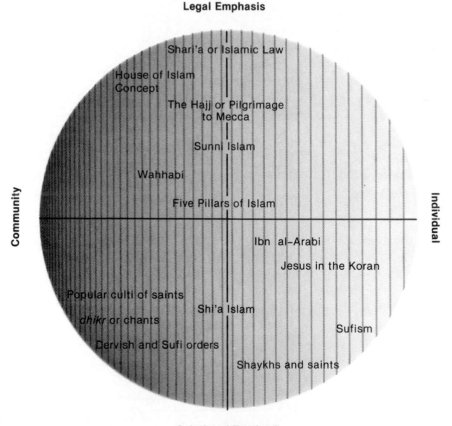

Main Themes in Islam

Muslims praying in Afghanistan.

tiny minority are wandering desert dwellers. The largest single Muslim nation is tropical Indonesia, where the faith of Muhammad is superimposed on an East Asian culture. Other Muslims in great numbers are farmers and craftsmen in India and Pakistan; businessmen in the cities of Turkey, Iran, or Malaysia; blacks in sub-Saharan Africa, where Islam is growing. Even in the Arab countries, where Islam originated, the population is largely urban or engaged in intensive, sedentary agriculture in fertile strips like those along the Nile and the Two Rivers. Normative Islam, in fact, has historically been preeminently a faith of citified, mobile, internationally minded people, sometimes conquerors but more often urban businessmen, and through them it has spread from culture to culture.

Partly because of this base, Islamic culture has a quite visible unity as well as a great diversity. From Morocco to Java, the Muslim mosque presents a distinctive atmosphere. Few would mistake a mosque for a church, synagogue, or Hindu temple. The **mosque,** a place of prayer to the infinite Lord, has no picture, image, altar, flowers, or candles—only a vast, clean, cool, austerely beautiful empty space. The floor may be spread with rich carpeting, and the walls and ceiling or dome, with the delicate, fantastic tracery of arabesque. But nowhere will realistic representational art be found. Only a bare niche in the wall serves to orient prayer in the direction of Mecca; only a modest affair like a seat atop a staircase serves as pulpit.

On the streets of a Muslim country, the pervasive influence of the religion is felt too. Five times a day—sunrise, noon, afternoon, just after sunset, at dark—a crier, called the **muezzin** (nowadays, he is often replaced by a recording and a loudspeaker system), summons the faithful to prayer from the minaret, the tower attached to every mosque. His plaintive cry replaces the bells of Christendom. Then believers prostrate themselves in prayer in shops and homes, wherever they are, as well as in mosques.

In the markets, veiled women are not seen as much as formerly, but they are still common in some parts of the Muslim world. Although the Muslim admonition against alcoholic drink is not always strictly observed, it is in coffee shops and teahouses rather than pubs or bars that one sees the men gathered of an evening to discuss the affairs of the day. Finally, if one is at all familiar with the local language, one will be struck by the frequency of expressions such as "If Allah wills" in daily conversation.

For the heart of Islam is submission to the total will of Allah, or God. (*Allah* is not the name of a god, but simply means "The God"—the one and only God.) God's will for humanity, Muslims believe, was most fully given in the Koran, the book revealed through the prophet Muhammad. The word *islam* means "submission," and the name tells us that the central idea of this faith is simply full and complete submission to the will of God; an adherent of the faith is called a *Muslim,* one who has made the submission.[1]

So it is that the muezzin in his five-times-daily cry says:

> God [Allah] is great! God is great!
> There is no god but God,
> And Muhammad is his prophet!
> Come to prayer! come to prayer!
> Come to abundance! come to abundance!
> (*At dawn, he here adds:*
> Prayer is better than sleep!
> Prayer is better than sleep!)
> God is great! God is great!
> There is no god but God!

That is the central motif of Islam—the greatness of God alone. Because **Allah** is great and sovereign, all the world and all the affairs of humankind belong only to him. For this reason Islam does not lavishly embellish the "religious" sphere with rites and symbols and priesthood; if Allah is truly great, Islam says, he can be worshipped anywhere by anyone in the simple forms prescribed by the Koran and tradition. If God is truly sovereign, what he has commanded for all of society—law, ethics, government—is just as important as the religious commandments and inseparable from them. For this reason, Islam is experienced as a total and indivisible way of life. It is deeply consistent with the basic premise of the faith—the absolute sovereignty of God over all situations and over every atom of the universe—that whenever feasible Muslims not only establish Muslim worship but create Muslim societies under Muslim rulers based on Koranic law. Modern conditions have often mandated reinterpretations of this ideal. But the Koran remains the fountainhead of the true law and true culture, and a summons to submission in every area of life, the "secular"—political, economic, and family life—as well as in such conventionally religious matters as how one says prayers.

MUHAMMAD

At the core of Islam lies the experience and faith of Muhammad (570–632) himself. He lived in Arabia and was born and raised in the city of Mecca, a commercial center already sacred to the Arabs. Its holy sanctuary, which drew numerous pilgrims, was the home of many polytheistic gods—of moon, stars, and the days of the year, chiefly—and the resting place of a sacred stone, probably meteoritic, considered to be from heaven. The area around this place of worship was a neutral zone where representatives and merchants of many tribes, often warring, could meet in peace.

Muhammad came from a respected merchant family of modest means that was part of the prestigious Quraysh tribe, custodians of the sacred places of Mecca. According to tradition, he became a camel driver as a young man. When he was twenty-five, he entered the service of Khadija, a wealthy widow much older than he. Before long he married her, and she bore his daughter Fatima.

Muhammad was always a serious, thoughtful, and rather withdrawn man. But until he was about forty, his life was not outwardly much different from that of the other merchants of the sacred city. At that age, however, he found himself going into the mountains more and more to devote himself to meditation.

About the year 611, Muhammad began to have a remarkable series of experiences in these solitary meditations in mountain caves. A mysterious darkness would come over him, then the luminous figure of the archangel Gabriel would appear and recite words to him, which he could remember clearly. These words were first of all about the unity of God—that there is but one single god, "Lord of the worlds," who abominates idolatry and will judge the earth on a day of fire and anxiety; this God calls upon all humanity to accept his sovereignty.

For ten years (611–21) Muhammad implored his fellow Meccans to obey this call to acceptance of the oneness of God, but with little success. Indeed, it seemed to many that his fervent message threatened the lucrative polytheistic cultus, and Muhammad found his position in Mecca untenable. In 622 he accepted an invitation from the city of Yathrib (now Medina) to teach there. His journey to Yathrib, called the *Hijra,* is the date from which the Muslim calendar starts; it marks the beginning of Muhammad's public and organizational work on a large scale.

It may be helpful to consider for a moment the context of this work. The Near East in Muhammad's day was dominated by the political, economic, and ideological rivalry of three great powers; the Byzantine and Ethiopian empires, which were Christian, and the Persian, which was Zoroastrian but harbored influential minorities of Jews and non-Orthodox Christians. The Byzantine and Persian empires, archfoes, fought interminable and debilitating wars, which usually ended in standoffs.

In this situation, Arabia was by no means the barbaric backwater sometimes imagined. But it was nonaligned, a no-man's-land between superpowers. There were Christians and Jews in Arabia who were thought to lean, respectively, to Byzantium and Persia. But the merchants of Mecca and Yathrib, well aware of world affairs through trading contacts in the great imperial cities, realized that their well-being required them to avoid overdependence on either side.

Yet many were also well aware that the religions of the great powers were more "modern" than their own polytheism. Belief in a sovereign deity—whether the Christian God or Ahura Mazda or the God of the Jews—was clearly the new progressive thing upon which great civilizations were being built. Moreover, "new occasions teach new duties," and the prosperous, individual-enterprise Meccan merchants found the old sense of identity in the tribe breaking down deep within them. A new doctrine and ethic was called for, emphasizing mercantile values, individual responsibility, and the sacredness of the individual betokened by personal judgment and immortal life. The new teaching might draw from Zoroastrianism, Judaism, and Christianity, or at least parallel them, in its idea of one God and moral choice. But it had to be politically independent of other ideologies. Some, called Hanifs, had already moved in this direction; they are not fully understood, but apparently they were a pious though not highly organized people who shunned the worship of idols and affirmed a generalized monotheism. Other Arabs to the north were Christian. But in this situation there was lacking an Arab prophet, one who as an Arab would bespeak the common national and spiritual concerns of the Arabs.

That is what Muhammad did visibly in the ten years that remained to him, and he did it so well that his words carried conviction far beyond the Arab world. Using Medina as a base, he brought all Arabia, including Mecca, under his control. He became at once the religious leader of the Arabs and their political ruler and military commander. Right up to the end of his life, which occurred just after his return from his triumphal progress to Mecca in 632, the strange revelations continued. Together they make up the text of the Koran, the Holy Scripture of Islam.

THE KORAN

Unlike the Judaeo-Christian Bible, the **Koran** is not a collection of diverse material from over a thousand years. It was all delivered in a period of no more than twenty-two years through one man in communications from God through his angel. It is not a book of history, or a life of Muhammad, or a philosophical treatise. It is a book of proclamation: proclamation of the oneness and sovereignty of God, of his coming judgment, of the need to submit to him. In passing, it also presents a Muslim view of previous religious history, especially of the earlier prophets such as Abraham, Moses, and Jesus. From time to time it gives instructions to the faithful, upon which Muslim law is based.

To Muslims, the Koran is a miracle—the most convincing miracle of all as validation of their faith. It is said to be untranslatable, but to be in the original Arabic of exquisite, incomparable beauty of rhythm and expression. That one man, and he illiterate according to tradition, could be the merely human author of "the Glorious Koran, that inimitable symphony, the very sounds of which move men to tears and ecstasy,"[2] seems to Muslims incredible. The Holy Koran, they deeply believe, is the full and complete message of the infinite Divine Mind to humanity. Thus, it is not only studied, but chanted, memorized, and recited on all sorts of occasions, venerated both as words and as a book. Even its way of speaking is divine; it represents the personal *style* of Allah and so transmits something of God's essence. Its very choice of rhythm, metaphor, and rhetorical method, in other words, reveals something of how God thinks and feels, just as do its contents. So significant is the Koran to Islam that it makes a distinction between other religions that have comparable scripture—even if not equal to the Koran—and the "idolatrous" religions that do not. The former, especially Jews and Christians, are called "People of the Book" and are considered of higher status and closer kinship to Muslims.

Admittedly, it is sometimes not easy for those who are neither Muslims nor Arabists to appreciate, on the basis of translations, the rapturous terms in which the Koran is praised. Even allowing for the elements of rhythm and allusive eloquence that are presumed to have been lost in translation, one may feel an initial disappointment. The book may seem disorganized, repetitious, or platitudinous.

It is necessary to bear in mind always the Koran's purpose—to proclaim the oneness and sovereignty of God. It does not develop a philosophy or tell a story because those are not its purposes. The Koran is intended only to state one basic truth; it repeats itself to reinforce that one simple truth. As A. J. Arberry has put it, it is like being surrounded by a gallery of paintings on the same subject.[3] If the accounts of some matters common to other faiths, such as the lives of Abraham or Jesus, seem twisted as they appear in the Koran, it must be remembered that Muslims are not, after all, Jews or Christians. They are under no obligation to regard the versions the latter consider authoritative to be fully authentic or complete.

The Koran begins with the following prayer, which well sums up its basic spirit and message:

> In the Name of Allah, the Compassionate, the Merciful
> Praise be to Allah, Lord of the Creation,
> The Compassionate, the Merciful, King of Judgment-day!
> You alone we worship, and to You alone we pray for help.
> Guide us to the straight path,

The path of those whom You have favoured,
Not of those who have incurred Your wrath,
Nor of those who have gone astray.[4]

The book continues to describe the wonders of creation; how God made human-kind from the union of the sexes, out of clots of blood, and through the mysterious development of the embryo. God, it says, created man of ideal form. It exhorts humans not to deny but to show gratitude for this panorama of mercy and marvel, for when the judgment comes, wrongdoers will not be asked about their sins, but will be known by the expression on their faces. The deniers of the Lord's blessings then will suffer in hell, but those who have regard for the divine majesty will find themselves in surroundings fit for heroes: gardens of flowing springs, lush fruits, and dark-eyed damsels. Like the paradises of most religions, this one has the brightly colored, gemlike, antipodes-of-the-ordinary quality of dream, poetry, and sensuous youthful joy. But the deeper meaning of the Koran's message is less reward and punishment than the inescapable fact of Allah himself:

Roam the earth and see how Allah conceived Creation. Then Allah will create the Second Creation. Allah has power over all things; He punishes whom He will and shows mercy to whom He pleases. To Him you shall be recalled.
　Neither on earth nor in heaven shall you escape His reach; nor have you any beside Allah to protect or to help you.[5]

And again:

To Allah belongs the east and the west. Whichever way you turn there is the face of Allah. He is omnipresent and all-knowing.[6]

The fundamental faith of the Koran, then, is consistent monotheism. It is expressed in the coming judgment, the absolute sovereignty of Allah over all things, over both the making and fortunes of the present world, and the issue of who will be brought into joy in the Second Creation. That Muhammad is the envoy of God and the last, or seal, of the prophets is not in Muslim eyes an addition to consistent monotheism but the way God guarantees that this truth shall be known.

For Muslims believe that Islam is the ultimate religion, the complete religion. It is the religion of Abraham, the primal monotheism of the beginning, come back in finalized form. It is the ultimate form of religion because it is in fact the simplest and clearest. It is just the essence of religion, plain and perfect submission to the absolute God in all areas of life.

The Koran indicates that before Muhammad a series of prophets, all to be greatly honored, labored to call humankind back to this perfect islam, or submission. They included Abraham, Moses, Ishmael, Idris (Enoch), and Jesus. But it was through Muhammad that the final, complete message came, superseding all that went before—it was the culminating message of God for humankind.

The role of Jesus in the Koran and in this series of prophets usually puzzles Christians. The Koran makes Jesus the greatest before Muhammad. He was called to preserve the Torah of the Jews and was a wise teacher of deep inward holiness. (This last quality has made him especially beloved of the esoteric mystics of Islam.) Jesus has, to say the least, been far more highly regarded by Muslims than Muhammad has been by Christians.

The Koran accepts the virgin birth of Jesus and calls Mary one of the greatest among women, but it says Jesus was born under a palm tree rather than in a stable. It mentions the Last Supper, but it denies that Jesus was actually crucified. It says that people only thought he died on the cross; instead, he was taken directly to heaven. It does not make Jesus the "Son of God," for in Muslim eyes such a concept would be polytheistic and idolatrous.

However different the life and meaning of Jesus may here appear, in looking at Islam and the Koran Christians may, in the words of Seyyed Hossein Nasr, "come to understand how the sun of their own spiritual world is also a shining star in the firmament of another world."[7]

One of the loveliest passages of the Koran reads:

> God is the light of the heavens and the earth.
> The likeness of His light is as a niche,
> Wherein is a lamp, the lamp in a glass, the glass like a glistening star, kindled from a
>   blessed tree,
> An olive neither of the east nor of the west,
> Whose oil would almost shine had no fire touched it.
> Light upon light: God guides to His light whom he will:
> God brings similitudes for men and God has knowledge of all things.[8]

In all ways then the light of God is added to light; the final revelation is not inconsistent with what was presented by earlier prophets, even though the other "People of the Book" may have distorted their heritages. But Islam gives the final luster of a perfect glass to the light of God agelessly hidden in the lamp of the world.

All the way through, then, the central message of Islam is oneness: the unity of the line of true prophets, the oneness of final prophet and book, the oneness of the People of God, the one submission to be made, and finally the supreme oneness of God.

Islamic submission to oneness is expressed in part through avoidance of *shirk,* idolatry, or putting other gods beside the One. It is typified by the avoidance of images and often of any representational art in Muslim religion and culture. This is not a condemnation of the world of created things, for Islam has little asceticism of that sort. It extols the joys of marriage and the table, and paradise itself is described in sensual terms. But these are gifts of God, to be accepted and enjoyed for themselves with gratitude. They are not to be worshiped or even artistically recreated as symbols for God, who needs no such help.

The submission of Islam is not just a private, personal matter. It is not meant to be the sort of following of inner "leadings" which often merely indulges whims and sanctifies self-inflation. To be sure, Islam has not lacked colorful but dubious figures who have claimed special divine calls. But the tradition has tried hard to combat the human proclivity to mix piety and egotism through the *shari'a,* or law. Islam makes the Koran not only a book of God's self-revelation, but also a source of practical regulations covering such matters as marriage, almsgiving, relations with non-Muslims, and punishment of criminals.

Shari'a is the Koran as it is explicated and expanded by recognized jurists who depend in this process upon *hadith,* traditions based on extra-Koranic sayings and examples in the life of Muhammad. Through the use of analogy, and by determining consensus, legal scholars decide how Koranic law is to be applied to concrete cases before them. Muslim law, then, provides an obligatory and objective measurement of whether a person really submits to God, or only says he does but loves more the idols of his own fantasies.

The submission is made even more objective by the concept of the community, or house, of Islam, a ready-made political, economic, and juridical, as well as purely "religious," unit in the world. Insofar as the Shari'a ideal is actualized in it, willing participation in the House of Islam and following its norms is one with Islamic submission to Allah. For the ideal of submission in all areas of life logically implies joining oneself to others who make the same submission; doing so is a test of real sincerity. (As the New Testament also recognizes, it is easy to think one loves God, but to dislike others who also love God.)

Out of the community ideal of Islam comes the concept of *jihad,* or holy war, which is designed to defend Islam and allow its social practice, though not to force individual conversions, which is forbidden. Since Islam in principle is a community as well as a religion, presumably only an absolute pacifist would be able to reject the theory of jihad out of hand, since other communities also fight to defend or expand their ways of life. However, many Muslims interpret the jihad as allegorical of the spiritual struggle.

THE FIVE PILLARS OF ISLAM

Let us examine some aspects of traditional and normative Islamic life based on Shari'a as derived from Koran and hadith. These center around the Five Pillars of Islam: the confession of faith, prayer five times a day, giving of alms to the poor, fasting in the month of Ramadan, and the *hajj,* or pilgrimage to Mecca.

The first of the five pillars is to say, "There is no god but God (Allah), and Muhammad is the *rasul* (Prophet or messenger) of God." This statement sums up in a few words the simple Muslim faith. The basic concept of the oneness of God has been discussed. When Muhammad is called the rasul or messenger of God, it means exactly this—that he is God's appointed spokesman, the mouthpiece through which God chose to deliver his call for submission and his final commandments to the world. True, Muhammad is also considered a paragon of virtue and fountain of wisdom, so that his sayings and acts, as transmitted by tradition, are basic precedents in Muslim Law. But he is not a saint, seer, wonder-worker, divine incarnation, or

---

Fundamental Features of Islam

Theoretical

Basic World View	The world is for humans but under the absolute rule of God.
God or Ultimate Reality	God, sovereign, personal, revealing himself and giving specific guidance to humanity.
Origin of the World	Created by God.
Destiny of the World	To be destroyed on the Last Day, the day of judgment.
Origin of Humans	Created by God.
Destiny of Humans	To be judged on the Last Day and receive reward or punishment in the Second Creation.
Revelation or Mediation Between the Ultimate and the Human	The revelation in the Koran given through Muhammad, the last and greatest of the prophets.

Practical

What Is Expected of Humans: Worship, Practices, Behavior	To worship and serve God in accordance with his commandments; to observe the Five Pillars and the rest of Shari'a.

Sociological

Major Social Institutions	The whole Islamic community; the local Friday Mosque community; the *uloma,* or body of teachers and preachers; Sufi orders; the ideal of the Islamic society.

---

even a profound mystic like the Buddha or a peerless philosopher like Confucius. It is emphasized that Muhammad's birth was biologically normal, and that he performed no miracles except the delivery of the Koran itself. The Koran attributes virgin birth to Jesus and miracles to earlier prophets—Moses changed a staff into a serpent; Jesus is said by the Koran not only to have been taken up into heaven, but also to have caused some clay birds to come to life and fly away. These are appropriate to the son of Mary, for he is the prophet of mystic and marvelous holiness; similar powers are recognized, as we shall see, in numerous Muslim *wali,* or saints. But Muhammad's own calling was not to this sort of thing but simply to be the spokesman of God. His miracle is the Koran itself; its production by a man like him in enigmatic circumstances and the wonderful emergence of the Islamic community around him are considered sufficient evidence of his authority. Muhammad needed dispense no other, more trivial, miracles as calling cards.

The second of the pillars is prayer, done five times a day. In the next part we shall examine how these formal prayers are done.

The third pillar is almsgiving. The fundamental obligation is to give a relatively small but variable percentage of one's wealth to the needy within the Muslim community; expanded, it covers good works and comradely attitudes in general, a helping hand and friendly smile for one's neighbor. This pillar reaffirms the social and ethical dimensions of Islam. The Muslim faith strives to remember it is a community of submission and service, working for a more just world, not just a personal path to salvation. Strictly speaking, almsgiving should be done out of religious commitment rather than compulsion (although it was collected, from Muslims only, as a tax in traditional Islamic states). But many modern reformers have seen in the almsgiving principle a rationale for social welfare programs or socialism as an application of the Islamic community ideal under contemporary conditions.

The fourth pillar of Islam is the fast of Ramadan. Ramadan is a lunar month of about twenty-eight days in the Muslim calendar; during this period the faithful are neither to eat nor drink between daybreak and dark, but to give attention to prayer and religion. Commonly, family and friends will gather at night to dine as soon as it is permitted, and there are traditional Ramadan dishes. Often the meal will be combined with reading aloud from the Koran and prayer, and will continue far into the night. The daylight hours will be for rest and further prayer. At the end of Ramadan there is, as one might expect, a festive celebration which commences when the first sliver of a new moon indicates the end of the month of fasting and the beginning of the next month.[9]

Because the Muslim calendar is lunar, the occurrence of Ramadan moves progressively through the seasons. When it falls in the short, cool days of midwinter it is relatively easy to endure, but amidst the long summer days of a hot, dry climate, going without food or even a sip of water provides a stern test of Muslim loyalty. Understandably, some partially successful attempts have been made in recent times to reinterpret Ramadan in view of the exigencies of modern urban life. For innumerable devout Muslims, however, Ramadan remains a strenuous test of faith, softened by support from culture and tradition and the "we're all in it together" mood of a Muslim society's observance. For many, too, the opportunity for a deepening of one's life of prayer and Koranic study is genuinely welcome.

The fifth pillar is one known to almost everyone who has heard anything about Islam: the pilgrimage to Mecca called the *hajj.* Mecca, the immemorially holy city and birthplace of Muhammad, is the focal point of Islam. As though aligned along rays to a sun, Muslims at prayer face toward this vale in the Arabian Desert, and once in a lifetime their feet are to take them down that ray to the holy place. Every year a million or more Muslims gather at Mecca in the month of pilgrimage; this assembly affords like nothing else that sense of unity and identity for which Islam is justly famous.

Not all Muslims, of course, make the pilgrimage even once. Minors, the elderly, the infirm, and those without financial means are among those exempted from the obligation. For those who do go on the hajj, the rewards are substantial, not only in spiritual fulfillment, but in prestige within the Islamic family. Back in his home community, wherever it lies between Mauritania and Indonesia, the returned pilgrim may add the title *hajji* to his name and will be afforded special honor.

The pilgrimage is properly made in Dhu-al-Hijjah, the last month of the Muslim calendar. The pilgrimage is thus a meeting of sacred ultimates—a return just before the beginning of a new year to the place where Islamic history began.

Muslim belief about Mecca and the hajj combines the city's pre-Islamic role as a sacred center, a sanctuary for combative tribes, and a place of polytheistic worship, with beliefs about Abraham and the revelation through Muhammad. According to traditional Muslim belief, Mecca is the navel of the world, the spot where creation began. Abraham (Ibrahim in Arabic), the primal prophet of the original pure monotheistic religion, was then called by God to proceed from Palestine to the valley where Mecca is now located.

This he did, together with Hagar his wife and Ishmael (Ismail) his son, forefather of the Arabs. On one occasion, Hagar was lost in the desert with Ishmael and ran desperately about looking for water for the infant, until she found that a well had sprung up where Ishmael had struck the sand with his heel. Later, Abraham under God's instructions built the cubical shrine at Mecca—the Kaaba—with the help of Ishmael. In the corner of the Kaaba was placed the Black Stone brought from heaven by the angel Gabriel. On another occasion, in a variant of the account of the sacrific of Isaac in the Judaeo-Christian Bible, Abraham was commanded by god to sacrifice his son Ishmael. As they went to the place of sacrifice, Satan three times appeared to Ishmael and tempted him to reject his father's demand, but Ishmael kept faith and refused. At the last moment, a ram was substituted for the boy.

The Kaaba is now the center of the great open-air mosque of Mecca and is the real focal point of all Muslim worship. Other mosques have a niche in a wall facing in the direction of Mecca; this mosque, because it *is* the focal point, surrounds the Kaaba, or Holy House, which stands at its center. The Kaaba itself is covered with black-and-gold cloth and has a gold-encrusted door, seldom opened. Around it is a broad marble pavement, where pilgrims circumambulate the shrine, and beyond this, platforms for prayer.

In Muhammad's day the Kaaba contained 360 images of heathen gods (so far had the faith of Abraham declined). But the prophet had these destroyed. Now the Kaaba holds nothing but a few lamps. Yet for Muslims, whose faith is in the infinite God alone, in its emptiness the shrine is all the more holy. The Kaaba is said to be an exact replica of the house of God in paradise above, around which angels circle as the faithful on earth circle the earthly Kaaba. Heaven, tradition says, is closer to earth at Mecca than anywhere else, so prayers are heard best from there. Nothing comes between the Kaaba and the abode of Allah; airplanes are not allowed to pass over it, and it is said that even birds will not fly above the Holy House. Nearby is Zamzam, the well of Hagar and Ishmael, reputed to have curative powers.

Interestingly, Muhammad developed his teaching about Meccan pilgrimage during the time he was at Medina, when it was by no means clear that he would ever be reconciled with his home city. The teaching may, of course, have had political motives aimed at appeasing his kinsmen. Yet it also suggests that for the exile Mecca had the quality of many pilgrimage centers of being "the center out there"—a place remote from the center of present action on the worldly plane, yet a place of access to ultimate origins and ultimate goals. So has Mecca ever been.[10] Indeed, after the time of Muhammad Mecca's role as a commercial center declined, and the holy city has since depended economically almost entirely on its sacred role.

The carrying out of the hajj is marked by many careful rituals. As he (or she, as women also undertake the hajj) approaches the city, probably from the seaport and airport city of Jaddah on the coast, the pilgrim stops to separate himself from the ordinary world by ablutions, as before prayer. He then dons special white garments; thereafter, until the rites are completed he must abstain from killing man, beast, or plant, from sexual activity, and from cutting hair or nails.

Upon arriving at the sacred site, he kisses (or if that is not possible because of the crowd, touches) the sacred Black Stone. He then circumambulates the Kaaba seven times.

Next he runs seven times up and down a colonnade between two hills about 450 yards apart. The usual explanation is that this commemorates Hagar's running about looking for water for Ishmael.

Then the pilgrim proceeds outside Mecca to Mina, where he probably finds quarters in a vast tent city with a temporary population of a million or so; this gathering in itself gives him an experience of the power and unity of Islam. The next day he and the other pilgrims all proceed to Mount Arafat, upon which they must stand between noon and sundown. There, seated on a camel, Muhammad gave his farewell sermon on his own last pilgrimage to Mecca.

This "standing at Arafat" is the culminating act of the hajj, and the one act that cannot be omitted. It is the archetypal assembly of the faithful as a united army drawn out of all kindreds and tongues in submission to God. It is said to bring to mind the gathering of all peoples for judgment on the Last Day, and it repeats the first assembly that Muhammad himself commanded so heroically.

After this, the final rites represent a process of desacralization. Returning to Mina, the pilgrim throws rocks at three stone pillars said to represent devils, recalling the three temptations of Satan which Ishmael rejected.

On the last day of the formal sacred pilgrimage time, the pilgrim will sacrifice a ram or goat in a certain field; part of the meat is supposed to be given to the poor. On the same day throughout the Muslim world, an animal is similarly sacrificed. Its head is pointed toward Mecca, and as the Muslim cuts its throat, he says, "In the name of Allah." This recalls the ram substituted for Ishmael in Abraham's rite.

Next, in Mecca, the pilgrim has his hair cut. The hair, a token of oneself, is left behind as a sign of his dedication. He circumambulates the Kaaba a final time.

Most pilgrims will then proceed on to Medina, although this is optional. There, in this second most sacred city of Islam, they visit Muhammad's mosque and tomb. Some Muslims desire to come to Medina to die and be buried there with the prophet and his family.

The hajj is a collection of diverse traditional acts. Some may seem very Islamic and meaningful; some, like the running and stoning of the "devils," rather primitive and bizarre. Yet Muslims find them all spiritually significant, though none more so than the mere fact of the pilgrimage itself. Many Muslims, including the most mystical, have found deep inward meanings in all the traditions; stoning the pillars, for example, is made to represent striking down sinful desires within one's self.

Perhaps the best explanation is that of the great medieval theologian al-Ghazali.[11] He pointed out that the hajj is meant to be a supreme act of Islam, of submission and self-abnegation. That in it which is less than rationally appealing or satisfying to refined feeling can do much to purify out the egotism which easily lingers in a heart that considers itself refined. The hajj is an act of sheer devotion and of sheer identification with the inscrutible mind of God and with the Islamic tradition. It affirms that at the center of true religion is the finite human facing the infinite mystery of God, not the satisfaction of human inclinations.

PRAYERS AND MOSQUES

Hundreds upon hundreds of the faithful, line up rank on rank, bowing and prostrating in unison in the mosque at noon Friday and spill over into the plaza in front of it. This is a common sight in Islamic lands that never fails to impress visitors. It expresses eloquently the unity and devotion of Islam.

Equally impressive, and even more frequent, are the five-times-a-day prayers said regularly by believers wherever they are. The manner of saying these prayers and preparing for them is carefully prescribed by Islamic law; their combination of legalistic form and tenacious, fervent faith is close to the spiritual heart of Islam.

The five times a day when the faithful Muslim's mind and heart, perhaps prompted by the muezzin, turns away from the things of the world to prayer are the following:

1. Early in the morning, when dawn has become bright but before the sun has well risen
2. Noon or early afternoon
3. Late afternoon
4. Directly after sunset
5. Night, between darkness and dawn; usually about two hours after the sunset prayers

If the worshipper cannot perform the prayers at the time they are called, they may be done any time until the next prayer is proclaimed.

Before prayers, one must be in a state of purification. This is attained by formal washing: the hands and arms are washed up to the elbows, the mouth and nostrils are rinsed, and the feet are bathed to the ankles, all thrice. Mosques and most homes will have water available in tanks, urns, or fountains for this purpose;

one may also wash in an oasis. If sufficient water is not present, sand may be used.

Several further conditions should be met, if possible, out of respect for this sacred action. One should pray in a clean place free of defilement; for this reason many Muslims use special small carpets, prayer rugs, which they spread over the place of prayer. One must be modestly dressed; for women, this means the body must be entirely covered except face, hands, and feet. Before beginning, one must articulate in one's mind the intention to say the right prayers. Finally, one must pray facing in the direction of Mecca.

The prayers begin and end with the petitioner standing upright but include bowing and prostration. They are said in Arabic, the language of Muhammad and the Koran, rather than the vernacular language of the one who prays.

The Muslim first stands to say *Allahu-akbar,* "God is greater [than all]." Then still standing he recites the *al-Fatiha,* or opening verse of the Koran, given on page 299, and another short chapter of the scripture. He then bows and says thrice or more, "Glory to the Lord, the Exalted." He stands, saying, "God hears him who praises him. Our Lord praise to you." He then kneels, touching the forehead to the ground, to say, "Glory to my Lord, the most High" thrice or more. Finally he stands saying again *Allahu-akbar.* This whole procedure is called a *raka,* and it is the basic unit of prayer; it is repeated a varying number of times, depending on the time of day. The whole is concluded by a prayer, not from the Koran, asking God to exalt and bless Muhammad and his followers.

We have dwelt in some detail with the prayers and their performance because they provide an intimate perception of Islam as it is lived and practiced day by day, and an incomparable view of its spirit. The rules surrounding the prayers may suggest that Muslims are burdened with an onerous task in fulfilling this basic obligation of their religion. Certainly, the prayers are not meant to be a trivial, lightly regarded part of one's life, but a constant punctuation of every day recalling one to his or her first identity and responsibility. But for the devout, they are a welcome expression of faith and an added dimension to daily life. They remind the believer that he or she is a Muslim, one who worships and serves God before anything else.

Furthermore, they remind the person who prays that to be a Muslim means to be a part of the worldwide community which, like any real community, has its traditions, its rules, and its center. One expresses this identity by doing one's prayers not haphazardly, but at the same time, in the same way, and facing toward the same center, as one's comrades in the community. The prayers, then, rank with the *hajj* in creating a deep sense of Muslim identity. It may be noted that, although one may say the prayers with a special intention for some personal need and may pray at any other time on behalf of one's personal petitions, there is no prayer here for individual needs, such as for daily bread or for personal favors. The Muslim knows that one's relation to Allah should be first of all one of faith, praise, gratitude, obedience, and identity with the Islamic community, and that God knows one's special needs before one can ask.

The prayers may be said individually wherever one is. But Muslims have always preferred to say them congregationally whenever possible. The mosque is the ideal

An illustration from *The Book of Kings* entitled *Sohrab Looking Again at the Tent of Roustem* by Firdousi.

Mosque in Isfahan, Iran.

Kaaba, the cubical temple of Mecca, a focus of pilgrimage.

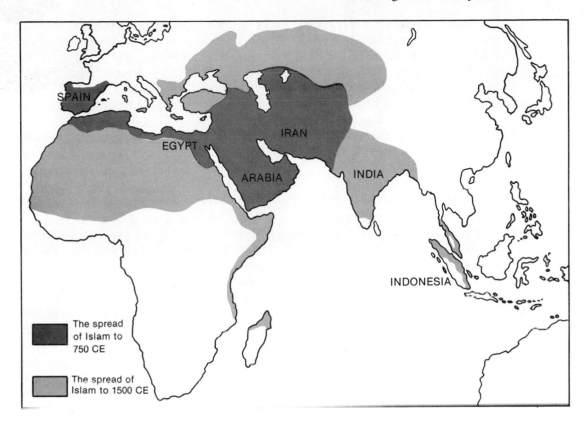

The spread
of Islam to
750 CE

The spread of
Islam to 1500 CE

MAP 9–1.   The Building of the House of Islam

place for corporate prayers, and the noon prayers on Friday are generally recited there. This is the major weekly Muslim service; in it certain additional prayers are offered, and two sermons, separated by a short break, are delivered by the *Imam,* or learned teacher, retained by the mosque.

Women are expected to pray but are exempted from congregational prayers. They may pray in the mosque in a separate section from the men, but more often pray at home.

The typical architecture of the mosque was originally inspired by the Arab house with its large courtyard and by the basilica-type Christian churches of conquered lands, some of which were converted into mosques. But the mosque has developed into a unique religious structure that represents sublimely the spirit of Islam. Far simpler in ornamentation than most churches and temples of other faiths, yet imposing and monumental, the mosque well reflects the austerity and majesty of Islam and its God.

The feature of a mosque that will first attract the attention of most visitors to the Islamic world are the minarets. These are the high towers beside the mosque proper. They are usually capped with the star and crescent moon, which is the symbol of Islam, said to be derived from the moon and single star that lighted the Prophet's way on his Hijra from Mecca to Medina. Great centers of worship may have as many as six minarets standing by the shorter and squatter building of the mosque. As we have seen, it is from the minaret that the muezzin cries out the call to prayer five times daily.

Approaching the mosque, the visitor enters a wide courtyard. It will probably contain water to be used for ablutions before prayer, and it is a favorite meeting place of the community. Indeed, mosques with their attached structures have traditionally functioned at once as virtually every sort of public building. Schools and libraries were and are connected with them, and their spacious facilities have served in the past as a place for gathering armies and as courts of justice. While modern states have felt that separate sites are more appropriate for such activities, their traditional affiliation with the mosque reminds us of the close alliance of Islam with the political, educational, and social life of the community.

The interior of the mosque characteristically possesses a clean, cool, open ambiance, yet the nonrepresentational ornamentation is sufficient to add a note of transcendent richness. The floor is covered with mats or carpets, often highly decorative. The walls and ceilings may be adorned with stunning arabesque designs or calligraphed Koranic verses. But no furniture to speak of appears except the *minbar,* or seat at the top of steps, which serves as a pulpit. Occasionally, a screened box provides protection for a worshipping ruler. A niche called the *mihrab* points prayer in the direction of Mecca. By its architecture and appearance, the mosque well expresses the two orientations of Islam—to God and to the community of believers—symbolized by Mecca, which is its earthly center.

The mosque also expresses well an already-mentioned feature of Muslim life: its focus in the city or town. The rhythm of Muslim religious obligations, the daily prayers called by the muezzin, the ablutions and fasting, the *hajj* which usually followed trade routes, and the law courts all seem to fit the outlook and pattern of life of the urban trader or craftsman. Even Muslim farmers have generally wanted to live in villages with mosques. In particular, the Friday noon prayers are supposed to be said in a Friday Mosque, a great mosque theoretically large enough to hold the entire community, in contrast to smaller edifices which may be used for daily prayers. The Friday Mosque idea again affirms that Islam is meant to be lived in community, and it perceives the city as the ideal earthly expression of community.[12]

HISTORIC ISLAM

In 632, the year of the Prophet's death, all these themes were coalescing to form the new faith of the newly unified Arab people. Returning from his triumphal pilgrimage to Mecca, Muhammad preached a farewell sermon and shortly after died with his head in the lap of Aisha, his favorite wife. He was mourned, yet his death came at a propitious moment.

Through a brilliant combination of diplomacy and militancy, Muhammad had united Arabia under his command. He was the charismatic hero of the hour; he died before his hour of supreme glory had had a chance to pall.

His religious mission was apparently fulfilled; the revelations that he delivered were gathered to form the Koran within twenty years of his death. Unlike other religious founders, Muhammad died a popular hero among his people, a ruler, a successful diplomat, politician, and general. He was also a mystic visionary, but there was nothing ethereal about him. Instead he seemed to his people a man larger than life in many senses: warmhearted, full of cheerful humor, a planner of stratagems, a marshall who rode into battle with his troops and held his following together by the force of his personality when all seemed darkest—yet also a seer deep in prayer and vision alone in the desert, a rock of convinced faith and principle, and of a trustworthy and sympathetic nature. From this complex and extraordinary man came the Islamic faith, a faith which seems at once made for humans as they are, with their needs for politics, laws, wars, and sexual expression—and made for God as he is at his most magnificent: personal, creative, sovereign, and glorious, calling humans to total submission.

Inspired by fresh memories of Muhammad striding through Arabia, the Arabs were ready, at the moment of his death, to carry Islam out of his native land, and this they did under new leadership with a rapidity that ever since has amazed the world. The caliphs ("deputies" of the Prophet as temporal ruler), who were successors of Muhammad, within a century ruled from Spain and Morocco to the Indus in the East. They came near to conquering Europe, but they were finally stopped by Charles Martel at the battle of Tours in 732. The weary Byzantine Empire reeled before their sway and lost vast provinces once Christian Egypt, Palestine, Syria, and part of Asia Minor. The Persian Empire collapsed entirely and passed to Muslim faith and sovereignty. After 750, Baghdad was the seat of the caliph who ruled all this realm except Spain; that imperial city typifies the fact that early expansive Islam was fundamentally a faith of urban merchants and men of affairs.

The years of the Baghdad caliphate (750–1258) and of the Cordova caliphate in Spain (755–1236) were the glorious years of early Islamic civilization. These centuries were the Dark Ages in Europe; but in the caliphates, art, science, and philosophy matured—thanks in part to Muslim revival of ancient Greek wisdom and the transmission west of lore from India. Modern mathematics has roots in the Arabic system of numbers and the zero, which the Muslims may have borrowed from India but whose use they explored. The Greek classics, including the philosophy and science of Plato and Aristotle, came back to Europe in the late Middle Ages and the Renaissance by way of the Muslim world. Muslim philosophers of the Baghdad caliphate, such as Avicenna (980–1037), and of Cordova, such as Averroës (1126–98), had no small influence on Christian and Jewish thought. Averroës, for example, searched out profoundly the relationship of reason and revelation, and held that both are valid ways of knowing, a quest upon which the works of Maimonides and Thomas Aquinas are partially built.

After the wars that Christian Europe called the Crusades, which engendered bitter feelings and much misunderstanding between the two faiths not yet healed, and after the fall of the caliphates, Islam broke down into smaller units. Most of the Arab lands ended up as parts of the Turkish-ruled Ottoman Empire (though the Turks are not Arab). The Turks finally took Constantinople (modern Istanbul) and ended the lingering death of Christian Byzantium in 1453. Farther east, Persia and the Mughul Empire in India became splendid Islamic civilizations.

But gradually, it seemed, the Muslim world grew stagnant. By the nineteenth century most of it was under European influence or direct colonial rule. The reasons for this decline from the brilliant and dynamic early life are complex. In part it was due to external factors: the incursions of conquerors such as Genghis Khan and the European advances in technology and world exploration. Internally, Shari'a, as case after case it became more and more fixed, had a stultifying effect. The control of law believed to have divine sanction inevitably made society static, putting a premium on conformity rather than innovation and new ideas.

In the twentieth century, however, Islam has shown a new burst of life. It has served as a vehicle for identity from North Africa to Indonesia and has recovered something of its old dynamic sense of the unity of the diverse peoples who are followers of the Meccan prophet.

Thus, the role of Islam as both a political and spiritual force in the world is by no means over. The new shapes of oil economics and geopolitics are, in the last decades of the twentieth century, giving parts of the Islamic world a leverage and comparative prosperity they have hardly known since the Middle Ages. At the same time, in recent decades some Muslim nations have modified Islamic law with legal codes borrowed from elsewhere and have made pragmatic revisions of it in the light of modern conditions—although practice varies from the thorough-going secularization of Turkey under Kemal Ataturk to Saudi Arabia, where traditional law largely remains in force. (For instance, the traditional law that allowed a man up to four wives if he treated them equally and to divorce a wife virtually at will is no longer observed in much of the Muslim world.) Out of this combination of new power, prosperity, and flexibility we may well see creative new forms of Islamic faith and culture emerge. At the same time, modernity has also produced a powerful fundamentalist reaction. We shall examine the features of modern Islam in more detail later.

FEATURES OF CLASSIC ISLAMIC CIVILIZATION

As we have seen, Islamic religious culture comes most fully to flower in urban settings. Never was this more true than in the classical Golden Age of Islamic civilization, when fabled cities like Baghdad or Granada in Spain were centers of brilliant culture as well as flourishing political and commercial hubs. Let us examine some characteristics of life in these communities.

A traveler to a great classical (or modern) Muslim city accustomed to such capitals as Paris, London, or Washington might first be struck, and perhaps a little disappointed, by the lack of monumental grandeur and imposing vistas. True, the Islamic city will be dominated by the impressive domes and minarets of its principal mosques and perhaps by a castle fortress, like the Alhambra of Granada. But streets, especially in residential areas, will tend to be narrow and twisting and often lead to dead ends. Houses, rather than presenting an ostentatious facade, will likely display only a rough whitewashed wall with a gate and balconies on the upper stories. The main business and shopping section will be in the *suq* in many Muslim areas, a covered street lined with shops, displaying a fascination within that is not apparent from any outside vantage point.

For the significant reality about the Islamic city which interprets its distinctive features is that the mazelike exterior is, so to speak, full of secrets. Just as Islam tells us that the created world veils and reveals the great secret of the universe—the power and sovereignty of Allah—so the city conceals, while expressing to the discerning eye, its more mundane social structures. Each of the little urban nooks and crannies created by the seemingly chaotic web of streets may house a subcommunity of practitioners of a particular craft or trade. Even more important, behind each wall and gate is the intimate world of a family. Beyond the gate is a courtyard and around it the house, with its quarters for women, children, and servants. For in a society in which women have traditionally been veiled and enclosed, and in which education of young children frequently took place in the home, the house was a private realm with profound meaning for the personal lives of those who resided in it. Much business was conducted in its court; here, at prosperous homes, would arrive merchants, storytellers, wandering holy men, officials, and teachers, bringing the world to the home.

Among the other important motifs that governed classical Islamic civilization already noted, was the close relation in Islam between religion and law and the historical role of Muslims as conquerors and then rulers of their portion of the world. This reality had two important, but rather different, effects. First, it meant that Islamic law, with its often benign but ultimately conservative effects, firmly shaped the contours and limits of this civilization. For even the most powerful ruler, whether caliph or Ottoman sultan, was in theory supposed to be only an upholder of the existing law and to innovate nothing.

Second, it meant that the courts of kings and caliphs were immensely influential centers of cultural creativity. The average person thought of them as *Arabian Nights* realms of splendor and wonder. The reality may have been a little less fabulous, but the wealth, power, and entertainments of Baghdad and Granada at their height were the marvel of the world. Courts patronized poets, artists, musicians, philosophers, and theologians, and they drew talent and sophisticated appreciators of culture to their circles. In turn, because lines of trade and communication ran from the capitals like Baghdad, and later Cairo, Delhi, Isfahan, and Istanbul, to the far-flung reaches of the Islamic world, those cities served as centers of cultural dissemination. The fact that Islam was a religious culture of a relatively few great capitals and had relatively great political cohesion during much of its most creative period has much to do with the considerable uniformity of Islamic culture, as does the fact that it was a faith of well-traveled soldiers and traders.

Another very important motif, intrinsic to Islam and related to court and mosque alike, is the prestige given to scholarship because of the importance of the law and so of its right interpretation. Members of the *ulama,* or body of learned men, adorned courts and presided in mosques; they also founded universities and searched out the philosophical underpinnings of faith. Because the language of scripture and its legal commentaries was Arabic, in whatever part of the world they dwelt they had to work in that language. The immense authority of Arabic scholarship also worked powerfully on behalf of Islamic cultural homogeneity. For although popular religion and culture might vary considerably, this factor meant that the "great tradition" of learning and "correct" interpretation would diverge far less, even when the Islamic world was not politically united.

The Muslim antipathy to representational art has also played a potent role in creating a highly distinctive Islamic culture. Although not directly Koranic, the idea that representation led to idolatry early became almost universal in the Muslim world. Though observed with varying degrees of literalness in various times and places, it has meant that Islamic art has been essentially decorative, and pen and brushwork have been largely limited to calligraphy and book illustration—the latter being the medium wherein representational art has been accepted by all but the strictest. Islam has also accepted representation in such relatively minor forms as household tiles, figurines, and china, but never in monumental sculpture or painting. However, gifted Muslim artists have explored the acceptable media to the limits and have created a remarkable artistic heritage.

Islamic calligraphy and painting derives its power—and its Islamic validity—from its capacity to reveal the secret that the power and sovereignty of God is everywhere, and so truth and paradisal beauty lurk beneath contrary appearances. Calligraphed lines from the Koran join with arabesques to adorn the clean walls and domes of mosques. The latter display the transcendent beauty of the One God; the former add, also through the medium of beauty, that the same God can be known and is known above all through the revealed words of the scripture. For example, Sura 68 of the Koran tells us it is "by the pen, and what it writes," that we are blessed and not cursed. But Islam universally holds that it is no sin and much virtue to make those words as appealing to the eye as possible through art and so to impress even more strongly their power.

So also the paintings that illumine the pages of books and sometimes the walls of schools and tombs give more a sense of conveying mystical rather than ordinary reality. They are flat and two-dimensional, with perhaps a gold background suggesting eternity rather than depth perspective. The saints and kings are mythic figures; the birds and gazelles creatures from paradise. In the same way as the arabesque, these ostensibly representational works actually do not show the world as it is but as it appears to one whose eyes are opened to the presence of the God within and above all that is, and so they preserve a sacred, not a worldly or idolatrous, vision. The famous Persian carpets also often have a comparable sacred message: the spot in the center upon which the elaborate design focuses is an opening from time into eternity.

In Islamic literature, poetry has been of far more importance than prose, for the two most influential literary languages of Islam—Arabic and Persian—lend themselves well to poetry and have highly exalted poetic feeling. Besides religious verse, they both have an exceedingly rich storehouse of secular verse: humorous, amorous, bacchic, and historical, together with odes celebrating the deeds of princes and warriors.

Perhaps because of these associations, poetry was not well regarded by the most exactingly orthodox Muslims. The great exception, of course, is the Koran itself, which, though not always strictly poetry, is composed with unique and powerful patterns of rhythm and rhyme. But the position of the Koran in Islamic letters is paradoxical. As the text with which traditional Muslims learned to read, of which they had memorized long passages, and which they constantly heard recited, its majestic cadences must have been deeply embedded in their conscious and unconscious minds. Yet the Koran was held to be beyond either imitation or criticism; to attempt either was presumptuous sacrilege. Thus, save in commentaries and pious treatises where it is directly quoted, one does not see an immediate influence of the Koran on literary theme or style.

For these reasons, one finds little good religious poetry associated with mainstream Islam. Rather, it is in the mystical tradition, above all in Persia, that the spiritual verse of Islam flowers. As much influenced by the secular poetry of wine and love as by the Koran, these songs of the spirit boldly use the language of intoxication and carnal passion to speak of the relation of the soul to God, the supreme Friend and Lover. They celebrate the "inebriate of God" beside himself with divine love, yet still able to express that love in soaring verse.

Islamic mysticism came also to express itself in elegant books. The most famous example is *The Conference of the Birds* by Farid ad-Din Attar (1119–1230), an allegory relating the quest of thirty birds for the Simurgh, a mythical bird who represents God. When they finally found that splendid being, the questing avians asked him to explain the mystery of the unity and multiplicity of reality. The Simurgh answered (in a mystical image that would be questioned by orthodox Islam) by saying that his form was a sunlike mirror. He who looks at God sees himself reflected there in all his many parts, yet the mirror is one.

The scientific work of the Golden Age of Islamic civilization has rightly been much acclaimed. Learned Arab men of the Baghdad Caliphate and Spain preserved classical Greek and Roman scholarship and transmitted to Europe much of importance from farther East, such as the concept of the zero in mathematics which had been developed in India. They also made substantial advances in such varied fields as astronomy, optics, medicine, geography, and chemistry. All this, as we have said, occurred during the Dark Ages of Europe. Had it not been for the world of Islam, ancient learning would undoubtedly have been lost to a much greater extent than it was, and important advances that set the stage for modern science would not have been possible.

Although the highest intellectual life for the Muslim remained the divine sciences, understanding the mystery and majesty of God and the application of his revealed law, the openness of the conquering Arabs toward what remained of Greek natural science in the Middle Eastern countries they ruled was remarkable. As one might have expected, conservatives were highly dubious of such foreign and unrevealed lore. Yet more than enough men were of the opinion that all learning about the creation of Allah was good and to his glory, and that science and logic could assist in the understanding of God. For them natural and theological queries were complementary rather than at odds. A story tells us that the ninth century Caliph al-Ma'mun had a dream in which Aristotle appeared to him and, after some philosophical discourse, told him to treat scientists as gold and to hold to the Oneness of God—the fundamental Muslim doctrine. The great philosopher al-Ghazali, sometimes blamed for the decline of Islamic science because of his emphasis on mystical intuition, strongly affirmed that the study of Greek logic was a necessary preliminary to the study of doctrine and religious law.

Islamic philosophy had to deal with the impact of Greek thought, to find what it could use of Plato, Aristotle, and the Neoplatonists, and what seemed no longer applicable in the light of new revelation. Interestingly, the Islamic appropriation of Greek ways of thinking followed the sequence of the latter's own development, from rationalism to Neoplatonic mysticism.

A very significant early school of Islamic thought was the *Mu'tazila,* founded by Wasil ibn Ata (699–749). It exhibited a strong rationalist tendency. What God does is always what is best according to reason, and reason is equal to revelation and superior to tradition as a source of truth, according to the Mu'tazila thinkers. They explained away anthropomorphic language about God in the Koran and contended that scripture was created in time, in opposition to the view of those who considered themselves more orthodox that it is the eternal Word of God. The Mu'tazila were supported by the same Caliph Ma'mun (r. 813–833) who entertained Aristotle in his dream. But their supremacy was short-lived.

A reaction that was to condition all subsequent mainstream Islamic theology set in through the writings of Abul-Hasan al-Ash'ari (873–935). He taught that divine actions cannot be explained in terms of human reason. God is simply absolute power and grace, mysterious rather than reasonable on the human level, to be adored and obeyed. This view won the allegiance of both political and spiritual leaders, and it set the stage for more and more emphasis on the basic Islamic concepts of God's oneness and sovereignty. It led toward determinism or predestination in theology and pantheistic tendencies in mysticism—in either case, the sole controlling reality in the creation is God, whether viewed in terms of his ever-present will or of his ever-present being.

In the eleventh and twelfth centuries, two scientist-philosophers at opposite ends of the Muslim world labored vigorously to revive the rational approach and in the process profoundly affected European thought. Both ibn-Sina (980–1037) in Persia, known to the West as Avicenna and ibn-Rushd (1126–98) in Spain, known as Averroës, were deeply influenced by the Greek tradition. Both wrote important scientific and medical works, as well as pure philosophy, and both strove to assert the primacy of reason and science over revelation, although toward the end of his life Avicenna moved more and more in a mystical direction. But that thinker provocatively held to such assertions as the eternality of the universe and that only the soul survives death. Believing the Greeks had conclusively proved these matters by reason, he required that the Islamic doctrines of creation and resurrection be interpreted in a nonliteral way.

Al-Ghazali, following in the Ash'arite tradition that the ways of God are beyond searching out, attacked these positions in such works as *The Incoherence of the Philosophers,* in which he tried to show that the notion of matter as eternal and uncreated does not even stand up to reason, and furthermore that reason itself is a poor guide to ultimate things. Averroës responded with, among his many books, *The Incoherence of the Incoherence,* strongly reasserting reason, though he was able to find a position somewhat more closely approximating orthodoxy than Avicenna's on the resurrection, whereof he contended that while reason and science make it incredible that one's literal physical body could be resurrected, God could supply a new likeness of it on the Last Day.

Averroës's mind, though, was wide-ranging and free. He asserted the superiority of Islam over Plato's idea state because the former seeks the happiness of all, not just a philosophical elite; but he also showed himself unorthodox when he regretted that Islam did not afford women the same equality he thought (incorrectly) Plato did in his *Republic.*

However, such a liberal outlook was not to be characteristic of subsequent Islamic thought. Instead, the devout antirationalism of Ash'arism and al-Ghazali, more and more colored by Sufi mysticism, was predominant in the last great classical school, that of Shihab al-Din al-Suhrawardi (1155–91), ibn al-Arabi (1165–1240), and Sadr al-Din al-Shirazi (d. 1640). While Avicenna and Averroës were much studied by them, they pursued a high Neoplatonism, influenced also by Zoroastrian concepts of light and darkness, which portrayed a multilevel reality within the sole being of God. It was modeled on the unity and diversity of the human being; the universe became understood as a "macrohuman." We shall examine the greatest of these mystical philosophers, al-Arabi, in connection with Sufism.

Classical Islamic civilization, then, created a world of rich diversity and brilliance but all constrained by the sometimes flexible parameters of a world view whose touchstone was the Koranic revelation.[13]

SUNNI ISLAM

We shall now examine some of the variations of belief and practice within Islam. The most important division today is between the *Sunni* and *Shi'a* traditions. Sunni Islam is the normative Islam of most places except Iran. Shi'a Islam is the official

Islam of Iran, is dominant in southern Iraq, and is represented by minorities in Lebanon, Pakistan, India, Yemen, and elsewhere.

Sunna means "well-trodden path," and it refers to the consensus of traditional legal and social practices, as well as referring to the majority Islamic community which claims to be founded on the authentic and correct consensus tradition. It is a tradition given to accommodation of differences and tolerance within the overall Islamic perspective, often citing as its precedent the Prophet's saying, "Differences of opinion within my community are a blessing." The 85 percent or so of the world's 800 million Muslims who are Sunni nonetheless maintain considerable overall homogeneity of belief and practice without a centralized organization or authority, for while some nostalgia for the caliphate remains, Sunni Islam today is self-governing in each Muslim country.

In Sunni Islam the fundamental authority, after the guidance of the Koran, is Muslim law. It is interpreted not by a single individual but by a consensus of learned men who base their decisions on tradition, hadith, and analogy. Although al-Azhar University in Cairo has long been considered the most venerable repository of such learning, Sunni interpretation is decentralized. Its tone is one of putting most emphasis on the basic Five Pillars of Islam and on a rather formal—though deeply felt—style of devotion. Its legal bent stresses putting all of life under God and the Koran. Different schools of law interpretation obtain within Sunni Islam, though they are not competitive but recognized alternatives. Sunni Islam also embraces some submovements; one is the *Wahhabi* movement, dominant in Saudi Arabia, a conservative, puritanical reform dating from the eighteenth century.

SHI'A ISLAM

Shi'a Islam, the Islam of Iran, southern Iraq, and minorities elsewhere, is different in tone and more complex. Shi'ites believe that after Muhammad there was intended to be a succession of *Imams,* divinely appointed and authoritative teachers of Islam, to guide the faithful. The first was Ali, Muhammad's cousin, and after him Ali's eldest son, Hasan, and then Ali's second son, Husain. There were then nine others in family succession, down to the twelfth, who was born in 869.

All of these, except the last, died mysteriously and are said by Shi'ites to have been killed at the instigation of various caliphs. From the Shi'a point of view, the caliphates represent dark usurping powers seeking to destroy the true spokesman in each generation of the house of the prophet of God. The twelfth Imam, the *Imam Zaman,* or Mahdi, the Imam for All Time, is said to be still living but invisible. In the fullness of time he will reappear to bring justice to the earth. Subsects of the Shi'a recognize only part of the lineage, or variations on it. Understandably, colorful claimants to the title of Mahdi have appeared from time to time in Muslim history.

Shi'a devotion puts most emphasis on Husain, the third Imam and the most worthy and tragic of all. In the sixty-first year after the Hijra, he and his companions were killed by the forces of the Caliph Yazid in a great battle at Karbala, in southern Iraq. The death of this splendid young hero has been made by Shi'a into an event that demands eternal recompense by fervent mourning and reenactment. Husain's shrine at Karbala is a mighty place of pilgrimage.

The death of Husain is celebrated by Shi'ites in the first ten days of the Muslim year, the festival of Muharram. During these days Shi'a communities exhibit great religious fervor. At the end of the old year, black tents are set up in the streets, with memorial arms and candles to remind passersby of the martyr. On the first day of Muharram, the devout cease from bathing or shaving. The story of Husain is vividly recited from pulpits in the tents; the listeners respond with wailing and tears. Occasionally, groups of men roam the streets venting their anguish by inflicting sword wounds on themselves, dragging chains, dancing wildly, and pulling out their hair.

The climax of this remarkable commemoration of a hero's death is on the tenth day of Muharram. The battle of Karbala and the death of Husain are enacted in a colorful passion play, with horsemen in bright costumes charging and recharging each other, battering their comrades in sport with wooden staves. The crowd becomes more and more excited; finally, Husain is taken and is seen to suffer excruciatingly from thirst while the cruel foemen make sport of him. At last he is beheaded.[14]

The atmosphere of Shi'a Islam, as reflected in the Muharram and the beliefs about the mysterious martyred or hidden Imam, is clearly different in tone from that of Sunni Islam. The Shi'a world, far from being one in which submission to the revelation of Allah steadily and progressively triumphs, is a darker sphere where treachery and cruelty are all too likely to prevail on the outer plane. Heroes and true prophets of God suffer and die in anguish, while ruthless imposters sit upon thrones; the number of true faithful is small compared to that of frauds, and the faithful are known chiefly by the fervor of their righteous wailing for the evils of this hard world and the keenness of their hope in God's inward, invisible plans.

The Shi'a mentality is conditioned by centuries of experience of being almost always a religious minority within Islam, save under the Fatimid dynasty, which ruled medieval Egypt and surrounding areas in the tenth and eleventh centuries, and in Iran since the Safavid dynasty made it the official faith early in the sixteenth century. But history as old as Islam itself lies behind the Shi'a experience.

When the Shi'a movement began, it appeared on the surface as more of a political than a religious caucus. It was the party (*Shi'a* means "party" or "faction") supporting Ali and his descendants for the caliphate over against the line recognized by the Sunni majority. According to the Sunni tradition, Muhammad left no designated successor. Upon his death, the community selected Abu Bakr, the Prophet's closest companion and father of his wife Aisha, to be its leader. He died after only two years, but he appointed as his successor Umar (r. 634–44), the real organizer of the Arab empire. From then on, the control of the empire by Meccans, of the Umayyad and later (after 750) of the Abbasid house, was clear, despite a brief and challenged caliphate by Ali himself from 656 until his assassination in 661.

According to the Shi'a account, Muhammad appointed Ali as his successor before his death, but while the latter was still mourning the Prophet's passing and before he could assume active leadership, a clique within the Companions of the Prophet had advanced the elderly Abu Bakr to the fore, and Ali's party felt compelled to accept him temporarily in order to prevent division at this critical juncture for Islam, despite knowing it was contrary to Muhammad's wishes. The bitterness of the Ali party was only increased by the attack during Ali's caliphate mounted against him by Mu'awiyah, governor of Syria, an exceptionally able ruler to whose banner the majority of Muslims turned as Ali's rule appeared weak and precarious. But the Ali party won sympathy from the discontented, especially the Bedouin tribesmen, with its demands for social justice and its opposition to the increasingly luxurious aristocracy of the empire. Further, the movement's emotional tone was, as we have seen, deepened when Ali's son Husain was cut down trying to raise a revolt against the Umayyads with a small, ragtag but heroic army in 680. The Shi'a faction also had roots in ancient antagonism on the part of south Arabians and their powerful allies in Iraq and Iran where Ali found support—regions where Shi'a is still strong— against the north Arabian Mecca-Medina power base of the ruling Islamic establishment in the Caliphate era.

As Shi'a Islam persisted despite failure in the military and political arenas, its theoretical concept of the Imam grew more and more exalted. The Sunni caliph was viewed as "successor" to Muhammad only in the latter's role as administrative leader of the Islamic community. No caliph presumed to share the Prophet's unique religious vocation as mediator of divine revelation. But Shi'a concepts of the Imam made his a unique and divinely blessed spiritual office, though they varied from conservative doctrines in which he was little more than a caliph to extremest theologies that saw him as virtually an incarnation or manifestation of God himself on earth and so even greater than Muhammad. What might be called the Shi'a mainstream was satisfied to hold that, by divine grace, the Imam is without sin, has various sorts of superhuman wisdom and power, and is able to interpret the Koran infallibly. However, since the "hiding" of the Imam, these extraordinary functions have been exercised by him through the visible spiritual leaders of Shi'a sects and nations who participate in some way in the Imam's prerogatives. The basic difference between Sunni and Shi'a Islam on the question of authority is clear: for Sunni Islam it derives from *imja,* "consensus," of the community; for the Shi'a it is entirely centralized, in theory, in the Imam or his deputies, whom the faithful are to hear and obey. But the upshot has been somewhat paradoxical. The Sunnis, through the consensus principle, tend toward rigid adherence to tradition and support of established Muslim rules. Shi'ites, who as we have seen were more often than not an oppressed minority, tend in following their almost-divine leaders to accept considerable innovation if it is believed to be specially revealed through the Imam. They are predisposed to mistrust and sometimes oppose the state, and they are inclined to partisan factions under leaders believed to be the Imam or Mahdi, or his envoy or precursor.

We are not surprised to find, then, that most sectarian movements within Islam have been Shi'a. The considerable majority of Shi'ites accept the standard list of twelve Imams before the "hiding" of the twelfth, and they are therefore called

"Twelvers," Ashariyah. Like the Shi'a of Iran, they hold to the "moderate" position concerning the Imam outlined above. But a smaller faction, generally called Ismailis though sometimes also "Seveners," accept only the first seven and differ on the identity of the last. The Twelvers contend that the younger son of the sixth Imam inherited his dignity since the elder son, Ismail, was guilty of the sin of drinking wine. But Ismailis assert that the succession did pass to Ismail, and moreover they claim that he was the last visible Imam, but that his son Muhammad at-Tamm will return as the Madhi.

The Ismaili system of belief has been deeply influenced by esotericism of Gnostic and Zoroastrian background. It holds that the Koran contains veiled doctrines in which concepts of the Neoplatonic sort of emanations, levels of reality, and the mystic significance of the number seven are important. Ismailism takes a cyclical view of history and views all actual, public religions relativistically.

Ismaili history is fascinating, for it shows how easily the sort of radical social attitudes engendered by Shi'a move from idealism to fanaticism and from anarchy to absolutism. In the ninth century, an Ismaili order called the Qarmatians arose in southern Iraq and Bahrain. The Qarmatians practiced communal living, holding all things in common and serving one another's needs. But they also defied the Caliphate, engaged in terrorism against those they regarded as their foes. They achieved such exploits as, in 930, sacking Mecca and temporarily carrying off the Black Stone of the Kaaba.

The Qarmatians prepared the way for something even greater: the rise of the Ismaili Fatimid dynasty. At once imperial and revolutionary, this house perceived its mission in highly ideological terms. Its ruler was himself the quasi-divine Mahdi, or coming Imam, and his task was to destroy the hated usurping caliphate in Baghdad, convert Sunni Muslims to the true faith, and establish a world empire under the world's true sovereign. Originating in North Africa (though claiming descent from Muhammad's daughter Fatimah), the Fatimid house conquered Egypt in 969, where they made Cairo their capital and built a great university and mosque. Besides armies, which tried to press ever closer to Baghdad, the Fatimids sent out missionaries to spread subversion and terror as well as to make converts in the lands of the enemy. But after reaching a high point in 1059, when they actually held Baghdad for a year, the Fatimids went into decline, harried not only by the Caliphate, itself in decline, but also by the rising power of Turks and Christian crusaders. Their regime was also made ultimately untenable by the fact that the majority of Muslims simply could not accept Ismailism or the legitimacy of Fatimid claims. Ismaili believers themselves came to lose faith in them, and the dynasty ended in 1171.

It left a grim progeny in the order called Assassins, which flourished in the mountains and, through secret agents, in the cities of Iraq and Iran and adjacent areas from 1099 to 1266. Founded by a fervent Ismaili missionary and a deposed claimant to the Fatimid throne, the Assassins lived by raiding and terrorism, believing that the murder of those considered enemies was a religious duty. The name derived from the hashish they allegedly took to steel themselves for their bloody deeds. They were finally put down by invading Mongols, who also took Baghdad in 1258, ending the Caliphate there and indirectly allowing Islamic culture to flourish all the more elsewhere—in Persia, India, Egypt, and later Turkey. (A strictly religious, nonpolitical caliphate was set up in Cairo, where it remained until 1517; thereafter the title was taken by the sultans of the Ottoman Empire who held it till 1926, when the ancient dignity of Commander of the Faithful and Successor of the Prophet vanished from the earth.)

The Ismailis today survive in several groups. The Druzes, a people of highly esoteric and initiatory faith centered in southern Syria, believe their creed was founded by al-Hakim, the sixth Fatimid ruler, who in 1017 proclaimed himself the latest incarnation of God. In 1021 he disappeared. Though others opine that he was deranged and murdered, the Druzes ever since have taken him at his word and regard him as the hidden Imam. Other Ismaili sects are centered in India and Yemen. The best known, with a following in the millions, is the Nizari movement, whose spiritual leader is now known as the Aga Khan. Aga Khan III (1877–1957) was much celebrated in this century as a philanthropist, sportsman, and Indian statesman.

But despite its wide dispersal and political origin, undoubtedly it is no accident that Shi'a Islam has its oldest roots in the Valley of the Two Rivers, where anciently New Year's (which Muharram really is) included rites of battle with chaos by the hero Marduk and wailing for the dead Tammuz. (One is reminded of the enacted battle and wailing for Husain.) Shi'a is also strong in formerly Zoroastrian Iran, with its belief in a cosmic battle of good and evil, a hidden coming prophet, and an apocalyptic reversal to which the faithful looked forward. Christian and Manichaean influences on Shi'a cannot be excluded either, for Husain emotionally becomes virtually a suffering saviour.

ISLAMIC MYSTICISM

A discussion of Islam would be superficial if it dealt only with its outward, official history and practices and left out the mystical wing, which has frequently given the faith of Muhammad another face. This tradition is known to the West as Sufism; and its practitioners, as Sufis. Their God is the same God as that of the Koran and the tradition. But they seek not only to follow his external commandments, but to know him intimately and even to lose themselves in love and loss of self into the depths of his being. Around the Sufis' mystic quest have clustered a number of auxiliary practices, many of great beauty: spiritual masters, parables and wisdom tales, spiritual fraternities, schools of meditation, and techniques of attaining ecstasy through music, chanting, and dance.

Sufis believe their approach is grounded in the inner experience of the Prophet himself. Muhammad clearly prayed deeply and knew God intimately, even experiencing trance and rapture. Certain verses of the Koran support the quest for mystical awareness of God everywhere: "To Allah belongs the east and the west. Whichever way you turn there is the face of Allah."[15]

Another suggests the esoteric side of things: We are told that Allah took his servant from a holy mosque to a farther mosque to reveal certain divine signs.[16] According to some traditions, this last passage refers to God's mysteriously transporting Muhammad in a single night from Mecca to Jerusalem, and then taking him up into heaven to show him sights not seen by other mortals. Second-hand accounts of this journey probably helped inspire Dante's *Divine Comedy*.[17]

Thus Sufis believe not only that their way is that of Muhammad himself, but many of them also believe—just as in a sense Muhammad's declaration was but a restoration of the true primordial faith of Abraham and of Eden—that Sufism is really a timeless path known to the wise in all generations.

Doubtless there is truth to this, represented historically by the parallels and possible influence between Sufism and Asiatic shamanism, Greek Neoplatonism, Christian monasticism, and the lore of Hinduism and Buddhism. But within Islamic history, Sufism became visible as a movement about a century after Muhammad. Like Shi'a but in a different way, Sufism was a reaction against the luxury and corruption, the loss of original desert simplicity and pure faith, which many serious Muslims saw overtaking the newly triumphant Islamic world of the caliphates.

The origin of the word *sufi* is disputed, but the majority of scholars attribute it to the Arabic word for wool, *suf,* alluding to the coarse wool garments worn by ascetics seeking a more inward way, as a mark distinguishing them from those content with outward conformity to Islam.

Sufi inwardness made of greatest importance one's personal relation of faith and love to God, a love which was its own reward. Never has this attitude been more eloquently expressed than by the mystic Rabi'a al-'Adawiya of Basra (d. 801), a former slave who had been trained as a flute player. At night she would pray thus:

> Oh my Lord, the stars are shining and the eyes of men are closed, and kings have shut their doors, and every lover is alone with his beloved, and here am I alone with Thee.

She said also:

> I saw the Prophet in a dream, and he said to me, "O Rabi'a, dost thou love me?" I said, "O Prophet of God, who is there who does not love thee? But my love to God so possessed me that no place remains for loving or hating any save Him."

And again:

> It is a bad servant who serves God from fear and terror or from the desire of a reward. . . . Even if Heaven and Hell were not, does it not behoove us to obey Him?[18]

This is a pure Sufi spirit echoing down through the ages. As time went on, this sheer love of God came to be more and more organized, with particular practices and doctrines and societies shaping the lives of those who followed its path.

Thus, Abu Yazid al-Bistami (d. 874) described the stages of the spiritual life leading up to *fana,* complete passing away of the separate individual self into God. The fana state was often manifested in ecstatic spiritual intoxication; in that state, al-Bistami, hardly knowing whether it was he or God in him whose words they were, did not shrink from such expressions as "I am your Lord," "Praise be to me, how great is my majesty," or "My banner is greater than that of Muhammad." The conventional were duly shocked.

Finally, in 922, one of these God-possessed persons of uninhibited rapture, al-Hallaj, was executed at Baghdad for saying "I am the Truth"—"Truth" being an attribute of Allah. The tragic al-Hallaj had taken Jesus, in Islam the exemplar of the inward mystic, as his model of the God-incarnate man, and he was sentenced to the same fate as Jesus: crucifixion.

At the same time, a reaction in favor of a more orthodox Sufism set in. Junayd of Baghdad (d. 911) emphasized that the claims of mystical experience cannot be given priority over normative moral and customary demands of religion, and that the nature of love itself demands that, even in the mystic's "identity" with God, there be also a difference between him and God.[19]

The great al-Ghazali (1058–1111), who had been a conventional Muslim scholar until he experienced and then sought to interpret the mystic path, made Sufism a respectable part of Islam. He interpreted Sufi inwardness as an attitude to accompany the outward acts and bring them to life, as we have seen in his treatment of the hajj.

The philosopher and Sufi master ibn al-Arabi (1165–1240), a spiritual follower of al-Ghazali, moved in the direction of a pantheist philosophy as the intellectual expression of what the Sufi "knows" and enacts. For him, as we have seen, God was not only the source of all, but the sole reality. Within the divine, however, are gradations; between the human and the divine is a realm of images that reflect in the human imagination—angels, the Day of Judgment, and so forth—and on these images religious visions and events are grounded.

The Sufi way has made much of *shaykhs,* spiritual teachers and masters, and *wali,* saints. Drawing initially from Shi'a sources, Sufis also have talked of hidden holy ones and of a coming Mahdi, or apocalyptic teacher-saviour. According to Sufism, the saints are different from the prophet Muhammad but are in their own way nearly as great. For a Sufi to attain *wilaya,* sainthood or being a "friend of God," was as good a goal as outward Islam, submission.

Indeed, by the tenth and eleventh centuries the twin goals of sainthood and submission came together, as the notion gained force in Sufi circles that one should submit to one's shaykh, or spiritual guide. The *shaykh,* called farther east around India a *pir* or *murshid,* was more or less an Islamic parallel to the Hindu guru. The very self-abnegation of submitting to his commands "as a dead body in the hands of its washers" was an experience of egolessness and bore its own spiritual reward, whether the guide was wise or not.

Many were wise, and their wisdom was often expressed in peculiar tales and gnomic wisdom. We are told, for example, that a certain man fell down in a seizure on a street of perfume sellers. People tried to revive him with various of the sweet odors of the tradesmen, but to no avail. Finally someone thrust sharp, pungent, ammonious ordure before his nose, and he arose. The implication is that only by the different, even the disconcerting, can the walking dead be brought to life.[20] Shaykhs have employed the methods of differentness with their paradoxes and their chanting, dancing, and trances.

Since the labors of al-Ghazali, Sufi masters generally have emphasized doing the normative devotions of Islam, but with a special mind to the inward as well as the outward aspects. But beyond that, there are special ecstatic techniques for knowing God which the shaykhs taught: practices such as *dhikr* (or *wird*), reciting the beautiful names of God on beads, or even whirling dances like those of the dervishes, or feats of shamanistic fervor like rending garments, eating glass, or cutting oneself without pain to show one's divine absorption.

Practices such as these were developed by the great Sufi orders which spread across Islam after the tenth century. They still exist, although since around 1900 their power has diminished. For the most part they were not celibate monastic orders, although in some instances an inner core of devotees or leaders might— whether officially married or not—exemplify a level of commitment comparable to that of monks or abbots in other faiths. But for the bulk of lay adherents, the orders were more like lodges: One would receive a formal initiation by a shaykh or pir of the order and then would practice its devotion corporately and privately. Some Sufi orders, especially in the Turkish Empire, had political and revolutionary overtones. Some have been suppressed by modern Islamic governments because the whole Sufi attitude was considered by modernizers to inculcate a medieval, superstitious, nonproductive mentality; ironically, at the same time Sufism has been discovered and much appreciated by many outside of Islam.

Sufi orders with their saintly masters were and are a great proselytizing force for Islam. It was primarily in their gentler, more mystical form that Islam entered

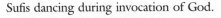

Sufis dancing during invocation of God.

India and Indonesia. It is easy to speculate that, apart from its empathetic presentation by such mystic saints, Islam might have had but little success in these cultures, which are so differently oriented from Arabia. Today, Sufi orders are having great success in spreading Islam in Africa.

The prestige of the shaykh made much of Islam into a cult of personalities. Shaykhs became saints who had cosmic as well as temporal meanings. It was said to be the saints who kept the world together generation after generation. In an invisible hierarchy were varying degrees of saints: "successors," "pegs," "pillars," and finally the *qutb,* the "pole" or "axis" of the universe. There is only one *qutb,* according to a popular tradition, in every generation, and when one dies he is replaced by another. The members of this hierarchy are the true pivots upon which the world in its inner life turns. They may not be known to the general public—indeed, a saint in his humility may not even know himself that he is a saint, much less an axis of the world—but should he fail in the mysterious work his inward sanctity enables him to do, the social order and the earth itself would fall apart. Finally, Sufis spoke of the enigmatic leader and guide of the saints themselves, al-Khidr, "the Green One," a generally invisible but immortal and ever-youthful guide who appears at time of need in the dreams or waking sight of the sincere questor on the mystic path.[21]

The Muslim public knew well the reputations of the more visible saints. It flocked to their presences and, after their deaths, to their tombs. In the heyday of popular Sufism—the twelfth through nineteenth centuries—legends of saints were rife, and pilgrimages to their holy places rivaled Mecca in popularity. Many of them are still much frequented. In Shi'a areas, the shrines of Imams, like that of Husain himself at Karbala in Iraq, are thronged. Countless village mosques contain the tomb of a local saint, unmarked by image or picture but well known and visible because of its coffin shape, inscription, and the many colored flags on the building.

In the valley of Bamian in Afghanistan, famous for its ancient Buddhist monastic caves, but whose population is now strongly Muslim, I came across a shrine of an "ice-burning saint." According to the local legend, this mystic had once come with his disciples into the valley and begged for fuel with which to cook food for himself and his band. But the villagers, not recognizing him for what he was, hardened their hearts against his request. The saint then sent a disciple into the nearby mountains to get some ice, and by a miracle he caused the ice to burn and used it for firewood. Thereupon, the awestruck villagers believed in him and besought the holy man to stay, which he did. When he died, the shrine was built over his tomb, a modest domed edifice of mud with a wall around it, all festooned with red banners. I saw bearded men of the village circumambulate the tomb inside the walls muttering dhikr as they went; in setting out, each stooped to pass under a table holding the Koran.

One sensed here both the devotional power of popular Islam and the basic similarities of the central Asiatic myths and culti of men or power, whether in shamanistic, Hindu, Buddhist, Muslim, or Christian forms—for the wizard saint has been a constant in all the many faiths which have swept across the wild mountains, deserts, and forests of that vast area of the earth.

Islam generally believes that the saints have power to perform miracles. Muhammad did none, except the miracle of the Koran itself. But the saints have a different calling from that of the public envoy of God, one at once more arcane and more popularly appealing. They must work wonders to show the transcendence of spiritual attainment over the material and do works of mercy which help hold the universe together. They are masters of the realm of archetype and dream that lies above this world and below God, as written in the philosophy of al-Ghazali and ibn al-Arabi. The *baraka,* or numinous power of the saints, rests eternally over their tombs and relics, and for this reason pilgrims to these sites are often healed and blessed.

ISLAM IN THE WORLD TODAY

In the closing decades of the twentieth century, Islam finds itself second only to Christianity in number of active members among the religions of the world. The devastation of Buddhism and the traditional religions of China by Communist revolutions leaves no doubt about that status. Moreover, as we have seen, Christianity today appears to be shorn of the overconfidence with which it began the century, though it still possesses much strength. But Muslims have little hesitancy in viewing the position of their faith and of Islamic culture at century's end as far stronger than at its beginning.

In 1900, the Muslim world was notoriously in decline compared to Europe and America. It was sunk in poverty and technologically backward. Most of it was subject to humiliating European colonial rule: The Dutch controlled Indonesia; millions of Indian Muslims as well as Hindus lived under the British flag; France ruled vast reaches of Muslim North Africa. The only large sovereign Muslim states were the Ottoman (Turkish) and Persian empires, which sprawled over much of the Middle East. They were anachronistic and corrupt regimes; if anything more oppressive than colonial rule to their long-suffering subjects, and moreover, despite nominal independence, subservient to Europe in many ways. Finally, Islamic faith itself in 1900 was not at its best. Intellectually, it was seldom in touch with the modern world, and on the popular level it was pervaded by the sort of mysticism that many observers considered neither authentic Islam nor able to meet modern needs.

But in the last quarter of this century, this situation has changed dramatically. Rarely since the stunning spread of Islam in its first century have the fortunes of a religion changed so remarkably in so short a time. Virtually all Muslim lands— except those in the Soviet Union—have attained independence. The old Ottoman and Persian empires are now Turkey (much diminished in size) and Iran. With the new names have come new regimes and far-reaching changes. Some Muslim countries have achieved great wealth, mostly from petroleum. Prior to the Persian Gulf War of 1991, Kuwait and Saudi Arabia reached levels of per capita income among the highest in the world. Islam is growing rapidly, both through a high birthrate in many places and through missionary efforts. Emigration and the establishment of Islamic centers have given the religion a new visibility around the world. Islam is also experiencing vigorous intellectual ferment and powerful movements for simplification and purification of the faith and its practice.

Change is uneven, of course. The House of Islam includes not only some of the richest nations in the world, but also some of the poorest, such as Bangladesh. Some aspects of its resurgence have seemed, at least to outsiders, as more like rampant nationalism accompanied by religious zealotry than real spiritual awakening. But such matters are not always well judged by outsiders, and they require considerable perspective in time before their ultimate meaning can be discerned. However one assesses it, Islam seems in a period of religious ferment and renewal associated with nation-building and expanding confidence comparable to the Protestant Reformation in the Christian world. The Reformation also produced much war and bigotry, yet nonetheless helped wrench Europe into new stages of historical development.

Not infrequently, the resurgence of traditional Islam has been associated with the self-assertion of underprivileged classes in Muslim countries, whether rural peasants or urban masses, against the westernized elite who typically dominated the governments and economies of these countries in their early period of modern nationhood, especially the first three decades after World War II. While those elites have often done much to promote nation-building and the development of modern (that is, Western-type) industry, transportation, education, and political institutions, these benefits have not always been readily apparent to those not of the elite class, whereas their disruptive effect on traditional village, family, and Islamic moral and spiritual values have been all too much so. Moreover, the elites are commonly perceived as inwardly contemptuous of traditional values and unduly eager to cultivate the ways and friendships of non-Muslim Europeans and Americans.

The political and social upsurge of traditional Islam that became so evident in the late 1970s, most conspicuously in the Iranian revolution of 1979, was the explosive outburst of long-pent-up hostility by nonelites against the dominant class. Often led by fiery Muslim fundamentalist preachers and mystics, the dispossessed understandably seized upon pure Islam as the symbol for what they stood for and stood against; Islam was their faith and culture, the true life-soul of a land that was truly theirs. They insisted, then, that the Shari'a become the law of the state as well as the mosque.

We shall now survey the situation of Islam around the world in the late twentieth century. Saudi Arabia incorporates the land where the faith began and contains its holy cities of Mecca and Medina. Islam there is firmly established. The strict Wahhabi sect, which rejects mysticism of the Sufi sort and demands a state based on literal interpretation of the Koran and Shari'a, dominates it. Under its influence, plays, cinema, alcoholic drinks, and excessive intermingling of the sexes are forbidden. Yet Saudi Arabia, convulsed by new wealth and inevitable social change, is striving

A little girl with a picture of the Ayatollah Khomeini in
front of the occupied U.S. Embassy in Tehran, Iran, in 1979.

to become both a modern nation and a conservative Muslim one at the same time;
the final result of this experiment remains to be seen.

In the other Arab countries, the picture is more varied. Traditional religious
attitudes mix with new social ideas. The movement often labeled Arab Socialism,
represented in several countries by the Ba'ath Party, seeks to combine Arab nationalism
(aimed at eventual unification of the Arab peoples into one nation) with Koranic
concern for justice and fair distribution of goods expressed through modern forms
of governmental social activism. But progress in this direction has been uneven
and its implementation diverse in character. In Libya, for example, the regime of
Muammar al-Qaddafi has conjoined ideological socialism with strong nationalism
and support of Islam to the extent that local government is in the hands of imams.
In neighboring Tunisia, on the other hand, the government, while nominally socialist
and Muslim, has taken a far more moderate stance and indeed has pioneered in
finding ways to adapt Islamic usages to modern conditions. In 1990, an Islamic
party was elected to power in Algeria, long a "moderate" state.

To the north of the Arab world lies Turkey, homeland of the Turks, the non-Arab race whose sultan long ruled most of the Arabic-speaking peoples in the days of the Ottoman Empire. By the nineteenth century this sprawling imperial state was slipping from the sultan's grasp. Turkey was the "Sick Man of Europe." Despite reforms, culminating in the "Young Turks" coup d'état of 1908, conditions only seemed to get worse in the empire's internal and external position. But after World War I, Turkey lost its empire and set off in a radically new direction under the iron rule of Kemal Ataturk (1881–1938). The sultans of the Ottoman Empire had claimed the ancient title of Caliph of Islam, but Ataturk sought to establish a westernized and militantly secular state. He ended religious courts and schools, put secular law in place of the Shari'a, abolished the Caliphate and Sufi orders, and forbade religious garb outside places of worship. Secularization dealt with matters large and small; Sunday was made the weekly holiday instead of Friday, and the wearing of the fez, a hat traditionally associated with the old Turkey and with Islam, was outlawed. The substitution of the Roman alphabet for the Arabic in the writing of Turkish helped detach the nation from the world of Islam. But after Ataturk's death, the deislamicization program was gradually relaxed and the continuing support of the religion by the peasantry showed the persisting strength of faith.

As we have already observed, toward the end of the twentieth century the wholesale promotion of secularization and westernization, which had been advocated by Ataturk as a solution for the problems of Muslim lands, was definitely an idea whose time had come and gone. It had had influence outside of Turkey; the father of modern Turkey was a hero to some of the early Ba'ath leaders, and the fathers of several other major Muslim countries, such as Pakistan and Indonesia, which gained independence or underwent transformation in mid-century, paid him the tribute of emulation. They too made no pretense of being orthodox believers, but while appealing to the general ideal of Islamic nationhood, they favored "progress" at whatever cost to the particulars of the tradition. But it was against the policies of these leaders that the reaction of the late 1970s—which of course has earlier roots—was largely directed.

New and strident voices said that Islam, far from being an awkward roadblock to modernization, was as good (indeed better) an ideological framework for building a just social and economic order as Western socialism or capitalism, and at the same time it was a sure rampart against the corroding influences (chiefly from the West) that traditionalists saw threatening family life and pride in one's land and culture. Four principles have been fundamental to the Islamic resurgence since the late 1970s:

1. The Shari'a, or systematized code of Islamic law based on the Koran and the traditions, must be the fundamental law of the state.
2. To ensure that state policies and actions are consistent with the Shari'a, Muslim teachers and scholars should have an important role in government, thus achieving what in the West would be called a union of church and state.

3. Wealth must be fairly distributed in accordance with Islamic ideals of justice and brotherhood.

4. Outside (non-Muslim) influences in society must be resisted, and the lifestyle of the people should conform to Islamic rules and values, as in matters of dress, family life, education, and the role of women.

To the east of the Arab world, Iran in the early 1980s presented the most dramatic example of the Islamic resurgence. Under the leadership of the Ayatollah (a high-ranking religious teacher sharing in the mystique of the Shi'a Imam) Khomeini, the Shah Muhammad Pahlavi was toppled in 1979 and an "Islamic Republic" was established, in which the Shari'a would be normative and the clergy like Khomeini would have a decisive role. The resplendent monarchy had lost popular support for reasons such as those suggested above. In its place came the classic revolutionary scenario of ecstatic mobs, reprisals, serious economic and social disruption, and the emerging outlines of a state more egalitarian, more isolationist, and more founded on Islamic law than what went before.

In the Indian subcontinent, the same resurgence of strict, traditionalist Islam has brought comparable problems and prospects to its multitudes. Pakistan, founded as an Islamic state at the time of the independence and partition of the former British Indian Empire in 1947, retained a legal system based on the English and followed the "progressive" course for a while; but in 1979 the Shari'a also became law under pressure of the Islamic resurgence. Prayer rooms were set up in factories and cinemas, and radio and television programs were censored to free them of anything obnoxious to Muslim faith and morals—a pattern similar to that elsewhere. In the Republic of India, the 10 percent Muslim minority, influenced by the spirit and literature of the resurgence, has become more assertive, and this has perpetuated tensions and even riots between Muslims and the Hindu majority.

Farther east, in Malaysia, the Islamic resurgence threatens the delicate racial balance that has held that nation together. Malaysia is 50 percent Malay Muslim, 35 percent Chinese, and 15 percent Hindu and others. Since independence from Britain, its government has been controlled by a wealthy, sophisticated urban class of Malays who have held their Muslim faith in moderation and maintained good relations with the Chinese, who dominate the economy. But a fundamentalist movement, with its own militant political party inspired by zealous preachers, has arisen among the poorer Malay peasants of the countryside. It gives voice to the simple, devout countryman's resentment of both Chinese and worldly urban Malays, and it calls for a rigorously Islamic state on the puritanical model of others we have already discussed. This would, of course, provoke strong opposition from the large Chinese minority, who are not Muslim at all and have no desire to live under such a regime but whose economic life is bound up with Malaysia.

Islam in Indonesia has long been regarded as somewhat superficial. It came late to the vast island nation and sat lightly on top of a spiritual culture still deeply permeated by the Hindu and Buddhist influences that preceded it and above all by an indigenous bent toward spiritism and shamanism. It was the mystical, Sufi side of Islam, most congenial to the Indonesian temper, which won clearest support. Here too, however, a strict Muslim party and movement have been gaining support.

At the other end of the earth, in Europe, Islam is represented in several ways. European Turkey, now a small enclave around the great city of Istanbul, is predominantly Muslim. Elsewhere in Southeastern Europe, in lands once ruled by the Ottoman Empire, Muslim populations remain: 70 percent of the people in Albania and much smaller numbers in Yugoslavia, Bulgaria, and Greece. Adverse historical circumstances, however, have diminished the influence and vitality of these populations: Ataturk's secularism in Istanbul; in the Balkans, independence from Turkey under Christian regimes, then, except in Greece, rule by unsympathetic Communist governments. In Albania from the 1960s through 1990 all places of worship have been closed and all religious observances prohibited, the most extreme antireligious policy of any state in the world. Relaxation of this policy seems on the way in the last decade of the century.

In Western Europe, the population of Muslims has grown considerably since World War II as a result of immigration. Turks work in German factories, Pakistanis have settled in England, and Algerians have come to France in great numbers, reversing former lines of European expansion. This, together with a greatly increased business and diplomatic presence from Islamic countries, has dotted Western Europe with mosques and Islamic centers, even though Muslims do not, of course, represent more than a small minority.

In North and South America, the situation is comparable. While Muslim immigration has been less, important diplomatic and commercial relationships between the American countries and Islamic counterparts have brought Muslims to the great cities of the Western Hemisphere, and Muslim donations have built impressive Islamic centers in Washington, Los Angeles, New York, and elsewhere. These have enabled many Americans for the first time to observe the practice of Islam and engage in dialogue with Muslims without leaving their homeland.

Mention should also be made of the "Black Muslims," a movement of African Americans that originally possessed staunchly separatist doctrines, but which has been approaching closer and closer to normative Islamic faith and practice. Formerly called the Nation of Islam, this movement is now the American Muslim Mission and is open to both whites and blacks. Splinter movements have continued the separatist approach.

Despite its sometimes troubled past, then, Islam entered the final decades of the twentieth century full of vigor and faith, confident of a powerful future.

SUMMARY

Islam is a religion with a highly distinctive cultural and spiritual atmosphere. The word *islam* means "submission"; the faith centers on the submission of individuals and communities to the absolute sovereignty of Allah, God, in all areas of life.

Muhammad, the Prophet of Islam, was a trader from Mecca who began at the age of forty to receive lines of powerful and beautiful Arabic while meditating in a cave. These lines included words of warning to repent, moral admonishments, and above all revelations of God's greatness. They were recorded by scribes and after the Prophet's death were compiled into the Koran, the book believed by Muslims to be the last and greatest divine revelation to humanity, just as Muhammad is seen as the last and greatest in a line of prophets sent to restore the simple, primal religion of justice and pure monotheism. Muhammad's spiritual purification movement also became a political movement. This is understandable since the Koran emphasizes that while conversion to Islam should never be by force, its faith and moral strictures should be practiced in a society that abides by them and seeks to implement them in all human spheres of activity, including the political and economic. By the time of Muhammad's death, most of Arabia had been united under his banner; within a century Islamic forces had spread across much of Africa and Asia to create an empire ruled by a caliph, or "successor" to Muhammad in the political realm. The caliphs reigned over a brilliant Islamic civilization for several centuries, but finally their realm was replaced by several regional Muslim empires, such as the Moghul, Persian, and Ottoman. Still later, after the experience of European colonial rule in some places, these were succeeded by the numerous Islamic nation-states of today.

The practice of Islam centers on what are commonly called its Five Pillars: reciting the creed that states that there is no god but Allah, and Muhammad is his Prophet; praying five times daily; giving alms; keeping a fast during the month of Ramadan; and once in one's life, if possible, making the pilgrimage to Mecca. The daily prayers are said according to certain set procedures, facing in the direction of Mecca; thus, like the pilgrimage, they reinforce the communal sense of Islam. On Friday noon they are customarily said congregationally in a mosque, accompanied by sermons. The mosque, with its austere ornamentation and its niche in the direction of Mecca, together with its traditional role as community, educational, and judicial center, is a beautiful expression of the spirit of Islam.

Islamic culture has been shaped by several factors: the predominance of the city, the court, and trade in its social and economic world; and the discouragement of representational art and of religious poetics imitative of the Koran. Its art has therefore emphasized ornamentation and calligraphy; within these limits it has developed splendid forms that well suggest the universal presence of God. Its poetic and prose literature has been chiefly developed within the mystical traditions; it often borrows boldly from verses of love and intoxication to describe the relation of the soul to God. During the Golden Age of the Caliphate, science, philosophy, and theology were extensively cultivated. Learned men not only preserved the best of classical thought, but made important advances which were finally transmitted to Europe.

Islam is divided into two main groups. Sunni Islam emphasizes the traditional path of Islamic life as interpreted by the consensus of scholars and the community. Shl'a Islam, while following the traditional path, also puts its faith in the authority of Imams who are Muhammad's hereditary successors. Now the true Imam is said to be in hiding but will emerge at the apocalyptic moment. Shi'a Islam has been productive of most sectarian movements within Islam; it predominates in Iran and southern Iraq.

Islamic mysticism, called Sufism in the West, focuses on the presence of the divine oneness everywhere and offers paths to the attainment of union with God. Several great orders of Sufis are spread across the Muslim world. Their practices include chanting, dancing, whirling, and meditation. The role of the shaykh, or spiritual mentor, is very important. Great mystics have often been venerated, in life and after death in their tombs, as great saints capable of working miracles. The literature of Sufism is often of remarkable beauty and has won much admiration both in the Islamic world and outside it.

In the world today, Islam is experiencing much vitality, particularly in comparison to its situation in the nineteenth century. It is growing, Muslim nations are becoming wealthy and important, and there are many signs of spiritual revitalization. Early in the twentieth century, Muslim countries such as Turkey sought to meet the demands of the modern world by secularization, but later, as in the Iranian revolution of 1979, a militant and fundamentalist Islam sought to impose conservative values and an alternative Islamic social order to capitalism and communism. This resurgent Islam is a major force in the world of the late twentieth century.

QUESTIONS FOR REVIEW

1. Describe the "feel" and characteristics of Islamic society.

2. On the basis of the thematic chart, discuss the ways in which Islam relates to the individual and to the community, and the ways in which its legalistic and mystical (or sainthood) aspects are expressed.

3. Summarize the life of the prophet Muhammad, placing it in the context of his times and assessing the nature of his immense impact on both religion and history.

4. Talk about the Koran as a book of revelation, referring to its style, content, message, and meaning.

5. Outline the faith and practice of the Five Pillars of Islam: the statement of faith, prayer, alms, fast of Ramadan, and pilgrimage to Mecca.

6. Describe how the Muslim's five daily prayers are done and what they mean.

7. Describe the characteristic architecture, arrangements, and use of the mosque.

8. Describe the history and main features of such principal areas of Islamic culture as art, poetry, prose literature, science, philosophy, and theology.

9. Explain the difference between Sunni and Shi'a Islam, and summarize the history of the Shi'a movement.

10. Discuss Islamic mysticism or Sufism, explaining where it has been in tension with mainstream Islam and in what ways it has deepened and widened its life.

11. Survey the position of Islam in the modern world, giving especial attention to its varied responses to the changes wrought by modernization, including the resurgence of Islamic fundamentalism.

12. Discuss the prospects of dialogue between the three great monotheistic faiths: Judaism, Christianity, and Islam.

SUGGESTED READINGS ON ISLAM

General

*CHRISTOPHER, JOHN B., *The Islamic Tradition*. New York: Harper & Row, 1972. A brief introduction covering all cultural aspects of Islamic civilization.

*CRAGG, KENNETH, *The Call of the Minaret*. London and New York: Oxford University Press, 1956. A brilliant and empathetic treatment of Islamic theology, with frequent comparisons to Christian concepts.

*————, *The House of Islam*. Belmont, CA: Dickenson, 1969. A splendid introduction.

DENNY, FREDERICK M., *An Introduction to Islam*. New York: Macmillan, 1985. A very good introductory textbook.

MARTIN, RICHARD C., *Islam: A Cultural Perspective*. Englewood Cliffs, NJ: Prentice-Hall, Inc., 1982. An excellent shorter introduction to Islam and the Islamic cultural world.

MORGAN, KENNETH, *Islam: The Straight Path*. New York: Ronald Press, 1958. A collection of popular papers by contemporary Muslims: a good introduction to the Islamic faith.

RAHMAN, FAZLUR, *Islam*. Chicago: University of Chicago Press, 1979. A solid textbook by a prominent Muslim scholar, oriented toward history.

WATT, WILLIAM MONTGOMERY, *What is Islam?* London: Longmans, 1968. An excellent overview by a distinguished Islamicist.

*WILLIAMS, JOHN ALDEN, *Islam*. New York: Braziller, 1961. A useful anthology of Muslim literature.

The Koran

ARBERRY, A. J., *The Koran Interpreted*. 2 vols. New York: Macmillan, 1955. Probably the most readable and literary English version.

*DAWOOD, N. J., TRANS., *The Koran*. Baltimore: Penguin Books, 1968. Also recommended: a sound and accessible translation.

*PICKTHALL, MOHAMMED, *The Meaning of the Glorious Koran*. New York: Mentor, n.d. An interesting translation by an English convert to Islam.

Islamic Mysticism

*ARBERRY, A. J., *Sufism*. New York: Harper Torchbooks, 1970. A brief, authoritative, and well-written introduction.

SCHIMMEL, ANNEMARIE, *Mystical Dimensions of Islam*. Chapel Hill: University of North Carolina Press, 1975. A definitive work on the subject.

*SHAH, IDRIES, *The Sufis*. Garden City, NY: Doubleday, 1964. Attractive, moving, readable, much influenced by the author's own point of view.

*SMITH, MARGARET, *Readings from the Mystics of Islam*. London: Luzac, 1950. Beautiful translation of original sources.

*TRIMINGHAM, J. SPENCER, *The Sufi Orders in Islam*. London and New York: Oxford University Press, 1971. Scholarly; gives an incomparable insight into an important aspect of Islamic life.

David Rosenfeld. Photo Researchers

CHAPTER 10

Looking Over the Spiritual Horizon:
RELIGION TODAY AND TOMORROW

CHAPTER OBJECTIVES

After studying this chapter, you should be able to

- Present an overview of contemporary religious movements.

- Discuss perspectives on the future of religion in a technocratic age.

We have surveyed the religions of humankind past and present. We have encountered a remarkable diversity among them, and we have noted what they all have in common.

Some of what we have looked at seemed very much rooted in the past, if not irrevocably locked there. The past may give religion a romantic patina, or sprinkle it with the blood of grisly sacrifices that we are glad are gone, but it is still the past. We may in wistful moods wish we could revisit the living temples of ancient Greece, or hear the Buddha speak, but we do not expect that their like will be seen again, unless all things do recur in infinite time and, as a poet says of the wonders of Mycenae:

> It may be that no splendor passes evermore from Earth,
> But that, through endless incantations—subtle, strange, divine—
> It knows in far-off time and space a new resplendent birth:
>
> In what age, in what world, shall this proud lion find again—
> Deep in the sea of stars—his race of gods and godlike men?[1]

But on a shorter scale, it may indeed seem that much of human religion is trapped beyond renewal in the past, and that even living religion is a carryover from the past into the present, relating modern experience to ancient maps.

Is religion, then, an anomaly that cannot be expected to survive much longer? At least since the eighteenth century eminent voices have predicted the withering away of religion. This is not a book of prophecy and will not attempt to foretell the future. But we can indicate that the relation of religion to its times is usually more complex and mysterious than appears on the surface.

Religion always comes into a present as something out of the past. Both the temple and the voice of the prophet, in differing ways, point to a world simpler and more pristine than the ambivalent world of the day. In this simpler world of mythic time, or of scripture or vision, the works of the gods are more evident and moral values clearer. For religion to appear today as something from the past, and somewhat out of joint with the present, is nothing exceptional in itself. Nor is it any new thing for prophets to appear who proclaim that at least the extant religion is ready to be superseded. So spoke the Buddha, in effect, of the old brahminism and its rites, and Muhammad, of the old gods of stars and moon.

In all the countless religious changes earth has seen, the religious quest has been renewed, but it has not seldom changed course and set out in unexpected directions. Often its new forms have at first hardly seemed like "religion" at all, compared with the older elaborate structure. At first the Buddha's methods may have seemed more like an ancient version of psychotherapy, and the cause of Muhammad more like a radical political movement than like institutions that would in time show equivalents to heavensful of gods and the temples of the Nile. These and other new movements seemed more like breaths of fresh wind, which swept away all the old gods and cleaned the skies, leaving None or only One.

But the "Death of God" is no new thing. God or the gods have died many times, but a new God or new gods have soon been born and have arisen to fill the vacuum. Their names may hardly yet have the glow of the old and holy, and they may come from segments of society little involved in the religious commerce of the previous age. The Buddha was of kshatriya rather than brahmin caste; Muhammad was from Arabia rather than one of the main religious powers; Jesus was from Galilee. But it is often something that appears "noncompetitive" in the power structure of the day which bears the future, like obscure tiny furry mammals in the age of giant reptiles.

Religion is changing today. It is not changing at as fast a rate as it has at some periods in the past, for there are no great new movements afoot that look as though they might replace Buddhism, Islam, or Christianity in the manner these replaced their predecessors. Moreover, conservative as well as innovative forces are at work in all faiths. Even the vaunted modern technology, which some have said will create a new secular world in which religion can no longer have a place, works both sides of the street. The urbanization and industrialization it has brought have indeed disrupted the traditional religion-based lifestyles of millions, but technology has also greatly facilitated such traditional religious practices as pilgrimage (now via jumbo jet) to Rome or Mecca, the publishing of scriptures for a mass readership, and mass preaching by means of radio and television.

FACTORS AFFECTING RELIGION TODAY

As our survey of the history of the world's religions has tried to make evident over and over, the shape and strength of religions can be much affected by the social, political, and economic worlds in which they live. What are some of those factors in the world of the late twentieth century?

The prospect of a nuclear holocaust has been a spectre haunting the minds of millions since the first atomic bombs exploded in 1945. If this were to happen, the effect on religion, as on all other aspects of life, for the survivors would be incalculable. Much would depend on who the survivors, if any, were and on what values—on what religions or religious surrogates—they came to put the blame for the devastated cities and food supplies, the hunger and radiation sickness, perhaps the nuclear winter. However, at the time of writing, at least, this particular threat seems to be in recession as an immediate concern. Among many such forces, both good and bad, technological and ecological realities cry for human and religious response. Here are some examples.

The Technological Revolution

The technological innovations of the last two hundred years have changed the lives of most people more than any change since the discovery of agriculture some ten thousand years earlier. From the steam engine to the computer, from railways to jets and telegraph to television, they have transformed not only how we live but how we work, how we relate to the world, and also how we understand what the world is. The contemporary electronics engineer, computer programmer, or technology-assisted businessperson or farmer are very different from the archaic agriculturalists in terms of how they interact with the physical universe.

As we have already indicated, this immense change thus far has pluses as well as minuses for religion. Religious persons and institutions have been able to make much use of technological aids, especially those of the transportation and communication revolutions, to advance their cause.

Most religious language, however, comes out of a pre-technological revolution world. Religion generally comes to the present as something out of the past, judging the present in terms of earlier and presumably simpler and purer values. This is tacitly expected, so it gives religious relevance a "grace period" or time-lag. Many people are not bothered that religious language reflects a world of shepherds, kings, and wandering holy men rather than multinational corporations, democracies or dictatorships, and television evangelists. They will argue, no doubt rightly, that the fundamental human problems and spiritual realities are the same in both worlds. But the question remains whether the "lag" can persist indefinitely without mounting calls for radically new forms of religion, as far-reaching as those that accompanied the agricultural revolution millenia ago.

The Ecological and Population Crises

These two interrelated problems are both direct or indirect products of the technological revolution, showing that its results have not all been benign. As an unwanted result of medical and food-production advances, together with the persistence of older attitudes toward family life, the earth's population has been growing at an astounding rate, from 1 billion to more than 5 billion since 1850. The world would be hard-pressed to feed this many even with optimal use and distribution of resources. But that has been far from the case, with the wealthy quadrant of the earth's nations consuming much more than their share. Thus, millions—perhaps billions—are doomed to subsistence living at best and face the continual threat of famine.

It seems that humans, no differently than all other animal species, insist on filling their ecological niche to the maximum, not for quality of life but for the quantity that can be sustained, even if at the most marginal level. (If the world today with all its technological marvels had only the population of 1000 C.E.—about 250 million—or even the billion of 1850, it could be a veritable paradise for all. Instead, it looks like nearly 6 billion in 2000, with famine, plague, and death as near as they were a thousand years ago for a good many.

At the same time, the very effort to feed these people—as well as to earn profits for the well-placed by such means as cutting tropical rain forests to graze cattle or grow cash crops and using ever-increasing amounts of hazardous agricultural chemicals—is devastating the ecology of the earth. Together with other effluvia of

Ecological Crisis: Sahara Desert sand dunes blanketed with grass to prevent sand from shifting to nearby acres of fertile land.

an industrial and technological age, it is killing the oceans and warming the air to melt polar ice, sink cities, and turn fields into deserts. There seems no way out but very difficult changes in the lifestyles of millions, from drastically reducing the consumption of meat and nonnutritional crops such as coffee, tea, and tobacco (all very inefficient in the use of now-scant farmlands in terms of people fed per acre) to massive conversion to nonpolluting fuels. Otherwise, nature will do the job for us in her usual ruthless and indiscriminate way or humans—no less ruthless—will fight it out until the numbers are reduced to an acceptable level.

It would seem that religion, with its proud claim to be the moral voice of humanity, would have much to say about resolving these interlocking crises in a humane way and about the spiritual worth of the sacrifices that will be needed to solve them with compassion rather than with callousness or the cannon. But here is where the making of judgments, referred to in Chapter 1, can come in. While prophets calling for a new environmental/ecological ethic—prophets desperately concerned like those of old who warned humanity of doom to come unless they repented—can be found in all religions, the large-scale response of religion has been far more mixed. Prophecy has been mingled with religion serving other roles: offering other-worldly escape to people oppressed or overwhelmed by the battered world in which they find themselves, even aligned with those perpetrating the battering of the planet and its impoverished masses for the sake of gold. In fairness, though, it must be said that the majority of religious leaders are well-meaning. But they are as baffled by the unprecedented situation as everyone else and find it as hard as anyone to change customary attitudes and styles of living. They also recall, rightly, that religion *is* supposed to offer meaning and goals to human life that are not just limited to this world but go beyond it—so they can say, if this world passes away, all is still not lost. But this attitude still faces the challenging task of fitting in with an ethic of compassionate responsibility toward the world and those enmeshed in its toils.

Gender Inequity

Bound up with these problems is a growing sense that the relative roles of women and men in society, including their roles in religious life, need to be profoundly rethought and reordered. In Chapter 1 we referred to the quite justified insistence of critics dissatisfied with a purely descriptive approach to world religions that questions like the role of religion in the oppression of women must be addressed. Looking first at religion itself, they correctly point out that the teaching and institutional power of the major religions are almost exclusively male, from their founding to the present. All of the religious founders, saviours, and authoritative teachers are male, and the chief God is generally designated male as well. Virtually all the scriptures and creeds are penned by men or were received by divine inspiration through men, and it goes without saying that religious power-structures—priesthoods, the ministerial profession, the office of the religious teacher or jurist, even the role of prophet or shaman—have been effectively controlled by men, though women have sometimes been given a certain place within them.

Furthermore, in their views of God, nature, and society, religions stand accused of promoting teachings that effectively put and keep women in subordinate roles, concerned with home and family while men concern themselves with the larger affairs of public and religious life. One way or another, all major religions have traditionally said that God, the gods, heaven, or dharma intended women and men to have distinct roles, with men in the position of dominating public life and exercising leadership and women structurally in a place of greater dependence and obedience, especially within the all-important arena of family life. The reader must decide whether she or he believes this is as it should be. But one cannot deny that in most societies these traditional religious precepts are bound up with social, political, and economic patterns that have still given women little more than minority representation in the worlds of culture, business, and government.

Yet it is also clear that in the matter of gender inequity (and also inequity based on sexual orientation) discontent is reaching critical mass in both religion and society, and change is in process. How far it will go, and what the ultimate product will look like, is impossible to say at this point. Probably there has never been a society, or religion, with real gender equality in decision making or access to the sacred, though some tribal societies may have come closer to it than "civilization." Thus, we have no working model for large-scale gender equality in either religion or society, and those who labor for such institutions will need to plan for a future that rejects the absolute authority of the past and devises its own models. In a moment we will see how this is being done in some religious contexts.

Will gender equality make a difference to the other current problems we have cited: the prospect of nuclear holocaust, those the technological revolution has spawned, the ecological and population crises? It is hard to say because, again, we have no model of such a society to use as a benchmark. Some argue that women inherently approach life and its problems with attitudes grounded in compassion, human sensitivity, nurturance, and a feeling for interdependency, in contrast to the male proclivities for law, order, individualism, and individual responsibility. The latter values, they say, have their place but easily lead into a "control mentality," with oppression of the weak (including women), rampant exploitation of the earth, and war. They need desperately to be at least counterbalanced by women's values. Only then can the present crises, which stem in no small part from hyperinflation of male values, be managed. Only then will heretofore strong and weak become truly sensitive to each other, the earth be seen as our mother rather than an object to be raped, and humanity attain the level of cooperative interdependence necessary to give the planet a viable future. Even overpopulation, they say, is directly related to women's lack of effective control over their bodies and their lives.

Others reply that men and women are not really *that* different. The special values attributed to women in the preceding paragraph are simply those that become important as survival strategies to all repressed classes, male or female, and both men and women take on the second set of values when their hand is on levers of real power. They point to the fact that as women have, in recent years, moved in considerable numbers into vocations such as business, law, and politics, and in certain countries have attained the top presidential or prime ministerial positions, more often than not their policies and values have not been conspicuously different from those of their male colleagues. On the other hand, they say, not a few men today do exemplify compassion, sensitivity, and a sense of human interdependency. Like it or not, they say, the need for change is a human need, not a gender issue. By all means, some of them would say, let women and men find equality in all institutions, even religion, but don't expect this of itself to bring in the millenium—that will require profound change on the part of both sexes.

Other, more conservative voices would argue that if women and men are really no better than each other except in values attuned to particular stations (we need nurturance in the home, individualism in business, a sense for law and order in the capital) then traditional values and roles are really best after all.

But while the jury (comprised of both men and women) is still out on some of these issues, two things are certain. The first is that far-reaching changes *will* occur in the 1990s and the twenty-first century in the roles of the two genders in society, the state, and religion. No large and complex society can really stay static for long in any case, and the pressures for change plus the potentially destabilizing problems that face us are clearly too great to allow things to remain as they are. In fact, the changes, though perhaps as yet only in their preliminary stages, are obviously underway all around us. The second certainty is that women will consequently have a major—possibly even a primary—role in solving, or trying to solve, the immense crises of war, technology, ecology, and population that the next century will have to deal with, as it confronts the debit side of the twentieth century's legacy. Women may also have a major role in restructuring religion to dwell effectively in a world of such challenges. How successful women—together with men—are in a world of such awesome trials will have very much to do with the future of gender, and religion, in centuries to come.

Here then are some religious responses to these issues of power in the contemporary world. They include religious liberalism and fundamentalism, religious feminism, new religious movements, and quasi-religious secularism.

RELIGIOUS TRENDS TODAY

Liberalism

A "liberal" approach to a religion may be defined as one which contends that its tradition formulae need not be interpreted literally or solely in terms of their interpretation in previous eras, but rather must be understood in light of the best current standards of reasonable thought and scientific truth. Religious liberals are also characteristically concerned about social justice issues as much as those of personal experience or salvation, and they are inclined to take positions similar to those of political liberals toward them—though of course exceptions can occur.

Religious liberalism is nothing new. Thinkers who have tried to put their religion in language harmonious with that of the leading philosophy and science of their day have no doubt existed as long as religion; we have mentioned such schools as the Mu'tazila in Islam, the medieval Christian scholastics with their recovery of Aristotle as a philosophical foundation, and the Neo-Confucians in China. But in the late nineteenth and twentieth centuries the movement has been especially forceful because of the unprecedented array of new scientific ideas, from evolution to psychoanalysis, it must deal with. It has also been more forcefully concerned with social reform than in most periods in the past.

Yet as the century draws to a close, the picture of religious liberalism is unclear. Powerful liberalizing forces have been at work. Despite some opposition in high places, the Roman Catholic Church is far more liberal than before Vatican II. Major movements such as "feminist theology" and "liberation theology," liberal by our definition though they go beyond conventional liberalism, have made profound and probably irreversible changes in religious consciousness in Christianity, Judaism, and elsewhere. Under the influence of persons such as Gandhi, Hinduism has done much to liberalize the roles of castes and of women.

At the same time, liberal Protestant denominations are in decline, and new spiritual movements around the world seem little concerned with the conventional philosophy/science/reform liberal program. They are more likely, one way or another, to push for radical (that is, "striking-at-the-root") changes in theology or society than the thoughtful but often fairly comfortable way of the conventional liberal. The latter, after all, have been seen in highly respectable "mainline" churches, universities, or brahminical circles more often than among those actually suffering from the way things are, however genuine their compassion is toward them. Moreover, the world of the conventional liberal is in disarray as society fragments and people seem less sure what "conventional wisdom" is, with science plagued by ecological guilt and the politics of both liberals and conservatives thrust into an unfamiliar new stage by the precipitous collapse of Marxism as a credible force in the late 1980s, just as the ecological "contradictions of capitalism" are coming true. All this has cut some ground from under the conventional liberal in favor of radical—or radical conservative—options.

Traditionalism and Fundamentalism

These are both terms used to designate people who do *not* believe that religion should be reinterpreted to fit prevailing views, but rather that its authority is independent of the world in which it lives and must be presented in the same language in season and out. Change in a religion believed to be true is a contradiction in terms, and it must therefore be denied symbolically by allowing little if any change in religious language, moral values, or practice. Traditionalism is the stance of those who adhere to a religious form still living and continuous with a long past but perceived to be beleaguered today, as among Roman Catholic "traditionalists." Similarly, fundamentalism puts additional stress on the infallibility—as true now as ever—of the religion's written sources; today they also tend to see their world under seige.

The appeal of traditionalism and fundamentalism in a world of confusing change and uncertain prospects is obvious. For many, it is important that at least one area of life seem secure, linked to one's roots in the past and able to stand still while everything else is reeling. Indeed, many people in this camp argue vehemently that the only sure answers to the complexities of modern life lie in "traditional values," and that by returning to them and building society on them we can reverse those trends that have made the world a dismaying place. Thus, as we have seen, Islamic "fundamentalists," as in the Iranian revolution, have determined to resist pernicious outside influences by restoring the authority of Islamic law in all areas of life. In the West, many Christian fundamentalists call for a return to strict Christian morality to counter the moral chaos in the world. (It is often less clear, however, what fundamentalists would do about the technological revolution, from which they have greatly benefitted around the world, or its demographic and ecological spawn. These, critics say, will require more than the exhortations to personal morality and the focus on issues such as sexuality or abortion with which fundamentalists tend to feel most at home.)

Much has been made of the late-twentieth-century revival of traditionalism and fundamentalism in several religions, and certainly they have been highly visible forces. However, careful analysis has sometimes revealed that this is not because those groups have been successful in winning over large numbers of "liberals" so much as that they have done much better at retaining the numbers they have long had and have acquired a new confidence manifesting itself in a conspicuous political and media presence in many countries. But the real size and staying power of their following in the difficult years ahead remains to be seen.

Religious Feminism

We have already presented issues raised by critics of traditional religion concerned with gender equality. Now we need to look at the responses of these critics who still believe there is nonetheless much of great value in the world's religious heritage. Not a few critics believe that religion can be reformed and indeed can be a powerful engine in the reforms needed generally to correct traditional oppression of women in many societies.

They point out that although religions have characteristically embraced and legitimated oppressive social structures, with males on top in family and the state, in their core experience of salvation or enlightenment most religions are remarkably gender-free. Women and men can be saved and inwardly transformed and can become saints and bodhisattvas if not bishops or mandarins. Thus, there is no gender inequality at religion's absolute heart.

They note also that in most religions there is a tradition of social as well as spiritual liberation (the Exodus of ancient Israel from slavery, the Islamic *jihad* on behalf of justice) and set this alongside the conservative side of religion that tends to uphold existing social norms, however repressive. This means, they say, that religion can be an instrument for powerful, overcoming social change that liberates women and all others who suffer wrong. The model exists and can be transferred to the cause at hand.

Within religious institutions, change is happening. Though they were very much the exception in the past, today a high percentage of the leading saints and spiritual teachers in Hinduism are women. Buddhism in the West, unlike the East, has significant female leadership. In many Christian denominations, women are now eligible for ordination, and the number of women ministers is growing at a rate that suggests parity with males in a generation or so. Even in those churches that do not ordain women, they have notably greater voice and spiritual freedom than, say, in 1950. Women are now ordained to the rabbinate in all but Orthodox Judaism. Along with women's ordination are coming changes in the language of worship and even translations of scripture to remove "sexist" connotations.

For some feminist critics that is enough. They will be content with traditional

Emergent leadership of women in religion: Barbara Harris became the first female bishop in the history of the Anglican church in 1989.

Judaism, Christianity, Buddhism, Hinduism, or another faith so long as women have equal access to leadership and the grosser abuses of the past in language and religion's social role are alleviated. They generally look to the positive "liberation" side of religion we have cited, and they want to keep great religious traditions intact because they basically believe in their core nonsexist salvation experience and they believe they can still be used as mighty vehicles for the social and spiritual liberation of women and others.

But for others, most traditional religion is hopelessly compromised by sexism at its very core, with its male Gods and scriptures and patriarchies. No amount of cosmetic change in contemporary worship language or lately invented women's ordinations can save them from such an unbalanced heritage in the eyes of these more radical religious feminists. They contend instead that a new genuinely feminist religion—maybe even a new kind of religion—needs to be discovered. For this reason some, aligned with the "Neo-Pagan" movement, are experimenting with worship of the Goddess, or Goddess and God together, rather than the old God commonly spoken of as "He." They are developing new songs and rituals and modes of worship to go with such a new religion, one frequently oriented toward peace and nature as well as women's spirituality.

To *their* critics in turn the whole idea of a new religion, or a newly remodeled form of old paganism concocted to meet current ideological requirements, is somewhat ridiculous. Any genuine religion, they say, has to be based on divine revelation or authentic long-standing tradition; the notion of a new self-made or self-discovered religion, if not downright blasphemous, is at least naive about what religion is and how it works. Further, the radicals should not so easily give up the immense social power and liberating language of the traditional great religions but should work from within them.

So the argument goes. It is not resolved, but surely the religious world can never again be the same as it was before such bold criticisms and proposals were openly made.

New Religious Movements

Widespread discussion of new and unconventional religions has been another feature of the twentieth-century scene. We have looked at the colorful and significant new religions of Japan and Africa. In the United States, attention has been devoted to groups such as the "Hare Krishnas," the Unification Church ("Moonies"), and UFO cults. Although most such controversial new movements are quite small compared to the established faiths, they are of intrinsic interest and may be indicative of emergent religious needs and trends.

Groups of this sort are sometimes spoken of as "cults" or "sects," though those terms need to be used with caution since they are usually taken as pejorative and can easily lend themselves to stereotyping a movement. We need to realize that not all unconventional religions are the same, and moreover that they can and do change over years and generations. Nonetheless, new religious movements generally have certain features in common. These derive from the fact that, as small and sometimes denigrated alternatives to the dominant spirituality, they need to have a living, immediate, experiential attraction powerful enough to focus the latent alienation many followers will have and to countermand the family, ethnic, and community ties they own toward established religion.

This means that new religious movements are likely to have a strong, charismatic central figure who draws people into his or her presence and contrasts with the more institutional leadership of normative religion. The new religion's social expression may be in a close-knit, supportive group that is like a surrogate family or community. Practice may be centered on a single, simple technique—meditation, chanting, ritual, a form of prayer—that for some at least induces directly felt changes

Oil painting by woman devotee of Hare Krishna.

of consciousness or benefits in life. Finally, the group's teaching may be sufficiently different from the normative religion to offer a significant contrast.

When a movement like this attains reasonable success, it tells us several things about the religious environment. First, traditional spiritual cohesion is weakening, permitting a sense of actual or potential pluralism that allows experimentation. Second, many people sense a spiritual identity within themselves which is different from that offered by the traditional faith. Third, for them, immediate experience is more important than the social ties sanctified by the established faith of family and ethnic group. Fourth, especially in the case of people joining intensive groups, there is a need for a surrogate family, perhaps surrogate parents, suggesting a lack felt in those institutions. Last, and most important, it tells us that people sense times are changing, and therefore customary institutions no longer have the legitimacy they once had; the claim that God is working something new for a new age can be taken seriously.

It should not be thought, though, that these characteristics are unique to the contemporary world. There are many new religions today, but there have always been many, probably more than we will ever know, for no doubt some in ages past have vanished without a trace. Yet their relative rise and fall is a barometer of how free people feel, whether out of alienation or confidence, to separate themselves from conventional faith.

Secularism

One of the big topics of discussion in contemporary sociology of religion is "secularization," that is, whether religion is losing force in society and, on a more subjective level, as a real power in the minds of people. Some say it is obvious that it is, pointing to the dramatic fall in recent decades in church attendance and other religious participation in places like Western Europe and East Asia and the fact that religion no longer has the near-monopoly it once had in the educational and artistic worlds. Skeptics of secularization point to the persistence of high levels of religious activity in other places, such as the United States and the Islamic world, and say that religion may not really have been quite as powerful in the past as is commonly supposed either.

Whichever side is right, plain secularism—a lack of interest in religion and a willingness to live one's life just in terms of this-world's goals and values—is yet another powerful option in the complicated current religious scene. Sheer indifference will limit the gains of liberals, traditionalists, fundamentalists, and new religionists alike, and secular values—saying that what is important is what gives people a good life here and now as measured by worldly relationships and assets—will be there to challenge their values based on heaven, hell, and sacred experience. Secularism could, in fact, point to one possible religious future.

RELIGIOUS FUTURES

We will end our discussion with a glance at such possible religious futures.

Secularism

First, *secularism*. It may be that the secularism described above will increase to crowd out religious values rather thoroughly, especially on the higher levels of education and culture, leaving us with a lingering folk religion at best. Some indications point in this direction. Even in the United States, where local religious participation remains high, faith is not the part of intellectual and national cultural life it once was and is less a factor in education than in the past. Yet this scenario must contend with the oft-demonstrated power of religion to revive itself and the prospect that the ecological and other crises of the next century could create the kinds of tensions and yearnings that go into religious revivals.

New Religions and New Religious Founders

Could one of the new religious movements mentioned above become a new world religion? Could a new religious founder in the pattern of the Buddha or Jesus arise to proclaim successfully a new religion for our time? Probably not. The age of originating great founder religions, and of their faiths sweeping nations and continents as of old, seems to have come and gone. Undoubtedly many people will be converted from one religion to another in the future as they are today. But the very individualism and pluralism that is so much a feature of contemporary faith ought to suggest that not all will go the same direction at the same time. Further, it is hard to imagine a *new* founder in our day having quite the sacred mystique and transcendence of the Buddha or Jesus in theirs, at least in the eyes of the public. Our news media, with their TV cameras and investigative reporters, create different sorts of images than in days when news traveled more slowly and easily adapted itself to mythic models before it was finally written down. We still live largely in the world constructed by the great religious founders, but we will not see their like again.

Syncretism

Some have suggested that world religion might become syncratic, that is, taking the "best" elements of each to form a new universal religion. But as appealing as this idea may seem to some, it does not reflect the way religion really works in history. To be sure, as the world becomes more of a global village, more and more exchanges of ideas and even practices may occur between faiths, as they have in the past. The rosary, for example, is a practice that seems to have originated in the Middle East and been picked up by several faiths. To see this happening wholesale, though, so that all religions are caught up in a "super-religion" is to overlook the integralist and exclusivist drives in all religion that counterbalance that tendency. There are always those who believe strongly—as the traditionalists and fundamentalists exemplify—that their faith must maintain its own purity and integrity. Moreover, in difficult times the trend is usually toward that mentality or toward the emergence of equally rigorous new religious movements.

The religious future, then, may be not too different from the past, with its indications every which way. Then again, it may not. Something totally surprising and unexpected may happen. We will see.[2]

In the present book, however, our task has been the fascinating historical and descriptive one. We have traced out some of the paths religion has followed through the years, and some of us may have found that just to be in the presence of all this variegated richness is in itself an awareness-expanding, even a religious, experience.

To feel this way before the past and present is a good prelude for turning to the future.

QUESTIONS FOR REVIEW

1. What is your view of the current religious scene? Is religion in permanent decline, or is it undergoing radical change?
2. What understandings have you gained from your study of diverse faiths that will aid you in your own spiritual development?

Glossary

Advaita Vedanta   Philosophy emphasizing nondualism; teaches that all is really Brahman; what appears as other than Brahman is maya, or Brahman's appearance in forms not absolute in themselves.

Allah   "The God"; the Muslim title for the one sovereign God.

Amidism   Pure Land Buddhism.

Anatman   No self or no ego; the Buddhist teaching that there is no separate individual human self; humans are instead an impermanent collection of parts, the five skandhas (form, sense, perception, karmic impulses, consciousness).

Ancestral spirits   The souls of ancestors, believed by many peoples to continue to take an active interest in their communities, and capable of great harm if displeased.

Ancestrism   The veneration of ancestors as semi-deified figures to whom offerings and worship are presented.

Anglican   The post-Reformation term for the Church of England and its daughter churches throughout the world, such as the Episcopal church in the United States; it retains both Catholic and Protestant features.

Animism   Belief in the widespread presence of souls or spirits, both of the departed and animating natural objects.

Apocalyptic   From the Greek for "disclosure" or "revelation"; refers to teachings that characteristically claim to be a special revelation and predict a time of troubles followed by dramatic action by God to defeat evil and establish righteousness.

Apostle   From the Greek for "a person sent forth," one of the twelve disciples of Jesus and Paul after beginning their missionary work subsequent to the life of Jesus on earth.

Arhant   One who has obtained complete enlightenment, without becoming a saviour of others as a bodhisattva or Buddha; the term especially characteristic of Theravada Buddhism, where the latter vocations are seen as unique to the one Buddha of a world or age.

Arminianism   Belief that one has free will to decide for or against faith in Christ, in contrast to a strict Calvinist view of divine election and predestination.

Ash'arism   The immensely influential school of Muslim theology that emphasizes that the ways of God are beyond human understanding; human knowledge of God, it says, can only be based on revelation.

Ashrama   In Hinduism, a stage of life, or a retreat under the guidance of a guru.

Atman   The soul or essence of one's self, said to be actually nothing other than Brahman.

Avatar   An animal or human form taken by a god on earth; an incarnation of God, like Rama or Krishna.

Ayatollah   In Shi'ite Islam, a legal and religious teacher regarded as possessing very great learning and righteousness, whose authority is believed to be backed by that of the infallible hidden Imam.

Bardo   The dharmakaya plus the heavenly or transcendent-but-with-wondrous-forms expression of the Buddha-nature in Tibetan.

397

Bar Mitzvah   Rite of passage for a young man, when he is able to read the Hebrew scriptures in synagogue or temple, thereby undertaking the obligation of the Law; in Reform and Conservative Judaism, an equivalent Bat Mitzvah may be held for women.

Bhagavad-Gita   Classic quasi-scriptural text emphasizing karma-yoga and bhakti.

Bhakti   Spiritual path based on love for one's chosen deity.

Bodhisattva   "Enlightenment being"; in Mahayana, a being on the path to enlightenment who has taken a vow to help all other beings and who works through wisdom and compassion for them in the world; in Theravada, a Buddha in a past lifetime when he is on the way to Buddhahood; in both, a future Buddha.

Brahman   The universal being; God, understood to be not so much personal as source and essence of all existence.

Brahmin   The priestly caste.

Buddha   An enlightened or awakened one.

Caliph   Leader of Islam regarded as successor of Muhammad in his capacity as temporal (political, this-worldly) ruler of the faithful.

Calvinism   The Reformation teaching and practice of John Calvin, who emphasized God's sovereignty in calling whom he will to salvation—a concept often called divine predestination.

Canonization   In the Roman Catholic Church, the procedure by which the Pope officially recognizes a person as a saint.

Canon of Scripture   The proper selection and order of books to make up a scriptural authority; in the case of Christianity, of the Old and New Testaments.

Cao Dai   A spiritualistic and syncretistic new religious movement in Vietnam.

Caste   Social group traditionally believed to be an expression of dharma and based on relative purity; caste may determine with whom one may eat, and one's residence, marriage, and occupation.

Chakras   In some yogic teaching, centers of spiritual power along the spinal column, which can be opened by raising the kundalini.

Chan   Chinese Buddhism, influenced by Taoism, emphasizing meditation, interaction of master and disciple, and nature; Zen in Japan.

Ch'ondogyo   An important new religious movement in Korea which has advocated worship of the God of Heaven, a combination of features of all major Korean spiritual traditions, and social reform.

Conditioned reality   Reality as we ordinarily experience it, limited and constrained by space, time, and the patterns of thought and feeling that shape our response to it.

Conservative Judaism   School of Judaism teaching that the principles of the Law are important, but practice may be modified to meet contemporary conditions.

Cosmic religion   Religion centered on nature—the turn of the seasons, sacred places such as holy trees and mountains.

Cult   A minority religion characteristically centered on a charismatic leader and combining teachings and practices from several sources.

Cultus   A particular form of worship or devotion.

Dao   Way, Existence, Nature, or God; the Chinese term for infinite Reality.

Denomination   In Protestant Christianity, a church organization comprised of a number of local churches, having a distinctive and autonomous structure, and probably some distinctive doctrines and forms of worship, while recognizing itself as only a part of the larger church of Christ on Earth; e.g. Methodist, Baptist, or Presbyterian churches.

Deus otiosus   "Hidden god"; term used for a creator god who after making the world withdraws from it, leaving day-to-day affairs in the hands of secondary gods and spirits.

Devotionalism   Emphasis on deeply felt prayer and meditation.

Dharma The cosmic order, which works for righteousness, and to which the righteous adhere; one's own duty.

Dharmakaya The expression of the Buddha-nature as essence of the universe, a term and meaning really identical in Mahayana with Nirvana or the Void. Called the Clear Light of the Void in *The Tibetan Book of the Dead.*

Divine Dark Mystical term for God beyond all words and concepts.

Doctrine A statement expresses basic beliefs of a religion in propositional form.

Ecstasy In religion, in a state of powerful rapture, trance, or alteration of consciousness believed to open one to spiritual experience, inspiration, or possession.

Ecumenical Movement The modern movement for mutual understanding among the branches of Christianity, toward increasing cooperation among them, with the hope of eventual Christian reunion.

Eightfold Path Right understanding, thought, speech, action, livelihood, effort, mindfulness, and concentration, or *samadhi*—the fundamental ideals of Buddhist life and practice as taught by the Buddha.

Eschatology Doctrines concerning the "last things": death, heaven, hell, judgment, resurrection of the dead, the end of the present world.

Evangelicalism Term widely used to refer to those forms of Protestantism that emphasize the supreme authority of Scripture and salvation by faith—sometimes expressed by a powerful conversion experience—in the atonement of Jesus.

The Exodus The journey of the Israelites under Moses out of Egypt to the Promised Land.

Fana Sufi term for mystical absorption in the Divine.

Four Noble Truths The truth of suffering; the truth of attachment as the cause of suffering; the truth of the end of attachment; and the Eightfold Path as the way to end it—the basic Buddhist teaching as presented by the Buddha in his first sermon.

Friday Mosque A mosque large enough to hold the entire population of a community, designated as the place for its Friday noon service.

General Council A meeting of bishops recognized as authoritative in teaching Christian belief and practice by the Eastern Orthodox and Roman Catholic churches; the former accepts only the first seven, the latter a longer list including the Second Vatican Council of 1962–65.

Guru In Hinduism, a spiritual teacher or guide; the disciple's relation to the guru is generally considered sacred.

Hadith Traditions of what Muhammad did or said which, in Islamic law and traditional scholarship, are believed divinely inspired and have great authority, together with the Koran, in establishing orthodox teaching and practice.

Hajj The Muslim pilgrimage to Mecca.

Hanifs Believers in one God who predated Muhammad, including Abraham and some pre-Islamic Arabs.

Hasidism Popular Jewish mystical and devotional movement beginning in eighteenth-century Eastern Europe.

Hatha Yoga The yoga of physical postures.

Hermit In religion, a person who lives alone in an isolated place to devote himself or herself to prayer and meditation.

High God A sovereign deity who created the world or humankind, and who may sustain the moral law, but who may not be involved in everyday affairs.

High Holy Days Rosh Hashana and Yom Kippur; see text for description.

Hijra Muhammad's flight from Mecca to Medina in 622 C.E.; the date from which the Muslim calendar begins.

History History is not just the story of what has happened. It is also a perspective on what it means to be human. It involves two key assumptions: that we can isolate some past events as far more important than others and that human life in this world is moving along an irreversible time-stream. We may speak of the movement when these realizations really sink in and begin to shape people's attitudes as the "discovery of history." That was a moment which, in turn, had immense consequences for religion.

Holy Communion   The rite of consecrating and consuming bread and wine in remembrance of Jesus' Last Supper with his disciples before the crucifixion; the principle service of worship in Roman Catholic, Eastern Orthodox, and some Protestant churches; also called the Eucharist (ancient and sometimes Anglican term, now often used in ecumenical contexts), Divine Liturgy (Eastern Orthodox), Mass (Roman Catholic), Lord's Supper (Protestant).

Imam   A trained Muslim teacher and preacher; in Shi'a Islam, a supernaturally endowed supreme teacher and leader of Islam who is a hereditary successor of the Prophet.

Incarnation   Becoming flesh; the Christian doctrine that in Jesus Christ, God (i.e., God the Son, the second person of the Trinity) took on flesh and became a human being.

Initiation   A process, often arduous, through which a person passes, usually in a traditional programmatic way, to acquire spiritual power and social status within a community, whether as adult member or as shaman.

Islam   "Submission" in Arabic; name of the religion.

Ismailis or "Seveners"   A minority within Shi'a who differ from the Twelvers on the identity of the seventh Imam, who, they believe, is the last and hidden one. Ismailism has incorporated many esoteric elements into its beliefs.

Jainism   Ancient Indian religion emphasizing the attainment of freedom from karma and material existence, as taught by sage-ascetics.

Jewish festivals   Major feasts and festivals include Passover, Shavuot, Sukkot, Purim, and Hanuka; see text for descriptions.

Kaaba   The cubical temple of Mecca that is the focus of pilgrimage.

Kabbala   Medieval system of mystical philosophy.

Kami   Shinto deities.

Karma   Cosmic and personal cause and effect by which one's thoughts and deeds determine what happens to one, whether good or bad, including one's future rebirths. In moksha, one transcends karma.

Karma-yoga   Attaining liberation through selfless work in the world and following one's own dharma.

Kingdom of God or Kingdom of Heaven   The reign or rule of God where God's will is done and his power is evident, which Jesus said is both present and coming through his ministry.

Koan   In Chan or Zen, an enigmatic riddle or saying intended to challenge ordinary rational thought and help one realize one's true nature.

Koran (sometimes Qur'an)   The sacred scriptures of Islam.

Kundalini   In some yogic teaching, coiled power at the base of the spine which can be raised for spiritual growth.

Li   Confucian term for rites, propriety, courtesy; suggests that doing things with correct form has religious and cosmic meaning.

Lingam   The sacred pillar that symbolizes Shiva.

Lotus Sutra   A sutra of Indian origin extremely influential in Chinese and Japanese Buddhism, especially Tian tai, Tendai, and Nichiren. It emphasizes simple devotion and the universal grace of the Buddha.

Lutheran   The Reformation teaching and practice of Martin Luther, who emphasized the sole authority of scripture and "justification by faith," the receiving of God's saving grace through inward faith, as cornerstones of Christianity; the term is used more in America than in Europe.

Magi   Order of priests or seers in ancient Persia and the Hellenistic world.

Mahayana   The "Great Vehicle," Buddhism of the northern tier of Buddhist countries, including China, Tibet, and Japan; emphasizes the bodhisattva, the

Buddha-nature in all things, and the use of many methods and paths to enlightenment.

Mandala In Buddhism, a meditation diagram showing arrangements of buddhas and bodhisattvas.

Mantra A set of sacred words or syllables chanted or meditated on to bring spiritual power or to unite one with the deity they represent.

Martyr From Greek for "witness," one who dies for a faith or cause.

Matsuri Shinto festival.

Maya Brahman manifest in the world of forms; illusion when these forms are seen as other than Brahman.

Messiah The "Anointed One"; in the Judaism of Jesus' time, an expected deliverer and Sublime King who would defeat the enemies of the Jews and establish a divine reign of righteousness. The word *Christ* is a direct Greek translation.

Middle Way The Buddha's path understood as avoiding attachment to all extremes or conditioned, partial realities, conceived of as coming in pairs of opposites.

Mihrab The niche indicating the direction of Mecca in a mosque.

Minaret The tower beside many mosques from which the muezzin calls out the times of prayer.

Minbar The seat atop a short flight of steps in a mosque from which the imam delivers sermons.

Moksha Spiritual liberation.

Monasticism The way of life of the monk or nun, a person who characteristically is celibate (unmarried for religious reasons), without personal possessions, and lives a regulated life of prayer, work, study, and service in a community of such persons. The residence may be called a monastery or convent and is under a superior (abbot, prior, father superior, mother superior) to whom the others owe obedience. Distinctive garb is usually worn by monastics.

Mosque Place of Muslim public worship.

Mount Arafat The hill outside of Mecca where Muhammad gave his farewell sermon in that city and where the faithful on pilgrimage stand throughout the afternoon.

Muezzin One who calls the faithful to prayer from the minaret of the mosque at the proper times.

Mu'tazila An early rationalist school of Islamic thought.

Mysticism Experience or teaching about direct inward experience of divine reality.

Myth A story which expresses something of the fundamental worldview of a society in narrative form.

Neo-Confucianism Confucian philosophy of the twelfth century and after which stressed its metaphysical aspects.

Neolithic "New Stone Age"; the period of the development of archaic agriculture.

Nirvana Unconditioned reality, experienced without form or limit when all attachments have been negated and the fires of craving blown out; the ultimate Buddhist goal.

Ontological From ontology, the philosophical study of being or reality.

Orthodox Correct in doctrine; the name of the ancient churches of the East which recognize the first seven General Councils.

Orthodox Judaism School of Judaism that emphasizes a strict following of the Law as traditionally interpreted.

Paleolithic "Old Stone Age"; the cultural stage of hunting and gathering before agriculture.

Patriarch A title given the bishop of certain ancient and important cities; in particular, the Patriarch of Constantinople (Istanbul) is the senior official of the Eastern Orthodox Church.

Phenomenological approach Looking at religion in a way that tries to set aside one's own prior beliefs and biases to see the phenomena just as they are.

Pluralism The condition, especially apparent in the modern world, in which many different options for belief and lifestyle exist together in the same society.

Pope The Bishop of Rome who, as successor of St. Peter, is believed by Roman Catholics to be head of the Church on Earth and representative of Christ.

Practical form of religious expression A religion's form of worship, prayer, meditation, pilgrimage, and the like. To find a religion's practical expression, start by asking yourself, "What do they *do?*"

Prajnaparamita "Wisdom that has gone beyond"; the highest intuitive-enlightenment wisdom in Mahayana; also, the name of a goddess who personifies it.

Prophet In the Biblical tradition, one who speaks on behalf of God in the context of a particular historical situation.

Purgatory In Roman Catholic teaching, an after-death state in which sins insufficient to warrant eternal punishment in hell are purged away, so that the soul can eventually enter heaven.

Pure Land Form of Buddhism strong in China and Japan emphasizing the believer's entry into paradise (the Pure Land) through faith in the vow of the Buddha Amitabha (Emiduo or Amida) to save all who call upon his name. Called Jodo in Japanese.

Rabbi A Jewish scholar or teacher, particularly the spiritual leader of a congregation.

Ramadan The month of the Islamic calendar during which Muslims fast from sunrise to sundown.

Rasul Muhammad's calling in relation to God; means prophet, envoy, messenger, apostle, ambassador, or spokesman.

Reform Judaism Liberal interpretation of Judaism that emphasizes ethics over following the Law legalistically.

Ren Confucian term for virtue.

Resurrection A raising from the dead.

Rita The Vedic term for the cosmic law or order.

Sabbath The seventh day of the week (Saturday) and Jewish weekly holy day, marked by observant Jews with many special practices and by strict abstention from work.

Sacraments Certain rites believed directly to convey God's grace and to be generally necessary to Christian salvation. Many Protestant churches celebrate the sacraments of baptism and Holy Communion, while Roman Catholic and Eastern Orthodox churches acknowledge five additional sacraments: confirmation, marriage, holy orders, penance, and extreme unction ("last rites").

Sadhu A "holy man" or renunciant who has set aside worldly goals for the sake of the spiritual life.

Saint In Christianity, a person recognized by a church as of exceptional holiness.

Samadhi The highest state of concentration or meditation, when the mind is one with the divine.

Samsara The wheel of rebirth; the world.

Samskaras Hindu "sacraments" or "rites of passage" performed at definite stages of life, from birth through entry into adulthood.

Samgha The Buddhist monastic order.

Shakti Spiritual power, often identified with the female consort of a Hindu deity.

Shaman A person who in many primitive societies through special initiation has powers of spirit-control, divination, healing, and contacting the gods, usually exercised through elaborate performances and in a trance state.

Shari'a The body of Muslim Law.

Shaykh A Sufi, or mystical Islamic, spiritual teacher and guide.

Shi'a Islam The "party" of Ali; the minority, some 10 to 15 percent of all Muslims, who traditionally believe that Islam should be headed by a divinely guided Imam who is a hereditary successor of the Prophet through Ali, Muhammad's cousin.

Shinto "Way of the Gods"; the native polytheistic religion of Japan.

Shirk Idolatry, putting anything else in the place of God; the ultimate and unforgivable sin in Islam.

Sikhism Indian religion emphasizing monotheism and equality; worship centers on its sacred scripture, the Holy Granth.

Skandhas Basic constituents of reality in Buddhist thought; five of them—form, sense, perception, reactions, and consciousness—make up a human being.

Sociological form of religious expression A religion's forms of group life, leadership, relation to outside society, governance, and interpersonal relations. To find a religion's sociological expression, start by asking yourself, "How do they relate to each other?" and "How are they organized?"

Soul The principle of life and consciousness, commonly believed to have a destiny separate from the physical body.

Sufism The mystical tradition in Islam.

Sunna The body of established Islamic faith, morals, and practice, established by consensus of jurists and the faithful.

Sunni Islam The majority body of Muslims who stress sunna and consensus.

Synagogue A Jewish congregation and its meeting place, where worship consists of prayer and instruction rather than the sacrificial offerings of the temple.

Taboo A prohibition, as against eating a certain food or going to a certain place, enforced through fear of anger of gods or spirits if the forbidden act is done.

Talmud A vast, authoritative commentary on the Law composed by rabbis, completed about the sixth century C.E.

Tantrism Spiritual path emphasizing initiation, esoteric rituals, and sexual symbolism.

Tathagata "One who has gone thus" or "come thus"—a title of the Buddha emphasizing his passing from worldly existence into Nirvana.

Tenrikyo One of the modern New Religions of Japan; monotheistic.

Theoretical form of religious expression A religion's stories, concepts, ideas, doctrines. To find a religion's theoretical expression, start by asking yourself, "What do they *say*?"

Theravada "Way of the Elders," the school of Buddhism emphasizing the historical Buddha and a conservative adherence to his teachings as Theravadins understand them; predominant in the Buddhist countries of South and Southeast Asia.

Three Refuges or Three Jewels The Buddha as the ideal teacher; the Dharma as his teaching or "gospel," and the Sangha, or order of monks, as the ideal community—three ideals which a person affirms on formally becoming a Buddhist or a monk.

Torah The common Jewish term for the first five books of the Bible containing the Law.

Totem An animal or plant believed to have a special spiritual relation to a particular tribe or subgroup.

Trikaya The three "bodies" or forms of expression of the Buddha-nature.

Trinity The doctrine that there are three "persons," the Father, the Son (Christ), and the Holy Spirit, in the one God.

Twelvers (Ashariyah) The majority of Shi'ites, who accept the first twelve of the Imams in the line of Ali, believing that the Twelfth has gone into hiding to return as the Mahdi, or messianic saviour, who will establish a paradisal reign on earth just before the end of the world and the judgment.

Ulama Collective term for Muslim religious scholars and teachers who, by consensus, establish correct teaching.

Unconditioned reality The opposite of conditioned reality; reality in its absolute nature equally present in all times and places and not limited in any way.

Upanishad The last and most philosophical of the Vedas, centering around the message that Atman is Brahman; one's true self is the universal divine Reality.

Vajrayana Diamond or Thunderbolt Vehicle; the esoteric or Tantric school of Buddhism emphasizing initiation, mantras, visualizing, and a special elaborate set of symbols and pictures.

Varnas Major groupings of castes in Hinduism; literally, "colors." The four varnas are brahmins, priests; kshatriyas, rulers and warriors; vaishyas, craftsman and merchants; and shudras, farmers and peasants.

Vedas The ancient Hindu scriptures in Sanskrit and comprised of the Rig Veda, Brahmanas, Aranyakas, and Upanishads. The first three parts are concerned mainly with the words, rituals, and meaning of the sacrificial rites of the brahmin priests.

Vipassana meditation Theravada method of meditation that aims at analyzing one's experience until one realizes through it that conditioned reality is impermanent, unsatisfactory, and has no "self."

Word, or Word of God (1) Jesus Christ as manifestation of God; (2) the Scripture understood as directly revealed by God. (An emphasis on the "Word" aspect of Christianity usually entails an emphasis on scripture, preaching, and a relation of inward faith to Jesus Christ.)

Yang and Yin The interacting cosmic principles, respectively masculine and feminine.

Yoga A spiritual path designed to unite one with God or one's true self; in a more restrictive sense, spiritual exercises involving postures, breathing, and meditation.

Zionism The movement to establish a Jewish homeland in Palestine.

Zoroastrianism Monotheistic religion of Persian origin; adherents are called Parsees in India.

PHOTO CREDITS

Notes

Chapter 1

[1] Different terms are used in most traditions for this category; the following are only examples. It should be made clear that these "conditioned" categories are not necessarily evil; they are just arenas of ignorance and separateness and therefore where evil or sin is possible.

[2] Joachim Wach, *Sociology of Religion* (Chicago: University of Chicago Press, 1944), pp. 17–34.

[3] See, for example, Nancy Auer Falk and Rita M. Gross, *Unspoken Worlds: Women's Religious Lives* (Belmont, CA: Wadsworth Publishing Co., 1989).

[4] A book on ethics in world religions which combines description and critique is Denise Lardner Carmody and John Tully Carmody, *How to Live Well: Ethics in the World Religions* (Belmont, CA: Wadsworth Publishing Co., 1988).

[5] In this book B.C.E. (Before the Christian or Common Era) and C.E. (Christian or Common Era) are used rather than B.C. and A.D.

Chapter 2

[1] For the meaning of the term *cosmic religion,* see Mircea Eliade, *Cosmos and History* (New York: Harper & Row, 1959); and *The Sacred and the Profane* (New York: Harper & Row, 1961).

[2] For further anthropological discussion of the American Halloween, see Victor W. Turner, *The Ritual Process* (Chicago: Aldine, 1969), pp. 172–74.

[3] "'Internal Conversion' in Contemporary Bali," mimeographed, 1961, p. 3. Cited in Robert N. Bellah, *Religion and Progress in Modern Asia* (New York: Free Press, 1965), p. 176.

[4] James G. Frazer, *The Belief in Immortality* (London: Macmillan, 1913), Vol. 1, pp. 72–73, quoting A. J. Kruijt.

[5] Paul Schebesta, *Among the Forest Dwarfs of Malaya* (London: Hutchinson, 1927), pp. 185–87.

[6] Frazer, *Immortality,* pp. 250–54.

[7] Mircea Eliade, *Shamanism: Archaic Techniques of Ecstasy,* trans. Willard R. Trask, Bollingen Series LXXVI, Bollingen Foundation (1964), 190–97.

[8] Peter Freuchen, *Book of the Eskimos* (New York: Fawcett World Library, 1965), pp. 168–71.

[9] See, for example, Peter L. Furst, ed., *Flesh of the Gods: The Ritual Use of Hallucinogens* (New York: Praeger, 1972); Michael J. Harner, ed., *Hallucinogens and Shamanism* (London and New York: Oxford University Press, 1973); and Barbara G. Myerhoff, *Peyote Hunt: The Sacred Journey of the Huichol Indians* (Ithaca: Cornell University Press, 1974).

[10] *Shamanism: Archaic Techniques of Ecstasy,* by Mircea Eliade, trans. by Willard R. Trask. Bollingen Series LXXVL Copyright © 1964 by Bollingen Foundation. Reprinted by permission of Princeton University Press from pages 60–61.

[11] See Eliade, *Shamanism;* and Andreas Lommel, *Shamanism: The Beginning of Art* (New York: McGraw-Hill, 1967), pp. 11–12.

[12] Franz Boas, *The Religion of the Kwakiutl, Columbia University Contributions to Anthropology,* 10, part 2 (New York: 1930), 1–11. Summarized in Claude Lévi-Strauss, *Structural Anthropology* (Garden City, NY: Doubleday, 1967), pp. 169–73.

[13] Ichiro Hori, *Folk Religion in Japan* (Chicago: University of Chicago Press, 1968), pp. 203–6.

[14] Frank G. Speck, *Naskapi* (Norman: University of Oklahoma Press, 1935), pp. 83–84.

[15] See John Batchelor, *The Ainu and their Folk-Lore* (London: Religious Tract Society, 1901), pp. 483–95; and Joseph M. Kitagawa, "Aimu Bear Festival (Iyomante)," *History of Religions,* 1, no. 1 (Summer 1961), 95–151.

[16] For a critical assessment of hunting ritual and its relation to hunting reality, see Jonathon Z. Smith, *Imagining Religion* (Chicago: University of Chicago Press, 1982), pp. 57–65.

[17] James Mooney, "The Ghost-Dance Religion and the Sioux Outbreak of 1890," *Annual Report of the Bureau of American Ethnology,* 14, no. 2 (Washington, DC: 1896), pp. 721, 724. Cited in Eliade, *The Sacred and the Profane,* p. 138.

[18] Mircea Eliade, *Myth and Reality* (New York: Harper & Row, 1963), pp. 104–5.

[19] T. C. Hodson, *The Naga Tribes of Manipur* (London: Macmillan, 1911), pp. 104–5.

[20] Michael J. Harner, *The Jivaro: People of the Sacred Waterfalls* (Garden City, NY: Doubleday, 1972), p. 147.

[21] Mircea Eliade, *Patterns in Comparative Religion* (New York: Sheed & Ward, 1958), pp. 344–45.

Chapter 3

[1] Betty Heimann, *Facets of Indian Thought* (London: George Allen & Unwin, 1964).

[2] Robert S. Ellwood, *Religious and Spiritual Groups in Modern America* (Englewood Cliffs, NJ: Prentice-Hall, Inc., 1973), p. 217.

[3] See A. L. Basham, *The Wonder that Was India* (New York: Grove Press, 1959), Chapter 2.

[4] There is a collection of similar words, confusing at first, that are built on this root. Brahma is the creator god of some Indian mythology. Brahman (the neuter form) is used in philosophical writing from the Upanishads on to refer to the impersonal Absolute. The Brahmanas are sacred ritual texts that are a part of the Vedas. Brahmans are the priestly caste, presumably so-called because they possessed mysterious and magical power like that by which the world is sustained. For the sake of clarity, in this book the common spelling *brahmin* will be used for the priests.

[5] R. Gordon Wasson, *Soma: Divine Mushroom of Immortality* (New York: Harcourt Brace Jovanovich, 1969). See also R. Gordon Wasson, "What Was the Soma of the Aryans?" in *Flesh of the Gods,* ed. Peter T. Furst, pp. 201–13.

[6] Mircea Eliade, *Yoga: Immortality and Freedom* (New York: Bollingen Foundation, 1958), Chapter 3.

[7] Swami Prabhavananda and Frederick Manchester, trans., *The Upanishads: Breath of the Eternal* (New York: Mentor Books, 1957), pp. 123–24. Copyright © 1957 by the Vedanta Society of Southern California. Reprinted with permission.

[8] Ibid., pp. 18–19.

[9] On this period and the following, see Basham, *The Wonder That Was India.*

[10] Swami Prabhavananda and Christopher Isherwood, *How to Know God: The Yoga Aphorisms of Patanjali* (New York: Mentor Books, 1969); Eliade, *Yoga;* and Alain Danielou, *Yoga: The Method of Reintegration* (New York: University Books, 1955).

[11] Swami Prabhavananda and Christopher Isherwood, *The Song of God: Bhagavad-Gita* (New York: Mentor Books, 1951), p. 37. Copyright © 1944, 1951 by the Vedanta Society of Southern California. Reprinted with permission.

[12] Ibid., pp. 40–41.

[13] Ibid., p. 79.

[14] Ibid., p. 67.

[15] Ibid., p. 69.

[16] Ibid., pp. 91–93.

[17] On Shankara and Advaita Vedanta, see Eliot Deutsch, *Advaita Vedanta: A Philosophical Reconstruction* (Honolulu: East-West Center Press, 1969); Eliot Deutsch and J. A. B. van Buitenen, *A Source Book of Advaita Vedanta* (Honolulu: University of Hawaii, 1971); Y. Keshava Menon and Richard F. Allen,

The Pure Principle: An Introduction to the Philosophy of Shankara (East Lansing, MI: Michigan State University Press, 1960); and Swami Prabhavananda and Christopher Isherwood, *Shankara's Crest-Jewel of Discrimination* (New York: Mentor Books, 1970).

[18] See Rai Bahadur S. C. Vidyarnava, trans., *Siva Samhita* (Allahabad, India: Lalit Mohan Basu, 1942); Eliade, *Yoga;* and A. Bharati, *The Tantric Tradition* (Garden City, NY: Doubleday, 1970).

[19] Swami Prabhavananda, *Srimad Bhagavatam: The Wisdom of God* (New York: Capricorn Books, 1968), pp. 199–200. Copyright © The Vedanta Society of Southern California. Reprinted with permission.

[20] See Milton Singer, "The Great Tradition of Hinduism in the City of Madras," *Anthropology of Folk Religion,* ed. Charles Leslie (New York: Vintage Books, 1960). The spirit of Krishna devotion is evident in the "Hare Krishna" movement in America with its fervent bhaktic singing and dancing. This movement derives from a Krishna devotional tradition started by Sri Chaitanya (c. 1486–1533) in Bengal. He and the movement regard Krishna as the supreme, personal God, and not as just an avatar of Vishnu or an expression of an ultimately impersonal Absolute like Advaita Vedanta.

[21] See Wendy O'Flaherty, *Asceticism and Eroticism in the Mythology of Siva* (London: Oxford University Press, 1973).

[22] See Ernest A. Payne, *The Saktas* (Calcutta: YMCA Press, 1933); and John G. Woodroffe, *Shakti and Shakta* (Madras: Ganesh, 1951). See also David R. Kinsley, *The Sword and the Flute: Kālī and Krskna, Dark Visions of the Terrible and the Sublime in Hindu Mythology* (Berkeley: University of California Press, 1975).

[23] Rabindranath Tagore, trans., *Songs of Kabir* (New York: Macmillan, 1917), pp. 45–46, 112. Hari is a name for Vishnu. Karim means a Muslim wonder-working saint. Ram is, of course, Rama. A *pir* is a Muslim Sufi teacher comparable to a Hindu guru.

[24] Trilochan Singh and others, *Adi Granth: Selections from the Sacred Writings of the Sikhs* (New York: Macmillan, 1960; London: George Allen and Unwin, © 1960; reprinted New York: Samuel Weiser, Inc., 1974), p. 30. Reprinted by permission of George Allen and Unwin, Ltd., and Samuel Weiser, Inc.

[25] See Mrs. Sinclair Stevenson, *The Heart of Jainism* (New Delhi: Munshivam Manoharlal, 1970; Oxford University Press, 1st ed., 1915); William de Bary, *Sources of Indian Tradition* (New York: Columbia University Press, 1958, 1966), Chapters 4, 5; and P. S. Jaini, *The Jaina Path of Purification* (Berkeley: University of California Press, 1979).

[26] See R. C. Zaehner, *The Dawn and Twilight of Zoroastrianism* (London: Weidenfelt & Nicolson, 1961).

[27] See R. C. Zaehner, *The Teachings of the Magi: A Compendium of Zoroastrian Beliefs* (London: George Allen & Unwin, 1956; New York: Macmillan, 1956), pp. 53–55.

[28] Jacques Duschesne-Guillaume, *The Hymns of Zarathustra* (Boston: Beacon Press, 1963), is a good translation of the Gathas. The bulk of the Zend Avesta is translated in *The Sacred Books of the East.*

[29] Rustom Masani, *The Religion of the Good Life* (New York: Collier Books, 1962), gives an account by a Parsee of their present-day beliefs and practices.

Chapter 4

[1] On the life of the Buddha, see E. J. Thomas, *The Life of the Buddha as Legend and History* (London: Routledge and Kegan Paul, 1927); and the shorter summary in Richard H. Robinson, *The Buddhist Religion: A Historical Introduction* (Belmont, CA: Dickenson, 1970).

[2] Edward Conze, *Buddhist Scriptures* (Harmondsworth, Middlesex, England: Penguin Classics, 1959), pp. 55–56. Copyright © Edward Conze, 1959. Reprinted by permission of Penguin Books Ltd.

[3] Conze, *Buddhist Scriptures,* pp. 186–87.

[4] In some sources this tradition is called *Hinayana* ("Little Vessel"). That term, however, originated as a derogatory label used by Mahayanists for the other camp in debate, and is not used by Theravadins themselves. It seems more courteous to keep to the word *Theravada.*

[5] In the early centuries C.E., Mahayana was strong in the areas of central Asia that are now Kashmir, Afghanistan, and surrounding regions; from this part of the world it spread to China. But it has been replaced there by Islam. It was also strong in medieval times in much of Southeast Asia, including the Khmer Empire centering in present Cambodia, with its great Buddhist temples of Angkor Wat (originally Hindu, then Mahayana, then modified to Theravada), and in present Indonesia (where it has been replaced by Islam). The story of the interaction of Hinduism, Theravada, and Mahayana in Southeast Asia up to early modern times is a very complex one.

[6] On the role of the monk, see Jane Bunnag, *Buddhist Monk, Buddhist Layman* (London and New York: Cambridge University Press, 1973); Robert C. Lester, *Theravada Buddhism in Southeast Asia* (Ann Arbor: University of Michigan Press, 1973), part 2; Richard F. Gombrich, *Precept and Practice: Traditional Buddhism in the Rural Highlands of Ceylon* (London: Oxford University Press, 1971); and Melford E. Spiro, *Buddhism and Society* (New York: Harper & Row, 1970), part 4.

[7] A stimulating discussion of monastic initiation is found in Paul Levy, *Buddhism: A 'Mystery Religion'?* (London: The Athlone Press of the University of London, 1957).

[8] The order of some of the lokas varies in different sources; this list follows Lester, *Theravada Buddhism*, pp. 39–41.

[9] The techniques of samadhic meditation are vividly described in B. A. Maitreya, "Buddhism in Theravada Countries," in Kenneth Morgan, ed., *Path of the Buddha* (New York: Ronald Press, 1956), pp. 113–52. Original texts are found in Edward Conze, *Buddhist Meditation* (New York: Harper & Row, 1969).

[10] For a personal account of the practice of vipassana meditation, see Eric Lerner, *Journey of Insight Meditation* (New York: Schocken Books, 1977).

[11] On the concepts and practices of popular Buddhism in Theravada lands, see Bunnag, *Buddhist Monk, Buddhist Layman*; Lester, *Theravada Buddhism*; Gombrich, *Precept and Practice*; Spiro, *Buddhism and Society*; Maitreya, "Buddhism in Theravada Countries"; and King, *A Thousand Lives Away* (Cambridge, MA: Harvard University Press, 1964).

[12] See Jerrold Schecter, *The New Face of Buddha* (New York: Coward-McCann, 1967).

[13] A scholarly translation of the Lotus Sutra is Leon Hurvitz, *The Scripture of the Lotus Blossom of the Fine Dharma* (New York: Columbia University Press, 1975).

[14] On Nagarjuna and his philosophy, see T.R.V. Murti, *The Central Philosophy of Buddhism* (London: George Allen & Unwin, 1955); and Frederick J. Streng, *Emptiness: A Study in Religious Meaning* (Nashville: Abingdon Press, 1967).

[15] On prajnaparamita thought, see two books by Edward Conze: *Buddhist Thought in India* (Ann Arbor: University of Michigan Press, 1967), pp. 198–204; and *The Prajnaparamita Literature* (The Hague, Netherlands: Mouton, 1960). These books contain references to the author's more technical scholarship in this area.

[16] There is no general introductory book in English on the bodhisattva. For easily accessible summaries, see Robinson, *Buddhist Religion*, pp. 54–63; and Edward Conze, *Buddhism in Essence and Development* (New York: Harper Brothers Publishers, 1959), pp. 125–30.

[17] There are few adequate books in English on Mind Only. See Conze, *Buddhist Thought in India*, pp. 250–60; and D. T. Suzuki, *Studies in the Lankāvatāra Sutra* (London: Routledge, 1930). On a closely-related school based on the Avatamsaka Sutra, see Francis D. Cook, *Hua-yen Buddhism: The Jewel Not of India* (University Park, PA: Pennsylvania State University Press, 1977).

[18] For an account of most of the Buddhas and bodhisattvas of practical importance in Mahayana art and devotion, see Alice Getty, *The Gods of Northern Buddhism* (Oxford: The Clarendon Press, 1928). See also Walter E. Clark, *Two Lamaist Pantheons* (Cambridge, Mass.: Harvard University Press, 1937).

[19] Fascinating accounts of Tantric apprenticeships can be found in Herbert V. Guenther, *The Life and Teaching of Naropa* (London: Oxford University Press, 1963); and W. Y. Evans-Wentz, *Tibet's Great Yogin Milarepa* (London and New York: Oxford University Press, 1969).

[20] Translations include Francesca Fremantle and Choguam Trungpa, *The Tibetan Book of the Dead* (Berkeley and London: Shambhala, 1975); and W. Y. Evans-Wentz, *The Tibetan Book of the Dead* (New York: Oxford University Press, 1927, 1960).

Chapter 5

[1] Marcel Granet, *Chinese Civilization* (New York: Meridian Books, 1958), pp. 170–79.

[2] See Judith M. Treistman, *The Prehistory of China* (New York: Natural History Press, 1972), pp. 47, 111–16.

[3] In this chapter, the Pinyin System of transliteration of Chinese into the Roman alphabet is used. This system, adopted by the People's Republic of China, is quite phonetic for English if one remembers that q = ch and x = sh, approximately. In some cases, the older Wade-Giles form is given in parentheses. It will be the one found in many books.

[4] The standard translation of the complete set of nine books is the nineteenth-century work of James Legge (Oxford: The Clarendon Press, various dates), although, of course, its scholarship has now been superseded in various particulars.

[5] See Harlee G. Creel, *Sinism* (Chicago: Open Court, 1929).

[6] For translations of the *Xiao Jing,* the "Classic of Filial Piety," see James Legge, *Hsiao King* (Oxford: Oxford University Press, 1899); and Sister Mary Makra, *The Hsiao Ching* (Annapolis: St. John's University Press, 1961).

[7] Creel, *Sinism.*

[8] Arthur Waley, *The Way and Its Power* (London: George Allen & Unwin, 1934), Introduction.

[9] From Witter Bynner, trans., *The Way of Life: According to Lao Tzu* (New York: The John Day Co.). Copyright © 1944 by Witter Bynner (renewed 1972). Reprinted by permission of The John Day Co., publishers.

[10] Ibid., pp. 25–26.

[11] Ibid., pp. 26–27.

[12] Ibid., p. 35.

[13] See Burton Watson, *Chuang Tzu: Basic Writings* (New York: Columbia University Press, 1964); and A. C. Graham, *Chuang Tzu: The Inner Chapters* (London: George Allen and Unwin, 1981).

[14] Fung Yu-lan, *A Short History of Chinese Philosophy* (New York: Macmillan, 1960), chapters 19–20, contains a good brief summary of the Daoism of this period.

[15] The best introduction to religious Daoism, as well as to other aspects of Daoism, is Holmes Welch, *Taoism: The Parting of the Way* (Boston: Beacon Press, 1965). See also Michael R. Saso, *Taoism and the Rite of Cosmic Renewal* (Pullman: Washington State University Press, 1972), which provides a striking description of modern religious Daoism, together with useful and informed comments on the history and meaning of religious Daoism. Peter Goulart, *The Monastery of Jade Mountain* (London: John Murray, 1961), offers a vivid if uncritical picture of Daoist life in mainland China in the decades before the Communist revolution. The same can be said of John Blofeld, *The Secret and Sublime: Taoist Mysteries and Magic* (London: George Allen & Unwin, 1973). Two older multivolumed works, J.J.M. de Groot, *The Religious Systems of China,* 6 vols. (Leiden: E. J. Brill, 1892–1910; reprinted Taipei: Literature House, 1964); and Henri M. Doré, *Researches into Chinese Superstitions,* 13 vols., in English (Shanghai: Tusewei Press, 1914–38; reprinted Taipei: Chéngwen Publishing Co., 1968), provide an immense wealth of material on the Daoist pantheon and related rites and beliefs, as well as on other matters, although the scholarship and attitudes are dated.

[16] See Mircea Eliade, *The Forge and the Crucible* (New York: Harper and Brothers, 1962), chapter 11.

[17] The best general book on Chinese Buddhism is Kenneth Ch'en, *Buddhism in China* (Princeton, NJ: Princeton University Press, 1964). Also useful is Arthur F. Wright, *Buddhism in Chinese History* (Stanford, CA: Stanford University Press, 1959). For the actual life of Chinese Buddhist monasteries and popular devotion, see Holmes, Welch, *The Practice of Chinese Buddhism, 1900–1950* (Cambridge, MA: Harvard University Press, 1967); and J. Prip-Möller, *Chinese Buddhist Monasteries* (New York: Oxford University Press, 1937, 1967).

[18] See Wright, *Buddhism in Chinese History,* pp. 36–37.

[19] This area is well portrayed in Wolfram Eberhard, *Guilt and Sin in Traditional China* (Berkeley: University of California Press, 1967).

[20] The standard treatment is Heinrich Dumoulin, S. J., *A History of Zen Buddhism* (New York: McGraw-Hill, 1965). For a readable history presented through the lives of the great Ch'an/Zen masters, see Thomas Hoover, *The Zen Experience* (New York: New American Library, 1980).

[21] The most useful translations are John Blofeld, *I Ching* (New York: Dutton, 1968); and Richard Wilhelm, *I Ching, or Book of Changes* (New York: Pantheon Books, 1950).

[22] Arthur Waley, trans., *Monkey: Folk Novel of China by Wu Ch'eng-En* (New York: Grove Press, 1958); Anthony Yu, trans., *The Journey to the West,* 4 vols. (Chicago: University of Chicago Press, 1977–1983).

[23] Rennselaer W. Lee III, "General aspects of Chinese Communist Religious Policy, with Soviet comparisons," *China Quarterly,* 19 (July–September 1964), 161–73. Selection reprinted in Laurence G. Thompson, *The Chinese Way in Religion* (Encino, CA: Dickenson, 1973), pp. 232–35.

[24] The best sources on religion in China to date of their publication are Richard C. Bush, Jr., *Religion in Communist China* (Nashville: Abingdon Press, 1970), which emphasizes the situation of Christianity but also has a useful chapter on Islam; and Holmes Welch, *Buddhism under Mao* (Cambridge, MA: Harvard University Press, 1972), dealing with Buddhism. Little is known about the state of Daoism,

and the significance of Confucianism lies mainly in the role that attacks on it and veiled defenses of its principles have played in internal Communist debate. See also *China Notes* (published since 1963), a quarterly newsletter on religion in China published by the Division of Overseas Ministries of the National Council of Churches of Christ in the United States of America.

[25] The best translations are Donald M. Philippi, *Kojiki* (Tokyo: University of Tokyo Press, 1968); and W. G. Aston, *Nihongi* (London: George Allen & Unwin, 1896, 1956).

[26] See Daniel C. Holtom, *The Japanese Enthronement Ceremonies* (Tokyo: Kyo Bun Kwan, 1928; Sophia University, 1972); and Robert S. Ellwood, *The Feast of Kingship* (Tokyo: Sophia University, 1973).

[27] See Kenzo Tange and Noboru Kawazoe, *Ise: Prototype of Japanese Architecture* (Cambridge, MA: MIT Press, 1965); Felicia G. Bock, "The Rites of Renewal at Ise," *Monumenta Nipponica,* 29, no. 1 (Spring 1974), 55–68; and Robert S. Ellwood, "Harvest and Renewal at the Grand Shrine of Ise," *Numen,* 15, no. 3 (November 1968), 165–90.

[28] See Aston, *Nihongi,* part 2, pp. 65–67, for the traditional account.

[29] See Joseph M. Kitagawa, *Religion in Japanese History* (New York: Columbia University Press, 1966), pp. 38–45.

[30] See Yoshito S. Hakeda, trans., *Kukai: Major Works* (New York: Columbia University Press, 1972).

[31] Harper Havelock Coates and Ryugaku Ishizuka, *Honen the Buddhist Saint* (Kyoto: Choinin, 1925).

[32] Alfred Bloom, *Shinran's Gospel of Pure Grace* (Tucson: University of Arizona Press, 1965).

[33] Masaharu Anesaki, *Nichiren the Buddhist Prophet* (Cambridge, MA: Harvard University Press, 1916).

[34] See James W. White, *The Sokagakkai and Mass Society* (Stanford, CA: Stanford University Press, 1970).

[35] See Robert N. Bellah, *Tokugawa Religion* (Glencoe, IL: The Free Press, 1957); Warren W. Smith, *Confucianism in Modern Japan* (Tokyo: Hokuseido, 1973).

[36] This division is based on that in Harry Thomsen, *The New Religions of Japan* (Tokyo and Rutland, VT: Charles E. Tuttle, 1963), which is the most readable general introduction to the subject. See also Robert S. Ellwood, *The Eagle and the Rising Sun: Americans and the New Religions of Japan* (Philadelphia: Westminster Press, 1974).

[37] Material on Korean religion can be found in C. A. Clark, *Religions of Old Korea* (New York: Garland, 1981; 1st ed., 1932); and Byung-Kil Chang, *Religions in Korea* (Seoul: Korean Overseas Information Service, 1984). But no English source is equal to Frits Vos, *Die Religionen Koreas* (Stuttgart: Verlag W. Kohlhammer, 1977). On special topics see Roger Janelli, *Ancestor Worship in Korean Society* (Stanford University Press, 1982); and two highly readable books by Laurel Kendall, *Shamans, Housewives, and Other Restless Spirits* (Honolulu: University of Hawaii Press, 1985) and *The Life and Hard Times of a Korean Shaman* (Honolulu: University of Hawaii Press, 1988).

Chapter 6 (no footnotes)

Chapter 7

[1] Transliterated into Roman letters, the name of God, called the tetragrammaton, is YHVH. The pronunciation must have been something like Yahweh or Yehveh. The name *Jehovah* of the King James Bible is an older attempt at pronouncing the same name by supplying the vowels of the title *Adonai,* "The Lord." Devout Jews, of course, would not make the attempt to pronounce the name; as in the Bible, God is spoken of not by name but by terms like Adonai.

[2] See Gershom G. Scholem, *Major Trends in Jewish Mysticism* (New York: Schocken Books, 1961), pp. 156–204.

[3] Colorful accounts of Hasidism can be found in the writings of Martin Buber and in Herbert Weiner, *9½ Mystics* (New York: Holt, Rinehart & Winston, 1969).

[4] See Howard Sacher, *The Course of Modern Jewish History* (New York: World, 1958).

[5] Rabbi Nahman of Bratslav (1772–1811), cited in Arthur Hertzberg, ed., *Judaism* (New York: George Braziller, Inc., 1961), pp. 91–92. Reprinted with the permission of the publisher. Copyright © 1961 by Arthur Hertzberg.

[6] The meaning of the Sabbath is vividly described in Herman Wouk, *This Is My God* (Garden City, NY: Doubleday, 1959), pp. 55–66. See also Abraham Joshua Heschel, *The Sabbath: Its Meaning for Modern Man* (New York: Farrar, Strauss, and Giroux, 1951).

[7] Wouk, *This Is My God,* pp. 96–99, contains a particularly colorful account of Purim.

Chapter 8

[1] See Robert M. Grant, *A Historical Introduction to the New Testament* (New York: Harper & Row, 1963).

[2] See John Bright, *The Kingdom of God* (Nashville: Abingdon Press, 1953).

[3] For a presentation of the theory that Jesus was involved with political revolutionaries, see S.G.F. Brandon, *Jesus and the Zealots* (New York: Scribner, 1967).

[4] See Günther Bornkamm, *Paul,* trans. D.M.G. Stalker (New York: Harper & Row, 1971); John Knox, *Chapters in a Life of Paul* (London: Adam and Charles Black, 1954); and Richard Longenecker, *Paul: Apostle of Liberty* (New York: Harper & Row, 1964).

[5] See John Marsh, *The Gospel of St. John* (Harmondsworth, England: Penguin Books, 1968); and Oscar Cullmann, *The Johannine Circle* (Philadelphia: Westminster Press, 1975).

[6] See Dom Gregory Dix, *The Shape of the Liturgy* (London: Dacre Press, 1945), pp. 36–45.

[7] J.W.C. Wand, *A History of the Early Church* (London: Methuen & Co., 1937), p. 97.

[8] See Robert M. Grant, *The Formation of the New Testament* (New York: Harper & Row, 1965).

[9] From the Epistle of St. Ignatius of Antioch to the Romans, vv. 4 and 7. Francis X. Glimm and others, *The Apostolic Fathers* (New York: Christian Heritage, 1947), pp. 109–10.

[10] See Hermann Dorres, *Constantine the Great,* trans. Roland Bainton (New York: Harper & Row, 1972).

[11] See Helen Waddell, *The Desert Fathers* (Ann Arbor: University of Michigan Press, 1957); Justin McCann, *Saint Benedict* (Garden City, NY: Doubleday, 1958); and David Knowles, *Christian Monasticism* (New York: McGraw-Hill, 1969).

[12] See George G. Coulton, *Medieval Panorama* (New York: Macmillan, 1938); and two works of readable history by H. Daniel-Rops, *The Church in the Dark Ages,* trans. Audrey Butler (New York: Dutton, 1959); and *Cathedral and Crusade: Studies of the Medieval Church 1050–1350,* trans. John Worthington (New York: Dutton, 1957).

[13] On spiritual dissidents in the Middle Ages, see Steven Runciman, *The Medieval Manichee* (Cambridge: Cambridge University Press, 1960); and Norman Cohn, *The Pursuit of the Millenium* (New York: Oxford University Press, 1970).

[14] A readable life of Luther is Roland H. Bainton, *Here I Stand* (New York: Abingdon-Cokesbury Press, 1950). For the entire period see Harold J. Grimm, *The Reformation Era 1500–1650* (New York: Macmillan 1973).

[15] See George Harrison Williams, *The Radical Reformation* (Philadelphia: Westminster Press, 1962).

[16] See Charles Williams, *The Figure of Beatrice* (London: Faber, 1943).

[17] Two books that provide real insight into the soul of Eastern Orthodox spiritually, especially in old Russia, are Jon Gregerson, *Transfigured Cosmos* (New York: Ungar, 1960); and *The Way of a Pilgrim, and The Pilgrim Continues His Way,* trans. R. M. French (New York: Seabury Press, 1974).

[18] These characteristics are based in part on those in the article by Richard P. McBrien, "Roman Catholicism," in *The Encyclopedia of Religion,* Vol. 12 (New York: Macmillan, 1987), pp. 437–39.

Chapter 9

[1] Formerly, the religion was often called *Muhammadanism* and its followers, *Muhammadans* by Occidentals, in analogy to Buddhism or Christianity. But Muslims object to this label and never use it themselves, saying that they do not worship or idolize Muhammad but rather submit to God's will as revealed in his prophetic ministry. Today these feelings are rightly respected, and the proper terms *Islam* and *Muslim* are generally used.

[2] Mohammed Maramduke Pickthall, *The Meaning of the Glorious Koran* (New York: Mentor Books, n.d.), p. vii.

[3] A. J. Arberry, *The Holy Koran* (London: George Allen and Unwin, 1953), pp. 26–27.

[4] N. J. Dawood, trans., *The Koran*, 4th rev. ed. (Harmondsworth, England: Penguin Classics, 1974), p. 15. Copyright © N. J. Dawood, 1956, 1959, 1966, 1968, 1974. Reprinted by permission of Penguin Books, Ltd.

[5] Ibid., p. 194.

[6] Ibid., p. 336.

[7] Sevyed Hossein Nasr, "Jesus Through the Eyes of Islam," *The Times* (London), July 28, 1973.

[8] Kenneth Cragg, trans., *The House of Islam* (Belmont, CA: Dickenson, 1969), p. 39. Reprinted by permission of the publisher.

[9] A vivid account of Ramadan, and of much else of Islam in an Iraqi Shi'a setting, may be found in Elizabeth Warnock Fernea, *Guests of the Sheik* (Garden City, NY: Doubleday, 1969).

[10] For an illuminating discussion of pilgrimage, which indirectly casts much light on the meaning of the hajj, see Victor Turner, "The Center Out There: Pilgrim's Goal," in *History of Religions,* 12, No 3 (February 1973), 191–230.

[11] G. E. von Grunebaum, *Muhammadan Festivals* (New York: Henry Schuman, 1951), pp. 44–47. The entire discussion of the hajj in this book, pp. 15–19, is very useful.

[12] See Xavier de Planhol, *The World of Islam* (Ithaca, NY: Cornell University Press, 1959), pp. 6–7.

[13] For useful overviews of many aspects of Islamic culture, see Bernard Lewis, ed., *Islam and the Arab World* (New York: Knopf, 1976).

[14] See the account in von Grunebaum, *Muhammadan Festivals,* pp. 87–94. Fernea, *Guests of the Sheik,* contains a colorful firsthand account of the first ten days of Muharram, pp. 216–66.

[15] Dawood, *The Koran,* p. 336.

[16] Ibid., p. 228.

[17] See J. R. Porter, "Muhammad's Journey to Heaven," *Numen,* 21, fasc. 1 (April 1974), 64–80.

[18] From Margaret Smith, *Rabi'a the Mystic* (New York: Cambridge University Press, 1928), pp. 22, 99, 100. Reprinted by permission of the publisher.

[19] See the discussion of Junavd in R. C. Zaehner, *Hindu and Muslim Mysticism* (New York: Schocken Books, 1969).

[20] Idries Shah, *Tales of the Dervishes* (New York: Dutton, 1970), p. 143.

[21] See the discussion of Muslim saints in Fazlur Rahman, *Islam* (Garden City, NY: Doubleday, 1968), pp. 162–65; and in von Grunebaum, *Muhammaden Festivals,* pp. 67–84.

Chapter 10

[1] "Golden Mycenae," in Donald S. Fryer, *Songs and Sonnets Atlantean* (Sauk City, WI: Arkham House, 1971). Reprinted by permission of the publisher.

[2] For further discussion of these possibilities, see the author's book *The History and Future of Faith* (New York: Crossroad, 1988).

Index